Fodor's

SO-AZV-943

SEE IT

SPAIN

**FODOR'S
TRAVEL PUBLICATIONS**

NEW YORK • TORONTO
LONDON • SYDNEY • AUCKLAND

WWW.FODORS.COM

228

CONTENTS

359

303

83

254

UNDERSTANDING SPAIN

Understanding Spain is an introduction to the country, its geography, economy, history and its people, giving a real insight into the nation. Living Spain gets under the skin of Spain today, while The Story of Spain takes you through the country's past.

UNDERSTANDING SPAIN

In Spain loyalties are first to home towns and villages, then to regions and only lastly (and not always very strongly) to the country itself. This means there are immense cultural variations and no 'typical' Spain, so your experiences will be truly different depending on which area you visit. The historical cocktail of Iberian, Roman, Celtic, Visigothic, Moorish, Jewish and Christian civilizations has produced a unique blend of architecture and culture, with some of the most astonishing festivals in the world. In short, there are many Spains to enjoy.

LANDSCAPE

Spain is perhaps Europe's most diverse country geographically, taking in the deserts of Andalucía, the green lushness of Galicia with its Norwegian-like fiords, the plains of Castile and the peaks of the Pyrenees. This is the highest country after Switzerland, and at its heart is the mighty Meseta, a little-populated agricultural plateau that covers nearly half the country. Lack of water plays a continuingly controversial role in Spain so the major rivers—the Ebro, Duero, Tajo (Tagus), Guadiana and Guadalquivir—are vital lifelines. The country also includes the Balearic Islands and the Canary Islands, plus the tiny outposts of Ceuta and Melilla in Africa.

LANGUAGE

Language is a divisive and controversial subject in Spain. Franco deliberately tried to eradicate the Catalan, Galician and Basque tongues, and impose Castellano (Castilian, regarded by the rest of the world as 'Spanish') on the entire country. With the transition to democracy, the various regions have used their traditional tongues— distinct languages, not dialects—as an emblem of their fight for autonomy: Català (Catalan), Basque and Galician are also official languages of Spain. Other Spanish languages include Bable in Asturias and various dialects of Fabla in Aragón, plus many regional variants (people in the Balearics and Valencia speak a close cousin of Catalan).

In this book you will find examples of Spain's linguistic diversity in place names. Larger cities and towns in the autonomous regions mainly have two names: a Castellano version and their original name. Since democracy, local names have regained the ascendancy, particularly in the Basque country and Catalonia, but also in areas such as Valencia and Galicia. Touring through the regions, you will see place-names in the local language and also in Castellano, with street signs and public information also using Catalan, Basque, Galician or Valencian, as well as Castellano. This book has been guided by what you will find on the spot; where local language names predominate, we have used them. This may vary within a region, where for some places the locals use Castellano, and for others the original language name. In some regions differences are slight, Alacant becoming Alicante, for example, but in others they are quite different, with Donostia (Basque) doubling as San Sebastián (Castellano) or Iruña (Basque) for Pamplona (Castellano).

SPANISH TODAY

Spanish has proved to be absorbent: The bedrock vocabulary comes from Latin but the Visigoths in the fifth century AD introduced Germanic words (*werra* became *guerra*—war), the Muslim conquest in the eighth century added Arabic words (*berenjena*—aubergine, *almacén*—shop), French pilgrims to Santiago de Compostela in Galicia brought elements of their language from the 11th century onwards and during the 15th and 16th centuries the Aragónese domination of Italy brought Italian words. Spain also has one of the world's more unusual languages in Silbo, a whistled speech system from La Gomera in the Canary Islands. The newer Spanglish is a hybrid of Spanish and English used increasingly in Spain.

CLIMATE

Spain's climate varies greatly and it is certainly not universally Mediterranean. Central Spain has hot summers and bitter winters, but is constantly pretty dry. Rainfall is increasingly scarce the farther south you travel, and given the fiercely hot summers there are very real fears of desertification. The north is cool, wet, and verdant thanks to the Pyrenees and Picos de Europa cordilleras.

ECONOMY

Disintegration and Francoist mismanagement following the Civil War (1936–39) have largely been overcome and, despite the economic crisis of 2009, the now-famous soundbite *España va bien* (Spain's doing well) generally still holds. Spain has particularly benefited from European Union (EU) grants (the high-speed AVE train link from Madrid to Seville and Barcelona is one example).

The key industries are tourism and agriculture, especially wine, cereals, oranges and olives, despite the drift of the rural population from the countryside to the cities, which has caused an increase in ghost towns. Hothouse agriculture is growing fast. Manufacturing—especially cars—is also important and Spanish companies, from clothing giant Zara to the world's biggest lollipop manufacturer, Chupa Chups, are increasingly conspicuous on the international stage. Though connections with South and Latin America are strong, Spain's principal trading partners are other EU countries. At home, unemployment and low pay remain problems and deregulation of industries such as gas, electricity and telephone has been a painful process. The worldwide economic downturn hit Spain's real estate and construction bubble harder than other EU countries. Recovery has been slow and will continue into 2011.

DEMOGRAPHY AND RELIGION

While Spain remains an essentially Catholic country, church attendance is dropping. Religious freedom is guaranteed by the 1978 Constitution. The birth rate is also dropping, which has huge social implications for the still strongly traditional family-dominated way of life. Spain's population of around 40 million will start to drop within the next couple of decades (some experts predict a 10 million decrease within 50 years at current levels) and in some regions, such as Asturias, the replacement rate is already at crisis point. Into this demographic hole are pouring immigrants from South America and Africa.

POLITICS

Spain is a constitutional monarchy (and has a much-respected and hands-on monarch in Juan Carlos I) with a central parliament but with power devolved to 17 autonomous regions, some more autonomous than others and several with strong separatist ambitions.

After a rocky 20th century, Spain has become an important player on the world stage, partly due to former prime minister Aznar's foreign policy. His successor, the socialist José Luis Rodriguez Zapatero, won elections in 2004 after terrorist attacks in Madrid, and has introduced modern laws such as those permitting same-sex marriage. He has continued a good relationship with the UK and overcame a rocky start with the Bush administration after wasting no time in honouring his electoral promise to pull Spanish troops out of Iraq. Zapatero and Obama, both progressives, see eye to eye across the board. The biggest ongoing conundrums are how to deal with the Basque pro-independence group ETA and immigration.

Opposite *Consuegra's windmills, immortalized by Cervantes*
Below *Gaudi's benches in Barcelona (left); flamenco (right)*

I CANTABRIA
2 EUSKADI / PAÍS VASCO
3 NAVARRA / NAFARROA
4 CASTILLA-LEÓN
5 LA RIOJA
6 VALÈNCIA

THE REGIONS OF SPAIN

Spain is divided into 17 autonomous administrative regions; in this book we have grouped some regions and places for convenience. The distant Canary Islands, which are 1,100km (680 miles) from the mainland, are not covered.

Madrid has a stately exterior and a spectacular nightlife and its central position makes it a perfect base for exploring the rest of the country.

Around Madrid is not an actual region, but a more convenient grouping of a number of historic places that are in easy reach of the capital and make great excursions if you are based in Madrid.

Galicia, Asturias and Cantabria offer a gently green and pleasant land quite different from the usual stereotype of arid, sun-drenched Spain.

Euskadi and Navarra are politically controversial, linguistically unique and fiercely independent. Navarra, half Basque and half Spanish, remains separate from Euskadi, the Basque Autonomous Community.

Barcelona, not a region in its own right but the capital of Catalonia, is the peninsula's chic city and the modern cosmopolitan melting pot of the country.

Catalonia, Valencia and Murcia claim the glorious coastline that inspired Dalí and Sorolla, gave the world paella and set the pace for the tourist industry.

Castile-León and La Rioja have largely agricultural areas with elegant cities such as Avila and Salamanca and the mountainous wilderness of the Sierra de Gredos. La Rioja and Ribera de Duero are Spain's top wine regions.

Castile-La Mancha and Extremadura enjoy bleakly beautiful, green landscapes, and in the impressive ruins at Mérida provide a step back in history to the days of the ancient Romans.

Andalucía is the archetypal Spanish destination for bullfighting, flamenco, tapas, sun, sea, sand, fiestas, whitewashed villages and extreme heat.

The Balearic Islands—pocket-size Spain—offer a taste of everything that can be found on the mainland, including superb food and beaches, fine walks and intriguing archaeological monuments.

Above *Exquisite ceramic tiling in Seville's Plaza de España*
Above right *The Puente Nuevo spans the gorge of the Río Guadalevín*
Below right *Bilbao's Guggenheim Museum*

HOW TO GET THE BEST FROM YOUR STAY

Though Spain is a large country and its road and rail network can sometimes be a bit patchy, getting around is reasonably easy, so focusing on more than one region or type of holiday is a definite possibility.

Since the 1960s, Spain has probably been best known for its beaches, and it's true that the coasts of Andalucía, Catalonia and the Balearic Islands in particular are still lovely to visit despite the millions who flock to them each year. However, there is much more to the country, particularly in the inland rural areas: In the Sierras, Alpujarras, Pyrenees and Picos de Europa, as well as national parks such as Doñana, Spain has wonderful wilderness areas. These are often excellent places to experience a more old-fashioned Spanish lifestyle. Conversely, Spain has many fascinating modern cities: Madrid's nightlife is legendary, as is the successful regeneration of Barcelona and Bilbao, all of which also have superb art collections. Meanwhile, in the south, the Moorish architecture of the Córdoba/Seville/ Granada triangle is a reminder that Africa has historically been much closer than London.

Perhaps the best way to see Spain is to try to time your trip to coincide with one of its many major fiestas, such as *Las Fallas* in March in Valencia, or the *Semana Santa* (Holy Week) celebrations in Andalucía. These are the ideal times to enjoy a slice of 'real' Spain in the company of the locals. There are also thousands of tiny village fiestas around the country—these receive less international attention but are just as atmospheric. Whatever you choose to do, you'll enjoy it best if you adopt the Spanish attitude to life: Be spontaneous, don't expect everything to happen to an exact timetable, and make time for a decent lunch every day.

UNDERSTANDING SPAIN

MADRID

Art The Golden Triangle of the Prado (▷ 74–75), Reina Sofía (▷ 77) and Thyssen-Bornemisza (▷ 78–79). museums contains inexhaustible collections of treasures.

Park Join the locals for a Sunday pre-lunch wander around the capital's Parque del Retiro (▷ 82).

Cafés The ambience of the establishment Café Gijón (▷ 97) and alternative Café Comercial (▷ 97).

Shopping Bring back a typically Spanish souvenir, a cape from Capas Seseña near Plaza Mayor (▷ 90).

Eating Salvador on Calle de Barbieri has an unchanging menu of Madrid's finest dishes (▷ 98).

AROUND MADRID

Memorials Philip II's greatest architectural legacy, El Escorial (▷ 109), and Segovia's Roman aqueduct (▷ 113).

Eating (1) Nothing beats roast lamb on one of Chinchón's balconied restaurants…

Eating (2) …unless it's the roast suckling pig (*cochinillo*) in Segovia's, Mesón de Cándido, upstairs if possible (▷ 127).

Children Tasty food and dressing up on the summer Strawberry Train outings from the capital to Aranjuez.

GALICIA, ASTURIAS AND CANTABRIA

Art The cave paintings in the Cuevas de Altamira, known as the 'Sistine Chapel of prehistoric art' (▷ 136).

Countryside A hike or drive in the dramatic Picos de Europa mountains, home to some of Europe's most endangered wildlife (▷ 140–141 and 152–153).

History The town of Covadonga, the place where the Christian Reconquest of Spain began in 722 and now an important religious spot for pilgrims (▷ 134).

Food Delicious Asturian cider and a plate of Galician *pulpo* (octopus) with paprika.

Music Forget your preconceptions and enjoy a concert featuring the traditional Galician bagpipes.

EUSKADI, NAVARRA AND ARAGÓN

Museum The Guggenheim in Bilbao lives up to all the hype, both inside and out (▷ 172).

Bulls Best not to run with them, but the San Fermín fiesta in Pamplona in July is a perfect chance to see these enormous beasts in action (▷ 182).

History The town of Gernika-Lumo, where Hitler's airforce helped Franco bomb Spanish civilians (▷ 178).

Scenery Enjoy the best of the Pyrenean scenery at the Parque Nacional Ordesa y Monte Perdido (▷ 181).

Fiesta Aragón's Las Tamboradas festival is a different take on the Easter celebrations, marked by hours of religious drumming.

Above *Detail of the glorious Nativity Facade of the Sagrada Familia church in Barcelona*

Opposite *The myriad arches of the Mezquita in Córdoba*

BARCELONA

Wandering The Barri Gòtic's medieval maze-like streets are full of shops and cafés to explore (▷ 216–217).
Work in progress Gaudí's unfinished Sagrada Família dazzles visitors to the city with its sheer scale and detail (▷ 228–229).
Streetlife There's something for everyone on Las Ramblas, from performance artists to Europe's best food market, the celebrated Mercat de la Boqueria (▷ 237).
Performance Risen from the ashes of a 1994 fire, the Teatre del Liceu (▷ 239) is as splendid and atmospheric as it was before.
W Hotel (▷ 248). Known as the Hotel Vela (sail) for its sail-like silhouette, Ricardo Bofill's skyscraper, complete with a terrace bar overlooking the Mediterranean expanse and a Carles Abellán restaurant, dominates the waterfront.

CATALONIA, VALENCIA AND MURCIA

Fiesta You won't forget the bomb-like fireworks and burning gigantic models at Valencia's Fallas (▷ 448).
History The Jewish quarter in Girona shows a way of life that was once central to Spanish culture (▷ 260).
Religion Montserrat is home to the Black Virgin and was a stronghold of Catalán resistance under Franco (▷ 261).
Eating Restaurant El Bulli in Roses is a delicious laboratory of tastes (▷ 282).
Drinking You can sample *cava*, Catalan sparkling wine on one of the region's many bodega tours.

CASTILE-LEÓN AND LA RIOJA

Cathedral Spain's loveliest and most spectacular Gothic cathedral is in Burgos (▷ 290–291).
Architecture Beautiful but restrained, Salamanca's elegant buildings are all around the city (▷ 300–303).
Drinking The wines in La Rioja are the best known outside Spain, but new wine-growing regions are proliferating everywhere.
Fiesta Hold your breath as El Colacho, a brightly dressed man, does his annual jump over a line of babies for luck in Castrillo de Murcia, the Sunday after Corpus Christi.
Sightseeing This is the best region to see Spain's monumental castles, such as La Mota (▷ 293).

CASTILE-LA MANCHA AND EXTREMADURA

Buildings Cuenca's hanging houses defy gravity and contain fine art galleries and restaurants (▷ 328).
Villages Rural, simple and uneventful, La Alcarria (▷ 325) was described by Nobel Prize-winning Spanish author Camilo José Cela as 'a beautiful region which people have apparently no desire to visit'.
Ancient history The country's finest Roman ruins at Mérida are surprisingly complete and still in use (▷ 332).
Books Live out your Don Quixote fantasies at Consuegra (▷ 329), Campo de Criptana (best for the windmills) and El Toboso (home of Dulcinea).
Tranquillity Enjoy the peace of the monastery of Yuste (▷ 331), where Charles V, Holy Roman Emperor (1500–88, Charles I of Spain) retired.

ANDALUCÍA

Religious building Islam meets Christianity in Córdoba's unique cathedral-mosque (▷ 355).
Spain-ish Multicultural Gibraltar has an unmistakably British atmosphere (▷ 359).
Architecture Granada's Alhambra is a breathtaking leap back into the country's Moorish past (▷ 364–365).
Sunset Watch the sunset with a glass of fine *manzanilla* sherry and a plate of enormous *langostino* prawns at Sanlúcar de Barrameda (▷ 352).
Celebrations Seville underlines the twin faces of Spain's national character with the riotous Feria de Abril hard on the heel of the austere Holy Week celebrations (▷ 448).

BALEARIC ISLANDS

Lifestyle Enjoy the peaceful old town of Eivissa (Ibiza) by day and its party atmosphere by night (▷ 405–406).
Mystery The archaeological remains on Menorca are evidence of the Mediterranean's thriving prehistoric megalithic culture.
Wilderness Leave the crowds behind and explore Formentera by bicycle (▷ 407).
Railway The Sóller railway on Mallorca is a delightful reminder of the more stylish days of travel.
Eating The cafés serving *pa amb oli* (bread with tomato, oil and usually garlic) in Palma de Mallorca offer a range of simple but delicious possibilities.

TOP EXPERIENCES

Tapas—from spicy chorizo sausage and *morcilla* (black pudding) to simple tortilla (potato omelette) and croquettes, these delicious tidbits can be a full meal.

Flamenco—the chance to enjoy a spontaneous display in Andalucía or Madrid; the smaller the venue, the better the chance of a high-quality performance.

Parque Nacional de Doñana (▷ 368–369), Europe's greatest natural wetland and a habitat for many endangered birds.

The lively fiestas—the holy week celebrations (Semana Santa) with processions of hooded penitents are the most spectacular (▷ 448).

A soccer match at the Bernabéu Stadium in Madrid or the Camp Nou in Barcelona, especially if you can get tickets for a Real Madrid–Barcelona *clásico* (Classic).

Vintage Spain—exploring some of the country's wonderful wine regions, especially La Rioja and Penedes (in Catalonia).

Spain's Moorish legacy, especially at the Alhambra in Granada (▷ 364–365) and the Mezquita in Córdoba (▷ 355–356).

Gaudí's Barcelona—from the still unfinished Sagrada Família (▷ 228–231) to his colourful Park Güell (▷ 225)

Above Gaudí's gatehouses at Park Güell, Barcelona
Left Wine barrels at the Muga winery, Haro
Below The medieval Moorish palace of the Alhambra, Granada

and the facades of Casa Milà and Casa Battló (▷ 215).

The Santiago de Compostela pilgrimage route, or at least a part of it; whether by foot, bicycle or horse, it's the perfect way to enjoy the delights of northern Spain.

The nightlife, especially in Madrid, a city that it is said never sleeps.

A *menú del día*, the inexpensive three-course meal that most restaurants offer at lunchtime from Monday to Friday and the reason the Spanish have a proper lunch.

The Pyrenees, higher and drier in Spain than in France—superb for walking and mountain sports from the Basque country to the Costa Brava.

Parque Nacional de Ordesa y de Monte Perdido (▷ 194–195 is a bite-sized Grand Canyon, a good one-day outing with dizzying heights and pellucid streams.

The Basque country's moist green hills and famously delicious culinary riches form an enchanted world.

The Costa Brava has tiny and intimate sandy inlets surrounded by rocky cliffs and washed by the pristine waters of the Mediterranean.

LIVING SPAIN

UNDERSTANDING   LIVING SPAIN

Following the expulsion of the Moors in 1492 and the union of the powerful kingdoms of Aragón and Castile, Spain established the borders that still define the country geographically. However, more than 500 years later, arguments still persist about whether the Spanish nation really exists. More than any other European nation, Spain is a country of regions. In the south, you will find that the people are proud of Andalucía and its historical and cultural significance to the rest of the country. Take a trip up the eastern coast, however, through Murcia and Alicante, and as you enter the region of Valencia, you will soon become aware that more and more people are speaking a different language: Valencià. Farther along the coast, in Catalonia, you will see how the Catalan flag dominates town squares, and maps of the Països Catalans (Catalan Lands) appear on posters in the streets. As you go west and cross into northern Spain the scenery changes, from the typically dry Spanish plains of Castile to the green, rolling hills of the Basque country and Galicia. The people here are proud of their own languages and traditions, and most do not regard themselves as Spanish at all. With Catalonia's controversial new Autonomy Statute (still under scrutiny in Spain's Constitutional Court) leading the way, 21st-century Spain seems destined to become an increasingly more decentralized confederation of Autonomous Communities..

ZERO TOLERANCE
A plaque in Puerta del Sol in the heart of Madrid marks 'Kilómetro cero' or Kilometre Zero and grandly states 'All roads in Spain originate at this point'. Madrid used to be a nondescript, rural town perched on top of an unfriendly plateau, until King Felipe II (1527–98) decided in 1561 that, for purely geographical reasons, it should be the capital city of the new united Spanish kingdom.

Barcelona is older, Seville is prettier and historically more important, and the king's court was based for centuries at nearby Toledo. But Madrid is right in the middle of the country, and for this reason alone it was given the opportunity to develop into one of the world's major cities and to become the place where Spain officially begins.

Clockwise from left to right *San Fermín festival in Pamplona; poster advertising a bullfight; the Rock of Gibraltar has been a talking point between Spain and Britain for many years*

PLEASE, SIR

The north of Navarra is on a linguistic border between two languages — an inevitable flashpoint in a country where, thanks to a long history of linguistic repression, language can be a highly sensitive issue.

Parents in San Juan, a small district of Pamplona, were determined that their children should be taught in the local language of Euskera. However, as there were only 17 new students one year (and the law in this region states that for this to happen at least 18 students must be speakers of Euskera), the local government ordered that classes were to be given in Spanish.

The enraged parents, pointing out that no such equivalent rule existed for Spanish, took their children out of school and set up their own classes. The issue was resolved only after the arrival of a new Euskera-speaking family in the district who conveniently made up the required number of students.

ROCK ON

The people who live on the Rock of Gibraltar (Flatlanders, as the local Andalucíans wryly call them) are proud of its status as a British overseas territory. Cross over from the southern Spanish town of La Línea — passing through the world's only aircraft runway regulated by traffic lights — and all of a sudden you will find yourself in a world of quaint pubs and red telephone boxes and a shopping street that would not look out of place anywhere in England's green and pleasant land. In 2002 the Gibraltarians voted by a large majority to reject the proposal by the British government to increase political ties with Spain. The socialist government took a more conciliatory stance than their predecessors, and noted that the Spanish would respect the wishes of the Gibraltarians. Unlike many Spaniards, the islanders themselves do not regard Gibraltar as a part of Spain.

¡VIVA ATHLETIC!

As in the rest of Europe, football (soccer) is big business in Spain. However, perhaps more so than in any other country, it is also about politics and identity. The statistics say that, after the two giants, Real Madrid and FC Barcelona, the most successful soccer team in Spanish history is Athletic de Bilbao; the Basque team from the northern industrial city has notched up 23 Spanish cups and 9 league titles in its 105-year history. But hiding behind the statistics is an extraordinary fact: Athletic has never had a non-Basque player. In these days of highly paid sport superstars, the club stubbornly sticks to its rule that all players must come from the Basque region. Although the Basque country tends to produce very good footballers, this policy is beginning to take its toll, and the club has been trophy-less since 1984.

BULLFIGHTING

In Barcelona in 2004, 250,000 people signed a petition calling for the abolition of bullfights. In a secret ballot, the majority of local councillors proved to be in favour. Although ratified by the Parlament de Catalunya in 2010 and yet to be made law, Catalonia was declared Spain's first 'anti-bullfighting region'. The year 2010 could witness Barcelona's last season of tauromachy.

Is bullfighting a cruel spectacle or an ancient and noble tradition? The answer often depends on where you are in the country.

The Catalan anti-bullfight motion has passed successfully through the Catalan Parliament and only awaits final approval and legal enactment. Meanwhile Barcelona's Plaza de Toros Monumental, once Spain's second most important bullring, may have seen its last season.

Spain is a country of striking natural contrasts, contained by the windswept shores of Finisterre (which means the end of the earth) in the far west and the placid coastline of the Mediterranean in the east, and by the vast mountain ranges of the Pyrenees in the north and the Sierra Nevada in the south. It is defined as much by the rugged beaches of the Costa Brava and the ancient forests of Galicia as by the flat, arid plains of La Mancha. Europe's third largest country is a beautiful, dramatic place that has inspired painters and poets for centuries. The area's wildlife includes the Iberian lynx, considered Europe's most scarce wild cat, and the more humble, yet also endangered, Spanish donkey. The economic boom of the 1960s and the demands of an unfettered travel industry, as well as Spain's rapid evolution from a rural society to a resource-hungry industrial economy, has left its mark on the environment. Only recently has Spain come to regard its natural inheritance as something to be nurtured and protected.

OCEAN

The Blue Flag is an EU-supported initiative that marks out the best beaches and marinas in Europe and South Africa, judging them on their amenities, services, environmental friendliness and cleanliness.

Currently 493 beaches and 78 marinas on the Spanish coastline have been awarded a Blue Flag, and the difference between having one and not having one can be the difference between a large slice of the tourist pie or remaining in relative anonymity.

There are seven Blue Flag beaches in Barcelona and two in Sitges, and Blue Flags have also been awarded to several beaches in some of the heavily visited tourist areas, such as Benidorm, Marbella, Málaga, Alicante, Zapillo in Almería and Cortadura in Cádiz.

Clockwise from left to right *A deserted beach on the wild coast of the Costa de la Muerte near Finisterre; a photogenic goat at the Sierra de Aitana Safari Park; the pink-tinged Isla de Portichol lies offshore from Cabo de San Martin, Costa Blanca*

WILDLIFE

On a cold winter morning in 2001 shepherd Pep Colell awoke to find his flock of sheep had been mauled by a wild animal. He soon found out who was to blame for this mishap: During the previous year, the government had re-introduced wolves to the Pyrenees in an effort to return these reviled but often misunderstood creatures to their natural habitat. Wolves once roamed freely here, living off the livestock that was sent out to pasture by the local population, who regarded these predators with fear and disgust. However, due to the destruction of the wolves' natural environment, they were all but wiped out. The reintroduction campaign began with five pairs, and to the delight of ecologists (but not the farmers) it has been successful. It is estimated that the Iberian wolf population is now stable, with 1,500 to 2,000 wandering northern Spain.

DOÑANA

The Parque Nacional de Doñana, in western Andalucía, is Europe's pitstop for migrating birds. Spanning more than 300,000ha (741,300 acres) of virgin forest, marshland and sand dunes, it is the largest of Spain's 13 protected national parks.

Doñana's position as the last undeveloped territory at the end of the European continent makes it the perfect place for migrating birds to stop off for food and rest on their journey to Africa for the winter. Ornithologists have been noticing unusual amounts of southern hemisphere species in Doñana, including buzzards, flamingos and African spoonbills.

It seems that due to the effects of global warming, and perhaps to the attractions of the national park terrain, many of Europe's migrating birds have decided to cut their journey short and take their winter break here instead.

ABANDONED VILLAGES

'Abandoned village needs owner,' read an advertisement in Spain's national press. The village of Matillas in the region of León came with a number of old, empty farmhouses, a functioning well and a small chapel. The only drawback was its isolated situation and complete lack of amenities.

There are about 3,000 empty villages like Matillas around Spain, victims of the unstoppable demographic transformation of Spanish society from a collection of villages to a modern, urban country.

Many of these villages, such as Cantabria's Bárcena Mayor in the valley of the Saja river, have been restored as summer sanctuaries and second homes by affluent urbanites.

Nearly 80 per cent of Spain's population now live in cities, compared with around 45 per cent at the beginning of the 20th century, leading to steep increases in property prices and lower standards of living in the cities.

AGRICULTURE

Next time you enjoy a plate of Spanish tomatoes in winter, spare a thought for where they came from. Almería has become the greenhouse of Europe, as vast tracts of sheeting stretch like a huge sea of plastic across the landscape, allowing the intensive farming of fruit and vegetables year-round. This is an arid land that film-makers have often used as a stand-in for the deserts of Egypt or Mexico (director Sergio Leone's spaghetti westerns should perhaps have been called paella westerns), but whose climate guarantees sunshine almost every day.

Intensive farming has undoubtedly brought wealth to the region, but the 30,000ha (74,130 acres) of plastic greenhouses have brought problems, too. Apart from the eyesore factor, environmentalists point out that the demands of such intensive farming, especially the contamination of scarce water supplies, could lead to the destruction of the region's ecosystem forever.

The extraordinary cave paintings discovered in 1879 at Altamira, in the north, have been called the Sistine Chapel of palaeontological art. Clearly, Spain's intimate relationship with the visual arts goes back a long way. Spain has always been a country of great artistic energy. Its artists, inspired perhaps by the sharp clarity of Spanish light and by the dramatic landscapes, as well as by its turbulent, multicultural history, have been at the forefront of artistic innovation for centuries. In Spain, the need to build and the search for beauty seem to go hand in hand. The Moorish occupation left several perfect structures dotted across the south of the peninsula, notably the imposing Alhambra in Granada and the profusion of arches of the mosque at Córdoba. The rest of the country is studded with jewels of Romanesque and Gothic architecture; it has more UNESCO World Heritage Sites than any other European nation. Today Spain's artists, architects and filmmakers infuse their work with a sense of their rich cultural heritage, creating new visions that remain at the cutting edge of artistic achievement.

DALÍ—A SURREAL MUSEUM

Surrealism may have been invented in Paris, but an ordinary town in northern Catalonia claims to be its true home. The Dalí Museum in Figueres (▷ 259) attracts about a million visitors a year, intrigued by the man who turned Surrealism from an élite revolutionary manifesto into a mass-market phenomenon, while keeping its tongue firmly lodged in its cheek. Salvador Dalí (1904–89) was born in Figueres, and despite touring the world, he never underplayed the influence of his birthplace on his art.

The Dalí Museum displays some of his emblematic works and is one of Catalonia's most visited museums, a Surrealist theme park with giant eggs, flying Cadillacs, and a red sofa in the shape of Mae West's lips.

Clockwise from left to right *The Basque sculptor Agustín Ibarrola's painted forest in Oma; Pedro Almodóvar, the Spanish film director whose unique style has brought admiration from Hollywood; Pablo Picasso, c1937*

THE PICASSO INDUSTRY

In 2000 Citroën introduced its new car: the Citroën Picasso. An offended art world was quick to point out that the great man never owned a car, let alone endorsed one, but that didn't stop it becoming a best seller worldwide.

Picasso's unmatched influence on the world of art has almost as much to do with his image as with his work. The diminutive Andalucian used a curious mix of machismo, arrogance and aesthetics to become the ultimate figure of the artist as superman.

Picasso the brand is a more recent phenomenon. His eye for an iconic image — the dove of peace, for example — has meant that his prints have outsold those by any other artist. It is a small step from the print to the T-shirt, but from there to the perfume (Paloma Picasso), the cognac (Hennesey) or the car takes more of a leap of the imagination.

LAS MENINAS

What is the greatest painting ever created? An impossible question and one that is open to great subjective interpretation, but many Spanish art historians think they have the answer: *Las Meninas* (The Maids of Honour), the informal portrait of the daughter of King Philip IV, with her maids of honour, by the Spanish artist Velázquez (1599–1660).

The painting is a playful and technically brilliant meditation on the role of the artist as the creator of reality and of the spectator as a participant in that reality. A trip to the Prado in Madrid (▷ 74–76) will quickly confirm its popularity, as hordes of camera-toting visitors, wide-eyed art students and security guards surround the painting from dawn to dusk, while its subjects — the princess and the artist, who has painted himself into the scene — gaze back implacably across the centuries.

AGUSTÍN IBARROLA'S ENCHANTED FOREST

If you stumble across a forest where the trees take on strange forms, their bark covered in swirls that sometimes become eyes or rainbows, don't worry, you haven't entered an enchanted forest, you are in Agustín Ibarrola's biggest work of art. Ibarrola (born 1930) is the last surviving member of the extraordinary generation of Basque sculptors, including Eduardo Chillida (1924–2002) and Jorge Oteiza (1908–2002), who found a new sculptural language by fusing organic forms with twisted metal and rough stone. Critics have identified this art form with the Basque love of nature and tradition. Ibarrola's forest, in Oma, is his attempt to create a dialogue between man and nature. Politics have often interrupted him, as his stand against the violence of Basque separatist terrorism has led to attacks on the forest.

ALL ABOUT ALMODÓVAR

From a small town in the region of La Mancha, principally famous for its cheese and windmills, a shy young man went to Madrid to work for a telephone company. Pedro Almodóvar was overweight and overwhelmed by the Madrid of *la movida*, the heady atmosphere that surrounded the post-Franco nightlife in the capital. Yet he soon began to revel in the sense of freedom and to nurture ambitions of directing movies. With a 16mm camera and the help of a new-found circle of friends, Pedro began to shoot his first film, a depiction of the lively urban characters he had befriended.

Flash forward 30 years and Pedro Almodóvar has Hollywood at his feet, has created a unique cinematic style and even become an adjective used to describe the combination of contained hysteria and melodrama that is key to his work.

The happy-go-lucky, fiesta-loving Spaniard of popular imagination is a dying breed in a country with one of the most turbulent economies in Europe and steep rises in the cost of living. Cultural shifts caused by demographic changes, immigration, the social position of women and a highly competitive workplace that no longer accepts *trabajo fijo* (a job for life) have rendered obsolete the image of Spain as a country that moves at a different, slower rhythm from the rest of Europe. But Spain is, and has always been, a country that thrives on deep contradictions. The religious fervour of the millions who greeted Pope John Paul II on his visit to Madrid in 2003 contrasts with the minor role that the church now plays in Spanish society. The family continues to be at the heart of Spanish life, with more than 15 per cent of families caring for an older relative and the majority of young people staying at home into their 30s, yet Spain has been at the forefront of legislation allowing same-sex marriages. Spaniards go to the theatre as much as to the bullfight and take vacations in places such as Prague as frequently as driving to the south of Spain. But a closer look at these changes shows that many of them are only skin-deep. It is perhaps impossible to understand Spaniards in the 21st century without understanding their history and cultural traditions.

SIESTA

It seems that the Spanish have always practised that sacred ritual of slumber that divides the working day into two manageable chunks, thanks to the traditional two-hour lunch break and the fact that time still seems to stand still between 2 and 4pm across the country.

Spain is not totally immune to the yuppie. Dr. Ignacio Buqueras i Bach of the Fundació Europea is an anti-siesta activist who says that Spain needs to ditch the midday shutdown in order to increase its level of productivity and improve business with countries that adhere to the 9–5 standard. Of course the fact that Spaniards on average sleep an hour less than their European counterparts means the siesta is more than a cultural relic. It's often a necessity.

Clockwise from left to right *Tarifa is only a few kilometres from Africa; an ornate statue of the Madonna and Child in Barcelona; King Juan Carlos I and Queen Sofia*

LA MUJER

Spain is a notoriously matriarchal society, where the most fervent prayers are saved for *La Virgen* (The Virgin Mary), and the importance of the mother figure cuts across all social classes. This idealization of women has often gone hand in hand with social and political repression, particularly in rural areas, where images of black-clad widows and poorly paid menial workers have endured.

Yet, arguably it is women who have most benefited from the dramatic changes that have taken place in Spanish society, where old taboos about women's role in the workplace have been swept aside in the more recent past.

Spain now has one of the lowest birth rates in Europe, an indication that most young women have chosen to put their career ahead of having a family.

PATERAS

Spain's most attractive beaches are also the setting for some of its saddest stories. Tarifa, the most southerly point in mainland Spain, and a magnet for windsurfers and for those who like their beaches wild and untouched, is only 15km (9 miles) from the African coast. However, that short distance was too far for the estimated 4,000 Africans who have died in the last five years in attempts to reach Europe by sea in makeshift crafts.

Spain has always been a bridge between civilizations, yet immigration is a fairly new phenomenon, as it is only in the last 20 years (during which it is estimated that the immigrant population has quadrupled) that many economic migrants have opted to make Spain their final destination, instead of a means of getting farther north.

THE PINK PRESS

All the rage on Spanish television in 2010, *Survivors* marooned a group of people on an island where one of them was voted out every week. *Mujeres Ricas (Rich Women)* is another hot new series showcasing interviews with the affluent.

Spain's gossip has been maintained by the classic magazines *HOLA!* and *Pronto*, with their TV equivalent *Corazón Corazón*. The public has also flocked towards salacious magazines such as *Cuore* and TV shows like *Sálvame/ Sálvame Deluxe* starring Belen Esteban as the 'Queen of the People'.

This circle is kept in motion by the *prensa rosa* (pink press), hugely popular gossip magazines, and the television shows that entertain millions. The need for a constant supply of celebrities to populate these magazines and TV shows suggests that Andy Warhol's theory of universal 15-minute fame may be coming true.

THE KING AND I

In a country not known for respect for people in power, criticism of the king is rare. This is probably because, to many Spaniards, Juan Carlos I (*b*1938) embodies the spirit of the *transición* — Spain's evolution from dictatorship to democracy. Ironically, it was dictator General Franco (1892–1975) who decided that the young prince would prove a suitable successor to carry on his vision of Spain as a Catholic dictatorship. However, Juan Carlos played his cards well. When he took over from Franco in 1975, he revealed that Spain would be a constitutional monarchy with the king as a figurehead rather than a politician.

Juan Carlos's decisive role in preserving the Spanish democracy during the unsuccessful military uprising of 1981 along with his easygoing personality have enabled him to maintain his popularity through a dynamic period of Spain's history.

Spain's economy has fallen on hard times since the World Bank declared it the eighth largest in the world in 2005. In 2007 the annual growth rate stood at 2.9 per cent and Spain appeared to be catching up with the traditional economic powerhouses in the north of Europe. After joining the European Community (now the European Union) in 1986, Spain's economy experienced a decade of growth that reached the economic goals required for joining the Euro currency in 2002. Since then, with Spain's property sector in crisis, unemployment has risen from 7.6 per cent in 2006 to a staggering 19.5 per cent in December of 2009. Comparisons with the economic woes of Greece persist. Spain's debt is lower than Greece's as a percentage of GDP, but its high unemployment rate combined with a stagnant real estate market indicate that Spain will take longer to pull out if its present economic crisis. Meanwhile, bright spots such as Bilbao continue to boom, with new construction projects by famous architects materializing almost daily, while Barcelona's new W Hotel towers sail-like over the waterfront since opening in October, 2009. Small, practical, technology-based enterprises such as Barcelona entrepreneur Ignacio Giral's www.mequedouno.com, an internet marketing service for sales of random objects from TVs to toothbrushes may yet save the day for Spain's struggling economy.

E-TRAVEL
Every year millions of tourists travel to Spain, the second most-visited country in the world, on one of the low-cost airlines. The trailblazer was easyJet, followed by Ryanair, who all but saved Catalonia's Girona airport from bankruptcy.

Cut-price airlines now account for more than half of the national market, but price wars between carriers and hotels, with the internet as their motor, is not all good news for an industry that employs 15 per cent of the country's workforce. The Spanish Tourist Board is critical of the current 'more for less' ethos. 'Spain needs to become an expensive tourist destination,' says its CEO Raimon Martínez Fraile. 'Those in the industry should not drop their prices, but offer higher quality instead.'

Clockwise from left to right *Colourful fishing boats at Cudillero; waterfall at Hotel Hacienda Na Xamena, Ibiza; Zara store in El Diagonal, Barcelona; a fisherman mending his net on a beach in the Costa del Sol*

ZARA

On 23 May 2001 Andrés Ortega became the richest man in Spain when his extraordinarily successful firm, Inditex, which includes Zara, the world's biggest clothing chain, was floated on the Madrid stock exchange.

Ortega opened the first Zara in 1975 in A Coruña, and there are now more than 1,060 shops in 68 countries, and hundreds more outlets selling the offshoot men's, children's and homeware lines.

Yet, despite being one of the richest men in the world, Ortega is a mystery. He has very rarely given interviews and until recently there were no known photographs of him. He lives in a modest apartment, only occasionally paying surprise visits to the local factory to make sure things run smoothly.

'FROM BAGS TO RICHES'

Barcelona advertises its events through PVC banners and flags hung from lampposts and buildings across Spain's cultural capital. Thirty thousand square metres (322,800sq ft) of this plastic was used in 2004 alone, but thanks to the local design outfit Demano, a large percentage is saved from the landfill and used as the base material for its cult range of bags, each named after a famous Barcelonese street.

From a humble cottage industry, started in 1999 by designers Eleonora Parachini, Marcela Manrique and Liliana Andrade, Demano now produces thousands of colourful items a month, sold in outlets from New York to Japan. The range now also includes canvas saved from building rehabilitation.

EXPAT ECONOMY

The Spanish housing boom of the 1990s and the first years of this century were both based on and contributed to the growth of the Spanish economy.

For more than 200,000 EU citizens, affordable property and an unbeatable climate helped to establish important concentrations of primarily German, Dutch and British nationals in areas such as the Costa Brava, the Balearic Islands and the Costa del Sol.

This investment was never embraced by local residents who found themselves priced out of their own homes in annual property value leaps of more than 50 per cent. The market eventually stagnated when prices reached prohibitive levels and mortgages began to outstrip property values, causing buyers to turn their attention to cheaper parts of Europe such as Portugal, Croatia, or Turkey. After bottoming out in late 2009, Spain's economy stabilized in the first quarter.

PRESTIGE AND THE FISHING INDUSTRY

Apart from being the worst ecological disaster to strike Europe since Chernobyl, the sinking of the Prestige oil tanker off the coast of Galicia in 2002 also showed how dependent the local economy is on the fishing industry. The wild seas off the coast here are some of Europe's most important fishing areas, while the rocky coastlines and estuaries provide a rich stock of shellfish. More than 12 per cent of the area's population rely on the fishing industry for their income, including a wide range of support industries. After the Prestige disaster, the government introduced a compensation scheme aimed at re-activating the local economy, and some more lateral thinking fishing communities have lowered their own quotas and implemented direct-to-public marketing schemes in the hope of achieving a more sustainable sea for future generations.

The sounds of Spain are diverse, and every region has its own rich musical tradition. Celtic bagpipes are played in Santiago—the capital of Galicia—while Islamic-influenced melodies are performed by gypsy musicians in Andalucía. Some pieces of music instantly evoke the popular essence of Spain, as with Joaquín Rodrigo's 1940 *Concierto de Aranjuez*, the 1925 *Andaluzas* by Enric Granados or the paso dobles that are improvised at bullfights and local fiestas. Musicians such as the legendary classical guitarist Andrés Segovia (1894–1987) or the cellist Pablo (Pau) Casals (1876–1973) became internationally famous, using their musical heritage within a wider European classical tradition. Flamenco is a wholly Spanish phenomenon that sprang up amid the poorest communities, a music of intense emotional complexity that would surprise those who have only experienced the watered-down version available in the tourist *tablaos* (flamenco bars). Since the days of the catchy summer hit *¡Y Viva España!* in 1973, Spanish pop has tended to lag behind the rest of Europe, copying rather than innovating, but it began to establish a voice of its own in the 1980s and has now adapted to new musical tendencies, with major festivals and recording artists, such as pop sensation Enrique Iglesias, at the forefront of the music scene.

Clockwise from left to right *Musicians play in Plaça de les Olles, Barcelona; Jordi Savall performs at the Fez Festival of World Sacred Music in 2010; the dramatic and passionate flamenco is centuries old*

CAMARON DE LA ISLA
In flamenco, suffering and music are fused to create a sound that expresses the deepest emotions. The *cante jondo* (deep song) is a vocal style that lays bare the singer's soul, a breathless attack on all notes of the musical scale that can sound like a controlled scream of pain. It is said that to sing true flamenco you must have suffered.

Camaron de la Isla is widely regarded as the greatest singer of the *cante jondo* in recent times. He was born into a poor, gypsy family, but his uncompromising vocal style earned him fame and fortune. Happiness was to elude him, however, and after a lifetime of excess he died of a drug overdose in 1992 aged 41.

IBIZA

Dancers at the coolest parties in London during the late 1980s noticed a new sound in the town: Balearic beat, a mix of soul, reggae and early Chicago house that was popular in the clubs of Ibiza. This hedonistic musical style helped to kickstart a revolution in British nightlife which was followed by the rest of Europe, and which has made Ibiza the world capital for DJs, music producers and lovers of dance music.

Twenty years on, the club scene on Ibiza has become a phenomenon (not always welcomed), with a million 20-something visitors cramming on to this small Mediterranean island every summer, many of them to hear the world's leading DJs in clubs like Space, Privilege, Amnesia and Pacha.

OPERA SINGERS

While the greatest composers have come from other parts of Europe, Spain has always had a strong tradition of singers who have made their names in some of the world's toughest opera houses, maybe due to the special feeling that Spaniards have for strong tones and melody.

The 20th century saw the emergence of two of opera's greatest voices: Plácido Domingo (b1941) from Madrid, famous for his roles in Puccini and Verdi operas, and José Carreras (b1946) from Barcelona, who had made his debut in London in 1974.

They soon became regarded, alongside Italy's late, great Luciano Pavarotti (1935–2007), as the greatest tenors of the age, rivals in the world of opera until they became the Three Tenors.

JORDI SAVALL & COMPANY

Viola de gamba master Jordi Savall, born in Barcelona in 1941, became early music's first star during the first decade of the 21st century, performing with his wife, soprano Montserrat Figueras, children Arianna and Ferran Savall, and their groups La Capella Reial de Catalunya Hesperion XXI and Le Concert des Nations. From research to recording fame the Savall dynasty reaches directly for the spirit through hauntingly intercultural music performed amid dazzling architecture.

'The synagogue of Toledo, the Cordoba mosque, the Cistercian Abbey of Narbonne are all absolute works of art,' explains Savall. 'Music can touch the universal human soul beyond individual religious beliefs…we try to transmit a universal spiritual message.'

'MIX IT UP'

The country's ever-more-varied ethnic melting pot has led to a new musical genre—*mestizaje*—or 'mix of styles'. The pioneers were Ketama, the Madrid-based band of gypsies whose elegant fusion of flamenco and jazz rhythms became the soundtrack of late 1990s Spain.

Mano Chao, a French-born Barcelona resident, set the tone for the new wave with 2000's Clandestino, a blend of reggae, rap, mariachi and flamenco that became an international best seller.

Ojos de Brujo are the current darlings of world music enthusiasts. Their combination of visceral Spanish rock and hip-hop is a dominant feature of their music. Spanish rap in general has come of age with outfits such as Solo Los Solo, and Arabic-Spanish music is heard from Cheb Balowski and 08001.

There is a popular myth that when two or more Spaniards get together they are either planning their local fiesta or having it. It is certainly true that no other European country has such a wealth of fiestas, a legacy of Spain's strong sense of rural tradition as well as the sociable nature of its people. Although many fiestas just look like a good excuse for a party, they often have a profound mystical, religious or historical significance. In Valencia, the *Fallas* (elaborate cardboard, wood and paper mâché sculptures) are burned in a celebration from medieval times announcing the arrival of spring. In Buñol, the Tomatina, where revellers pelt each other with fresh tomatoes, is a tradition whose origins remain a mystery—it's just good fun. The historical significance of Los Moros y Cristianos (Moors and Christians) fiesta is clear, as elaborately costumed villagers re-enact the surrender of the Moorish troops to the Catholic kings—but this being Spain, they end up dancing together. A more arcane tradition is the ritualized burial of the sardine that takes place across northern Spain to end the week-long festivities of Carnival, a fiesta suppressed by Franco due to its pagan origins, but are now major annual attractions in Cádiz and Sitges.

Above Left *The origins of Buñol's Tomatina are a mystery*
Above right *The running of the bulls in Pamplona*

DEATH IN THE MORNING

Like millions of his compatriots, American student Matthew Peter Tassio was fascinated by writer Ernest Hemingway's portrayal of thousands of young men wearing the distinctive red scarves and running with the bulls during Pamplona's San Fermín celebrations.

In his 1926 novel *The Sun Also Rises*, Hemingway (1899–1961) depicted the event as a drunken frolic and masculine rite of passage and described the unique cocktail of joy and adrenaline unleashed during the festivities that take over Pamplona, the capital of Navarra, in the second week of July.

Tassio, however, was seemingly unaware of the dangers involved and the skill needed to successfully guide a bull weighing 600kg (1,320lb) along the slippery, cobblestone streets, and he was struck down and killed by one of the beasts on 13 July 1995.

HE AIN'T HEAVY…

Semana Santa (Holy Week) provides the perfect opportunity for the Spanish to indulge their love of spectacle, as well as a chance to express the fascination with death and suffering that is evident in Spanish rituals.

During Easter, the huge baroque icons in churches are taken out and are paraded around the streets by groups of young men who are bent double under their weight.

In Seville it is considered to be a privilege to be part of the *cofradia* (the group that carries each statue) and only the strongest and most devoted men are chosen for the task. Much of Seville's social life revolves around the *cofradias* and *hermandades*, with coveted memberships passing down from generation to generation. These brotherhoods raise money for charities and disaster relief as well as participating in ceremonies and processions.

THE STORY OF SPAIN

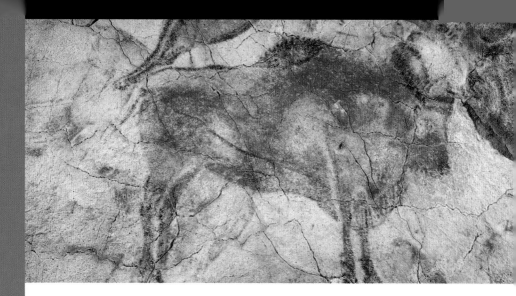

Bone fragments found in several locations in Spain suggest that humankind's remote ancestors wandered around here a million years ago. Their descendants, Stone Age cave-dwellers, created the fascinating cave drawings of Altamira, in Cantabria. By 1000BC, Iberian tribes were mingling with immigrant Celts. Phoenician traders landed in southern Spain and founded Gadir (Cádiz) in 1100BC. Their objective was gold and silver from the mines of the legendary kingdom of Tartessos. Greek colonists settled in Empúries, in the northeast, around 600BC. In 237BC the great Carthaginian general Hannibal (247–182BC) swept through Spain from North Africa and marched across Gaul (France) and the Alps to attack Rome in the Second Punic War. The Romans landed at Empúries in 218BC to cut him off from possible reinforcements. The plan worked. Carthage lost the war and by 206BC all Hispania (Spain) had become a Roman territory. Intermittent tribal revolts disturbed the peace until the empire crumbled in the fifth century. In AD410 the Vandals, a Germanic warrior tribe, wrought havoc in Spain. The Christianized Visigoths, pushed out of Gaul by the Franks, followed them, gradually taking control of the entire peninsula by the early seventh century.

VERY OLD MASTERS

In the 1870s Marcelino de Sautuola, a well-to-do Spaniard with a penchant for archaeology, started digging around in the caves of Altamira, west of Santander on the northern Spanish coast, and discovered the oldest Stone Age cave drawings ever seen.

The expressive but subtle red and black images of bison, horses, wild boar, deer and other creatures date at least to 12,000BC, possibly 20,000BC, and cover the walls and ceiling of an inner cave that has been nicknamed the Sistine Chapel of Prehistory.

Also depicted is a series of images of people and handprints of the artists. The semi-nomadic people who created these pictures lived by hunting the animals they drew, so perhaps they were sufficiently easy prey to allow them time for such artistic pursuits.

Clockwise from left to right *The Altamira cave paintings give a glimpse of Stone Age life and are recreated in the Neocueva at the Museo de Altamira; the remains of a Roman village at Castelló d'Empúries; the hump-backed Puente Romano at Cangas de Onís*

UNDERSTANDING   THE STORY OF SPAIN

FAMILY CONQUEST

In 218BC the Roman consul Publius Cornelius Scipio, having failed to engage Hannibal near Marseille, sent his army to Empúries in northeast Spain under the control of his brother, Gnaeus. A year later he joined Gnaeus and they marched south. All went well until the Carthaginians, led by Hasdrubal, launched a counter-offensive and in 211BC decimated the Romans, slaying the Scipio brothers.

Undeterred, the Romans came back for more. Publius's 25-year-old son, also called Publius, made a daring march south of the Ebro River in 209BC, took New Carthage and turned the tables. A brilliant general, the young Scipio also knew how to win hearts and minds. His generous treatment of the locals won them to his cause and by 206BC Hispania had passed to Rome.

THE CELTIBERIANS ARE REVOLTING

The Romans didn't have it all their own way, as Celt-iberian and Basque tribes frequently rose in revolt. In particular, the Celtiberian hill settlement of Numantia (Numancia) in northern Spain created a problem. In 137BC the Numantines captured a Roman army of 20,000 men, whom they spared after negotiating a peace treaty with their commander, Mancinus.

Imperial fury knew no bounds, however, and in 134BC Rome sent Scipio Aemilianus to put an end to the indigenous effrontery once and for all.

There was nothing gentle about Scipio, who had already razed Carthage to the ground. He besieged Numantia, starved its inhabitants out (most preferred to take their own lives rather than fall into Roman hands) and then destroyed the town.

SPANIARDS GO TO ROME

In return for gold (spectacular Roman mines survive at Las Médulas), grain and conscripts, Rome granted Spain the Pax Romana (Peace of Rome). Many Spanish families flourished in this environment and brought forth great names like Trajan. Lucius Annaeus Seneca the Younger (4BC–AD65), born in Córdoba, was a gifted philosopher and a humane politician. Tutor to Emperor Nero, he later all but ruled in his name.

The good times ended when he and his poet nephew Lucan (cAD39–65) were forced to commit suicide after conspiring against the increasingly despotic Nero. Before his downfall, Seneca introduced celebrated Spanish poet Marcus Valerius Martialis, otherwise known as Martial (AD38–103), to court.

THE BARBARIANS BARGE IN

By AD410 Roman Hispania had all but ceased to exist. The Vandals pillaged their way south to dominate the southern Baetica province, which they called Vandalus (Land of the Vandals), and the Swabians occupied the northwest.

The Toulouse-based Visigoths, in the pay of the Romans, also ranged across the country bringing to heel these rival Germanic tribes, but it was only in the early sixth century, when the Franks crushed them in Gaul, that they made a serious move south. Toledo became their capital and by AD624 they had taken control of the entire peninsula. But Visigothic Spain was fragile. Succession to the throne usually took place amid a bloodbath and the economy was at a standstill. Spain was ripe for invasion.

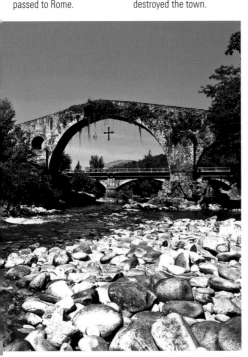

From the Arabian desert burst forth an unprecedented crusade in the early eighth century as armies of a new faith, Islam, blitzed across the Middle East and North Afria. In 711 they attacked Spain and swept away all before them until halted by the Franks at Poitiers in France in 732. Pockets of Spanish territory escaped Moorish occupation and by 801 the Franks had helped push them out of Barcelona. In 929 Emir Abd ar-Rahman III declared Al-Andalus (Muslim Spain) a Caliphate (Muslim state) and his capital, Córdoba, entered its golden age. Western Europe's most dazzling city, blessed with extraordinary monuments (in particular the Mezquita), an enormous library, luxuriant gardens and great wealth, attracted Arab, Jewish and Christian scholars alike. The Moors modernized Roman-era agriculture and introduced new foods such as oranges and rice. By 1031 the Caliphate had split into rival *taifas* (small kingdoms). The emboldened Christians then pounced from the north. Castile's leader, Alfonso VI, seized Toledo in 1085 and soon established control over other parts of central Spain. The Reconquista (Reconquest) was finally gathering momentum, but the Muslims would prove to be far from a spent force.

THE DEMISE OF BAD KING RODERICK

Legend has it that Visigothic King Roderick's biggest mistake was to rape a young damsel by the name of Florinda. Her father, Count Julian, wanted revenge and urged the Muslim governor of North Africa to raid Spain. In AD711 Tariq ibn Ziyad, governor of Tangier, landed with 10,000 troops, mostly Berbers, at the promontory that was later named after him—Jebel Tariq (known today as Gibraltar). He was confronted by what Muslim chroniclers described as a 90,000-strong Christian host. Roderick watched from an ivory throne as Tariq spurred on his troops with the promise of paradise and a warning that to the rear lay only defeat and the sea. 'God is Great!' they cried and carried the day.

Clockwise from left to right *Córdoba's Great Mosque is supported by more than 850 columns of granite, jasper and marble; the pilgimage cathedral of Santiago de Compostela rises above the pantiled rooftops; Gibraltar was named Jebel ('mountain' in Arabic) Tariq, after the general who led the 711 invasion*

THE WAY OF ST. JAMES THE MOOR-SLAYER

In AD42 disciples of the apostle St. James (Santiago; see below) whisked away their master's decapitated corpse from Palestine, following his execution by Herod Agrippa. It is said they landed at Padrón, in Galicia. There the saint was buried and forgotten until in 810 word spread that his remains had been unearthed. These were dark days for Spain's Christians, but miraculously, St. James's ghost started appearing on the battlefields, riding boldly through Moorish lines, slaughtering the enemies of Christ.

The church of Santiago de Compostela was founded where the saint was buried and has become the most revered European site of Christian pilgrimage after Rome. Medieval hoteliers did brisk business with the devout of Europe along the arduous Camino de Santiago (Road to Santiago).

MEDIEVAL MUSINGS ON ARISTOTLE

Abu Walid Muhammad ibn Rushd (1126–98), known in the West as Averroës, was one of the greatest thinkers in Al-Andalus (Muslim Spain), but largely ignored in the Islamic world. Versed in law, medicine and theology, he also attained the post of first doctor in the court of Caliph Abu Yaqub Yusuf in 1182. Averroës, a senior official in Córdoba and Seville, wrote extensive commentaries on Aristotle and, in *On the Harmony of Religions and Philosophy*, explored the nature of reason and faith.

However, Orthodox Muslims regarded his intellectual dabblings as dangerous and he was exiled in 1195.

Snubbed by Islamic co-religionists, his writings were translated into Latin and were then debated enthusiastically by many prominent European thinkers during the 13th and 14th centuries.

THE SCOURGE OF GOD

Muhammad ibn Ami Amir (938–1002) rose from obscurity to become the senior adviser to Caliph al-Hakam II. He committed adultery with the Caliph's wife, and was mentor to al-Hakam's son, Hisham.

After al-Hakam's death, Muhammad's relationship with the young new caliph, Hisham, aided his wide military ambitions.

Taking the name Al-Mansour (the Victorious), he launched 52 campaigns against the Christians, sacking cities from Barcelona to Santiago de Compostela. He was never defeated.

At night during the campaigns his servants would collect battlefield dust from his clothes. When the Scourge of God, as Castile's King Alfonso X later named him, died, he was buried and sprinkled with that same earth.

THE LIFE OF EL CID

To the Moors he was El Cid (Lord), to the Spaniards he was El Campeador (heroic warrior), and to Hollywood he was great movie material. Born Rodrígo Díaz de Vivar, near Burgos in 1043, he backed the wrong side in the succession squabble of Castile after Ferdinand I's death in 1065. He was banished in 1076 and embarked on a mercenary career, employed by Moorish or Christian princes, whichever suited him. Finally, tiring of adventures, he settled in the seaside city of Valencia, which he first had to wrest from the Moors in 1094, and remained the city's lord and master until his death in 1099.

His tale inspired the epic *Poema de Mio Cid* and, in 1636, French dramatist Pierre Corneille (1606–84) wrote *Le Cid*, a masterpiece of French classical tragedy.

The fall of Toledo shook the Seville *taifa* (small kingdom) into turning to the fanatical Almoravid rulers of Morocco for aid. Their arrival in 1091, followed by the Almohads (a Muslim movement from the Atlas Mountains in North Africa) around 1160, blunted the Christian sword. In the north, Catalonia and Aragón joined under the Crown of Aragón in 1137. Aragón had taken Zaragoza from the Moors, but then the Almohads swept the Castilian army away in the Battle of Alarcos in 1195. The shock prompted the creation of a coalition of Christian kings under the leadership of Alfonso VIII of Castile, which struck back in 1212 in the Battle of Navas de Tolosa, the turning point in the Reconquista (Reconquest). The Christians had to move quickly. In 1229, James I of Aragón seized the Balearic Islands from the Moors; Castile took Córdoba, followed by Seville; and by 1248 all of Valencia had fallen to James. Portugal followed and Al-Andalus was reduced to the Emirate of Granada, ruled from the sumptuous Alhambra. An outbreak of the plague in 1348 and again in the 1380s totally crippled the country. Civil wars rocked Catalonia and later Castile. Finally Isabella of Castile married Ferdinand of Aragón in 1469, and together, under the name of the Catholic Monarchs, they assaulted the last Muslim redoubt of Granada in 1492 and unified Spain.

Clockwise from left to right *A 13th-century depiction of troops en route to the Crusades; Las Damas Tower at the Alhambra Palace in Granada; the 12th-century Pont Vell spans the River Ter at Besalú*

THE TERUEL LOVERS

In Teruel they tell the tale of Isabel de Segura and the penniless Juan de Marcilla.

When Juan's request to marry Isabel was turned down in 1212 by her father, he left to seek his fortune, with a promise that she would wait five years for him to return wealthy.

The five years passed and Isabel married another. Juan returned, rich and famous, and begged her for one kiss. The chaste Isabel refused his request and Juan, heartbroken, died on the spot.

At his funeral a veiled woman slumped over his coffin. People who tried to pull her up found she had died — it was Isabel. They were buried together.

LEARNED ALFONSO AND THE BIRTH OF SPANISH

Alfonso X (1221–84) could hardly have guessed that the rough Castilian tongue he promoted over Latin would one day become Spanish, the world's third most spoken language after Chinese and English. Dubbed El Sabio (the Learned), Alfonso presided over a cultural flowering. He gave Salamanca University its charter and established the prestigious Toledo School of Translators. Here, Christian and Jewish intellectuals translated great Arabic works, ranging from astronomy to poetry, into Castilian. Alfonso started work on a vernacular history of Spain and wrote numerous songs—he considered himself an accomplished troubadour (folksinger). He also realized that to cement monarchical power required centralization and national unity, for which a national culture was indispensable. The vehicle for this would be a new Castilian literature.

THE DARING DEEDS OF JAMES I

Count-King James I (1213–76) of Catalonia and Aragón, known as *El Conqueridor* (The Conqueror), embarked on a campaign of conquest that converted Spain's northeastern confederated kingdom into a thriving and successful Mediterranean trade empire.

To open the way for Barcelona's mercantile ambitions, he seized Mallorca from its Moorish masters in 1229, forcing open a passage east to Italy.

Six years later Ibiza and Formentera fell. Next he turned his attention south to the wealthy Moorish kingdom of Valencia and by 1245 it was his.

So impressed was James with his own feats that he wrote *El Llibre dels Fets (The Book of Deeds)*. His successors, Peter II (1240–85) and Alfonso III (1265–91), were chips off the old block, respectively adding the Mediterranean islands of Menorca and Sicily to the spoils.

THE ETERNAL UNREST OF COUNT ARNAU

Catalán ballads from the Pyrenees relate the tale of the wicked Count Arnau of Mataplana, probably a mythical character, but thought by some to have lived in the 13th century.

Like many political masters before and since, Arnau abused his position of power to satisfy his sexual appetite. He was a particular fan of the convent of Sant Joan de les Abadesses, where he regularly romped with the abbess. Then the evil count fell in love with a local girl who sought refuge in, of all places, the convent. When Arnau cornered his unsuspecting prey, she died of fright. Suddenly consumed by remorse, the lascivious noble retired to the mountains and, so the story goes, his eternally damned soul still rides at night by the full moon.

THE SURRENDER OF BOABDIL

On 2 January 1492, Boabdil, the last Moorish ruler of the Emirate of Granada, descended from the dazzling Alhambra Palace to hand over the keys of his besieged city to the Catholic Monarchs, Ferdinand and Isabella. As Boabdil turned to look back, his mother, Sultana Aixa, delivered her legendary "You weep like a woman for what you could not defend as a man". After almost 800 years Muslim rule in Spain had ended.

Boabdil was guaranteed safe conduct to Morocco, and Muslims who stayed behind were granted freedom of worship—a promise soon broken. The Catholic Monarchs brought the chains from freed Christian prisoners from Granada to Toledo, where they still hang in the church of San Juan de los Reyes.

SPAIN AT ITS ZENITH

Shortly after the fall of Granada the Catholic Monarchs Ferdinand and Isabella were in ebullient mood, and in April 1492 they commissioned Christopher Columbus to sail west in search of the East. What he found was a whole new world, the Americas, and the first Spanish colonies were soon set up in Cuba and Hispaniola (Dominican Republic). That same year, Ferdinand and Isabella expelled from Spain all Jewish residents who did not convert to Christianity. About 200,000 left. Carlos I (1500–56), grandson of Isabella and Ferdinand, ascended the throne in 1516. Three years later he inherited the Austro-Hungarian Habsburg crown, and became Charles V, Holy Roman Emperor. His lands stretched from Austria across Germany to the Netherlands, from Burgundy to Spain, and to America. His reign was also the time of the Conquistadores, starting with Hernán Cortés, who conquered the Aztecs in Mexico in 1520. Others followed, taking what would become Chile, Ecuador, Colombia and Texas. American gold and silver, new crops (potatoes and tomatoes) and chocolate poured into Spain. Charles presided over the expansion of the greatest empire ever seen. Spanish armies were universally feared, but his constant European wars bled Spain's coffers.

THE INQUISITION, JEWS AND WITCHES

Fray Tomás de Torquemada (1420–98) was Queen Isabella's confessor when Pope Sixtus IV appointed him as head of the Castilian Inquisition in 1483. Its charter was to root out heresy and Torquemada was behind the decision to expel Jewish residents from Spain in 1492; a curious act, since he was the son of *conversos*, Jewish converts to Christianity.

He presided over many harsh trials, and the Inquisition became feared for its liberal use of torture and *autos da fé*, the ritual burning at the stake of heretics. There were some chilling cases: In 1612, 40 Basque women accused of witchcraft were hauled before the Inquisitorial tribunal of Logroño. Twelve of the women were burned at the stake.

Clockwise from left to right *Explorer Christopher Columbus is commemorated by this column in Barcelona; Queen Isabella interviews Christopher Columbus; Hernán Cortés, conquerer of Mexico*

UNDERSTANDING THE STORY OF SPAIN

THE QUEEN IS QUITE MAD

Queen Isabella's daughter, Juana, would have preferred a contemplative life in a monastery, but instead her stern parents had her married to a Habsburg prince, Philip the Handsome (Felipe el Hermoso), Duke of Burgundy, in 1496. The marriage was a success in some ways—they had six children—but Philip was renowned for his infidelity, and Juana became extremely jealous. It is even said she would permit only unattractive women to serve in the palace in case Philip's eye roved.

Called on to succeed her mother in 1504, Juana returned to Spain from Flanders with her ambitious husband, who declared his wife mad. Philip's death in 1507 didn't help matters as Juana took to touring around with his coffin. She was eventually locked up in the small town of Tordesillas, where she languished for 46 years.

CORTÉS AND THE AZTECS

Hernán Cortés (1485–1547), privateer and adventurer, landed in Mexico in 1519. When he reached Tenochtitlán, the Aztec capital and the present location of Mexico City, he stood transfixed. A great temple dominated the biggest city in the world, which was home to around 200,000 inhabitants. The Spaniards found a complex society where gold was considered the excrement of the gods, bird feathers were prized as jewels and blood-curdling human sacrifices were a ritual part of life. Thinking Cortés a god, Emperor Moctezuma welcomed him and his men, who repaid his hospitality by slaughtering their hosts.

The Aztecs expelled the Spaniards from their lands in 1520, but Cortés returned the following year. Arrows proved no match for firearms and he quickly became governor of the new colonial territory.

THE REFORMING SAINT

At the age of seven St. Teresa de Ávila (1515–82) ran away with her brother, Rodrigo. Their intention was to head for Moorish lands and sacrifice themselves to Christ, but their uncle stopped them outside Ávila.

Thirteen years later Teresa joined the Carmelite order. After an inexplicable illness that left her paralyzed for three years, she had visions of Christ. Some of her confessors thought these were the work of the devil, but others believed her. Teresa decided her vocation was to reform the Carmelite order. The Carmelites were not amused, but in 1562 she founded the Carmelitas Descalzas (Shoeless Carmelites). The faithful take comfort from her spiritual texts, such as *The Interior Castle*. She died in Alba de Tormes and her remains lie in the convent church of La Anunciación.

EUROPE'S FIRST ENCOUNTER WITH CHOCOLATE

Hernán Cortés was one of the first Europeans to sip a bitter cocoa drink known as chocolate. Soon after he had subdued the Aztecs, cocoa bean shipments began to arrive in Spanish ports. Some of the first loads came to Galicia, and the Maragatos, people dedicated to the transport trade in northwest Spain, brought it to the town of Astorga. There the first Spanish chocolatiers, spotting a niche market, made drinking chocolate mixtures following mostly Aztec recipes.

This strange new beverage (the edible version came later), made of toasted and ground cocoa beans mixed with sugar, was for a long time the preserve of the rich, and until the 19th century Astorga remained the major Spanish base for its manufacture.

Felipe II (1527–98) inherited an enormous part of his father Charles V's empire: Spain, the Netherlands and the American colonies. Under his reign Spain expanded its American territories and, in 1580, absorbed Portugal. But Felipe also inherited a disastrous economy. War debts ate up most of the American gold and farmers suffered under heavy taxes. Commerce and banking were largely in foreign hands. In 1561 Felipe established the royal court permanently in the village of Madrid, but he was destined to keep warring. His troops put down rebellions in Andalucía and attempted to do the same in the Netherlands. In the Atlantic, English raiders harassed Spanish colonial shipping. When Elizabeth I started aiding the Dutch, Felipe ordered the invasion of England. The rout of the Spanish Armada in 1588 was the humiliating result. Despite these troubles, the Siglo de Oro (Golden Century) of Spanish arts began during Felipe's reign. Even after his death, as Spain's decline gathered pace under his ineffectual successors, Velázquez (1599–1660) was painting his best works and Cervantes (1547–1616) was writing his most mordant prose. In 1700 the last Spanish Habsburg ruler, Carlos II, died heirless.

ADVENTURES OF CERVANTES

Universally credited as the author of the first modern psychological novel, Cervantes suffered no shortage of grist for the mill. *Don Quixote* might be a grand tale, but the life of its creator, Miguel de Cervantes Saavedra (1547–1616), makes an even better read. At the age of 19 he was on the run, fleeing to Italy to avoid a term in prison for assault. He later lost the use of an arm in the Battle of Lepanto, took part in raids on Tunis and was captured by corsairs and sold into slavery in Algiers. Back in Spain in 1580, he was in and out of prison for unproven charges ranging from fraud to murder. After all the drama he settled in Madrid, where he spent his final years writing *Don Quixote*, which was published in 1605.

Clockwise from left to right *El Escorial was Felipe II's magnificent palace complex;* Don Quixote, *and his faithful squire Sancho Panza; the* Virgen de Guadalupe *is revered by pilgrims from around the world*

A GREEK IN TOLEDO

Cretan artist Domenikos Theotokopoulos (c1541–1614) took a gamble and went to Toledo in 1577, hoping to get a commission on El Escorial, Felipe II's palace northwest of Madrid. Although he had trained in Venice under Tintoretto, he was not chosen, but El Greco (The Greek), as he became known, decided to stay in Toledo. In Spain's religious capital there was no shortage of clients and money, and he was sufficiently possessed of confidence to command high prices for his unique, ethereal works.

He liked the high life, but things turned sour in later years as patrons became scarce, although possibly some of his best work dates from this period. Probably his most famous painting is the *Burial of Count Orgaz* (1586), in the church of Santo Tomé, Toledo.

DEMISE OF THE SPANISH ARMADA

On 21 July 1588, the invincible Armada left A Coruña on the Enterprise of England, due to meet up with the Duke of Parma's Flanders-based Spanish invasion force.

The Armada clashed with the English fleet in the first great naval battle of the modern era, but the duke's troops failed to show up.

On 7 August the English, led by Sir Francis Drake (c1540–96), launched fire ships towards the Spanish fleet off Calais. As chaos ensued, the nimble English vessels attacked the Spaniards. Outgunned, the Armada was forced by prevailing winds to sail through the Straits of Dover and beyond any possible meeting with Parma.

More than half the fleet was sunk by Atlantic gales on the ignominious journey back to Spain.

A DANGEROUS DREAM-WEAVER

In 1587 an obscure, 19-year-old Madrid maiden, Lucrecia de León, came to the royal court's attention for her extraordinary dreams, seemingly a portent of much evil that would befall Spain.

Don Alonso de Mendoza, a powerful cleric and not well disposed to King Felipe II, started transcribing the dreams.

In her apocalyptic reveries Lucrecia saw the lands of Spain overrun, foretold the demise of the Armada fleet and predicted an early end for an unjust Felipe. Was she really dreaming or was she part of an anti-royal plot?

The King's counsellors considered Lucrecia and her supporters to be a growing danger and the Inquisition imprisoned them in 1590. Five years later she received 100 lashes and was exiled from Madrid.

THE VANITY OF VELÁZQUEZ

Undoubtedly talented, Diego Velázquez (1599–1660), the Seville-born court artist, considered himself worthy of nobility. His extraordinary talent for realism made him the brightest star of the 17th-century Spanish artistic firmament. He depicted both kings and dwarfs with equal dignity and compassion. Probably his most celebrated work is *Las Meninas* (1656), a portrait of Philip IV's family (now in Madrid's Prado Museum, ▷ 74–76). It throws an interesting light on the character of the artist.

He spent years lobbying for a noble title—a daring request for a mere artist—and in *Las Meninas* he has the gall to depict himself with the royal family *and* adds to his vest the cross of the Order of Santiago! The hint was taken and he received his noble title just before his death.

Carlos II died childless and left the throne to a Frenchman, the Bourbon Philip V (1683–1746). Austria was displeased and launched the War of the Spanish Succession (1702–13), which resulted in Spain losing its Italian and Dutch territories, parts of Catalonia, Gibraltar and Menorca. Spain later became embroiled in the Napoleonic wars, at first siding with France and losing much of its navy in the 1805 Battle of Trafalgar. French troops occupied the country in 1808 and for five years Spanish irregulars fought alongside the Duke of Wellington to dislodge them. Throughout the 19th century the country was torn by conflict as conservatives battled liberals and republicans, and the Carlists (supporters of Carlos, pretender to the Spanish throne) started two civil wars over who should be king. The colonies deserted and the last of them—Cuba, Puerto Rico and the Philippines—were snapped up by the USA in a humiliating blow to the Spanish navy in 1898. Mining and industry were starting up in the Basque country and Catalonia, but with the inevitable prosperity came urban crowding, social unrest and the first stirrings of worker organizations.

MADRID'S BEST EVER MAYOR

Madrid remembers fondly the *rey-alcalde* (king-mayor) Carlos III, who brought enlightened rule from 1759 to 1788. He constructed roads, finished the Royal Palace, began a botanical garden and built the Palacio de Villanueva as a natural sciences museum (later the Prado, ▷ 74–76).

Best of all, he cleaned up the filthy streets (visitors had long remarked upon Madrid's stench). His minister, Squillace, promptly banned the wearing of full-length capes, sometimes used to hide weapons, arguing that, since the streets were cleaner, they were no longer needed to keep muck off clothes. The people of Madrid rioted. The law was repealed and Squillace lost his job.

Clockwise from left to right *An engraving from 1816 of the Battle of Trafalgar shows the British defeating the French and Spanish navies; Carlos III signing the decree authorizing trade with Asia and the Philippines; Madrid's 200-year-old Botanical Gardens fronting the Prado building; Goya's mystery woman, La Maja Desnuda c1800*

GOYA AND THE MYSTERIOUS *MAJA*

Who is the coy lady stretched out naked on a couch in *La Maja Desnuda*? And why does she appear in identical pose, fully clothed, in *La Maja Vestida*?

Behind the portraits is Francisco José de Goya y Lucientes (1746–1828), a provincial boy from Aragón who became Spain's most powerful artist of the 18th and 19th centuries.

In his eventful life he painted and sketched the savagery of the bullfight, the atrocities of war, the dandies of his age and, during a period of deep depression, grotesque depictions of his nightmares (his so-called *Pinturas Negras*/*Black Paintings*). And the comely lady *(maja)*? Some say it is the fiery Duchess of Alba, with whom Goya is said to have had an amorous adventure. But no one is telling…

THE BATTLE OF TRAFALGAR

'"It's for the blood", a sailor aboard the *Trinidad* explains to Pablos as they spread sand around the cannons. "For the blood?" Pablos turns pale.'

So the great Spanish writer Benito Pérez Galdós (1843–1920), in his historical novel, *Trafalgar*, prepares us for the mighty clash off southern Spain between British Admiral Lord Horatio Nelson (1758– 1805) and the French-led fleet on 21 October 1805. Nelson's 29-strong fleet decimated the Franco-Spanish line of 33 vessels in a daring two-pronged attack. Nelson and 1,500 British sailors perished, but 14,000 French and Spaniards were also killed and 20 of their warships were captured. Britannia now ruled the waves and Napoleon's dream of invading Britain was dashed.

BORROW'S BIBLES

In early 1836 a young English adventurer and linguist by the name of George Borrow (1803–81) arrived in Badajoz, in Portugal. He had been sent by the British and Foreign Bible Society to disseminate the New Testament in Spanish; in other words, to spread the Protestant word in an arch-Catholic bastion.

During the next four years Borrow wandered the length and breadth of the country, preaching about the Bible and engaging with all manner of interesting characters. He was frequently thwarted and certainly Protestantism never took a hold in Spain.

Borrow's experiences in the country, all recounted with rakish good humour, formed the basis of his book *The Bible in Spain*, a rare and engaging account of 19th-century Spain.

THE ROCKY REIGN OF ISABEL II

When her father, Ferdinand VII, died, Isabel (1830–1904) was just three years old. Ferdinand's brother, Carlos, challenged her right to the throne and launched the first Carlist war, but Isabel eventually took the reins in 1843 at the young age of 13. She went on to produce nine children from an unhappy marriage, but her rocky reign was studded with positive developments: the arrival of the railways, radically improved roads, a new National Library and a water system for Madrid. However, right up until she was forced to leave Spain after the revolution in 1868, her rule was marred by rebellion and coups and marked the end of absolutism in Spain. The role of parliament and the military had become paramount. Isabel died in exile in Paris.

Tension in Spain's cities and among the landless rural poor rose in the 1900s as socialism and anarchism gained big followings and nationwide trade unions were formed. Tempers flared in Barcelona when Catalán reservists were called up in 1909 to fight in Morocco, with mobs running amok during the *Setmana Tràgica* (Tragic Week) in July. Spain stayed out of World War I and enjoyed a boom, but the 1920s ushered in more unrest and the six-year dictatorship of General Miguel Primo de Rivera (1870–1930). King Alfonso XIII had him removed in 1929 but two years later went into exile himself as Spain became a republic. First the left (1931–33), then the right (1933–36) held power, while street violence between extremists of both sides increased. The Wall Street Crash had also shaken the fragile economy. Election of the left-wing Popular Front in February 1936 led General Francisco Franco (1892–1975) to head an army revolt in July. The ensuing Civil War raged until Franco's victory in April 1939. Repression and hunger marked the first Franco years, but US aid (in exchange for military bases) in the 1950s and tourism in the 1960s dragged Spain out of the mire. With Franco's death in 1975 came the rebirth of democracy.

GAUDÍ'S GIDDY HEIGHTS

'There are no straight lines in nature,' declared Antoní Gaudí (1852–1926), 'so why should there be in architecture?' Guided by this premise, the Spanish architect embarked on one of the most fantastical eras of European design. Embracing the art-nouveau style that his fellow Catalans called Modernisme, he created many buildings, ranging from the wavy Casa Milà apartments to the unfinished Sagrada Família church in Barcelona (▷ 228–231).

This project became his obsession. As funding ran low, he poured his life savings into it. He slept on site and viewed his work as a divine mission. When he was run over by a tram in 1926 he looked more like a vagrant than Catalonia's best-known architect.

Clockwise from left to right *In Picasso's* Guernica *a wounded horse represents the Spanish people; statue of Pablo (Pau) Casals, the Catalán cellist and nationalist; the distinctive towers of Gaudí's Sagrada Família church in Barcelona*

BIZARRE BUDDIES— BUÑUEL AND DALÍ

When rebellious Luis Buñuel (1900–83) and bizarre Salvador Dalí (1904–89) met it was art at first sight. Buñuel was interested in film, Dalí mostly in himself, but he was producing hallucinatory paintings of a disquieting nature.

In Paris together, they worked on various projects before coming up with the surreal short films *Un Chien andalou* (1929) and *L'Age d'or* (1930). *Un Chien andalou* has remained a classic of barely comprehensible cinema.

Buñuel went on to become an important movie director, working mostly in exile in Mexico, while Dalí progressed from one crazy idea to the next, avidly promoting himself and falling into a tortured lifelong relationship with Gala, his Russian muse and wife.

THE BURGOS TRIAL

For General Franco, the result of a show trial of 16 Basque Separatist Group (ETA) terrorists in a Burgos military court in December 1970 should never have been in doubt. At least six death sentences were on the cards for the group, which since the 1960s had carried out terrorist attacks against the regime in support of Basque independence. Heavy publicity before the trial sparked demonstrations across Spain, and the presiding judge allowed the accused to detail police torture they had suffered. Repressive measures against demonstrators were stepped up and the trial finally went behind closed doors. On 28 December 1970, the death sentences were duly announced, but under international pressure General Franco commuted them three days later.

GUERNICA AND PICASSO

The Spanish Civil War (1936–39) was not just an internal conflict. For Nazi Germany it was a testing ground for new styles of warfare, including the aerial bombing of civilians.

On 26 April 1937, as townsfolk crowded into the busy market in the Basque town of Guernica, bombers of Hitler's Condor Legion unleashed a devastating air raid. About 2,000 people died and the world was horrified. Later that year the Republican government in Madrid commissioned a painting from Pablo Picasso for the Paris Exposition, called simply *Guernica*.

Picasso used his characteristic disjointed, post-Cubist style to express the horror of that day. The painting became an anti-Franco symbol and was despatched to New York in 1939 as part of a fund-raising tour for Spanish war relief, finally returning to Spain in 1981.

'IT IS BETTER TO DIE STANDING…

…than to live on your knees.' So cried the whirlwind of the Spanish Communist Party (PCE), La Pasionaria, during the Spanish Civil War.

Dolores Ibarruri (1895–1989), born to a modest family in Gallarta in the mining region of Vizcaya, joined the communists at an early age and stayed with the party for the rest of her life. To some she was a hero, to others a cynical Stalinist ready to sacrifice comrades in repeated purges.

Towards the end of the war, Ibarruri escaped to the USSR and for 38 years lived in communist countries in eastern Europe. There she rose to the presidency of the PCE and broadcast to Franco's Spain.

When she eventually returned home to Spain in 1977 she was elected to parliament and there continued an active political life until her death in 1989.

Under King Juan Carlos I, Spain returned to democracy in 1978 with a new constitution. The country held its breath during a bungled coup in 1981 (see right), and in 1982 voted in a socialist government under Felipe González. The country joined the European Economic Community in 1986 and staged the Barcelona Olympics and Seville Expo in 1992. In 1996 power went to the right-wing Partido Popular, led by José María Aznar. During his term of office, unemployment dropped and economic growth accelerated. José Luis Rodriguez Zapatero, leader of the Socialist Party, was elected prime minister in 2004, after the terrorist attacks in Madrid and re-elected in 2008. Whether Zapatero will be the Socialist Party's candidate in 2012 is a theme of lively debate as of mid-2010.

Above left *Santiago Calatrava's communications tower at the Olympic complex in Barcelona*
Above right *King Juan Carlos I signs the 1978 Spanish constitution*

MADRID MOVES ON THE WILD SIDE

'When Franco kicked the bucket, boredom in the capital ended,' says one writer about Madrid's *movida*, a whirl of hash-and-cocaine partying and sex involving a group of young, hip rebels in the years after Franco's death in 1975.

Led by the likes of the then undiscovered film-maker Pedro Almodóvar and now long-forgotten musicians Alaska and Radio Futura, *madrileños* (Madrid residents) let their hair down in reaction to the straitjacketed years of dictatorship. Artist Andy Warhol praised the new permissive atmosphere and socialist mayor Enrique Tierno Galván, who pumped public money into theatre and free music concerts, declared: 'Go out and get stoned!' Such tolerance is largely gone but *madrileños* are still famous for partying.

ATTEMPTED COUP TO CATALAN AUTONOMY

Supporters of the failed military uprising of February 1981 have watched in dismay as socialists governed for 14 years and *patrias chicas* ('little countries', under the Franco regime) morphed into fully fledged Autonomous Communities. The Constitutional Court remains blocked over the legality of Catalonia's autonomy statute drafted in 2006. Catalonia's president has promised a grave constitutional crisis should the text, which defines Catalonia as a nation and Spain as a federal state, be significantly altered. As always, the right-wing Partido Popular supports a hard line on separatism while the Spanish left generally favours granting Autonomous Communities whatever their elected representatives decide.

ON THE MOVE

On the Move gives you detailed advice and information about the various options for travelling to Spain before explaining the best ways to get around the country once you are there. Handy tips help you with everything from buying tickets to renting a car.

ON THE MOVE SPAIN

ARRIVING BY AIR

Spain is well served by international airlines and the advent of budget providers makes flying there from some European countries, relatively easy. There are major international airports at Madrid and Barcelona and several smaller international airports in other regions, including Alacant (Alicante), Málaga and Bilbao (Bilbo).

AIRLINES

Spain's main national and international carrier is Iberia, though most other major carriers, such as British Airways, American Airlines, KLM and Lufthansa, operate services to at least the two main airports.

AIRPORTS

Madrid Barajas airport (MAD) is 12km (8 miles) northeast of central Madrid. There are four terminals. International airlines operating from Terminal 1 include easyJet, Aer Lingus, Air Europa, Air Canada, Delta Airlines, Continental, Ryanair and US Airways. Terminal 2 has services from Air France, Alitalia, KLM and Spanair, among others. Terminal 3 is largely dedicated to domestic flights, while the beautiful new Terminal 4 is used by Iberia, British Airways, American Airlines and others.

Domestic regional flights and Air Nostrum, a subsidiary of Iberia, operate from Terminal 3. Visitor Information (tel 902 404 704) can be found at the main information desk in the main hallways of all terminals.

Most of the major car rental companies have offices in the Arrivals area of all terminals. Hotel reservation desks are in all main terminals and there are shops in the Arrivals areas of both main terminals. Money exchange offices are at Arrivals in terminals 1, 2 and 4. Those in Terminal 1 are open 24 hours a day. ATMs are available in both terminals. There is a selection of bar/cafés in all terminals, and restaurants in Terminal 4.

The largest left-luggage site is opposite the Arrivals lounge outside Terminal 1 (call the general information line: 902 404 704). It can accommodate large pieces of luggage; identification will be required. There is another left-luggage site at Terminal 2, and at Terminal 4. Lockers cost between €4 and €6.

A free bus transfer service operates between all terminals. **Barcelona airport** (BCN) is 12km (8 miles) southwest of the city at El Prat de Llobregat. It has four

terminals. The über-splendid new Terminal 1, complete with shops, spas and gourmet dining options, handles most international flights by non-Spanish airlines, including Virgin, easyJet, Air France and KLM. Terminal 2A handles international flights by both Spanish and non-Spanish airlines

Terminal 2B handles flights by Spanish airlines, such as the national carrier Iberia, as well as Air Europa, and non-Spanish airlines in the Oneworld and Star Alliance groups, including British Airways and Lufthansa. Iberia flights to Madrid operate from Terminal 2C.

Alamo, Avis, Hertz, Europcar and Sixt have rental desks in both main terminals. The pick-up point is across the main access road in front of the relevant terminal. There is a hotel reservation desk in Arrivals in Terminal B (a short walk from Terminal A), and there are tourist information offices in the Arrivals halls of terminals 2A and 2B (tel 93 478 47 04 and 93 478 05 65, open Mon–Sat 9.30–8, Sun 9.30–3).

Terminals 1, 2A and 2B also have shops, including newsstands, bookstores and shoe shops. A bank, ATMs and money changing facilities are in the Arrivals halls of Terminals 1 and 2. There are excellent restaurants in Terminal 1 and cafeterias in Terminals 2A and 2B Left luggage is in Terminals 1 and 2B.

Alacant (Alicante) airport (ALC) is 9km (5.5 miles) southwest of the city. It has only one terminal. The information desk is at the check-in area of Departures, and car rental desks are near the baggage reclaim in Arrivals; these include Avis, Europcar and Hertz. A small selection of duty-free shops is supplemented by a number of other stores, including souvenir shops, newsstands and a music store.

There is a post office (open Mon–Sat 9.30–1.30) and bureau de change and ATM facilities in the Arrivals area. Bars, restaurants and fast-food options are available. There is a lost luggage desk in the Arrivals hall.

Málaga airport (AGP) is 8km (5 miles) southwest of the city. There are two terminals, 1 and 2, adjoined and just a short walk apart. Both have information desks in Arrivals and there is an additional one in Terminal 2 Departures. Europcar, easyCar, Avis, Hertz and Budget all have rental desks at the airport, as do several local companies, such as Málaga Car and Sur Rent.

There is a small selection of shops, including newsstands and snack bars. Arrivals in Terminal 2 has money changing facilities, a bank and several ATMs. There are bars, cafés and restaurants in Terminal 1 and other food outlets in Terminal 2 two floors up. There are no left-luggage facilities at the airport.

Bilbao (Bilbo) airport (BIO) is 12km (7.5 miles) north of central Bilbao. It has one terminal with an information desk in Arrivals on the lower floor. Car rental desks are in the arrivals area as well as a desk where you can reserve hotels. There is a visitor information desk upstairs in the terminal building on the Departures floor. Souvenir shops are in the Departures area two floors up.

The BBK bank near the information point outside the terminal building is open from 6am to 11pm. There is a small coffee shop and snack bar on the lower floor outside the terminal building. Another small coffee shop is one floor up from ground level and additional restaurants and coffee shops are two floors up in the Departures area.

The lost luggage desk is on the lower floor near the bank and the information desk.

TRANSFERS FROM AIRPORT TO CITY

Distance to city	Madrid	Barcelona	Alacant (Alicante)	Málaga	Bilbao (Bilbo)
	12km (8 miles)	10km (6 miles)	9km (5.5 miles)	8km (5 miles)	12km (7.5 miles)
Taxi	Taxi stands outside arrivals area at all four terminals. Price: around €30. Journey time: 20–25 min.	Taxi stands directly outside terminals A and C; to the right when you exit Terminal B. Price: €25–€30. Journey time: 20 min.	Taxi stand in front of terminal building. Price: €20–€25. Journey time: 20 min.	Taxi stands directly outside both terminals. Price: €12–€20. Journey time: 15 min.	Taxi stand just to the right on the ground level outside the main terminal building. Price: €25. Journey time: 15 min.
Bus	To Avenida de América. Line 200 for Terminals 1–3; Line 204 for Terminal 4 Price: €1. Frequency: every 10–15 min from 5.20am to 11.30pm. Journey time: 30–35 min.	Price: €5. Frequency: every 12–13 min from 6am–midnight. Journey time: 25–30 min.	Bus stop outside arrivals building. Price: €1. Frequency: every 40 min from 6.30am to 11.10pm. Journey time: 40 min.	Price: €1.20. Frequency: every 30 min from 6.30am–midnight. Journey time: 20 min.	Price: €1.30. Frequency: every 30 min from 6.20am–midnight (from Bilbao 5am–10pm). Journey time: 40 min.
Metro	From Terminal 2, accessed from walkway leading to Parking Area 2. Goes into city on Línea 8. Operates from 6.05am–2am. Price: €2. Journey time: 40 min.	N/A	N/A	N/A	N/A
Train	A train line is presently under construction and due for completion in early 2011.	Price: €3. Frequency: every 30 min from 6am–10.30pm. Journey time: 30 min. A ten-ride T10 metro card (€8) is the cheapest way to Barcelona from the airport.	N/A	Price: €1.50. Frequency: every 30 min from 6.59am–11.59pm (from Malaga 5.30am–10.30pm). Journey time: 13 min.	An airport train connection is under construction scheduled for completion in 2011.

CAR RENTAL

Check your rental car thoroughly before you set off. The smallest marks, scratches or anomalies are worth pointing out, even if they are then dismissed as unimportant by the company's representative. Ensure that any significant damage is marked down on the rental form, or you could face a substantial damage penalty surcharge.

Some rental companies send their cars out with full tanks of fuel; you need to return the vehicle the same way. It is significantly cheaper to fill the tank before returning it, as the fuel prices charged by the rental companies can be as much as double the usual price. Other companies send the cars out almost empty (with just enough to get you to a filling station) and these should be returned empty—more difficult to judge than bringing them back full.

Unless you are using the car for minor trips out of the city, it is cheaper to get an unlimited kilometre package. Some companies, such as easyCar, do not offer this, allowing you only 100km (60 miles) per day and then surcharging for every kilometre over that total. You may need to do some calculations to work out which is cheaper to rent, depending on your requirements.

» To rent a car you need your driver's licence—an international driver's permit is often more useful—and money, or a credit card, for the deposit. If you are leaving cash, the deposit can be quite a significant amount.

» There may be a minimum age (often 21, sometimes higher) and a requirement that you have been driving for at least a year. Some firms may also choose to impose a maximum age limit.

» If you rent when you get to Spain, look for local firms in the telephone book under *Alquiler de coches* or *Automóviles alquiler,* or ask at the information office.

Above *Car rental signs in the sun*
Opposite *Ferries service the islands*

USEFUL TELEPHONE NUMBERS AND WEBSITES

Airports
» Madrid Barajas 902 404 704
» Barcelona 902 404 704
» Alicante 902 404 704
» Málaga 902 404 704
» Bilbao 902 404 704

Airlines
» Iberia, tel 902 40 05 00; www.iberia.com
» British Airways, tel 902 11 13 33; www.britishairways.com
» American Airlines, tel 902 11 55 75; www.aa.com
» KLM, tel 902 22 27 47; www.klm.com
» Lufthansa, tel 902 22 01 01; www.lufthansa.com

Ferries
» Brittany Ferries (UK), tel +44 (0)8703 665 333; www.brittany-ferries.com
» P&O Ferries (UK), tel +44 (0)8716 645 645; www.poferries.com
» Trasmediterránea, tel 902 45 46 45; www.trasmediterranea.es

Trains
» RENFE, tel 902 24 34 02 (international), tel 902 24 02 02 (national); www.renfe.es

Car rental offices
» Avis; www.avis.com
» Budget; www.budget.com
» easyCar; www.easycar.com
» Europcar; www.europcar.com
» Hertz; www.hertz.com
» Málaga Car; www.malagacar.com
» Sur Rent; www.sur-rent.com

Taxis
» Madrid Barajas airport Officina Municipal del Taxis, tel 915 88 96 32
» Barcelona airport, tel 93 303-3033
» Alicante airport, tel 965 25 25 11 or 965 91 01 23
» Málaga airport Radio Taxi, tel 952 04 08 04 Unitaxi, tel 952 33 33 33
» Bilbao airport Radio Taxi, tel 94 480-0909

ARRIVING BY FERRY

The main international ferry access routes to Spain are from the UK and operate into the north-coast ports of Bilbao and Santander. Other international services run from the southern coast of Spain to North Africa and ferries go to the Balearic Islands from the Spanish mainland. There are no scheduled boat connections between Spain and North America, although many cruise ships visit Spanish ports.

PLYMOUTH (UK) TO SANTANDER

Brittany Ferries (tel +44 (0)8709 076 103; www.brittany-ferries.com) operates a ferry between Plymouth and Santander. The ships sail twice a week from mid-March to mid-November only. The journey takes a full day (21 hours). You can opt for a cabin or seat only.

Santander's ferry terminal is in the heart of the city. There are no money exchange facilities as such at the terminal, so it's best done on board the ferry. Once the ferry has docked, the local police enforce a temporary traffic flow system to allow arriving vehicles to leave the terminal area.

PORTSMOUTH (UK) TO BILBAO (SANTURTZI)

P&O Ferries (tel +44 (0)8716 645 645; www.poferries.com) sails twice a week year round, except January, when there are two sailings in the month. The journey takes 34 hours and cabins only are available.

Ferries dock at Santurtzi, a port about 20km (12 miles) to the northwest of central Bilbao. It is on the RENFE train system (www.renfe.es) on Línea C1 Bilbao-Santurtzi. Services run every 10 to 20 minutes from about 5am to 11.15pm. The cost is €2.75 one way and the journey takes about 20 minutes. The A-3115 bus service from Bilbao calls at the port, and taxis are also available. To drive into the city, take the A8.

MINI-CRUISES

On both the Santander and Bilbao ferry services there is a mini-cruise option where you can get return travel and a day in the destination city at a discounted rate.

ISLANDS AND NORTH AFRICA

Trasmediterránea (tel 902 45 46 45; www.trasmediterranea.es) is the main ferry operator to the Balearic Islands, the Canary Islands and across to North Africa. They have many offices throughout the mainland coastal region and the islands and in Madrid and Barcelona. Services to the Balearic Islands depart from Barcelona and Valencia and call at Palma (Mallorca), Eivissa (Ibiza) and Maó (Menorca). Services to the Canary Islands depart from Cádiz, then inter-island ferries run from Las Palmas on Gran Canaria. Services to North Africa depart from Almería to Melilla and Nador, from Málaga to Melilla and from Algeciras to Ceuta and Tangier.

TIPS

» Driving on busy roads immediately after arriving can be very stressful. Take time on the ferry journey to familiarize yourself with a map of the city, picking out any substantial landmarks and the major roads you will take, to help navigate.
» Even in heavy traffic do not be panicked by other drivers; do things more slowly and more deliberately than you are used to at home.
» Driving is on the right-hand side of the road.

ARRIVING BY TRAIN

There are international train services to Spain from several European countries, including the UK, France, Portugal and Germany. Journey times are generally long and the fares are quite high compared with some of the budget airline flights. However, if you prefer going overland or want to see more than one European country during your visit, then the international train services, with their high levels of comfort and service, are a good choice. Although you can travel to other stations, particularly in some of the bigger cities in the north of Spain, most international services go to Madrid's Chamartín and Barcelona's Sants stations. The Spanish national rail company, RENFE, operates services throughout the country.

RAIL JOURNEY TIMES
(times given are dependent on connections and time of travel)
London to Madrid:
from 18 to 23 hours.
London to Barcelona:
from 18 to 20 hours.
Paris to Madrid:
from 13.5 to 17.5 hours.

Paris to Barcelona:
from 12 to 15 hours.
Rome to Madrid:
from 22 to 27 hours.
Rome to Barcelona:
from 18.5 to 22.5 hours.

For more information on Europe-wide rail travel check out www. alleuroperail.com; www.raileurope. co.uk or www.seat61.com.

Madrid's Chamartín station is around 5km (3 miles) to the north of central Madrid along Paseo de la Castellana. It is on the Metro system, Línea 10, and there are regular buses and a taxi service into the city. It has a wide range of shops and services, including cafés, bars, restaurants, souvenir shops and banks.
    Several of the major car rental companies have offices here for pick-up and drop-off.

Barcelona's Sants station is near Plaça de Espanya on the western side of the city about 5km (3 miles) from the central Plaça Catalunya transportation hub. You will find a tourist information office here (open Mon–Fri 8–8, Sat–Sun 8–2), as well

as taxis, ATMs and a hotel reservation desk. A very frequent bus service runs from outside the station to Plaça de Catalunya and the station is also on the Metro system, on Línea 5 and Línea 3. It is also on the commuter rail line.

ARRIVING BY CAR

Driving into Spain from France and Portugal is very easy—in fact, you may not notice that you have crossed the border at all. There are customs points at all border crossings, varying in size depending on whether it is a main motorway (expressway) access point, such as at Portbou and Hondarribia, or a small mountain crossing point in the Pyrenees, for example. You must stop if requested by a border guard. Although these crossings are usually not manned, you must slow down to pass through these areas. The southern crossing from Andorra into Spain is more obviously controlled, and usually takes time to clear. Again, stop if indicated to do so by a border guard and your vehicle may be searched.

MAIN DRIVING ROUTES
On entering Spain you will almost certainly need to head south, as few roads go east to west across the Pyrenees. To make quick progress from east to west there is a motorway (expressway) link running in that direction to the south of the Pyrenees, from Bilbao, via Zaragoza, to Barcelona (following the A-8, AP-68, AP-2 and AP-7). Throughout the rest of Spain, the main roads tend to head to Madrid or along the north, east and south coasts. The A-8/E-70 goes west along the northern coastline from Donostia (San Sebastián), at the main western border crossing, to Oviedo. From the main eastern border crossing at La Jonquera, the AP-7/E-15 heads south through Girona to Barcelona and on to Valencia and beyond.

Above *Madrid's local and suburban train service*
Opposite *The main road through the countryside around Jaén*

Spain is a large country and getting around it can require patience, no matter what form of transport you use. The excellent rail network and extensive local and national bus services make getting around easy enough for independent visitors, especially if you stick to the main towns and cities. Safety standards on public transport are generally high. If you want to stray into some of the more rural areas, you will almost certainly need a car.

The main motorway (expressway) network radiates from Madrid and covers the coastlines. There are inland areas that are some distance off the network, though they are served by a usually good system of national routes.

For some of the best driving experiences, it is worth exploring the labyrinth of backcountry minor roads. They are usually quiet, pass through beautiful parts of rural Spain and have no tolls. Motorways are significantly faster than the national routes. They are generally toll-free, except in parts of the north and east; here truck drivers travel on the national roads to avoid the tolls, slowing traffic down and making driving on some of them a stressful experience. The highways are generally quiet, even during rush hours away from the main city hubs, and they are in excellent condition.

Driving in the biggest cities can be difficult and parking is a problem, though it is certainly nowhere near as bad as some other European cities. The smaller, provincial cities are easier to navigate, especially if you avoid the rush hour.

The Spanish rail network is comprehensive and has several levels of service, from high-speed, long-distance, intercity trains to local trains that call at every station, covering a wide area of rural Spain.

The main rail operator, RENFE, covers the whole of the country, while FEVE also operates along the north coast (and a short stretch in Murcia). Train journeys are usually an economical way of getting about, though the best high-speed services are quite expensive. They are often a better option than flying, unless you are short of time or are touring across the country in one go.

Domestic flight coverage has historically been rather limited, and fares have been high. New generation low-cost airlines such as Vueling (www.vueling.com) and Clickair (www.clickair.com) have improved the situation considerably, and it's now possible to find reasonably priced fares to most destinations. The other main airlines for domestic flights include Iberia and its subsidiary Air Nostrum, Air Europa and Spanair. Air Berlin also operates services connecting the Spanish mainland with Mallorca.

Almost the whole of Spain takes a break during July and August, so getting around on any form of public transport, or by car, becomes far more of a problem.

Plan in advance, reserve ahead where possible and be prepared for delays and waits at stations, airports and on the roads.

GETTING AROUND IN MADRID

Madrid is an easy city to negotiate, with a first-rate public transport network, including a very efficient bus service, an excellent Metro and plenty of taxis. As Madrid's sights are quite spread out, any visit to the city is going to involve using public transportation at some stage.

BUS

The bus system is efficient and far-reaching, with regular schedules to all parts of the city and its suburbs. Finding your way is made easy as the various routes and stops are shown at every bus stop on a plan. There are two types of buses—the standard red bus and the yellow microbus. Both operate between 6am and midnight, and charge €1 for each one-way ride in the city, though the *abono* or Metrobús ticket giving 10 rides costs €9. You can buy the *abono* (also valid for the Metro system) from the Empresa Municipal de Transportes (EMT) office at Calle Cerro de la Plata 4 (tel 902 50 78 50, open daily 8–2), from any EMT kiosk or Metro station in the city and from some newsstands and tobacconists.

Night buses (locally known as *búhos*, meaning owls) operate from Plaza de la Cibeles to many suburbs between midnight and 6am and the tickets cost the same as during the day.

The night bus service is not as punctual as the daytime one. Bus information offices are located in Plaza de la Cibeles and Puerta del Sol, where you can pick up route maps and schedules.

METRO

The Metro system, one of the oldest in Europe, has been modernized. It is easy to follow, and lines converge at Puerta del Sol. The 13 lines each have a different colour and number on maps and at stations.

The latest addition is line 12 Metrosur, an extension southwest of the city reaching as far as Parque Europa. Metrosur is accessed from Puerta del Sur station on Línea 10.

The system is split into zones, with most of it in Zone A, while the outlying areas and lines are in zones B1, B2 and B3. The one-way fare for any journey is €1 but you can buy an *abono* or Metrobus ticket (see Bus).

There is a separate Metrosur multi-ride ticket giving 10 trips on the Metrosur line and the interconnecting Línea 10 stations, also for €9.

The Metro system runs from 6am to 2am; schedule information and a full Metro map are available from www.metromadrid.es (tel 902 44 44 03). You can also pick up maps at any station.

The Metro trains operate around every three to six minutes from Monday to Friday; this extends to every 15 minutes after midnight, and there are slightly fewer trains on weekends. It is very reliable and the best way of getting around the city quickly, but it's best to avoid the rush hours, generally 7–9.30am and 8–10pm, when it gets very busy.

TAXI

Taxis can be called by a hotel or hailed on the street quite easily. Official taxis are white with a red diagonal stripe, and a green light on the roof shows when they are free.

Beware of pirate taxi cabs, which charge higher fares and can be less trustworthy. The prices for official taxis are reasonable, so if you need to get somewhere quickly then it is certainly worth considering.

The standard base taxi fare is €2.10 (€2.30 Mon–Fri 10pm–6am, €3.10 weekends), with a charge of €0.98 to €1.17 for every further kilometre. There is a supplement payable for journeys to certain places, such as the rail station (€2.95) or airport (€5.50). Make sure the meter is turned on and set at the base fare for your journey, otherwise you will pay more. You can ask for a receipt if you have any queries.

The major private taxi companies in Madrid are TeleTaxi (tel 913 712 131; www.tele-taxi.es) and Radio Taxi (tel 914 473 232).

TRAIN

Chamartín, north of Plaza de Castilla, is the terminus for northern destinations. It is linked by a through line with Atocha, the southerly station at the bottom end of the Jardín Botánico (Botanical Gardens).

There is also a Metro link, No. 8, Chamartín to Plaza de Castilla; then take No. 1 to Atocha RENFE. Cercanías refers to local and suburban trains, *largo recorrido* to intercity and long-distance trains.

DRIVING

Try to avoid driving in Madrid—it's always busy, often dangerous, and navigating and driving at the same time is challenging.

BICYCLING

The Bike Spain bicycle store at Plaza de la Villa 1 (tel 91 559 0653; www.bikespain.info) rents out mountain bicycles at €20 per day, but be careful—the city's motorists pay little attention to bicyclists.

GETTING AROUND IN BARCELONA

Getting around Barcelona is no problem thanks to a comprehensive public transport network, and its old quarter is easily accessible by foot. The Metro system is backed up by a local RENFE train network, a bus service and countless taxis. It is also a pleasant enough city to bicycle and walk around. Don't drive unless you must.

BUS

Barcelona's buses are red and white. Bus stops are indicated either by signs or bus shelters. Hold your arm out to flag down the driver. You can buy a one-way ticket from the driver, but if you have a travel card or multi-ride ticket, you can use the machine just behind the driver to validate your journey (see Travel Cards). A one-way ticket for a journey costs €1.35.

To get off the bus, press the red button to let the driver know that he needs to call at the next stop. If you don't know where your stop is, state the name of your destination to the driver when you get on.

Daytime buses run from 5am to midnight; on Fridays and Saturdays they run until 2am. The NitBus night service runs along 15 routes, designated N0 to N16. Buses leave from various points around Plaça de Catalunya and run from 10.30pm to 6am. Check out www.emt-amb.com or www.tmb.net

METRO

The Metro system, identified by a white M on a red diamond background, is made up of six lines (L1 to L5 and L11) and provides good coverage of the city. Each line has a separate colour to aid identification.

Lines operate 5am–midnight Monday to Thursday and Sunday, and 5am–2am Friday and the day before a public holiday, and all night on Saturdays. The six Metro lines are supported by two rail services operated by Ferrocarrils de la Generalitat de Catalunya (FGC), U6 and U7, which serve the outlying areas around Sarrià and Tibidabo.

A one-way ticket for a Metro journey costs €1.35, available at any Metro station or sales outlet, but you can buy one of a number of travel cards that give discounted multi-trip travel (see below). Metro trains run every three to six minutes on average. Check out www.tmb.net for further information.

TRAVEL CARDS

Several travel cards are available. The T-Dia allows unlimited travel on the Metro or connected train and bus services for one day (from €5.80 for one Zone to €15.85 for all six).

Another popular travel card is the T-10, which allows 10 one-way trips or combined trips on bus, FGC or the Metro (€7.85).

You must validate one unit of a travel card per journey by inserting it into the automatic machine at the entry to a station or on the bus. It costs from €7.85 for one zone to €32.10 for six zones. There is a time limit: from 1 hour 15 minutes for one-zone cards to 2 hours 30 minutes for six-zone cards, during which any single one-way journey must be completed, but permits changing from Metro to bus or FGC and vice versa.

Cards can be bought from any Metro station, TMB bus kiosk, newsstands, FGC stations, lottery shops and Servicaixa banks. You can also buy travel cards for two to five consecutive days of unlimited travel.

TRAIN

Barcelona has four commuter lines run by RENFE around the city and its suburbs. Check at the RENFE website—www.renfe.es—or go to www.tmb.net and look under the train and Metro information section.

TAXI

There are plenty of taxis around Barcelona and you should be able to flag one down on the street quickly. Official taxi ranks can be found at the main rail stations, airport and around the main city streets. Taxis are black and yellow. Ensure the taxi has a meter and that it is set to its minimum fare at the start of the trip. The minimum fare for weekdays from 7am to 9pm is €2, then €0.86 per kilometre. On Saturdays and public holidays it is €2.10, then €1.10 per kilometre. Supplements: €3.10 to the airport; €1 per hand-luggage size bag. The two largest taxi firms are Radio Taxi 033 (tel 933 03 30 33) and Co-operativa de Radio Taxi Metropolitana de Barcelona (tel 932 250 000). Further information is available at www.emt-amb.com

BICYCLING

Dedicated bicycle lanes in the city make bicycling a feasible alternative. Amics de la Bici (tel 933 39 40 60; www.amicsdelabici.org) is an excellent organization with a website listing rental companies and routes.

Left *The Barcelona trixi taxi*

DRIVING

Spain is generally easy to drive around. There's a good network of motorways (expressways) and dual carriageways (divided highways); about half of these are toll roads *(autopístas)* and the rest are free *(autovías)*. There are also national roads *(nacionales)* and smaller roads *(comarcales)*. Many roads, particularly the main motorways, are quiet outside the rush hour.

If you are tempted to skip the tolls and head for the main national routes, be warned that many truck drivers think the same way so these roads can be very busy and very slow. If you have the time and the inclination to explore, tackle the amazing network of country back roads and lanes. They take you through glorious countryside at a more relaxed pace that allows you to enjoy the scenery, and are almost always traffic free. Driving is on the right.

SPEED LIMITS

» The maximum speed limit on motorways (expressways) is 120kph (75mph); 80kph (50mph) for vehicles towing trailers. The minimum speed on motorways is 60kph (37mph).

» Two-lane roads or roads with overtaking lanes 100kph (62mph); 80kph (50mph) for vehicles with trailers.

» Roads outside built-up areas 90kph (56mph); 70kph (43mph) for vehicles with trailers.

» Towns and built-up areas 40kph (31mph).

OVERTAKING

» Other drivers are usually considerate and aware of overtaking cars.

» If you are behind a slow vehicle it might flash its passenger side indicator lights to let you know the road ahead is probably clear enough to overtake. Don't take this for granted; check ahead yourself as it may simply be indicating its own intention to turn off the road.

» Many country roads are straight and flat, but dips can hide oncoming cars.

» Watch for the No Overtaking signs *(prohibido adelantar)* and obey them at all times.

ROUNDABOUTS

Unless otherwise indicated, traffic coming on to the roundabout from the left has priority.

CITY DRIVING

Driving into Madrid or Barcelona or any of the larger cities is not a great idea for the less confident driver. While Spanish drivers are generally considerate, the volume of traffic and the pressure of navigating can make it a less than enjoyable encounter. One-way systems, narrow streets, lack of parking spaces and aggression can make driving in the city an anxious experience. It is best to plan your driving route beforehand as much as possible.

SEATBELTS

» Seatbelts are compulsory for driver and front-seat passenger and for rear passengers if the vehicle is fitted with them.

» It is illegal to carry a child under the age of 12 years in the front passenger seat unless he or she is big enough to use the seatbelt.

WHAT TO BRING

» You need a driver's licence to drive in Spain. Licences from the United States, Canada, the UK and other EU countries are valid.

Above *Cars negotiating hairpin bends on a mountain road in Mallorca*

» An international driving permit (IDP) is not required in any EU member state, including Spain, as all European licences should now be recognized throughout Europe without any other supporting documents. US nationals will require an IDP. An IDP may also prove to be useful in some situations for Euopean nationals. They are available from major motoring organizations in your home country.

» It is compulsory to carry your licence with you at all times, as well as the vehicle registration document and at least third-party insurance. If the vehicle is not registered in your name, you should have a letter from the registered owner that gives you permission to drive it.

» Your insurers should also provide you with a Green Card (proof of insurance) before you travel if your insurance policy requires it.

» It is compulsory for drivers to carry the following equipment in the vehicle at all times:
— 2 self-standing, warning triangles (to be placed at least 50m/55 yards behind and in front of the vehicle in the case of breakdown);
— a green safety jacket;
— 1 set of spare headlight and rear light bulbs;
— 1 set of spare fuses for lights and electrics;
— 1 spare wheel;
— 1 spare fan belt.

» If you have rented a car, ensure that this equipment is provided and is functioning before you leave the rental office.

» It is illegal to carry spare fuel, but don't let your tank get too low; you could be fined if you run out.

ACCIDENTS

» If you witness an accident, you must attend to the incident and the people involved, and call emergency services as soon as possible.

» If the passengers are not seriously injured it is not necessary to contact the police, but if you are in doubt as to the extent of any injuries it is advisable to contact the police as a precaution.

» If you are involved in an accident, you must use your warning triangles to alert other traffic (place them the same distance before and after the car as for a breakdown—see earlier). Only the one behind is necessary on two-lane roads.

» If you can move your car to a safe position, do so.

» Notify the appropriate emergency services as soon as possible. There are SOS phones by the side of all main roads, though you may have to walk some distance to find one.

» Do not wait in your car; move well away from the vehicle and off the road, but stay within sight of the car so that you can see when the emergency services arrive.

» It is your responsibility to get your car removed as soon as possible, but vehicles must be towed only by an official breakdown vehicle.

DRINKING AND DRIVING

Spain has a legal blood alcohol limit of 0.5g per 1,000cc (0.3g for professional drivers and new drivers), which is strictly enforced.

If you are stopped by a police unit, it is compulsory to comply with the alcohol tests. Failure to do this is a serious offence and can lead to fines of up to €600 and loss of your licence. The same applies to the use of any drugs that may impair your ability to drive properly.

FINES AND SPEEDING OFFENCES

Speed cameras are fairly common in Spain and the hefty fines are strictly enforced. The police will issue an on-the-spot fine to foreign drivers (which entitles you to a 30 per cent discount), but you have to pay it there and then or, if you do not have enough cash, be accompanied to the nearest town to get the cash. Make sure you get a receipt.

USE OF LIGHTS

» During daylight hours, headlights should be used only when visibility is reduced, such as in rain or fog, or when driving through poorly lit tunnels (a blue and white dipped headlight sign at the entrance to the tunnel tells you if you have to do this). There is another sign at the end of the tunnel with a dipped (low-beam) headlight and question mark to remind you to turn them off.

» Rear fog lamps are only to be used when visibility is severely reduced.

» During the night, from sunset to sunrise, headlights are necessary outside built-up areas and in poorly lit tunnels.

» In built-up areas or other tunnels, dipped headlights should be used.

» Drivers from the UK with right-hand drive vehicles must use headlight adjuster patches to correct the headlight beam, to avoid blinding other drivers. These are available from motoring stores and at ferry terminals in the UK.

» Motorcyclists must use dipped headlights during the day.

» A crash helmet is compulsory.

» A replacement set of bulbs is required.

ROAD SIGNS

No parking (clearway)

Maximum speed

No overtaking

No right turn

No left turn

No half-turns

Toll motorway

Motorway

Two-lane highway

Vehicular road

Maximum advisable speed

Parking

Road narrows

Two-way traffic

Steep verge

Roadworks

Farm animals

Loose rocks

Roundabout

Only permitted direction

Minimum speed limit

Animal-drawn traffic lane

Pedestrian lane

Snow chains obligatory

Give way

Stop

Give way to oncoming traffic

Priority over oncoming traffic

FUEL

» The types of fuel normally available are Super, Normal, *Sin Plomo* (unleaded) and *Gasoleo* (diesel).

» Fuel is generally around €1.30 per litre for unleaded Super 98, €1.18 for Super 95.

» Many filling stations in the countryside and some in cities still offer an attended service. If you would like a full tank of unleaded, for example, ask for *Sin Plomo, lleno* (pronounced yay-no).

» All filling stations accept major credit cards, such as Visa and MasterCard.

TOLLS

The motorway (expressway) network in Spain is a mixture of toll and non-toll sections. Most toll booths have a simple digital display on the side that indicates the amount payable in euros. You can pay at all toll booths with a credit card, even for very small tolls. If you have the correct change in coins you can use the auto toll lane (indicated by a basket sign above the lane); throw the money into the basket and it is counted before the barrier is raised.

If you are driving a right-hand-drive car, the booth window will be on the passenger side, which can be awkward if you are driving alone.

SERVICE STATIONS

The bigger service stations offer a range of services other than just fuel, such as souvenir shopping, cafés and mini-supermarkets. On the whole, prices at these are higher than you would find in towns and cities, and the quality of the food on offer tends to be quite poor. Many non-motorway service stations are close to towns or villages, so if you are hungry you may prefer to go there instead.

PARKING

Parking areas are known as *aparcamientos* in Spanish ('parking' is also used) and are usually signposted in cities and towns with a large, white P on a blue background, sometimes with a neon sign beneath saying *libre,* which means free spaces.

In the larger cities and towns parking areas may be the only option, as well as the best option, as street parking can be a real problem and it is not always clear what the street parking restrictions are.

STREET PARKING

» Every Spanish city has street parking available but it is almost always on meters, which can be expensive if you intend to stay there all day.

» Some cities, such as Barcelona, have colour-coded parking zones, which make on-street parking even more complicated.

» Meters accept only coins and there is always a minimum fee and maximum stay, which is usually two hours.

» Free street parking can be found farther away from central city areas, but be sure to look for the parking restriction signs, usually mounted on lamp-posts, showing the times when parking is permitted.

» Never leave anything of value on view in the car. It is better to secure anything you leave in the car in the boot (trunk). This is particularly true if you are parking on backstreets.

CITY PARKING

All cities have well-signposted parking areas; many in central areas are underground. They are often accessed via narrow and steep ramps alongside the main streets. These parking areas are generally safe, though you should always ensure you lock any valuables away.

Charges vary widely from city to city and from one parking area to another within a city. A general guideline is that the nearer to the historic area they are, the more expensive they become. They can charge anything from €5 to €15+ per day. The fees are charged on an hourly basis. After collecting a ticket at the barrier on the way in, you can then pay either at the automatic ticket machines before returning to your car or at the manned ticket office at the exit barrier.

Above *A parking meter in Seville displaying the internationally recognized blue symbol*

TRAFFIC WARDENS AND PARKING FINES

Many traffic officers work the streets, so if you do fall foul of the parking restrictions you are likely to be caught and issued a fine.

If you return when the warden is still there, it may be worth trying to dissuade him or her from issuing the fine, but if the ticket is already written it stands.

TIPS

» Familiarize yourself with a map of the city and pick out any obvious places (such as castles or palaces) and features (such as rivers or main boulevards) that can help to guide you on the move.

» Try to work out which road you will be arriving on and turn the map in this direction as you approach the outskirts; it makes it easier to work out whether to go left or right.

» When in the city slow down, take your time and don't be rushed by other drivers.

» Most drivers are used to dealing with the unexpected, so if, for example, you are in the wrong lane when you get to an intersection, indicate and patiently move your way across. The traffic will stop for you eventually.

» Be aware of traffic lights as they are often small and poorly placed for visibility.

USEFUL DRIVING TERMS

a la derecha right	**encender las luces** switch on lights
a la izquierda left	**espere** wait
abierto open	**estacionamiento reglamentado** limited parking zone
altura máxima maximum height	**fin de…** end of…
arcenes sin afirmar soft verges	**hielo** ice (on road)
¡atención, peligro! danger	**mantenga su derecha** keep right
autopista de peaje toll road	**mantenga su izquierda** keep left
autovía motorway (expressway)	**obras** roadworks ahead
bajada peligrosa steep hill	**paso a nivel (sin barreras)** level crossing (no gates)
calzada resbaladiza slippery road	**paso de ganado** cattle crossing
cambio de sentido change of direction	**peaje** toll
cañada animals crossing	**peatones** pedestrian crossing
carretera comarcal secondary road	**precaución** caution
carretera cortada road closed	**prohibido adelantar** no overtaking
carretera nacional main road	**prohibido aparcar** no parking
ceda el paso give way	**puesto de socorro** first aid
centro town centre	**salida** exit
cerrado closed	**salida de camiones** works exit
cruce peligroso dangerous crossing	**substancias peligrosas** dangerous substances
curvas en…km bends for…km	**todas direcciones** all directions
despacio drive slowly	**travesía peligrosa** dangerous crossing
desprendimientos loose rocks	**zona peatonal** pedestrian zone
desvío diversion	
dirección prohibida no entry	
dirección única one-way traffic	

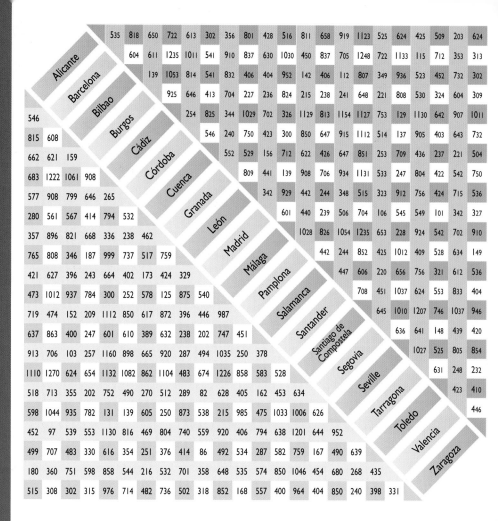

	Ali	Bar	Bil	Bur	Cád	Cór	Cue	Gra	Leó	Mad	Mál	Pam	Sal	Sant	SdC	Seg	Sev	Tar	Tol	Val	Zar
Alicante		535	818	650	722	613	302	356	801	428	516	811	658	919	1123	525	624	425	509	203	624
Barcelona	546		604	611	1235	1011	541	910	837	630	1030	450	837	705	1248	722	1133	115	712	353	313
Bilbao	815	608		139	1053	814	541	832	406	404	952	142	406	112	807	349	936	523	452	732	302
Burgos	662	621	159		925	646	413	704	227	236	824	215	238	241	648	221	808	530	324	604	309
Cádiz	683	1222	1061	908		254	825	344	1029	702	326	1129	813	1154	1127	753	129	1130	642	907	1011
Córdoba	577	908	799	646	265		546	240	750	423	300	850	647	915	1112	514	137	905	403	643	732
Cuenca	280	561	567	414	794	532		552	529	156	712	622	426	647	851	253	709	436	237	221	504
Granada	357	896	821	668	336	238	462		809	441	139	908	706	934	1131	533	247	804	422	542	750
León	765	808	346	187	999	737	517	759		342	929	442	244	348	515	323	912	756	424	715	536
Madrid	421	627	396	243	664	402	173	424	329		601	440	239	506	704	106	545	549	101	342	327
Málaga	473	1012	937	784	300	252	578	125	875	540		1028	826	1054	1235	653	228	924	542	702	910
Pamplona	719	474	152	209	1112	850	617	872	396	446	987		442	244	852	425	1012	409	528	634	149
Salamanca	637	863	400	247	601	610	389	632	238	202	747	451		447	606	220	656	756	321	612	536
Santander	913	706	103	257	1160	898	665	920	287	494	1035	250	378		708	451	1037	624	553	833	404
Santiago de Compostela	1110	1270	624	654	1132	1082	862	1104	483	674	1226	858	583	528		645	1010	1207	746	1037	946
Segovia	518	713	355	202	752	490	270	512	289	82	628	405	162	453	634		636	641	148	439	420
Seville	598	1044	935	782	131	139	605	250	873	538	215	985	475	1033	1006	626		1027	525	805	854
Tarragona	452	97	539	553	1130	816	469	804	740	559	920	406	794	638	1201	644	952		631	248	232
Toledo	499	707	483	330	616	354	251	376	414	86	492	534	287	582	759	167	490	639		423	410
Valencia	180	360	751	598	858	544	216	532	701	358	648	535	574	850	1046	454	680	268	435		446
Zaragoza	515	308	302	315	976	714	482	736	502	318	852	168	557	400	964	404	850	240	398	331	

The above chart lists major points on Spain's road network. Use the chart to gauge the distance in kilometres (green) and duration in hours and minutes (blue) of a car journey.

Right *These spaces are reserved for people with disabilities (minusvalidos)*
Opposite *The Costa Blanca Express pulling into a station in Alicante*

TRAINS

The major rail network in Spain is run by RENFE (tel 902 24 02 02; www.renfe.es/ingles) and it covers much of the country with its extensive 12,000km (7,440 miles) of track. There are different types of train services, which all serve different purposes, travel at different speeds and often have several different names. It isn't straightforward but it is comprehensive.

DIFFERENT TYPES OF TRAIN

» Local (Cercanías) These services operate around major cities, including Barcelona, Madrid, Bilbao, Seville, Málaga and Valencia, calling at most local stations, and are generally slow but pleasant.

The trains are usually red and white and some have double decker carriages (cars). They offer a simple ticket one-way (ida) or return (ida y vuelta), and are usually a better and faster, though slightly more expensive, option than taking the bus. Make sure to double-check that the train actually stops at your destination as there are semi-fast services, which skip certain stations.

» Regional This is a comprehensive network of services covering the entire country. It has reasonable prices, comfort and access to smaller towns, as well as the major cities, without the express speed.

» Long-distance (Diurno, Estrella, Talgo, Intercity). These trains generally run at high speed between major cities on journeys over 400km (250 miles). They are very spacious and comfortable. Passengers board the trains by following a check-in procedure similar to that used at airports.

The standard long-distance services are Diurno and Estrella, which often cost substantially less than the other services, such as Talgo. These trains stop only at the largest cities.

There are several derivatives of the long-distance service operating between certain cities, such as the Euromed service between Barcelona and Alicante, stopping at Tarragona, Castellón and Valencia; the Alaris between Madrid and Valencia; and the Altaria between Madrid and Albacete, and Madrid and Alicante.

Star Trains and Hotel Trains offer sleeping facilities on overnight services. Hotel Trains are the more comfortable. Intercity and Talgo run frequently and have greater levels of comfort between the major cities.

» AVE This is the ultimate in speed and luxury, but these services currently run only on the Madrid–Seville, Madrid–Ciudad Real–Puertollano, Barcelona–Madrid and Madrid–Zaragoza routes. They have cafés, telephones, music and video entertainment on board and tourist-, first- and club-class seating. These fast trains take just 2 hours 35 minutes to go between Madrid and Seville compared with 3 hours 15 minutes on a normal long-distance service, but may cost more. The fares between Madrid and Seville are €80.70 (Turista), €121 (Preferente) and €145.20 (Club) one-way. The fastest Madrid–Barcelona AVE gets you from Atocha station in Madrid to Sants station in Barcelona in 2 hrs, 38 minutes. The fares are listed at €134.50 (Turista), €201.70 (Preferente), and €242 (Club) but cheaper fares are often available for specific dates reserved by internet. You get a 20 per cent discount on a return (round-trip) ticket if your return journey is within 60 days of the outward trip. .

» FEVE This modern, independent rail network (tel Asturias 985 982 381; Cantabria 942 209 522; Castilla y León 987 271 210; Galicia 981 370 401; Murcia 968 501 172; País Vasco 944 250 615; www.feve.es) operates services along the north coast of Spain from Bilbao to Ferrol and inland from Bilbao to León, plus

some smaller, local routes in Murcia, Palencia and A Coruña. It runs on a narrower gauge track than RENFE trains. It has offices in Santander, Bilbao, Gijón and Oviedo, and offers two types of service—the local one, also known as Cercanías, and Regionales for longer trips between the bigger cities. You can buy books of 10 tickets and monthly tickets, as well as the usual one-way and return.

SPECIAL FARES

Discounts are generally available to ISIC Student Card holders and seniors.

BUYING TRAIN TICKETS

Every station has a ticket office (*despacho de billetes*) or ticket machine (*máquina del billetes*). The ticket machines accept notes (bills) as well as coins for payment. For long-distance trains, it is advisable to reserve in advance as they are a very popular way of getting around the country.

At the ticket offices prices are displayed on a digital readout on the cash register, making it easier to know the cost if you don't speak the language.

You should double-check your tickets if you want a return to make sure you were properly understood when asking for it. In Spanish, a one-way ticket is an *ida*, pronounced ee-dah, and a return ticket is an *ida y vuelta*.

FINDING YOUR PLATFORM

Most major stations have information screens giving details of the platforms where trains arrive and depart, though it is not unusual for these screens to be out of order. The best way is to ask the ticket officer to point the way; the Spanish word for platform is *andén*. The screens, especially at provincial stations, tend to show only the final destination of the train, so you need to know this if you are getting off in between. At the major city stations, the indicator boards in the main foyers give detailed information for each train, including all the station stops.

At some stations you need to walk across the track to get to the platforms as there are no underground walkways. Find the official crossing points at the ends of the platforms or outside the ticket office area. Be very careful and check both ways several times before crossing. Trains have right of way.

RAIL STATIONS

Apart from the big city stations, rail stations generally consist of just a ticket office, a small newsstand and a drinks machine. You can ask for general information at the ticket office. At larger stations you can expect to find toilets, cafés, bars, newspaper stores, souvenir shops and clothes stores. The major city stations, such as Madrid and Barcelona, have restaurants and a wider range of stores, left-luggage desks, car rental offices, tourist information desks and hotel reservation desks. You may even be able to get a shoe-shine.

CLASSES OF TRAVEL

Club, Preferente, Turista, Camas (beds) and Literas (bunks) classes are available, though the better standards of ticket generally apply only on the fast, long-distance services and the sleeping accommodation only on overnight services.

ON-BOARD FACILITIES

These vary considerably depending on the service you are using. You should find the following on these services:
Cercanías Basic facilities; often don't even have toilets.
Regional Basic facilities such as toilets, though some services offer newspapers and perhaps a trolley buffet service.
Grandes Líneas (long distance) Cafeteria/restaurant, video, telephone, newspapers, music and toilets.

RAIL PASSES

Inter Rail passes: The Inter Rail Pass is useful if you intend to travel extensively around Spain by rail

within the allocated time of your ticket. If you are not going to use it regularly, you may be better off buying individual tickets. Check out www.interrailnet.com and www.raileurope.co.uk (www.raileurope.com for North American visitors).
» There are two types of Inter Rail ticket: Inter Rail -26 for those under 26 on the day the card is first used; Inter Rail +26 for those over 26, with no upper age limit; children aged 5–11 are entitled to a 50 per cent reduction on the price for adults in first or second class. Children under four travel free.
» These tickets are available to permanent residents of any European country, as well as Morocco, Algeria and Tunisia.
» You will need a passport or Residency Certificate (*tarjeta de residencia*) showing residence in one of these countries for more than six months. The pass must be bought no more than 60 days before the first date of use.
» Supplements are payable on some services, such as AVE and Talgo.
» Interail also offers a single-country pass (Inter Rail One Country Pass) which allows travel for between three and eight days within a one-month period. There are discounts for under-26s and children.

Spain FlexiPass: Available only to US visitors and others permanently resident outside Europe. It is valid for first- and second-class unlimited rail travel for anything from three to ten days during a two-month period on main line, AVE and international routes to Paris, Zurich and Milan. It includes discounts on various ferry routes, hotel reservations and car rental. It can be bought in Spain as well as abroad.

Eurail Pass: This is available only to US visitors and others permanently resident outside Europe, Algeria, Byelorussia, Estonia, Latvia, Moldova, Morocco, Russia, Tunisia and the Ukraine, and valid for international rail travel in Spain, as well as in 16 other European countries. Choose between passes valid for one country; the Select Pass for travel within three to five bordering countries; or the Global Pass for travel throughout all 17 participating countries. It is also valid for ferries between Italy and Greece (HML and Adriatic Navigation) and between Finland and Sweden (Silja Line). Options include first or second class, from two weeks' travel to one, two or three consecutive months' travel, a Eurail YouthPass for under 26s, a Eurail SaverPass for groups of two to five. Children aged four to eleven travel half price; under fours go free, unless they require a separate seat or bed. Passes must be bought before arrival in Spain.

INTER RAIL PRICE CHART

	DURATION	INTER RAIL -26	INTER RAIL +26
One Country Pass	3 days in 1 month	€109	€147
Global	1 month	€399	€599
Prices are for second-class travel; first class is also available			

INTER RAIL ZONE

Europe is divided into eight zones and you can travel in one, two, three or all zones, depending on which rail pass you buy (see above). The eight zones are:

Zone A	Great Britain, Ireland
Zone B	Finland, Norway, Sweden
Zone C	Austria, Denmark, Germany, Switzerland
Zone D	Croatia, Czech Republic, Hungary, Poland, Slovakia, Bosnia
Zone E	Belgium, France, Luxembourg, Netherlands
Zone F	Morocco, Portugal, Spain
Zone G	Greece, Italy, Slovenia, Turkey (includes the Ancona/Bari/Brindisi to Corfu/Igoumenitsa/Patras ferry route)
Zone H	Bulgaria, Macedonia, Yugoslavia, Romania

The chart below shows the duration in hours and minutes of a train journey between these destinations in Spain.

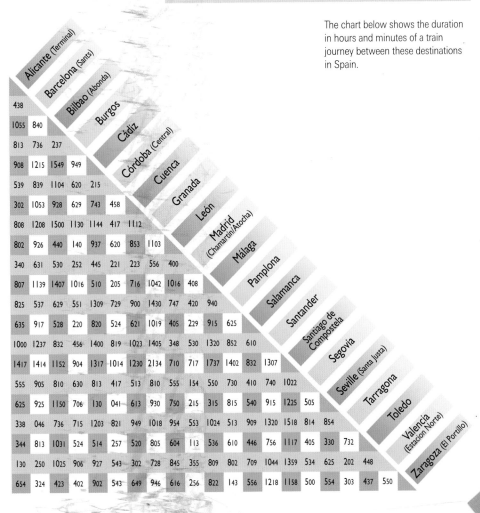

	Alicante (Terminal)	Barcelona (Sants)	Bilbao (Abonda)	Burgos	Cádiz	Córdoba (Central)	Cuenca	Granada	León	Madrid (Chamartin/Atocha)	Málaga	Pamplona	Salamanca	Santander	Santiago de Compostela	Segovia	Seville (Santa Justa)	Tarragona	Toledo	Valencia (Estación Norte)	Zaragoza (El Portillo)
Barcelona (Sants)	438
Bilbao (Abonda)	1055	840
Burgos	813	736	237
Cádiz	908	1215	1549	949
Córdoba (Central)	539	839	1104	620	215
Cuenca	302	1053	928	629	743	458
Granada	808	1208	1500	1130	1144	417	1112
León	802	926	440	140	937	620	853	1103
Madrid (Chamartin/Atocha)	340	631	530	252	445	221	223	556	400
Málaga	807	1139	1407	1016	510	205	716	1042	1016	408
Pamplona	825	537	629	551	1309	729	900	1430	747	420	940
Salamanca	635	917	528	220	820	524	621	1019	405	229	915	625
Santander	1000	1237	832	456	1400	819	1023	1405	348	530	1320	852	610
Santiago de Compostela	1417	1414	1152	904	1317	1014	1230	2134	710	717	1737	1402	832	1307
Segovia	555	905	810	630	813	417	513	810	555	154	550	730	410	740	1022
Seville (Santa Justa)	625	925	1150	706	130	041	613	930	750	215	315	815	540	915	1225	505
Tarragona	338	046	736	715	1203	821	949	1018	954	553	1024	513	909	1320	1518	814	854
Toledo	344	813	1031	524	514	257	520	805	604	113	536	610	446	756	1117	405	330	732
Valencia (Estación Norte)	130	250	1025	906	927	543	302	728	845	355	809	802	709	1044	1359	534	625	202	448
Zaragoza (El Portillo)	654	324	423	402	902	543	649	946	616	256	822	143	556	1218	1158	500	554	303	437	550

DOMESTIC FLIGHTS

Flights within Spain vary wildly in price and can be major money savers if booked via the internet at off-peak hours. The late-evening Madrid-Sevilla and Madrid-Barcelona connections cut AVE prices in half. If you add in the time needed to get to airports and check in, then on shorter inland trips it can be as quick to travel by train, especially as trains tend to go to the heart of cities and towns.

Flight service frequency varies considerably from every 15 minutes between Madrid and Barcelona in peak times to twice a day or so between provincial capitals.

If you need to fly from one provincial capital to another, your journey may be routed via Madrid, at which point you will need to change aircraft, lengthening your journey time.

BUYING TICKETS

After many years when Spain's main carrier, Iberia, had the domestic airline market all to itself, the arrival of Spanair and Air Europa has helped stimulate more competition and keener prices.

For the most popular services, such as the Puente Aéreo shuttle between Madrid and Barcelona, there is an automatic self-ticketing system, which allows passengers to buy tickets as little as 15 minutes before their flight departs. Advance reservations offer lower prices. Reserve at least a week in advance.

At some airports, such as Madrid and Barcelona, there are express check-in services where you can get your boarding card and seat allocation by scanning your ticket. Spanair also has a ticket-buying and check-in service at the Nuevos Ministerios Metro station in Madrid.

MAIN DOMESTIC CARRIERS

» **Iberia** (www.iberia.com), Spain's national airline, operates services to all the main regional airports around the Iberian peninsula. At peak times during the day it flies a shuttle every 15 minutes between Barcelona and Madrid.

» **Air Nostrum** (www.airnostrum. es), a subsidary of Iberia, operates some of the Iberia services to the Balearic islands.

» **Air Europa** (www.aireuropa.com) serves an extensive list of cities and the Balearic and Canary islands, in addition to flights to other parts of Europe and the Americas.

» **Spanair** (www.spanair.com) operates international flights as well as national flights to a range of regional airports and the larger cities.

» **Vueling** (www.vueling.com) is a new low-cost internet company that operates national and some international services from Barcelona and Madrid.

» **Clickair** (www.clickair.com) is the newest low-cost airline; it operates domestic and international flights from its base in Barcelona.

» **Ryanair** (www.ryanair.com) now flies from Barcelona's El Prat airport (since 1 September 1010) to destinations in Spain and Europe including Gran Canarias, Lanzarote, Ibiza and Málaga.

LUGGAGE ALLOWANCE

» 20kg (44 lb) in standard class.
» 30kg (66 lb) in business class.
» Hand luggage allowance is 10kg/ 22 lb (6kg/13 lb with Spanair and Air Europa).

DOMESTIC AIRPORTS AND SERVICES

	IBERIA	AIR EUROPA	SPANAIR	VUELING	CLICKAIR
Alacant (Alicante)	yes	yes	yes		yes
Almería	yes				
Asturias	yes	yes	yes		yes
Badajoz	yes	yes			
Barcelona	yes	yes	yes	yes	yes
Bilbao (Bilbo)	yes	yes	yes	yes	yes
A Coruña	yes				yes
Donostia (San Sebastián)	yes				
Fuerteventura	yes	yes	yes		
Granada	yes	yes		yes	
Gran Canaria	yes	yes	yes	yes	yes
Ibiza	yes	yes	yes	yes	yes
Jerez de la Frontera	yes	yes	yes	yes	
Lanzarote	yes	yes	yes		
León	yes				
Logroño	yes				
Madrid	yes	yes	yes	yes	
Maó (Mahón)	yes	yes	yes	yes	yes
Málaga	yes	yes	yes		
Melilla	yes				
Murcia	yes				
Palma de Mallorca	yes	yes	yes	yes	yes
Pamplona (Iruña)	yes				
Reus	yes				
Santa Cruz de la Palma	yes				
Santander	yes				
Santiago de Compostela	yes	yes	yes	yes	
Seville	yes	yes			yes
Tenerife	yes	yes	yes		
Valencia	yes	yes	yes	yes	yes
Valladolid	yes				
Vigo	yes		yes		yes
Vitoria (Gasteiz)	yes				
Zaragoza	yes	yes			

National Express Eurolines (tel 08717 818 181 in the UK, www.eurolines.com) is one of the major operators, offering multi-day passes that cover travel to some 31 countries. Youth fares are available for the under-26s.

North American visitors can book via the European website.

INTERNATIONAL BUS JOURNEY TIMES

(all times are approximate)
London to Barcelona—25 hours.
London to Madrid—28 hours.
Paris to Barcelona—15 hours.
Munich to Madrid—31 hours.

Above *A EuskoTran tram running alongside a Bilbobus in Bilbao. Both transportation systems are part of an efficient citywide network*

BUSES AND TAXIS

Spain has a very good bus network at local, regional, national and international levels, so you should be able to travel just about anywhere you want to go and it is generally less expensive than going by train.

In a city, if convenience and speed are important, then a taxi is a pretty straightforward way of quickly getting exactly where you want to go.

LOCAL AND REGIONAL BUSES

Many villages throughout Spain are accessible only by bus. The local train network is comparatively sparse, so going by bus can often be the best, if not the only, way to get directly to a small village or town, especially in a remote area.

Local bus services tend to emanate from the bigger towns and regional capitals, so you may find yourself having to travel via one of them to get between villages.

There are plenty of bus companies running services, and the best way to find out where a particular bus departs from is to ask at a visitor information office or at the main bus station. Comfort levels vary widely on these services and there are usually no facilities on board.

You can buy a ticket at the station prior to departure or, more often, on the bus itself.

NATIONAL BUSES

There are many bus companies running services to and from major cities. These services tend to depart from main bus stations, though some companies operate out of their own bus garages. They are popular, but also numerous, so advance booking is rarely necessary, though it's a good idea if you are touring around in the height of the visitor season, when all of Spain seems to be on the move. Advance tickets must be purchased from the bus station.

The quality of service and facilities does vary from one coach operator to another, but they tend to be comfortable, and there are basic facilities on board.

INTERNATIONAL BUSES

There are services running into Portugal, France, the UK and other western European countries from many of the major Spanish cities, including Barcelona and Madrid. These offer excellent conditions on modern buses and can be cheaper than other forms of international travel, though the journey times are lengthy (see above right).

TAXIS

Generally, catching a taxi in Spain is fairly stress-free as long as you take into account some of the basic rules of taxi travel anywhere.

» Always check to see that the meter is working, switched on and set to the minimum fare before the journey commences.

» If there is no meter or it is not working, fix a price beforehand with the driver.

» If you do not speak the language, write the price down on a piece of paper.

» If the taxi has a meter, it helps to have a general idea of where you are heading on a city map, to prevent the driver taking you around every backstreet to run the meter up.

» Bogus or crooked taxi drivers do exist, so stay on your guard, especially at night.

» You can hail a taxi out on the street, as well as catching one from an official taxi stand.

» At airports and rail stations you must wait at the official rank, but taxis arrive quite frequently.

» Taxis that are free have their roof sign lit up.

» It is up to you whether you tip the driver. Around 10 per cent of the fare is usual.

» Outside of the cities and the major towns, it can often be difficult to find taxis out on the street.

» The best place to find one is the train or bus station.

While visitor services in the main cities and some of the more modern attractions out in rural areas are active in providing suitable disability access, Spain is on the whole quite poorly equipped compared to other European and North American countries.

Things are improving all the time, though, and new public buildings are now legally obliged to include facilities for people with disabilities.

BY TRAIN

Most RENFE trains have space for passengers using wheelchairs. Guide dogs accompanying people with impaired vision travel free of charge at any time on all long-distance *(largo recorrido)* lines — normally, you pay 50 per cent of the ticket price to take an animal on such a journey.

At major stations, there is usually a member of staff to provide assistance getting on to and off trains, and wheelchairs are available for use at most main stations.

BY AIR

All of the major airports are quite well equipped for visitors with disabilities, with lift (elevator) access to all floors and assistance available if needed; just ask at the main information desks.

BY BUS

Few buses beyond the major cities have easy access for wheelchairs. In the main cities, wheelchair accessible buses display the international wheelchair sign. There are taxis with wheelchair ramps available in the main cities.

BY FERRY

If you are going to Spain by ferry from the UK, Brittany Ferries (tel +44 (0)8709 076 103; www.brittany-ferries.co.uk) sail from Plymouth to Santander and cater for visitors with special needs or disabilities.

Their ports have disabled parking provision, wheelchair access and wheelchair accessible toilets. They also have a limited number of wheelchairs for passenger use in the terminals, and can provide special cabins on board, as long as they are notified in advance and the ships have lift (elevator) systems.

AROUND TOWN

The older parts of Spain are particularly difficult for people with disabilities. Generally, the old towns and villages have high, uneven, cobbled paving, often steep streets and narrow doorways. Some of the bigger attractions, such as castles and museums, have made an attempt to address the issue, but coverage is patchy.

Bigger cities, especially Madrid and Barcelona, are more disability friendly. Pavements (sidewalks) are ramped on many street corners, particularly in the more modern quarters. The older quarters, though, tend to have very narrow streets, often cobbled, and allow traffic, making it a bit of an obstacle course in a wheelchair. The quieter streets are sometimes easier to negotiate. Major museums and other public attractions have some facilities for those with disabilities, and many public parks are also accessible.

Access to cathedrals and churches varies considerably, but on the whole it is difficult, with rough sets of stone steps being the principal problem.

For specific information on the region or city you intend to visit contact the Spanish Tourist Board (www.tourspain.es) who can give you information on individual attractions.

Right *Sign showing wheelchair access on to the beach at Port Bou*

USEFUL INFORMATION SOURCES FOR VISITORS WITH DISABILITIES

» ONCE is the high-profile Spanish organization for the visually impaired. It can supply information on access for visitors with visual impairment around Spain. You can contact it on www.once.es or alternatively call its Madrid office (tel 915 32 50 00).

» www.makoa.org has a vast number of resource links for people with disabilities, including information on travel; look under Travel and Recreation Resources.

» Global Access (www.globalaccessnews.com) is a website containing a huge range of links useful for visitors with disabilities around the world, and includes Barcelona and Seville.

» UK: RADAR, 12 City Forum, 250 City Road, London EC1V 8AF (tel +44 (0)20 7250 3222; www.radar.org.uk).

» US: SATH, 347 5th Avenue, Suite 610, New York City, NY 10016 (tel +1 212/447-7284; www.sath.org).

» US: Mobility International, Suite 343, 132 E. Broadway, Eugene, OR 97401, tel 541/343-1284, www.miusa.org

ACCESSOS FÀCILS I SEGURS

ACCESOS FÁCILES Y SEGUROS

SAFE AND EASY ACCESS

REGIONS

This chapter is divided into ten regions of Spain (▷ 8). Region names are for the purposes of this book only and places of interest are listed alphabetically in each region.

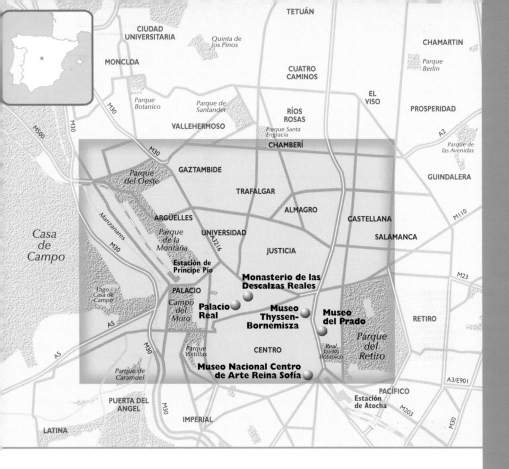

MADRID

Madrid sits high on a lofty plain in the very heart of Spain. This buzzy, vibrant, modern capital offers visitors fantastic opportunities for shopping, nightlife and culture, and is home to some of the finest museums in Europe. The greatest of these is undoubtedly the Prado, renovated and expanded, with a magnificent collection of Old Masters. Nearby, the fashionable Reina Sofía, now expanded with a sleek new annex, displays Picasso's *Guernica*, arguably the most important painting of the 20th century. The third museum of the so-called Golden Triangle, the elegant Thyssen-Bornemisza, offers a superb art collection which spans seven centuries.

The old kernel of the city is surprisingly small but deeply atmospheric, with a warren of narrow streets connecting charming squares. Tucked away down hidden passages you'll find ancient convents for blue-blooded nuns, tile-lined tapas bars, and old-fashioned restaurants serving the classic local stew, *cocido madrileño*. To the west of the old centre lies the glittering royal palace, the opera house, and the former royal hunting grounds of the Casa de Campo, now a magnificent public park. The broad, busy Gran Vía bisects the city from west to east, and is lined with grand turn-of-the-20th-century buildings, most now converted into shops, cinemas and restaurants. To the north of Gran Vía lie the bohemian neighbourhoods of Chueca and Malasaña, and to the south are the once-shabby, but now rapidly gentrifying La Latina and Lavapiés districts. The Puerta del Sol is the city's transportation hub, and the gateway to the lively nightlife neighbourhood of Santa Ana, where historic theatres and literary haunts still survive among the new, fashionable bars and restaurants. The Parque del Retiro to the east is the city's loveliest park, with a central boating lake and manicured gardens. Beyond it is Salamanca, a chic district of smart avenues with elegant hotels and expensive boutiques.

MADRID

300 m
300 yds

MADRID • CITY MAPS

Museo del Traje
Plaza Cardenal Cisneros
Escuela T S de Ingenieros Aeronauticos
Hospital Clinico San Carlos
Plaza Cristo Rey
AVENIDA DE FILIPINAS
Glorieta Guzmán El Bueno
CALLE
CEA
DE
Islas Filipinas
ARAPILE

AVENIDA JUAN DE HERRERA
AV. PUERTA DE HIERRO ARCO VICTORIA
Casa del Brasil
Museo de América
CALLE DE LOS REYES CATÓLICOS

Universidad Nacional de Educación Física
AVENIDA MARTIN FIERRO
CALLE DE EL PARDO

AVENIDA DE SÉNECA

Parque del Oeste

PASEO DE RUPERTO CHAPI
Glorieta Maestro

GAZTAMBIDE
Mercado

Centro Cultural Galileo

Plaza Cancilleria

PASEO PINTOR ROSALES
PASEO DE CAMOENS
PASEO DE MORET
CALLE ISAAC PERAL

Cuartel General del Aire

AVENIDA DE VALLADOLID

Plaza de Moncloa

ALCÁNTARA
Estación Salida Teleférico
CALLE MARQUÉS DE URQUIJO
Convento Trinitarias
Mercado
Argüelles

ARGÜELLES

CALLE ALBERTO AGUILERA

UNIVERSIDAD

Servicio Histórico del Ejército
Palacio Duque de Liria

Monumento Infante Isabel
Antiguo Cuartel del Conde Duque
Ventura Rodríguez

Ermita de San Antonio de la Florida

PINTOR
Parque de la Montaña
Templo de Debod

ROSALES

Plaza Cristino Martos
Torre de Madrid

Teatro San Pol

Río Manzanares
PASEO DE LA FLORIDA

Casa de Campo

PASEO DEL MARQUES DE MONISTROL

Museo Cerralbo

Plaza de España
PRINCESA

Mon a Cervantes

ESTACIÓN DE PRINCIPE PÍO

Palacio del Senado

Lago Casa de Campo

EMBARCADERO

Puente del Rey

Jardines de Sabatini

Real Monasterio de la Encarnación

PASEO AZUL

Príncipe Pío
Glorieta San Vicente

CUESTA DE SAN VICENTE
Palacio Real

Teatro Real
Plaza Isabel II

Plaza de Oriente

PASEO DEL
Glorieta los Patines
Lago
AVENIDA DEL ANGEL

Campo del Moro
Plaza de la Armería

PALACIO

San Nicolás de los Servitas
Plaza de la Villa
Ayuntamiento

Catedral de Nuestra Señora de la Almudena

Ermita
Muralla Árabe

VIADUCTO
BAILEN

Arzobispal Castrense
San Pedro el Viejo

Glorieta Azorín
Parque de Atenas
Parque Emir Mohamed I

Feria del Campo

Santa Cristina
Puerta del Angel
Plaza Santa Cristina

Servicio Geológico del M O P T

AVENIDA DE PORTUGAL

AVENIDA DE EXTREMADURA

Centro Estud Hidrográficos

PASEO DE LA VIRGEN DEL PUERTO
Glorieta Boccherini

CALLE DE SEGOVIA
Viaducto

Plaza de la Paja
San Andrés

Capilla Cristo de los Dolores

Parque Vistillas

San Francisco

Alto de Extremadura

Molino de Vientó

Basílica de San Francisco el Grande

GRAN VIA DE SAN FRANCISCO

Parque de Caramuel

PASEO DE LA ERMITA DEL SANTO

PASEO DE LOS MELANCÓLICOS

V de la Paloma

SEGOVIA

Glorieta Puerta de Toledo

A
B
C

66

Parque Santa Engracia
Rios Rosas
CHAMBERÍ
Ministerio Defensa
Monumento de Isabel La Católica
Archivo Histórico Nacional

CALLE
Bretón
Calle
Herreros
PASEO
Zurbano
CALLE DE SERRANO
Pedro
de
Valdivia
CALLE DE VELAZQUEZ

Canal
Murillo
BRAVO
ABASCAL
Plaza Dr Marañón
Gregorio Marañón
CALLE MARIA
DE
MOLINA

Cortés
CALLE DE
Alonso Cano
JOSE
Convento San Vicente
Garcia
Paredes
LA CASTELLANA
Viriato
Museo Lázaro Galdiano
Convento P. Dominicos
Santa Monica

TRAFALGAR
Sinagoga
Glorieta Pintor Sorolla
Museo Sorolla
PASEO GENERAL MARTINEZ CAMPOS
ALMAGRO
Glorieta Emilio Castelar
CALLE DIEGO DE LEON
Convento Esclavas del Sagrado Corazón
San Francisco de Borja
La Virgen Peregrino
Santa M de Carmelo

CALLE ELOY GONZALO
Iglesia
Plaza Santa Feliciana
Calle Sagunto
PASEO DE EDUARDO DATO
Pte Enrique de la Mata Gorostizaga
Museo de Arte Infantil
CALLE DE JUAN BRAVO

Glorieta Ruben Dario
Museo de Escultura Abstracta
Ruben Dario
Museo de Escultura al Aire Libre
CASTELLANA
San Andrés Flamencos
Fundación Juan March

CALLE DEL General Arrando
Monasterio Convento Visitación Santa Maria
Calle de Zurbarán
CALLE JOSE ORTEGA Y GASSET
Plaza Marques de Salamanca

San José de la Montaña
Calle de Caracas
Calle Fernando El Santo
Santa M de Monte Carmelo

SAGASTA
Plaza Alonso Martinez
Alonso Martinez
Ayala
SALAMANCA

Plaza de Dos de Mayo
Museo Municipal
Jardines Arquie Riv
Museo Romántico
Colón
Mercado
RECOLETOS
Hermosilla

San Feo de Sales
JUSTICIA
Plaza de Colón
Centro Cultural Villade Madrid
CALLE DE GOYA
La Concepción

Convento de San Plácido
Iglesia de San Antón
Palacio de Justicia Bárbara
Museo de Cera
Jardines del Descubrimiento
Biblioteca Nacional
Príncipe de Vergara

San Antonio Alemanes
Chueca
Santa Bárbara
Calle de Piamonte
Museo Arqueológico Nacional
Archivo Heráldico
Plaza de Toros

San Martin
Gran Via
Calle de Augusto Figueroa
Calle del Almirante
ESTACIÓN DE RECOLETOS
Palacio Marques de Salamanca

Casa de las Siete Chimeneas
Calle de Prim
Palacio de Buenavista
Casa de América
San Manuel y San Benito
CALLE DE O'DONNELL

GRAN VIA
San José
Plaza de Cibeles
Palacio de Comunicaciones
Plaza de la Independencia
Puerta de Madrid

Monasterio de las Descalzas Reales
SOL
Calatravas
ALCALA
Banco de España
Museo Naval
Museo Artes Decorativas
Alfonso XII
Glorieta Sardana

Real Academia de Bellas Artes de San Fernando
Palacio la Zarzuela
Museo Thyssen-Bornemisza
La Bolsa
Paseo de la Argentina
Palacio Velázquez

Puerta del Sol
CARRERA DE SAN JERÓNIMO
Palacio del Congreso
Museu del Boen Retiro
Palacio de Cristal

Casa de Correos
Teatro R Victoria
Plaza de las Cortes
Plaza Canovas del Castillo
Cason del Buen Retiro

Plaza Mayor
Teatro Español
CORTES
Ateneo
Museo del Prado
San Jeronimo El Real
Parque del Retiro

CENTRO
Casa Museo Lope de Vega
Jesús de Medinaceli
JERÓNIMOS

Colegiata de n Isidro el Real
San Sebastián
Convento Trinitarias
San Roberto
CaixaForum Madrid
La Rosaleda

San Millán y San Cayetano
Antón Martín
Real Jardín Botánico
PASEO REINA CRISTINA

Conservatorio de Música
Ministerio Agricult Pesca y Alimentac
Ministerio Educación y Cultura
Viveros Municipales

Convento de Santa Isabel
Museo Nacional Centro de Arte Reina Sofía
Atocha RENFE
Museo Etnologia
Observatorio Astronómico

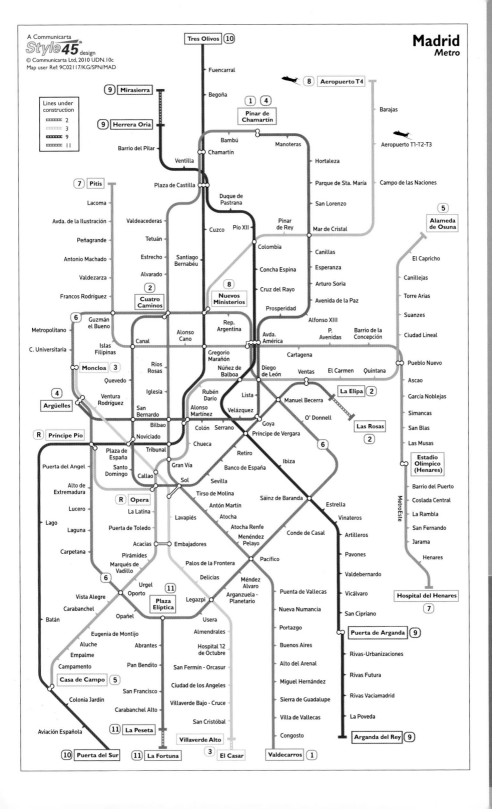

Madrid Metro

CAIXAFORUM MADRID

www.laCaixa.es/ObraSocial

A remarkable contemporary building houses Madrid's newest cultural space. The CaixaForum offers a varied programme, which includes everything from events for children to free concerts, workshops, art exhibitions and much more. A full programme is available online, or pick up a leaflet at tourist offices.

➕ 67 E5 ✉ Paseo del Prado 36, 28014 Madrid ☎ 913 30 73 00 🕐 Daily 10–8 ✋ Free, charge for some activities 🚇 Atocha 🚌 🚊

CAMPO DEL MORO

In 1890 Queen María Cristina of Habsburg relandscaped the gardens of the Palacio Real (▷ 81) along the lines of a Romantic English park, renaming them The Moor's Field after the Arab general Ali Ben Yusuf, who supposedly set up camp here while laying siege to the city in 1109. The grotto near the main gate conceals the entrance to a tunnel built for Felipe II as a short cut to the Casa de Campo (see below). You can see the royal carriage horses being exercised every day around noon, but the Museo de Carruajes (Carriage Museum) is closed indefinitely for restoration.

➕ 66 B4 ✉ Paseo de la Virgen del Puerto, 28071 Madrid ☎ 914 54 87 00 🕐 Apr–Sep Mon–Sat 10–8, Sun 9–8; Oct–Mar Mon–Sat 10–6, Sun 9–6 ✋ Free 🚇 Opera 🚌 25, 33, 39, 41, 46, 68, 69, 75

CASA DE CAMPO

This vast green lung, on the western side of Madrid, is a tract of wooded countryside. During the Civil War Franco's troops were based here, and signs of trenches are still visible. Once a royal hunting ground, it was opened to the public in 1931, and has a combined zoo and aquarium housing 600-plus species (daily 11–dusk), the Parque de Atracciones amusement park (Jul–Aug Mon–Fri noon–1am, Sat noon–2am, Sun

noon–midnight; Sep–Jun Sat–Sun and festivals noon–9), and a boating lake. The best way to arrive is by taking the *teleférico*, or cable-car (tel 915 41 74 50), from the Paseo del Pintor Rosales on the edge of Parque del Oeste.

➕ 66 A3 ℹ Calle Marqués de Monistrol, Avenida de Portugal, 28011 Madrid ☎ 914 79 60 02, 915 12 37 70 for zoo 🚇 Lago, Batán 🚌 33, 39, 41, 65, 75, 84

CATEDRAL DE NUESTRA SEÑORA DE LA ALMUDENA

Madrid's Roman Catholic cathedral shares a clifftop setting with the adjoining Palacio Real (▷ 81), and has wide views across the city from the terrace. It was consecrated in 1993 by Pope John Paul II and officially opened a year later. The interior is impressive, resembling a medieval church, with (modern) stained-glass windows and painted, vaulted ceilings. The Chapel of the Almudena has a late 15th-century statue of the Virgin. Less pleasing to the eye are the facade and dome.

➕ 66 C4 ✉ Calle de Bailén s/n, 28071 Madrid ☎ 915 42 22 00 🕐 Cathedral: daily 9–7.30. Closed during services. Crypt: daily 10–2, 5–8 ✋ Free 🚇 Opera 🚌 3, 148

COLEGIATA DE SAN ISIDRO EL REAL

The Church of San Isidro, one of the city's most important baroque monuments, dates from 1534, when Jesuits founded a monastery on the site and, later, a prestigious school, the Colegio Imperial. San Isidro served as the city's cathedral until

the completion of the Almudena. The barrel-vaulted interior is impressive, if a little gloomy. The remains of San Isidro, Madrid's patron saint, are in a reliquary above the high altar.

➕ 67 D5 ✉ Colegiata de San Isidro, Calle de Toledo 37–39, 28005 Madrid ☎ 913 69 20 37 🕐 Mon–Sat 7.30–1, 6.30–8.30, Sun 9–2. Closed during services ✋ Free 🚇 La Latina, Tirso de Molina 🚌 17, 18, 23, 35

ERMITA DE SAN ANTONIO DE LA FLORIDA

www.munimadrid.es/ermita

The walls, vaults and cupola of the Chapel of St. Anthony are decorated with superb frescoes by Francisco de Goya (1746–1828), who is buried here. The church was designed by Italian architect Felipe Fontana in 1792 and completed eight years later. An identical chapel was built in 1925 so that the *ermita* (hermitage) could function exclusively as a museum.

The frescoes themselves, dating from 1798, were considered revolutionary in both technique and subject matter. The vaults are adorned with sensuous angels and cherubim. The central scene, in the cupola, depicts St. Anthony of Padua bringing a murdered man back to life to clear the name of his father, wrongly accused of the crime. The models for the frescoes were members of the Spanish Court.

➕ 66 B3 ✉ Glorieta de San Antonio de la Florida 5, 28008 Madrid ☎ 915 42 07 22 🕐 Tue–Fri 10–8 (until 2.30 in Aug), Sat–Sun 10–2 ✋ Free 🚇 Príncipe Pío 🚌 41, 46, 75

Right *Madrid's Royal Palace is best viewed from the Campo del Moro (Moor's Field)*
Opposite *San Antonio de la Florida church*

www.patrimonionacional.es

➕ 67 D4 ✉ Plaza de las Descalzas
Reales 3, 28013 Madrid ☎ 914 54 88 00
🕐 Tue–Thu, Sat 10.30–12.45, 4–5.45,
Fri 10.30–12.45, Sun 11–1.45. 🎫 Adult
€5, child (5–16) €2.60; combined
admission with Real Monasterio de la
Encarnación available, adult €6, child
€3.50 🚇 Sol 🚌 3, 5, 15, 20, 50, 51, 52,
53, 150 🚐 Compulsory 1-hour guided
tour departs every 15 min 🛍 Small
shop, selling art books, guides to
Madrid, decorative religious objects and
mementoes

TIPS

» The guided tour is in Spanish, but
your guide may be English speaking. Be
prepared to wait for up to 15 minutes
while a sufficient number of visitors
assemble for the tour.

» To get the most out of your visit, focus
on the overall impact of the artistic
treasures rather than trying to locate
particular exhibits.

Below *The austere brick and stone facade
of the monastery*

MONASTERIO DE LAS DESCALZAS REALES

The monastery has been a working convent since its foundation more than
400 years ago. The building was originally a palace, and in 1554 Felipe II's sister,
Juana de Austria, stayed here while acting as regent for her brother. She had
the palace adapted for use as a convent, and the Franciscan nuns who live here
were originally nicknamed *las descalzas reales* ('the royal barefooted women') on
account of their aristocratic backgrounds. The convent has an impressive display
of paintings, sculptures, tapestries, *azulejos* (painted tiles) and gold and silver
liturgical objects. The only way to see them is on a guided tour.

OUTSTANDING FRESCOES

The Grand Staircase is one of the first stops, and one of its highlights. The
stunning frescoes that cover the walls, arches and balustrades were painted at
the end of the 17th century by José Ximénez Donoso (1632–90) and Claudio
Coello (1642–93). To the right is the Balcón Real (Royal Balcony), with a splendid
portrait of Felipe IV and his family. The staircase leads to the Upper Cloister,
which is surrounded by chapels. Look for the Chapel of the Virgin of Guadalupe,
which has 68 oil panels painted in 1653 by Sebastián de Herrera Barnuevo. The
altar facing is made of wood, bronze and glass, and the statue of the Virgin,
though not the original, dates from the 16th century.

TAPESTRY ROOM

Next is the antechoir, with its late 15th-century *Virgin and Child*, one of the
oldest works of art in the convent. You then go through the choir and to the
16th-century Redeemer's Staircase, which leads to the Tapestry Room. Here
is a superb set of 20 Brussels tapestries dating from the 17th century, not all
of which are on show. They were commissioned by the Infanta Isabel Clara
Eugenia. The cartoons for the tapestries were prepared by Peter Paul Rubens
(1577–1640) and include the famous *Triumph of the Eucharist* (*c*1625).

PAINTINGS

The Spanish and Italian Picture Room has an excellent collection of paintings,
among them *St. Francis*, attributed to Zurbarán (1598–1664), and *The Tribute
Money* by Titian (1490–1576).

MUSEO DE AMÉRICA

www.museodeamerica.mcu.es

This unusual museum, northwest of central Madrid, gives a fascinating insight into the native cultures of the American continent as seen from a Spanish perspective.

The exhibition is spread over two floors and divided into five themed areas: the tools of knowledge and understanding, from the Age of the Discoveries to the 18th century; the societies as they really were; the evolution of American societies, from tribal communities to nation states; religion; and communications, from pictograms to music. The majority of the pre-Columbian objects on show here were recovered in the 18th and 19th centuries by scientists on overseas expeditions, and the collections embrace textiles, ceramics, tools, weaponry, paintings and sculptures.

The Quimbayas treasure in Area 4 is the largest collection of pre-Columbian goldwork ever discovered. For most visitors, this is the star exhibit. The collection, which includes objects around 1,000 years old, was donated by the Colombian government in 1892.

✚ 66 B1 ✉ Avenida Reyes Católicos 6, 28040 Madrid ☎ 915 49 26 41 🕒 Tue–Sat 9.30–3, Sun 10–3 ✋ Adult €3, under 18 free. Free Sun 🚇 Moncloa 🚌 1, 12, 16, 44, 46, 61, 82, 83, 132, 133, C 🍴 Small café 🛍 The ground-level shop sells postcards, mementoes and books, but most if not all of these are in Spanish

MUSEO CERRALBO

www.museocerralbo.mcu.es

When Enrique de Aguilera y Gamboa, the 17th Marquis of Cerralbo, died in 1922, he left his palace and its entire contents, including 30,000 works of art, archaeological objects and curios, to the state. It was another 40 years, however, before it opened to the public as a museum.

Apart from being a professional politician, the marquis spent more than 30 years of his life touring the world in search of artistic treasures. As a result, the rooms in this former palace are crammed with furniture,

Above *Balconies adorn the 19th-century curved corner facade of the Museo Cerralbo, formerly the home of the 17th-century Marquis of Cerralbo*

paintings, sculptures and objets d'art. Everything is exactly as the old marquis left it, so you also gain an insight into the life and tastes of a 19th-century Spanish aristocrat.

The paintings on display in the Picture Gallery and Billiard Room include works by El Greco, Ribera, Zurbarán, Titian, Tintoretto and Veronese. The Ballroom is the most opulent room in the mansion, and is decorated with marble, mirrors and a ceiling fresco, *History of the Dance*, by Máximo Juderías Caballero (1867–1951). A 16th-century porcelain moulding of the Nativity by Italian sculptor Andrea della Robbia (1435–1525) decorates the Porcelain Room; *The Ecstasy of St. Francis* by El Greco (1541–1614) hangs in the Sacristy (ground level); and the marquis' roll-top desk and wall telephone are in the Red Room.

✚ 66 C3 ✉ Calle de Ventura Rodríguez 17, 28008 Madrid ☎ 915 47 36 46 🕒 Closed for restoration; due to reopen in early 2011 🚇 Plaza de España, Ventura Rodríguez 🚌 1, 2, 44, 46, 74, 75, 133, 138, 148, C

MUSEO LÁZARO GALDIANO

www.flg.es

On his death in 1947, José Lázaro Galdiano, publisher, patron of the arts and insatiable collector of paintings

and objets, bequeathed his palatial home and its contents to the state. The legacy amounts to what must be one of the most important private collections of its type in the world. The collection contains furniture, gold and silver pieces, clocks and watches, jewellery, various ornaments and pieces of armour.

The Spanish paintings on display include works by (or attributed to) El Greco, Zurbarán, Murillo, Claudio Coello, Velázquez and Goya. There are European paintings by Bosch, Dürer, Rembrandt, Van Dyck and Rubens, and by the English artists Reynolds, Constable, Gainsborough, Turner and Lawrence. The museum has been completely overhauled.

Look for the 16th-century rock-crystal cup that belonged to Emperor Rudolph II of Austria; the second-century BC Celtic diadem (headband) found at Ribadeo; and a 13th-century crozier (bishop's staff) from France.

✚ 67 F1 ✉ Calle Serrano 122, 28001 Madrid ☎ 915 61 60 84 🕒 Wed–Mon 10–4.30. Closed Tue ✋ Mon-Sat €4; free Sun 🚇 Núñez de Balboa 🚌 12, 16, 19, 51, 89

MUSEO NACIONAL CENTRO DE ARTE REINA SOFÍA

▷ 77.

INFORMATION

www.museodelprado.es

➕ 67 E4 ✉ Paseo del Prado s/n, 28014 Madrid ☎ 913 30 28 00/902 10 70 77 (within Spain) 🕐 Tue–Sun 9–8. Last entry 30 min before closing; visitors are requested to start leaving the galleries 10 min before closing ✋ Adult €8, under 18s free. Free Tue–Sat 6pm–8pm, Sun 5pm–8pm, also 2 May, 18 May, 12 Oct, 19 Nov and 6 Dec 🚇 Banco de España, Atocha 🚌 9, 10, 14, 19, 27, 34, 37, 45 🎧 Audioguide in Rooms 1 and 51 for €3.50. For licensed private guides, ask at the visitor office. Free floorplan 🍴 Catalogue €36.10; guidebook €18.53 ☕ Self-service café-restaurant and upstairs bar. The former is rather overpriced. The bar is more pleasant, but its range of drinks and snacks is limited 🛍 Several sales points, with art books in a number of languages, books on Spain, CD-ROMs and guides to the Prado, plus assorted souvenirs

INTRODUCTION

The museum is in the so-called Golden Triangle of museums, which includes the nearby Reina Sofía and Thyssen-Bornemisza (▷ 77 and 78–79 respectively). The main entrance to the central Villanueva building is the Goya door at the north end. The labyrinthine layout and continuing renovations of this vast space result in constant room changes, so pick up a free floorplan as you enter. Generally, however, the first level contains most of the must-see pieces, by Velázquez, Goya and other major Spanish artists, while Italian Renaissance masters and sculpture are on the ground level. A separate exhibition space is the revamped former Casón del Buen Retiro ballroom. In 2007, Rafael Moneo's new extension, which incorporates the cloister of Los Jerónimos, opened to great acclaim. The new space now accommodates temporary exhibitions.

The Prado, which means 'meadow' in Spanish, is architecturally impressive in its own right, built in a neoclassical style under architect Juan de Villanueva. Although construction started in 1785, the building has been constantly extended, most recently in 1918 and then again in the 1950s and 1960s. The current renovation schedule has proved controversial, for although the Prado has been notoriously under-resourced for decades, it is seen as a cultural benchmark for Spain in general and Madrid in particular. (There was a national scandal in 1993, when the museum's roof developed major leaks in its key exhibition rooms, putting the showpiece *Las Meninas* at risk.)

The core of the collection was brought together over several hundred years by Spanish royalty, in particular Isabel, Carlos V, Felipe II and Felipe IV. It was Felipe IV who commissioned *Las Meninas* and who sent Velázquez and Rubens abroad to buy works by Italian, Flemish and English artists. It thus represents the personal taste of the monarchs, making it much stronger in some areas than others. There are also a large number of paintings here that were collected in the late 19th century from convents and monasteries in and around the capital. The Prado itself was established as an art gallery in 1819; it had originally been intended as a museum for natural sciences. It has had an eventful history, once occupied by Napoleonic troops as a barracks, then looted by locals after they left, and closed during the Spanish Civil War, when its collections were sent away for safekeeping.

WHAT TO SEE

GROUND LEVEL

The Annunciation by Fra Angelico (Room 49)

This picture is a superb encapsulation of early Renaissance Florentine painting by Fra Angelico (c1400–55). It shows both the expulsion of Adam and Eve from Paradise and the moment when the Virgin hears she is to bear a son. The architectural setting, masterly perspective and naturalistic details are all typical of the period, when painting was moving increasingly towards realism.

The Garden of Delights by Hieronymus van Aeken Bosch (Room 56A)

The Prado has an unmatched collection of work by Bosch (c1450–1516). The artist's most famous work is the triptych Garden of Delights (1504). It is divided into creation, earthly pleasures (and sins) and, finally, hell—a satirical view of the cyclical nature of humanity.

The Adoration of the Shepherds by El Greco (Room 61A)

This piece is typical of El Greco's later Mannerist work, with the awkward hands and posture, elongated bodies and strong use of yellow and crimson. This night-time adoration, using a powerful *chiaroscuro* (light and shade) technique, was painted towards the end of El Greco's career (1612–14) and was earmarked for his own funerary chapel. The crowded arrangement, full of stylized bodies, was said by critic José Ortega y Gasset to look 'ready to ignite'.

Christ Washing the Disciples' Feet by Tintoretto (Room 75)

Startling depth of perspective and dazzling use of light and shade draw the viewer deep into this scene from the days before Christ's death. Christ kneels in the right foreground, almost subservient to the three-dimensional effect given by the table and architectural background.

FIRST LEVEL

Artemesia by Rembrandt (Room 7)

The widow Artemesia here prepares to drink her husband's ashes, a thoughtful expression on her face. The composition, with its golden light playing on the central figure and air of grandeur and solemnity, is quintessential Rembrandt.

The Three Graces by Rubens (Room 9)

These luscious nudes, with their ample curves and glowing flesh, are utterly characteristic of Rubens' work. The artist kept the painting, which portrayed his wife (43 years the younger), all his life; it was acquired by Philip IV after Rubens' death.

TIPS
» The Prado is free Tuesday to Saturday 6pm to 8pm, and Sunday 5pm to 8pm.
» The Madrid Card (€48, €61 and €74 for one, two or three days) includes 40 museums such as the Prado, Thyssen, and the Reina Sofia.
» If you have only a limited amount of time, concentrate on the works by Velázquez and Goya (first level).

Opposite A statue of artist Velázquez fronts the main entrance to the Prado
Below left The Marquesa de Santa Cruz by Goya (1805)
Below A statue of Goya (1746–1828) stands outside the museum

GOYA

REGIONS MADRID • SIGHTS

75

Las Meninas by Velázquez (Room 12)

This is court painter Velázquez' best-known work, painted in 1656 under the original title of *La Familia de Felipe IV*, which refers to the court companions of the monarch's children. Although the royal Infanta Margarita is in the middle (the work was originally intended to hang in the king's private study), *Las Meninas* is full of endless interest, including plays on perception and perspective, an aristocratic self-portrait placed cheekily close to royalty, and copies of Rubens' works within the painting. The proportions are so perfect that Velázquez may have used a camera obscura to achieve the effect.

Black Paintings by Goya (Rooms 38 and 39)

The *Pinturas Negras* series of 14 works was never really meant for public consumption, having been painted by Goya on the walls of his home after he moved there in 1819; it was only long after his death that they were transferred to canvas and bequeathed to the Prado. These violent and disturbing images — including *The Witches' Sabbath* and *Saturn Devouring One of his Sons* — were painted during Goya's later years when he was deaf. Like his *Disasters of War* series and *The 3rd of May 1808* (painted 1814; also in the Prado), they underline his views on the atrocities of war and man's inhumanity to man.

SECOND LEVEL

The Clothed Maja and The Naked Maja by Goya (Room 89)

These two matching versions of the same subject — a reclining woman, clothed and then naked — were actually painted at different times (both c1800) and are among Goya's most talked-about works (▷ 39). The sensual nature of the paintings (the pose of the arms behind the head was a recognized sexual come-on) attracted the attention of the Inquisition. The model was initially thought to be the rich and powerful Duchess of Alba, with whom Goya almost certainly had a passionate affair. Although this theory is now discounted, there is speculation that the artist simply added a different 'head' to the Duchess's 'body'. Whatever the truth, the clothed *maja* (a term for a lower-class woman) was once hung over the naked version to give a striptease effect when lifted.

Above *The labyrinthine Museo del Prado contains many must-see Spanish pieces*
Right Las Meninas *by Velázquez (1656)*

MUSEO NACIONAL CENTRO DE ARTE REINA SOFÍA

Spain's national modern art museum opened in 1992 and is the largest exhibition space in Europe after the Pompidou Centre in Paris. Pride of place goes to Picasso's masterpiece, *Guernica* (1937), but the gallery also has an exceptional collection of work by his contemporaries, including Juan Gris, Joan Miró and Salvador Dalí.

The austerity of the facade is modified by the glass lifts (elevators), which allow visitors a view over the rooftops. A stunning new extension, designed by Jean Nouvel, opened in 2005. It contains the library and is mainly used for temporary exhibitions. The collection, in light and airy galleries, is arranged chronologically and thematically, beginning on the second level with the Basque and Catalán schools of the early 20th century. Art from the post-war period can be found on the fourth level, while the first and third levels are used for temporary shows.

GUERNICA

The focus of the permanent collection is Pablo Picasso (1881–1973). Most visitors make a beeline for *Guernica*. This huge canvas was the artist's response to the aerial bombing of the town of Gernika-Lumo (▷ 178) by the Germans, who were allies of General Franco during the Civil War. The impact of the painting was such that it still aroused controversy when it was first exhibited here in 1992. A bulletproof screen was installed to protect the painting against maverick right-wing attacks, but this was removed three years later and visitors can now see the painting as it was meant to be seen.

Room 6 shows some of Picasso's earlier work, including the Blue Period painting *Woman in Blue* (1901).

WORKS BY OTHER ARTISTS

The work of Madrid-born painter Juan Gris (1887–1927) is in Room 4. The whole of Room 7 is devoted to the Catalán artist Joan Miró (1893–1983). The artistic evolution of Salvador Dalí (1904–1989) during the 1920s and 1930s is explored in Room 10, where *The Great Masturbator* (1929) is representative of his work during this period.

The post-war generation of Spanish artists is also represented, along with European artists such as Robert and Sonia Delaunay, Max Ernst, Henry Moore and Francis Bacon, and leading American artists Ellsworth Kelly, Barnett Newman, Donald Judd and Bruce Naumann.

INFORMATION

www.museoreinasofia.es

⊞ 67 E5 ✉ Calle de Santa Isabel 52, 28012 Madrid ☎ 917 74 10 00 🕐 Mon, Wed–Sat 10–9, Sun 10–2.30. Closed Tue and public holidays 💷 Adult €6, under 18 free. Free Mon, Wed, Thu, Fri 7–9, Sat.2.30–9 and Sun 🚇 Atocha 🚌 All routes to Atocha 🎧 Audiotour €4. Free guided tours (Spanish only) Mon and Wed at 5, and Sat at 11; advance reservation required, tel: 915 27 72 05 📖 Official guide €22. Regularly updated, informative floorplan (English and Spanish) free 🍴 Café-restaurant and bar in basement. Drinks terrace 🍹 🎦

TIPS

» Out of season, the best time to visit the Reina Sofía is early on Sunday morning, when entry is free and there are relatively few visitors.

Below *Two external glass lifts (elevators) are a focal point of the museum*

INFORMATION

www.museothyssen.org

✚ 67 E4 ✉ Paseo del Prado 8, 28014 Madrid ☎ 913 69 01 51 🕐 Tue–Sun 10–7 👆 Permanent exhibition: adult €8, over 12 €5, under 12 free if accompanied by an adult. Temporary exhibitions: adult €8, over 12 €5. Combined permanent and temporary exhibition ticket: adult €13, over 12 €5 🚇 Banco de España 🚌 10, 14, 27, 34, 37, 45 🎧 Audiotours €5 📖 Guidebook €6. Floorplan free ☕ Café serving snacks, plus daily fixed-price menu and à la carte dishes 🏪 Museum publications, art books, guides to Madrid, posters, postcards

Above *Inside one of the museum's airy galleries*

Opposite left *The Thyssen-Bornemisza collection's elegant home*

Opposite right *The museum shop is a good place to buy art books*

INTRODUCTION

Displayed in a building specially adapted for the purpose, the collection is arranged in chronological order to take you on a fascinating journey through the history of Western art, from the 13th to the 20th centuries. The exhibition has an overall coherence, making it less overwhelming than the Prado, and the layout and clear signing make it easy to find your way around.

The tour begins on the second level, as the oldest paintings benefit most from the low ceilings and natural light, while 20th-century art can be found on the ground level.

German financier and industrialist Baron Heinrich Thyssen-Bornemisza began collecting Old Masters in the 1920s, and by the time of his death in 1947 he had acquired more than 500. His son, Hans Heinrich (who died in 2002), shared his father's love of art and eventually diversified into modern movements, including the 20th-century avant-garde.

In 1988 some 775 paintings were loaned to the Spanish government, which bought them outright five years later for the knockdown price of €350 million (their true value was estimated at closer to €1 billion). Hans Heinrich's wife, Carmen Cervera, a former Miss Spain, has offered a substantial part of her own collection of paintings to the museum.

WHAT TO SEE
THE BUILDING

The handsome 18th-century palace itself formerly belonged to the Duque de Villahermosa, after whom it is named. It was designed by Antonio López Aguado and is considered to be an impressive example of the Madrid neoclassical style. Contemporary architect Rafael Moneo (born 1937) was responsible for restoring and adapting the original palace building to the specific requirements of the gallery in the late 1980s, and for this he won a design award from the Madrid City Council.

SECOND LEVEL
Portrait of Giovanna Tornabuoni by Ghirlandaio (Room 5)
Painted in 1488 by the Florentine master Domenico Ghirlandaio (1449–94) this is the Thyssen's most famous portrait. By the late 15th century it had become acceptable to portray secular subjects, and this is an idealized and serene profile of a young girl, elaborately dressed and wearing a magnificent gown. The text behind her back reads: 'If the artist had been able to portray the character and moral qualities there would not be a more beautiful painting in the world.'

Young Knight by Carpaccio (Room 7)
One of the earliest full-length portraits, probably painted around 1510, this languid and beautiful young man is by the Venetian artist Vittore Carpaccio (1460–1523). The plants, animals and figures that surround the central figure are allegorical.

St. Jerome in the Wilderness by Titian (Room 11)
Painted about 1575, this is a late masterpiece by the Venetian painter Titian (c1488–1576). It reveals his unsurpassed handling of colour, tone and light and is a superb example of his late work displaying clearly its almost impressionistic brushwork.

FIRST LEVEL
Expulsion, Moon and Firelight by Thomas Cole (Room 29)
The Thyssen has one of the best collections of American painting outside the USA and this huge landscape by Thomas Cole (1801–48), a member of the Hudson River school, perfectly highlights the vision of America as a virgin land shared by 19th-century painters of this movement.

Les Vessenots by Van Gogh (Room 33)
Spanish museums are not, on the whole, strong on Impressionism, but the Thyssen's superb collection goes far towards filling the gap. Vincent van Gogh (1853–90) painted this vivid picture at Auvers-sur-Oise, northwest of Paris, in the last year of his life; it displays the explosive colour and brushwork typical of his late work.

GROUND LEVEL
Man with a Clarinet by Picasso (Room 41)
This painting from Picasso's Cubist period is a parallel study with the pictures by Georges Braque and Piet Mondrian which hang on either side of it.

GALLERY GUIDE

SECOND LEVEL
Rooms 1–2: Italian Primitives
Rooms 3–4: 15th-century Dutch religious
Rooms 5–9: Italian and Northern Renaissance
Room 10: 16th-century Dutch
Rooms 11–15: 16th- to 17th-century Italian, Spanish/French late Renaissance and baroque
Rooms 16–18: 18th-century Italian
Rooms 19–21: 17th-century Dutch and Flemish

FIRST LEVEL
Rooms 22–27: 17th-century Dutch landscapes, interiors and still life
Room 28: 18th-century French and British schools
Rooms 29–30: 19th-century North American
Room 31: 19th-century Romanticism and Realism
Rooms 32–33: Impressionism and Post-Impressionism
Rooms 34–40: Fauve movement and Expressionism

GROUND LEVEL
Rooms 41–44: Experimental European— Cubism, Dadaism, Constuctivism
Room 45: Post-World War I European
Room 46: North American 20th-century abstract Expressionism
Rooms 47–48: 20th century Realism, Surrealism and Pop Art

MUSEO SOROLLA

http://museosorolla.mcu.es
This house-museum is devoted to the life and work of the artist Joaquín Sorolla y Bastida (1863–1923). Born in Valencia, Sorolla trained in Madrid before making his way to Rome on a scholarship in 1885. He exhibited his work all over Europe, but was especially admired in the United States.

His first New York show (in 1909) attracted 160,000 visitors and won him enough commissions to build the house in Madrid where he lived for the last 13 years of his life with his wife and three children. His widow, Clothilde, donated it to the state and it opened as a museum in 1932.

The 250 paintings and drawings here reveal why the artist is often tagged 'the Spanish Impressionist' and 'the painter of light'. Although highly regarded as a portraitist, he is best known for his seascapes and for the gentle evocations of a rural life that was fast disappearing even in his lifetime.

➕ 67 E1 ✉ Paseo del General Martínez Campos 37, 28010 Madrid ☎ 913 10 15 84 🕐 Tue–Sat 9.30–8, Sun 10–3 💷 Adult €3, under 18 and over 65 free. Free on Sun, 18 May, 12 Oct and 6 Dec 🚇 Iglesia or Rubén Darío 🚌 3, 5, 7, 14, 16, 27, 40, 45, 61, 147, 150

MUSEO THYSSEN-BORNEMISZA
▷ 78.

MUSEO DEL TRAJE

http://museodeltraje.mcu.com
This museum is a must for anyone interested in fashion and costume. The collection offers a enticing glimpse into the evolution of dress throughout Spain's history, from earliest times until the present day.

Highlights include the superb, if poignantly small, funerary outfit of the Infanta Doña Maria, who died in 1235 at the age of five. Admire a sumptuous, silver, silk-brocade frock-coat, which dates from around 1740, and has a flaring skirt and exquisite embroidery. The shoes are also fascinating—impossibly tiny by modern standards and curiously

unformed. In the 18th century, shoes for left and right feet were exactly the same shape. Traditional regional dress from different parts of Spain is also represented, including typical costumes of fishermen, shepherds, tinkers and other trades.

You might have admired Goya's portraits of Madrid's artisans in the Prado: Here you can see the neat jackets and high-waisted skirts of the typical Spanish *majo* and *maja*. (*Majos* were usually people from artistic, and often lower-class backgrounds, who took great care with their appearance. They appear often in Goya's works.)

The exhibit outlining the rise of haute couture is largely dedicated to the great 20th-century Spanish designer, Balenciaga, whose original pieces were almost sculptural in form. In a fun touch, visitors walk down a 'catwalk' as they exit.

The museum opened in 2004 in a striking, revamped 1970s building which once held Spain's contemporary art collection. The interior was attractively modernized, and the exterior was refurbished and the museum now overlooks pretty gardens studded with fountains. The restaurant Bokado (▷ 96) is currently one of the hottest in the city with the fashionistas.

➕ 66 A1 ✉ Avenida Juan de Herrera 2, 28040 Madrid ☎ 915 50 47 00 🕐 Tue–Sat 9.30–7, Sun 10–3 💷 €3, free after 2.30 Sat, Sun 🚇 Moncloa or Ciudad Universitaria 🚌 46, 82, 83, 132, 133, G 🚻 ♿

PARQUE DEL OESTE

This landscaped park is one of Madrid's largest (98ha/242 acres) and most attractive green spaces, laid out at the beginning of the 20th century to a design by the city's head gardener, Cecilio Rodríguez. Less formal than the Retiro (▷ 82), it is one of the best places in the city for a stroll in summer.

Visitors can walk along the leafy pathways and avenues, admire the Rosaleda (Rose Garden; created in the 1950s), stop for a drink on one of the terrace cafés lining Paseo de Pintor Rosales (this was the preferred Madrid walk of US author Ernest Hemingway) or go for a ride on the *teleférico*, the cable-car linking the park with the Casa de Campo (▷ 71).

Also in the park is the Egyptian Templo de Debod (Apr–Sep Tue–Fri 10–2, 6–8, Sat–Sun 10–2; rest of year Tue–Fri 9.45–1.45, 4.15–6.15, Sat–Sun 10–2). Dedicated to the gods Amon and Isis, the temple dates from the fourth century BC. It was installed in Madrid in 1970, donated by the Egyptian government in recognition of work carried out by Spanish archaeologists and engineers in removing historic monuments from Abu Simbel prior to the construction of the Aswan Dam.

➕ 66 B1 ✉ Paseo del Pintor Rosales, 28008 Madrid 🕐 24 hours 💷 Free 🚇 Plaza de España, Argüelles, Moncloa 🚌 74, 84, 93 🅿 Many dotted around the park

PALACIO REAL

The Royal Palace is the official residence of the royal family. While only a fraction of the 3,000 rooms are in daily use, around 25 of the state apartments are open to the public. These are decorated with frescoes, gilded stucco, Spanish marbles and silk wall-hangings, and are crammed with priceless *objets d'art*.

The current Palacio Real stands on the site of the ninth-century Moorish Alcázar (fort), which, with some modifications, became the preferred royal palace after Felipe II moved his court to Madrid in 1561. In 1734 the palace burned down, and it was rebuilt by Italian architect Battista Sacchetti. It occupies a superb cliff-top site overlooking the Río Manzanares and the Casa de Campo (▷ 71), and the views to the Sierra de Guadarrama mountains are stunning.

THE ROOMS

The most impressive room on the tour is the Throne Room, designed by Giovanni Battista Sacchetti and completed in 1772. The velvet wall-hangings were made in Genoa and decorated with gilded silver thread. Covering the ceiling is the allegorical masterpiece, *The Apotheosis of the Spanish Monarchy*, by Giovanni Battista Tiepolo (1696–1770). The Throne Room is still in use, although the present King and Queen prefer to stand during audiences.

The Gasparini Room, named after its Neapolitan designer, Matteo Gasparini, was the king's robing room. The restored silk hangings are embroidered with arabesques to match the equally spectacular ceiling, which is encrusted with stuccoed fruit and flowers. The Banqueting Hall dates from 1885. It was created for Alfonso XII by joining together three rooms from the queen's apartments. The ceiling frescoes formed part of the original design, although most of the contents were introduced later. The dining table seats up to 164 guests and can be dismantled for balls and receptions.

For a small extra fee (€1), visitors can admire the new Paintings Gallery, which contains a fine collection of works dating from the 15th century

PALACE PRECINCTS

The Royal Armoury (reached from the courtyard) has one of the finest collections of arms and armour in Europe. Opposite is the Royal Pharmacy, most of whose exhibits date from the reign of Carlos IV.

INFORMATION
www.patrimonionacional.es
✚ 66 C4 ✉ Calle de Bailén, 28071 Madrid ☎ 914 54 88 00 🕐 Apr–Sep Mon–Sat 9–6, Sun 9–3; Oct–Mar Mon–Sat 9.30–5, Sun 9–2 🎫 Adult €8 or €10 with guided tour, child (5–16) €3.50, under 5 free Ⓜ Opera 🚌 3, 25, 39, 148 ☛ Guided tour €10, departs every 10 min in groups of about 30. Audioguide in variety of languages €3 📖 Official guidebook 🍽 Café-bar 🎁 Gift shop on ground floor

TIPS
» The palace frequently closes for state visits and other formal occasions. Check at the visitor information office.
» The Changing of the Guard ceremony takes place in the Plaza de Armas at noon on the first Wed of the month, Feb–May and Sep–Dec.
» The entrance and ticket office are on Plaza de Armas.

Opposite *A small statue of a seated figure in the gardens of the Museo Sorolla*
Below *Statue of Felipe IV before the long facade of Palacio Real*

PARQUE DEL RETIRO

Madrid's most central green space has been popular with the public for more than 150 years. The Retiro, or Retreat, extends over some 130ha (320 acres), and its main gate is opposite the huge Puerta de Alcalá. You can walk through the numerous shady avenues and pathways, enjoy the formal gardens or take a rowing boat out on the lake.

The park is peppered with statues and monuments of all kinds, and for this reason it is often described as an open-air sculpture gallery. The most unusual monument (near the Rose Garden) is dedicated to Lucifer, the fallen angel (hence the statue's name—El Angel Caído). It is the 1878 work of Spanish sculptor Ricardo Bellver (1845–1924), and is said to be the only public statue of the Devil in the world.

Note that the park should be avoided late at night.

✚ 67 F4 ✉ Plaza de la Independencia s/n, 28009 Madrid ☎ 915 88 16 36 ◷ Apr–Sep daily 6am–midnight; Oct–Mar daily 6–11 ✋ Free 🚇 Retiro, Ibiza 🚌 2, 14, 19, 20, 26, 28, 51, 52, 68, 69

PLAZA DE CIBELES

Presiding over one of Madrid's busiest traffic intersections (Calle de Alcalá, Paseo de Recoletos and Paseo del Prado) is the city's best-loved monument and most photographed landmark. The Fuente de Cibeles (Cibeles Fountain), designed in 1777 by court architect Ventura Rodriguéz, was completed 15 years later. The Greek goddess of fertility is seated on a chariot pulled by two lions, which represent the Spanish provinces of Castile and León. Today's square dates from 1895, and it is surrounded by buildings of architectural note. The Palacio de Comunicaciones (Mon–Fri 8.30–2, 5–7, Sat 8.30–2), known as Our Lady of Communications because it resembles a cathedral, was designed by Antonio Palacios and Joaquín Otamendi in 1904 as the General Post Office. Partly hidden from view by its gardens on Paseo de Recoletos are the General Army Barracks, built as the Palacio de Buenavista in 1777 for the Duchess of Alba, a renowned beauty and former lover of the painter Francisco de Goya (1746–1828).

On the other side of the Paseo is the baroque Palacio de Linares, designed in 1872 by Carlos Collubi. It is currently the Casa de América (guided visits only, Sat–Sun 10, 10.30, 11, 11.30, 12, 12.30, 1, 1.30, 2pm; €7; tickets must be reserved one day before visit), showcasing work of artists from Latin America.

✚ 67 E4 ✉ Plaza de la Cibeles, 28014 Madrid ✋ Free 🚇 Banco de España 🚌 10, 12, 14, 15, 20, 27, 34, 37, 45

PLAZA MAYOR

This handsome square is still Madrid's most impressive public space. Plaza Mayor was originally known as Plaza de Arrabal (Outskirts Square) because it lay just outside the city walls. About 20 years after the court moved to Madrid in 1561, Felipe II chose this site as a focal point of his new capital, but only the Casa de la Panadería was completed during his reign. It was the property of the baker's guild, and its facade has always been decorated with frescoes. Felipe III revived the Plaza Mayor project in 1617, and his bronze statue stands guard over it. The square was designed for processions, plays, pageants, tournaments, public executions and even bullfights. The most macabre ceremony held here was the auto da fé, the ritual burning of condemned heretics before the judges of the Inquisition, a practice that continued until 1680. Plaza Mayor also served as a marketplace.

Traffic is banned, so you can wander at will. A stone's throw away is the world's oldest restaurant, Botín, founded in 1725. The author Ernest Hemingway loved its roast suckling pig. Las Cuevas de Luís Candelas is a traditional tavern named after a 19th-century bandit who took refuge in its cellars. Calle de Toledo, the old road to Toledo, has unusual shops—look for Casa Hernanz (No. 18), which sells rope espadrilles, mats and baskets. The Christmas market in December has a richly festive atmosphere.

✚ 67 D4 ✉ Plaza Mayor, 28012 Madrid ✋ Free 🚇 Sol 🚌 5, 15, 51, 52, 150

Below *A verdant avenue (left) and monument to Alfonso XII (right) in Parque del Retiro*
Opposite *The Cibeles Fountain, with the goddess in her chariot*

Left *Bullfight at Plaza de Toros*
Opposite left *Puerta del Sol, heart of the city*
Opposite right *Kilometre Zero, centre of Spain*

Spain's greatest admiral, the Marqués de Santa Cruz, who defeated the Turks at the Battle of Lepanto in 1571.

➕ 66 C4 ✉ Plaza de la Villa, Calle Mayor, 28005 Madrid 👣 Free 🚇 Opera, Sol 🚌 3

PUERTA DEL SOL

Since the 15th century the 'gateway of the sun' has been the city's heart and, technically speaking, the centre of Spain, as all distances are measured from here. By day Sol is the hub of an important shopping district, and after dark it becomes a popular meeting place for those out for a night on the town.

In the 17th century the space in front of the Convento de San Felipe el Real (now a McDonald's outlet) was known as *el mentidero* (gossip shop), because it was here that the flotsam and jetsam of Madrid society would gather to exchange scandal and gossip.

Puerta del Sol is now home to the Casa de Correos, headquarters of the Comunidad de Madrid, or regional government. Dating from 1768, it is the oldest building on the square and was designed by the French architect Jacques Marquet. Used initially as a post office (hence its name—*correos* means 'post'), the Casa de Correos was subsequently occupied by the Ministry of the Interior and, following the Civil War, by General Franco's secret police.

On the paving in front of the building is the marker for *Kilómetro Cero* (Kilometre Zero), the point from which all distances in Spain are measured. Another of the city's landmarks, the statue of a bear eating the fruit of an arbutus tree (the symbol on Madrid's coat of arms), stands at the foot of Calle del Carmen.

➕ 67 D4 ✉ Plaza Puerta del Sol, 28012-3 Madrid 👣 Free 🚇 Sol 🚌 3, 5, 15, 20, 51, 52, 53, 150

PLAZA DE ORIENTE

Elegant Plaza de Oriente was laid out in the 19th century, specifically to allow uninterrupted views of Sacchetti's Palacio Real (▷ 81). Greener than the average city square, it has been a haven of peace and quiet since it was made pedestrians-only in the 1990s. The plaza is best appreciated from the terrace of the Café de Oriente, in one of the houses forming a stately crescent on its eastern side.

Also included in this row is the Teatro Real, Madrid's opera house, which was completed in the mid-19th century during the reign of Isabel II (there are tours every half-hour, Tue–Sun 10.30–1.30, Wed–Mon 10.30–1, €4). At the heart of the geometrical garden is one of Madrid's finest monuments, an equestrian statue of Felipe IV that was based on sketches by artist Diego Velázquez (1599–1660).

➕ 66 C4 ✉ Plaza de Oriente, 28013 Madrid 👣 Free 🚇 Opera 🚌 3, 25, 39, 148, 500

PLAZA DE TOROS DE LAS VENTAS

This is the home of Las Ventas, the country's premier bullring, with a capacity of around 22,500. It was officially opened in 1934, although *corridas* (bullfights) had been taking place there since 1931. Whatever your feelings about bullfighting, it is difficult not to be impressed by the

sheer scale of the place. If you do want to learn more, visit the Museo Taurino (Mar–Oct Tue–Fri 9.30–2.30, Sun 10–1; Nov–Feb Mon–Fri 9.30–2.30), next to the stables. Here you will find all sorts of bullfighting memorabilia, including posters, paintings and the heads of a number of bulls that were killed during fights. Guided tours of the bullring are also available (Tue–Sun 10–2; €5; Tauro Tour tel 915 56 93 27).

➕ 67 off F3 ✉ Calle de Alcalá 237, 28028 Madrid ☎ 913 56 22 00 🚇 Ventas 🚌 12, 21, 38, 53, 106, 110

PLAZA DE LA VILLA

Once a Moorish market, this traffic-free square contains some of Madrid's finest civil architecture and has been the seat of local government since the 17th century. During the Middle Ages Madrid was governed from the Iglesia de San Salvador on Calle Mayor. However, by the 17th century these premises were deemed unworthy of Spain's capital city, and in 1644 the church was demolished so that work could begin on the much more imposing Casa de la Villa (Town Hall). This stands on the western side of the square and can be visited on a weekly guided tour (Mon 5pm). Opposite is the Casa y Torre de los Lujanes, the oldest-surviving private residence in Madrid, dating from the late 15th century.

In the middle of the square is a 19th-century statue commemorating

REAL ACADEMIA DE BELLAS ARTES DE SAN FERNANDO

http://rabasf.insde.es

Although it receives relatively few visitors, the Academy of Fine Arts museum has an outstanding collection of Spanish and European paintings, Spanish sculptures and engravings, spread over three floors. Highlights of the Spanish collection are the works by Francisco de Goya (1746–1828), including two self-portraits, an equestrian portrait of Fernando VII, *Scene from the Inquisition* (c1816; a protest against the revival of that institution) and *The Burial of the Sardine* (1814), a brilliant evocation of a Madrid carnival tradition that is still observed today.

Of European artists represented in the museum, pride of place belongs to Peter Paul Rubens (1577–1640) and one of his best-known works, *Susanna and the Elders* (1607). *Spring* (1573), by Giuseppe Arcimboldo (c1530–93), is the only work on show in Spain by this Italian artist. Other treats are the 19th- and 20th-century sculptures, as well as the priceless collection of Goya etchings. The sister National Institute of Calcography (Mon–Fri 10–2, Sat 10–1.30) houses displays of copper and brass engravings.

🚇 67 D4 ✉ Calle de Alcalá 13, 28014 Madrid ☎ 915 24 08 64 🕐 Tue–Fri 9–7, Sat–Mon 10–2.30 ✋ Adults €5, under 18 free; free to all on Wed (includes entry to Museum of Calcography) 🚇 Sol or Sevilla 🚌 3, 5, 15, 20, 51, 52, 53, 150

REAL JARDÍN BOTÁNICO

www.rjb.csic.es

With its cooling fountains, shady pathways and strategically placed benches, the Royal (Real) Botanical Garden, just a stone's throw from the Prado (▷ 74–76), is ideal for quiet contemplation.

The garden was founded by Carlos III in 1774, and opened seven years later. It is the oldest and most important place for botanical research in Spain. Unaccountably neglected for decades, the garden was given a new lease of life in 1981 to coincide with its bicentenary and is now one of the city's most valued attractions. The wonderful tree collection includes the arbutus, the emblem of Madrid, and there is a herbarium and rose garden.

Another highlight is the Puerta Real (Royal Gate) on Paseo del Prado, which was the original entrance to the gardens. Dating from 1781, the gate is regarded as one of the finest examples of neoclassical architecture in Madrid.

🚇 67 E5 ✉ Plaza de Murillo 2, 28014 Madrid ☎ 914 20 30 17 🕐 May–Aug daily 10–9; Apr, Sep 10–8; Oct–Mar 10–7; Nov–Feb 10–6 ✋ Adult €2.50, under 10 free 🚇 Atocha 🚌 10, 14, 27, 34, 45

REAL MONASTERIO DE LA ENCARNACIÓN

www.patrimonionacional.es

Like the Monasterio de las Descalzas Reales (▷ 72), the Monastery of the Incarnation was established as a convent exclusively for women from royal or noble families. The nuns were originally known as *margaritas*, after their patroness, Queen Margaret of Austria, wife of Felipe III and founder of the convent in 1611. Originally the monastery was connected to the Arab fortress where the Royal Palace now stands. Although the facade is original, architect Ventura Rodríguez restyled the interior after a fire in the 18th century. Paintings and sculptures by a number of distinguished 17th-century artists are on display here.

The guided tour is compulsory and lasts 45 minutes. You are shown a dozen or so rooms, starting with the *portería* (reception hall), which has one of the finest paintings in the convent, *The Handing Over of the Princesses on the River Bidasoa*, by an anonymous Flemish artist. The cloisters, decorated with 17th-century tiles from Talavera are beautiful. The *Relicario* is the macabre highlight of the tour—a dimly lit room filled with the bones and hair of scores of saints and martyrs in specially made cabinets.

Cristo Yacente (Recumbent Christ), a sculpture by Gregorio Fernández (1576–1636), is in the Sculpture Hall; the monstrance in the reliquary (1619) is made of gilded bronze and rock crystal; and the ceiling frescoes in the church are by Zacarías González Velázquez (1763–1834).

🚇 66 C4 ✉ Plaza de la Encarnación 1, 28013 Madrid ☎ 914 54 88 00 🕐 Tue–Thu, Sat 10.30–12.45, 4–5.45, Fri 10.30–12.45, Sun 11–1.45 ✋ Adult €3.60, child (5–15) €2 🚇 Opera 🚌 25, 39, 500

AROUND ROYAL MADRID

From convents for blue-blooded nuns to the extravagant royal palace, this walk takes in some of the city's most opulent monuments. On the way, you'll pass the splendid opera house and royal gardens. The walk culminates in the vast, café-filled Plaza Mayor.

THE WALK

Distance: 1.5km (1 mile)
Allow: 3 hours, including visits to convents and palace
Start at: Plaza de las Descalzas, map 67 D4
End at: Plaza Mayor

HOW TO GET THERE

From Puerta del Sol Metro stop, take Calle Arenal and turn right to find the Plaza de las Descalzas.

★ Plaza de las Descalzas is a small, rather nondescript square, but it can be found easily by following signs for the Convento de las Descalzas Reales (▷ 72). This 16th-century convent was established for blue-blooded nuns by Juana of Austria, who was widowed at 19. Behind the dour facade, a lavish building unfolds, with trompe l'oeil frescoes and expensive tapestries.

When you leave the convent, take Calle San Martín (the short street opposite the main door of the convent) to Calle Arenal, one of Madrid's main arteries, and turn right. Walk until you reach Plaza Isabel II, a small square with a metro stop and several bus stops. It is overlooked by the imposing bulk of the back entrance to the Teatro Real, the city's prestigious opera house.

Make your way to the front of the Teatro Real, by taking the narrow street Calle Felipe V, which curves to the right, and passes the Taberna del Alabardero, a café-bar and restaurant, on the right.

❶ The Teatro Real overlooks splendid Plaza de Oriente, Madrid's grandest square. The vast Royal Palace stands opposite the Teatro Royal, and in the centre is a monumental fountain, topped with a 17th-century bronze of Felipe IV astride a rearing horse. There are several delightful, if expensive, cafés with terraces on the square where you can sit and enjoy the spectacle.

Head north, via little Calle de Pavia (on your left, skirting the gardens, if you are facing the Teatro Real), which passes a little shop selling dance clothes and tutus for children.

❷ The Real Monasterio de la Encarnación (▷ 85) is easy to spot, with its restrained neoclassical facade, just beyond the gardens. A highlight of the tour of this royal monastery, also established for aristocratic nuns, is the reliquary, where the bones, hair and nails of saints are kept in gorgeously decorated caskets. Famously, the reliquary contains a phial of the blood of San Pantaleón, which miraculously liquefies every year on the anniversary of the saint's martyrdom, 27 July. It is said that if it liquefies at any other time, the country is in grave danger.

Retrace your steps towards the Plaza de Oriente, but continue walking down Calle Bailén, to find the entrance to the Palacio Real (Royal Palace, ▷ 81) on your right.

❸ The Spanish royal family don't live in this enormous palace, but use it on state occasions. Take the tour of the ornate salons and visit the armoury and pharmacy.

When you exit the Palace, turn right down big, busy Calle de Bailén, and then left onto Calle Mayor, keeping the large, red-brick edifice of the Capitanía General on your right.

❹ Calle Mayor was once the main street of the old city, and leads past little Plaza de la Villa, now easy to miss, but once an important meeting point. It is overlooked by Madrid's restrained 17th-century city hall (Ayuntamiento), and a pair of handsome palaces from the 15th and 16th centuries.

Continue past the pretty, glass market of San Miguel, and turn right down the passage which heads through an archway into Plaza Major.

The walk ends here in this expansive, arcaded square at the heart of old Madrid. Pull up a chair at one of the many terrace cafés and, while enjoying a drink, contemplate the square's terrible history—it was here that executions took place, and where the Inquisition held the terrifying *autos de fé*. It all seems impossibly distant under the bright blue skies of modern Madrid.

WHEN TO GO
Any time of year is good, although it may be too hot in July and August to enjoy the walk. Also, note that opening hours (in shops, cafés, restaurants and museums) are reduced during August.

WHERE TO EAT
LA TOJA
A great place for seafood, tucked inside one of the arches leading into

Above *The Mercado de San Miguel is the only traditional food market of its kind in the city*
Opposite *Plaza de Oriente is Madrid's grandest square*

the Plaza Mayor. Go for tapas and a chilled beer at the bar, or sit down in the *comedor* for a more substantial seafood meal.
✉ Calle del Siete de Julio 3 ☎ 913 66 30 34 🕐 Daily 1–4, 8–midnight

LA TABERNA DEL ALABARDERO
Choose from tapas at the bar, or splash out on the refined Basque cuisine in the dining room. There's a small terrace in summer.
✉ Calle Felipe V ☎ 915 47 25 77 🕐 Daily 1–4, 9–midnight

CAFÉ DE ORIENTE
Chic café/restaurant on the square, with sublime views of the palace and the opera house.
✉ Plaza de Oriente 2 ☎ 915 41 39 74 🕐 Daily 8.30–1.30

EL MOLLETE
A classic, old-fashioned Spanish bar with a separate dining room which has enjoyed a long and colourful history. *Menú del día* (€10).
✉ Calle de la Bola 4 ☎ 915 47 78 20 🕐 Mon–Sat 9–5, 8–1

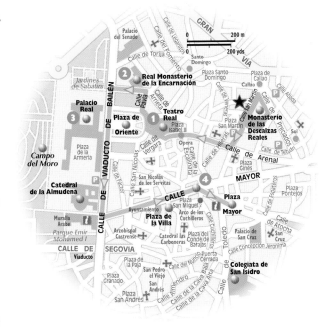

AROUND PLAZA SANTA ANA

The area around Plaza Santa Ana is known to *Madrileños* as the Barrio de las Letras, a reference to its historic reputation as a meeting point for the city's writers, dramatists, thinkers and poets. In recent years, it's become one of the main nightlife areas, with countless tapas bars, restaurants and clubs, but its old-fashioned streets recall the golden age of Cervantes and Lope de Vega.

THE WALK
Distance: 1.5km (1 mile)
Allow: 2 hours, including visit to museum
Start at: Plaza Puerta del Sol, map 67 D4
End at: Plaza Santa Ana

HOW TO GET THERE
Nearest Metro: Sol.

★ The Plaza Puerta del Sol is Madrid's main transportation hub with crowds ebbing and flowing from the metro stations and bus stops day and night. Where Calle Carmen joins the square to the north, there is a bronze statue of the bear and the Madroño or arbutus tree, often translated as 'strawberry tree'. This iconic city symbol is interpreted as a reference to Madrid's fertility and wildlife abundance in 1561 when Felipe II established the royal court here. Across the square, the Casa de Correos, now the seat of the city government, is the very centre of Spain. A marble plaque on the wall marks *Kilómetro Cero* (Kilometre

Zero), the point from which all distances in Spain are measured.

Leave the square by Carrera San Jerónimo (to the left, if you are facing the Casa de Correos), passing Casa Mira (a traditional bakery and confectioner) on your right.

❶ The street widens into the circular Plaza de las Canalejas. Just beyond it on the right is the Teatro Reina Victoria, built in 1916, with stained glass and ornamental tilework. Opposite is the pink, frothy Palacio de Miraflores, built in the 18th century for the Count of Villapaterna.

Immediately after the palace, take the left fork, Calle Zorrita, tucked behind the modern bulk of the Palacio del Congreso (the Spanish parliament). Turn left onto Calle Jovellanos to find the Teatro de la Zarzuela.

❷ The theatre is dedicated to the popular operettas *(zarzuelas)* which

Madrileños love. Opposite is a fine little tapas bar, Casa Manolo, which must be one of the few places in Madrid where politicians and opera-singers can be found eating side by side.

Turn back down Calle Jovellanos, and then left down Calle Zorrita to emerge onto Plaza de las Cortes.

❸ From here you can admire the magnificent neoclassical facade of Spain's parliament building. Across the street is the belle-époque Hotel Palace, one of the city's grandest historic hotels.

From Plaza de las Cortes, take small Calle San Agustín and turn immediately right onto Calle de Cervantes.

❹ This is the heart of the Santa Ana neighbourhood, home to the city's writers and artists since the 16th century, and which still has a faint whiff of bohemia. Immediately on the right, you will see the entrance to the delightful home (Casa-Museo) of Lope de Vega (1562–1635), the great poet and dramatist of the Golden Age. The house contains few hints of his colourful life (including several naval campaigns and a love affair with an actress which culminated in the playwright's banishment from the kingdom), but is a charming spot, with a tiny garden scented with orange blossom.

Leaving the museum, turn right and then immediately left onto Calle Quevedo, named after the satirical writer Francisco Quevedo (1580–1645), famous for his biting wit. Passing the Basque cider house Zerain on your left, continue to the corner of Calle Lope de Vega where you will see the old brick walls of the Trinitarias convent across the street.

5 A white marble plaque attests that Cervantes, the creator of Don Quixote, was buried here (his remains were subsequently lost).

Continue uphill along Calle Lope de Vega, and turn right on Calle León. (The delicatessen Casa González at No.12 is a great spot to buy presents and also try some great wines along with simple tapas.) Turn left when you reach Calle Prado, and walk uphill until you reach Plaza Santa Ana. It is overlooked by the prestigious Teatro Español, where the premiere of Federico García Lorca's *Yerma* in 1934 was greeted with howls and boos. This square is the heart of this neighbourhood, and surrounded with bars and cafés.

WHEN TO GO
Begin this walk in the morning and avoid August and Sundays when everything is closed.

WHERE TO EAT
CASA MANOLO
The *croquetas* are famous throughout the city, but it's also great for the classic local breakfast of *chocolate con churros* (fried dough strips).

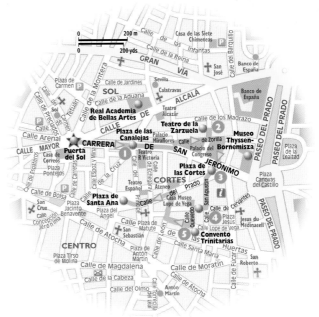

✉ Calle Jovellanos 7 ☎ 915 21 45 16
🕓 Tue–Sat 9am–midnight, Mon 9am–5pm

CASA GONZÁLEZ
A gem of a deli and bar offering wine, cheese and cured meats.
✉ Calle León 12 ☎ 914 29 56 18
🕓 Mon–Thu 9am–midnight, Fri–Sat 9am–1am

CERVECERÍA ALEMANA
A classic bar and Hemingway haunt with marble tables and lace curtains.

✉ Plaza Santa Ana 6 ☎ 914 29 70 33
🕓 Daily 11am–midnight, until 2am Fri and Sat

PLACE TO VISIT
CASA-MUSEO LOPE DE VEGA
✉ Calle Cervantes 11 ☎ 914 29 92 16
🕓 Tue–Sun 10–3

Opposite *A portrait of playright Lope de Vega in his one-time home, now a museum*
Below *Plaza Puerta del Sol, where this walk starts*

SHOPPING

ABC SERRANO
www.abcserrano.com
The range of shops here includes
a home furnishings store, plenty of
fashion, gifts and jewellery shops,
a wine merchant and hairdresser.
There is a café, a bar and a restaurant
on the rooftop terrace. They also
organize special activities for children
at weekends.
✉ Calle de Serrano 61, 28006 Madrid
☎ 915 77 50 31 🕑 Mon–Sat 10–9;
restaurants open until midnight 🚇 Núñez
de Balboa, Rubén Darío 🚌 5, 9, 14, 19, 27,
45, 51, 61, 74, 150

AGATHA RUIZ DE LA PRADA
www.agatharuizdelaprada.com
This Spanish designer has built her
name on original and bold clothing.
The ladies' collection includes
some incredible dresses, all in her
trademark bold, brilliant colours
and prints. There are also shoes,
jewellery, children's clothes and
toys, plus towels, feather quilts,
chairs, tables and crockery for the
home. Prices start at around €50 for
a T-shirt.

✉ Calle Serrano 27, 28001 Madrid
☎ 913 19 05 01 🕑 Mon–Sat 10–2, 5–9
🚇 Serrano 🚌 1, 9, 19, 51, 74

CAPAS SESEÑA
www.sesena.com
The cape is a classic Spanish
garment, with a long history in
Madrid. This specialist shop, which
opened in 1901, is the place to buy
handmade wool capes. Capes are
enjoying a resurgence in the fashion
world, even if you don't go to the
opera. The bilingual website allows
you to customize your own version.
✉ Calle de la Cruz 23, 28012 Madrid
☎ 915 31 68 40 🕑 Mon–Fri 10–2, 5–8,
Sat 10–2 🚇 Sol 🚌 3, 5, 20, 50, 51, 52,
53, 150

CASA DE DIEGO
This popular Madrid store has been
around since 1850 and stocks any
fan the heart could desire. Other
accessories, such as umbrellas and
handmade shawls, are also stocked.
✉ Puerta del Sol 12, 28013 Madrid
☎ 915 22 66 43 🕑 Mon–Fri 9.30–8, Sat
9.30–1.30, 4.45–8 🚇 Sol 🚌 3, 5, 20, 50,
51, 52, 53, 150

CASA MIRA
Luis Mira opened this sweet shop
in 1842, and the family still prepares
home-made, all-natural *turrón*
(nougat), delicious marzipan, ice-
cream and flaky biscuits (cookies).
✉ Carrera de San Jerónimo 30, 28013
Madrid ☎ 914 29 88 95 🕑 Mon–Sat
10–2, 5–9, Sun 10.30–2.30, 5.30–9 🚇 Sol
🚌 3, 5, 9

CASA Y CAMPO
www.casaycampo.com
In this large store selling anything you
might require for home decoration,
you can find design classics such as
imitation 1960s toasters.
✉ Calle del Pradillo 60, 28002 Madrid
☎ 915 10 38 10 🕑 Mon–Fri 10.30–2.30,
5–8.30, Sat 11–2.30, 5–8.30 🚇 Alfonso XIII
🚌 3, 9, 40, 43, 72, 73

EL CORTE INGLÉS
www.elcorteingles.es
This department store has it all:
fashion, shoes, accessories, furniture,
electronics, books, art, jewellery and
music, and there's also an in-house

Above *Loewe's shop on Calle de Serrano*

travel agent. The food hall offers great quality. The restaurant and cafeteria are on the top floor.

✉ Calle de la Princesa 56, 28008 Madrid ☎ 914 54 60 00 🕐 Mon–Sat 10–10 🚇 Argüelles 🚌 1, 21, 44, 68, 69, 133

CUENLLAS

A popular delicatessen among Madrid's connoisseur gourmets, where the shelves are full of delicacies. There's also a great variety of Spanish wines. If you prefer to try before you buy, the company manages a restaurant and tapas bar next door where you can sample the products.

✉ Calle de Ferraz 3, 28008 Madrid ☎ 915 47 31 33 🕐 Mon–Fri 9.30–2, 5.30–9, Sat 9.30–2 🚇 Argüelles 🚌 74

THE DELI ROOM

This shop acts as a showcase for young Spanish designers. On the stainless steel racks and shelves you will find beautifully tailored creations of Ailanto, Josep Font's funky and vibrant off-the-peg line and Jocomomola: Sybilla's 1960s-inspired range. There is a great selection of iconic T-shirts.

✉ Calle Santa Bárbara 4, 28004 Madrid ☎ 915 21 19 83 🕐 Mon–Sat 11–2, 5–8

DURÁN JOYEROS

www.duranjoyeros.com
This is one of Madrid's most exclusive jewellers. All the leading international brands are represented in the collections, including the watchmakers Baume Mercier, Longines, Cartier and Breitling. When it comes to fine jewels, there are both classic and modern pieces on display. There's also a branch at Calle de Serrano 30.

✉ Calle de Goya 19, 28001 Madrid ☎ 914 26 40 30 🕐 Mon–Sat 10–2, 5–8.30 🚇 Serrano 🚌 1, 9, 19, 21, 51, 53, 74

FANN

Interior decoration is combined with art, stationery, fashion and a cafeteria here. The store markets art reproductions and original paintings. Items include puzzles, address books, pens and other items of stationery

with illustrations by contemporary Spanish artists.

✉ Calle de Velázquez 24, 28001 ☎ 914 35 72 23 🕐 Daily 10–9 🚇 Velázquez 🚌 1, 9, 19, 21, 51, 53, 74

FARRUTX

www.farrutx.com
This Mallorcan brand's shoes, for both men and women, are of an exceptionally high quality and have been created using the latest methods—reflected in the price. There are also accessories, such as bags and belts.

✉ Calle de Serrano 7, 28001 Madrid ☎ 915 76 94 93 🕐 Mon–Sat 10–2, 5.30–8.30. Closed pm in Aug 🚇 Retiro 🚌 1, 9, 19, 51, 74

EL FLAMENCO VIVE

www.elflamencovive.com
One of the best flamenco stores in Madrid. New releases are stocked alongside old songs, books, biographies, collectors' items, sheet music and even some instruments such as the traditionally made flamenco guitar.

✉ Calle Conde de Lemos 7, 28013 Madrid ☎ 915 47 39 17 🕐 Mon–Sat 10.30–2, 5–9 🚇 Ópera 🚌 3, 50

FNAC

www.fnac.es
A four-floor store stocking all the latest music and literature, one of FNAC's strengths is the foreign-language section. It also sells TVs, cameras, software and games, and hosts occasional concerts and exhibitions. Customers are welcome to use the small reading lounge and cafeteria. Concert tickets are also available here.

✉ Calle de Preciados 28, 28013 Madrid ☎ 915 95 61 00 🕐 Mon–Sat 10–9.30, Sun noon–9.30 🚇 Callao 🚌 1, 2, 46, 74, 75, 133, 146, 149

JOCOMOMOLA

www.jocomomola.com
The design team at this store in the distinguished Salamanca district has targeted the higher end of the market with one elegant collection. However, there's a more

contemporary feel in the label Jocomomola, which is aimed at younger women. The accessories, shoes, hats, umbrellas, casual wear and bedlinen are of particular interest, but the watches, jewellery, glasses, belts and the home range shouldn't be missed either.

✉ Callejón de Jorge Juan 12, 28001 Madrid ☎ 915 75 00 05 🕐 Mon–Fri 10–2, 5–9, Sat 11–3, 5–8.30 🚇 Serrano, Callao 🚌 1, 9, 19, 51, 74, 89

LOEWE

www.loewe.com
Loewe is one of the more prominent luxury brands in Spain, something which is reflected in the prices. Leather is the main theme, and this is a particularly good place to find high-quality shoes and bags. There's also a selection of fine clothes and accessories such as wallets, belts, suitcases and scarves. For Loewe's collection for men, try the branches at Serrano 34 and Gran Vía 8.

✉ Calle de Serrano 26, 28001 Madrid ☎ 915 77 60 56 🕐 Mon–Sat 9.30–8.30 🚇 Serrano 🚌 1, 9, 19, 21, 51, 61, 74

LOTTUSSE

www.lottusse.com
High-quality shoes for both men and women are available here. The shop sells its own line of products, as well as brands such as Timberland and classic styles from Sebago. There's a wide selection of accessories, including bags, suitcases, wallets, key rings and belts.

✉ El Jardín de Serrano, Calle de Goya 6–8, 28001 Madrid ☎ 915 77 20 14 🕐 Mon–Sat 10–9 🚇 Serrano 🚌 1, 9, 19, 21, 51, 53, 74

LA MALLORQUINA

A traditional Spanish sweet (candy) shop and pâtisserie with more than 100 years' experience in the business. Downstairs is a selection of pastries, croissants, cakes and sweets, and upstairs there is a cafeteria. A good place to stop for a coffee.

✉ Calle Mayor 2, 28013 Madrid ☎ 915 21 12 01 🕐 Daily 9am–9.30pm 🚇 Sol 🚌 3, 5, 15, 20, 50, 51

MERCADO DE CHAMARTÍN

http://mercadodechamartin.com

A popular market, this is well known for quality at reasonable prices. There is an enormous selection of vegetables, the best fruits from all over the country, fresh fish and seafood, meat, chicken and plenty more besides.

✉ Calle de Bolivia 9, 28016 Madrid ☎ 914 57 53 50 ⓓ Mon–Fri 9–2, 5.30–8.30, Sat 9–2 🚇 Colombia 🚌 7, 16, 29, 51

MERCADO DE FUENCARRAL

www.mdf.es

Known as a bastion of Madrid's rather grungy street culture, this is not a market as such but rather a mall for youth and urban wear and a springboard for young designers. Jeans, sports shoes, body piercing, tattoos, retro clothing, studded belts and leatherwear, music: You name it, they have it.

✉ Calle Fuencarral 45, 28004 Madrid ☎ 915 21 41 52 ⓓ Mon–Sat 10–10 🚇 Tribunal

PETRA'S INTERNATIONAL BOOKSHOP

www.petrasbookshop.com

Browse through the stock of books here while enjoying a cup of herbal tea. Quality used books in several languages are traded. You can reserve conversation classes and take part in language exchanges here, too.

✉ Calle de Campomanes 13, 28013 Madrid ☎ 915 41 72 91 ⓓ Mon–Sat 11–9 🚇 Ópera, Santo Domingo 🚌 25, 39, 44, 133, 147

PIAMONTE

www.piamonteshop.com

You will find an enormous selection of handbags (purses) here for every occasion: party bags, or something innovative or classically stylish. The final touches to an outfit are not overlooked and you can also choose from hats, shawls and costume jewellery. The designers featured are Isabel Marant, Locking and Shocking, La Casita de Wendy and Josep Font, among others. It also produces its own line of bags. Other branches can be found at Calle Piamonte 16

(tel 915 23 07 66) and Calle Lagasca 28 (tel 915 75-55 20).

✉ Calle Marqués de Monasterio 5, 28004 Madrid ☎ 915 75 55 20 ⓓ Mon–Fri 10.30–2, 5.30–8, Sat 11–2, 5–8. Closed Sat pm in Aug 🚇 Colón 🚌 5, 14, 27, 37, 45, 53, 150

PIEDRA

All Piedra's pieces are arranged for easy admiration. There's no shortage of things that sparkle, gold and silver jewels, as well as semiprecious stones. Don't miss the beautiful necklaces and earrings; you'll find modern designs and antique pieces.

✉ Calle de Zurbano 43, 28010 Madrid ☎ 913 19 89 49 ⓓ Mon–Fri 10–2, 5–8, Sat 10.30–2 🚇 Rubén Darío 🚌 5, 7, 16, 40, 61, 147

EL RASTRO

www.elrastro.org

This is one of the capital's most intriguing street markets. Antiques, handmade clothes and jeans line Calle Ribera de Curtidores, and Plaza del General Vara del Rey is the place to go for second-hand clothes, leather and furniture. Get there early to avoid the crowds and watch your bag carefully. The area is good for bars and tapas.

✉ Plaza de Cascorro, 28005 ☎ 915 40 40 10 ⓓ Sun and public holidays 9–3 🚇 Tirso de Molina 🚌 17, 18, 23, 35

RESERVA Y CATA

www.reservaycata.com

This well-stocked vintner's has a passion for Spanish and Portuguese wines. There is a great selection of liqueurs from Spain and abroad, malt whiskies and some top-class olive oils and vinegars as well as red, white and sparkling wines. Tastings, dinners and shows are organized.

✉ Calle Conde de Xiquena 13, 28004 Madrid ☎ 913 19 04 01 ⓓ Tue–Sat 12–3, 5–10 🚇 Colón 🚌 5, 14, 27, 37, 45, 53, 150

SMITH & ROW

The modern and innovative collide with classical style here, with exquisite pieces for the home and gifts. The porcelain is fine, as is the Bohemian and Murano glassware.

✉ Calle Lagasca 65, 28006 Madrid ☎ 915 15 82 10 ⓓ Mon–Fri 10–2, 5–8.30, Sat 10–2 (also Sun 10–2 in Jul and Aug) 🚇 Núñez de Balboa 🚌 9, 19, 51, 61, 89

ENTERTAINMENT AND NIGHTLIFE

ALPHAVILLE

All the films shown on the four screens here are in their original version with subtitles in Spanish.

✉ Calle Martín de los Heros 14, 28008 Madrid ☎ 915 59 38 36 ⓓ Screenings daily around 4.10, 6.15, 8.20 and 10.30; session Fri–Sat at 12.50am 🖐 €6.50, Mon €5 🚇 Plaza de España 🚌 1, 2, 44, 74

AUDITORIO NACIONAL

www.auditorionacional.mcu.es

There are two concert halls here with great acoustics, and up to four concerts daily.

✉ Calle del Príncipe de Vergara 146, 28002 Madrid ☎ 913 37 01 40 (information); 913 37 03 07 (box office) ⓓ Box office: Mon 4–6, Tue–Fri 10–5, Sat 11–1 🖐 €6–€29 🚇 Prosperidad, Cruz del Rayo 🚌 1, 9, 16, 19, 29, 52, 73

BASH/OHM/WEEK-END

www.tripfamily.com

On weekdays this massive club is Bash, on Friday and Saturday it's Ohm, and Sunday is a house night, popular with gay partygoers.

✉ Plaza Callao 4, 28013 Madrid ☎ 915 31 01 39 ⓓ Mon–Wed 11pm–3am, Thu–Sun midnight–7am 🖐 €15 (includes one drink) 🚇 Callao 🚌 1, 2, 46, 75, 133, 146

CASA PATAS

www.casapatas.com

One of the better places for live flamenco shows features both established stars and up-and-coming artists. There is also a restaurant.

✉ Calle de Cañizares 10, 28012 Madrid ☎ 913 69 04 96 🖐 €20 🚇 Antón Martín Tirso de Molina 🚌 6, 26, 32, 50, 65, N14

CLAMORES

www.salaclamores.com

An old jazz nightclub, well known among jazz-lovers in Madrid, Clamores has a superb sound system. Tables are set around the stage so guests can relax, enjoy a drink and listen to the music. It often features interesting new artists.

✉ Calle de Alburquerque 14, 28010 Madrid ☎ 914 45 79 38 ⏱ Daily 7pm–3am 💶 €5–€25 🚇 Bilbao 🚌 3, 37, 40

GALILEO GALILEI
www.salagalileogalilei.com
This spacious hotspot (a cinema in its past life) aims to offer something for everyone, from magic shows to live jazz, flamenco and salsa. Big and not-so-big names in contemporary Spanish music have made it their regular home and art and photography exhibitions regularly adorn the walls, making Galileo Galilei a Madrid institution. Most concerts start at 9.30pm.

✉ Calle Galileo 100, 28003 Madrid ☎ 915 34 75 57 ⏱ Daily 6pm–3am 💶 €10–€20 🚇 Islas Filipinos or Canal 🚌 2, 12

GULA GULA
www.gulagula.net
This highly entertaining revue restaurant is famous in the city for its outrageous drag shows, popular with both the gay and gay-friendly crowds. There is no charge for the show, but you must purchase a meal that is actually rather good.

✉ Calle Gran Via 1, 28013 Madrid ☎ 915 22 87 64 ⏱ Shows: nightly 9pm, Fri and Sat 9pm and midnight 💶 €25 for cold buffet or main meal or €30 for both (reservations essential) 🚇 Banco de España, Sevilla, Gran Via 🚌 146

HONKY TONK
www.clubhonky.com
A central bar with live pop, rock and soul concerts throughout the week. It can be packed during weekends. It is popular with an older crowd.

✉ Calle de Covarrubias 24, 28010 Madrid ☎ 914 45 61 91 ⏱ Jun–Sep daily 10.30pm–5am; Oct–May 9.30pm–5am 💶 Free 🚇 Alonso Martínez 🚌 3, 21, 40, 147

IMAX MADRID
www.imaxmadrid.com
This IMAX cinema has three projection systems. The playlist features both Spanish and original-version films. Fill up before or after

the film at the cinema's cafeteria or restaurant. There's even a terrace and the parking is free.

✉ Parque Enrique Tierno Galván, Calle Meneses s/n, 28045 Madrid ☎ 914 67 48 00. Reservations: 902 10 12 12, 902 40 02 22 ⏱ Screenings daily; times vary 💶 One session €12–€15 (depending on show) 🚇 Méndez Alvaro 🚌 8, 102, 148

JOY ESLAVA
www.joy-eslava.com
Joy Eslava is one of Madrid's oldest and most popular nightclubs, the scene of parties and social events. The music is diverse, in keeping with its clientele. A strict dress code is enforced; dress to impress.

✉ Calle del Arenal 11, 28013 Madrid ☎ 913 66 37 33 ⏱ Daily 11.55pm–6am 💶 €18–€22 (includes one drink) 🚇 Sol, Ópera 🚌 3, 50

NUEVO APOLO
The place to go to see the city's principal music theatre shows and the best contemporary plays, as well as modern dance.

✉ Plaza Tirso de Molina 1, 28012 Madrid ☎ 913 69 06 37; 902 48 84 88 (advance sales) 💶 Around €25–€45 🚇 Tirso de Molina 🚌 6, 26, 32, 57

PACHÁ
www.pacha-madrid.com
The world-renowned club Pachá goes from strength to strength. Dress to impress the picky bouncers or pick up a flyer offering admission from many of the city's bars for a smoother entry.

✉ Calle Barceló 11, 28004 Madrid

Above *Siroco showcases live music*

☎ 914 47 01 28 ⏱ Wed–Sat 11.30pm–6am 💶 €18 🚇 Tribunal, Alonso Martinez 🚌 3, 10, 21, 35, 149

LA RIVIERA
www.salariviera.com
A whole host of renowned bands and artists has performed here. The music genres vary but tend towards pop, rock and techno. There's a great outdoor terrace open in summer. In winter the venue closes soon after the concerts have finished, except on Friday to Sunday nights when it stays open as a nightclub.

✉ Paseo Bajo Virgen del Puerto s/n, 28005 Madrid ☎ 913 65 24 15 ⏱ Fri–Sun midnight–5am 💶 From €20 for concerts, €12 for nightclub (includes one free drink) 🚇 Puerta del Ángel 🚌 25, 31, 33, 36, 39, 50, 69

SEGUNDO JAZZ
www.segundojazz.com
This bar draws its loyal regulars from Madrid's jazz-lovers. There are live shows and during weekends other genres of music are performed. The atmosphere is relaxed and the discerning crowd is mostly aged 30 or older. A civilized evening.

✉ Calle del Comandante Zorita 8, 28020 Madrid ☎ 915 54 94 37 ⏱ Daily 9pm–3am 💶 Free 🚇 Nuevos Ministerios, Cuatro Caminos 🚌 68, 69, 149

SIROCO
www.siroco.es
This two-floor music venue showcases bands playing pop, rock,

breakbeat, acid house, hip-hop and funk. All the action is downstairs; escape the chaos upstairs.

✉ Calle San Dimas 3, 28015 Madrid ☎ 915 93 30 70 🕐 Thu 9.30pm–5.30am, Fri–Sat 9.30pm–6am 💳 €5–€10 (some include a drink) 🚇 San Bernardo, Noviciados 🚌 21, 147

TEATRO DE LA ABADÍA
www.teatroabadia.com
La Abadía features the works of major international playwrights (mainly English) alongside classic Spanish drama.

✉ Calle de Fernández de los Ríos 42, 28015 Madrid ☎ 914 48 11 81 🕐 Closed Jul and Aug 💳 €20–€25 🚇 Quevedo 🚌 2, 16, 61

TEATRO DEL CÍRCULO DE BELLAS ARTES
www.circulobellasartes.com
This auditorium, concert space, cinema and exhibition halls has a playlist that includes dance and ballet, contemporary works and drama, mostly in Spanish. There are special performances for children.

✉ Marqués de Casa Riera 2, 28014 ☎ 913 60 54 00 💳 €20 and €25 🚇 Banco de España 🚌 2, 14, 27, 51, 52

TEATRO FERNÁN-GÓMEZ
http://teatrofernangomez.esmadrid.com
A varied schedule concentrates on contemporary drama, contemporary dance, zarzuela (Spanish light opera) and ballet. Flamenco is frequently staged here.

✉ Plaza de Colón s/n, 28046 Madrid ☎ 914 80 03 00 💳 €20–€45 🚇 Colón 🚌 5, 14, 21, 27, 45, 53

TEATRO HÄAGEN-DAZS CALDERÓN
www.teatrohaagen-dazs.es
This is Madrid's largest theatre. It mostly stages operatic and musical productions sponsored by a large ice-cream company.

✉ Calle de Atocha 18, 28012 Madrid ☎ 902 00 66 17 💳 €30–€40 🚇 Tirso de Molina, Sol 🚌 6, 26, 32

TEATRO DE MADRID
www.teatromadrid.com
Teatro de Madrid comes highly

recommended for ballet-lovers; its flamenco productions are also first class.

✉ Avenida de la Ilustración s/n, 28029 Madrid ☎ 917 30 17 50 (box office); 917 40 52 74 (information) 💳 €10–€25 🚇 Barrio del Pilar, Herrera Oria 🚌 67, 83, 124, 130, 134, 142, N9

TEATRO REAL
www.teatro-real.com
Madrid's opera house presents all operatic styles and offers a first-class schedule, including a number of ballet productions. It also has a nouvelle cuisine restaurant, open for dinner in the theatre's splendid former ballroom.

✉ Avenida de la Ilustración s/n, 28035 Madrid ☎ 917 30 17 50; 902 22 16 22 (advance sales) 💳 From €2.40–€280 🚇 Ópera 🚌 25, 39

SPORTS AND ACTIVITIES
CANAL ISABEL II
www.cyii.es
This reservoir is the centre of a sports and leisure complex, which includes facilities for golf and football. Alternatively, you can go jogging, walking or take the children to the play area.

✉ Avenida Filipinas 54, 28003 Madrid ☎ 915 33 17 91 🕐 Daily 8–11 💳 Free 🚇 Ríos Rosas, Cuatro Caminos 🚌 2, 12

ESTADIO SANTIAGO BERNABÉU
www.realmadrid.com
Real Madrid's home ground holds 80,000 spectators. Most games are played on Saturday and Sunday.

✉ Avenida Concha Espina 1, 28036 ☎ 913 98 43 00 🕐 Tue–Sun 10.30–8.30 💳 Around €32–€160 🚇 Santiago Bernabéu 🚌 14, 43, 120

ESTADIO VICENTE CALDERÓN
www.clubatleticodemadrid.com
Home to first division Atlético de Madrid soccer club. Games are mostly played on Sunday.

✉ Paseo Virgen del Puerto 67, 28005 Madrid ☎ 913 66 47 07 🕐 Mon–Fri 10–2, 5–8 💳 Tickets: around €40 🚇 Pirámides, Marqués de Vadillo 🚌 17, 18, 23, 34, 35, 36, 50, 116, 118, 119

EL OLIVAR DE LA HINOJOSA
www.golfolivar.com
At this public sports complex there are 18- and 9-hole golf courses plus practice area, the Spanish racquet game of pádel, tennis, a gym and a sauna. There is a snack bar and restaurant with terrace.

✉ Avenida de Dublín s/n, Campo de las Naciones, 28042 Madrid ☎ 917 21 18 89 🕐 Daily 8.30am–10pm 💳 Green fee €49. Club rental €11.70 🚇 Campo de las Naciones 🚌 104, 122

PLAZA DE TOROS DE LAS VENTAS
www.las-ventas.com
This is one of the most important bullrings in Spain. The major season begins during the San Isidro Festival in May (▷ 95) and bullfighting is held daily thereafter. Guided tours are available.

✉ Calle de Alcalá 237, 28028 Madrid ☎ 913 56 22 00 🕐 Bullfights: Sun and holidays around 5pm; May–Sep during festivals daily at 7pm 💳 €4.50–€127 🚇 Ventas 🚌 12, 21, 38, 53, 106, 110, 146

TELEFÉRICO
www.teleferico.com
Take a ride in a cable-car for magnificent views over Madrid. The ride ends in Casa de Campo (▷ 71) park.

✉ Paseo del Pintor Rosales s/n, 28008 Madrid ☎ 915 41 74 50 🕐 Summer daily from noon; winter weekends only; phone for times 💳 Single €3.55, return €5.15; child under 3 free 🚇 Argüelles 🚌 21, 74

HEALTH AND BEAUTY
AGUA Y BIEN
www.aguaybien.com
Have a sea-salt hydro massage or a hot-stone foot treatment, make use of the thermal swimming pool, sauna and Scottish or oil showers, and finish off with a glass of freshly squeezed juice. There are also a number of other treatments on offer.

✉ Calle Martínez Villergas 16, 28027 Madrid ☎ 914 03 31 73 🕐 Mon–Fri 9.30am–10pm, Sat–Sun 9.30–3 💳 90-min thermal circuit €18; full massage €35; thermal pool €14 🚇 Barrio de la Concepción 🚌 21, 53

BAÑOS DE ROSALES
www.balneariosamsara.com
This spa offers a one-hour thermal circuit that includes relaxation, Roman hot baths, body care with hot stones, aromatherapy and steam baths.

✉ Calle Romero Robledo 28, 28008 Madrid ☎ 902 10 81 47 🕐 Mon–Sat 10–10, Sun 10–3 💷 1-hour thermal circuit €28 Ⓜ Moncloa, Argüelles 🚌 1, 21, 44, 68, 69, 74, 133

FOR CHILDREN
AQUÓPOLIS
www.aquopolis.es
This aquatic park is fun for children. There is a restaurant, a cafeteria, souvenir shops and a solarium.

✉ Avenida de la Dehesa s/n, 28691 Villanueva de la Cañada ☎ 918 15 69 11 🕐 Jul–Aug daily 12–8; Jun, Sep 12–7 💷 Adult €21.95, child (4–9) €16.95 🚌 Free buses from Plaza España 🚗 Take the M-503 from Madrid; leave Exit 41 for Majadahonda. Head to Boadilla del Monte and Brunete; follow signs to Villanueva de la Cañada

CASA DE CAMPO
An enormous park, ideal for a drink on the terrace or a boat trip on the lake, also has a zoo, an amusement park, fair pavilions and bullfighters' school. Sports events and concerts also take place here.

✉ Casa de Campo, 28011 Madrid ☎ 914 79 60 02 🕐 Some areas close at night 💷 Free Ⓜ Casa de Campo 🚌 33, 65

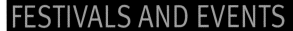

FESTIVALS AND EVENTS

FEBRUARY–MARCH
EL ENTIERRO DE LA SARDINA
The Burial of the Sardine is an entertaining parade which forms part of Carnaval.

PARQUE DE ATRACCIONES
www.parquedeatracciones.es
There are more than 40 attractions divided into five different adventure zones. Music concerts every night in summer. Snack bars and restaurants, serving pizzas, hamburgers and sandwiches, as well as fine dining.

✉ Carretera de Extremadura (NV), Entrada al Parque Atracciones, 28011 Madrid ☎ 914 63 29 00 🕐 Summer daily; winter weekends only; phone for times 💷 Adult €29, child (3–7) €22. Reduced admission for those not taking rides Ⓜ Estación Batán 🚌 33, 65

PARQUE WARNER
www.parquewarner.com
A spectacular movie theme park boasts plenty of action and fun in its five themed areas: Super Heroes World, Movie World Studios, Cartoon Village, Hollywood Boulevard and Old West Territory. There's a range of restaurants, and a pet day-care service. Don't miss the actors recreating scenes from popular Warner Bros movies such as *Lethal Weapon*.

✉ Carretera N-IV, Exit Km 22, 28330 San Martín de la Vega ☎ 902 02 41 00 🕐 Summer daily; rest of year weekends only; phone for times. Closed Nov–Mar 💷 Adult €38, child (5–10) €29 🚗 From Atocha direct to park 🚗 Take Carretera de Andalucía (N-IV) and exit at Km22. Follow the signs from here

MAY
FIESTAS DE SAN ISIDRO
Two-week festival celebrating the feast of Madrid's patron saint.
🕐 One week either side of 15 May

ZOO ACUARIUM
www.zoomadrid.com
The aquarium has a spectacular tropical fish collection and daily dolphin, seal and sea lion shows. There's a restaurant and snack bars or take a picnic. Kiddy cars and prism binoculars are available for rent.

✉ Casa de Campo s/n, 28011 Madrid ☎ 915 12 37 70 🕐 Mon–Fri 10.30–7, Sat 10.30–8; late night visits during summer 9.30–midnight 💷 Adult €18.65, child (3–7) €15.10 Ⓜ Casa de Campo 🚌 33

Below *The Teleférico gives superb views*

PRICES AND SYMBOLS

The restaurants are listed alphabetically (excluding El, Le, La and Les). The prices given are the average for a two-course lunch (L) and a three-course dinner (D) for one person, without drinks. The wine price is for the least expensive bottle.

For a key to the symbols, ▷ 2.

19 SUSHI BAR

www.19sushibar.com
Dynamic chef Álex Moranda has made a name for himself at some of Spain's top fusion restaurants for years, and his own restaurant, 19 Sushi Bar, has proved a big hit with fashionable *Madrileños*. Try superb contemporary Japanese cuisine, which includes innovative dishes such as the melt-in-the-mouth baby squid tempura. Desserts include a scrumptious, calorific chocolate and ginger mousse.
✉ Calle Salud 19, 28013 Madrid ☎ 915 24 05 71 🕐 Mon–Sat 1–4.30, 8–12. Closed Aug ✋ L €35, D €45, Wine €13 🚇 Gran Vía 🚌 1, 2, 46, 74, 146, 202

LA ANCHA

www.laancha.com
La Ancha is a traditional restaurant and serves Spanish dishes, including steak, fresh fish and stew.

Reservations are advisable.
✉ Calle Príncipe de Vergara 204, 28002 Madrid; Calle Zorrilla 7 ☎ 915 63 89 77; 914 29 81 86 🕐 Mon–Sat 1.30–4, 9–12 ✋ L €40, D €45, Wine €12 🚇 Concha Espina 🚌 16, 29, 52

ASADOR DE LA ESQUINA

For Real Madrid fans, this might be a little slice of heaven: a traditional restaurant serving excellent local cuisine with views over the legendary Bernabéu Stadium. There is a terrace for outdoor dining in the summer. The lamb chops are a house specialty and the home-made desserts are superb.
✉ Avenida Concha Espina 1 (Bernabéu Stadium, gate 46) ☎ 914 43 06 75 🕐 Daily 1–4, 8–12. Closed during matches ✋ L €50, D €55, Wine €15 🚇 Santiago Bernabéu 🚌 43, 120,150

LA BARDEMCILLA

www.labardemcilla.com
This tapas bar is regularly full, its house specials of ham croquettes and cod are popular. Reserving a table is advisable. It's owned by the famous Bardem family (including Oscar-winning actor, Javier Bardem).
✉ Calle de Augusto Figueroa 47, 28004 Madrid ☎ 915 21 42 56 🕐 Mon–Fri noon–5, 8–1.30, Sat 8–1.30 ✋ Tapas

from €3, *raciones* (small plates) from €8 🚇 Chueca 🚌 3, 40, 149

BOKADO

www.bokadogrupo.com
Bokado is run by two celebrated Basque chefs, Jesús and Mikel Santamaría, famous for their elaborate *pintxos* (upmarket canapés). The restaurant is located inside the Museo del Traje (▷ 80) and offers superb, contemporary Basque cuisine, with the emphasis on seafood. The adjoining cafeteria has some of the famous *pintxos* and a good value set menu at lunchtimes (€18). The garden terrace is beautiful.
✉ Avenida Juan de Herrera 2 ☎ 915 49 00 41 🕐 Tue–Sat 1.30–4, 9–12 (also Sun 1.30–4 in winter) ✋ L and D €55, Wine €14 🚇 Moncloa or Ciudad Universitaria 🚌 46, 82

LA BOLA TABERNA

www.labola.es
La Bola really is best known for its *cocido madrileño* (a soup-style stew with noodles, chick peas, meat and vegetables). Reservations are advisable as this place is popular. Credit cards are not accepted.
✉ Calle de la Bola 5, 28013 Madrid

Above Boquerones en vinagreta

☎ 915 47 69 30 Ⓦ Mon–Thu 1–4, 8.30–11, Fri–Sat 1–4, 8.30–12, Sun 1–4 ♨ L €35, D €45, Wine €12 Ⓜ Santo Domingo 🚌 25, 39

CAFÉ COMERCIAL

This is one of the city's oldest cafés. It has a long bar and a large, airy (apart from the smoke) space to drink coffee, have a slice of cake and relax.

✉ Glorieta de Bilbao 7, 28004 Madrid ☎ 915 21 56 55 Ⓦ Mon–Thu 8am–1am, Fri–Sat 8am–2am, Sun 10am–1am ♨ Coffee and cake €5 Ⓜ Bilbao

CAFÉ GIJÓN

www.cafegijon.com
Established in 1881, this café has been a social hub for artists and intellectuals throughout its existence. The restaurant represents Spain's many regions with grilled meats and fish such as hake or cod. There's a sizeable wine list to choose from, too.

✉ Paseo de Recoletos 21, 28004 Madrid ☎ 915 21 54 25 Ⓦ Daily 9am–2am ♨ L €36, D €50, Wine €17 Ⓜ Colón 🚌 5, 14, 27, 37, 45, 53, 150

CAFÉ DE ORIENTE

www.cafedeoriente.es
The chef creates contemporary dishes such as green peppers stuffed with cod, fish and seafood soup, grilled sirloin, lamb and hake with clams in a green sauce.

✉ Plaza de Oriente 2, 28013 Madrid ☎ 915 41 39 74 Ⓦ Café: daily 8.30am–1.30am. Restaurant: Mon–Fri 1–4, 9–12, Sat–Sun 1–4 ♨ L €40, D €75, Wine €18 Ⓜ Ópera 🚌 25, 39

CAFÉ SAIGÓN

www.elcafesaigon.es
Old Indochina is the theme at this attractive restaurant, with its original Vietnamese sculpture and rattan furnishings set amid palms. The menu is mainly Vietnamese, with some Thai and Chinese dishes, and includes summer rolls, stir fries and noodle dishes. International visitors should note that the spicier dishes have been toned down for Spanish palates. Reserve well in advance, particularly for the terrace, as this is very popular with the fashion pack.

✉ Calle María de Molina 4 ☎ 915 63 15 66 Ⓦ Daily 1.30–4, 8.30–12 ♨ L €30, D €45, Wine €14 Ⓜ Gregorio Marañón 🚌 7, 12, 14, 16, 27, 40, 147, 150

EL CAPRICHO DE LA CAÑERÍA

This traditional Spanish tavern prepares excellent marinated anchovies. At the bar, a range of tapas is available alongside more substantial dishes. Hearty *Madrileño* cuisine, from *cocido* (chickpea soup) to *lentejas* (lentils), is served in the *comedor* behind the bar.

✉ Calle de Doctor Castelo 14, 28009 Madrid ☎ 915 04 61 79 Ⓦ Mon–Thu 12–5, 8–12, Fri–Sat noon–1am, Sun 12–5 ♨ Canapés around €3.25; tapas around €6 Ⓜ Ibiza 🚌 2, 15, 20, 26, 61, 63, 68

CASA CAROLA

www.casacarola.com
At this traditional Spanish restaurant *cocido madrileño* (soup with noodles, chick peas, meat and vegetables) is served only at lunchtime, as is the local custom. It's considered to be one of the best places to try this authentic local dish in the city.

✉ Calle de Padilla 54, 28007 Madrid ☎ 914 01 94 08 Ⓦ Daily 1–4, 9–11.30. Closed Aug ♨ L €29, D €33, Wine €11 Ⓜ Núñez de Balboa 🚌 1, 29, 52, 74

CASA LUCIO

www.casalucio.es
Madrid's rich and famous are regular customers here. The chef makes simple but delicious dishes, using the finest ingredients. One of the most notable is *huevos rotos* (scrambled eggs with fries), which is tasty, if a little expensive. Reserve a table in advance. Valet parking.

✉ Cava Baja 35, 28005 Madrid ☎ 913 65 32 52 Ⓦ Sun–Fri 1–4, 9–12, Sat 8.30–12 ♨ L €35, D €50, Wine €13 Ⓜ La Latina 🚌 17, 18, 23, 35, 60

CASA MINGO

www.casamingo.es
Casa Mingo is a large, traditional tavern in Moncloa serving popular dishes from the Asturias region. Reservations are not taken, so it's wise to arrive early. Credit cards are not accepted.

✉ Paseo de la Florida 34, 28008 Madrid ☎ 915 47 79 18 Ⓦ Daily 11am–midnight ♨ L €25, D €35, Wine €12 Ⓜ Príncipe Pío 🚌 41, 46, 75

LA CASTAFIORE

This is a special place where the waiters serenade you while you dine. The food is enticing.

✉ Calle Marqués de Monasterio 5, 28004 Madrid ☎ 915 32 21 00 Ⓦ Mon–Sat 2–4.30, 9.30–1 ♨ L €35, D €45, Wine €12 Ⓜ Banco de España 🚌 1, 2, 5, 20, 37, 51, 52, 53, 74, 146

CASTELLANA 179

www.castellana179.com
A sophisticated restaurant in Chamartín, Castellana 179 serves satisfying Spanish dishes and home-made desserts. A favourite with well-heeled local business people, it has a fine selection of after-dinner cigars.

✉ Paseo de la Castellana 179, 28046 Madrid ☎ 914 25 06 80 Ⓦ Mon–Sat 2–4.30, 9–12.30 ♨ L €35, D €50, Wine €13 Ⓜ Plaza Castilla 🚌 5, 27, 147, 149

CHOCOLATERÍA SAN GINÉS

A classic spot for an early breakfast after a night out. As 6am approaches, the café fills up, as this is when many of the city's nightclubs close. *Churros* (fritters) and *porras* (a larger version of the same) come in generous portions. Hot chocolate, coffee and assorted refreshments are also available. No credit cards.

✉ Pasadizo San Gines 5, 28013 Madrid ☎ 913 65 65 46 Ⓦ Daily 6pm–6am ♨ Hot chocolate and *churros* €5.50 Ⓜ Sol, Opera 🚌 3, 50

COMBARRO

www.combarro.com
This is one of Madrid's best fresh fish and seafood restaurants, with a blistering wine list. The fish and shellfish are brought daily from Galicia, and prepared to authentic local recipes.

✉ Calle de Reina Mercedes 12, 28006 Madrid ☎ 915 54 77 84 Ⓦ Daily 1.30–4, 9–12, Sun 1.30–4. Closed Aug ♨ L €50, D €65, Wine €14 Ⓜ Núñez de Balboa 🚌 1, 29, 52, 74

CORNUCOPIA

www.restaurantecornucopia.com

This is a very charming, contemporary restaurant, with three boldly painted dining areas which double as galleries for temporary art exhibitions. The menu offers a wide range of modern Mediterranean cuisine, and—unusually for Madrid—also includes an excellent selection of imaginative vegetarian and vegan dishes. There are good-value set menus during the week, and the restaurant also functions as a café in the afternoons. The cakes are fabulous.

✉ Calle Navas de Tolosa 9, 28013 Madrid ☎ 915 21 38 96 🕐 Daily 12–12 ✋ L €22, D €28, Wine €12 🚇 Callao

EL COSACO

www.restauranteelcosaco.com

A classic Russian restaurant, where the prices are as palatable as the food. It fills up quickly at weekends, so reservations are advisable. There is live Russian music on Thursday evenings.

✉ Plaza de la Paja 2, 28005 Madrid ☎ 913 65 35 48 🕐 Tue–Sun 2–3.30, 9–12, Mon 9–12 ✋ L €35, D €45, Wine €10 🚇 La Latina 🚌 31, 50, 65

CURRITO

www.restaurantecurrito.es

This traditional Basque restaurant in Casa de Campo has built its reputation over the years by virtue of the excellent meat and fish it offers its customers. Reservations are recommended.

✉ Paseo de la Gastronomía s/n, Casa de Campo, 28023 Madrid ☎ 914 64 57 04 🕐 Mon–Sat 1.30–4, 9–12.30, Sun 1.30–5 ✋ L €60, D €65, Wine €16 🚇 Lago 🚌 25, 33, 36, 39

FAST GOOD

www.fast-good.com

Burgers are laced with olive tapenade and gorgonzola, paninis are made of a special, half-baked bread and the ham sandwich uses the best *pata negra* (prime-cut, Iberian ham). This is part of Ferran Adriá's empire (see El Bulli, ▷ 282).

✉ Hotel NH Eurobuilding, Calle Padre

Damián 23, 28036 Madrid ☎ 913 43 06 55 🕐 Daily 8am–11pm ✋ L €10.50, D €15, Wine €3.50 for individual 8.5cl bottles of Rioja 🚇 Cuzco

EL INGENIO

www.restauranteingenio.com

You'll find traditional Spanish cuisine on the menu here, with salads, croquettes, wild mushrooms with *aioli* (garlic mayonnaise), vegetable stew, soups, dried butter-bean dishes and fresh cod. Menu of the day €15. Reserving a table is advisable.

✉ Calle de Leganitos 10, 28013 Madrid ☎ 915 41 91 33 🕐 Mon–Sat 1.30–4, 8.30–12 ✋ L €17, D €25, Wine €12 🚇 Santo Domingo 🚌 1, 2, 44, 46, 68, 74, 75, 133, 148

JOCKEY

www.restaurantejockey.net

This traditional restaurant is one of Madrid's finest. It has won awards over the years, and famous people have dined here. The elegant interior is dotted with equestrian objects. The menu features traditional dishes with an exotic touch. Reserving a table is advisable, and men are required to wear a jacket and tie.

✉ Calle Amador de los Ríos 6, 28010 Madrid ☎ 913 19 24 35 🕐 Mon–Sat 1.30–4.30, 9–12. Closed Sun, holidays and Aug ✋ L €95, D €125, Wine €18 🚇 Colón 🚌 5, 14, 27, 45, 150

LOMBOK

As well as a long list of wok and stir-fry dishes, specialties include sautéed duck breast with rice and apple and various fusions of East meets West.

✉ Calle Augusto Figueroa 32, 28004 Madrid ☎ 915 31 35 66 🕐 Mon–Thu 1.30–4, 9.30–12, Fri–Sat 9pm–1am ✋ L €15, D €35, Wine €14 🚇 Chueca

MICOTA

www.micota.com

Micota is creative in its grilled cuisine. The house specials include nachos, assorted pâtés, salads, fondue (cheese or beef), grilled meats and a plethora of starters. Children have their own menu. There is a no-smoking section.

✉ Calle de Castelló 18, 28001 Madrid

☎ 915 77 76 71, 902 19 39 63 🕐 Daily 1–5, 8–12 (Sat–Sun until 1am) ✋ L €10, D €20, Wine €8 🚇 Príncipe de Vergara, Velazquez 🚌 21, 29, 53, 142

MONTEPRÍNCIPE

www.restaurantemonteprincipe.com

Montepríncipe is owned by a couple, one Basque and the other from the Asturias region. Exquisite traditional recipes create delicious fare at reasonable prices. Reserve a table in advance, especially during weekends.

✉ Calle San Andrés 31, 28004 Madrid ☎ 914 48 83 10 🕐 Tue–Sat 2–3.30, 9–11.30, Sun 2–3.30 ✋ L €40, D €50, Wine €10 🚇 Bilbao 🚌 21, 147, 149

NODO

www.restaurantenodo.es

The appeal of Nodo is enduring, mainly owing to its original Asian fusion cuisine. Reservations are advisable at this fashionable, yet reasonably priced, place.

✉ Calle de Velázquez 150, 28002 Madrid ☎ 915 64 40 44 🕐 Sun–Thu 1.30–4, 9–12, Fri–Sat 1.30–4, 9–1 ✋ L €25, D €40, Wine €12 🚇 República Argentina 🚌 7, 16, 19, 51

O'PAZO

www.opazo.es

A top choice if you fancy fresh fish or seafood, this is one of the most prestigious Galician restaurants in the city. Meat doesn't feature on the menu, except for a delicious Iberian ham starter.

✉ Calle Reina Mercedes 20, 28020 Madrid ☎ 915 34 37 48 🕐 Mon–Sat 1–4, 8.30–12. Closed Aug ✋ L €60, D €75, Wine €18 🚇 Santiago Bernabéu 🚌 5, 43, 149

SALVADOR

This welcoming restaurant was founded by a *torero* (matador), and retains an authentic taurine atmosphere, with old photographs of famous bullfighters on the walls. The *rabo de toro* (oxtail) is considered among the best in the city. Ask for a more secluded table upstairs.

✉ Calle de Barbieri 12, 28004 Madrid ☎ 915 21 45 24 🕐 Mon–Sat 1.30–4, 9.30–11.30. Closed Aug ✋ L €25, D €45, Wine €12 🚇 Chueca

EL SENADOR
www.restaurantesenador.com
This well-established traditional restaurant serves Segovian cuisine. The tender roast suckling pig is recommended. Reserve in advance.
✉ Plaza de la Marina Española 2, 28013 Madrid ☎ 915 41 22 21 🕐 Mon–Sat 1–4, 8.30–12, Sun 1–4. Closed Jul–Aug Sun 🍴 L €42, D €60, Wine €12 Ⓜ Santo Domingo, Ópera 🚌 25, 39, 148

SERGI AROLA GASTRO
www.sergiarola.es
Ferran Adrià graduate (and most likely to succeed) Sergi Arola's tasting menus (midday, short and long with wine pairings) and superb by-the-glass wine list of some 500 little-known winemakers has been a hit in Madrid since his 2007 opening.
✉ Zurbano 31, 28010 Madrid ☎ 913 10 21 69 🕐 Mon–Fri 2–5, 9–11.30 🍴 L €95 D €125 Wine €24 Ⓜ Alonso Martinez

THAI GARDENS
www.thaigardensgroup.com
Thai Gardens incorporates the essence of Thailand in its menu of tasty dishes and its decoration.

✉ Calle de Jorge Juan 5, 28001 Madrid ☎ 915 77 88 84 🕐 Sun–Thu 2–4, 9–12, Fri–Sat 2–4, 9–2.30 🍴 L €38, D €55, Wine €13 Ⓜ Serrano 🚌 1, 9, 19, 51, 74, 89

EL TOMILLAR
This is an agreeable place for tapas. Stand at the bar or sit at a table.
✉ Calle Profesor Waksman 14, 28036 Madrid ☎ 914 58 29 10 🕐 Daily 8am–1am. Closed Sun Jun–Sep 🍴 Tapas around €4 Ⓜ Santiago Bernabéu, Cuzco 🚌 11, 40, 150

TRES ENCINAS
www.tresencinas.com
Seafood is the order of the day, although there are good meat dishes served here, too. There is valet parking, and you can take your order away with you. The kitchen here, conveniently, is open all day.
✉ Preciados 33, 28013 Madrid ☎ 915 21 22 07 🕐 Daily 1pm–midnight 🍴 L €42, D €48, Wine €14 Ⓜ Callao 🚌 44, 75, 133, 146, 147

LA VACA VERÓNICA
www.lavacaveronica.es
A charming, romantic restaurant,

near the Prado. Pasta with crayfish and filet Veronica are house specials. Reserving a table is advisable.
✉ Calle de Moratín 38, 28014 Madrid ☎ 914 29 78 27 🕐 Sun–Fri 2–4, 9–12, Sat 9–12 🍴 L €25, D €35, Wine €12 Ⓜ Antón Martín 🚌 6, 10, 14, 26, 27, 32, 34, 37, 45

EL VERGEL
www.elvergel.com
El Vergel has a restaurant, shop and library aimed at meat-free lifestylers.
✉ Paseo de la Florida 53, 28008 Madrid ☎ 915 47 19 52 🕐 Daily 1pm–midnight 🍴 3-course menu (lunch and dinner, including wine) €10, weekends €14 (not including wine) Ⓜ Príncipe Pío

VIRIDIANA
www.restauranteviridiana.com
One of Madrid's very popular classic restaurants, Viridiana's innovative chef is Abraham García.
✉ Calle Juan de Mena 14, 28014 Madrid ☎ 915 31 52 22 🕐 Mon–Sat 1.30–4, 8.30–12 🍴 L €60, D €75, Wine €16 Ⓜ Retiro 🚌 19

Above *Traditional paella includes chicken or rabbit, fish, prawns and shellfish*

PRICES AND SYMBOLS

The prices are for a double room for one night including breakfast, unless otherwise stated. All the hotels listed accept credit cards unless otherwise stated. Note that rates can vary widely throughout the year.

For a key to the symbols, ▷ 2.

ABALÚ MADRID

www.hotelabalu.com

This establishment has been dramatically transformed into a chic, designer hotel. Each room is boldly and individually decorated, and some rooms have a Jacuzzi and even a home cinema. It's located in a lively nightlife district, and is popular with a hip, young, budget-conscious crowd.

✉ Calle Pez 19, 28004 Madrid
☎ 915 31 47 44 🖐 €95–€125 ⓘ 15
🛗 🚇 Noviciado 🚌 47

AC SANTO MAURO

www.hotelacsantomauro.com

A 19th-century palace in the Chamberí district which has avant-garde architectural detail. What was originally the library now houses a contemporary restaurant with a summer terrace. Facilities include 24-hour room service, a bar, internet access, free minibar (although beer is the only alcohol on the list), sauna, a car rental service and a 24-hour laundry.

✉ Calle de Zurbano 36, 28010 Madrid
☎ 913 19 69 00 🖐 €245–€365 excluding à la carte breakfast (€29) ⓘ 51 (4 non-smoking) 🛗 🏊 Indoor 🏋 🚇 Alonso Martínez 🚌 7, 40, 147

ADLER

www.adlermadrid.com

An elegant and classically stylish hotel in a chic neighbourhood, the five-star Adler is perfect for a romantic weekend. It's close to the lovely Retiro gardens, and handy for Barrio Salamanca's chic fashion boutiques and smart restaurants. The bedrooms are plushly furnished with beautiful fabrics, and most have charming wrought-iron balconies. The hotel restaurant serves Mediterranean cuisine.

✉ Calle Velázquez 33, 28001 Madrid
☎ 914 26 32 20 🖐 €305–€495 ⓘ 45
🛗 🚇 Velázquez 🚌 1, 9, 19, 21, 51, 53, 74

ASTURIAS

www.hotel-asturias.com

This hotel is conveniently central, close to Puerta del Sol and not far from Huertas and its many bars and restaurants. The rooms are well turned out: simple, classic decor, with private bathrooms, safety deposit boxes and satellite TV. There's also a bar, TV lounge and restaurant that specializes in traditional Spanish dishes.

✉ Calle de Sevilla 2, 28014 Madrid ☎ 914 29 66 76 🖐 €95–€125 excluding breakfast (€9) ⓘ 175 🛗 🚇 Sevilla 🚌 5, 15, 20, 51, 52, 53, 150

CASA DE MADRID

www.casademadrid.com

At the Casa de Madrid, an 18th-century *palacio* on a beautiful square opposite the opera house, there are just seven opulent, romantic rooms. It feels like an aristocratic, private home—perhaps because it was just that until recently, and is still the globe-trotting owner's pied à terre while in the capital. Antiques,

Above *The Indian Room, Casa de Madrid*

artworks from around the world, and whimsical objets d'art fill the rooms.
✉ Calle de Arrieta 2, 28013 Madrid ☎ 915 59 57 91 🖐 €230–€285, suite €395 🛏 6 rooms, I suite 🚇 Ópera

CHIC&BASIC COLORS

www.chicandbasic.com

A welcoming little *hostal*, which offers small but brightly painted rooms, with contemporary design and modern facilities including plasma TVs—all for a very reasonable price. There is a free self-service snack bar and internet access. The location, in the heart of the lively and atmospheric Santa Ana neighbourhood, is perfect for sightseeing as well as nightlife.
✉ Calle Huertas 14, 28012 Madrid ☎ 914 29 69 35 🖐 €60–€93 🛏 15 🔁 🚇 Sol 🚌 6, 26, 32

CLEMENT BARAJAS HOTEL

www.clementhoteles.com

This modern, four-star hotel is located in a lively little suburb near the airport, and is a good option for those arriving late at night, or departing on early morning flights. The rooms are stylishly decorated in cool shades of cream and beige, and all come with plenty of bathroom goodies, as well as dressing gown and slippers. There are shops, restaurants and bars nearby, but the hotel also has its own good restaurant, a casual brasserie, and a buffet breakfast is served. There is a free, 24-hour shuttle service to the airport.
✉ Avenida General 43, 28042 Madrid ☎ 917 46 03 30 🖐 €75–€220 🛏 72 🔁 🚇 Barajas 🚌 105, 114

DE LAS LETRAS H&R

www.hoteldelasletras.com

This handsome hotel occupies a fine neoclassical building on Madrid's biggest avenue, the bustling Gran Vía. The interior is a fashionable mix of ultra-modern amenities and original details, including pretty painted tiles. Bedrooms range from the good-value basic doubles to the luxurious suites, but all are individually decorated and adorned with quotes from famous writers.

There's a restaurant and spa area.
✉ Gran Vía 11, 28013 Madrid ☎ 915 23 79 80 🖐 €132–€305 🛏 103 🔁 🚇 Gran Vía 🚌 1, 2, 74, 146, 202

GRAN HOTEL CONDE DUQUE

www.hotelcondeduque.es

The Conde Duque has a superb central location, close to busy Calle de Fuencarral, but set back in a quiet square. The rooms are elegant and traditional, with the main focus on comfort. Facilities include 24-hour room service, internet access and laundry services.
✉ Plaza Conde Valle Suchil 5, 28015 Madrid ☎ 914 47 70 00 🖐 €145–€380 excluding breakfast (€25) 🛏 143 (34 non-smoking) 🔁 🚇 San Bernardo 🚌 21, 147

HOSTAL BARRERA

www.hostalbarrera.com

This spotless, family-run *hostal* is a good option for those travelling on a budget. It is conveniently located for visiting the principal three museums of the Golden Triangle and on the edge of the popular nightlife district of Santa Ana, with its tapas bars and restaurants. The bedrooms are impeccably clean, but on the small side. It can be a little noisy, so bring ear plugs.
✉ Calle Atocha 95, second floor, 28012 Madrid ☎ 915 27 53 81 🖐 €65–€85 🛏 14 🔁 🚇 Anton Martín 🚌 6, 26, 32

HOTEL URBAN

www.derbyhotels.es

This is the latest offering from the luxury hotel group Derby, and like Barcelona's Hotel Claris (▷ 249) the Hotel Urban features valuable pieces of Egyptian, Asian and tribal art in its halls and public areas. The rest of the architecture and decor is cutting-edge. But Philippe Starck chairs and keepsake toiletry sets aside, the rooms themselves are a tad on the cramped side for a five-star and double-glazing does little to block out the traffic noise below. That said, the breakfasts are excellent, staff superb, and for the ultimate in a 'designer hotel' experience the Urban is the best in Madrid.

✉ Carrera de San Jerónimo 34, 28014 Madrid ☎ 917 87 77 70 🖐 €185–€475 excluding breakfast (€21) 🛏 96 (15 non-smoking) 🔁 🏊 🛁

INGLÉS

www.hotel-ingles.net

This two-star hotel dates from as far back as 1853, and is close to Madrid's Art Triangle (the Prado, Thyssen-Bornemisza and Reina Sofía) and lively Calle de las Huertas. The area can be quite noisy at night, especially if your room looks out onto the main street. Guest rooms are comfortable and fitted with satellite TV and direct telephone lines.
✉ Calle de Echegaray 8, 28014 Madrid ☎ 914 29 65 51 🖐 €85–€125 excluding breakfast (€6) 🛏 58 🔁 🛁 🚇 Antón Martín, Sevilla, Sol 🚌 6, 26, 32, 57

ME BY MELIÁ

www.mebymelia.com

The Spanish hotel chain Meliá has revamped the historic Grand Hotel Victoria, which overlooks buzzy Plaza Santa Ana. It's now one of the most fashionable accommodation options in the city, with a sought-after roof-terrace nightclub, a glitzy restaurant, a fabulous spa, and a range of plush, contemporary rooms. All rooms are equipped with essential amenities, including martini bars, WiFi and Aveda toiletries. One floor, called The Level, offers ultra-luxurious suites, including a panoramic duplex which occupies the uppermost tower.
✉ Plaza Santa Ana 14, 28012 Madrid ☎ 917 01 60 00 🖐 €150–€310 🛏 192 🔁 🚇 Sol 🚌 6, 26, 32, 50, 65

MEDIODÍA

www.mediodiahotel.com

A two-star hotel opposite the Atocha train station, close to the Reina Sofía and Prado museums and just a stroll away from Parque del Retiro. It's good value for money, is well connected by public transportation, and there's a range of tapas bars and restaurants on the square.
✉ Plaza Emperador Carlos V 8, 28012 Madrid ☎ 915 27 30 60 🖐 €85 excluding breakfast (€5) 🛏 174 🔁 🚇 Atocha 🚌 6, 19, 27, 34, 59, 68, 69, 141

MENINAS

www.hotelmeninas.es

This attractive, modern hotel occupies a 19th-century building conveniently close to the Opera House and the Royal Palace. The bedrooms are pristine and modern, with white minimalist decor complemented by hot pink accents. Some feature small balconies. Non-smoking rooms and wheelchair-accessible rooms are available.

✉ Calle Campomanes 7, 28013 Madrid ☎ 915 41 28 05 ♨ €115–€195 ⓘ 37 ⓢ ⓜ Ópera ⊟ 29, 35

ÓPERA

www.hotelopera.com

The Opera is about as central as it gets. Rooms include a minibar, safe deposit boxes, internet access and hairdryer, and the hotel also has a bar, a cafeteria (serving fixed-price menus), a laundry service and business facilities. Spanish and international dishes are served at the Café de la Ópera; the restaurant's waiters (professional singers) perform for guests as they serve.

✉ Cuesta de Santo Domingo 2, 28013 Madrid ☎ 915 41 28 00 ♨ €75–€220 excluding breakfast (€14) ⓘ 79 (59 non-smoking) ⓢ ⓜ Ópera ⊟ 25, 39

PETIT PALACE LA POSADA DEL PEINE

www.hthoteles.com

This hotel opened in 2005, but it occupies an old inn *(posada)* which dates back to the early 17th century. The hotel elegantly combines original details with sleek contemporary fittings, particularly in some of the public spaces where the ancient beams have been retained. Bedrooms are uncompromisingly modern, with stylishly minimalist decor.

✉ Calle Postas 17, 28012 Madrid ☎ 915 23 81 51 ♨ €110–€350 ⓘ 69 ⓢ ⓜ Sol ⊟ 3, 50

RITZ

www.ritz.es

The Ritz is one of the most beautiful and emblematic of Madrid's hotels. It has played host to royalty and countless aristocrats, writers and musicians. The bold interior features old tapestries, elegant chandeliers, marble bathrooms, exquisitely embroidered linen sheets and a wealth of antiques. The hotel benefits from a garden terrace, and the restaurant serves traditional Spanish cuisine on its daily menu. Children are well provided for with a range of facilities and a babysitting service.

✉ Plaza de la Realtad, 28014 Madrid ☎ 917 01 67 67 ♨ €355–€690 excluding breakfast (€34) ⓘ 165 (two floors with non-smoking rooms) ⓢ ⓜ ⊟ 10, 14, 27, 34, 37, 45

ROOM MATE ÓSCAR

www.room-matehotels.com

This is the newest of a small chain of hip hotels which offer chic contemporary design at a modest price. This hotel is well located right in the heart of the city, on an attractive square just off the busy Gran Vía. It offers a range of rooms (standard, executive and junior suites, all wheelchair accessible), which have been futuristically decorated by hot Spanish interior designer Tomás Alía. Ask for a room

with balcony overlooking the square.
Buffet breakfast and WiFi access is
included in the price. There is a café-
restaurant.

✉ Plaza Vázquez de Mella 12, 28004
Madrid ☎ 917 01 11 73 💶 €90–€195,
junior suite €140–€160 🛏 75 ⬡
Ⓜ Gran Vía

SENATOR GRAN VÍA
www.senatorhoteles.com
The Senator Gran Vía is in the
heart of the city. Its interior is a blend
of functionality and urban style.
Guests can expect a CD player, iron,
free minibar (beer is the strongest
alcohol available), coffee-making
equipment, cable TV and bathrobes.
Services include a laundry, room
service, internet access and two
meeting rooms. The bar-restaurant
serves buffet breakfasts and dinners.

✉ Gran Vía 21, 28013 Madrid ☎ 915
31 41 51 💶 €95–€310 excluding
breakfast (€15) 🛏 136 (18 non-smoking)
⬡ Ⓜ Gran Vía 🚌 1, 2, 3, 46, 74, 146, 149

SOL MELIA BARAJAS
www.solmelia.com
Forget your preconceptions about
soulless 'airport' hotels, and nurse
your jetlag at the Sol Melia, which
is located a stone's throw from
Madrid's Barajas airport. The
extra-spacious rooms, full-channel
satellite TV, plush carpet throughout,
extra-comfy beds and in-room
writing desks (with stationery) will
make you nostalgic for the days
when good hotels were judged on
the standard of their amenities and
extras and not the latest in 'designer'
detailing. The resort-size outdoor
pool is set in an enormous expanse
of leafy garden and is incredibly well
maintained: pull up a sunbed, order
a drink from the terrace bar and
wait for your next flight in style. Free
shuttle service to and from airport
every 15 minutes.

✉ Avenida de Logroño 305, 28042 Madrid
☎ 917 47 77 00 💶 €94–€235 excluding
breakfast (€20) 🛏 229 (40 non-smoking)
⬡ 🏊 Outdoor

Opposite *The Ritz Hotel, Madrid*
Above *A luggage trolley*

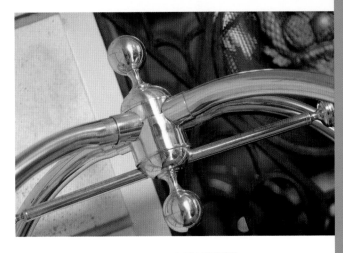

TIROL
www.hotel-tirol.com
A comfortable three-star hotel in the
middle of the Argüelles business
district. The terrace is a great place
to sample a cocktail in summer.
Hotel amenities include interactive
TV, internet access, car-rental
facilities, an express dry-cleaning and
laundry service, safety boxes, airport
transfers and transportation to the
IFEMA Trade Centre. There is a babysitting service.

✉ Calle Marqués de Urquijo 4, 28008
Madrid ☎ 915 48 19 00 💶 €145
excluding buffet breakfast (€14) 🛏 95
⬡ Ⓜ Argüelles 🚌 1, 21, 44, 69

TRAFALGAR
www.hotel-trafalgar.com
Trafalgar is a three-star hotel not far
from lively Calle de Fuencarral and its
shops, and convenient for peaceful
Plaza de Olavide. All in all, this a good
option for those watching their euros
but still keen to stay somewhere
pleasant. The building is modern
and the rooms comfortable, with TV,
direct-dial phone, safety deposit box,
private bathroom and hairdryer. Other
features include a coffee bar, money
exchange, laundry, meeting rooms
and a restaurant serving Spanish
dishes.

✉ Calle Trafalgar 35, 28010 Madrid
☎ 914 45 62 00 💶 €90–€155
🛏 48 (non-smoking upon request)
⬡ Ⓜ Quevedo, Iglesia, Bilbao, Canal
🚌 3, 16, 37, 61, 149

WELLINGTON
www.hotel-wellington.com
This luxury hotel is in a handsome
building with a neoclassical interior
and attractive wall hangings.
Amenities include a laundry
service, 24-hour room service, a
hairdresser, internet access and
meeting rooms. The elegant guest
rooms have a safety deposit box,
minibar and satellite TV. The Goizeko
Wellington restaurant specializes in
Basque cuisine.

✉ Calle de Velázquez 8, 28001 Madrid
☎ 915 75 44 00 💶 €275–€430 excluding
breakfast (€28) 🛏 259 (53 non-smoking)
⬡ 🏊 Outdoor Ⓜ Velázquez, Retiro
🚌 1, 9, 19, 51, 74

ZENIT ABEBA
www.zenithoteles.com
This modern, four-star hotel is perfect
for shoppers as it is just a stone's
throw from Goya and Serrano streets
in the chic Salamanca district.
The decor is functional and the
rooms are comfortable. Facilities
include a laundry service, bureau
de change, business services, lobby
bar, babysitting upon request and
breakfast room service. The guest
rooms are quite spacious and feature
a safety deposit box and TV (satellite
and Canal+).

✉ Calle de Alcántara 63, 28006
Madrid ☎ 914 01 16 50 💶 €95–€260
excluding buffet breakfast (€12) 🛏 89
⬡ Ⓜ Diego de León 🚌 12, 26, 48,
56, 68

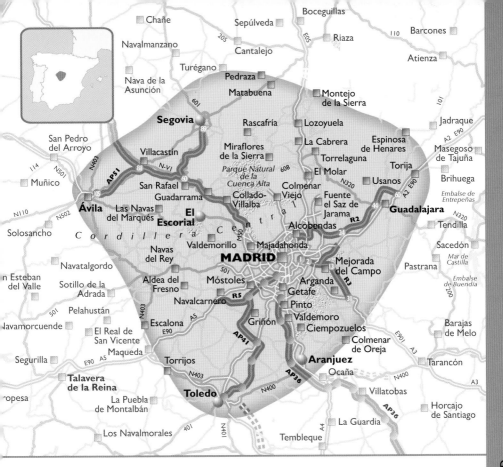

AROUND MADRID

Within an hour or two's drive of Madrid are some fascinating towns and historic sights. There is a clutch of splendid royal palaces, including the austerely beautiful palace-monastery of El Escorial, burial place of kings since the 16th century. Nearby is the sumptuous 18th-century palace of La Granja de San Ildefonso, built to rival the French palace of Versailles, which overlooks spectacular, fountain-filled gardens. There's more royal extravagance at the Palacio Real de El Pardo, originally a relatively humble royal hunting lodge, which was lavishly expanded in the 18th century.

At Aranjuez, southeast of the capital, there is yet another plush royal residence, a frothy baroque concoction, which also enjoys some luxuriant and refreshing gardens spread along the banks of the river—a lush retreat from the searing summer heat.

Madrid is perfectly placed for a quick escape to the hills: The great granite ridge of the Sierra de Guadarrama lies north of the city, and offers endless opportunities for hiking, climbing, birding, picnicking and even skiing.

The region also boasts some enticing towns and cities, little time capsules which offer an alluring glimpse of old Castile. In Segovia, you can admire the famous Roman aqueduct, and explore the ancient streets before tucking into the celebrated local specialty—roast suckling pig. Ávila, enclosed within its monumental walls and towers, is another historic gem, packed with splendid churches, monasteries and monuments. At Chinchón, the arcaded Plaza Mayor has barely changed in five centuries. Its old-fashioned *mesones* (inns) and taverns are always packed at weekends with day-tripping families from the capital. But perhaps the most beguiling and atmospheric of all the cities near Madrid is Toledo, with its warren of narrow streets and pretty squares stuffed with reminders of a long and illustrious history—among them, the vast cathedral, Visigothic churches, synagogues and mosques.

ALCALÁ DE HENARES

www.turismoalcala.com

Alcalá de Henares is home to Spain's fifth-oldest university, and retains at its heart a charming town centre and vibrant student life.

Cobbled Calle Mayor, the longest porticoed street in Spain, is lined with buildings dating from the 15th to the 19th centuries and has a 1950s reconstruction of the birthplace of Miguel de Cervantes (1547–1616), author of *Don Quixote* (Tue–Sun 10–6, last visit 5.30). Also on Calle Mayor is the Hospital de Antezana (daily 10–2, 4–8), the oldest hospital in Europe, which opened in 1483.

The town's highlight is Colegio Mayor de San Ildefonso (Mon–Fri 11–7, Sat–Sun 11–7.30), one of the best-preserved Renaissance universities in Europe (1508). The Patio de Santo Tomás de Villanueva was named in tribute to the university's first student, who was later sanctified by the Roman Catholic Church. Look out for swan crests above the arches, a reference to the university's founder, Cardinal Cisneros—*cisne* means 'swan' in Spanish.

Also striking are the Capilla and Paraninfo, both of which contain impressive Mudéjar timber ceilings and carvings. The Paraninfo was where the university's finals used to be taken; today, it is where Spain's most important literary award, the Cervantes Prize, is presented annually to the best Spanish-speaking writer.

The Monasterio de San Bernardo, near the other end of the Calle Mayor, in addition to its impressive oval dome, has a copy of the *Biblia Poliglota Complutense*, the first version of the Bible to be translated into the three languages of antiquity: Latin, Hebrew and Greek.

✚ 469 G5 ☷ Callejón de Santa María 1, 28801 Alcalá de Henares ☎ 918 89 26 94

ARANJUEZ

▷ 108.

ÁVILA

www.avilaturismo.com

Although no single thing stands out in Ávila, its intimate collection of historic buildings and streets makes it a worthy World Heritage Site. The town is a Castilian masterpiece, and the combination of medieval buildings and new chic—typified by trendy restaurants, bars, cafés and shops—makes it hard to fault.

In the 11th century, Alfonso VI built a 2.4km (1.5-mile) wall, with 88 towers and nine gates, around what is now the old town. The whole complex still stands, making it the biggest and best-preserved fort in Europe. A walk along the walls is a must, and the price includes an excellent guide in English (Apr–15 Oct daily 10–8; 16 Oct–Mar Tue–Sat 11–8; €4.50). For stunning views of the walled town at sunrise or sunset, head west to Los Cuatro Postes, a monument 1.5km (1 mile) out of town.

Dominating the walls at their eastern end is the massive early Gothic cathedral (summer Mon–Fri 10–7.30, Sat 10–8, Sun 12–6.30;

winter Mon–Fri 10–5, Sat 10–6, Sun and festivals 12–6; €5), which is built into the fortifications. The interior is notable for its carved walnut choir stalls, the locally quarried mottled red and white granite of the apse and transepts, and the tomb of Don Alfonso de Madrigal, a 15th-century bishop known as El Tostado (The Toasted One) for his dark skin. The modern blue stained glass gives the nave a lighter, brighter feel.

The Monasterio de Santo Tomás, outside the walls south of town, is a sumptuous example of so-called Isabelline architecture, characterized by late-Gothic structures and decorated with the more curvaceous lines and motifs of Moorish design.

Finally, don't forget to sample *yemas*, the local dish. These cakes are a gooey mixture of sugar and egg yolks.

✚ 469 F5 ☷ Avenida de Madrid 39, 05001 Ávila ☎ 920 22 59 69

BUITRAGO DEL LOZOYA

www.buitrago.org

Buitrago sits at the heart of the Sierra Norte on a bend of the Río Lozoya, commanding good views over both mountains and river. Its main attraction is the Museo Picasso (Tue, Thu–Fri 11–1.45, 4–6, Wed 11–1.45, Sat 10–2, 4–7, Sun 10–2).

Local hero Eugenio Arias, friend to Pablo Picasso, amassed a sizeable collection of the great artist's works, many of them created specifically for him. All these are now exhibited at the museum, which, although quite small, is a treasure trove of sketches, sculptures and books.

The nearby Iglesia de Santa María was built in 1321, but was largely destroyed by a fire in 1936. Restoration began in 1980, and elements of the region's three main religions—Christianity, Islam and Judaism—were included.

✚ 469 G5 ☷ Calle Tahona 11, 28730 Buitrago del Lozoya ☎ 918 68 16 15

Left The impressive defensive walls surrounding Ávila
Opposite Colegio Mayor de San Ildefonso, University of Alcalá de Henares

INFORMATION

www.aranjuez.es

✚ 469 G6 ⓘ Plaza San Antonio 9, 28300 Aranjuez ☎ 918 91 04 27

TIP

» The Museo de Faluas Reales (Museum of Royal Barges), near the Casa Labrador, contains a dazzling array of royal watercraft, including a sumptuous 17th-century Venetian barge encrusted with gilded nymphs.

ARANJUEZ

Listed as a World Heritage Site by UNESCO, Aranjuez, a green oasis in arid Castile-La Mancha, is magically set on the banks of the languid Rio Tajo. In 1560, Felipe II awarded it the title *Real Sitio y Villa de Aranjuez* (Royal Site and Town of Aranjuez) but its royal connections date back much further. The Catholic Kings, Ferdinand and Isabel, regularly summered here, and Carlos I established a Royal Forest to pursue his passion for hunting.

ROYAL PALACE

Felipe II, who ordered the construction of the elaborate Palacio Real (Apr–Sep Tue–Sun 10–6.15; Oct–Mar 10–5.15), the royal palace which still dominates Aranjuez, cemented the town's royal relationship once and for all. The palace he commissioned, using the same architects as the palace-monastery at El Escorial (Juan Bautista de Toledo and Juan de Herrera), was a comparatively modest and restrained affair. It was completed under Ferdinand VI, but it was the Bourbon king Carlos III (1716–88) who added two new wings and ordered the lavish embellishment which characterizes the building today. The interior is a dazzling whirl of gilt and marble, the halls and salons filled with precious paintings and works of art. Among the most extravagantly decorated rooms are the Sala de Fumadores (Smoking Room) with intricate hand-painted ceiling and walls, the scarlet Salón de Baile (Ballroom), the extraordinary Salón de Espejos (Mirror Room), and the Sala de China (Porcelain Room), created in 1763 entirely from porcelain produced in the royal porcelain factory in Madrid.

The apotheosis of the royal family's lavish lifestyle and decadent tastes can be seen in the smaller but no less impressive Casa del Labrador, in the gardens to the east of the palace. In summer, the grounds are every bit as impressive as the palace, with grand, tree-lined avenues radiating out for miles. Of the gardens, the Jardín de la Isla is the most accessible and the best.

TOWN CENTRE

The heart of the town is so well kept and manageable that it provides a perfect foil to the overwhelming intricacy of the palace rooms and gardens, and has patios and squares offering an abundance of places to relax and unwind. An excellent visitor information office, which houses a small, state-of-the-art visitor information facility with audiovisual displays, can be found between the palace and the town.

Below *The elaborate Palacio Real still dominates the town of Aranjuez*

EL ESCORIAL

The Monasterio de San Lorenzo de El Escorial is the final resting place for nearly every Spanish monarch from Charles V (1500–58) to Alfonso XIII (1886–1941). Quite apart from its political pedigree, it's also an architectural triumph, and its collection of objects and antiques is impressive.

El Escorial dates back to 1557, when Felipe II declared it the site for a major monastery where he could build a mausoleum to his father, Charles V. It is also said to commemorate the joint Spanish-English victory over France at the Battle of St-Quentin. In the centuries that followed, the monastery became a thriving intellectual and social hub.

THE TOUR

The palace-monastery is a huge, horizontal granite edifice that took barely 20 years to complete. The tour begins with the Bourbon apartments, although the luxury-loving Bourbons preferred their summer palace at Aranjuez and rarely visited El Escorial. The apartments contain some fine tapestries, executed to designs by Goya. The Habsburg apartments are cosier and more intimate, attractively decorated with blue-and-white tiles.

The tour also takes in fine paintings by such masters as José Ribera (1591–1652) and Francisco de Zurbarán (1598–1664) in the vast painting collection housed in the Salas Capitulares (Chapter Halls); the Sala de Batallas (Hall of Battles) 55m (180ft) long, with a painting of the same length depicting the Battle of St-Quentin; and the gold and black Panteón Real, where nearly all of Spanish royalty is buried.

The highlight is the vast Basílica, with 42 altars (of which only two were available to commoners) and an enormous altarpiece, *El Cristo Blanco* (1556–57), by Benvenuto Cellini (1500–71), exquisite, despite the somewhat puritanical present-day addition of a silk scarf to cover Christ's modesty.

THE TOWN

The cobbled town of San Lorenzo has a variety of restaurants, tranquil hidden squares and shops selling local crafts. The Museo de Arquitectura (Museum of Architecture) explains the massive undertaking involved in constructing the palace-monastery.

INFORMATION

www.patrimonionacional.es

🕂 469 G5 ✉ Avenida de Juan de Borbón y Battenberg 1, 28200 San Lorenzo de Escorial ☎ 918 90 59 02/03 🕙 Apr–Sep Tue–Sun 10–6; Oct–Mar Tue–Sun 10–5 💵 Adult €10 with guide, €8 without, over 65 €6, child (5–16) €3.50–€4, under 5 free 🚉 Escorial, 2km (1.2 miles) south ☞ Tour route marked with arrows, or join Spanish guided tour (extra €1); English tours if sufficient numbers. Bourbon Apartments with guide only (advance reservation essential): Tue–Fri 4, 5, Sat 10, 11, 12, 4, 5 (also Apr–Sep Fri–Sat 6); tour extra €3.60. Audiotours (€3) 📖 🏛

Above El Escorial was designated a World Heritage Site in 1984

CHINCHÓN

www.ciudad-chinchon.com

The town square of Chinchón is the Plaza Mayor to top them all, surrounded by two- and three-storey, 18th-century wood-beamed balconied buildings. Many of the balconies belong to restaurants, bars and cafés, and give the best views of the bullfights that take place in the square below in the summer. The Iglesia de Nuestra Señora de la Asunción, complete with a Virgen painted by Francisco de Goya (1746–1828), and Chinchón's 16th-century castle, now a private house, with a moat and drawbridge, are other notable buildings.

✚ 469 G6 🛈 Plaza Mayor 6, 28370 Chinchón ☎ 918 93 53 23 ❓ Leaflet on village and surrounding area from visitor information office

LA GRANJA DE SAN ILDEFONSO

www.patrimonionacional.es

La Granja, built between 1721 and 1734 by Felipe V, is one of a number of grand royal palaces scattered around Madrid, but arguably has the best location, in the foothills of the Sierra de Guadarrama.

It is, however, the gardens, that are a masterpiece of design and engineering. Felipe V wanted French-style gardens to rival those at Versailles, and they include no fewer than 28 fountains incorporating 496 jets. Ten of them stand alone, including *Los Baños de Diana* (The Baths of Diana), *Los Vientos*

(The Winds) and *Los Dragons* (The Dragons). The others are arranged in three groups: *Las Ocho Calles* (The Eight Avenues), *La Cascada* (The Waterfall) and *La Carrera de Caballos* (The Horse Race). The gardens also feature a maze. If you can, watch the fountains being illuminated (16 Jul–3 Sep Sat 10.30pm–11.30pm). They are switched on (water supplies permitting) on Wednesdays, Saturdays and Sundays at 5.30pm.

✚ 469 G5 ✉ Plaza de España 17, 40100 Real Sitio de San Ildefonso ☎ 921 47 00 19 🅲 Palace: Apr–Sep Tue–Sun 10–6; Oct–Mar Tue–Sat 10–1.30, 3–5, Sun and holidays 10–2. Gardens: Jul–Aug daily 10–9; May, Jun, Sep 10–8; Apr 10–7; Oct, Mar 10–6.30; Nov–Feb 10–6 🍴 Adults €5 with guide, €4.50 without, child (5–16) €2.50, under 5 free; EU nationals free Wed. Gardens free; fountains additional charge €3.40, child €1.70 🎫 Admission includes 1-hour guided tour of palace and gardens in Spanish (access to palace on tour only). Audioguides in Spanish, English, French, Italian and German €2 📖 Guides in Spanish, English, French, German and Italian €3.50 or €7 🎫

GUADALAJARA

Guadalajara, whose name derives from the Arabic Uad-al-Hayar (River of Stones) became one of the most important Islamic cities in northern Spain. In 1085 it was retaken by Alvar Fanez de Minaya under Alfonso VI. The town's most famous building, El Palacio de los Duques del

Infantado, was built in 1461. Its striking facade, clad with hundreds of little pyramids and topped by a frieze of Gothic tracery, is a mixture of Mudéjar and Renaissance architecture. It is now home to the local fine arts museum, the Museo Provincial de Bellas Artes (Tue–Sat 10–2, 4–7, Sun and holidays 10–2), and has a magnificent cloister.

✚ 469 H5 🛈 Plaza de Los Caídos 6, 19001 Guadalajara ☎ 949 21 16 26 🅲 Closed Sun afternoons

MANZANARES EL REAL

www.manzanareselreal.org

It is the town's location that makes Manzanares El Real a great place to spend a day or two. The historical highlight is undoubtedly the 15th-century castle (Mon–Sat 10–5.30), meticulously restored and one of the best examples of Castilian military architecture in Spain.

The mountains surrounding the town are best explored from the visitor office (Centro de Educación Ambiental; daily 10–6) of the Parque Regional de la Cuenca Alta de Manzanares, signposted off the main road just to the west. You can pay a guide to lead you on walks.

La Pedriza mountain is a huge, granite outcrop that glows red and gold at sunset.

✚ 469 G5 🛈 Ayuntamiento (Town Hall), Plaza del Pueblo 1, 28410 Manzanares el Real ☎ 918 53 00 09

PALACIO REAL DE EL PARDO

www.patrimonionacional.es

The Palacio Real de El Pardo has been a royal retreat for around five centuries and was Franco's official residence from 1940 to 1975. Originally a hunting pavilion for Enrique IV in the 15th century, it was restyled in the 18th century by Carlos III. Carlos commissioned architect Francisco Sabatini (1722–97) to extend the existing palace and to plan additional buildings. Sabatini also supervised the alteration of the interior, including the series of superb frescoes on the ceilings by Francisco Bayeu (1734–95) and Mariano Salvador Maella (1739–1819), and the tapestries based on drawings by Francisco de Goya (1746–1828).

Franco's combined bedroom and dressing-room contains Spain's first ever television, which was imported from Italy. The palace now holds conferences and is a guesthouse for visiting dignitaries. The Marquesitas pâtisserie on Plaza de Caudillo serves locally made cakes, also called *marquesitas*.

➕ 469 G5 ✉ Calle Manuel Alonzo s/n, 28048 El Pardo ☎ 913 76 15 00 🕐 Apr–Sep Mon–Fri 10.30–6, Sat–Sun 10–1.30; Oct–Mar Mon–Fri 10.30–4.45, Sat–Sun 10–1.30 ✋ Adult €4, child (5–16) €2.30, under 5 free 🎧 Compulsory 1-hour guided tour; usually in Spanish, but can be in English if sufficient numbers 📖 Guides in Spanish, English, French, German and Italian €8 🏬 Museum shop 🚗 El Pardo is badly signposted if driving into Madrid from the north or northwest. It is well signed off the M-30 at the 24km (15-mile) point if you're to the west of Madrid driving northwards

SEGOVIA

▷ 112–113.

SIERRA DE GUADARRAMA

www.turismomadrid.es

The Sierra de Guadarrama is Madrid's answer to the Alps or the Pyrenees, with miles of hiking and cycling trails, thousands of climbing routes and a few ski runs.

Generations of Spanish kings have liked the Guadarrama so much that they've seen fit to build their most majestic palaces within an open window of the views, including El Escorial (▷ 109), La Granja (▷ 110) and Valle de los Caidos (see below).

Madrileños come on summer weekends to escape the heat of the city, and in the winter months the pistes are busy with skiers and snowboarders from the capital. Because of the area's proximity to Madrid, the best place to get details is the information office in the capital itself. Manzanares El Real (▷ 110) is great for walkers and rock-climbers, Cercedilla is frequented by walkers and mountain-cyclists, and places for skiing are Puerto de Navacerrada, Cotos and Valdesquí.

➕ 469 G5 ℹ Plaza Mayor 27, 28012 Madrid ☎ 915 88 16 36

TOLEDO

▷ 114–117.

VALLE DE LOS CAIDOS

www.patrimonionacional.es

Valle de los Caidos (Valley of the Fallen), General Franco's most prominent architectural legacy, is essentially a huge underground basilica marked by a 120m-high (390ft) granite cross. Built by prison inmates and professional workers in the 1940s and 1950s, it is dedicated to those who died in the Spanish Civil War.

To one side under the cross is a series of wide, empty arcaded courtyards featuring the monument's *hospedería* (once a trendy inn) and what used to be a monastery. On the other side, far below the cross, is a granite patio of giant proportions, with little to indicate what it signifies. The answer lies underground below the cross, in the cavernous basilica. This is also lined in granite and is as dark and foreboding as a crypt, with 'torches' lining the walls of the vaults leading to the altar; a funicular departs from above the basilica to the base of the cross (currently closed). The grave of Francisco Franco Bahamonde, the man himself, is here, as is that of José Antonio Primo de Rivera, a Fascist politician executed in 1936.

➕ 469 F5 ℹ Carretera Guadarrama-El Escorial, Valle de los Caidos s/n, 28209 Valle de Cuelgamuros, San Lorenzo de El Escorial ☎ 918 90 56 11, 918 90 13 98 🕐 Apr–Sep Tue–Sun 10–6; Oct–Mar 10–5 ✋ Adults €5, child (5–16) €2.50, under 5 free; combined admission for El Escorial and Valle de los Caidos: adult €11, child €5 🎧 Audiotours in Spanish, English, French, German and Italian €2 ☕ Café Apr–Sep 🏬 Museum shop

Opposite *The Anis distillery in Chinchón (left); Manzanares el Real castle (right)*
Below *The basilica of Valle de los Caidos, with its huge cross*

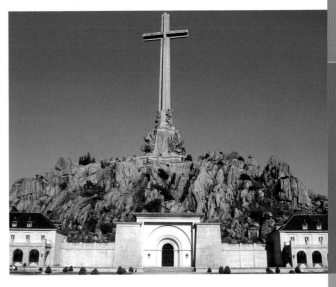

REGIONS | AROUND MADRID • SIGHTS

INFORMATION

www.infosegovia.com
www.turismocastillayleon.com
✚ 469 G5 🚹 Plaza Mayor 10, 40001 Segovia ☎ 921 46 03 34 🕐 Apr–Sep, Easter and public holidays daily 9–8; Oct–Mar 9–2, 5–8 🚌 Segovia

INTRODUCTION

Now an icon of Spain, Segovia's aqueduct is still standing virtually intact some 2,000 years after it was built. The Alcázar was extensively rebuilt in the 19th century as a Gothic fantasy, and has to be seen first-hand—inside and out—to be appreciated. In addition, Segovia is home to a wealth of smaller gems, as well as restaurants and cafés that take the region's obsession with pork to a new level.

WHAT TO SEE

THE CATHEDRAL

Segovia is perched on a lofty, rocky outcrop, 1,000m (3,300ft) above sea-level. Nicknamed the Stone Ship, it is dominated by the 'mast' of the cathedral's massive tower and, at its western end, by the 'prow' of the Alcázar. The former was begun in 1525 in late-Gothic style, inheriting a Hispano-Flemish cloister from an earlier church and supporting the east ambulatory with an explosion of flying buttresses. It is known as the Lady of Cathedrals and has a vast dome.

✉ Plaza Mayor 🕐 Apr–Sep daily 9–6.30; Oct–Mar 9–5.30

THE ALCÁZAR

www.alcazardesegovia.com

In the Middle Ages, the Alcázar became a popular residence of the monarchs of the region. When the court moved to Madrid in 1561, the Alcázar was used as a prison and in 1762 it become the Royal Artillery School. A fire in 1862 damaged the roofs and framework, but restoration began in 1882, resulting in the extravaganza of turrets and towers seen today. Perched on a rocky bluff, it is an enchanting fairytale vision—so much so, that Disney apparently chose it as a model for their first theme park. Highlights of the interior are the Mudéjar ceilings, some of which are copies of those destroyed in the fire. There is also a small collection of weapons and armour. The steep climb up the watchtower is rewarded with staggering views over the mountains.

✉ Plazuela de Juan Gras ☎ 921 46 07 59 🕐 Daily 10–6 💶 Adult €4, child €3 (access to tower 2) 🎧 Guided tour €1

THE AQUEDUCT

Perhaps the most impressive of all Segovia's monuments is its aqueduct, which dominates the Plaza del Azoguejo. Built during the first and second centuries AD, it is the tallest surviving aqueduct in Spain and remained in use until the middle of the 20th century. Now reduced to a stretch of 728m (796 yards) at the eastern end of the city, it stands 28m (92ft) high and was built in a double tier of massive granite arches.

Amazingly, the aqueduct was constructed without the use of any kind of cement: each of the 20,400 stone blocks were meticulously arranged to achieve the perfect marriage of balance and strength.

MUSEO DE ARTE CONTEMPORÁNEO ESTEBAN VICENTE

www.museoestebanvicente.es

Other places to visit include the Museum of Contemporary Art, with its permanent art exhibition and temporary displays, in the Palacio de Enrique IV. The 12-sided Convento de Santa Cruz La Real, now a university, was built in the 13th century by the Knights Templar and contains a chapel where candidates for knighthood kept vigil over their armour.

✉ Plazuela de las Bellas Artes s/n ☎ 921 46 20 10 🕐 Tue–Wed 11–2, 4–7, Thu–Fri 11–2, 4–8, Sat 11–8, Sun and holidays 11–3 💶 Adult €3, under 12 free

CHURCHES

The city also boasts some remarkably beautiful churches, including the Iglesia de San Esteban, topped with a six-storey, Italianate belltower, and the charming, Romanesque church of San Martín, with a covered portico and a Mudéjar belltower. On the hillside outside the city walls is the 13th-century Templar church of La Vera Cruz (the True Cross), which offers spectacular views over Segovia from the belltower.

MORE TO SEE

CASA DE LOS PICOS

The House of Spikes, a grand, 15th-century mansion, is remarkable for the diamond-shaped designs which decorate its facade. It is now a cultural centre which hosts temporary exhibitions; visitors can admire the graceful courtyard.

✉ Calle Cervantes

TIP

❱❱ Make sure you try the local dishes, *cochinillo asado* (roast suckling pig) and *ponche segoviano* (a rich cake drizzled in *ponche*, a well-known Spanish liqueur), in one of the many restaurants that cluster around the Plaza Mayor.

Opposite *The Roman aqueduct was built without the use of mortar*
Below left *A field of sunflowers in the countryside near Segovia*
Below right *Market stalls in front of the cathedral*

AROUND MADRID • SIGHTS

REGIONS

113

INFORMATION

www.toledoweb.org

➕ 469 G6 ℹ Plaza del Consistorio 1, 45003 Toledo ☎ 925 22 08 43

🕐 Tue–Sun 10.30–2.30, 4.30–7, Mon 10.30–2.30 🚉 Toledo

INTRODUCTION

The walled city of Toledo is built on top of a hill, surrounded on three sides by the Tajo (Tagus) river, and overlooks the Castilian plains. The older part of the city is easy to wander around—in fact, a car is a disadvantage—and at a real push you can see most of the major sights in a day. That said, an overnight stay is recommended as the city is best enjoyed in the early morning and in the evening, when the crush of visitors has died down.

Toledo first became important under Roman rule, when Toletum (as it was then known) was allowed to mint its own coins. Parts of the Roman city walls still remain, as does a circus, which could hold 13,000 people. Visigoths conquered the city in the sixth century AD and turned it into their capital (it replaced Seville), but were vanquished by the invading Moors in AD711. Toledo consequently became—not for the first time—a major cultural hub as well as a political power base.

After Alfonso VI conquered the city in 1085, the mixed Christian, Jewish and Muslim population gave it an international cultural role; the scholars of the Escuela de Traductores de Toledo (Toledo Translators' School) could be said to have made the whole Renaissance possible with their translations of philosophical and scientific works from Arabic and Hebrew into Latin and Castilian. Their work ended dramatically in 1492 with the onset of religious persecution and the expulsion of the Jewish population from Spain.

The royal court was moved to Madrid 70 years later by Felipe II, and the city soon went downhill, losing its once-thriving textile industry and its reputation for making swords and daggers. Yet Toledo retained enough of its historical atmosphere to attract El Greco, and during the Golden Age also inspired many other artists and writers. Its fortunes have seen an upturn since the relatively recent advent of a hugely successful tourist industry, at least partly due to the city's proximity to Madrid.

WHAT TO SEE

ALCÁZAR DE TOLEDO

Every culture that has ruled Toledo has built a fortress on this site—most of which have been burned down or destroyed—and all dominated the city's skyline, as does the present-day version. This rather austere fortress was built by Charles V in the 16th century, partly using the same architect, Juan de Herrera (1530–97), who was responsible for El Escorial (▷ 109). Rebuilt to Franco's specifications, the fortress really hit the international headlines at the start of the Spanish Civil War, when thanks to its key strategic role it underwent a very destructive 70-day siege. It now houses an army museum featuring models, photos and equipment from those dark days. Included is a re-creation of the famous telephone conversation between the colonel in charge of the Alcázar at the time and his son, who had been kidnapped by enemy forces; in it the father tells the poor lad to face death bravely as he has no intention of bartering his life for a surrender. Tragically, the boy was shot.

✚ 117 C1 ✉ Cuesta del Alcázar ☎ 925 22 16 73 🕑 Closed indefinitely for restoration

CATEDRAL

Toledo's cathedral, one of the world's finest Gothic buildings, took 267 years to erect (1226–1493) on the site of a destroyed mosque. This is the spiritual heart of the Spanish church and for centuries its archbishops were extraordinarily powerful in national politics.

Among its art treasures the Transparente stands out, a baroque marble, jasper, bronze and alabaster altarpiece. The Treasure Room has a 15th-century monstrance that weighs 225kg (500lb) and was made with gold brought back from the Americas by Christopher Columbus. It is still carried through the streets of Toledo during the Fiesta del Corpus Christi (▷ 125). Other highlights include the paintings *Twelve Apostles* (1605–10) and *Spoliation of Christ* (1577–79) by El Greco, and *Arrest of Christ on the Mount of Olives* (1798) by Francisco de Goya, as well as a Mudéjar ceiling in the chapterhouse and the story of the fall of Granada carved into the wooden choir stalls. It is also one of the few places in the world that celebrates Mass in the tongue of Mozarabic, originally spoken by Christian inhabitants of Moorish Spain.

✚ 117 B1 ✉ Calle del Cardenal Cisneros 1 ☎ 925 22 22 41 🕑 Cathedral: daily 10.30–12, 4–6. Museum: Mon–Sat 10.30–6.30, Sun 2–6.30 💶 €7

Above left *Houses along Toledo's main square, Plaza de Zocodover*
Above right *Ceramic detail*
Opposite *Panoramic view over Toledo, the spiritual capital of Spain*

BARRIO SEFARDÍ (JEWISH QUARTER)

Although only two of Toledo's original 11 synagogues stand today, there is still a surprising amount to see in the former Jewish *barrio* and the city remains an important Jewish cultural base, especially for Sephardic Jews. The 14th-century Sinagoga del Tránsito (Tue–Sat 10–2, 4–9, Sun 10–2) was once an important house of worship for the city's large Jewish population, until they were expelled from the city—and Spain—in 1492. The building has a superb Mudéjar interior and houses the Museo Sefardí, which holds an important collection of Sephardic objects, costumes and manuscripts.

The nearby Sinagoga de Santa María la Blanca (daily 10–6) is a late 12th-century synagogue. It was the setting for a massacre of Jewish citizens in 1391, and was converted into a Christian church in the early 15th century, but retains its Jewish and Moorish character thanks to sensitive restoration.

✚ 117 A2

MUSEO SANTA CRUZ

Originally a 16th-century hospice, this building now houses a museum of art and sculpture. The facade itself is the finest exhibit on show, a perfect example of the Plateresque style. Inside, apart from El Greco's *The Assumption of the Virgin*, there are paintings by Goya, Flemish tapestries, war standards from the 1571 Battle of Lepanto and Visigoth objects. Look for the typical Toledo armour and swords.

✚ 117 C1 ✉ Calle Miguel de Cervantes 3 ☎ 925 22 10 36 🕐 Mon–Sat 10–6.30, Sun 10–2 ✋ Free

IGLESIA DE SANTIAGO DEL ARRABAL

This beautifully restored church is Toledo's finest Mudéjar building; the ornate Gothic pulpit was used by San Vincente Ferrer, the altarpiece is 16th-century and the tower is styled after a minaret.

✚ 117 B1 ✉ Real del Arrabal 1 ☎ 925 22 06 36 🕐 During Mass ✋ Free

MORE TO SEE
MONASTERIO DE SAN JUAN DE LOS REYES

Founded by Fernando V and Isabel I at the end of the 15th century and restored after Napoleon's troops damaged it in 1808, this still working Franciscan monastery has fine cloisters.

✚ 117 A1 ✉ Calle de los Reyes Católicos 21 ☎ 925 22 38 02 🕐 Daily 10–6 ✋ Adult €2, under 8 free

TIPS

» Street parking is a nightmare, so head for the underground parking area near the Alcázar.

» The view from the Toledo *parador* (state-run hotel) is fantastic (El Greco painted his famous *View of Toledo* from roughly this spot in about 1597). If you want to stay, reserve well ahead (tel 925 22 18 50; www.parador.es).

Opposite *The spires, towers and rooftops of Toledo*

Below *Stained-glass window in Toledo's cathedral*

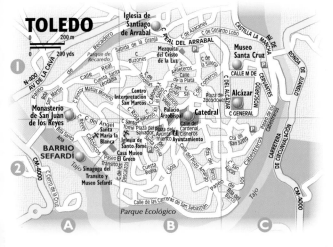

REGIONS | AROUND MADRID • SIGHTS

THROUGH THE GRANITE MOUNTAINS OF THE SIERRA DE GUADARRAMA

La Pedriza del Manzanares, a mountain-sized monolith of granite at the heart of the Sierra de Guadarrama, is arguably the most impressive natural wonder of the entire region. Not only does it provide literally thousands of climbs up hundreds of rock faces, but it also offers some of the best walking in Spain, including the GR-10 long-distance path. The route described here follows a short section of the GR-10 through some typical granite scenery to reach one of the most unusual features on the entire route, a lone 500-tonne rock that lies at the bottom of the valley, right next to the Majadilla stream. The waypoints in the directions refer to numbered marker posts along the GR-10 route.

THE WALK
Distance: 5.6km (3.5 miles)
Allow: 1.5 hours
Ascent: Approximately 250m (820ft)
Start/end at: Canto Cochino (Pig's Edge) map 469 G5
Parking: There is ample parking at the start/end point

HOW TO GET THERE
The Parque Regional de la Cuenca Alta del Manzanares (also referred to as La Pedriza) is signed off the M-608 just west of Manzanares. Follow signs past the visitor centre

(Centro de Educación Ambiental) and continue on a narrow road to the hills. After a while you come to El Canto Cochino and a large parking area. Continue past this and a bar, then go down a short hill to a smaller parking area on the banks of the Río Manzanares.

★ From the parking area (Waypoint 1), cross the footbridge over the Río Manzanares and turn immediately left. Bear right, away from the river, to follow a track through the woods.

❶ On this section of the walk, pines intermingle with Arizona cypresses. Keeping the forest buildings (Waypoint 2) and the fence around them to your right, continue along this path until you reach the bank of the Arroyo de la Majadilla stream just to your right.

After following this upstream for around 600m (650 yards), the path veers up and away from the stream for about 900m (980 yards) before rejoining it at a narrow footbridge.

❷ Along the stream, the permanent availability of water supports willow and poplar trees; the rock faces higher up, unable to store water, nurture just a few juniper bushes.

From the footbridge (Waypoint 3), head away from the stream up a short, steep path towards the Refugio Giner de los Ríos. At the top of this slope is the Fuente de Pedro Acuña (spring of Pedro Acuña)—the water is clean, cold and delicious, making it a great place to fill up empty water bottles.

❸ The Refugio Giner de los Ríos shelter was built early in the 20th century and was paid for by public subscription; one of the donors was Alfonso XIII, who gave 500 pesetas.

At the spring (Waypoint 4), head left and continue to follow the side of the valley across more open, tussocky slopes, picking your way along the narrow, rock-strewn path. Thicket predominates in these sunny areas, with plentiful lavender and heather. It can become wet after very heavy rain, but it's nothing a good pair of boots can't handle. Continue for 800m (875 yards) to reach the El Tolmo boulder, buried deep on the banks of the stream.

❹ The remarkably smooth-faced granite boulder named El Tolmo is thought to have fallen from a breach

in the crag high above. If you look closely, you can make out the metal bolts drilled at intervals into the overhang below the boulder—these are used by climbers as a means of clipping their ropes on to the face, but you only have to note how smooth the rock is and how much it overhangs to realize that such a route defies every known law of physics. During the 19th century, the hide-outs of the area sheltered numerous local bandits.

From El Tolmo (Waypoint 5), you can either continue to follow the path

(and river) upstream to the pass and viewpoint at Collado de la Dehesilla (1,453m/4,767ft) before returning the way you came, or you can just head straight back. The pass is a further 1.2km (0.75 mile) up a slightly steeper path than before. It was once nicknamed Collado de la Silla (which means saddle-shaped pass), and the old name is still preserved on some maps of the region.

WHEN TO GO

This walk is fine most of the year, though there's always a chance of snow from November to March. The best times are spring (April and May) and autumn (September and October) as temperatures in the summer can be sizzling.

WHERE TO EAT

There is a bar in Canto Cochino and another above, between Canto Chino and Charca Verde. You can eat (and sleep) in the Refugio Giner de los Ríos (tel 659 02 17 54; www.refugioginer.com; open weekends, all year; half-board €22).

Opposite *Cattle grazing on high pastures*
Above *Climbers are drawn to this region*
Left *A footpath through the Sierra de Guadarrama*

REGIONS AROUND MADRID • WALK

AROUND TOLEDO

Toledo's deeply atmospheric old quarter is a delight to stroll around. This walk takes in some of its most emblematic monuments, including the spectacular cathedral, several sights associated with the great 16th-century painter El Greco who spent much of his life here, and culminates with a pair of beautiful Mudéjar synagogues.

THE WALK

Distance: 2km (1.3 miles)
Allow: 4 hours, including visits to monuments
Start at: Plaza de Zocodover, map 117 B1
End at: Calle de los Reyes Catolicos

HOW TO GET THERE

Plaza de Zocodover is easily found at the entrance to the old city. If you are coming from the bus station or the train station, take Calle Venencio González up the hill and it will lead you directly to Plaza de Zocodover.

★ Begin the walk at Plaza de Zocodover, on the edge of the tight warren of alleys which comprises Toledo's historic centre. There are numerous cafés and bars here, for breakfast or refreshment.

Turn down busy Calle del Comercio. This is still, as it has been for centuries, one of Toledo's main shopping streets. It is lined with traditional houses, with geranium-filled balconies, below which are numerous shops selling damascene work and glittering swords. Beautifully framed at the end of the street is the graceful spire of Toledo's enormous cathedral. Head towards the spire, then turn left down Arco de Palacio, which is overhung by a passage connecting the Archbishop's Palace to the cathedral.

Arco de Palacio opens up into Plaza de Ayuntamiento, where you can buy admission tickets for the cathedral. There is also a tourist information office here—it's a good idea to pick up a map, as it is easy to get lost in the maze of tiny streets.

❶ Enter the great, hulking cathedral (▷ 115), one of the largest in the world. It was begun in the 13th century and incorporates the remains of a sixth-century Visigothic cathedral and an enormous mosque which once stood here. The sacristy contains a fine painting collection, with works by several Old Masters. After exploring the cathedral, return to Plaza de Ayuntamiento, a handsome ensemble of Gothic and Renaissance buildings, which includes the city hall *(ayuntamiento)*.

Take Cuesta de la Ciudad, a narrow passage directly opposite the city hall, which emerges onto Calle Trinidad.

❷ To the left is the new Centro Interpretación San Marcos, an audiovisual exhibition which traces Toledo's fascinating history with interactive exhibits.

Continue walking down Calle Trinidad, and take the right fork at little Plaza el Salvador. This is Calle Santo Tomé which will bring you to the Iglesia de Santo Tomé, topped by a red-brick, Mudejar belltower.

❸ This church contains *The Burial of the Count of Orgaz* (1586), a masterpiece by El Greco, which is hung above the Count's tomb. The painting depicts the burial of Don Gonzalo Ruíz, posthumously awarded the title of Count, who was famous for his charity and good works. It was said that Saints Stephen and Augustine descended from Heaven to attend the burial. El Greco introduces contemporary elements to the story, and among the mourners at the graveside are numerous important figures from Toledano society.

When you leave the church, turn left down Calle Samuel Levi. On the left, you will pass the Casa-Museo El Greco (closed for restoration), an elegant 16th-century mansion which never actually belonged to El Greco, and was in fact home to Samuel Levi, treasurer to Pedro I of Castille. This is the heart of Toledo's ancient Jewish quarter and, if you turn left on leaving the Casa-Museo de El Greco, you will arrive at the Sinagoga del Tránsito and adjoining Museo Sefardí (▷ 117).

❹ The Sinagoga del Tránsito is one of two surviving synagogues, which were converted into churches after the explusion of the Jews from Spain in 1492. The museum traces the history of the important Jewish community who once lived and worked here. Opposite the synagogue is a small garden, which offers pretty views over the River Tajo below.

Finally, turn up Calle de los Reyes Católicos (keep the river on your left) to reach the Sinagoga Santa Maria La Blanca (▷ 117), the city's other surviving synagogue, which retains a magical forest of white horseshoe arches inside.

WHEN TO GO
This walk is suitable at any time, although start early during the summer when the heat can be overwhelming. Some of the sights are closed for a few hours around lunchtime.

WHERE TO EAT
LOCUM
www.locum.es
Classic regional cuisine prepared with original touches in a charming 17th-century mansion. Near the cathedral.
✉ Calle Locum 6 ☎ 925 22 32 35
🕐 Wed–Sun 1.30–4, 8.30–midnight, Mon 1.30–4

CIRCULO DEL ARTE TOLEDO
www.circuloartetoledo.org
In a strikingly converted church. Great for coffee, breakfast, lunch or drinks.
✉ Plaza de San Vicente s/n ☎ 925 21 29 81 🕐 Daily 10am–midnight (until 2am Fri and Sat)

ASADOR ADOLFO
www.grupoadolfo.com
A classic, this is one of the most stylish restaurants in town. Fine, regional cuisine.
✉ Calle de la Granada 6 ☎ 925 25 24 72 🕐 Tue–Sat 1–4, 9–midnight, Sun 1–4

Opposite *The Alcázar fortress dominates the skyline of Toledo*
Right *Santa Maria La Blanca is one of two surviving synagogues in the city*

PLACES TO VISIT
CENTRO INTERPRETACIÓN SAN MARCOS
www.clavesdetoledo.com
✉ Calle Trinidad 7, 45001 Toledo ☎ 925 22 16 16 🕐 Tue–Sat 10.30–7.30, Sun 10.30–1.30

CASA-MUSEO EL GRECO
✉ Calle Samuel Leví s/n, 45002 Toledo ☎ 925 22 40 46 🕐 Tue–Sat 10–2, 4–6, Sun 10–2

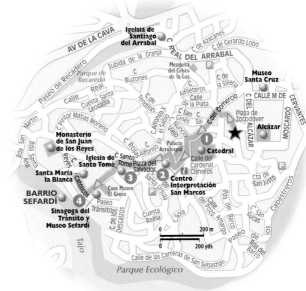

ALDEA DEL FRESNO
SAFARI PARK

Established by naturalist Félix Rodríguez de la Fuente, the park functions as a refuge for illegally trafficked animals as well as a place of education and entertainment. The animals live in semi-liberty, in conditions which closely resemble their original habitats. There are antelopes, bears, lions, jaguars and giraffes, as well as a huge variety of birds. The Park offers special displays featuring birds of prey. There is also a small, more traditional zoo, and a small waterpark in summer.

✉ Carretera de Extremadura, M-507, Km 22 (50km/31 miles from Madrid) ☎ 918 62 23 14 ⏰ Easter–Sep daily 10.30–8 🚌 From Madrid take the N-V, exit 32 at Navalcarnero, and follow signs

CENTRE COMERCIAL MADRID-XANADU
PARQUE DE NIEVE MADRID-XANADÚ

www.madridsnowzone.com
Spain's only indoor ski park has two pistes ideal for children and beginners. There is a ski lift, and instruction is available (Spanish only). The park can be found in a shopping and entertainment centre on the outskirts of Madrid. Clothing and equipment can be rented.

✉ Carretera Extremadura (N-V) Km 23,5, 28939 Arroyomolinos ☎ 902 36 13 09 ⏰ Sun–Thu 10am–midnight, Sat–Sun 10am–2am 💶 Adult 1 hour €20, child 1 hour €17

CUENCA
GRES TALLER DE CERÁMICA

In an attractive stone house in the heart of Cuenca's magnificent old quarter, this art studio produces some beautifully designed ceramic and porcelain pieces in original forms and bold, bright colours.

✉ Calle Alfonso VIII 27, Cuenca ☎ 969 22 94 41 ⏰ Mon–Sat 10.30–2, 5–8.30

EL ESCORIAL
HÍPICA PRADOS MONTEROS

www.hipicapradosmonteros.com
At this stables in the Sierra de Guadarrama about 12km (8 miles) north of El Escorial, you can take horse-riding lessons or take part in organized excursions into the rugged mountains. These last from between one and three days (a minimum of five participants is necessary). Basic Spanish is essential.

✉ Calle Fuencisla 8, 28480 Los Molinos ☎ 918 55 05 37 💶 From €15 for basic 1-hour hack, full-day outing around €90

LA PESQUERA
COMPLEJO RURAL MULTIOCIO LA PESQUERA

www.complejolapesquera.com
This vast rural activity centre is found in the southwest corner of Cuenca province. Numerous outdoor activities are provided, including quad-biking, canyon descent, hiking, horse-riding, paintball and even motocross. Activities are available to day visitors, but accommodation is also provided in double and triple rooms within the complex, or in self-catering houses in the village.

✉ Calle Arrabal 35, 16269 La Pesquera ☎ 962 16 20 26 💶 Prices vary according to activity: 1-hour quad bike €40, bike hire from €3 per hour, paintball session €20

PUEBLONUEVO DEL BULLAQUE
PARQUE NACIONAL DE CABAÑEROS
www.parquenacionalcabaneros.com
This vast National Park is a paradise for hikers, birdwatchers and nature-lovers. It incorporates some of the best preserved Mediterranean forest in Europe and encompasses a large swathe of the Montes de Toledo, located southwest of the city of Toledo. A small section of the park is freely open to hikers, with four signposted walking itineraries, but the park visitor centre (Casa Palillos, 5km/3 miles from the village of Pueblonuevo del Bullaque) can arrange hikes and special jeep trips into the remarkable interior. This visitor centre is a good place to begin your visit, as it provides a wealth of information on the varied flora and fauna found within the park's boundaries.
✉ Park information office: Carretera Abenojar-Torrijos s/n, 13194 Pueblonuevo del Bullaque ☎ 926 78 32 97 🕐 Park information office: 9–2, 3–7 (4–8 in summer)

PUERTO DE NAVACERRADA
PUERTO DE NAVACERRADA ESTACIÓN DE ESQUÍ
www.puertonavacerrada.com
This is a small ski station, about 80km (50 miles) north of Madrid, but it's convenient for a day trip from the capital. It has been modernized and offers good facilities for a resort of its size. There are 16 pistes (7 red, 5 blue, 4 green), making it ideal for beginner and intermediate skiers. There is a ski school, plus a handful of hotels and refreshment options.
✉ Puerto de Navacerrada ☎ 902 88 23 28 🕐 Nov–Mar daily 9–5

SEGOVIA
LA ABADÍA
In an old house with a modern look, tapas are served all day, and at night Spanish bands liven the place up. Blues and jazz concerts often feature on the bill.

✉ Calle Colón 5, 40001 Segovia ☎ 921 46 24 00 🕐 Tue–Fri 8am–12am, Sat 12–12. Closed Mon ✋ Free

ALCÁZAR DE SEGOVIA
www.alcazardesegovia.com
This 12th-century fortress with fine views was once the residence of the Spanish royal family. The General Military Archives and Arms Museum are housed here, and the tower and gardens are open to visitors.
✉ Plaza de la Reina Victoria s/n, 40003 Segovia ☎ 921 46 04 52 🕐 Apr–Sep daily 10–7; Oct–Mar 10–6 ✋ €4; access to the tower €2

BAR SANTANA
www.barsantana.com
One of the best spots in Segovia to listen to live music. Rock, pop and blues concerts are regularly scheduled and there are exhibitions that change every two weeks.
✉ Calle Infanta Isabel 18, 40001 Segovia ☎ 921 46 35 64 🕐 Daily 10am–3am ✋ Free

CAJA SEGOVIA FS
www.cajasegoviafutbolsala.com
Caja Segovia FS club plays indoor soccer in the top national league at this pavilion, which holds 2,800 spectators. Bar and cafeteria on site.
✉ Pabellón Municipal Pedro Delgado, Polígono Residencial Nueva Segovia, 40006 Segovia ☎ 921 44 43 25 🕐 Games: Sat at 6.30pm (no games in Aug) ✋ Tickets: €7

CERVANTES
www.cervantes.com
One of the most popular bookshops in the city sells antiquarian books. Subjects range from literature and religion to travel and cookery.
✉ Calle Cervantes 14, 40001 Segovia ☎ 921 46 24 85 🕐 Jul–Sep Mon–Sat 10–1.45, 5–8.30; Oct–Jun 10–1.45, 4.30–8

MERCADILLO LOS HUERTOS
This is a traditional street market where you can find all kinds of vegetables and fruits from around the province. There are also stands selling flowers, eccentric clothing and typical pastries. Take a look at the

local handmade pots and pans.
✉ Plaza de los Huertos s/n, 40001 Segovia 🕐 Thu 9–2

REGALOS PALMA
A craft store in the city's busiest street. Excellent for souvenirs, plus Talavera ceramics, bronze pieces, traditional Castilian pottery and porcelain figures. There are also painted fans in a wide range of designs, T-shirts and bags.
✉ Calle de Isabel La Católica 5, 40001 Segovia ☎ 921 46 22 19 🕐 Mon–Sat 10–1.30, 4–8.30

TEATRO JUAN BRAVO
www.teatrojuanbravo.org
The theatre first opened in 1917 and was refurbished in the 1980s. Dramas, classical music, ballet and children's shows, mainly in Spanish, are on the bill here. An exhibition hall displays paintings and crafts.
✉ Plaza Mayor 6, 40001 Segovia ☎ 921 11 33 00. Advance sales: 902 10 12 12 ✋ From €7

TOYS
A popular disco-bar on a street lined with bars and clubs (in fact Calle Infanta Isabel is better known simple as '*Calle de los Bares'*), this is a relatively spacious venue laid out over two floors. It's a good place to start the night, with a young crowd happily dancing to cheerful Spanish pop. It's fun, and a big favourite with local students. There is a huge TV in the main bar, where sports events are screened.
✉ Calle Infanta Isabel s/n, 40001 Segovia 🕐 Daily 9am–4am

TOLEDO
ADOLFO COLLECTION 1924
This is the latest offering from the prestigious Toledano restaurant group Adolfo, a sleek, classy designer tapas bar-cum-wine shop, where you can sample some divine designer treats accompanied by fine Spanish and international wines in the bar upstairs, or purchase some delectable regional goodies and fine wines at the small shop downstairs. As well as a selection

CAFÉ TEATRO EL PÍCARO

www.picarocafeteatro.com

This is a good place for drinking, dancing and listening to live music, as well as afternoon coffee. At night, cocktails are served and the three floors are open for drinking, hanging out and dancing. Live concerts are regularly staged in the evening.

✉ Calle Cadenas 6, 45001 Toledo ☎ 925 22 13 01 🕐 Sun–Thu 3pm–4am, Fri–Sat 3pm–6am 💷 Free–€10 🚌 1, 3, 4, 5, 6

CAFÉ-TEATRO TRISKEL

The Triskel hosts music concerts during weekends and on Thursday nights. Mainly a mid-20s crowd.

✉ Plaza de Cuba 7, 45004 Toledo ☎ 667 50 78 89 🕐 Daily 9pm–6am 💷 Free 🚌 5

CALZADOS TENORIO

High-quality leather shoes for men, women and children are sold in this shop in Santa Bárbara district. There is also an excellent selection of leather bags, belts, wallets and sports shoes.

✉ Avenida del Río Guadarrama 39, 45007 Toledo ☎ 925 23 06 49 🕐 Mon–Sat 10–1.30, 5–8.30 🚌 6, 9

CASA CUARTERO

www.casacuartero.com

A highly recommended deli and wine shop, founded in 1920, selling tasty local goodies. There are cured hams and sausages, cheeses (including excellent Manchego cheese from the region), honeys, jams and marmalades, saffron, and of course *mazapán* (marzipan)—the typical Toledan sweets. The wine selection is very good, and the friendly and informed staff are happy to make recommendations. It's well located close to the cathedral.

✉ Calle Hombre de Palo 5, 45001 Toledo ☎ 925 22 26 14 🕐 Mon–Fri 10–2.30, 4.30–8.30, Sat 10–8.30 🚌 1, 4, 5, 10, 11

CASA TELESFORO

Marzipan, a famous Toledan delicacy, is handmade here following original Arabic recipes. The shop's version is

of more than 300 wines, the delicatessen section offers everything from artisanal cheeses and olive oil to spices, honey and pastries.

✉ Calle Nuncio Viejo 1, 45002 Toledo ☎ 925 22 42 24 🕐 Daily 12–12

ARTE TOLEITOLA

Toleitola specializes in the traditional Toledan art of *damasquinos*, and has a wide range of beautiful objects created using this tradition. It also offers other local souvenirs, including lovely ceramics and the famous Toledan swords.

✉ Calle Reyes Catolicos 3, 45001 Toledo ☎ 925 21 52 26 🕐 Mon–Sat 11–8 🚌 12

BERMEJO

www.bermejoswords.com

Bermejo is the oldest sword factory in the city. Here among a wide selection of steel swords you can watch the artisans at work. Products include reproductions of historic swords and daggers, as well as the swords used by matadors in bullfighting.

✉ Calle Airosa 5, 45003 Toledo ☎ 925 22 03 46 🕐 Daily 8–1, 3–6 (8–1 in Aug) 🚌 5, 6, 11

Above *The tower and gardens of Segovia's Alcázar are open to the public*

both elaborate and popular. There's also a café-restaurant attached.

✉ Plaza de Zocodover 7, 45001 Toledo
☎ 925 22 33 79 🕐 Daily 9am–12am
🚌 1, 4, 5, 7, 10, 11

CÍRCULO DEL ARTE TOLEDO

www.circuloartetoledo.org
There are art exhibitions, poetry readings, live gigs, theatre events and much more at Toledo's Circulo del Arte. It's housed in a former church, and has been beautifully transformed into a vibrant arts centre. The attractive café-bar (good for everything from morning coffee to late-night cocktails) has become increasingly fashionable over the last couple of years—arrive before midnight if you don't want to queue.

✉ Plaza de San Vicente s/n, 45001 Toledo
🕐 Daily 10am–midnight (until 2am Fri and Sat) 🚌 12

GARCILASO CAFÉ

www.garcilasocafe.com
Housed in a 16th-century chapel, this venue offers entertainment with DJs and live bands. During the day it serves tapas and regional dishes. At night the bar churns out cocktails and cool drinks.

✉ Calle Rojas 5, 45002 Toledo ☎ 925 22 91 60 🕐 Tue–Sun 12pm–5pm, 8pm–1am
✋ Free (cover charge for more popular shows) 🚌 2

JARDINES DE EL TRÁNSITO

These gardens are a good choice for a shady walk, and children should enjoy the play area. The gardens provide good views of Toledo's *cigarrales* (old country houses) and a monument to the painter El Greco.

✉ Paseo de El Tránsito, 45002 Toledo
✋ Free 🚌 2

SPIN

This play area next to Zoco Europa shopping mall offers morning activities for two- to three-year-olds. In the evenings the space is used for children's parties and as a nursery. Kids should enjoy all the fun games, and there's a cafeteria.

✉ Plaza de Paris s/n, 45003 Toledo ☎ 925 21 30 89 🕐 Mon–Thu 10–2, 4–9, Fri 10–2,

FESTIVALS AND EVENTS

MARCH–APRIL
SEMANA SANTA
Lavish and formal processions celebrating Holy Week.
✉ Toledo

MAY–JUNE
CORPUS CHRISTI
Solemn religious costumed procession paying tribute to the Blessed Sacrament.
✉ Toledo

JULY–AUGUST
VERANO
Music, folk and dance festivities.
✉ Segovia

AUGUST
VIRGEN DEL SAGRARIO
Fiesta in the name of the Virgin; outstanding fireworks.
✉ Toledo

OCTOBER
FERIA DE SANTA TERESA
Fiesta celebrating St. Teresa, a patron saint of Spain.
✉ Ávila

SAN FRUTOS
Parades, music and dance in the name of the city's patron saint.
✉ Segovia

4–10, Sat noon–2, 4–11, Sun 5–10 ✋ 30-min session: €3. 1-hour session: €4. 2-hour session: €7 🚌 4, 9

TEATRO DE ROJAS

www.teatroderojas.es
Comedies and dramas, operas, dance productions and classical music concerts, as well as children's performances (performances usually on Saturdays, with showings at noon and 5pm). The theatre also holds mini film festivals throughout the year. There are three auditoriums and regular art-house cinema screenings on Tuesday.

✉ Plaza Mayor s/n, 45001 Toledo ☎ 925 21 57 08; box office: 925 22 39 70 ✋ €7
🚌 1, 3, 4, 5, 6

TREN TURÍSTICO

www.zocotren.com
Take the 'Zocotren' train tour of the city's best attractions, starting and finishing at Plaza de Zocodover. On the way you'll pass a number of the city's main sights and get some spectacuar views. Recorded information is available in Spanish, English and French.

✉ Plaza de Zocodover, 45001 Toledo
☎ 925 23 22 10 🕐 Daily 11–dusk. Runs every hour; rides last 50 min ✋ Adult €4.50, child (5–12) €1.75 🚌 1, 4, 5, 7, 10, 11

VENTA DEL ALMA

Sit by the fire in winter or on the patio in summer at this nightspot. Venta del Alma is perfect for a coffee in the afternoon or a night of dancing.

✉ Carretera de Piedrabuena 35, 45004 Toledo ☎ 925 25 42 45 🕐 Sun–Thu 3.30pm–2.30am, Fri–Sat 3.30pm–5am (Jun–Sep 3.30pm–4.30am) ✋ Free 🚌 7

VILLA NAZULES HOTEL HÍPICA SPA

www.villanazules.com
To really get away from it all, consider a stay at this luxurious hotel, which has a gorgeous spa offering all kinds of health and beauty treatments, open to day visitors as well as hotel residents. If you prefer more active pursuits, the hotel also has horse-riding stables attached, as well as tennis courts, an outdoor swimming pool, and even a small carriage museum. Hiking, mountain-biking and treks on horse-back can all be arranged. It is located just a 10-minute drive from Toledo, surrounded by olive groves.

✉ Carretera Alomanacid a Chueca s/n, 45190 Almonacid de Toledo ☎ 925 59 03 80 🕐 Spa Mon–Sat 10–10, Sun 10–8 ✋ Rooms €110–€175 (excluding buffet breakfast €13). 90-minute circuit €40

PRICES AND SYMBOLS

The restaurants are listed alphabetically (excluding El, Le, La and Les). The prices given are the average for a two-course lunch (L) and a three-course dinner (D) for one person, without drinks. The wine price is for the least expensive bottle.

For a key to the symbols, ▷ 2.

ALCALÁ DE LOS HENARES

HOSTERÍA DEL ESTUDIANTE

www.parador.es
The *parador* in Alcalá de los Henares is located in the 17th-century Colegio de San Jerónimo. The restaurant, as the name suggests, is actually in the old student refectory, and has changed little with the passing of time. It's an atmospheric spot to enjoy delicious local specialties such as roast lamb and other meats, casseroles and country dishes such as *migas,* made with breadcrumbs, garlic, peppers and chorizo. There are also fish and egg dishes
⊠ Calle Colegios 3, 28801 Alcalá de los Henares ☎ 918 88 03 30 🕐 Daily 1.30–4, 8–10. Closed Aug ✋ L €40, D €45, Wine €15

ÁVILA

EL ALMACÉN

El Almacén is located in a beautifully converted warehouse, originally built in the 1880s for grain storage. Now it's one of the city's finest and most elegant restaurants, which boasts spectacular views of the storybook walled city of Ávila. Talented chef Isadora Beotas prepares sublime regional cuisine, reinventing age-old recipes with contemporary flair. The wine list is outstanding and desserts are mouthwatering creations.
⊠ Ctra de Salamanca 6, 05002 Ávila ☎ 920 25 44 55 🕐 Tue–Sat 2–4, 9–11, Sun 2–4. Closed Sep ✋ L €54, D €58, Wine €18

MÁXIMO

www.maximorestaurante.com
A former wine bodega, now a sleek, fashionable restaurant, Máximo serves refined contemporary Spanish cuisine. Although Castilla y León is most famous for its meat dishes, Máximo is perhaps the best place in the city for delicious and inventive seafood, brought freshly from Galicia every day. The *ensalada templada de zamburiñas*—a delicate mound of vegetables served with succulent Galician clams—is fabulous, but the local beef with foie gras is another excellent option.
⊠ Ctra de Salamanca 3, 05002 Ávila ☎ 920 25 78 37 🕐 Mon, Wed–Sat 2–4, 9–11, Sun 2–4. Closed 2 weeks in Aug ✋ L €40, D €42, Wine €16

GUADALAJARA

AMPARITO ROCA

www.amparitoroca.com
Named after a popular pasodoble, this excellent restaurant occupies a modern building on the outskirts of the city. The refined cuisine is based on the finest produce, and changes with the seasons. Go for the *menu de degustación* to enjoy some of the chef's specialties. These might include flavoursome rice cooked with shellfish and baby squid. Chocolate fans should finish with *cremoso de chocolate con naranja*—a perfect fusion of chocolate with orange.
⊠ Calle Toledo 19, 19002 Guadalajara

Above *Hostería del Estudiante is one of Spain's range of* paradores

☎ 949 21 46 39 ⏰ Mon–Sat 2–4, 9–11.
Closed Easter week and 2 weeks in Aug
🖐 L €55, D €60, Wine €16

SEGOVIA
AMADO
www.restauranteamado.com
Established in 1950, this traditional
restaurant offers fish, red meats and
roasted suckling pig or lamb. For a
starter, try the shrimps from Huelva,
the croquettes or the scrambled
eggs. The Segovia cake is especially
delicious. There's a varied wine list,
good service and a special fixed-price
menu for €20.
✉ Avenida Fernández Ladreda 9, 40001
Segovia ☎ 921 43 20 77 ⏰ Mon–Tue,
Thu–Sun 1–4.30, 8–11.30 🖐 L €30, D €45,
Wine €15

LA FRASCA
Enjoy beer, wine and tapas at this
lively bar close to the cathedral. The
summer terrace is especially lovely.
Sandwiches, baguettes, salads, and
raciones (large portions of tapas) of
Manchego cheese, fried calamari,
Spanish omelette, ham, tripe or
anchovies are also served.
✉ Plaza de la Rubia 6, 40001 Segovia
☎ 921 46 10 38 ⏰ Daily 9am–2am
🖐 Tapas €3–€9.50, salads €4–€8.50,
baguettes €4.50–€7.50

JOSÉ MARÍA
www.rtejosemaria.com
Close to Plaza Mayor, this tapas bar
and traditional restaurant specializes
in roast suckling pig which is raised
on their own farm. Other delicacies
include Iberian ham with olive oil,
crab and shrimp cream, and salmon
cooked in a sparkling wine sauce.
There's a great wine selection from
Spain and abroad. The sampler
menu costs €45. Private rooms
are available.
✉ Calle Cronista Lecea 11, 40001 Segovia
☎ 921 46 60 17, 921 46 11 11 ⏰ Daily
10am–midnight 🖐 L €45, D €50, Wine €15

MESÓN DE CÁNDIDO
www.mesondecandido.es
In business since 1884, this
landmark, family-run restaurant
upholds the traditions of the best

Castilian country cuisine. Don't
miss the roast suckling pig, which
is ceremoniously cut with the edge
of a plate. Other great main courses
include boar with apple, salt-crusted
trout and hake in a green sauce.
Finish with the Segovia punch cake
(tarta de ponche segoviana). The
wines are excellent too.
✉ Plaza Azoguejo 5, 40001 Segovia
☎ 921 42 59 11 ⏰ Daily 12.30–4.30,
8–11.30 🖐 L €55, D €60, Wine €16

MESÓN RESTAURANTE EL CORDERO
www.rte-elcordero.com
This old brick and stone building has
three dining rooms serving typical
regional dishes such as *judiones*
(large beans) from La Granja, roast
suckling pig or lamb, beef sirloin with
foie gras and truffle sauce, and salt-
crusted fresh hake or sea bass.
✉ Calle El Carmen 4–6, 40001 Segovia
☎ 921 46 33 45 ⏰ Daily 12.30–4, 8–11.30
🖐 L €30, D €45, Wine €14

TOLEDO
LA ABADÍA
www.abadiatoledo.com
A delightfully old-fashioned café
and bar in the historic heart of
Toledo, this offers everything from
breakfasts to more substantial meals
at lunchtimes, and tapas during the
day and in the evenings. It offers a
simple and inexpensive lunch menu
for children, too *(croquetas* and chips,
pasta etc). The vaulted stone bar on
the lower level is the place to try one
of the range of chilled draught beers.
✉ Plaza de San Nicolás 3 ☎ 925 25 11 40
⏰ Daily 9am–11pm 🖐 Tapas from €3.50,
Set lunch menu €14, Wine €12

ADOLFO
www.adolforestaurante.com
Adolfo, near the cathedral, is one
of the most exclusive restaurants
in town, serving local cuisine using
the best seasonal produce. Game is
used in the star dishes: venison in
red wine sauce, and rabbit with fresh
vegetables. The ample and elaborate
wine selection includes options
from the most renowned wine
areas in Spain. There are four dining

rooms, but advance reservations are
advisable to secure a table.
✉ Calle de la Granada 6, 45001 Toledo
☎ 925 25 24 72 ⏰ Mon–Sat 1–4, 8–12,
🖐 L €80, D €110, Wine €22 🚌 1, 3, 4, 5, 6

CASA AURELIO
www.casa-aurelio.com
A traditional restaurant serving
typical Toledan cuisine. The tables
are wooden and the ornaments
Castilian. Specials include Castilian
soup with egg and cured ham,
partridge stew and tangy venison
loins. For dessert, try cheeses from
La Mancha or classic regional
pastries. Free parking is available but
reserving is advisable. There are two
other branches in the city.
✉ Calle Sinagoga 1, 45001 Toledo
☎ 925 22 13 92 ⏰ Tue–Sun 1–4.30,
8–11.30 🖐 L €35, D €45, Wine €15
🚌 1, 2, 3, 4, 5, 6

HIERBABUENA
www.restaurantehierbabuena.com
Creative, seasonal menus are served
at this contemporary restaurant,
set in a typical historic city house.
During the hunting season (autumn
and winter), try game dishes such
as boar, partridge or venison. There
is also plenty of fish on the menu.
Home-made desserts and quality
wines accompany the meals. The
restaurant surrounds a sumptuous
inner patio. Choose à la carte, or from
the daily menu or gourmet sampler
menu. Reserving a table is advisable.
✉ Callejón de San José 17, 45003 Toledo
☎ 925 22 37 24 ⏰ Mon–Sat 1.30–4,
9–11.30, Sun 1.30–4. Closed Sun in Aug
🖐 L €38, D €42, Wine €14 🚌 1, 3, 4, 5, 6

VENTA DE AIRES
www.ventadeaires.com
House specials include cream of
crab soup, roast lamb and suckling
pig, partridge Toledan style and
scrambled eggs with peppers. For
dessert, the creamy custard and
crêpes are good, and the wine
selection is superb.
✉ Paseo del Circo Romano 35, 45004
Toledo ☎ 925 22 05 45 ⏰ Mon–Sat 1–5,
9–midnight, Sun 1–4 🖐 L €35, D €45, Wine
€15 🚌 1, 2, 4

PRICES AND SYMBOLS

The prices are for a double room for one night including breakfast, unless otherwise stated. All the hotels listed accept credit cards unless otherwise stated. Note that rates can vary widely throughout the year.

For a key to the symbols, ▷ 2.

ÁVILA

HOSPEDERÍA LA SINAGOGA

A simple but attractive little two-star hotel, located in the remnants of a 15th-century synagogue, this has modern rooms for a modest price. It's perfectly located in the heart of the old town, tucked down a tiny alley near the cathedral and all the main sights. Each of the rooms is named after a famous Jewish intellectual, and all are different. Furnishings are modern, but many original details, such as the brick arches, the central patio (now prettily glassed over) and wooden beams, survive. There's no restaurant in the hotel, but there are dining options nearby.

✉ Calle Reyes Catolicos 22, 05001 Ávila ☎ 920 35 23 21 📱 €78–€112 🛈 22 ♿

PALACIO DE LOS VELADA

www.veladahoteles.com

A magnificent 16th-century palace, in an incomparable position opposite the cathedral in Ávila's atmospheric old quarter, this is now the most luxurious, central hotel in the city. The spacious rooms, classically decorated with a mixture of antique-style and modern furnishings, are arranged around a magnificent glassed-over interior patio. There's a bar, a good, although rather formal, restaurant, and a less formal cafeteria on the patio. WiFi is available, and there's free internet access in the Cibercorner.

✉ Plaza de la Catedral 10, 05001 Ávila ☎ 920 25 51 00 📱 €140–€325 🛈 145 ♿

PARADOR DE ÁVILA

www.parador.net

The *parador* in Ávila occupies the 16th-century Palacio Piedras Albas, which is built into the city's famous walls. Some of the comfortably furnished rooms, decorated in pastel prints, look out over beautiful gardens. The best room is named

after the Conde de Benavides, with huge windows and a bathroom with Jacuzzi. The gardens are wonderful, with superb views of the monumental walls and beyond, and they are scattered with all kinds of curious archaeological finds from an early Christian baptismal font to Roman reliefs. The palace has had numerous royal visitors, from Charles V in the 16th century to the current Prince of Asturias (heir to the Spanish throne). There's an excellent restaurant and parking is available.

✉ Calle Marques de Canales y Chozas 2, 05001 Ávila ☎ 920 21 13 40 📱 €138–€260 🛈 61 ♿

SEGOVIA

LOS ARCOS

www.hotellosarcos.com

A modern, five-floor hotel in the city's shopping district which has good views of the historic quarter. Facilities include a laundry service, cocktail bar and room service. Rooms have a

Above *Although it is a day trip from Madrid, the best way to see Toledo is to stay there*

safe, TV, hairdryer, marble bathroom and minibar. The restaurant serves traditional local dishes.

✉ Paseo de Ezequiel González 26, 40002 Segovia ☎ 921 43 74 62 🖐 €65–€165 excluding buffet breakfast (€12) ⓘ 59
🆒 🍽

CORREGIDOR

www.hotelcorregidor.com

About a five-minute walk from the aqueduct and cathedral, this modern hotel is good value for money. The guest rooms have a TV, and the restaurant offers a daily menu as well as traditional à la carte dishes. The cafeteria serves breakfasts and assorted tapas.

✉ Carretera de Avila 1, 40002 Segovia ☎ 921 42 57 61 🖐 €65–€85 excluding buffet breakfast (€10) ⓘ 62 🆒

HOSTERÍA AYALA BERGANZA

www.partner-hotels.com

This 15th-century palace-turned-hotel has been declared an artistic historic monument. The rooms are pleasant and it's just three minutes' walk from the aqueduct. Each room is decorated in its own style, and all are well equipped. Amenities include a meeting room, tavern bar and garden terrace.

✉ Calle Carretas 5, 40001 Segovia ☎ 921 46 04 48 🖐 €120–€148 ⓘ 17 🆒

INFANTA ISABEL

www.hotelinfantaisabel.com

The building may be a century old, but this small, comfortable hotel has been totally renovated. The classic decor changes from room to room, but each comes equipped with a balcony, minibar, modem point, satellite TV and safe.

✉ Plaza Mayor 12, 40001 Segovia ☎ 921 46 13 00 🖐 €70–€135 excluding breakfast (€9) ⓘ 37 🆒

TOLEDO
AC CIUDAD DE TOLEDO

www.ac-hoteles.com

This modern hotel (built 1998) is in Los Cigarrales, an area known for its exquisite country houses, and has excellent views of the Río Tajo and the city. All rooms have

a minibar, satellite TV and internet connection. Other amenities include a hairdresser, a reading room and two meeting rooms.

✉ Carretera de Circunvalación 15, 45002 Toledo ☎ 925 28 51 25 🖐 €115–€195 excluding breakfast (€14) ⓘ 49 (25 non-smoking) 🆒 🍽 📶 7

ALFONSO VI

www.hotelalfonsovi.com

A luxurious option in Toledo, the Alfonso VI is located opposite the Alcázar, with rooms overlooking the city, a restaurant serving superb food and a typical tapas bar. The rooms are decorated with fine blue tiles and the furnishings are typically Castilian. The bathrooms are large and finished with marble.

✉ Calle General Moscardó 2, 45001 Toledo ☎ 925 22 26 00 🖐 €150–€160 excluding breakfast (€10) ⓘ 83 🆒

HOSTAL DEL CARDENAL

www.hostaldelcardenal.com

The 18th-century Hostal de Cardenal is in the city's old quarter and is surrounded by walls. It preserves its original style with glazed tiles, handicrafts, a terrace, rambling gardens and beautiful patios with fountains. The guest rooms contain antiques; each also has a TV, hairdryer and safe.

✉ Paseo de Recaredo 24, 45004 Toledo ☎ 925 22 49 00 🖐 €118–€138 excluding breakfast (€12) ⓘ 27 🆒 📶 1, 2, 3, 5, 6, 9

PARADOR DE TOLEDO

www.parador.es

This is one of the more romantic places to stay in Toledo, even though it's outside the central area at Los Cigarrales. A typical country house on a hill has been converted into a luxurious hotel, decorated in Castilian style, with great views of the surrounding landscape. Rooms have a hairdryer, minibar and satellite TV, and the *parador* has a bar, a garden, swimming pool and meeting rooms. The restaurant serves traditional regional cuisine and there's a terrace where non-guests can enjoy a coffee.

✉ Cerro del Emperador s/n, 45002 Toledo

☎ 925 22 18 50 🖐 €165–€175 excluding breakfast (€14) ⓘ 76 (2 non-smoking) 🆒 🏞 Outdoor

PINTOR EL GRECO

www.hotelpintorelgreco.com

The El Greco is in the historic Jewish quarter, surrounded by gardens and shops, and has good views of the Los Cigarrales district of old country houses dotted over the hills. The facade and inner courtyard of the 17th-century building are original, but the rest has been renovated. The comfortable rooms are furnished in rustic style and have satellite TV, safe, minibar, hairdryer and internet access. There is no restaurant.

✉ Alamillos del Tránsito 13, 45002 Toledo ☎ 925 28 51 91 🖐 €75–€130 excluding breakfast (€12) ⓘ 60 (2 non-smoking) 🆒 📶 2, 5

SANTA ISABEL

www.santa-isabel.com

This 15th-century house is in the town's historic district near the cathedral and opposite the Convento de Santa Isabel. It was renovated in 1990, although the facade has been preserved and the rustic style of the original building retained. All the rooms are comfortable and have small balconies. Other facilities include free WiFi, a reading room with a library, a TV room and 24-hour room service.

✉ Calle Santa Isabel 24, 45002 Toledo ☎ 925 25 31 20 🖐 €62–€75 excluding breakfast (€8) ⓘ 42 🆒 📶 2

SOL

www.hotelyhostalsol.com

Sol, in Toledo's historic quarter, is in a quiet area convenient for the major attractions. There is also an economical hostel here. The hostel rooms are smaller and have only showers; hotel rooms have a complete bathroom, satellite television and telephone. There is parking and a cafeteria.

✉ Calle Azacanes 8 & 15, 45001 Toledo ☎ 925 21 36 50 🖐 €32–€75 (hostal), €45–€90 (hotel), excluding breakfast (€6)
ⓘ 25 🆒 📶 1, 4, 5, 6

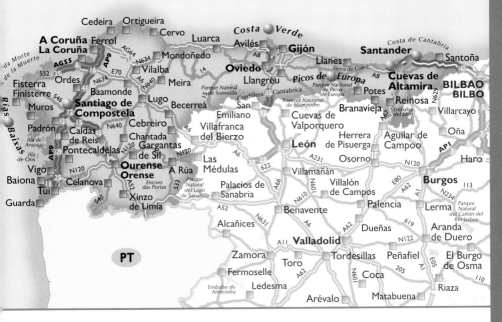

GALICIA, ASTURIAS AND CANTABRIA

Wild, wet, green and mystical, Galicia is one of Spain's most alluring and unspoiled regions. The magnificent Rias, huge fjord-like inlets which indent the Atlantic coast, are at their most dramatic to the north, where smugglers still prowl the secret coves. The southern Rias, known as the Rias Baixas, are less dramatic visually, but the glorious golden beaches and pine-fringed bays are a magnet for tourists. Inland, the land is chequered with tiny villages and neatly kept smallholdings. Most still have the traditional granaries, called *hórreos*, which resemble tiny granite chapels raised on pillars to keep out the rodents and the wet. The jewel of this region is the magical stone city of Santiago de Compostela, the culmination of the celebrated Camino de Santiago.

East of Galicia, the tiny principality of Asturias was the launching pad for the Christian reconquest of Spain and contains spectacular pre-Romanesque churches. Inland are the magnificent Picos de Europa, a beautiful mountain range scattered with traditional villages. The Costa Verde ('Green Coast') is dotted with charming ports and modest resorts, including pretty Ribadesella and Llanes. Asturias is famous for its dairy herds, which provide most of Spain's milk, along with some superb cheeses including the pungent Cabrales. While here, visit an old-fashioned *sidrería*, to enjoy a refreshing glass of cider, poured in the traditional manner from overhead.

Cantabria shares both the Picos de Europa and the Costa Verde with its diminutive neighbour. Even in the height of summer, it's possible to find secluded coves and you won't find the crowds as oppressive as along the crammed Mediterranean. It has its own string of picturesque little towns, such as Comillas and San Vicente de la Barquera, but none compare with Santillana del Mar, perhaps the prettiest Renaissance village in all Spain. Near here are the Cuevas de Altamira, which contain some of the finest prehistoric cave paintings in the world.

BAIONA (BAYONA)

www.turgalicia.es
www.baiona.org

Baiona (Bayona), at the southern end of the Rías Baixas (▷ 148), is one of the region's most popular seaside resorts and has a choice of sheltered beaches set around its bay.

The Playa de Santa Marta is a particularly good option, with impressive views of the former castle of the Count of Gondomar, begun in the 10th century and now a luxurious *parador* (state-run hotel). Here, a fortified wooded promontory with medieval walls juts into the ocean, still guarding this once important trading port.

It was into the small harbour below that Christopher Columbus's boat, *Pinta*, returned with news of the New World in 1493. The Praia de América beach is across the bay.

🕇 462 B3 🔢 Paseo da Ribeira s/n, 36300 Baiona ☎ 986 68 70 67

BETANZOS

www.betanzos.es

A sarcophagus supported by sculpted wild boars is one of the treasures on view in this medieval town, traditionally tagged 'dos Cabaleiros', meaning 'of the Knights'. The tomb is housed in the 14th-century Gothic Iglesia de San Franscisco, and contains the remains of nobleman Fernán de Pérez de Andrade, known as O Bo, or 'The Good', who died in 1470.

This former provincial capital stands on a steep hill at the head of the *ría* (estuary) that separates A Coruña (▷ 134) from Ferrol. Below, the Río Mendo and Río Mandeo almost encircle the town. Fragments of the medieval walls can be found at the base of this hill, which is topped by the town's main square, the Praza dos Irmáns G. Naveira. One of the town's best-preserved traditions is its markets. On the first and sixteenth day of each month fairs are held, during which local produce is sold. These are worth catching if you are in the area at the time.

O Pasatiempo, the 'encyclopedia park', has flower displays and murals

and sculptures representing world history and places.

🕇 462 B1 🔢 Praza de Galicia 1, 15300 A Coruña ☎ 981 77 66 66 🚊 Betanzos-Infesta

CANGAS DE ONÍS

www.infoasturias.com
www.cangasdeonis.com

For trekking and canyoning tours into the surrounding Picos de Europa, or descents along the nearby Río Sella, the pleasant, compact market town of Cangas de Onís makes an ideal base. Your first stop could be the Casa Dago (summer daily 9–9; winter daily 9–2, 4–7), with its typical Asturian mountain architecture. This building is home to the offices of the Parque Nacional de los Picos de Europa (▷ 140–141), and is a useful place to pick up information on the area.

Access to the town via the western end gives views of the ivy-covered Puente Romano (Roman bridge), one of the most photographed sights in Asturias, where a copy of King Pelayo's Cruz de la Victoria (victory cross) hangs suspended from the central arch. Pelayo made a wooden cross when heavily outnumbered by the Moors at Covadonga in AD724 (▷ 134); the Virgin Mary came to his aid and angels dropped rocks on his attackers. Pelayo was thus able to defeat the Moors in the first Christian success of the Reconquest. The original cross is now in the cathedral at Oviedo (▷ 139). Ermita de Santa

Cruz, with foundations dating from AD437, is also of interest.

Don't forget to sample the local cider, which is available in the numerous *sidrerías* (cider houses) in town.

🕇 463 F1 🔢 Jardines del Ayuntamiento 2, 33550 Cangas de Onís ☎ 985 84 80 05

CASTRO-URDIALES

www.castro-urdiales.net

Sandwiched between Santander and Bilbao, and set around a natural rock harbour, Castro-Urdiales has retained its traditional seafaring character. The port's fleet of wooden fishing boats is well known for its tuna and anchovy catches, and fills a waterfront edged by an attractive stone wharf.

A promontory juts out from the town's northern end, where the Gothic buttressed Iglesia de Santa María is the central feature. Across a Roman bridge, opposite, is a lighthouse built in the shell of a castle once owned by the crusading Knights Templar. Elegant town houses with glassed-in balconies add further style to the promenade.

From Playa Ostende, on the western side of the promontory, an impressive cliff walk leads back to town.

🕇 464 G1 🔢 Avenida de la Consitución 1, 39700 Castro-Urdiales ☎ 942 87 15 12 🚊 Bilbao and then bus to Castro-Urdiales

Opposite *Boats lined up along the waterfront of Castro-Urdiales*
Below *The Puente Romano (Roman bridge) spans the gorge at Cangas de Onís*

CEBREIRO

On a good day, Cebreiro's rural community—made up of traditional *pallozas,* or thatched stone huts—presents a tranquil view of surrounding pastoral lands. Perched in the mountains at 1,300m (4,264ft), this remote settlement bears the worst of the weather and is regularly blanketed with fog and snow. The huts are no longer inhabited but have been turned into a national monument. In summer a guide is on hand to offer information. A simple ninth-century church lies at the heart of the hamlet, and lower down is the steep pass of Pedrafita de Cebreiro, the final daunting challenge to weary pilgrims en route to Santiago de Compostela (▷ 144–147).

✚ 463 C2 🅸 O Cebreiro, 27672 ☎ 982 36 70 25

COMILLAS

www.turismo.cantabria.org
Comillas is an intriguing place with fascinating *modernista* architecture and the bonus of several beaches nearby. The main attraction is the Palacio de Sobrellano (Jun to mid-Sep daily 10–9; mid- to end Sep daily 10.30–2, 4–7.30; Oct–May Wed–Sun 10.30–2, 4–7.30), designed by Catalán architect Joan Martorell (1833–1906) for the Marquis of Comillas. The 1883 El Capricho folly (now a restaurant) that shares the hilltop is the work of Antoni Gaudí (1852–1926), the modernist architect.

✚ 464 F1 🅸 Ayuntamiento, 39520 Comillas ☎ 942 72 25 91

A CORUÑA (LA CORUÑA)

www.turismocoruna.es
Galicia's largest city is packed with seafaring history. It was from A Coruña that the disastrous Armada set sail for England in 1588, and that ships seeking the New World departed filled with emigrants. Local heroine María Pita, who reputedly raised the alarm against an English attack in 1589, is immortalized in a statue in the central colonnaded square named after her. The Torre de Hércules lighthouse, founded by the Romans, still warns shipping traffic from its rocky northern outcrop. The city is concentrated around an isthmus, with a port on one side and a beach on the other. The sweeping Praia del Orzán is the main beach. At its southern end is the Estadio de Riazor, the home stadium of soccer club Deportiva La Coruña. To its north is the interactive Museo Domus (summer daily 11–9; winter daily 10–7), which has family-friendly exhibits about the human body. Farther out on the headland is the Aquarium Finisterrae (Jul–Aug daily 10–9; rest of year Mon–Fri 10–7, Sun and holidays 10–8), with a massive tank and viewing area. Houses with glass balconies, a characteristic feature of A Coruña, overlook the port. The original city, La Ciudad Vieja, a twist of medieval streets, is close by. At its eastern edge, the Jardín de San Carlos, contains the grave of British general Sir John Moore, who died while retreating from the French in 1809 during the Peninsular Wars. The Romanesque churches of Santa María and Santiago are also in La Ciudad Vieja. Paseo Marítimo is a panoramic walkway flanking the southern end of La Ciudad Vieja. Explore the city's past in the Museo Historica Arqueolóxico, in the Castelo San Antón on a small spit south of the old town (Jul–Aug Tue–Sat 10–9, Sun 10–3; Sep–Jun Tue–Sat 10–7, Sun 10–2.30).

✚ 462 B1 🅸 Plaza de Maria Pita s/n, 15001 A Coruña ☎ 618 79 06 55 🅿 A Coruña

COSTA DE LA MORT

▷ 137.

COSTA VERDE

▷ 135.

COVADONGA

www.santuariocovadonga.com
Devoted pilgrims come here to take Mass in the Santa Cueva, the unique cave shrine where the Reconquista (Reconquest) allegedly started. The Asturian King Pelayo and his men are believed to have taken a fortified position in the cave before defeating 20,000 attacking Moors in AD724. A waterfall flushes through the rock face beneath the shrine into a clear pool below. A tunnel and a stone staircase access the shrine. The chapel was built in 1940. The Basílica, a striking, large, salmon-pink church, is the other main sight.

✚ 462 F2 🅸 Información Santuario y Real Sitio, Explanada de la Basílica, 33589 Covadonga ☎ 985 60 81 10

COSTA VERDE

Between Llanes in the east and Ribadeo in the west, the Atlantic-facing Costa Verde is every bit the green and pleasant land its name implies. Resorts are few and far between and remain on the small side, making the 'green coast' an altogether less commercialized stretch than Spain's Mediterranean seaboard. Its fringe is dotted with fishing ports, wide beaches and tiny coves separated by rocky cliffs, and the industrial towns of Gijón (▷ 137) and Avilés are the exceptions to its otherwise small-scale communities.

THE EASTERN SECTION

Llanes (▷ 138) marks the eastern edge of the Costa Verde. Dramatic cliff views give way in the west to some fantastic beaches, including the Playa de la Huelga, complete with its own rock arch, which can be reached from the hamlet of Villahormes.

West of Llanes is the fishing port of Ribadesella. The old town and port on the eastern edge of the river is a lively area of bars, restaurants and the *lonja* (market). On the opposite bank is the Cueva Tito Bustillo, an important archaeological site containing prehistoric art that was discovered in the 1960s. More than 80 other similar caves have been found across the Basque country, Cantabria and Asturias (Cuevas de Altamira, ▷ 136). The town is also a natural gateway to the Parque Nacional de los Picos de Europa (▷ 140–141), Cangas de Onís (▷ 133) and Covadonga (▷ 134).

Farther west is the small resort of La Isla, with one of the most popular beaches of the area, and the fishing villages of Villaviciosa and Lastres. North of the Ría de Villaviciosa, the village of Tazones overlooks the Bay of Biscay.

BEYOND CABO DE PEÑAS

The port village of Cudillero lies 31km (19 miles) from Avilés and is one of the most attractive in Asturias. Its painted houses cling to the surrounding cliffs and the wharfside flanks the main square. Beyond Luarca (▷ 138) is the secluded fishing port of Viavélez, a popular summer resort. The small towns of Tapia de Casariego and Castropol lie tucked into the eastern side of the Ría de Ribadeo.

INFORMATION

www.gijon.info

✚ 463 E1 ℹ Espigón Central de Fomento C/Rodriguez San Pedro s/n, 33200 Gijón ☎ 985 34 17 71 🕓 Jul to mid-Sep Mon–Fri 9–8, Sat–Sun 9–10; mid-Sep–Jun daily 9–8

TIP

» This is a great coastline to explore by car, but if you don't have your own transportation the FEVE rail line (independent of RENFE), running the length of the Costa Verde's rugged coastline, gives you pretty good access to all the best spots; check timetables in advance—the train is very slow.

Opposite left *Antoní Gaudí's El Capricho folly, in Comillas*
Opposite right *Lobster pots at Luarca*
Below *The rugged Costa Verde*

REGIONS GALICIA, ASTURIAS AND CANTABRIA • SIGHTS

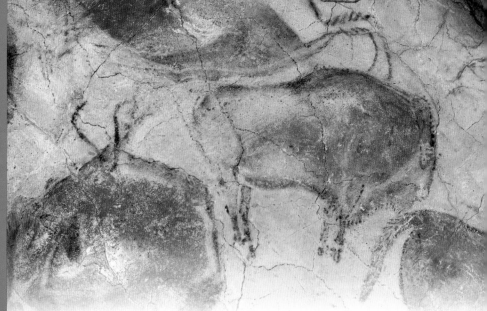

INFORMATION

http://museodealtamira.mcu.es

✚ 464 G1 ✉ Museo de Altamira, 39330 Santillana del Mar ☎ 942 81 80 05 ◎ May–Oct Tue–Sat 9–8, Sun and holidays 9.30–3; Nov–Apr Tue–Sat 9–6, Sun and holidays 9.30–3. Entry to the Neocueva is on a timed ticket; advance reservation available through the internet and is advisable, particularly during the summer 🖐 Adult €3, under 18 free ☛ Tours included in admission price (advance reservation advisable) 📖 Altamira Museum guidebook €4 ▢ Smart, modern and well maintained 🏛

TIPS

» Avoid Easter if you can, as this is the busiest time.
» Visits are currently suspended as a study into conservation conditions is being carried out. Write (email informacion@maltamira.mcu.es) or phone or visit the website for latest information.

CUEVAS DE ALTAMIRA

The Cuevas de Altamira are a truly extraordinary find. The painted images of bison, bulls, deer and horses, dating from between 10,000 and 25,000 years ago, were first discovered by a local man who followed his dog into the caves in 1868, but it wasn't until 1879 that their true value came to light when the cave paintings were rediscovered by Santander lawyer Marcelino de Sautuola.

On the ceiling of the caves are almost a hundred animals and symbols, created using a variety of techniques. The breadth, range and extent of movement in the composition led archaeologists, who did not believe prehistoric people capable of producing such fine art, to declare the work a fake. The authenticity of the paintings was later proved, and by the 1960s the caves were one of the country's most popular sights. Atmospheric changes caused by so many visitors began to threaten the images however, and the caves were closed in 1977. They have since been declared a UNESCO World Heritage Site, and visits have been limited since 1982 to 8,500 people a year.

Written applications must be made at least a year in advance for approved entrance to the real caves. Write to Centro de Investigación de Altamira, 39330 Santillana del Mar, Santander (tel 942 81 80 05).

ENJOYING THE PAINTINGS

Even if you don't get into the caves, the artwork can still be enjoyed at the Museo de Altamira, considered by many to be Europe's leading prehistory museum. Here, the outstanding feature is a faithful reproduction of the caves, the Neocueva, only 300m (330 yards) away from the original. The paintings capture the same textures, contours and variations in tone of the originals, and use identical pigments.

The subterranean reproduction cave is entered through the museum and visitors are shown a short explanatory film on the history of Altamira before entering. State-of-the-art technology describes the way of life of the inhabitants of the original cave. The adjacent museum provides further background history, with extraordinary visual displays, videos and film footage.

As you enter the cave computerized film footage recreates a cave scene with moving inhabitants. It is worth seeing the making of the cave exhibit before visiting the Neocueva to appreciate the extraordinary work that went into producing the paintings.

Above *Cave painting in the Neocueva*
Opposite left *Beira beach, Costa Morte*
Opposite right *Fishing nets at harbour*

COSTA DA MORTE (COSTA DE LA MUERTE)

Notorious for shipwrecks, treacherous cliffs and turbulent waters, the 'coast of death' has some of the most untainted, remote coastal scenery in Spain. It stretches from A Coruña in the north to Fisterra in the southwest (▷ 134 and below respectively), and the battering force of the Atlantic has sculpted inlets and rugged rock faces along its length. Scattered down the coast are attractive beaches such as Malpica de Bergantiñas and Laxe, and small fishing villages that huddle around pretty ports and dramatic headlands. Between the town of Camariñas, clustered behind a curving strip of sand, and Fisterra is the least populated section, known as *finisterre*, 'the end of the world'. At Cabo Vilán, 5km (3 miles) from Camariñas, is an impressive lighthouse (see walk, ▷ 151).

✚ 462 A1 🚹 Plaza de Maria Pita s/n, 15001 A Coruña ☎ 618 79 06 55 🚉 A Coruña

CUEVAS DE ALTAMIRA
▷ 136.

FISTERRA (FINISTERRE)
www.concellofisterra.com
This squat, stone village is perched at the end of a jagged peninsula. Its biggest attraction is its location, and for sheer natural drama little can beat it. When Roman legionnaires witnessed the sun dropping off the horizon from here, they named the spot *finis terre*, meaning 'end of the world', where in mythology

the country of the dead was to be found. Mar de Fóra is a wild, curving beach on the road to Corcubión. Some 4km (2.5 miles) out of town is Cabo Fisterra, set on a weatherbeaten outcrop surrounded by sea. Viste Monte do Facho, above the lighthouse here, has sweeping views of the Costa da Morte stretching northwards. The Romanesque Iglesia de Santa María das Areas is passed en route.

✚ 462 A2 🚹 Rúa Real 2, 15155 Fisterra ☎ 981 74 07 81

GARGANTAS DE SIL
www.turgalicia.es
The canyon of Gargantas de Sil is one of Galicia's finest natural sights. The wooded canyon, which extends over 16,000ha (39,520 acres), has a Mediterranean-like microclimate. It positively brims with lavender, cork-oak trees, oranges and olives, and provides good walking territory. The Camino de la Barca takes you through the middle of the forest to the Monasterio de San Esteban de Rivas de Sil. The Río Sil floods into the Embalse de San Estéban, a dammed hydroelectric lake stretching for 43km (27 miles), where you can take catamaran rides. The Ourense–Monforte de Lemos rail service follows seven of the canyon's length.

✚ 462 C3 🚹 Casa do Legoeiro, Ponte Romana, 32003 Ourense ☎ 988 37 20 20 🚉 Ourense

GIJÓN
www.gijon.info
Although Gijón is the biggest city in Asturias, its fine Cimadevilla (old fishermen's quarter) saves it from

being just an industrial sprawl. This beautifully maintained old town of Roman ruins, ramparts and regal buildings occupies a headland to the northwest of the surfer-friendly Playa de San Lorenzo, and separates the latter from the modern and not particularly interesting central part of town. The 15th-century Palacio Revillagigedo (Jun–Sep Tue–Sat 11–1.30, 4–9, Sun and public holidays 12–2.30; Oct–May Tue–Sat 11.30–1.30, 5–8, Sun and holidays 12–2), a fusion of neo-baroque and neo-Renaissance styles, is a natural starting point. Nearby is the arcaded Plaza Mayor and the impressive mid-19th-century Casa Consistorial government buildings; for great views climb the Torre del Reloj.

At the northern end of the peninsula, the grassy recreational area of Parque La Atalaya lends a refreshingly open feel to the city. Here, the sculpture *Elegy of the Horizon* (1990), by Eduardo Chillida (1924–2002), faces the Atlantic.

The Fuerte Viejo, an excavated Roman military complex on the western promenade, leads to the Parque La Atalaya. It has wide views and gives an insight into some of the archaeological work undertaken in Gijón's old town. Farther west is fashionable Puerto Deportivo, the city's main marina and port.

✚ 463 E1 🚹 Espigón Central de Fomento C/Rodriguez San Pedro s/n, 33206 Gijón ☎ 985 34 17 71 🚉 Gijón

LAREDO
www.laredo.es

Laredo has a crescent-shaped beach with 5km (3 miles) of white sands, an old quarter and a bustling fishing port, and is a popular holiday resort. La Salvé beach is one of the largest in Spain; for the best views of the strand, stroll along the Paseo Marítimo. Look for the fishing sculptures, monuments to the men and women of the town.

There is more to Laredo than just sand and sea. The Puebla Vieja (old town) lies at the foot of Monte Rastrillar. Behind the Puerto Pesquero (fishing quarter), narrow streets and shady squares cluster around the Gothic Iglesia de Santa María (open during religious ceremonies). A tunnel dating from 1860 links the town to the coast.

🚗 464 G1 🛈 Alameda de Miramar, s/n, 39770 Laredo ☎ 942 61 10 96

LLANES
www.venallanes.com

The small seaside town of Llanes has transformed its port with an open-air exhibit, *Los Cubos de la Memoria*. Here, concrete defences have been turned into a unique work by Basque artist Agustín Ibarrola.

From the port, a tidal stream flows through the town, past a number of big houses built by immigrants on their return from America.

The Gothic Basílica de Santa María and medieval walls lie at the heart of the town's old quarter. The Aula del Mar (Mon–Fri 5–7, Sat 11–2, 5–7,

Sun 11–2; open until 9pm in summer) is a modern museum dedicated to Llanes' relationship with the sea.

The Paseo de San Pedro walkway crosses the headland overlooking Playa del Sablón; a rock arch here frames the dramatic coastline. You can also walk to the more sheltered coves of Playa de Puerto Chico and Playa de Toró.

🚗 464 F1 🛈 Calle Alfonso IX, Edificio La Torre, 33500 Llanes ☎ 985 40 01 64 🚆 Llanes

LUARCA
www.ayto-valdes.es

This sleepy town, also known as Villa Blanca, is one of the prettiest along the northern coast.

The fishing port is the busiest part of Luarca, which is set around a snaking bay and surrounded by cliffs. A detailed mosaic at the wharfside *lonja* (market), where the catch is auctioned daily, tells the intriguing tale of how the local fishermen used to decide whether to go to sea. The men would be asked to stand by either a model house or a model ship; whichever had the most men next to it would provide the answer.

Around the waterfront area are seafood restaurants and typical Asturian *sidrerías* (cider bars). The main town is bisected by a pretty, meandering tidal stream crossed by a series of low bridges, and contains a number of shops.

🚗 463 D1 🛈 Calle los Caleros 11, 33700 Valdés ☎ 985 64 00 83 🌐 Summer only 🚆 FEVE station 2km (1.2 miles) out of town

LUGO
www.lugo.es

In the heart of Galica, Lugo is still completely protected by walls encircling the medieval inner city.

The walls are 10m (33ft) high, have 85 circular towers and stretch for nearly 3km (2 miles), providing a walkway. Inside the walls is the cathedral (daily 8.30–8.30), on the pilgrimage route to Santiago de Compostela.

Roman ruins include mosaics at the Domus Oceani (Tue–Sun 11–2, 5–7; until 8pm in Jul and Aug), and the remnants of a necropolis at the Centro Arqueológico de San Roque (Tue–Sun 11–2, 5–7). The colonnaded Praza Maior, the Museo Provincial (Mon–Sat 10.30–2, 4.30–8, Sun 11–2; closed in summer) and Parque Rosalía de Castro are the town's other main sights.

🚗 462 C2 🛈 Praza Maior 27 (Galerías), 27080 Lugo ☎ 982 23 13 61 🚆 Lugo

MONASTERIO DE OSEIRA (SANTA MARÍA DA REAL)
www.turgalicia.es

Santa María da Real, a vast and beautifully situated monastery,was founded in 1137. The structure has been restored and modified, and includes the Escalera de Honor and the three cloisters of Dos Cabaleiros, Dos Medallóns and Os Pináculos. The church, built between 1185 and 1240, is one of the jewels of Cistercian art.

🚗 462 C2 ✉ San Cristovo de Cea, 32136 Oseira ☎ 988 28 20 04 🌐 Daily 🖐 Adult €3 🕐 Tours at 10, 11, 12, 3.30, 4.30, 5.30

OURENSE (ORENSE)
www.turismourense.com

Known as the gateway to Galicia, the provincial capital of Ourense has a particularly attractive *casco viejo* (old town). At its heart is the cathedral, built in the style of Santiago's cathedral (▷ 145) and with a painted imitation of the latter's Pórtico de Gloria. Also in this southern section of the town are lively bars, thermal springs and a succession of stepped squares. The Museo Arqueológico (temporarily closed for renovation) is housed in one of the town's most striking buildings, the 12th-century former Palacio Episcopal, with an impressive heraldic facade.

Ourense, which straddles the Río Miño, is home to Fidel Castro's family. The splendid six-arched Puente Romano, originally built by the Romans, was reconstructed in the 13th century.
✚ 462 C3 ℹ Casa do Legoeiro, Ponte Romana, 32080 Ourense ☎ 988 37 20 20 🚍 Ourense

OVIEDO (UVIÉU)
www.ayto-oviedo.es

A trio of pre-Romanesque churches, all built in a simple regional style, is the highlight of a visit to the Asturian capital of Oviedo (Uviéu). The beautiful ninth-century churches of Santa María del Naranco and San Miguel de Lillo, regarded as among the best in Spain, sit just out of town on wooded slopes. Above, a massive statue of Christ crowns the hilltop, conjuring up images of Brazil's Rio de Janeiro. The third church, Iglesia Santjullano de los Prados, also ninth

century, is a short walk from central Oviedo. If you want to make the most of these out-of-town sights, detour to the Parque Recreativo Naranco, at the foot of the Christ statue, which has plenty of space and great views. In the city's compact old quarter is the Gothic cathedral, housing a cross that is reputed to have been the one carried by King Pelayo at Covadonga (▷ 134 and Cangas de Onís, ▷ 133).
✚ 463 E1 ℹ Plaza de la Constitución 4, 33003 Oviedo ☎ 984 08 60 60 🚍 Oviedo

PARQUE NATURAL DE SOMIEDO
www.infoasturias.com

The nearby Picos de Europa (▷ 140–141) may be more popular, but little-known Somiedo is a remarkable mountain and forest wilderness, a UNESCO Biosphere Reserve and a hiker's delight. It was declared a natural park in 1988 and covers 291sq km (112sq miles) around the tiny village of Pola de Somiedo, home to the 15th-century Palacio de los Flórez Estrada. An Ecomuseu (mid-Jul to Sep Tue–Sat 10.30–1.30, 5.30–8.30, Sun 10.30–1.30; Oct to mid-Jul Tue–Fri 11–2, Sat 11–2, 5–8, Sun 11–2) shows how villagers lived and worked traditionally.

The park contains a clutch of peaks exceeding 2,000m (6,500ft), of which El Cornón is the highest at 2,194m (7,196ft). There are many waymarked hiking routes; the four-hour PR.AS 14.1 up the Valle del Pigüeña is one of the most challenging of these.
✚ 463 D2 ℹ Oficina del Parque Natural, 33840 Pola de Somiedo ☎ 985 76 37 58

PICOS DE EUROPA
▷ 140–141.

PONTEVEDRA
www.turgalicia.es

Cobbled squares, such as the shady Praza de Leña with its distinctive stone cross, arcaded streets like those surrounding the Praza da Ferrería, and narrow lanes lined with squat stone houses, make this an ideal city to explore on foot. Stroll along the Almeda, a promenade area leading down from Praza de Espana, with tile artworks depicting typically Galician scenes. The town's old and new quarters are divided by the splendid baroque Capella da Virxe Peregrina (daily 9–2, 4–9), with its interesting scallop-shaped design. In the old town's *zona monumental* is the Museo de Pontevedra (Jun–Sep Tue–Sat 10–2, 5–8.30, Sun 11–2; Oct–May Tue–Sat 10–2, 4–7, Sun 11–2), housed in two fine mansions. Before its river became silted up, Pontevedra was one of the biggest ports in Spain. It claims to be the birthplace of Christopher Columbus (c1451–1506). Basílica Santa María, Praza de Alonso de Fonseca, has a fine baroque altar and carvings by Galician sculptor José Ferreiro.
✚ 462 B3 ℹ Calle General Gutierrez Mellado 3 Bajo, 36080 Pontevedra ☎ 986 85 08 14 🚍 Pontevedra

---

Clockwise from top left *Santa Maria del Naranco, Oviedo; Luarca port; Los Cubos de la Memoria, Llanes; monument to fishermen, Laredo*

INFORMATION

www.picosdeeuropa.com
✚ 464 F2 ℹ Casa Dago, Avenida Covadonga 43, 33550 Cangas de Onís, ☎ 985 84 86 14 🕐 Summer daily 9–2, 5–6.30; winter daily 9–2, 4–6.30
🚌 Cangas de Onís

INTRODUCTION

Dominating the skyline across three regions are the serrated peaks of the Picos de Europa, popular with walkers, trekkers and climbers. If you are less active or short of time, the park still has some of the most captivating driving in the country, with several medieval villages and towns to visit en route and a thrilling cable-car ride. Whichever way you choose to travel, a major advantage of exploring the Picos is its compactness and diversity of terrain, which allow even those on the shortest of visits to discover some truly wild country. The region is split into three upland areas: In the west, the Cornión Massif runs between the Cares and Sella rivers; at the eastern end is the Andara Massif; and in the middle is the most dramatic and wild region, the Urrieles Massif. The three are spread across Asturias, Castile-León and Cantabria, with a common meeting point at the 2,570m (8,430ft) summit of Tesorero.

There are many higher mountains in other parts of Europe, but the way the peaks of the Picos thrust up from the low Cantabrian coastal belt gives them a particular impact. They began forming around 300 million years ago and the carboniferous limestone was subsequently raised. Glaciers and rivers then carved and sculpted the valleys and gorges into the impressive forms seen today. The park's origins date back to 1918, when the Marquis of Villaviciosa, Don Pedro Pidal, set up Spain's first national park, Montaña de Covadonga. This covered much of the Cornión Massif, subsequently incorporated in 1995 into the far larger Parque Nacional Picos de Europa.

WHAT TO SEE

POTES

The medieval town of Potes, on the eastern edge of the park, has some of the better accommodation and eating options in the area, and is also a base for several adventure-tour companies.
✚ 464 F2

FUENTE DÉ

If you lack the time or energy to get high up into the Picos mountains, take the sensational cable-car ride from Fuente Dé, on the road from Potes. It climbs 753m (2,474ft) over 1.6km (1 mile) in a mountain bowl and is the third-longest cable-car in the world. Note, however, that there are long waits in the peak summer months.

➕ 464 F2

MAIN TOWNS

The main access point for the Picos de Europa is Cangas de Onís (▷ 133). The town is also the base of one of the park's information offices (see Information). The other main access routes are via Arenas de Cabrales in the north, a livelier place, and Potes in the southeast, perhaps the most enchanting of the Picos towns. Both have other park information offices. To the southwest of Cangas de Onís lies the cave shrine of Covadonga (▷ 134).

PICOS ADVENTURES

Getting into some parts of the mountainous interior does not require a great deal of commitment, as there are convenient road-linked trailheads. By far the most popular hike is from Poncebos to Caín along the 1,000m-deep (3,300ft) Cares Gorge (see walk, ▷ 154–155). Another well-known walk is the 28km (17-mile) Senda del Arcediano, an old Roman route that leads from the mountain pass of Puerto del Pontón, on the southwestern side of the Picos, to Amieva via Soto de Sajambre. Other good trekking access points include Fuente Dé, for the southern side of the Picos, and Buferrera, for lakeside walks and for reaching the northern flanks. The highest peak in the Picos is Torrecerredo, at 2,648m (8,688ft), although there are several others higher than 2,600m (8,500ft), including Peña Vieja and Llambrión.

Hiking is undoubtedly the best way to reach the most inspiring parts of the national park and there are plenty of adventure-tour operators based in the region's major towns that offer guided walks, along with kayaking, rock climbing and almost any other outdoor activity you can think of. The national park offices also have a series of free, relatively easy guided walks each day throughout the summer from July to September.

FLORA AND FAUNA

Brown bears, wolves, chamois and otters, capercaillie, eagles and vultures all star in the wildlife extravaganza with varying regularity. There are more than 700 species of flowering plant, best seen in the spring.

TIPS

» Driving around the Picos can be a bit hair-raising at times, especially along the narrow roads through the gorges. Take it really easy and expect large vehicles such as motor homes and trucks to be coming the other way around every corner.

» The roads get very busy in summer. In winter, snow regularly causes road closures, so check in at the park offices or visitor information offices to find out the latest conditions.

» Although this is a wild region, the influx of August visitors from around Spain and the rest of Europe can make the experience akin to weekend shopping at the supermarket. At this time it becomes impossible to find somewhere to stay.

» Don't underestimate the untamed nature of the higher peaks and mountains. The weather can turn in a few minutes and in poor conditions it can be challenging even to follow marked trails. Take a proper walking map and a compass (and know how to use them), a good waterproof jacket, warm underlayers and sufficient water and food.

Opposite top *Hiking in the Picos de Europa at Fuente Dé*
Opposite bottom *Café between Riona and Caín*
Below left *Hórreo, a typical Asturian granary, in the foreground between Cangas de Onís and Llastres*
Below *Herding cattle on the road to Cangas de Onís*

INFORMATION

www.riasbaixas.org

✠ 464 A2 🛈 Praza Santa Maria s/n, 36080 Pontevedra ☎ 986 84 26 90

🕐 Summer Mon–Fri 9–9, Sat–Sun 10.30–2, 4.30–8; winter Mon–Fri 9–8, Sat–Sun 10–2 🚉 Pontevedra

RÍAS BAIXAS (RÍAS BAJAS)

At the western edge of Galicia between Fisterra in the north and Baiona in the south are four sea inlets known as the Rías Baixas. Here the rivers of Vigo, Pontevedra, Arousa and Muros-Noia shape the indented coastline, where dramatic cliffs alternate with bays. A mild climate has created a luxuriantly green landscape, dotted with arable fields, fruit orchards and vineyards. Small archipelagos and sandbars shield the inlets, which are dotted with fishing boats and mussel rafts, and fishing towns nestle in their sheltered coves.

THE SOUTHERN RÍAS

The Illas Cíes stand almost like watchtowers over the entrance to the wedge-shaped Ría de Vigo, the most southerly of the four. The three islands, a protected natural park, can be reached by boat from Vigo (▷ 147), but tickets are limited, so reserve in advance in summer. Opposite Vigo are Cangas and Moaña, traditional seafaring communities. To the northeast the *ría* becomes narrower at Rande, where a suspension bridge with one of the longest spans in the world links Vigo with northern Galicia. At the head of the inlet is Arcade, one of Europe's major oyster beds.

The Ría de Pontevedra stretches from Punta Cabicastro in the north to Centoleira in the south, and is flanked by forested shores. Pontevedra (▷ 139) and the resort areas of Sanxenxo, Portonovo and O Grove are the most popular destinations here.

THE NORTHERN RÍAS

The largest of all the inlets is the Ría de Arousa, extending from Punta Covasa in the north to Cabo San Vincente in the south. Islands and islets dot its inland waters, the most picturesque of which include Illa de Sálvora, Illa de Arousa and Cotegada. Many seafaring towns have grown up around the coves and peninsulas of this *ría*, including the Ribeira and Cambados and the major port of Vilagarcía de Arousa. The town of Padrón, at the head of the Ría de Arousa, is famous throughout Galicia for its peppers, served locally as spicy tapas.

The most northerly of the Rías Baixas is the Ría Muros-Noia. Its two major stopping points are Muros on the north shore and Noia at its head. The main ports of Porto do Son and Portosín, on the south coast, reflect the nautical heritage that characterizes so much of this area.

Below *Detail on the doorway of the Church of San Martiño, Noia*

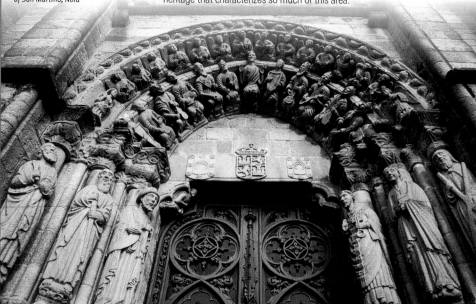

SANTANDER

For many, the first glimpse of Santander's broad bay, golden sands and busy waterfront will be from the deck of one of the summer ferry services that land visitors to Spain on the country's northern coast. The initial views across the Bahía de Santander, dotted with attractive islets and sandbars, are pretty special. On the western side of the bay is a cityscape of elegant esplanades, a fashionable waterfront and a busy port. On the eastern side is an entirely different kind of Spain of mountains and fields.

The city was almost entirely rebuilt after a fire in 1941 destroyed most of its buildings. It is now an agreeable mixture of university town, regional hub, travel terminus and refined resort. The 13th-century Gothic cathedral and Museo Marítimo (May–Sep daily 10–7.30; Oct–Apr 10–6), with its whale bones and aquarium, are the main sights.

THE BEACH SUBURBS

Santander's most obvious attraction is its beaches. The suburb of El Sardinero, a fashionable haunt with palm-lined boulevards, modern mansions and an equally elegant grand casino, has one of the best. The *playa* (beach) curves gently around a small neat bay to provide 2km (1.2 miles) of beautiful white sands. To the south, Playa Magdalena, an attractive sheltered strip of sand opposite Isla de la Torre, occupies the southern side of the headland that divides the two areas. It is another great spot, with beautiful views across to Playa del Puntal and Playa de Loredo. A ferry service connects Santander with Somo and Pedreña across the water, and with the eastern and often less crowded beaches. Tours of the bay and excursions up the Río de Cubas can be made.

PENINSULA DE LA MAGDALENA

The promontory jutting out between the main Santander beaches is the Peninsula de la Magdalena, seat of the former summer palace of Alfonso XIII (1886–1941) and a popular public open space. It is ideal for families as it has picnic areas and children's play parks, and backs on to Playa de Los Bikinis. A train runs tours around the headland and there is a curious collection of rafts sailed from South America to Australia on display.

INFORMATION

www.ayto-santander.es
www.turismodecantabria.com
✚ 464 G1 ℹ Paseo de Pereda (by the cathedral), 39001 Santander ☎ 942 20 30 00 🕐 Mid-Jun to mid-Sep daily 9–9; Easter to mid-Jun Mon–Fri 8.30–7, Sat–Sun 10–7; mid-Sep to Easter Mon–Fri 8.30–7, Sat and holidays 10–2 🚆 Santander

Above *The coastline around Santander*
Below *Part of the* Raqueros *monument on Santander Bay*

SANTIAGO DE COMPOSTELA

INTRODUCTION

The beautiful granite city of Santiago de Compostela, one of the three great shrines of medieval Christendom, has been welcoming *peregrinos* (pilgrims) for centuries. It lies at the end of the pilgrims' route, Camino de Santiago (The Way of St. James). Today, Santiago is capital of the autonomous region of Galicia, the seat of its parliament and governing institutions, and home to a prestigious 500-year-old university.

Legend tells that St. James preached in Spain before returning to his martyrdom in Judaea in AD44. His disciples brought his body back to Spain, where it lay hidden until 844. In that year the hermit Pelagius was supposedly guided to the burial place by a glowing field of light—the *campus stellae,* 'field of stars', from which the name Compostela derives. The burial ground was then visited by the king of Asturias, Alfonso II, who had seen the saint in a vision before starting his battle to oust the Moors from the peninsula. St. James led the Christians to victory, earning the title of Matamoros, the Moorslayer, and ensuring his place as the embryonic nation's patron saint. A monastery was founded at Compostela and the pilgrimage tradition was born, with up to 2 million on the move annually by the 12th century.

Start exploring in the Praza do Obradoiro, a huge expanse dominated by the cathedral. To the left is the Renaissance Hostal dos Reis Catolicos, a former pilgrim hostel and now a luxurious *parador* (state-run hotel). Opposite this stands the 17th-century Colegio de San Jéronimo, while the fourth side is occupied by the neoclassical Pazo de Raxoi, headquarters of the city council and the Galician government *(Xunta).*

Walk along the left side of the Catedral to reach the Praza da Inmaculada, backed by San Martiño Pinario ($\triangleright$ 146). This square is linked to the spacious Praza da Quintana, which backs on to the Catedral itself. South from here, and dominated by a fountain of horses, is the old silversmiths' square, the Praza das Paterias. From here you can stroll down Santiago's main streets, Rúa Nova, Rúa do Vilar and Rúa do Franco; cobbled and colonnaded in the Galician style, they are the heart of the medieval city, surrounded by a complex of streets, arcades and alleyways.

WHAT TO SEE

CATEDRAL DE SANTIAGO

www.catedraldesantiago.es

The various routes of the Camino de Santiago wind their way across Europe, leading ultimately to one point, a scallop shell carved into a flagstone in the paving in front of the Catedral de Santiago. From here, a majestic 17th-century double stairway fronts the ornate facade, crowned with a towering statue of St. James brandishing a staff and wearing his scallop shell symbol.

The frontage is flanked by two soaring baroque towers, designed by Santiago-born architect Fernando Casas y Novoa in the first half of the 18th century. Behind it lies the cathedral's highlight, the Pórtico de la Gloria. The 12th-century work of Master Mateo, this inner facade, the most outstanding example of Romanesque sculpture in Spain, consists of triple arches decorated with Christ, the Evangelists and St. James. Pilgrims give thanks on completing their journey by placing a hand on the central column, which represents the Tree of David—an act that has been repeated so often that a handprint has been worn into the stone.

Inside, the plain 12th-century Romanesque structure was designed to accommodate as many pilgrims as possible, the ambulatory behind the high altar giving them room to move around freely. In contrast with the clean, soaring lines

INFORMATION

www.santiagoturismo.com

✚ 462 B2 ⓘ Rúa do Vilar 63, 15705 Santiago de Compostela ☎ 981 55 51 29 🌐 Jun–Sep 9–9; Oct–May 9–2, 4–7 🚉 Santiago

Above *Detail of a scallop shell carved on a wall*
Opposite *Cathedral facade*
Below *Pilgrims and tourists near the cathedral in Praza do Obradoiro*

of the nave, the baroque high altar glitters with embossed silverwork and gilded figures surrounding a seated wooden statue of St. James, reached by pilgrims via a stairway. A passage leads to the crypt (part of the museum) beneath, where the remains of St. James are housed in a silver chest. The museum admission ticket also includes a visit to the rather neglected cloister, the glittering treasury, and the Panteón, which contains royal tombs belonging to the Kings of León and their families.

In front of the altar is a pulley system to lift the *botafumeiro*, the world's largest censer (incense-burner), used during special services to perfume the cathedral's interior. The pulley system is guided at such times by the expert *tiraboleiros*, or pullers.

✉ Praza do Obradoiro ☎ 981 58 35 48 🕐 Daily 9–9 🖐 Cathedral: free; museum €6

SAN MARTIÑO PINARIO

This Benedictine monastery is famous for its church, built in 1597, and is approached up graceful, curving steps. Behind the plateresque facade, the interior is dominated by an immense gilded baroque altarpiece, depicting St. Martin riding out alongside the apostle James. The 17th-century carved choir stalls are well worth a look.

✉ Praza da Inmaculada ☎ 981 58 30 08 🕐 Jul–Sep daily 11–7; Jun daily 11–1.30, 4–7; Oct–Jun Tue–Sun 11–1.30, 4–6.30 🖐 €3

MUSEO DAS PEREGRINACIÓNS

This fascinating museum traces the history of pilgrimage in general, and Santiago in particular. There are excellent displays and models, but the main focus is the Codex Calixtinus, a 12th-century travel guide for pilgrims, which recommended routes and lodgings along the route to Santiago. Don't miss the souvenirs taken home by medieval pilgrims—not so different from those on sale today.

✉ Rúa de San Miguel 4 ☎ 981 58 15 58 🕐 Tue–Fri 10–8, Sat 10–1.30, 5–8, Sun 10–1.30 🖐 Adult €3, under 18 free

Below *The Catedral de Santiago, part of the stunning architectural complex, Praza do Obradoiro*

SANTA MARÍA DE VALDEDIÓS

www.valdedios.org

For a glimpse of monastic life, stay at the hostelry at the 13th-century Cistercian Monasterio de Santa María de Valdediós. The simple accommodation includes a meal made and served by the monks. You can visit just for the day, but be sure you don't miss the Iglesia de San Salvador and its restored murals. The monastery was founded in 1200 by Alfonso IX of León around a ninth-century church. For six centuries it was a religious base, until it was deconsecrated in 1835. Three monks obstinately remained, the last one dying in 1862.

Restoration began in 1986 and in 1992 the community of monks returned, but the monastery's future is uncertain. The Vatican has ordered that the community move to another monastery. It is thought that another order of monks may take over Santa María de Valdediós.

➕ 463 e1 ✉ Monasteiro de Santa María de Valdediós, 33312 Villaviciosa ☎ 985 89 23 24 🕓 May–Oct Tue–Sun 11.30–1.30, 4.30–6.30; Nov–Apr Tue–Sun 11.30–1.30, Sat–Sun 4–5.30 ✋ Adult €2; child (7–12) €1

SANTIAGO DE COMPOSTELA

▷ 144–146.

SANTILLANA DEL MAR

www.santillana-del-mar.com

Grand mansions, sandstone churches, cobbled streets, shady alleyways and graceful arches make Santillana del Mar one of the northern coast's most popular rural villages. Its ochre-hued stone mansions are decorated with heraldic coats of arms, and some (such as the Villa and Cos family homes) feature mottoes. These houses seem at odds with the rest of this very rural setting. The village extends from the pedestrian-only main street, and stands in a dip between rolling hills covered with meadows and woodland.

The village gained its name from the relics of St. Juliana (in Latin Sancta Iuliana), brought here by Benedictine monks almost 1,200 years ago. They built a small shrine that was taken over by Augustinian monks in the 12th century and subsequently became a collegiate church (closed Mon). Only 2km (1.2 miles) away are the Cuevas de Altamira (▷ 136).

➕ 464 G1 ℹ Jesús Otero s/n, 39330 Santillana del Mar ☎ 942 81 88 12 🚉 Torrelavega, then bus

TUI (TUY)

www.concellotui.org

The fortified town of Tui (Tuy), with its sloping streets, makes for an interesting last stop before you hit the Portuguese border. The strategically placed cathedral has a vantage point overlooking the frontier, which was a hot spot of skirmishes during the Middle Ages. The tiny interior of the cathedral reflects the town's varied roots, with its Mozarabic arches and Gothic and Romanesque influences. Surrounding the cathedral is the old quarter. Interesting churches here include the Romanesque San Bartolomeu and Covento de Santo Domingo. The town's market day is Wednesday, when the main street fills up with stalls.

➕ 462 B3 ℹ Colón 2, 36700 Tui ☎ 986 60 17 89 🚉 Tui

VIGO

www.turgalicia.es

A superb coastal location and its status as Spain's leading fishing port have given Vigo a reputation for fine seafood. The Marisquería Bahía, on the main promenade (which in the summer months is occupied by oyster-sellers), claims to be the largest seafood restaurant in Spain. The town's Parque Castro is a great *paseo* (promenade) spot and looks out over the city. From Estación Marítima de Ría, visits can be made to the scenic Illas Cíes (▷ 142). Ferry services connecting Cangas and Moaña provide an alternative way of enjoying the pleasant scenery of the broad and sheltered Ría Vigo. Vigo itself is a good point of access to the Rías Baixas region (▷ 142).

➕ 462 B3 ℹ Calle Cánovas del Castillo 22, 36202 Vigo ☎ 986 43 05 77 🚉 Vigo

Above left *The collegiate church in Santillana del Mar*
Above right *Majolica plates in Santillana*

RÍAS BAIXAS

A drive through the Rías Baixas (▷ 142), an incomparable area of natural beauty at the western edge of Galicia. It takes you along a spectacular coastline backed by rolling hillsides and lush eucalyptus and pine forests. The four famous *rías* (sea inlets) shape a landscape of broad bays, sheltered coves and attractive fishing villages, home to some of Spain's best seafood, and form a fertile wine-growing region.

THE DRIVE
Distance: 214km (133 miles)
Allow: 1 day
Start at: Fisterra (Finisterre), map 462 A2
End at: Pontevedra, map 462 B3

★ The small fishing village of Fisterra (Finisterre ▷ 137) is in a spectacular location, clustered on the side of a rocky headland. Stone houses edge the quayside and a wide, sweeping, sandy bay lies on the edge of town. The Romanesque Iglesia de Santa María das Areas stands on its northern outskirts.

At the most extreme end of the rock-weathered peninsula, 3km (2 miles) out of town, is Cabo Fisterra. Above the lighthouse here is the Vista Monte do Facho, revealing dramatic views of the Costa da Morte (▷ 137 and 150), infamous for its shipwrecks and tragedies.

From the Cabo Fisterra lighthouse, drive back through Fisterra. Head out of town on the AC-552 signed for A Coruña. The road climbs gently past the bay to your right and snakes around a rocky coastline, with superb views back to Fisterra. Pass through Sardiñeiro de Abaixo and Corcubión on the same road before picking up the AC-550 signed for Muros. The road now largely follows this coastline, which has wide bays, pine-backed beaches and small fishing ports. After just over 51km (32 miles), a *mirador* (lookout point) overlooking the Ría de Muros-Noia is signed to your right. Eucalyptus trees line the road, which brings you into Muros.

❶ The little town of Muros is typically Galician in style, positioned on the northern side of the *ría* and centred on its fishing port. Arcaded, sunken stone houses and an attractive *ayuntamiento* (town hall)

line the main street. Many of the houses have traditional glassed-in balconies, to protect them from the wind and rain. Along with Noia, Muros is known as a 'granite town' for its ubiquitous use of this stone.

Drive through Muros, still on the AC-550, following signs for Noia. The road continues around the water's edge, passing through pretty whitewashed villages and climbing into Tal to give splendid views across the *ría*. Just beyond the Río Tambre crossing, about 88km (55 miles) into the journey, you enter Noia.

❷ Narrow streets and small squares hide behind Noia's main front. The Iglesia de San Martiño, at the heart of the old quarter, has a charming facade of smiling sculpted figures. Leave town on the AC-543 signed to Santiago de Compostela. The road climbs gently upwards past houses and then out of town over slopes of pine and eucalyptus trees. After around 1km (0.6 mile) you pick up the AC-301, signed right to Padrón. The road winds through pretty woods and open pastures.

❸ Padrón is where the remains of the apostle St. James (Santiago) were supposedly brought by boat. He is said to have preached Christianity in Spain for seven years before returning to Judaea. In the parish church by the bridge is the mooring stone of the legendary vessel.

Take the N-550 out of Padrón and follow signs for Vilagarcía de Arousa on the PO-548 through a series of roundabouts. Shortly before entering the town you pass Carril and a small island to your right.

❹ Vilagarcía is the main port of the Ría de Arousa. It is also the main town for the O Salnés district, which is famous for its wine.

Pass the port and continue on the PO-550 signed for Cambados. After passing through this stately town, capital of the Albariño wine-growing region, follow the signs for O Grove. You cross a narrow spit of land, with water on either side, to reach the O Grove peninsula.

❺ On a small headland linked to the mainland by a narrow causeway lies O Grove, one of Galicia's most popular resorts. To the north the resort opens out on to the Ría de Arousa, while views to the east are of the beautiful pine-covered island of A Toxa.

Leave O Grove on the same road that entered the headland and cross back over the causeway. On the other side, follow signs for Pontevedra along the coastal road. This takes you past signs for the aerodrome and on through Portonovo and Sanxenxo. From here continue to Pontevedra (▷ 139) on the coastal PO-308.

WHEN TO GO
Although this route is easy to follow at any time of year, avoiding the winter will give you a slightly better chance of missing the rain.

WHERE TO EAT
PULPERÍA PACHANGA
One of several good seafood restaurants along this coast.
✉ Rúa Castelao 29, 15250 Muros
☎ 981 82 60 48 🕐 Daily 10am–2am

TASCA TÍPICA
This restaurant is in an arcaded building in Noia's old quarter.
✉ Cantón 15, 15200 Noia ☎ 981 82 18 42
🕐 Daily 10am–2am

PLACE TO VISIT
ACQUARIUMGALICIA SUBMARINE TOURS
www.acquariumgalicia.com
✉ Acquariumgalicia, 36980 O Grove
☎ 986 73 15 15 🕐 Jul–Sep daily 10–9; Mar–Jun, Oct–Nov daily 10–8; Dec–Feb daily 10–6 🎟 Adult €10, child €7, under 6 free

Above *Pontevedra, once a major port before it silted up*
Opposite *The intricately sculpted facade of Iglesia de San Martiño in Noia*

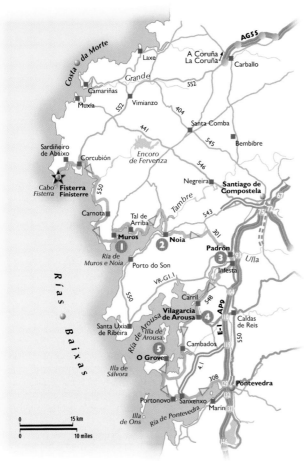

COSTA DA MORTE

Hauntingly known as the 'coast of death', this remote part of Spain has earned its reputation through a history of shipwrecks. In 2002, it was the scene of the sinking of the *Prestige* oil tanker. For all its dangers, the Costa da Morte retains a rugged, wave-swept beauty.

THE WALK

Distance: 10km (6 miles)
Allow: 3–4 hours
Total ascent: 350m (1,150ft)
Start/end at: Camariñas, map 462 A2
Maps and guides: Visitor office leaflet, Galicia on Foot, includes a brief description of the PR-G38 Costa da Morte route
Parking: Along waterfront in Camariñas

HOW TO GET THERE

Camariñas is about 57km (35 miles) north of Fisterra, off the AC-432.

★ Camariñas is well known for its fine tradition of lacemaking. A small notch in the coastline cups the port, which lies across the bay from the Ría de Camariñas inlet.

Start at the waterfront. With the sea on your left, walk along the promenade to the road junction at the far end. Turn left and follow signs for Ruinas Castello Soberano and Ruta Costa da Morte. Skirt the edge of the port, fork right up a slight ramp (signed Costa da Morte) and continue ahead past houses and a grassy area with an old anchor. Follow the road to the right and continue. When you reach three houses, follow the concrete road to the left between the two lower houses and head slightly downhill. At a Y-fork, take the right fork and you immediately reach another where the paved road heads uphill to the right and a flat gravel track goes left. Take the gravel track. The road bends left, then right, passing a track coming from the left. Continue to another meeting of tracks; turn right on to a four-wheel-drive track (the left track passes a lighthouse). Follow the track between stone walls. It eventually bends inland and comes to a small garden area. Follow the grassy track as it curves in a U-bend around the top of the garden (ignore the path up on the banking), and continue between stone walls and pine trees. Walk on to the next major intersection; turn left to head gently downhill towards the beach at Lago Pequeño.

❶ This beautiful little beach has a small lagoon that reveals itself at low tide. The beach was affected by the *Prestige* oil spill in 2002 but was painstakingly cleaned by an army of volunteers.

The track bends left around the back of the beach, passing a jeep track from the village. Follow it to the end of the beach; a trail marker points to the wooded trail that continues from here. The trail climbs above the bay to a waymarked track junction. Turn right and go up past pine trees. At the crest of the hill is a soccer stadium. At the track's T-junction, detour left and climb up Monte Farelo to the Capilla Virxe do Monte.

❷ According to legend, the Virxe do Monte (Virgin of the Hill) was the sister of the much-venerated Virxe da Barca de Muxía, protector of the region's fishermen. The views from the Capilla Virxe do Monte look south to Muxía and north to Cabo Vilán.

Return to the T-junction and continue straight alongside the stadium wall past an old stone granary store. Soon after the store, turn left on to an obvious smaller path. Shortly after, at the T-junction, turn right to follow the track near the cliff line above rocky beaches. These beaches were badly hit by the *Prestige* oil spill in 2002 and clearing efforts may have created new paths. Keep heading up the coastline towards the wind turbines at Cabo Vilán. Eventually, a path climbs up to the Cabo Vilán road next to the turbines.

❸ The turbines at the Parque Eólico Cabo Vilán were one of the first wind farms in Spain, and produce 1.2MW of energy thanks to the persistent strong winds that blow in mainly from the north.

From the track/road crossroads, a 4km (2.5-mile) return detour along the road to the left goes to Faro Vilán, the first electric lighthouse in Spain. Otherwise, continue straight across the road on to a wide track with Costa da Morte trail signs (beware of traffic). The track skirts right below the turbines and above the sandy bay of Enseada de Areliña. At the left-hand bend, a track heads off to the right. Ignore it and continue on the main track, climbing to the left. As you crest the saddle near the promontory, you reach a track junction. Turn right on to a surfaced road. (An extended, waymarked hike option continues straight on to Praia Reira, adding 5km/3 miles to the overall distance before returning to Camariñas.) Continue on the road past farm buildings (this road is not marked on most maps, so is very quiet). At the road intersection turn left, then almost immediately you reach another junction; turn right here, with open fields opposite. At the modern village crossroads, beyond a granary store, carry straight

on. At the second crossroads again continue straight ahead. When you reach the Camariñas church junction, go straight on and then head left at the fork on Rua Grixa. Continue straight through the village past Plaza Mayor to return to the waterfront and parking area.

WHEN TO GO
Galicia and the northwestern coast of Spain are well known for their year-round changeable weather. This route is open to the elements the whole way, so it is best avoided on wet or windy days.

WHERE TO EAT
There are no refreshments available en route outside Camariñas, so stock up well before you go. The walk is exposed for almost its entire length, so on hot days make sure you take plenty of water with you.

Opposite *Waves pound the rugged coastline*
Below *The wind turbines and lighthouse at Cabo Vilán*

REGIONS   GALICIA, ASTURIAS AND CANTABRIA • WALK

PICOS DE EUROPA

This drive is virtually a circular route of the Parque Nacional de los Picos de Europa, starting on the Asturian side, in the west, then taking you south and looping back to the park's eastern edge. Fantastic views, incredible mountains and dramatic gorges shape this vast landscape. It is a quite a long drive, with plenty to see, so you may prefer to use Potes as an overnight stopover en route.

THE DRIVE
Distance: 248km (154 miles)
Allow: 1 day
Start/end at: Cangas de Onís, map 463 F1

★ The compact little market town of Cangas de Onís (▷ 133) was the seat of the Asturian court following the start of the Christian Reconquest from Covadonga (▷ 134). Some elegant mansions remain, along with the Puente Romano, which spans the Río Sella. The park information office for the Picos de Europa (▷ 140–141) is on the main street in Casa Dago.

With the Roman bridge to your right, leave Cangas de Onís, taking the first right turn on to the N-625 (signed to Riaño). For the next 34km (21 miles) or so you travel through a landscape framed by high mountain peaks, gorges, cliffs and winding waterways to reach the mountain village of Oseja de Sajambre.

❶ On the left side of a steeply twisting valley beneath pyramidal peaks are the typical Picos-style stone houses that form the charming little village of Oseja.

Leave Oseja de Sajambre on the same road to pass through a rocky cleft and continue upwards through forested slopes. There are excellent views as the road leads to the top of the pass.

❷ At 1,290m (4,232ft), Puerto del Pontón is one of the high points of the route.

Continuing over the other side of the col, the road gently descends through wooded slopes, passing the picturesque Ermita de Pontón on the right. You then drive through a broad valley and soon gain views of the massive Embalse de Riaño. The road crosses a bridge putting this man-made lake on your right-hand side.

❸ The town of Riaño lies just above the reservoir. This small town, overlooking the huge lake, is stunning. It is the setting rather than the actual town that is the attraction here, although Riaño does have some amenities, including bars and a couple of hotels.

After following the lakeside, you come to a junction with Riaño and León signed to the right. To go into Riaño, take this turn; otherwise take the left turn signed for Puerto de San Glorio (on the N-621). The road continues past the lake, with the Sierra de Riaño off to your left. Forested slopes, high peaks and gorges fill the landscape, and you pass the communities of Portilla de la Reina and Llánaves de la Reina. Impressive cliff faces flank the narrowing gorge as it climbs higher.

❹ Puerto de San Glorio, at 1,609m (5,280ft), is the route's highest

point and gives splendid views of the central Picos de Europa and Cordillera Cantábrica.

A twisting road descends through a series of switchbacks. The drive then takes you through sloping farmland to the bottom of the valley. After 126km (78 miles) you enter Potes.

5 The lovely little town of Potes, with its arcaded front street and cobbled main square, is the eastern hub for exploring the Picos. Set beneath lofty peaks, it has some fine views and makes an ideal overnight stop, with a selection of restaurants, hostels and hotels to choose from.

To head to the cable-car at Fuente Dé, 21km (13 miles) to the west, drive through Potes, crossing the river via the stone bridge. Just after leaving town you will pass a sign on the right, which lets you know if the *teleférico* (cable-car) is operating. Shortly afterwards, you pass one of the Picos de Europa information offices on the right. The road then follows the Río Deva and heads through a wooded valley as it climbs gently upwards. As you get higher, there are stunning cliff-face views.

6 At Fuente Dé is a *parador* (state-run hotel) and the cable-car terminal beneath a band of towering rock. The *teleférico* takes you up some 753m (2,474ft) to the Mirador del Cable, with extensive panoramic views over the Río Deva, Potes and the central range of the Picos de Europa.

Return to Potes on the same road and head straight through town, following the signs for Panes on the N-621. The road enters the dramatic limestone Desfiladero de la Hermida gorge, where overhanging cliffs and rocky outcrops shield the sunlight. You pass through the small village of La Hermida, where the cliffs seem at their highest and a small shrine is carved in the cliff face to your left. As the canyon opens out into agricultural lands, you approach Panes.

7 A gateway town for the eastern edge of the Picos de Europa, Panes has a scattering of restaurants.

On leaving Panes, pick up the AS-114 signed to Arenas de Cabrales. The road winds alongside the Río Cares, crossing and then recrossing it, and passing wooded slopes and dramatic rock walls. From Arenas de Cabrales,

continue along the AS-114 to return to Cangas de Onís.

WHEN TO GO
The park roads are open year round, subject to weather conditions, although spring and autumn are the best times to drive them as in the summer months they are very busy.

WHERE TO EAT
EL BODEGÓN
✉ Calle San Roque, 39570 Potes ☎ 942 73 02 47 🕐 Jul–Sep daily 10–2; Oct–Jun Thu–Tue 10–2

HOTEL RESTAURANTE COVADONGA
www.hotelcovadonga.net
✉ Plaza de la Iglesia, 33570 Panes ☎ 985 41 42 30 🕐 Daily 1–4, 8.30–11

MESÓN EL ARCEDIANO
http://mesonelarcediano.webcindario.com/meson.htm
✉ 24916 Oseja de Sajambre ☎ 987 74 03 24 🕐 Daily 9am–midnight

WHERE TO STAY
CASA CAYO
www.casacayo.com
✉ Calle Cántabra 6, 39570 Potes ☎ 942 73 01 50

PLACE TO VISIT
FUENTE DÉ CABLE CAR
www.picoseuropa.net/liebana/fuentede.php
✉ 39588 Fuente Dé ☎ 942 73 66 10
🕐 Jul–Sep daily 9–8; Oct–Jun 10–6
🎟 Round trip: adult €15, child (6–12) €5. One way: adult €9, child (6–12) €3

Above *A church in the pretty village of Oseja de Sajambre*
Opposite *Puente Romano at Cangas de Onís*

REGIONS GALICIA, ASTURIAS AND CANTABRIA • DRIVE

CARES GORGE

Etched into a cliff face that at times rises vertically almost 800m (2,625ft) from the river below is the Garganta del Cares (Cares Gorge) trail, one of the highlights of any visit to northern Spain. At times the path burrows through the rock and passes through several short tunnels. The gorge itself is so deep that it has its own microclimate—during the wetter months, waterfalls cascade down the towering rock walls, while overhead, vultures, eagles, hawks and nuthatches are often seen here. This easy-to-navigate walk is ideal for anyone with a reasonable level of fitness and a head for heights.

THE WALK

Distance: 12km (7.5 miles) one way
Allow: 3–4 hours one way
Total ascent: 300m (985ft)
Start/end at: Poncebos
Maps and guides: The visitor office and park office in Cangas de Onís have a leaflet on the gorge route (Spanish only), which includes a detailed map at the back. This will be sufficient for most people, as the trail is extremely easy to follow.
Parking: There is limited trackside parking at the trail start point above Poncebos. Back in town, you can park across the bridge in the official parking area.

HOW TO GET THERE

Poncebos is 35km (21 miles) east of Cangas de Onís, off the AS-264.

★ There isn't much in Poncebos other than a hydroelectric substation and a straggle of hotels and restaurants aimed at hungry or tired hikers. Its great drawcard is its setting at the base of soaring limestone cliffs overlooking the fast-flowing Río Cares.

Start the walk from the parking area across the bridge, signed to Bulnes Funicular Railway. Go back across the bridge to the main road and turn left, signed to Bulnes and Senda de Cares. Walk up the road alongside the tumbling Río Cares, with the gorge ahead. Pass the Hotel Mirador de Cabrales and continue up the main road past a trail sign on the right and then through a tunnel (a detour path option around the tunnel heads off left here if traffic is a problem). The road then becomes a gravel track, which you should continue to follow. After about 100m (110 yards), pass wooden sheds on the right and immediately turn right, signed Ruta del Cares, for the start of the footpath.

❶ From the trail sign, the footpath zigzags up the mountainside to get high above the gorge. The lower four-wheel-drive track is extremely dangerous owing to a high incidence of rock falls, so do not be tempted along it.

The trail climbs quite steeply and then eases off at a point where there are goat pens behind stone walls on the right side. An obvious path winds its way ahead. Pass a track junction, where a right detour goes to Mirador del Naranjo. Continue past a rocky outcrop on the left (a popular if precarious photo spot), then a scree (rubble) slope area before climbing up to ruined buildings.

2 Set into the hillside and connected via stone stairways, these ruined old buildings were the base for the hydroelectric workers. There are several other smaller huts farther up the trail, but this was the main refuge. If the weather is poor, they offer some shelter.

The path climbs to the right of the buildings and continues to join the canal. It then continues gradually over a headland, with wonderful views ahead into the narrow cleft. Beyond a small, dilapidated building on the headland, the path drops down steeply past an isolated rock buttress on the left, high above the river. The path flattens out again below the canal, before eventually passing beneath a natural rock arch.

3 The limestone massifs of the Picos de Europa are riddled with caves and gorges where the water has carved its way through the porous rock. This rock arch, set high over the trail, is elliptical and was formed by water run-off from the summits above. There are memorable views down to the humid, forested sides of the river.

Soon you pass a metal-roofed canal service hut, right next to the canal and with a small water-release valve. The trail is now cut into the rock face, sheltering you from above. Cross a concrete ford where a small footbridge keeps your feet dry in rainy conditions.

Continue through a series of four rock tunnels with impressive views into the gorge ahead. Then pass another old building opposite a long gully on the other side of the river. Where the gorge narrows, the

vegetation increases at river level. Soon you come to a pair of workers' buildings on the right.

4 These two buildings mark the turn-around point for people who have opted to ride horses into the gorge from Caín.

The gorge narrows again and the path cuts through another rock tunnel with sheer drops on either side of it. Ahead, the trail is ramparted for a short section. The gorge opens out slightly and there is a larger pool in the canal. The path continues through the subtly changing canyon and crosses a series of bridges— Bolín, Rebecos and Trascamara— before emerging from the gorge just short of Caín.

If you have not arranged a car shuttle there is only one way back from Caín—retracing your route to Poncebos. You will find a four-wheel-drive taxi service in Poncebos, which for a sizeable fare will collect you and take you back from Caín, but if it is a good day the return walk is likely to be more pleasurable. The gorge looks distinctly different when going in the other direction.

WHEN TO GO
It should be possible to walk the Cares Gorge at any time of year, although snow and ice in winter can make the path treacherous and the implications of falling are severe indeed. The high gorge sides offer good protection from the sun at the height of summer, but it can still get hot. Avoid July and August if you don't want to feel as if you are on a conveyor belt of hikers.

WHERE TO EAT
Take refreshments with you and in summer plenty of water as it can get hot in the gorge and the canal water is not drinkable.

Right Mountain goats cope easily with the inhospitable terrain
Opposite The Garganta del Cares (Cares Gorge)

SANTOÑA AND MONTE BUCIERO

Rising majestically from the Cantabrian Sea across the Bahía de Santoña from Laredo, Monte Buciero's lofty heights give it the appearance of an island rather than a peninsula. The route through this rugged, beautiful and surprisingly quiet landscape takes in 17th-century castles, sea vistas, a breathtaking descent to a lighthouse, salt marshes and a bizarre view over a prison. The well-maintained and obvious track is easy to navigate and suitable for anyone who likes a circular walk of this length—the plunging detour down to the Caballo lighthouse can always be omitted.

THE WALK

Distance: 10km (6 miles)

Allow: 3.5–4.5 hours

Total ascent: 500m (1,640ft)

Start/end at: Santoña, map 464 G1

Maps and guides: This walk is very straightforward—just keep the sea on your right side. The visitor office has a brochure with several walks in the region, including this one. The website www.turismosantona. com has descriptions of walks and a map.

Parking: There is ample street parking along the parkside promenade in Santoña.

HOW TO GET THERE

Santoña is about 6km (4.5 miles) northwest of Laredo (▷ 138).

★ The bustling, traditional fishing port of Santoña enjoys an enviable position on the sheltered northern shore of a protected bay at the mouth of the Río Asón. It has long beaches, including Playa de San Martín, and a green promenade with views across to Laredo.

Start your walk at the far end of the promenade on the corner where the road turns sharply to the right. Climb the stone steps opposite, signed to Fuerte de San Martín; the fort is at the top of the steps.

❶ Built at the start of the 17th century for Felipe II, the Fuerte de San Martín protected the bay's entrance. It was subsequently burned down in a naval attack and then reconstructed in 1668, with further restoration work in 1863.

Continue up the road past the fort to a road junction. Turn right, signed for Fuerte de San Carlos and Faro del Caballo, and follow the road, enjoying the great views over the bay. At a fork, take the left route and continue uphill (there's a small sign on the pylon for Circuito del Buciero). Pass fishing cottages on the left. The road soon becomes a rocky track. Continue uphill past a ruined cottage on the left and an indentation in the rock, called Culo de Santa María (Bottom of Santa María). Hawthorns, bay trees, ilexes and madroñas surround the track, offering a little shade on hot days. Carry on through thicker woodland. The track now emerges into the open at a balcony overlooking a large rock pinnacle. Shortly after, the path turns right at Casa de la Leña, an old cottage where wood collectors once lived; by the mid-20th century, they had deforested the entire headland. The track continues along a grassy ridge into the woods. At the fork, take the right track uphill into the woods. At the left turn in the track, you reach the Mirador de Campolargo. The track descends into woods; continue along the main path to a crossroads, called Cuatro Caminos. Turn right here to reach the top of the stairway to Faro del Caballo.

❷ This detour down 780 extremely steep steps is breathtaking in every respect, as the path dives headlong towards the sea. The lighthouse itself is abandoned and disappointing, but in compensation the seascapes lift the spirits. The only way out is to walk back up all of those steps! You can skip this detour if you feel it is too energetic.

Back at the Cuatro Caminos crossroads, turn right and continue along the path as it descends. The track narrows to a footpath as you pass through trees painted with yellow trail markers. At the track's fork, take the more prominent route to the left. The path climbs through rocky scree and then descends sharply on a narrow mud trail beyond a rock outcrop. At the junction at the end of the narrow mud trail are two yellow spots marked on boulders. Turn right here on to the bigger track and follow the green arrow on the boulder on the right. The track zigzags down towards the sea and then broadens out significantly through trees. It then descends slowly and emerges from the trees above Faro del Pescador.

❸ Set back below track level, Faro del Pescador is a working lighthouse. There is no public access but the views are impressive.

Follow the road (as it is an access only road, there is almost no traffic). There are great views down to the arcing bay of Playa de Berria. At the road junction, turn left. The road contours around the headland until it overlooks El Dueso Prison.

❹ This must surely be one of the most sought-after locations for any prisoner. Surrounded by salt marshes and overlooking the beach and sea, this large prison complex can only be differentiated from a resort camp by its barbed wire-topped walls.

Follow the road around the prison wall until you reach a junction by some houses. Turn right and head downhill to a small concrete soccer pitch. Immediately after the pitch, turn left off the main road on to a smaller concrete track marked with cross-hatching. The track climbs quite steeply past a house topped with a trawler boat cabin, then steepens to a fork. Go straight on (right fork) past a house on the right. The track bends right in more open country and reaches an intersection. Turn right here and climb the cobbled hill to Fuerte del Mazo, or Fuerte de Napoleón as it is also known.

❺ The *fuerte* (fort) was constructed in 1811 by the French, but is not open to the public. The short footpath around the wall has views over Marismas de Santoña, a protected salt-marsh estuary that is home to more than 80 species of birds.

From the fort, head back down the

cobbled track. Continue straight on at the junction and after another 2km (1.2 miles) or so, the road emerges next to Fuerte de San Martín, at the top of the steps leading down to the promenade in Santoña.

WHEN TO GO
This trail is accessible year round. Although the hot sun can make it more taxing in summer, there are several shady sections that offer some respite. Take a hat and use high-factor sunblock as the coastal winds may fool you into thinking it is cooler than it really is.

WHERE TO EAT
There are plenty of shops in Santoña where you can stock up on food and water, but no other refreshment options along the route. Take plenty of water, especially during the hot summer months.

PLACE TO VISIT
FUERTE DE SAN MARTÍN
✉ Paseo Marítimo, 39740 Santoña
🕐 Jul–Aug daily 11–2, 6–9 💲 Free

Above *The view from this lighthouse along the route will inspire*
Opposite *Looking back towards Santoña, still a working fishing port*

WHAT TO DO

CANGAS DE ONÍS
CASA MUNICIPAL DE CULTURA DE CANGAS DE ONÍS
The city hall organizes periodic music concerts, conferences, exhibitions and activities for children. On warm summer evenings theatre, dance and folk music groups perform on the Plaza de Ayuntamiento.

✉ Calle La Cárcel 13, 33550 Cangas de Onís ☎ 985 84 86 01 🕑 Depends on the event

CARTELLE
O MUNDIL ASOCIACIÓN CABALISTA
www.omundil.com
Attractively set in the rural hills east of the provincial capital of Ourense, this horse-riding school provides lessons for beginners and those with more experience. Classes are open to children and adults. There is a guesthouse and restaurant on site, and the riding school also organizes

horse races throughout the year.

✉ Lugar de Nogueiró, 32824 Cartelle ☎ 988 49 11 11 🕑 One hour beginner's class from €15.

ISLA DE LA TOJA
CLUB DE GOLF LA TOJA
www.latojagolf.com
Although Galicia is not as well known for golf as other parts of Spain, it does boast several beautiful courses. If you want a game, this 18-hole golf course is beautifully set on the edge of the *ría* at O Grove, with sublime views across the sea.

✉ Illa da Toxa, s/n, 36991 Isla de La Toja ☎ 986 73 01 58 🕑 Greens fee €23

MALIAÑO
CENTRO COMERCIAL EROSKI
You'll find most of the well-known chains at this large shopping mall. The supermarket has a good selection of regional products: cheeses, *orujo* (strong liqueur) and

sobaos (a local pastry). On the upper floor there is a choice of restaurants, bars and cinemas.

✉ Carretera Santander–Bilbao, Alday s/n, 39600 Maliaño ☎ 942 26 96 26 🕑 Daily 10–10; shops closed on Sun

PONTE CALDELAS
GRANJA O CASTELO
www.caminoacaballo.com
Located 14km (9 miles) east of Pontevedra, this attractive rural farm provides both accommodation, either in the main house or in little bungalows, and runs wonderful horse-riding holidays. It focuses particularly on the Camino de Santiago, with horse-riding trips along both the Portuguese and French routes. These trips are of varying length (choose between 7, 10 and 21 days) and take place several times a year. They also offer a fun-filled activity weekend, which includes accommodation, a horse-

riding trek and a rafting trip.
✉ 36829 Ponte Caldelas ☎ 986 42 59 37, 608 38 13 34 🖐 Weekends from €175–€225 per person. Horse-riding holidays along the Camino de Santiago from €1,725 for 7 days. For a 20-day trip from Burgos to Santiago de Compostela €5,950

POSADA DE VALDEÓN
PANADERÍA CASARES
This traditional village bakery sells all kinds of interesting bread, freshly prepared each morning and containing no preservatives. It also sells *rosquillas* (ring-shaped pastries), marzipans and *empanadas* (pastries filled with tuna and tomato). On Saturdays, it makes *torata mantecada* (sweet bread roll).
✉ 24915 Posada de Valdeón ☎ 987 74 26 42 🕐 May–Sep Mon–Sat 9–2, 5–8, Sun 9–2; Oct–Apr Mon–Sat 9–2 🚌 Take the N-625 from León to Cistierna, then the N-621 to Riaño. Head to Oviedo via the Puerto del Pontón, then follow signs to Posada de Valdeón

POTES
ALBERGUE EL PORTALÓN
www.albergue-el-portalon.com
A beautiful 17th-century inn in the foothills of the Picos de Europa, this offers basic, youth hostel-style accommodation and is also a centre for all kinds of mountain activities. Professional guides will take you hiking, pot-holing or rafting, and many other activities, including horse-riding, can be arranged. Families might be interested in the special summer packages, which include bed and board plus a host of family-friendly adventures. These activities are held in Spanish, but many of the guides have at least a smattering of other languages. It's very popular with Spanish schools.
✉ La Vega de Liébana, Potes ☎ 942 73 60 48 🖐 Accommodation in rooms for 2, 4, 6 and 8. Half pension from €25–€40 per person. Prices for activities vary

FOTOGRAFÍA BUSTAMANTE
This shop in the main plaza is a useful stop if you are touring round the Picos de Europa area. There's a good selection of guides, maps and

information about the region, plus souvenir postcards, posters and photos of local landmarks.
✉ Calle Capitán Palacios 10, 39570 Potes ☎ 942 73 01 04 🕐 Mon–Sat 10–9

MERCADO DE POTES
Since the 13th century, Potes has hosted a traditional street market every Monday. Browse or buy some of the delicious regional products, such as the exquisite Picón Bejes-Tresviso cheeses, juicy apples and pears, and local liqueurs.
✉ 39570 Potes 🕐 Mon 9–2

SAN LÁZARO
SOCIEDAD DEPORTIVA COMPOSTELA
This soccer team once played in the first division of the Spanish national league, but is now struggling to make the second division.
✉ Estadio San Lázaro, Barrio San Lázaro s/n, 15703 San Lázaro ☎ 981 58 06 71 🖐 €15, €25, €30 🚌 6

SANTANDER
CAFÉ NAROBA
Large place decked out like an Irish pub but with some regional touches. A good choice for a coffee or beer from the wide selection on offer. Folk music is usually played and live bands perform once a month on Thursdays.
✉ Perines 42, 39007 Santander ☎ 942 37 12 60 🕐 Jul–Sep daily 6pm–1am (until 2am weekends); Oct–Jun daily 5pm–1am (until 2am weekends) 🚌 1, 2, 3, 5, 6, 7

CANELA
Located at the heart of Santander's thriving nightlife scene, Canela is hip, lively and filled with a friendly, crowd. It's also a top spot for cheap cocktails and live music on Tuesday.
✉ Plaza de Cañadío s/n, 39003 Santander. ☎ 942 27 42 60 🕐 Daily 9pm–late 🖐 Free

CAMPO DE GOLF DE MATALEÑAS
www.golfmatalenas.com
At this public nine-hole golf course no membership is required. Facilities include dressing-rooms, showers,

lockers, parking, bowling, restaurant, bar and cafeteria. Instruction is available.
✉ Avenida del Faro s/n, 39012 Santander ☎ 942 39 27 75 🕐 Daily 8am–10pm 🖐 Green fee: €20–€300. Rental bag of 35 balls: €2 🚌 9

CENTRO CULTURAL CAJA CANTABRIA
www.cajacantabria.com
The building may date back to 1907, but the facilities are up to date, with a good selection of classical music, theatre, film screenings and jazz. There are also two exhibition halls.
✉ Calle Tantín 25, 39001 Santander ☎ 942 20 43 00; advance sales 902 12 12 12 🖐 Varies 🚌 5C

LA DESPENSA
http://ladespensasantander.es.tl/
Housed in an old pharmacy, La Despensa is among an increasing number of trendy wine bars to hit the city scene. It offers a solid selection of Spanish wines-by-the-glass to down with equally trendy tapas.
✉ Calle Daoiz y Velarde 15, 39003 Santander ☎ 942 07 10 88 🕐 Mon–Sat 11–4, 7–1.30

FILMOTECA REGIONAL DE CANTABRIA
www.palaciofestivales.com/cine.html
An art-house cinema with three screenings a day and foreign films in their original version. Also a library, video room and exhibition halls.
✉ Calle Bonifaz 6, 39003 Santander ☎ 902 12 12 12 🕐 Jun–Aug Tue–Sat; Sep–May Wed–Sun 🖐 €2.50–€6 🚌 1

JOTA
Jota has a fine selection of watches, wallets, jewellery, bags and belts. It also sells clothes, handmade furniture, tableware and table linen. There's another branch at Calle de Becedo 1, next to the town hall.
✉ Calle Burgos 7, 39008 Santander ☎ 942 37 64 52 🕐 Mon–Fri 10–8, Sat 10.30–2, 5–8.30 🚌 1, 2, 3, 4, 5, 6, 7, 8, 9

Opposite *Once found only around A Coruña, Queso Tetilla cheeses are now a typical product of the whole region of Galicia*

LIBRERÍA ESTUDIO

One of the oldest bookshops in the city, this place sells everything from the latest best sellers and children's books to textbooks on architecture, philosophy, art and science. There is also a variety of travel guides, dictionaries and magazines. Another branch is at Calle Calvo Sotelo 21, 39002 Santander.

✉ Calle Burgos 5, 39008 Santander
☎ 942 37 49 50 ⏰ Mon–Fri 9.30–1.30, 4–8 (Jun–Aug 5–8.30), Sat 10–2, 5–8.30
🚌 1, 2, 3, 4, 5, 6, 7, 8, 9

MERCADILLO DEL TÚNEL

A good Sunday morning market for crafts, jewellery or eccentric clothing. Also for sale are antiques, furniture, antiquarian books, comics, landscape paintings, bags, clocks and porcelain figures. Come early.

Below *Browse the bookshops in Santander*

✉ Pasaje de Peña, 39008 Santander
⏰ Sun 9.30–2 🚌 1, 2, 3, 4, 5, 6, 7, 8, 9, 10

MERCADO DE LA ESPERANZA

This market occupies a huge, late 19th-century iron, stone and glass building. On the ground floor you can pick up fresh, locally caught fish, while on the upper floor there are meat, fruit and vegetable stands. Spanish sausage stands spill outside, and on Monday and Thursday there is a clothes market.

✉ Plaza de la Esperanza, 39002 Santander
☎ 942 22 05 29 ⏰ Mon–Fri 8–2, 5–7.30, Sat 8–2 🚌 1

PALACIO DE FESTIVALES

www.palaciofestivales.com
Shows and performances throughout the year include classical music, dance, opera, musicals and theatre.

There are also special film screenings.

✉ Calle Gamazo s/n, 39004 Santander
☎ 942 36 16 06 💶 €6–€40 🚌 1

SANTIAGO DE COMPOSTELA

A MOUGA

This traditional craft store in the historic quarter, has the best variety of hand-made ceramics and glassware, as well as antiques, vintage garments, silk shawls and linen quilts. You can pick up old photographs, cookbooks and traditional music, as well as wines, liqueurs and preserved foods here.

✉ Rúa de Xelmírez 26, 15704 Santiago de Compostela ☎ 981 56 07 96 ⏰ Mon–Sat 10.30–2, 4.30–8; closed Sep–May Sat pm
🚌 1, 2, 4, 8

AREA CENTRAL

www.acentral.com
This huge, two-storey shopping area has more than 160 shops. The Alcampo hypermarket is a good place for culinary souvenirs. For fashion, try Purificación García, Bershka and Zara. There are also jewellery shops, furniture shops and beauty salons.

✉ Polígono Fontiñas, Calle Sótano 1, 15707 Santiago de Compostela ☎ 981 56 08 45
⏰ Daily 9am–10pm; shops closed on Sun
🚌 11, 11bis, C2

AUDITORIO DE GALICIA

www.auditoriodegalicia.org
Santiago's most important venue for classical music concerts, and the permanent home of the Real Orquesta Sinfónica de Galicia, also hosts opera and dance.

✉ Avenida Burgos das Nácions s/n, 15705 Santiago de Compostela ☎ 981 55 22 90
💶 €10–€40 🚌 15

BEGON

Begon sells all kinds of furniture, including wooden tables and chairs, sofas and chests. It also stocks accessories for the home, such as frames, mirrors, paintings, vases, carpets, lamps and tableware. The shop specializes in brands like Baccarat and Valentí.

✉ Rúa Ramón Cabanillas 6, 15701 Santiago de Compostela ☎ 981 53 15 47

Mon–Fri 10–1.30, 4.30–8, Sat 10–2

1, 2, 4, 8

CASA DAS CRECHAS

www.casadascrechas.com

This beautiful space in the old quarter is a great place to enjoy a cool beer while listening to live music concerts (usually folk or Celtic).

Via Sacra 3, 15704 Santiago de Compostela ☎ 981 56 07 51 Daily noon–3.30am; winter daily from 4pm

Free 1, 2, 4, 8

CONVENTO SAN PELAYO

http://monasteriosanpelayo.com

The convent has become popular for the cake the nuns bake here: *torta de Santiago*, a succulent almond pastry. The nuns sell other confections as well.

Calle Ante-Altares 23, 15704 Santiago de Compostela ☎ 981 58 31 27 Mon–Fri 8.30–7, Sat 9–2.15, 3.30–7, Sun 9.30–11.30, 1–2.15, 4.30–7 1, 2, 4, 8

DADÓ-DADÁ

http://jazzclub.dadodada.com

A long-established jazz club, Dadó-Dadá features live acts most nights, as well as jam sessions every Tuesday. Jazz isn't the only sound you'll hear, though: the club also hosts classical and folk music performances, and even magic shows. It's an intimate space, with galleries overlooking the stage.

Rúa Alfredo Brañas, 19, Santiago de Compostela ☎ 981 59 15 74 Daily 8pm–3am

FOLLAS NOVAS

A well-known bookstore, especially among students, Follas Novas covers three floors and stocks a variety of subjects, including classic literature, children's books, paperbacks, travel guides and dictionaries.

Rúa Montero Ríos 37, 15706 Santiago de Compostela ☎ 981 59 44 06 Mon–Fri 9.30–2, 4.30–8, Sat 9.30–2, 4–8.30 1, 2, 5, 10, 11, 12, 15

SALA CAPITOL

www.salacapitol.com

This central theatre is one of the city's best venues for visiting pop acts. The

JUNE

SAN JUAN

Processions with giants and wonderful costumes, and fireworks all over the region.

Galicia

JULY

FIESTA DE LLANES

Asturian sports, tightrope walking and music.

Llanes

FIESTA DE SANTIAGO

▷ 448.

Santiago de Compostela

AUGUST

INTERNATIONAL SANTANDER FESTIVAL

Music and cultural festival.

Santander

programme features a whole range of musical styles—garage, hip hop, funk, electronica and much more. You might also catch comedians or cabaret, or even football matches shown live on an enormous screen. The website has full details of the programme.

Rúa Concepcion Arenal 5, 15702 Santiago de Compostela ☎ 991 57 43 99 From €14 1, 2, 4, 8

SALA NASA

www.salanasa.com

A modern theatre and music venue, Sala Nasa is devoted to local artists and new forms of artistic expression. It stages cabaret, folk, blues, flamenco and rock concerts.

Rúa San Lourenzo 51–53B, 15705 Santiago de Compostela ☎ 981 57 39 98 €3–€20 1, 2, 4, 8

VINOTECA O BEIRO

http://obeiro.com

This delightful, wood-panelled wine shop, just a stone's throw from the cathedral, offers a wonderful range of international and Spanish wines,

EL ROSARIO

Sea procession of fishermen in tribute to the Virgin.

Luarca

SEPTEMBER

AMERICAS DAY

Celebrates Latin-American emigrants.

All over Asturias 19 September

EXALTACIÓN DE LA CRUZ

Activities and entertainment, sports and games, with theatre for children and fireworks.

Potes 14–16 September

including a fine selection from Galicia. The well-informed staff are happy to make recommendations, or you can try the wines out in the adjoining bar (there are around 75 wines available by the glass). Tastings and other events are held.

Rúa Raiña 3, 15703 Santiago de Compostela ☎ 981 58 13 70 Daily 11–1.30, 6–1 1, 2, 4, 8

SOMO

ESCUELA CANTABRA DE SURF

www.escuelacantabradesurf.com

Learn to surf or bodyboard at this large and long-established surfing school, on the beach at Somo, on the outskirts of the Cantabrian capital of Santander. They offer a wide range of classes for all levels, as well as equipment rental. Accommodation can be arranged for longer courses. The summer Surfcamp starts at €80 per day per person, and includes instruction, equipment rental, accommodation and meals.

Paseo Marítimo S/N, Somo (Cantabria) ☎ 942 51 06 15 Surf lessons from €25 for two hours.

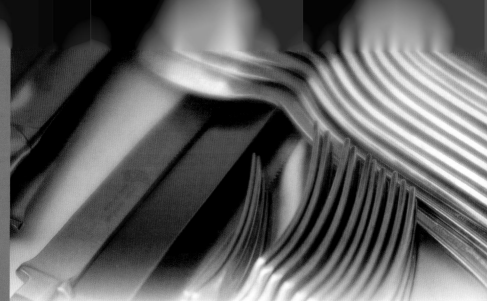

PRICES AND SYMBOLS

The restaurants are listed alphabetically (excluding El, Le, La and Les). The prices given are the average for a two-course lunch (L) and a three-course dinner (D) for one person, without drinks. The wine price is for the least expensive bottle.

For a key to the symbols, ▷ 2.

A CORUÑA
GAIOSO

www.gaiosorestaurante.com

In this elegant, modern restaurant in the heart of A Coruña's atmospheric old quarter, you will find original cuisine prepared with the finest local produce, resulting in such delectable dishes as scallops with sweet onion mousse, or monkfish with sea urchins and clams. The wine list is carefully chosen.

✉ Calle Puerta de Aires 4, 15001 A Coruña ☎ 981 20 02 74 🕒 Tue–Sat 1.30–3, 9–11.30, Sun 1.30–3. Closed 2 weeks in Feb/Mar and 2 weeks in Sep/Oct 🖐 L €38, D €46, Wine €16

CABEZÓN DE LA SAL
LA VILLA

www.restaurantelavillacabezon.com

A simple bar-restaurant in the centre of this old salt-mining town, this is a good option for classic local favourites. There is a well-priced

menú del día (under €10) available on weekdays, or go à la carte and try one of the local fish or meat dishes. The *cocido* (a meaty stew) is highly recommended. The bar serves tapas, and there's a little terrace overlooking the main square, good for morning coffee.

✉ Plaza de la Bodega s/n, 39500 Cabezón de la Sal ☎ 942 70 17 04 🕒 Tue–Sat 9am–midnight, Sun 10–4 (daily in Aug) 🖐 L €14, D €32, Wine €10

CANGAS DE ONÍS
LOS ARCOS

www.loslagos.as

Headed by chef Ramón Celorio, Los Arcos is a welcome antidote to the rather heavy cuisine of the region. A traditional *sidrería* (cider bar) serving tapas is attached. This restaurant is part of a simple but attractive hotel.

✉ Avenida Covadonga 17, 33550 Cangas de Onís ☎ 985 84 92 77 🕒 Daily 1.30–4, 8.30–12. Closed 10–20 Jan 🖐 L €35, D €45, Menu €30, Wine €18

EL CENADOR DE LOS CANÓNIGOS

www.hotellacepada.com

El Cenador is a luxurious place. The seasonal menu combines international and modern Spanish cuisine. The extensive wine list has only Spanish wines. The attached

hotel is modern and luxurious with views of the Picos de Europa.

✉ Hotel La Cepada, Avenida de Contranquil s/n, 33550 Cangas de Onís ☎ 985 84 94 45 🕒 Tue–Sat 1–4, 9–12, Sun 1–4 🖐 L €45, D €45, Wine €14

EL HUERTO DEL ERMITAÑO

www.elhuertodelermitanodecovadonga.com

This friendly restaurant by Covadonga's cave sanctuary serves regional cuisine such as *fabada* (sausage and bean stew) and traditional fish and meat dishes. Locals recommend this place as one of the best in the area. Stone walls and beamed ceilings provide a rustic, romantic setting.

✉ Real Sitio de Covadonga 25, 33589 Cangas de Onís ☎ 985 84 60 97 🕒 Jul–Oct daily 11am–midnight; Nov–Jun Sun–Thu 12–5, Fri–Sat 12–5, 8.30–12 🖐 L €23, D €42, Wine €12

EL MOLÍN DE LA PEDRERA

www.elmolin.com

This *sidrería* boasts rustic interior design with stylish modern touches, and a short, but well-chosen menu of creative tapas and more substantial dishes. Try the *faba asturiana*, a sturdy local stew with beans, flavoured with piquant chorizo and *morcilla* (black pudding). The desserts include a fluffy chocolate charlotte.

✉ Rio Güeña 2, 33550 Cangas de Onís ☎ 985 84 91 09 🕒 Thu–Mon 11–11. Closed Jan 🍴 L €25, D €30, Wine €12

CASTRO-URDIALES
MESÓN EL MARINERO
www.mesonmarinero.com

Linger over the succulent *marmita de langosta* (lobster stew) at this traditional tavern, which overlooks the picturesque fishing port in Castro-Urdiales. Choose a table by the window to enjoy the best views. Even if you aren't tempted by the splendid selection of seafood in the dining rooms you can't fail to be moved by the long tapas bar which groans with a seemingly unending array of *pinchos* (canapés). Staff are friendly and happy to make recommendations.

✉ Calle Correría 32 Bajo, 39700 Castro-Urdiales ☎ 942 86 00 05 🕒 Daily 10am–midnight 🍴 L €23, D €30, Wine €14

COMILLAS
GUREA
The restaurant is housed in an old townhouse, complete with thick wooden beams and columns. Although it's near the beach, the menu offers traditional mountain dishes as well as offerings from the sea. Classic Cantabrian recipes are found side-by-side with more adventurous fare, with dishes, such as hake with crayfish sauce, served with skewered prawns, asparagus and mushrooms, as well as the classic steak served with wild mushroom sauce.

✉ Calle Ignacio Fernández de Castro 11, 39520 Comillas ☎ 942 72 24 46 🕒 Mon–Sat 2–4, 8.30–11 (daily in Aug) 🍴 L €30, D €45, Wine €14

FISTERRA
O FRAGÓN
With a pretty setting opposite the fortress of San Carlos in this fishing town at the 'end of the world' (Fisterra), this traditional, wood-panelled tavern offers typical Galician cuisine. The house specialty is local fish, grilled barbecue style, but the menu offers plenty of other choices. Try to get a table out on the terrace

if possible, which enjoys wonderful views over the port with its busy fishing vessels.

✉ Rúa Ribeira, 15155 Fisterra ☎ 659 07 73 20 (mobile) 🕒 Thu–Tue 1.30–3.30, 8.30–10.30 🍴 L €24, D €35, Wine €12

GIJÓN
EL PERRO QUE FUMA
www.elperroquefuma.com

This attractive restaurant on the outskirts of Gijón is decorated in ochre and vanilla tones. Its name means 'the smoking dog', and the sign depicts a solemn spaniel smoking a pipe. The menu changes with the season, highlighting the best local produce, and focuses on modern versions of Spanish classics. The beef *canelone* with mango and yogurt sauce is delicious, as is the chocolate soufflé served with banana ice-cream. There's a great fixed-price lunch menu available from Tuesday to Friday (€18).

✉ Calle Poeta Ángel González 18, 33204 Gijón ☎ 984 19 34 93 🕒 Tue–Sat 1.30–4, 9–12, Sun 1.30–4 🍴 L €25, D €45, Wine €14

LA PONDALA
www.lapondala.com

La Pondala, established in 1899, is a classic in the region. The attractive restaurant is set in gardens in the village of Somió, 3km (2 miles) east of the Asturian capital of Gijón and is very popular for family gatherings. They serve typical local dishes like *guisos* (stews) and fresh *merluza* (hake), but the restaurant is most famous for classic paellas and other Spanish rice dishes.

✉ Avenida de Dionisio Cifuentes 58, 33203 Somió ☎ 985 36 11 60 🕒 Fri–Tue 1.30–3.30, 8–10.30. Closed 2 weeks in Jun and 2 weeks in Nov 🍴 L €35, D €45, Wine €14

LAREDO
CAMAROTE
Arguably the best shellfish restaurant in the resort of Laredo, Camarote is located a couple of streets back from the seafront. Always busy, with traditional marine decoration and cheerful waiters, it's very popular

with tourists and locals alike. They have their own *viveros* (fisheries) which produce a wide variety of shellfish, ensuring all the produce is spectacularly fresh. Try local dishes like the clam stew, or go for the simply grilled fish of the day.

✉ Avenida de la Victoria s/n, 39770 Laredo ☎ 942 60 67 07 🕒 Mon–Sat 1.30–4, 8.30–12, Sun 1.30–4. Closed Wed in winter 🍴 L €40, D €45, Wine €15

LUGO
MESÓN DE ALBERTO
wwww.mesondealberto.com

This classic restaurant occupies an elegant stone mansion in Lugo's historic centre. On the ground floor, the cosy bar serves a wide array of tapas, and is buzzing with locals. The upper floors have elegant, traditionally furnished dining rooms. The Mesón de Alberto is well known for its hearty traditional cuisine—succulent stews and roast meats from the Galician interior, as well as wonderful fresh shellfish and seafood from the coast. Try some of the delicious local cheeses. The wine list offers some fine local wines, including delicious Albariño wines which are perfect with seafood, and a selection from the rest of Spain.

✉ Calle Cruz 4, 27001 Lugo ☎ 982 22 83 10 🕒 Mon–Sat 1.30–4, 8.30–10.30 🍴 L €28, D €42, Wine €12

VERRUGA
www.verruga.es

This classic, family-run tavern in the heart of Lugo's historic centre has been going strong for more than 50 years. It's small, with just 14 tables, but you can also stand up at the bar. It's popular with locals, keen to sample Galician specialties such as the mouthwatering *caldo Gallego* (a hearty broth). Prime quality fish and meat are used in the simple recipes, and the desserts are all home-made.

✉ Calle Cruz 12, 27001 Lugo ☎ 982 22 95 72 🕒 Tue–Sat 1–4, 8–12, Sun 1–4 🍴 L €30, D €40, Wine €12

Opposite *You can eat well in this region*

OVIEDO

CASA CAMILA

www.casacamila.com

With a panoramic setting in the hills above Oviedo, this elegant hotel-restaurant has a wonderful terrace to enjoy the views down over the old town in the valley below. On the menu, you'll find classic local favourites, such as *fabada asturiana* (a sturdy and flavoursome pork and bean stew) or Asturian beef with chestnut purée, as well as good seafood. Go for the fixed-price *menu asturiana* (€28) which includes the famous *fabada* and is accompanied by Asturian cider as well as wine.

✉ Calle Fitoria 28, 33011 Oviedo ☎ 985 11 48 22 🕔 Wed–Sun 1.30–3.30, 9–11, Mon 1.30–3.30 🍴 L €30, D €45, Wine €14

OVIÑANA

CABO VIDÍO

www.cabovidio.com

This pretty, stone-built, rural hotel-restaurant is located a short drive west of the fishing town and tourist resort of Cudillero. The restaurant is glass-fronted on one side, offering views of the verdant gardens. The menu features creative versions of traditional Asturian recipes, and has a particularly fine selection of fresh seafood. The *calderetas* (local fish stews) are house specialties.

✉ Las Chavolas, 33156 Oviñana ☎ 985 59 61 12 🕔 Daily 2–4, 8.30–11 🍴 L €28, D €38, Wine €14

PONTEVEDRA

ALAMEDA 10

www.restaurantealameda10.com

A long-established favourite in the heart of Pontevedra, the Alameda serves refined Galician cuisine accompanied by an extensive selection of wines. The menu offers a wide range of dishes, including meat, fish and shellfish—this is a good place to try *percebes* (barnacles), which are a local delicacy. The bar area offers more informal dining.

✉ Calle Alameda 10, 36001 Pontevedra ☎ 986 85 74 12 🕔 Mon–Sat 1.30–3.30, 8.30–10.30 (restaurant) 🍴 L €30, D €45, Wine €15

POTES

PACO WENCES

In one of the main towns of the spectacular Picos de Europa, this rustically decorated, comfortable restaurant offers reliably good mountain fare. The house specialty is *cocido lebaniego*, a succulent stew which provides perfect comfort food for tired walkers, but the roast meats (including particularly fine local lamb) are also recommended. The restaurant can be found in the Hotel Valdecoro, near Potes.

✉ Calle Roscabado 5, 39570 Potes ☎ 942 73 00 25 🕔 Daily 1.30–3, 8.30–10. Closed Jan 🍴 L €35, D €40, Wine €12

RIBADESELLA

LA PARRILLA

The name means 'the grill' and that's how your fresh shellfish, fish and meat will be prepared at this simple restaurant. It may not look like much from the outside, perched as it is on the side of the main road out of town, but this old-fashioned *tasca* has a fine reputation for selecting its fresh produce with the utmost care. Try the *cigalas a la plancha*—grilled crayfish—or the fish of the day and don't miss the home-made charlotte for dessert.

✉ Calle Palacio Valdés 28, 33560 Ribadesella ☎ 985 86 02 88 🕔 Tue–Sat 2–4, 9–11, Sun 2–4. Closed one month in Oct–Nov 🍴 L €30, D€42, Wine €14

SAN SALVADOR DE POIO

CASA SOLLA

www.restaurantesolla.com

Tradition and modernity combine in both the architecture and cuisine at this stunning restaurant. Exciting young chef José González-Solla prepares sublime, inventive contemporary cuisine using the finest regional produce. A stone *pazo* (country house) has had a glassy refit with sleek minimalist furnishings. Garden views and excellent service complete the picture.

✉ Avenida Sineiro 7, 36005 San Salvador de Poio ☎ 986 87 28 84 🕔 Tue–Wed, Fri–Sat 1.30–4, 9–11.30; Thu and Sun 1.30–4. Closed 2 weeks at Christmas 🍴 L €55, D €65, Wine €18

SANTANDER

BODEGA DEL RIOJANO

This is a traditional place in the Zona Maritima that is worth a visit. It serves tapas (cheeses and Spanish sausages) or you can eat in the restaurant.

✉ Calle Río de la Pila 5, 39003 Santander ☎ 942 21 67 50 🕔 Tue–Sat 11.30–4.30, 7–12, Sun 11.30–4.30 🍴 L €20, D €38, Wine €12

BODEGUCA

A traditional restaurant where you can try the region's best-known dishes, all prepared as they would be at home. The desserts are excellent, especially the cheesecake.

✉ Calle Santa Lucía 61, 39003 Santander ☎ 942 21 89 52 🕔 Tue–Sun 1–4, 8–12. Closed Nov 🍴 L €25, D €45, Wine €14

LA BOMBI

www.restaurantelabombi.com

La Bombi is a long-established Santander restaurant that serves regional cuisine with the emphasis on seafood and fish. The service is excellent.

✉ Calle Casimiro Sáinz 15, 39003 Santander ☎ 942 21 30 28 🕔 Mon–Sat 1–4, 8–12 🍴 L €45, D €65, Wine €14

LAURY

www.restaurantelaury.es

A chic and modern seafood restaurant serving the freshest catch from the Bay of Biscay. It has its own aquarium, and you'll find king prawns, lobsters, shrimps and more on the menu. There is a superb wine cellar. Laury also serves as a tapas bar. Reserving a table is advisable.

✉ Avenida Pedro San Martín 4, 39010 Santander ☎ 942 33 01 09 🕔 Daily 12–4, 8.30–11.30 🍴 L €35, D €60, Wine €10

MACHINERO

www.machinero.com

This friendly restaurant is decorated simply and serves tasty regional dishes with a special touch. There are home-made desserts and a good wine selection. A cafeteria under the same roof serves pastries and sandwiches. There is a terrace for dining out in summer.

Compostela ☎ 981 55 85 80 🕐 Tue–Sat 1.30–3.30 and 9.45–11.30. Closed Oct–Mar 🖐 Set Menu only €75, Wine €24

CASTRO

www.castrohotel.com

Castro, a restaurant in a hotel of the same name, specializes in regional cuisine, with a good selection of fresh fish, seafood and meat dishes. The wine list comprises mainly Galician offerings. ✉ Rúa Formarís 22–23, 15884 Santiago de Compostela ☎ 981 50 93 04 🕐 Mon–Sat 8am–midnight. Closed 25 Dec and 6 Jan 🖐 L €25, D €42, Wine €15 🚗 From Santiago, head north towards A Coruña for 3km (2 miles). Castro is just beyond the Polígono del Tambre

FORNOS

Fornos is known for its good traditional Galician cuisine served in an elegant setting at reasonable prices. The house specials of seafood, fish and meats are a feast for the palate. Wheelchair access is provided at the main entrance and there is parking opposite. ✉ Rúa Hórreo 24, 15702 Santiago de Compostela ☎ 981 56 57 21 🕐 Mon–Sat 12.30–4.30, 8.30–12 🖐 L €24 *(menú de la casa)*, D €45, Wine €12

MONCHO VILAS

The best-loved dishes are Galician: stews, *empanadas* (deep-fried pastries) and the house special, Vilas-style beef. It's an old-fashioned, traditional place, now run by the third generation of the family who founded it. Some of the original recipes are still on the menu, but they have been joined by new dishes too. ✉ Avenida de Villagarcía 21, 15706 Santiago de Compostela ☎ 981 59 83 87 🕐 Tue–Sat 1–6, 8.30–12, Sun 1.30–4.30 🖐 L €35, D €48, Wine €10

SAN CLEMENTE

San Clemente is decorated in contemporary style, with two terraces for alfresco dining. The house specials are seafood, fish and traditional Galician cuisine. In addition, tapas and dishes from other Spanish regions are also served. A wide range of Galician wines and Riojas is available. There is a public parking area close by. ✉ Calle San Clemente 6, 15705 Santiago de Compostela ☎ 981 58 08 82 🕐 Tue–Sun 11am–1.30am; Aug daily 🖐 L €22, D €45, Wine €12

TOÑI VICENTE

www.tonivicente.com

Toñi Vicente is an authority on modern Galician cuisine and her superb restaurant has a well-deserved Michelin star. There's also an extensive wine list. ✉ Avenida Rosalía de Castro 24, 15706 Santiago de Compostela ☎ 981 59 41 00 🕐 Mon–Sat 1.30–3.30, 9–11. Closed Sun, Christmas 🖐 L €52, D €65, Wine €18

SANTILLANA DEL MAR
ALTAMIRA

www.hotelaltamira.com

A 16th-century mansion, rebuilt in the 19th century, is the setting for this simple yet classy restaurant. It has gained a reputation for its local game, cod and rice dishes. Dining on the summer terrace is a bonus. ✉ Calle Cantón 1, 39330 Santillana del Mar ☎ 942 81 80 25 🕐 Daily 1–4, 8–11 🖐 L €25, D €45, Wine €15

SAN VICENTE DE LA BARQUERA
MARUJA

www.restaurantemaruja.com

One of the prettiest resorts on the Costa Verde, San Vicente de la Barquera is still a thriving fishing port. Try the local catch at Maruja, which is perfectly located in the redolent old quarter and has been going since 1941. It prepares sophisticated dishes such as *buñelos de bacalo con salsa de erizos de mar* (cod puffs with sea anemones). The desserts are excellent, and include a superb chocolate and bitter orange tart. There's also a good wine list. ✉ Avenida del Generalisimo s/n, 39540 San Vicente de la Barquera ☎ 942 71 00 77 🕐 Mon–Sat 1.30–4, 8.30–12, Sun 1.30–4. Closed Wed in winter 🖐 L €45, D €55, Wine €16

✉ Calle Ruiz de Alda 16, 39009 Santander ☎ 942 31 49 21 🕐 Mon–Sat 1–4, 9–11.30. Closed two weeks in Oct 🖐 L €15, D €35, Wine €12

SANTIAGO DE COMPOSTELA
A BARROLA

www.restaurantesgrupobarrola.com

A Barrola, in the heart of the old city, is a great place to sample some of the best Galician seafood in town. ✉ Rúa Franco 29, 15701 Santiago de Compostela ☎ 981 57 79 99 🕐 Daily 10–5, 8.30–12 🖐 L €20, D €35, Wine €14

CAMILO

This well-established restaurant has specialized in seafood, fish, grills and tapas since 1942. There is a public parking area very close to the restaurant. ✉ Rúa Raíña 24, 15705 Santiago de Compostela ☎ 981 58 45 93 🕐 Daily 1–5, 8–12 🖐 L €35, D €44, Wine €12

CASA MARCELO

www.casamarcelo.net

Chef Marcelo Tejedor is currently recognized as one of Galicia's most innovative cooks. He's comfortable enough in his kitchen to offer just one set menu that changes daily. The result is extraordinary. ✉ Rúa Hortas 1, 15705 Santiago de

Above *Tables set for lunch*

PRICES AND SYMBOLS

The prices are for a double room for one night including breakfast, unless otherwise stated. All the hotels listed accept credit cards unless otherwise stated. Note that rates can vary widely throughout the year.

For a key to the symbols, ▷ 2.

CUDILLERO
CASONA DE LA PACA

www.casonadelapaca.com

A beautiful 19th-century mansion, built by Indianos (returning emigrants who had made fortunes in the Americas), this is now a rural hotel in the hills above the seaside resort of Cudillero. You can choose between elegantly furnished rooms in the main house, or self-catering accommodation in the annexe. This latter option is good for families, as some apartments have a small private garden. The house itself is surrounded by magnolias, camellias and oak trees. Breakfasts include freshly squeezed juices, local cheeses and charcuterie.

✉ El Pito, 33150 Cudillero ☎ 985 59 13 03 🌐 Closed mid-Dec to Feb 💶 €85–€110;

apartments €75–€95 ⓘ 19, plus 10 apartments

FUENTE DÉ
PARADOR DE FUENTE DÉ

www.parador.es

This comfortable hotel nestles at the foot of the Picos de Europa. Other features are a bar, access for visitors with disabilities, telephone, satellite TV, minibar, safe-box, children's play area, gardens and a shop.

✉ Carretera de Fuente Dé s/n, 39588 Fuente Dé ☎ 942 73 66 51 🌐 Closed mid-Nov to mid-Mar 💶 €85–€130 excluding breakfast (€14) ⓘ 78 (15 non-smoking) 🅿 🔲 The hotel is at the end of the main road from Potes to Fuente Dé

MESTAS DE PONGA
LA CASONA DE MESTAS

www.casonademestas.com

La Casona de Mestas is a simple but comfortable hotel in the heart of the Picos de Europa. La Casona's special feature is a hot-water spring that supplies the pool and hydro-massage baths. All the bedrooms have a private bathroom but no TV; there is a communal TV lounge.

✉ Las Mestas, Carretera Cangas de Onís–San Juan de Beleño, 33557 Mestas de Ponga ☎ 985 84 30 55 🌐 Closed 15 Jan–28 Feb 💶 €60–€75 including tax, excluding breakfast (€10) ⓘ 14 🅿 🔲 Indoor with thermal water

OVIEDO
DE LA RECONQUISTA

www.hoteldelareconquista.com

This opulent five-star establishment occupies a former hospice, including a magnificent 18th-century facade with a baroque marble doorway, and an interior cloister. Elegant rooms with large marble bathrooms are fully equipped and facilities include a restaurant and cafeteria, a sauna, a hairdresser and boutiques.

✉ Calle Gil de Jaz 16, 33004 Oviedo ☎ 985 24 11 00 💶 €255–€295 ⓘ 142 🅿

PONTEVEDRA
PARADOR DE PONTEVEDRA

www.parador.es

Pontevedra's parador, in an 18th-century pazo (unfortified manor house), is well placed for visiting the sights and for touring the rías.

✉ Calle Barón 19, 36002 Pontevedra
☎ 986 85 58 00 🖐 €135–€175 excluding breakfast 🛈 47 ♿

SANTANDER

APARTAMENTOS ARÁNZAZU
www.grupocastelar.com
These apartments are a good budget option. Apartments are for one or two people, and all have TV, bathroom and a kitchen area.
✉ Calle Mies del Valle 4, 39010 Santander
☎ 942 37 11 00 🖐 €45–€90 excluding breakfast (€5) 🛈 79 apartments ♿

HOTEL CENTRAL
www.elcentral.com
If turn-of-the-century charm is your style, then this small, independent and (as the name suggests) central hotel may be just the ticket. The roof terrace offers perfect views over the rooftops and out to sea.
✉ General Mola, 5, 39005 Santander
☎ 942 22 24 00 🖐 €80–€145 excluding breakfast (€6.30) 🛈 41 ♿

REAL
www.hotelreal.es
All rooms have views of the city and contain satellite TV, a minibar and modem connection. Facilities offered are a laundry, room service, bar, free entry to the casino and a cafeteria with terrace and garden. It also has a thalassotherapy centre.
✉ Calle Pérez Galdós 28, 39005 Santander
☎ 942 27 25 50 🖐 €135–€360 excluding buffet breakfast (€22) 🛈 123 ♿ 🍴

SANTIAGO DE COMPOSTELA

CASA GRANDE DE CORNIDE
www.casagrandedecornide.com
This bed-and-breakfast in a former farmhouse has been restored and turned into modern accommodation. The house also has an extensive library and a beautiful garden. Guests have the use of bicycles.
✉ Cornide, 15886 Cornide-Teo (near Santiago de Compostela) ☎ 981 80 55 99 🕐 Closed 7 Jan–28 Feb 🖐 €60–€105 excluding breakfast (€9) 🛈 11 🌳 Outdoor 🚗 From Santiago take the N550 towards Pontevedra. In Casalonga, 7km (4 miles) from Santiago, take the left turn after the

filling station on the left-hand side; the Casa Grande is 1km (0.5 mile) down this road

HOSTAL LA ESTELA
This small, family-run hostel is right opposite the *parador* (see below). Prices are reasonable despite the location. Half the rooms have their own bathroom, and all are simply furnished. There is no parking area or access for visitors with disabilities, and credit cards are not accepted.
✉ Calle Rajoy 1, 15703 Santiago de Compostela ☎ 981 58 27 96 🖐 €40–€45 for a room with bathroom, excluding breakfast (from €3) and including tax 🛈 14

REYES CATÓLICOS
www.parador.es
The luxurious Reyes Católicos is probably the best and most beautiful *parador* in Spain. Founded in 1499 by the Catholic Monarchs, Ferdinand and Isabella, as a hostel for pilgrims visiting the shrine of St. James (Santiago), it has a prime location in the heart of the old town. Reserve months in advance .The hotel has a parking area, but reserving a space in advance is recommended.
✉ Plaza del Obradoiro 1, 15705 Santiago de Compostela ☎ 981 58 22 00 🖐 €270–€290 excluding breakfast. Special offers (see website for details) and 35 per cent discount for over-60s in winter 🛈 137 ♿

VIRXE DA CERCA
www.pousadasdecompostela.com
All rooms in this beautiful hotel have private bathrooms, satellite TV and hairdryers. The hotel has private gardens and a launderette.
✉ Rúa da Virxe da Cerca 27, 15703 Santiago de Compostela ☎ 981 56 93 50, 902 40 58 58 🖐 €95–€150 excluding breakfast (€8) 🛈 43 ♿

SANTILLANA DEL MAR

ALTAMIRA
www.hotelaltamira.com
The Altamira has comfortable rooms, and is a well-priced alternative in town to the Parador de Santillana del Mar (see right).
✉ Calle Cantón 1, 39330 Santilla del Mar ☎ 942 81 80 25 🖐 €75–€115 excluding breakfast (€12) 🛈 32

CASA DEL MARQUÉS
www.turismosantillanadelmar.com
An aristocratic 16th-century palace, built by the first Marqués de Santillana in the heart of the most beautiful village in Cantabria, this is now a charming small hotel. Antique furnishings and portraits of the original noble owners give it a regal atmosphere. Each of the rooms is individually decorated, with classic prints and elegant rugs, although those on the first floor are generally more spacious and enjoy more light. There is no restaurant, but you'll find plenty of options on the doorstep. Parking is available for a fee (€8).
✉ Calle Cantón 24, 39330 Santillana del Mar ☎ 942 81 88 88 🕐 Closed Dec–Mar 🖐 €135–€205 🛈 15 ♿

PARADOR DE SANTILLANA DEL MAR
www.parador.es
Created from a pair of lovely old mansions in one of the quieter squares in Santillana, this *parador* is a mixture of old (15th- to 16th-century) and new sections.
✉ Plaza Ramón Pelayo 11, 39330 Santillana del Mar ☎ 942 02 80 28 🖐 €165–€175 excluding breakfast (€16) 🛈 28 ♿ Restaurant only

VIGO

PAZO LOS ESCUDOS
www.pazolosescudos.com
A 19th-century palace with glassy modern annexe right on the seafront, this is a luxurious option in Vigo. Rooms are a blend of tradition and modernity, with 21st-century amenities, including WiFi, and sleek contemporary furnishings. Most rooms overlook the lovely gardens or out to sea. The hotel gets its name from the collection of historic stone coats-of-arms from the original palace which are still displayed. There is an excellent restaurant, Alcabre, with a sea-facing terrace, serving Galician cuisine.
✉ Avenida Atlántida 106, 36208 Vigo ☎ 986 82 08 20 🖐 €155–€305 🛈 54 ♿

Opposite *The parador* Reyes Católicos

EUSKADI, NAVARRA AND ARAGÓN

Euskadi is Spain's greenest corner, a lush, mountainous region caught between the Pyrenees and the Atlantic. It's justly famous for its cuisine, and every bar, however humble, will usually provide an extraordinary array of *pintxos*, delicious nibbles which have justifiably been called 'miniature works of art'. This art reaches its apotheosis in San Sebastián (Donostia), the region's gourmet capital. The Basques have their own language, traditions and history, and Euskadi has a distinct charm all its own. Explore the big city delights of Bilbao, with its spectacular museums and buzzy bar life; wander through the elegant seaside resort of San Sebastián (Donostia), curled around a glorious, golden beach; and escape to untouched mountain villages and tiny fishing ports.

Navarra, next door to Euskadi, has a split personality. The mountainous north is distinctly Basque, evidenced in place names and local politics. The plains of the sun-baked south are closer to Castile culturally as well as geographically. The vibrant capital Pamplona, besides hosting the famous Fiesta de San Fermín, is a delightful spot to lose yourself, with its medieval warren of ancient churches and narrow passages. Navarra can claim just a short section of the Pyrenees, but this includes the lovely Valle de Roncal with its steep, cobble-stoned villages. The Camino del Santiago, a branch of which passes through Navarra, has endowed the region with some enchanting Romanesque churches, especially those at Sangüesa and Estella (Lizarra).

Neighbouring Aragón was once the most important kingdom on the Iberian peninsula but now is often overlooked by visitors. This is a shame, because it contains some spectacular corners. Not least of these is the Ordesa y Monte Perdido National Park which encompasses some of the most impressive peaks in the Pyrenees. A world away, in the arid plains to the south, towns and cities like Zaragoza, Teruel and Tarazona boast fine Mudéjar buildings, which feature the intricate brickwork characteristic of Islamic architecture but which was created for the new Christian rulers during the Reconquista.

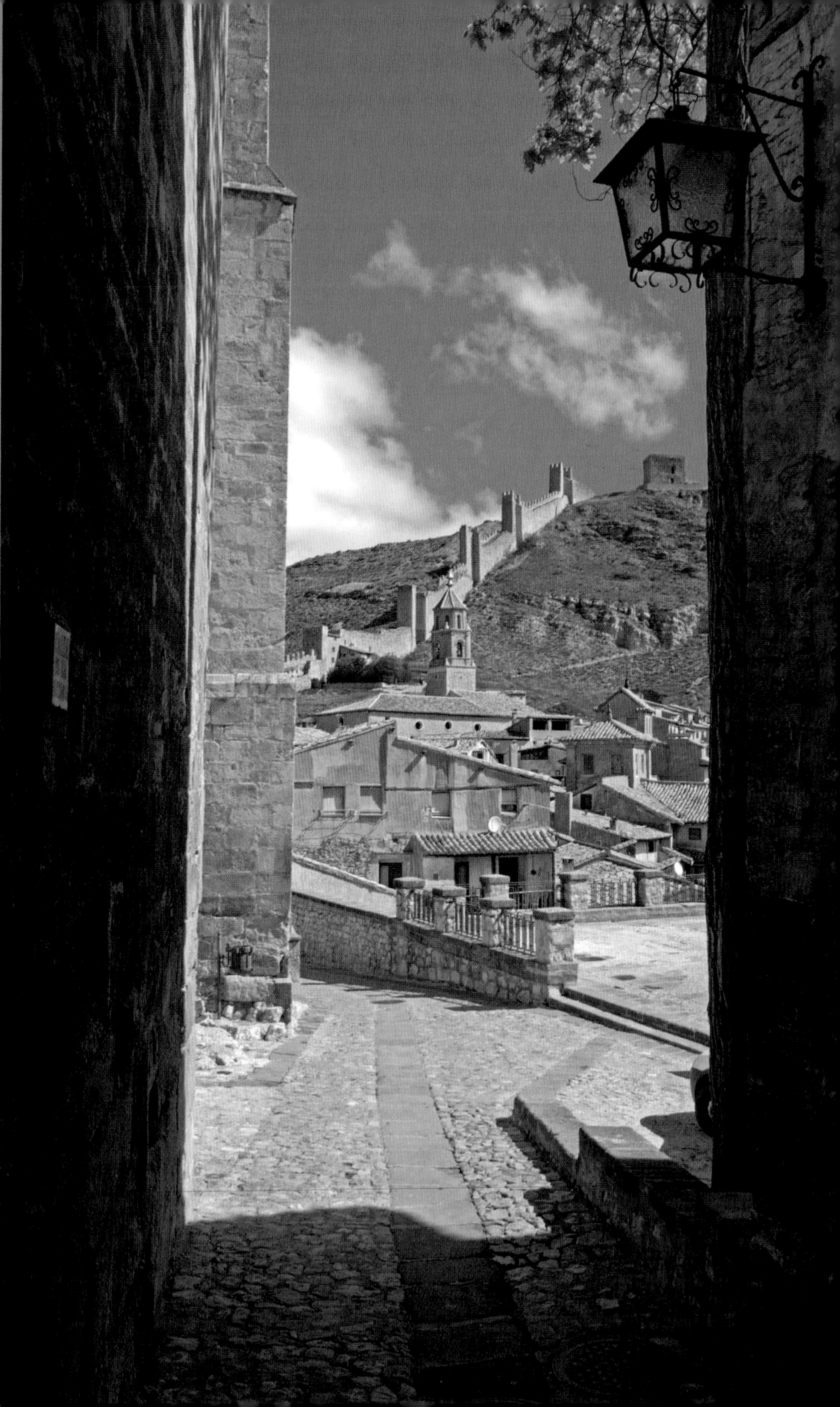

AINSA
www.villadeainsa.com
Built on a promontory overlooking
the confluence of the Ara and Cinca
rivers, Ainsa was once the capital
of a small kingdom formed by Garcí
Jiménez after he defeated the Moors
in 724 outside the city walls.

The arcaded Plaça Mayor in the
heart of the upper old walled town is
full of medieval charm, and entering
it is like taking a step back in time.
The unremarkable new town below
gives rise to a labyrinth of cobbled
streets, arches and alleyways, all
converging on the Plaça Mayor,
where outdoor cafés open in
summer. The Romanesque parish
church of Santa María, with its solid
belfry tower and cloisters, is Ainsa's
main focal point. You can climb the
belfry for wonderful views.
🔢 466 L3 🛈 Avenida Pirenaica 1, 22330
Ainsa ☎ 974 50 07 67

ALBARRACÍN
www.turismoaragon.com
On the northeastern edge of the
Montes Universales, along a ridge
above the Río Guadalaviar, the
medieval walls of Albarracín sweep
up the hillside. As you arrive from
Teruel you are treated to a panorama
of the town, rising before you in a
concave crescent. A patchwork of
ochre shades can be seen in the
perfectly preserved walls, which still
retain their turrets, while in town
there are distinctive tall buildings with
overhanging upper floors. The Plaza
Mayor is reached via the El Túnel
gate, and houses the 16th-century
ayuntamiento (town hall), the Palacio
Episcopal and the small cathedral,
which has a fine wooden retablo
(altarpiece) depicting the life of St.
Peter. Between 1170 and 1284 this
picturesque town was an entirely
independent state, known as the
kingdom of the Azagras.
🔢 470 J5 🛈 Calle Diputación 4, 44100
Albarracín ☎ 978 71 02 51

Opposite View of the medieval walls
of Albarracín

Right *The greystone town of Benasque*
attracts walkers, climbers and skiers

ALQUÉZAR
www.alquezar.org
The lively town of Alquézar, gateway
to the Sierra de Guara, is the main
base for exploring the mountains
and its sculpted gorges. In town, the
eighth-century Moorish fortress (the
alcázar that gave the town its name)
sits on a pinnacle overlooking the Río
Vero and is reached through a twist
of arcaded streets.

Within its defences stands the
Colegiata de Santa María la Mayor,
built by Christians in the 12th
century. The Gothic-Renaissance
church, designed by Juan de Moreto,
houses a collection of baroque art.
Only the cloisters remain from the
Romanesque period. Puente de
Villacantal, a bridge spanning the Río
Vero, was built by the Romans.
🔢 466 L3 🛈 Calle Nueva 14, 22145
Alquézar ☎ 974 31 89 40

BENASQUE
www.benasque.com
With the towering masses of Pico de
Aneto (3,404m/11,168ft) and Pico
Posets (3,371m/11,060ft) nearby, lies
this charming stone town.

The area has a mix of challenging
walking routes and easier going
terrain. Other popular outdoor
activities include skiing, mountain-
bicycling, horseback riding,
canyoning and paragliding.

In town cobbled streets, steeply
pitched roofs and wooden shuttered
windows reflect a typical Pyrenean
style. The 13th-century Iglesia
de Santa María la Mayor, the 16th-

century Casa Juste (a private fortified
house) and the Renaissance Palacio
de los Condes de Ribagorza, a private
house, are of particular interest.

If you're in the area on 23 June,
look for the Midsummer Night
Celebrations in Sahún, 6km (4 miles)
away. Bonfires are lit outside the
town and children come down from
the hillsides carrying burning pieces
of bark to add to the fires.
🔢 466 L2 🛈 Calle San Pedro s/n,
22440 Benasque ☎ 974 55 12 89
🔢 Monzón-Río Cinca, then bus to Barbastro
and Benasque

BERA DE BIDASOA
www.berakoudala.net
The industrial town of Bera (Vera) de
Bidasoa sits high up in the beech-
and pine-clad Valle Bidasoa, near the
French border.

Along the street that links Barrio
Alzate to the old quarter are some
of the region's most interesting
houses, including the old home of
Pío Baroja (1872–1956), a renowned
Basque writer.

The town is one of the so-called
Cinco Villas, or 'five towns', of the
Bidasoa basin, which spread over a
Palaeolithic massif. As the main road
here is busy with traffic crossing into
and out of France, it is necessary to
wander away from it to get a true
feel for the place. The Iglesia de
San Esteban, on a hill overlooking
the town, is worth a look for its
Romanesque organ.
🔢 465 J2 🛈 Paseo Eztegara 11, 31780
Bera de Bidasoa ☎ 948 63 12 22

BILBAO (BILBO)

INFORMATION

www.bilbao.net

464 H2 Plaza Ensanche 11, 48009 Bilbao 944 71 03 01 Mon–Fri 9–2, 4–7.30, Sat 9–2 Bilbao

INTRODUCTION

The Guggenheim is playing an important part in the makeover of Bilbao (Bilbo in Basque) following the collapse of the traditional steel and shipmaking industries in the 1980s. As a result, this modern city is fast becoming the 'in' place, and with a new tram system and Metro link, it is increasingly accessible. The Guggenheim is flanked at its eastern edge by the massive steel Puente de la Salve bridge and stands on the opposite riverbank to the Universidad de Deusto. Beyond the riverfront there is more than just modernism to this city: The interesting *casco viejo* (old town) preserves the older character of Bilbao and has a good selection of varied sights.

Bilbao had humble beginnings in the Middle Ages, but was made a borough in 1300 by Don Diego López of Haro, then Lord of Bizkaia. It grew rapidly on the backs of three industries: iron, fishing and farming. The surrounding iron mines had been worked since Roman times, but their 19th-century development as part of the industrial revolution brought extraordinary power and wealth into the area after the Carlist Wars ended in 1874. The city remains the Basque economic capital today. Its navigable estuary port provided a safer inlet than the ports on the coast itself, and the city established strong trading links with both Britain and America through the export of steel and the import of coal. Although these big industries suffered a decline in the 20th century, the modern city still thrives thanks to its financial and service sectors.

WHAT TO SEE
MUSEO GUGGENHEIM

www.guggenheim-bilbao.es

The gigantic mass of the shimmering Museo Guggenheim dominates its setting alongside the Río Nervión. With its towering, curving, titanium folds and huge glass windows it stands symbolically as a modernist introduction to the city. Designed by American architect Frank O. Gehry and opened in October 1997, this vast 24,000sq m (259,000sq ft) museum is a focus for modern and contemporary art. It has become Bilbao's most notable building, and is world renowned for its ground-breaking, iconoclastic design. At its main entrance is the much-loved *Puppy* statue, a huge creation made out of flowers and greenery. Originally intended as a one-off exhibit for the museum opening, it has remained in place, becoming an emblem of the city.

The monumental building revolves around a central axis, an empty space crowned by a metal dome. From this central point, glass lifts (elevators) and curved walkways connect 19 galleries. The permanent collection on show includes works from the last 40 years, including pop art, minimalism, conceptual art and abstract expressionism. Basque and Spanish contemporary art is also represented. The Guggenheim Foundation regularly sponsors impressive special shows. Temporary exhibitions and large-format works are displayed in a gallery 30m (100ft) wide, linked to the main complex via La Salve bridge.

✉ Avenida Abandoibarra 2, 48001 ☎ 944 35 90 80 🕒 Jul–Aug Mon–Sun 10–7.45; Sep–Jun Tue–Sun 10–7.45 💷 Adult €13 or €15.50 for combined ticket with Museo Bellas Artes, under 12 free

CASCO VIEJO

Farther along from the Guggenheim Museum, on the eastern bank of the river, is the *casco viejo*, Bilbao's old quarter and the medieval heart of the city. Here, among twisting streets and shady alleyways lined with lively tapas bars, is the Gothic Catedral Basílica de Santiago (Tue–Sat 10–1.30, 4–7, Sun 10.30–1.30) and the arcaded Plaza Nueva. This elegant, entirely enclosed square, reached via arched walkways, is flanked on every side by restaurants, old-fashioned shops and balconied apartments. Surrounding it are the lively bars and cafés of Siete Calles, meaning 'seven streets', the city's most renowned nightspot.

The Museo Vasco (Basque Museum; Tue–Sat 11–5, Sun 11–2) is in the nearby Plaza Miguel de Unamuno and includes Basque art, folk objects and photographs. In its cloisters is the *Idol of Mikeldi*, a third-century BC animal carving. Opposite the beautiful 1890s Teatro Arriaga, with its fake rococo semicircular facade, is the Parque de Arenal, a popular *paseo* (promenade) that includes a small open-air stage.

By the river, the huge, sleek, art deco Mercado de la Ribera was strikingly modern when it was built in the late 1920s. It made it into the *Guinness Book of Records* in 1990, as the largest covered market in Europe. It's been sadly neglected in recent years, but plans are afoot to restore it to its former glory.

Above *Paseo del Arenal*
Opposite *The Guggenheim Museum illuminated at night*
Below left *Bilbao is not a beautiful city but it has some fine old buildings*
Below *Fresh local fish on sale in Bilbao's fish market*

MUSEO DE BELLAS ARTES
www.museobilbao.com
In the newer town is the Museo de Bellas Artes, one of Spain's best regional galleries, with exhibits ranging from 12th-century Catalán masters to modern works. This museum has benefited enormously from the so-called 'Guggenheim Effect' which has transformed it from a quiet, provincial gallery into a thoroughly modern and interesting space which attracts thousands of visitors through its doors. There is a particularly good collection of work by Basque artists, with a couple of galleries dedicated to the two great 20th-century Basque sculptors, Jorge de Oteiza and Eduardo Chillida. There are also several rooms dedicated to Basque artists, as well as a number of paintings by Goya, El Greco and Murillo. It combines two older museums, the original 1908 museum of the same name and the Museo de Arte Moderno, founded in 1924. Opposite is the city's largest open space, the Parque de Doña Casilda de Iturrizar.
✉ Plaza del Museo 2, 48011 ☎ 944 39 61 37 🕓 Tue–Sat 10–8, Sun 10–2 ✋ Adult €6 or €13.50 for combined ticket with Guggenheim, under 12 free; free on Wed

MUSEO MARÍTIMO RÍA DE BILBAO
www.museomaritimobilbao.org
The city's Maritime Museum is housed, fittingly, on the banks of the river in an enormous contemporary building which resembles a vast, ocean-liner, complete with portholes. The museum traces Bilbao's maritime history with models, photographs, film clips, maps and hundreds of excellent audiovisual exhibits which vividly bring the past to life. As well as the interior galleries, you can also visit a section of the old locks, part of an ingenious system which once operated along the whole length of the river. The museum also accommodates beautifully restored historic sailing ships, which can often be seen at the water's edge with their tall masts and billowing sails.
✉ Muelle Ramón de la Sota ☎ 946 08 55 00 🕓 Tue–Sat 10–8 ✋ Adult €5, under 6 free

MORE TO SEE
ARTXANDA FUNICULAR
Reached from the Plaza Funicular, this gives great cityscape panoramas (daily 7.15am–10.30pm, €5).

PALACIO DE LA MÚSICA Y CONGRESOS EUSKALDUNA
This palace on the riverside by the Puente Euskalduna, at Avenida Abandoibarra 4, is a striking new building, designed to resemble a ship. It is a conference centre and the home of the Bilbao symphony orchestra (tel 944 31 03 10 for performance times). The new town's bustling main shopping street has some of the city's best department stores.

TIP
» Bilbao is justly famous for its restaurants and tapas bars. Don't leave without trying them out! The Casco Viejo is full of atmospheric bars.
» Bilbao's opera and classical music scene has always been first rate, with stars such as June Anderson singing *Norma* in the Palacio de Euskalduna or *viola de gamba* master Jordi Savall in the Teatro Arriaga.

Opposite and below left *The stunning Guggenheim Museum*
Below right *Crossing the Río Nervión which runs through the heart of Bilbao*

REGIONS EUSKADI, NAVARRA AND ARAGÓN • SIGHTS

CASTILLO DE JAVIER
www.turismonavarra.com

Looking out towards the Sierra de Leyre is this prettified castle, the birthplace of San Francisco Javier, Navarra's patron saint, in 1506. Although the 'stiff' flag flying from its mast accentuates its Disney-like appearance, the castle has experienced some serious battles. It was built in the 10th century but destroyed in 1516 at the command of Cardinal Cisneros after Javier's elder brothers fought against Fernando V. The castle was heavily restored in 1952. In the simple chapel is a statue of San Francisco, with four towering stained-glass windows, a 'smiling' Gothic crucifix and 15th-century wall paintings depicting the Dance of Death.

The castle is part of a wider, well-developed though somewhat commercialized visitor complex, with a bar-restaurant, hotel and picnic parks. The museum is open daily 9–12, 4–7 (6 in winter).

⊞ 465 K2 🚹 Plaza del Santo s/n, 31411 Javier ☎ 948 88 40 24 🕓 Apr–Sep daily 9–12.45, 4–7; Oct–Mar daily 9–12.45, 4–6 ✋ Free; donations accepted

CASTILLO DE LOARRE
www.castillodeloarre.com

The majestic castle of the kings of Aragón towers over the Ebro valley on a rocky outcrop. This is the region's finest fortress. Built on the remains of a Roman fort by order of King Sancho Ramírez I in the 11th

century, it became a monastery in the 12th century. Massive walls, complete with cylindrical towers and two entrance gates, surround the Romanesque church building. The views from the castle, especially its *mirador* (lookout point), are fantastic.

⊞ 466 K3 ✉ Castillo de Loarre, 22809 Loarre ☎ 974 38 26 74 🕓 Mid-Jun to mid-Sep 10–2, 4–8; Mar to mid-Jun, mid-Sep to Oct daily 10–2, 4–7; mid-Oct to Feb 11–3, 5.30–7.30 ✋ Free 📷 Guided tours in Spanish, English and French €4.50

COSTA VASCA
www.donostia.org

Stretching from Hondarribia (▷ 179) at the French border to Cabo Matxitxako in the west, the Costa Vasca is a dramatic sight, with its sea-swept cliffs, secluded bays, river inlets and Basque villages and towns. Donostia (San Sebastián) is the only city (▷ 177), but there are many other worthwhile stopping points.

Bermeo is tucked into a bay at the mouth of Río Oka, protected by the rugged Cabo Matxitxako headland. It is an active fishing port, and home to the Museo del Pescador, or Fisherman's Museum (Tue–Sun 10–1.30, 4–7), in the Torre del Ercilla. Elantxobe's cobbled streets are lined with traditional fishermen's houses tumbling down its steep hillside. The village's upper road has good views.

Farther east is Lekeitio, with beaches on either side of a river inlet island and glass-balconied houses. Getaria is linked to the giant rock known as El Ratón (the mouse) by

a narrow isthmus. A trawler fleet is based here and stocks the seaside restaurants. Nearby Zarautz has a wide, sandy beach with striped beach tents. It was popular with Madrid's high society in the 19th century and has the stylish Palacio de Narros, now a Franciscan convent. Many towns and villages in this region have *sidrerías* (cider houses) or offer tours to farms where the golden liquor is made.

⊞ 465 H1 🚹 Reina Regente 3, 20003 Donostia ☎ 943 48 11 66

DAROCA
www.daroca.org

Clustered within its crumbling walls and overlooking Río Jiloca, this once powerful medieval town is now a shadow of its former self, although its grand buildings remain, but it provides a memorable insight into Spanish history. Napoleon's troops destroyed large parts of the town in 1808 during the War of Independence, but 20 churches and convents remain in one form or another. The 13th- to 17th-century Renaissance Colegiata de Santa María is the most impressive, looming over the Plaza de España. The Puerta Baja, the old town gateway guarded by two mighty towers, features the coat of arms of Charles V. Parts of the defensive wall have been restored, but you can make out only a handful of the 114 towers that once punctuated it.

⊞ 467 P3 🚹 Plaza de España 4, 50360 Daroca ☎ 976 80 01 29

DONOSTIA (SAN SEBASTIÁN)

Donostia, capital of Gipuzkoa (Guipúzcoa) province, is set on the Cantabrian Sea along the dramatic, sweeping arc of the Bahía de la Concha. A devastating fire in 1813 destroyed almost the entire town; the old quarter seen today sprang up to replace it.

The arrival in 1845 of Isabel II, who came to see if bathing in sea water would help her skin condition, launched the city's 'summer playground' reputation among Spain's high society, and it remains a popular resort.

THE OLD QUARTER

Any visit should include a wander around the streets of the old quarter, which is focused on the Plaza de la Constitución. The arched, pedestrian arcades here are topped by triple-storey, uniformly white apartments, with golden window frames and blue balcony-door shutters. Each still bears a number from the days when they were viewing stalls over what was then the city's bullring. Set among excellent seafood restaurants, tapas bars and cafés are the Iglesia de Vicente, the city's oldest church, and the Iglesia de Santa María.

THE PORT

The old quarter's main streets all lead to the port, where yachts and pleasure cruisers moor alongside the red and green fleet of fishing trawlers. From here there are views out into the bay to Isla de Santa Clara and across to the Playa de la Concha and Playa de Ondarreta. Beyond them rises the park headland of Monte Igueldo. From the base a funicular train ascends to the summit. Clinging to the sea cliffs is an intriguing twisted iron sculpture, *El Peine del Viento* (1976), by Eduardo Chillida. Monte Urgull looms behind the old port. This park is dominated by its gigantic statue of Christ, Sagrado Corazón, and the Castillo de la Mota, built between the 13th and 15th centuries.

Aquarium Donostia (Jul–Aug daily 10–9; Easter–Jun, Sep daily 10–8; Sep–Easter daily Mon–Fri 10–7, Sat–Sun 10–8), at the far end of the port, has a superb acrylic foot tunnel through a tank full of sharks, rays and other exotic fish; the Museo San Telmo (currently closed for major renovations; due to reopen early 2011, but check the website) has a fine collection of Basque paintings.

INFORMATION

www.donostia.org

✚ 465 J1 🛈 Reina Regente 3, 20003 Donostia ☎ 943 48 11 66 🕐 Jun–Sep Mon–Sat 8–8, Sun 10–1.30, 3–7; Oct–May Mon–Sat 9–1.30, 3.30–7, Sun 10–2 🚉 Donostia–San Sebastián; there are two stations here, one for trains to and from Bilbao and the other for alternative destinations

TIP

» Finding somewhere to stay is very hard in summer and almost impossible during the jazz and film festivals, so make reservations well in advance.

Above Fishing trawlers line Donostia's port
Opposite left *Castillo de Loarre—castle of the kings of Aragón—high on its crag*
Opposite right *The Puerta Baja gateway at Daroca*

ELIZONDO

www.bidasoaturismo.com

The town of Elizondo sits at the base of the Valle Baztan on the way to France. Its main attractions are typical Basque homes and fortified palatial houses lining the main street and across the river. The mansions were built during the late Middle Ages when battles in the valley were a constant threat.

Among the most notable buildings are the baroque Palacio de Arizkunenea (Governor's Palace) and the arcaded *ayuntamiento* (town hall). The surrounding green hills are dotted with traditional farmhouses and orchards. Just across the river is the tiny village of Elbete, with two manor houses, Azkoa and Jarola, and the striking red and white Iglesia de Santa Cruz, in the typical hues of the Basque region.

➕ 465 J2 ℹ Palacio de Arizkunenea, 31700 Elizondo ☎ 948 58 12 79
🕐 Summer only

ESTELLA

www.turismonavarra.es

Estella's group of impressive monuments and its tranquil riverside setting make it one of the region's most appealing towns. Originally the ancient village of Lizarra, it is set on the banks of the Río Ega. The Palacio de los Reyes de Navarra, whose Romanesque bulk is offset by delicately columned windows, is on Plaza San Martín and is now the Museo Gustavo de Maeztu (Tue–Sat 11–1, 5–7, Sun and holidays 11–1.30).

Above it, reached via steep steps, is the Mudéjar-influenced facade of the Iglesia de San Pedro. Across the river is the Iglesia de San Miguel, on the Camino de Santiago pilgrimage route (▷ 144–145), with a doorway depicting St. Michael slaying Lucifer (now protected by a glass shelter).

Estella has its own annual bull-running festival, which is almost as spectacular as the famous Pamplona version (▷ 182–183) but less well known outside the region.

➕ 465 J2 ℹ San Nicolás 1, 31200 Estella ☎ 948 55 63 01

Above *Memorial to the Gernika Battalion, World War II, Pasealeku balcony in Gernika town*

FRAGA

www.fraga.org

With the so-called Monegros 'desert' to its west, Fraga can seem a refreshing oasis from the surrounding dry scrublands. Here, lush orchards of pear, apple, peach and fig trees line both banks of the Río Cinca, watered by irrigation channels built during Muslim rule between AD715 and 1149.

The layout of intricate streets in the old quarter, leading to the 12th-century Iglesia de San Pedro, was similarly influenced by this period. Fraga has its own traditional dress, dating back to this time and worn on Faldeta Day on 23 April. This festival was originally intended to celebrate the town's elderly women, who wore the typical Fraga dress of *bobiné* handkerchiefs, puffed sleeves and cosset cuffs. Now young people also take to the streets, wearing mantilla shawls and multilayered Fraga skirts.

The central Parque de La Estacada—an open area with woods—contains a swimming pool and play area.

➕ 466 L4 ℹ Plaza España 1, 22530 Fraga ☎ 974 47 00 50

GERNIKA-LUMO (GUERNICA)

www.gernika-lumo.net

Long established in the heartland of Basque nationalism, this famous town was immortalized by Pablo Picasso in his painting *Guernica,* now hanging in Madrid's Museo Nacional Centro de Arte Reina Sofía (▷ 77). The scenes in the Guernica painting capture the moment when German aircraft, with Franco's acquiescence, bombed and destroyed the town in 1937. It was a defiant act against the Basques, and all but wiped out the town and its people. It was here that the Basques had gathered for centuries to hold general assemblies under the Gernika Arbola, a symbolic oak tree where rulers were sworn in.

Now, there are three trees planted in the grounds of the Casa de las Juntas, seat of the Basque government and originally built in 1826 as a church parliament. The 'old tree' is more than 300 years old, the ceremonial 'current oak' was planted in 1860 and is a direct descendant of the old tree, and behind is the 'sapling', which will be their successor.

The Gernika Peace Museum (Museo de la Paz) (Jul–Aug daily 10–7; Sep–Jun Tue–Sat 10–2, 4–7, Sun 10–2) charts the bombing campaign and promotes peace.

The Europako Herrien Parkea, a sculpture park close to the assembly house, displays the work of Basque sculptor Eduardo Chillida (1924–2002) and British sculptor Henry Moore (1898–1986).

➕ 465 H2 ℹ Artekalea 8 E, 48300 Gernika-Lumo ☎ 946 25 58 92 🚉 Gernika

HONDARRIBIA (FUENTERRABÍA)

www.bidasoaturismo.com

The only remaining walled town in Guipúzcoa province is a huddle of wooden-beamed houses and a lively and colourful marine quarter at the mouth of the Río Bidasoa. Life here revolves around the water, so if you want to go scuba diving or sailing or take a relaxing boat trip, this is a good place to go. In the old town's Plaza de Armas is the sturdy 15th-century Castillo de Carlos V, now a *parador*. Opposite, the mainly Gothic Iglesia de Santa María has a fine baroque tower. Shuttle boats ferry passengers from the Cofradia de Pescadores to Hendaye, across the bay in France, where there is a superb beach.

Between the airport runways and Irun train station is the Parque Ecológico de Plaiaundi, a lush refuge for migrating birds (Tue–Sat 10–1, 4–7, Sun 10–1).

✚ 465 J1 🚹 Calle Javier Ugarte 6 bajo, 20280 Hondarribia ☎ 943 64 54 58

HUESCA

www.huescaturismo.com

Old Huesca is the main reason to visit this provincial capital, with its striking Gothic cathedral, grid of twisting streets and neat squares.

Here the *ayuntamiento* (town hall), a former Renaissance palace, has a massive canvas depicting the legendary saga of the *Campana de Huesca* (Bell of Huesca), painted in 1880 by José Casado del Alisal. On permanent loan from the Prado in Madrid, it shows Ramiro II, the monk who became king, and the infamous bell—the head of a nobleman who had refused to accept the king's title. On the same plaza stands the 13th-century cathedral, with a detailed facade consisting of 14 different sculpted figures. The cathedral contains an alabaster altarpiece by 16th-century Spanish sculptor Damián Forment (*d*1540). Nearby is the Mozarabic quarter and, opposite Plaza Allue, the Romanesque Iglesia de San Pedro el Viejo, whose cloisters have been beautifully restored. This is the burial place of the Aragonese kings.

✚ 466 K3 🚹 Plaza de la Catedral 1, 22002 Huesca ☎ 974 29 21 70 🚉 Huesca

JACA

www.aytojaca.es

Jaca is a convenient base from which to explore the nearby Pyrenees, and it is worth a visit in its own right. It was founded by the Romans and occupied by the Moors. The city returned to Christian hands following a mostly women-led battle in AD795, and soon became the first port of call for French pilgrims on their way to Santiago de Compostela (▷ 144–145). At the heart of the old quarter is the Romanesque cathedral, and close by deer graze in the grassed moat of the huge star-shaped Ciudadela (Citadel). This 16th-century fort, on the eastern side of town, is still used by the Spanish military, although part of it can be visited (daily 11–2, 4–7, tel 974 36 37 46 for guided visits).

The Paseo de la Canter, on the northwestern edge of town, has views over the Río Aragón and to the Puente de San Miguel, a medieval bridge that brought pilgrims into Jaca. Aragón's best ski resort, Astún-Candanchu, is nearby.

✚ 466 K2 🚹 Plaza de San Pedro 11–13, 22700 Jaca ☎ 974 36 00 98 🚉 Jaca

EL MAESTRAZGO

www.turismoaragon.com

The ancient domain of the crusading Knights Templar is surrounded by the rugged Sierra del Maestrazgo. This wild landscape of rocky peaks, gorges and valleys forms a bitterly disputed region, the frontier between Teruel in Aragón and Castelló de la Plana in Valencia that was fought over by Moors and Christians. Maestrazgo's capital, Morella (▷ 262), is an archetypical fortified hilltop town.

Southwards, Cantavieja is precariously perched on a spur 1,300m (4,265ft) high, but the Puerto de Villarroya (to the east on the A-226) is the high point of the Maestrazgo at 1,655m (5,430ft).

To the northwest, the restored walled village of Mirambel retains an ancient air. Set around the base of a rock 1,318m (4,323ft) high, Ares del Maestre is another spectacular town worth seeing. If you don't have time to explore the whole area, head to Valderrobres, southwest of Alcañiz, which is one of the easiest towns to reach.

✚ 471 L5 🚹 Nueva 47, 44560 Castellote ☎ 978 88 75 61

Below left *Huesca's Gothic cathedral glowing at sunset*
Below *Enjoying a traditional pastime—juego de las bochas*

Above *Snow-covered Monasterio de Leyre*
Right *Mary and Jesus altarpiece in the nave at Monasterio de Leyre*

MONASTERIO DE LEYRE

www.monasteriodeleyre.com

Set high on the forested slopes of the rugged Sierra de Leyre is this 11th-century Benedictine monastery, with its unusual pre-Romanesque crypt and the impressive Porta Speciosa, or 'pretty door'. This main entrance to the church is a 12th-century masterpiece of sculpture, depicting the Last Judgement, saints, monsters and martyrs. The monastery was repopulated in 1954 after Prime Minister Mendizabal expelled the monks in 1836 as part of his plan to recoup money following the Carlist Wars (▷ 38); there are currently 26 resident monks. During Mass and vespers the monks sing Gregorian chants. The rough-hewn low crypt has squat pillars and three naves, and the predominantly Romanesque church's main features are a beautiful sculpture of Santa María de Leyre and the soaring apses. The monks run a comfortable hotel here.

🚏 465 K2 ✉ Monasterio de Leyre, 31410 Yesa ☎ 948 88 41 50 🕐 Summer Mon–Fri 10.15–2, 3.30–7, Sat–Sun 10.15–2, 4–7; rest of year Mon–Fri 10.15–2, 3.30–6, Sat–Sun 10.15–2, 4–6.30 ♿ Adult €3, child (6–13) €1

MONASTERIO DE LA OLIVA

www.monasteriodeoliva.eu
www.larrate.net/LaOliva

The monastery was founded in 1143 by the kings of Navarra and sacked by Napoleon's troops during the War of Independence (1808–14) and then abandoned in 1836 following Prime Minister Mendizabal's takeover of religious buildings. Monks returned here in 1927.

Its 12th-century church has three naves and basic choir stalls, where the otherwise silent, white-robed monks sing during Mass and vespers. The only ornamentation here is on the capitals, which are sculpted in the shape of vegetables. Although the church is open at all times, the rest of the complex (including the spacious 14th-century cloister) can be visited only on a guided tour.

🚏 465 J3 ✉ Monasterio de la Oliva, 31310 Carcastillo ☎ 948 72 50 06 🕐 Monastery: Sun 9–11.45, 4–6.15, Mon–Sat 8.30–12.30, 3.30–6.15. Church: open at all times ♿ €3 🗝 Guided tours available on request

MONASTERIO DE PIEDRA

www.monasteriopiedra.com

Although monks no longer live here, the parkland surrounding this restored monastery helps make it one of Aragón's main attractions. Once a Moorish castle, it was set up as a monastery in 1194 by three monks from Poblet (▷ 262) on the orders of Alfonso II.

The monastery retains its magnificent Gothic cloisters with their pointed arches, and Sala Capitular. The church has a mixture of styles ranging from Roman to Mudéjar, and the old cellars are now the Museo del Vino. The park and its waterfalls can be explored via marked trails.

La Sala de Carruajes has a collection of old Spanish and English horse carriages.

🚏 465 J4 ✉ Monasterio de Piedra, 50210 Nuévalos ☎ 902 19 60 52 🕐 Monastery: summer daily 10.15–1.15, 3.15–7.15; rest of year daily 10.15–1.15, 3.15–5.15. Park: winter 9–6; summer 9–8 ♿ Combined ticket for park, museum and monastery: adult €7, under 4 free 🗝 Guided visit to monastery €5

MONZÓN

www.turismoaragon.com

The Knights Templar castle that crowns the crumbling hillside here dominates the area (closed Mon). Once a Moorish stronghold, this was the fortress home of Jaime I (1207–76), later king of Aragón, during part of his childhood.

Of the ruins, the Arab Torre del Homenaje (keep) is still intact, as is a group of four imposing, Cistercian-style buildings and a small chapel. Beneath the castle is the town itself, with its old quarter and the Plaza Mayor, the setting for the 16th-century Renaissance *ayuntamiento* (town hall).

🚏 466 L3 ℹ Plaza Mayor 4, 22400 Monzón ☎ 971 41 77 74 🚇 Monzón

PARQUE NACIONAL ORDESA Y MONTE PERDIDO

Towering, banded, tabletop mountains, deep valleys, unspoiled forests and an array of wildlife are features that make this park one of Spain's most highly rated wilderness areas. First established in 1918 as the Parque Nacional Valle de Ordesa, it was expanded further in 1982 to include Monte Perdido and other features, such as the Garganta de Añisclo. It now covers around 20,000ha (50,000 acres), and is also part of the much larger UNESCO Ordesa-Viñamala Biosphere Reserve.

PEAKS AND VALLEYS

The highest point of the park is the summit of Monte Perdido at 3,355m (11,004ft), part of Europe's biggest limestone range. Ascending this peak is a serious undertaking that requires sound mountaineering skills. However, there is an extensive network of gentler trails throughout the park.

The park can be divided into three sections. Valle de Ordesa, the most popular area, is reached via Torla, a charming stone village. Private vehicle access is not allowed past here during *Semana Santa* and from July to the end of September, when a shuttle bus takes hikers into the park itself at Pradera de Ordesa. Note also that visitor numbers are limited at each access point (see Tips). On the eastern side Bielsa serves as the entry point for the Valle de Pineta, while in the south, Escalona and Buerba are the main entry villages for the Garganta de Añisclo, a Grand Canyon-like chasm, or the Valle de Escuaín, with another beautiful gorge.

HIKING ROUTES

Trekking is the best way to see the wilderness. Top of the list for most visitors is the climb up to the Cola de Caballo waterfall at Circo de Soaso, a six- to seven-hour undertaking with a vertical ascent of around 680m (2,230ft).

Other good treks include Pradera de Ordesa to Tozal del Mallo (six to seven hours, 950m/3,110ft ascent, more difficult), and the Cañon de Añisclo from Puente San Úrbez to the waterfall at Fon Blanca (eight to nine hours, 680m/2,230ft ascent and fairly easy). If you find that your time is limited you can get to Fuentes de Escuaín from the village of Escuaín and back in about an hour and a half.

INFORMATION

www.ordesa.net

✚ 466 L2 ℹ Centro de Visitantes 'El Parador', Valle de Ordesa, Carretera Torla–Pradesa, 22376 Torla ☎ 974 48 64 21 🕐 Summer daily 9–1, 3.30–7

🚆 Sabiñánigo, Jaca 🚌 For bus services tel La Oscense in Sabiñánigo 974 48 00 45, or in Jaca 974 35 50 60; or Hudebus in Sabiñánigo 974 21 32 77

TIPS

» Take binoculars: you may see golden eagles, marmots, chamois and even rare bearded vultures.

» The park is heavily regulated during the summer months, when only 1,800 visitors are allowed in at any one time. If you want to reach it via Torla, get there early in the morning.

» Avoid summer if possible, as the trails are busy at this time and consequently lose some of their wilderness feel.

» The climb up to the Mirador de Calcilarruego is a 90-minute vertical ascent. The Sendero de los Cazadores along the southern rim of the canyon, called La Faja Pelay, is a gentle stroll with magnificent views. Mountain goats (chamois or isard) descend to the trail in the evenings.

Below *Ordesa National Park, one of the glories of the Pyrenees*

INFORMATION

www.pamplona.net

✚ 465 J2 ℹ Calle Eslava 1 (corner of Plaza San Francisco), 31001 Pamplona
☎ 948 20 65 40 ⏰ Mon–Sat 10–2, 4–7, Sun 10–2 🚉 Pamplona

INTRODUCTION

Pamplona (Iruña in Basque) is known for its 6–14 July San Fermín Fiesta bull run, but this city is far more than the annual, frantic, sometimes deadly stampede through its streets. Sprawled across the Río Arga basin, it is the cultural and political hub of Navarra and the pulsing heart of the Basque country. It has supreme monuments—including the immense, star-shaped Ciudadela and Gothic cathedral—as well as spacious parkland and a buzzing old quarter.

Roman general Pompeius founded the town in 75BC on the site of Iruñea, a Basque village. Pamplona was captured by the Moors in AD718 and became the northern front of the Reconquest. Many battles were fought here between the Moors and French, most notably the ambush of Charlemagne's rearguard troops, including his nephew Roland, on their way back to France in the Pyrenees, at Puerto de Ibañeta near Orreaga (Roncesvalles).

In 1423 Carlos III united the rival Franks and Navarrese districts of the city with the Privilegio de la Unión law, which effectively formed the basis for the modern-day city. It became the capital of Navarra under the Catholic Monarchs in the early 16th century, triggering many building projects, including the Citadel. The city's location on the Camino de Santiago pilgrimage route (▷ 144–145) ensured that it continued to grow in stature, and the 19th century saw another bout of major construction and conversion projects, many of which—such as the Escuela de San Francisco—used religious buildings reclaimed in 1836 by Prime Minister Mendizabal through his Law of Disentailment.

Above *Bull running in Pamplona, immortalized by Ernest Hemingway, who never ran with the bulls, in his 1926 novel* The Sun Also Rises
Opposite *A cloister decoration in the* Catedral de Santa María

WHAT TO SEE

CIUDADELA

The Ciudadela (Citadel), built between 1571 and 1645, is Pamplona's geographical, cultural and political heart and its biggest single building. Based on a fortress in Antwerp, Belgium, the complex's pentagonal shape is outlined by two deep, dry moats protecting an inner walled fortress. These days the only struggles taking place here are likely to be sporting ones, as much of it has been turned into parkland. It is also home to a music and exhibition centre.

CATEDRAL DE SANTA MARÍA

Although the cathedral's 18th-century, heavily columned, neoclassical front is not overly exciting, its interior is a rich Gothic affair. Originally a Romanesque structure, the cathedral was redesigned in the 14th and 15th centuries and the main facade rebuilt in 1783. Carlos III (1361–1425) and his wife Leonor (c1350–1415) are buried here in an exquisite alabaster tomb. The most impressive feature is the clean-lined French Gothic cloister, where the portals, Puerta del Amparo and Puerta Preciosa, feature sculptures of the death of the Virgin. From the cloister you can enter the Museo de Diocesano, housed in the old refectory and kitchen, which showcases religious art and objects from across Navarra.
✉ Calle Dormitaleria 🕐 15 Jul–15 Sep Mon–Fri 10–7, Sat 10–1; 1 May–14 Jul, 16 Sep–Oct Mon–Fri 10–1, 4–7, Sat 10–1; Nov–Apr Mon–Fri 10.30–1.30, 4–6, Sat 10.30–1.30; Sun phone for information: 948 22 29 90. Closed festivals 👋 Adult €5, child (7–12) €3

EDIFICIO BALUARTE (PLAZA DEL BALUARTE)

www.baluarte.com
The Palacio de Congresos y Auditorio de Navarra was built in 2003 by Patxi Mangado, Pamplona's most famous architect. A contemporary, minimalist structure made of granite from Zimbabwe with a concert hall lined with beechwood from the Navarran Pyrenees, this splendid venue is built into the remains of one of the five bastions of Pamplona's 16th-century citadel.

LA NAVARRERÍA

Pamplona's oldest quarter lies to the west of the cathedral and contains the best section of the remaining city walls. It's a predominantly pedestrian-only area of narrow, cobbled streets, tiny traditional shops, good restaurants, tapas bars and a few 18th-century palaces.

MUSEO DE NAVARRA

You can learn all about the old kingdom of Navarra at this museum, housed in a fine old hospital building with a Renaissance facade. The collection includes Roman mosaics and sculptures, archeological finds, Romanesque capitals from the old cathedral and frescoes from all over the region. The main treasure is an 11th-century Moorish casket from the Monasterio de Leyre (▷ 180).
✉ Cuesta de Santo Domingo ☎ 848 42 64 92 🕐 Tue–Sat 9.30–2, 5–7, Sun and holidays 11–2 👋 Adult €3; free under 18, Sat afternoon and Sun

PARQUE DE LA TACONERA

The pick of Pamplona's many green spaces has winding paths and sections of the old walls. The park is scattered with monuments to local personalities—a prettier bet is the neoclassical Fountain of Neptune, designed by Luis Paret. The 18th-century church at the end of the park is dedicated to San Lorenzo.

PLAZA DEL CASTILLO

Known as Pamplona's 'living room', the old quarter's central square formerly hosted bullfights and jousting matches; today, this wide space, ringed by arcades and porticoes, is the social hub of the city, with plenty of bars and cafés and a lively atmosphere.

TIP
» The city is packed to overflowing during San Fermín. There is nowhere to stay unless you reserve months in advance.

SAN FERMÍN AND THE BULLS

Fireworks on 6 July kick-start the raucous Fiesta de San Fermín, first brought to the world's attention by Ernest Hemingway in his 1926 novel *The Sun Also Rises*, and now firmly established as one of Europe's most spectacular parties. It features nine days and nights of non-stop live music, parades galore and, of course, the bulls. At 8am every morning, a thousand young men and a few dozen women, dressed in white with red neckerchiefs and sashes, try to outpace six fighting bulls and a herd of steers along an 825m (900 yard) course through the old quarter. Most barely see the bulls, fleeing too soon or being overtaken. Others see them all too closely; injuries are certain, fatalities thankfully rare. Although the bulls always survive the run, they meet their fate in the afternoon bullfight. Good vantage points for the *encierro* (running) are the Plaza Santo Domingo and the Plaza Consistorial.

OLITE

www.olite.es

A bizarre castle, remarkable churches and a real sense of medieval history make fortified Olite one of the most outstanding towns in the region. In the 15th century Carlos III built the Palacio Real castle, with its substantial towers, numerous turrets and perfectly restored walls, and it subsequently became home to the court of Navarra. The 14th-century Castillo Viejo, behind, is now a *parador.* Next to it is the Iglesia de Santa María la Real, with a striking Gothic facade and arched atrium. At the eastern edge of town is the medieval Iglesia de San Pedro. In August, medieval fairs are held with troubadours and falconers entertaining the crowds.

Underground, beneath the spacious Plaza de Carlos III, is a series of medieval arched tunnels that may have been used as a market or as a secret escape route.

✚ 465 J3 ℹ Plaza de los Teobaldos 10, 31390 Olite ☎ 948 74 17 03 🚉 Olite

OÑATI

www.onati.org

Given its isolated valley location, Oñati's collection of monuments may surprise you. Until the mid-19th century the village was independent of the rest of Gipuzkoa province. Its superb 16th-century Renaissance Universidad Sancti Spiritus (tel 943 78 34 53 for guided visits) has a facade adorned with sculpted figures and an inner chapel and cloister. Lectures ended here in 1901. The Iglesia de San Miguel, on Plaza de los Fueros, is a fine baroque church with 16th-century cloisters overlooking the river. The crypt houses the tombs of the counts of Oñati. Also on Plaza de los Fueros is the *ayuntamiento* (town hall), with its baroque facade and arched walkway.

✚ 465 H2 ℹ San Juan Kale 14, 20560 Oñati ☎ 943 78 34 53

ORREAGA (RONCESVALLES)

www.roncesvalles.es

Getting to this village high in the Pyrenees is a pretty drive north from Pamplona on N-135 through rural Basque villages like Burguete, where Hemingway's character Jake Barnes fishes for trout in *The Sun Also Rises.*

The village, founded by monks as a pilgrim sanctuary and hospital in 1332, has as its prized possession a silver statue of the Virgin in the Real Colegiata de Nuestra Señora, a French Gothic masterpiece. The Battle Window in the chapterhouse, an exquisite stained-glass window, depicts scenes from the Battle of Navas de Tolosa (1212), where the Christian armies defeated the Moors. The tiny 12th-century Iglesia de Santiago is also interesting. Up at the Puerto de Ibañeta a stone monolith marks the spot where Charlemagne found the body of his nephew Roland, killed by Basques in AD778.

✚ 465 J2 ℹ Antiguo Molino, 31650 Orreaga ☎ 948 76 03 01

PAMPLONA (IRUÑA)

▷ 182–183.

PARQUE NACIONAL ORDESA Y MONTE PERDIDO

▷ 181.

PUENTE LA REINA

www.turismonavarra.es

Puente la Reina has a unique location at the meeting point of two routes on the Camino de Santiago (the pilgrimage path to Santiago de Compostela, ▷ 144–145). Its principal landmark, a seven-span bridge constructed by the Romans and rebuilt in the 11th century, is also related to the *camino.*

Pilgrims on the parallel Camino Real Francés paths, from Orreaga (Roncesvalles) in Navarra and Somport in Aragón, would join forces here and leave town by crossing the Río Arga over the bridge. They would call in at the Iglesia de Santiago el Mayor, which has a Romanesque facade, and the small but lovely Knights Templar church, Iglesia del Crucifijo. The latter contains an image of *Nuestra Señora de los Huertos* and a 14th-century Gothic crucifix.

✚ 465 J2 ℹ Plaza Mena s/n, 31100 Puente La Reina ☎ 948 34 08 45

RODA DE ISÁBENA

www.turismoaragon.com

The Romanesque cathedral of this remote hill town deserves a visit. It is a grand fusion of styles, the result of work carried out between 1053 and 1067. Six columns with finely decorated capitals flank the superb entrance, and of special note inside are the sarcophagus of St. Román and a valuable organ built in 1653 by Fray Martín Peruga, considered to be the finest in Europe. Look for the superb frescoes on the crypt. The former refectory, or dining room, has been converted into a restaurant.

The winding streets in the town itself are intriguing to explore and there are excellent views from them.

✚ 466 L3 ℹ Fermin Mur y Mur 25, 22430 Graus ☎ 974 54 61 63 ❓ Visits by guided tour only (tel 974 54 45 03; tours depart six to ten times a day)

Clockwise from above *Medieval pilgrim bridge at Puente la Reina; detail of a statue in Orreaga's Colegiata; Iglesia de San Pedro, on tree-lined El Fosal square, Olite*

SAN JUAN DE LA PEÑA

www.monasteriosanjuan.com

The cave monastery of San Juan de la Peña sits underneath a bulging, overhanging cliff, surrounded by densely wooded slopes and *miradors* looking out to the Pyrenees. This simply styled Mozarabic monastery was declared a national monument in 1889.

Inside are preserved horseshoe arches and frescoes, but the most memorable part is the beautiful cloisters of the Romanesque church, with a rock ceiling. The capitals, some of bizarre animals, were sculpted by an unknown artist in the late 12th or early 13th centuries and are regarded as some of the best in Spain. The neoclassical, 18th-century Panteón Real was built by Aragónese nobles on the orders of Carlos III.

A connecting bus service runs during the summer to link the lower monastery with a 17th-century upper monastery, built as a replacement. It now contains the visitor centre and a chic hotel. Alternatively, you can walk there along forest trails, but it is uphill all the way. There are several woodland walks leading off from the upper monastery area (Walk, ▷ 192–193).

✚ 466 K3 ✉ San Juan de la Peña, 22792 Huesca ☎ 974 35 51 19 ◷ Mid-Jul to Aug daily 10–8; Jun to mid-Jul 10–2, 3–8; mid-Mar to May, Sep–Oct 10–2, 3.30–7; Nov to mid-Mar 10.30–2, 3.30–5.30 💶 €7, under 7 free. Tour guides available at no extra charge ❓ Visits are timed

SANGÜESA (ZANGOZA)

www.turismonavarra.es

Most people come to the Roman town of Sangüesa to see just one thing: the intricately sculpted facade of the Iglesia de Santa María la Real. The Last Judgement, The Twelve Apostles, Mary and even the Norse hero Sigurd can be found among the array of figures on the south portal of this 12th-century church. The town's Romanesque-Gothic Iglesia de Santiago was the first port of call in Navarra for pilgrims on their way to Compostela (▷ 144–145). The Palacio del Principe de Viana, overlooking Plaza de Las Aracadas, was home to the last Navarran monarchs, Juan de Labrit and Catalina de Foix, in the 16th century.

✚ 465 J2 ❶ Calle Mayor 2, 31400 Sangüeza ☎ 948 87 14 11

SOS DEL REY CATÓLICO

www.sosdelreycatolico.com

Teetering on a mountain ridge in the Valle de Onsella is the walled town of Sos del Rey Católico, a medieval maze and birthplace of Fernando V, one of the Catholic Monarchs. The town is crowned by the ruined Castillo. The castle isn't pretty inside, but there are magnificent views from the Torre del Homenaje. More attractive is the Renaissance Palacio de Sada (Jun–Aug daily 10–2, 4–8; Sep–May Wed–Sun 10–1, 4–7), birthplace of Fernando in 1452, and the Iglesia de San Esteban has a crypt decorated with murals dating from the 13th–14th centuries. The

irregular web of cobbled streets leading from the small Plaza Mayor is fascinating. One of Spain's most famous *paradors* is on the edge of town overlooking the valley below.

✚ 465 K3 ❶ Plaza Hispanidad s/n, 50680 Sos del Rey Católico ☎ 948 88 85 24

TARAZONA

www.turismoaragon.com

Winding alleyways, narrow streets and a plethora of Roman, Christian, Jewish and Moorish influences make Tarazona's upper town the focus of any visit. It also tags itself La Ciudad Mudéjar, after 400 years of Moorish rule from AD713 left their mark. This rich influence can be seen in the geometric brick patterns of the tower of the Iglesia de Santa María Magdalena, a major landmark. From here there are grand views over the Barrios Altos and Río Quiles below. The Plaza de Toros Vieja is best seen from the church; the perimeter of this 18th-century bullring is made up of ancient, balconied houses. At the heart of the old quarter is the *ayuntamiento* (town hall), with a finely sculpted facade featuring coats of arms. The cathedral was constructed between the 12th and 13th centuries, with another fine brick tower and Mudéjar cloisters.

Vía Verde del Tarazonica links Tarazona with Tudela, 22km (14 miles) away. The railbed is now a path for walkers and bicyclists.

✚ 465 J3 ❶ Plaza de San Francisco 1, 50500 Tarazona ☎ 976 64 00 74

REGIONS EUSKADI, NAVARRA AND ARAGÓN • SIGHTS

TERUEL

www.teruel.es

A legendary tale of true love is associated with this provincial capital, which contains some of the best Mudéjar work in the country.

Its *casco histórico* (old quarter) shelters the most interesting sights, on a high terrace overlooking the Río Turia. Now an industrial town, Teruel was fought over first by the Romans and then by the Moors. After Alfonso II recaptured Teruel for Christian Spain in 1171, many Muslims stayed and embellished the city with Mudéjar towers, five of which remain today. Most striking of these are the Torre del Salvador, which you can climb, and the Torre de San Martín (closed for building works). In the Iglesia de San Pedro is the tomb of the famous 13th-century 'Romeo and Juliet' lovers of Teruel, Juan Diego Martínez de Marcilla and Isabel de Segura (▷ 32).

The story goes that Juan Diego set off to seek his fortune, but on his return found Isabel on the point of being forced to marry another against her will. Juan Diego consequently died of a broken heart; at his funeral, Isabel kissed her dead lover and promptly died herself. The superb coffered ceiling of the cathedral reveals extensive Moorish influence.

In front of the train station and leading up to the Torre del Salvador is La Escalinata, a Mudéjar-style flight of steps.

➕ 470 K6 ℹ️ Plaza Amantes 6, 44001 Teruel ☎ 978 64 14 61 🚆 Teruel

TUDELA

www.tudela.es

Mudéjar art enlivens this agricultural settlement, most notable for its transitional-style cathedral. Tudela, on the banks of the Río Ebro, is the second city of Navarra and was a Moorish stronghold until 1147, when Alfonso I conquered it. The influence of the Moors is ever present in the streets of the old town and in the multihued patterning on many of the buildings. The cathedral (Tue–Sat 9–1, 4–7, Sun 9–1), constructed over the remains of a ninth-century mosque, reveals the change in style from Romanesque to Gothic. Set in the main facade is the Puerta del Juicio (Door of the Last Judgement). Near the cathedral, the entrance to the city council buildings has a collection of grand tapestries.

➕ 465 J3 ℹ️ Calle Juicio 4, 31500 Tudela, ☎ 948 84 80 58 🚆 Tudela

UJUÉ

www.turismonavarra.es

The Pyrenees form a backdrop to this medieval Navarra village balanced on a remote mountain ridge. Just getting there on the twisting road that climbs from San Martín de Unx is an adventure.

The fortified Castillo-Basílica de Santa María, above Plaza de Iñigo Aristia (named after Pamplona's first king and founder of Ujué), crowns the village maze of steep cobbled streets. The Gothic portal depicts the Last Supper and the Epiphany, and inside is the Romanesque *Virgen con el Niño*, a delicate, revered silver statue of the Virgin Mary with the baby Jesus. The village is renowned for its fresh almonds, on sale at shops in and around the Plaza de Iñigo Arista. A minor road from Ujué to Murillo el Fruto takes you along the Sierra de Ujué ridge, with stunning vistas of the Pyrenees and the La Ribera wine-growing region.

➕ 465 J3 ℹ️ Rua Mayor 1 bajo, 31390 Olite ☎ 948 74 17 03

VALLE DE ANSÓ

www.valledeanso.com

This valley, together with the Valle de Hecho to the east, forms one of Aragón's most attractive areas. The pretty Río Veral carves its way through dramatic mountain scenery to join the Río Aragón west of Jaca, and on its way flows through the village of Ansó. Here, you will find a small beach-like area that allows you to enjoy sun and sand in the mountains. The NA-176 minor road now connects this once isolated settlement with the nearby Valle del Roncal (▷ 187) and Hecho. Ansó is becoming an increasingly popular base with mountain-bicyclists, walkers and cross-country skiers.

➕ 465 K2 ℹ️ Plaza del Ayuntamiento, 22728 Ansó ☎ 974 37 02 25

VALLE DE HECHO

www.valledehecho.net

Like its twin to the west, the Valle de Ansó (see above), this is a magnificently carved valley surrounded by high peaks. It can be reached from Jaca (▷ 179) via the N-240 at Puente la Reina. The road then cuts through the valley, following the winding Río Aragón, to the historic village of Hecho. From here the kingdom of Aragón is believed to have grown. It is a particularly engaging spot, where traditional solid stone houses have high wooden balconies and immense eaves. A pleasant trek leads from La Mina, at the very top of the Valle de Hecho, to Lago Acherito; the walk takes 2–3 hours.

➕ 466 K2 ℹ️ Museo de Arte Contemporaneo 'Pallar d'Agustín', 22720 Hecho ☎ 974 37 55 05

VALLE DEL RONCAL

www.valleronçal.es

Slicing through the Pyrenean massif, this limestone gorge makes for an exciting drive past traditional stone villages. The village of Burgui clings to the hillside above the Río Esca. It has a fine medieval bridge, under which traditional *almadía* rafts sail once a year. A famous valley product is cheese; the Enaquesa Roncal cheese factory (tel 948 47 50 14 to arrange a visit) is near the Garde road. At Roncal a nature interpretation centre is found among a maze of cobbled streets. Below the jagged Peña de Ezkaurre rock, the gorgeous village of Isaba is the access point for hikes into the Belagoa and Belabarce valleys.

✚ 465 K2 ℹ Centro de Interpretación de la Naturaleza, 31415 Roncal ☎ 948 47 52 56

VALLE DE SALAZAR

www.valledesalazar.com.es

Snaking its way north from Sierra de Leyre, this enchanting valley brims with medieval history. At Lumbier, a dramatic gorge is carved by the Río Irati and can be explored through tunnels bored for the old timber trains. Farther north, at Puerto de Iso, there is a viewpoint opposite Foz de Arbayún, another magnificent gorge. Continuing towards France, you pass Izal, home to the valley's only remaining granary. In cobbled Escaroz, the valley's capital, pretty stone houses are interspersed with garden orchards. Just 2km

Opposite *Iglesia de San Miguel and Calle de San Francisco, Vitoria-Gasteiz*
Right *Entrance to the Valle de Roncal*
Below *Plaza de España, Vitoria-Gasteiz*

(1.2 miles) farther, at the confluence of the Río Anduña and the Río Zatoia, is Ochagavía, a quintessential Pyrenean village of whitewashed stone houses with red-tiled roofs. Perched on top of Ochagavía is the 13th-century Iglesia de San Juan.

✚ 465 K2 ℹ Centro de Interpretación de la Naturaleza, 31680 Ochagavía ☎ 948 89 06 41

VITORIA-GASTEIZ

www.vitoria-gasteiz.org/turismo

Elegant and fervently separatist, the Basque country capital of Vitoria (or Gasteiz, to give it its old Basque name) has mansions, tranquil parks and a poignant history. The atmosphere here is friendly, and it is also relatively off the beaten track. Founded as Nueva Vitoria in 1181 by Navarran King Sancho VI, it was sacked by the king of Castile in 1200. Wealth from the city's craft industries paid for the construction of glass-balconied houses, palaces and churches. Particularly notable among these are the 13th-century fortified Catedral Vieja de Santa María (guided visits only; daily half-hourly 11–1, 5–7; tel 945 25 51 35), whose west portal is a sculptural jewel, and the Iglesia de San Miguel, home to Vitoria's patron saint, the Virgen Blanca. The neoclassical Plaza de España and 40 tree-lined parks make this one of Spain's most naturally appealing places in which to live. Parque de la Florida, by the cathedral, is the most popular of these, although El Prado and Juan de Arriaga are equally delightful. Many of the old quarter's streets are lined

with lively bars and plastered with Basque political posters.

Of the city's many museums, the most unusual is the Museo Fournier de Naipes (Tue–Fri 10–2, 4–6.30, Sat 10–2, Sun and holidays 11–2), with around 20,000 historic playing cards.

✚ 465 H2 ℹ Plaza General Loma 1, 01005 Vitoria-Gasteiz ☎ 945 16 15 98 🚉 Vitoria-Gasteiz

ZARAGOZA

www.turismozaragoza.com

Zaragoza, 2,000 years old, is one of Spain's great monumental cities and contains one of its most sacred pilgrimage icons. The Basilica de Nuestra Señora del Pilar (daily 5.45am–8.30pm; museum daily 9–2, 4–6; panoramic tower Sat–Thu 9.30–2, 4–6, until 7 in summer) contains the column on which the Virgin is supposed to have appeared before St. James. Pilgrims flock to the amazing baroque building with its four towers and eleven cupolas covered in bright tiles; you can climb up the northwest tower. The basilica is flanked by Río Ebro and huge Plaza del Pilar. In the same square are the Renaissance *lonja* (market), with its fine facade, and the 14th-century Catedral de la Seo. About 15 minutes' walk west of the Plaza del Pilar is an 11th-century Moorish palace, the Palacio de la Aljafería (Jun–Sep Sat–Wed 10–2, 4.30–8, Fri 10–2; Oct–May Sat, Mon–Wed 10–2, 4.30–6.30, Fri 4–6.30, Sun and holidays 10–2).

✚ 465 K4 ℹ Plaza de Nuestra Señora del Pilar s/n, 50003 Zaragoza ☎ 976 39 35 37 🚉 Zaragoza

FROM THE ATLANTIC TO THE PYRENEES

This route explores the beautiful beach resorts and medieval towns of northern Spain's Atlantic coastline before heading inland to Pamplona and up into the Pyrenees. It takes you from the shores of Donostia (San Sebastián) to the vibrant streets of Pamplona, and then up to the heady heights and religious majesty of Orreaga (Roncesvalles).

THE DRIVE

Distance: 151km (94 miles)
Allow: 1 day
Start at: Donostia (San Sebastián), map 465 J2
End at: Orreaga (Roncesvalles), map 465 K2

★ The fashionable, cosmopolitan resort of Donostia (San Sebastián ▷ 177) is split in two by Río Urumea. In addition to palaces and religious monuments, there are superb beaches and large parks here.

Leave the city via the Puente de la Zurriola over the Río Urumea, the nearest bridge to the sea. With the sea on your left, pass the large Kursaal Palacio conference/theatre building on your left. Go along the Avenida de la Zurriola promenade and through traffic lights to a little roundabout; fork left here. The road bends right on to Avenida de Navarra. Follow the sign for the A-8 to Irun/Francia (France) as far as the junction and turn left on to the wide two-lane highway. At the next intersection, keep straight ahead on the A-8 towards Irun and France.

Go through the port area alongside the railtrack. Stay in the left-hand lane to follow the A-1 Irun/France route (ignore the highway turn-off). Go through an underpass and follow the A-8 out of the city. At the next intersection for the highway, turn right on to the A-8, signed Irun/Francia and Hondarribia. Continue towards Hondarribia on the N-10.

❶ Smaller and more inviting than Donostia, Hondarribia (Fuenterrabía ▷ 179) has cobbled streets and quaint medieval houses.

Leave town and follow signs initially for Donostia past the airport. At the junction, turn left towards Irun/France, and at the next roundabout follow signs for Irun/Pamplona. Stay in the left lane and immediately branch left on to the A-8 to Irun/Pamplona. Take the second exit off the next roundabout on to the N-121A to Iruña. Drive through a built-up area and on to Behobia. At the next roundabout, turn right and follow signs for the N-121A to Iruña.

The road starts climbing into the hills on the right side of a pretty valley, but is quite busy with trucks avoiding the highway tolls. Turn right off the N-121A towards Bera de Bidasoa. Drive past factories until you come to a T-junction, turning right here for Bera de Bidasoa (▷ 171).

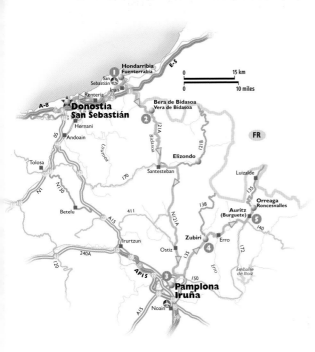

pilgrim's hostel welcomes the weary. Stay on the N-135 towards Burguete (Auritz) as the road climbs more steeply to Puerto de Erro. Follow the switchbacks down into the Erro valley. After crossing the river, climb back up to Puerto de Aurizberri. Pass through Espinal to Burguete.

⑤ Burguete is full of red and white Basque houses, and offered respite to Ernest Hemingway in 1925 when he was preparing *The Sun Also Rises* and in 1959 while he was writing *The Dangerous Summer*. There is also a pilgrim's hostel for walkers who have just made it over the Pyrenees.

From Burguete it's a short drive to Orreaga (▷ 184).

WHEN TO GO
Although it may be possible to drive this route at any time of year, the road to Orreaga from Pamplona can be affected by snow during winter. The visitor offices will be able to check weather and road conditions.

WHERE TO EAT
BODEGÓN ALEJANDRO
A traditional bodega serving superb local dishes at reasonable prices.
✉ Fermín Calbetón 4, 20003 Donostia
☎ 943 42 71 58 ⊙ Tue, Sun 1–3.30, Wed–Sat 1–3.30, 9–11.30

RESTAURANTE SAN FERMÍN
A wide selection of à la carte dishes.
✉ Calle San Nicolás 44, 31001 Pamplona
☎ 948 22 21 91

WHERE TO STAY
HOTEL AVENIDA
✉ Avenida Zaragoza 5, 31003 Pamplona
☎ 948 24 54 54

PLACE TO VISIT
AQUARIUM DONOSTIA
www.aquariumss.com
✉ Plaza Carlos Blasco de Imaz, 20003 Donostia ☎ 943 44 00 99 ⊙ Jul–Aug daily 10–9; Easter–Jun, Sep 10–8; Oct– Easter Mon–Fri 10–7, Sat–Sun and holidays 10–8 ♿ Adult €12, child (4–12) €6

Opposite *Monte Igueldo, Donostia*

② The small town of Bera near the head-waters of Río Bidasoa is traditional. It is renowned for whitewashed stone houses and its lovely 15th-century church.

Continue through Bera de Bidasoa and follow signs for the N-121A to Iruña/Pamplona. Go straight over a mini-roundabout. At the junction, turn left on to the N-121A. Keep climbing up the wooded valley with the river on your right, then pass through a series of tunnels and the village of Narbate as the valley opens up. At the N-121A/N-121B junction, turn right, staying on the former road towards Pamplona. Continue on the N-121A for a further 43km (26 miles), along the Valle de Ulzama and through the Puerto de Velate tunnel, to Pamplona. At the roundabout, take the first exit signed towards Pamplona. Continue straight ahead into central Pamplona.

③ Known as the 'city of the bulls', Pamplona (▷ 182–183) has much more going for it than its famous annual San Fermín street dash of man and beast. As the city is neatly

compact, it is easy enough to see its highlights in a couple of hours.

Leave Pamplona from Plaza Merindades and head east along Avenida de la Baja Navarra. Once out of the city, at the traffic lights near a park, join the right filter lane and turn right, following signs to Huarte and the N-135 to France. At the large roundabout turn left on to the exit for Huarte. At the next roundabout, take the second exit for the N-135, signed to France. Immediately, get into the left lane for the two-lane highway leading to the N-135 France road. The signing on this road is confusing—the NA-138, N-121A and N-135 all go to France. Continue to the roundabout and follow the NA-32. At the next roundabout take the exit for the N-135 to Zubiri. Turn right at the junction for the N-135 to Zubiri and France, which leads through open fields and beside the river to Larrasoaña and Zubiri.

④ Zubiri is surrounded by sumptuous countryside. St. James is said to have stayed here on his way to Santiago de Compostela, and a

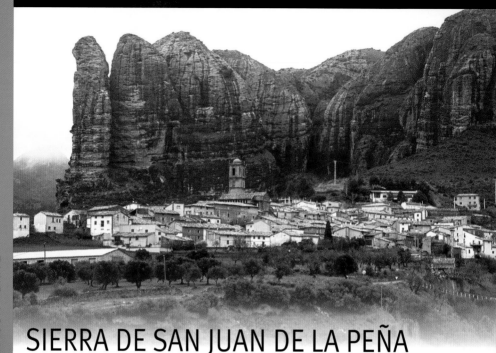

SIERRA DE SAN JUAN DE LA PEÑA

This drive provides historic sights and stunning natural scenery. From the craggy hilltop setting of Castillo de Loarre to the forest-cloaked slopes of San Juan de la Peña, it is a drive of many vistas. The orange spires of Los Mallos de Riglos and the snaking waters of the Río Gállego carve a landscape that is both fascinating and formidable.

THE DRIVE

Distance: 138km (86 miles)
Allow: 1 day
Start at: Huesca, map 466 K3
End at: Jaca, map 466 K2

★ Huesca (▷ 179) is not particularly attractive on the outskirts, but its old quarter has a collection of squares and streets rich in Aragónese art and architecture. Beyond its Gothic cathedral, the town makes a good starting point for exploring some of the region's nearby sights.

At the roundabout where Avenida de Monreal, Calle de San Juan Bosco and Avenida de la Paz intersect, follow the northwesterly exit, signed A-132 to Pamplona. You will pass a Repsol garage and a police station on your left. Pass under a bridge and

continue on the A-132 signed for Ayerbe. After 14km (9 miles) take the right turn signed for Bolea, Colegiata Bolea and Castillo de Loarre; you will also see a sign here, which informs you that you are on the Ruta de la Cereza (Cherry Route).

❶ The small rural village of Bolea is laid out around the 16th-century hilltop Colegiata and built on the remains of a Roman temple and Muslim fort. On the edge of the village a ceramic sign invites newcomers to visit the Colegiata and enjoy Bolea cherries, ham and wine. Climb up to the church for excellent views over the village, little touched by tourism, and to the plains beyond.

Leave Bolea on the same road, following the signs for Castillo

de Loarre and passing through agricultural landscapes and cherry orchards. The castle is signed to the right after 8km (5 miles), and the road leads up a winding set of switchbacks to the visitors' parking area.

❷ Towering over the Ebro valley beneath the Sierra de Loarre, Castillo de Loarre (▷ 176) was once the castle-eyrie of the kings of Aragón. During the 12th century it was used as a monastery. Massive walls and cylindrical towers still encircle the church, from where there are superb views.

Continue back down the hillside and on to the road towards Loarre. Passing this small village on your right-hand side, head towards

Ayerbe. Here, turn back onto the A-132, heading northwest and following signs to Pamplona. The scenery opens out to give dramatic views of the Los Mallos de Riglos sandstone spires. After 8km (5 miles), take the left turn for Agüero.

❸ The isolated village of Agüero shelters beneath towering cliffs of the Mallos range. On its outskirts is Iglesia de Santiago, a Romanesque jewel well worth a visit.

Return to the A-132 and continue north towards Pamplona and the Embalse de la Peña.

❹ The massive dammed lake of Embalse de la Peña is crossed by a bridge. Flowing south from it, through splendidly carved canyons and gorges, is the Río Gállego.

After crossing the lake, take the right turn signed for Monasterio de San Juan de la Peña. The road continues to hug the lakeside for a while and then heads through a broad forested valley. Stay on the A-1205, passing the village of Anzánigo with its medieval bridge, to reach Bernués.

❺ Bernués is a small, mainly agricultural community, lying on the edge of the Sierra de San Juan de la Peña.

Continue past the village and then take the left turn shortly afterwards on to the A-1603 for the Monasterio de San Juan de la Peña. The road narrows and climbs through lush pine woods.

❻ There are two monasteries here at San Juan de le Peña. You arrive first at the upper monastery, Monasterio Nuevo, built to replace the cave monastery below following a fire in 1675. This was later abandoned but has now been elegantly restored to house an interesting visitor centre. There are two sections, dedicated to the history of Aragón and the history of the monastery complex. You can walk down to the unusually located Monasterio de San Juan de la Peña (▷ 185), housed almost within its own cave beneath an overhanging cliff. The area is ideal for walks (▷ 192–193) and has superb views over the Pyrenees, the Valle de Ansó (▷ 186) and the Valle de Hecho (▷ 186).

From the parking area, follow the road past both monasteries and through Santa Cruz de la Serós to the N-240. Turn right on to this main road and on to Jaca (▷ 179).

WHEN TO GO
To avoid the weekend crowds, do this tour on a weekday—although note that the monastery is closed Monday from 16 October to 15 March.

WHERE TO EAT
There is a very pleasant picnic area with benches and a snack bar in front of the Monasterio Nuevo at San Juan de la Peña.

HOSPEDERÍA DE LOARRE
www.hospederiadeloarre.com
Serves a very good *menú del día*.
✉ Plaza Mayor, 22890 Castillo de Loarre
☎ 974 38 27 06 ✪ Daily 1.30–3, 8.30–10

PLACE TO VISIT
MONASTERIO DE SAN JUAN DE LA PEÑA
www.monasteriosanjuan.com
✉ San Juan de la Peña, 22792 Huesca
☎ 974 33 51 19 ✪ Jun–Aug daily 10–2.30, 3.30–8; 16 Mar–May and Sep–15 Oct daily 10–2, 4–7; 16 Oct–Feb Tue–Sun 11–2, 4–5.30 🎫 Adult €6 (includes admission to both monasteries), child (7–16) €5. Tour guides available at no extra charge

Above *Bolea, a simple rural settlement, remains unchanged by time*
Opposite *Agüero and Los Mallos de Riglos*

AROUND SAN JUAN DE LA PEÑA

Set among open parkland, forests and hills in the heights of the Sierra de San Juan de la Peña are two of the region's most notable monasteries. This circular walk combines several shorter trails emanating from the higher Monasterio Nuevo. It takes in woods, wildlife, both monasteries, the church ruins of San Voto and Santa Teresa, and wide views of the Pyrenees, with little altitude gain, so it is suitable for everyone.

THE WALK

Distance: Approximately 4km (2.5 miles)
Allow: 1–1.5 hours
Total ascent: 100m (330ft)
Start/end at: Monasterio Nuevo, San Juan de la Peña, map 466 K3
Maps and guides: The walk's leaflet *Paseos a Través del Monumento Natural de San Juan de la Peña* (Spanish only) is available from the Casa Forestal information desk, next to the Monasterio Nuevo. This is sufficient for walks along the well-signed trails. The booklet *Monumento Natural de San Juan de la Peña — Espacios Naturales Protegidos* (Spanish only) is a good guide to the area and its wildlife and is also available at Casa Forestal.
Parking: Free parking with toilets and picnic area at the Monasterio Nuevo.

HOW TO GET THERE

The Monasterio Nuevo is on the A-1603 mountain road between Bernués and Santa Cruz de la Serós (the latter is 4km/2.5 miles to the south of the main N240 between Jaca and Puente la Reina).

★ The baroque Monasterio Nuevo (▷ 191) was built between 1675 and 1714 to replace the old monastery below, which had suffered damage from a fire and falling rocks. The renovated building contains a visitor centre, which outlines the history of the monastery complex, and of the ancient kingdom of Aragón.

Facing the monastery, head to the right corner of the property (demarcated with a fence and a crumbling stone wall), crossing the grass. Where the wood begins, the green trail sign 'Balcón de los Pirineos 400m' points the way to a wide path along the side of the monastery. The track passes among silver pines and past a board giving information on the *castaño de Indias*, a tree planted by the monks as its seeds could be mixed with alcohol to make anti-inflammatory cures. A wide track continues to a fork just beyond the information board about holly. Take the right fork. The track eventually starts to climb gently, with information boards on silver pines and forest birds and another about weasels, foxes and badgers. At the top of the path you reach the Balcón de los Pirineos.

❶ Saving the view until the last few moments, this fenced area gives panoramas across the Aragón valley to the entire Pyrenean range. A brass arc dial on a marble stand identifies the peaks, from El Maladeta on the right to Navarra on the left. A board gives information on the eagles and vultures you often see flying in the valley.

Above *The awe-inspiring San Juan de la Peña range*
Left and opposite *The Monasterio Nuevo has a Churrigueresque baroque facade*

From the Balcón, and facing the Pyrenees, turn left to follow the footpath that is signed San Voto. The path follows the ridge edge safely, giving more views of the Pyrenees. The trail narrows and becomes rockier as it starts to descend gently, until you reach a sharp left bend and it descends more steeply into denser woods.

At a crossroads, follow the track straight over, signed 'San Voto'. Continue on the path through woodland to the junction with the road linking the two monasteries. Cross the road and bear right, ignoring the paved road and the first track on the right (this leads down to the cave monastery). Instead, follow the sign a little farther on for Paseo de San Voto. Continue past more information boards until you arrive at a track junction. Turn right on the track to reach Ermita de San Voto.

❷ This diminutive, ruined and overgrown church, built at the end of the 16th century on the orders of San Voto, stands on a promontory. Legend has it that this was the spot where a bolting horse miraculously stopped before the edge, saving its rider from certain death.

From the church, a narrow footpath drops steeply down to a stone stairway with wooden handrails. At the bottom is the Mirador de San Voto.

❸ From this balcony platform there are views over the Monasterio Viejo, sheltering under the bulging cliff face (▷ 185), and beyond to the heavily forested sierra.

Return up the stairway to the Ermita de San Voto. Go to the right of the church on a track, passing a board giving information on the church, to reach a track junction. Turn right and continue down the straight track through towering pines, past an old stone bench on the right. Just after the board on *jabalí* (wild boar), you come to a surfaced road.

Turn right and then immediately left at an overgrown arched ruin. Follow the track through woods and then across an open field to the Casa Forestal building. Go to the right of this and continue across the field to the wooden play area near the pond. From the pond edge, follow the track signed 'Paseo Santa Teresa, 350m', which heads back into woodland. It climbs gradually to Balconcillo de Santa Teresa.

❹ Balconcillo de Santa Teresa, another outstanding viewpoint, is also home to the ruined Ermita de Santa Teresa, which has just a couple of walls still standing. Built around the same time as San Voto, it was a place of contemplation for the monks and a strategic lookout over the Sierra Guara and Sierra Loarre, Mallos de Riglos and Río Gállego.

Retrace your route back to the Casa Forestal and bear right to return to the adjacent Monasterio Nuevo and the parking area.

WHEN TO GO
The walk is possible at any time of year, although the steep access road to San Juan de la Peña may be closed by snow or ice during winter. There is plenty of tree cover, so the summer heat won't affect you too much. Spring and autumn are perhaps the best times, when the woods are at their most beautiful. In July and August, especially during weekends, the area is very popular with locals and the parking areas can fill up.

WHERE TO EAT
RESTAURANTE MONJES NEGROS
The new monastery complex now contains a hotel with a stylish restaurant: There's also a café for light meals and snacks.
✉ Monasterio Nuevo, 22711 Jaca
☎ 974 37 44 22

REGIONS EUSKADI, NAVARRA AND ARAGÓN • WALK

PARQUE NACIONAL ORDESA

From the high peaks of the Valle de Benasque to the magnificent mountain scenery of the glacier-carved Parque Nacional Ordesa y Monte Perdido, this is a spectacular drive of geographical highs and lows. Winding waterways twist through deeply cut canyons to give a helter-skelter journey of giddy views. The landscape then opens out into pleasant rolling countryside as the drive takes you through typically lush Aragónese farmland. Medieval history and a beautifully preserved square make the town of Ainsa an obvious stopping point, where you can also enjoy some of the famous Aragónese cooking, such as pig's cheeks, roast lamb or mountain goat and a wide range of cheeses.

THE DRIVE
Distance: 109km (68 miles)
Allow: 4–5 hours
Start at: Benasque, map 466 L2
End at: Torla, map 466 L2

★ The pretty town of Benasque (▷ 171), with its traditional stone houses and historic buildings — including the Renaissance Palacio de los Condes de Ribagorza — is a popular base for exploring the

surrounding mountains. Walkers, climbers, skiers and bicyclists all flock here to enjoy the delightful landscape of the Pirineos. The town is geared for the outdoor enthusiast, with places to stay, guiding services and equipment shops. The 3,404m (11,168ft) Aneto peak, the highest in the Pyrenees and a demanding full day's walk up and back, will require crampons and a *piolet* (ice axe).

From the Barrabes outdoor shop, unmissable with the huge ice climbing image on its wall, head southwest out of town and cross the Río Esera. Continue on this road, past Eriste (starting point of the Taste of the Pyrenees walk — ▷ 196) and pass through the Valle de Esera, with its rock pinnacles, towering cliffs and sheer drops. Some 32km (20 miles) later you enter the village of Campo.

❶ The heart of the small rural village of Campo is set back from the main road. Narrow cobbled streets of compact stone houses lead to the Plaza Mayor. Nearby, just off Calle de San Antón, is an arcaded square of characterful buildings. Signed from the N-260 and down an alleyway is the fascinating Museo de Juegos Tradicionales, a museum dedicated to traditional games.

Leave Campo behind, following the same road until Ainsa is signed to the right. Following the N-260 through open countryside, you pass Foradada del Toscar, Samper and Banastón, from where there are views over the Embalse de Mediano. You will reach Ainsa, at the confluence of the Río Cinca and Río Ara.

❷ Overlooking this river confluence is Ainsa's attractive old quarter, on a hilltop promontory (▷ 171). Enclosed within ancient walls, the winding cobbled streets, flanked by stone houses with floral balconies, lead to the pretty main square and its Romanesque parish church. In the 11th century this city was the capital of a small kingdom formed by García Jiménez after he defeated the Moors.

Continue out of town on the N-260, following signs for Boltaña and/or Parque Nacional Ordesa y Monte Perdido. Beyond Boltaña the road winds through a forest-cloaked valley before entering a canyon of multi-layered rock. The road eventually narrows beneath a rising rock face, where there are plunging views of the Río Ara. The valley opens out soon after into fields and pastures. Just over 15km (9 miles) farther on, you enter the Valle de Broto, which leads to the pretty village of Broto. The impressive waterfall here can be seen from the bridge that crosses the Ara.

Leave Broto on the same road and climb a snaking pass. Shortly after, take the first right turn to Torla and follow this access road until you reach the village.

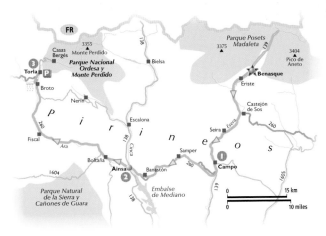

❸ Attractive Torla (▷ 181) is the main base for access to the Parque Nacional Ordesa y Monte Perdido. It is geared up for walkers, with *refugio* (overnight hostel) accommodation and hotels. The view of Torla's church, with the great rocky mass of Mondarruego (2,848m/9,344ft) rising up behind, is impressive.

As you enter town you will notice the big parking areas to your right. Torla is still some 8km (5 miles) from the entrance, but you must park here and catch a shuttle bus into Ordesa; note also that numbers of visitors are limited for conservation reasons.

WHEN TO GO
Summer is generally busy, but July is much better than August when Ordesa becomes crowded. June and September are ideal. Midweek is generally less crowded than weekends. In winter, snow drifts usually block access to the park.

WHERE TO EAT
Along the route the best stopping place is Ainsa, where a number of excellent restaurants spill out onto the attractive main square.

BODEGÓN DE MALLACÁN
Has won a number of awards for its traditional dishes.
✉ Plaza Mayor 6, 22330 Ainsa ☎ 974 50 09 77 🕐 Daily 10–1

LA PARRILLA
Specializes in Aragonese cuisine.
✉ Avenida de Francia s/n, 22440 Benasque ☎ 974 55 11 34 🕐 Daily 1–3.30, 9–11.30 (closes Sun pm 15 Sep–1 Nov). Closed May

PLACE TO VISIT
MUSEO DE JUEGOS TRADICIONALES
✉ Calle Pallerez s/n, 22450 Campo ☎ 974 55 01 36 🕐 Tue–Sat 11–2, 5–8, Sun 11–2 ♿ Free 🎟 Tours are an additional €2

Opposite *Although it is a popular base for visiting the national park, Torla has retained its old stone charm*
Below *Old bridge across the Río Cinca*

REGIONS EUSKADI, NAVARRA AND ARAGÓN • DRIVE

A TASTE OF THE PYRENEES

In an area renowned for its challenging and severe mountain terrain, this relatively short and easy circular walk takes in a traditional village yet also provides views of peaks over 2,000m (6,560ft) high, the spectacular Aigüeta de Grist (Eriste) canyon and the imposing walls of the Colladetas de Xinebro. On the way back down, you can enjoy the sweeping panoramas across Valle de Esera and Embalse de Linsoles to the summits beyond. Utilizing part of the GR-11 trail, the route crosses the simple and enchanting Puente de Tramarrius, where the frigid waters running off the Aigüeta de Grist tumble down to meet those from the Aigüeta de Saunc (Sahún).

THE WALK

Distance: 6km (3.7 miles)
Allow: 1.5–2 hours return
Total ascent: 190m (620ft)
Start/end at: Eriste (Grist), map 466 L2
Parking: Free parking spots are available along the lakeside, but note that they fill up early in the day during the summer season.

HOW TO GET THERE

Eriste (Grist) lies along the main A-139 4km (2.5 miles) south of Benasque on the north bank of the Río Ésera.

★ Strolling through the small, sleepy, traditional village of Eriste (Grist) makes for a gentle start to the walk. Note the Romanesque Iglesia de San Feliu, old houses with stone doorways and cobbled streets. From the main road and with your back to the lake, take the street leading up into the village from the Hostal de Los Pirineos. Go uphill past a building called the Grist and a 19th-century house on the right. At the main plaza, with the church to your right, take the right-hand exit (there is a *No aparcar* (no parking) sign on its wall) and walk along a cobbled street of three-floor houses with stone portals.

At the end of the street ignore the immediate left turn and continue ahead for another 20m (25 yards). Take the left exit (ignore the right turn that goes over a hump), then turn immediately left again into a narrow street that bends to the right to meet up with the trailhead. A map (Camin de Tramarrius) of the route up to the Refugio Ángel Orús and a wooden trail sign (PR-HU36 Puente de Tramarrius and Refugio Ángel Orús) point the way.

Follow the footpath under power lines, with views right across the Aigüeta de Grist waters to the hydroelectric pipeline that drops down from the 1,944m (6,378ft) peak of Tossal de Seira. The obvious trail bends west and you will soon see the

Above *Snow-covered Pyrenean heights above Eriste (Grist)*
Opposite left *The medieval Puente de Tramarrius*

2,116m (6,942ft) pyramidal peak of Tuca de Grist ahead.

The path becomes cobbled and winds through fields, before ascending more steeply to a fork. Take the right fork (the left has wooden poles across it) on to a cobbled path and continue to climb.

❶ The path then flattens out between fields, with Tuca de Grist ahead on the left, before climbing very gently to an information board about the *zorro* (fox). An adult fox can apparently eat up to 5,000 rats per year and is not a pest at all—a message no doubt aimed at hunters.

Continue up the trail, ignoring a left turn on to another trail indicated by a yellow and white cross on a boulder. The trail narrows and becomes rockier as you pass scrub bushes and small trees to arrive at a junction with a bigger track, with a sign (fallen over) to Eriste.

At the track junction, turn right on to the wider track (the left turn has a yellow/white cross on a post) and continue uphill. Ahead are views into the deep notch of the Grist valley. The trail continues to climb gently up to a fork. Stay ahead on the left fork (the right drops down to the river). Soon the track winds gently through a couple of S-bends.

❷ Across the river is the peak of Tossal del Seira, while ahead the river tumbles over miniature waterfalls. Straight ahead through the canyon stands a high mountain ridge, with Tuca Pula Chullá at the left end and Agulla del Xinebro at the right. Just before the riverbed, a small track leads off to the right and on to the Puente de Tramarrius.

❸ From this pointed-arch Roman bridge you can see the emerald-green run-off waters from the Aigueta de Grist and Aigüeta de Saunc plunging into a rock pool.

Cross the bridge and turn immediately right on to a jeep track, which climbs below scree slopes. Continue until you reach a track junction with trail signs for the Refugio Ángel Orús to the left, and for Eriste and Puente de Tramarrius pointing back the way you came. Turn right on to a jeep track and follow it as it descends to a fork.

Take the left fork and continue down the switchback jeep track, leading to another intersection. Here, the private right track leads a short distance to the top of the hydroelectric water pipe and ramshackle buildings. Continue down the main track through a series of switchback corners that give views of the surrounding peaks, Eriste and the Embalse de Linsoles.

Near the bottom, where the road is surfaced, you reach a junction where the track to the right is marked with *prohibido* (prohibited) signs (it leads to the hydroelectric station). Take the left track, which curves steeply down to the left. Follow the road past old workers' huts to the junction with the main Eriste–Benasque road. Turn right on to the road (beware of traffic) and walk past the hydroelectric station back to Eriste.

WHEN TO GO
It should be possible to walk this easygoing route any time of year, but good footwear is essential if there is snow. Most of it is along a deep valley, so is sheltered from the sun for much of the day. The July/August visitor season brings more hikers, although the trail is less frequented than many in the area.

WHERE TO EAT
Eriste (Grist) is the only place to find refreshment or resupply on the route and the choice is rather limited, so stock up at Benasque.

HOTEL ERISTE
www.hoteleriste.com
A chalet-style hotel serving local dishes, tapas and snacks.
✉ Carretera de Benasque s/n, 22469 Eriste
☎ 974 55 15 14 🅚 Closed Nov–Mar

Below *Wooden trail signs clearly show the way on this walk*

REGIONS EUSKADI, NAVARRA AND ARAGÓN • WALK

BERRIOPLANO

ARTSAIA
www.artsaia.com
A live music club with various stages playing different rhythms. Resident and guest DJs bring the latest electro pop and dance music to a young, happy crowd.

✉ Poligono Industrial Iruregaña s/n, Aizoain, 31195 Berrioplano ☎ 948 30 33 57 🖐 Varies according to performance 🚌 5km (3 miles) west of Pamplona on the N-121 via Berriainz

BILBAO

ARRIAGA THEATRE
www.teatroarriaga.com
Bilbao's most illustrious theatre has a grandiose facade and a busy calendar. Ballet, classical recitals and opera are performed by both national and international acts.

✉ Plaza Arriaga 1, 48005 Bilbao ☎ 944 16 35 33 🖐 From €8 🚇 Abando Interchange

ATHLETIC BILBAO FOOTBALL CLUB SAN MAMÉS
www.athletic-club.net
Athletic Bilbao's illustrious history speaks for itself, with 24 soccer league championships to its name. Locals are intensely proud of their 40,000-seat San Mames Stadium. Weekend matches take place regularly every two weeks from September to May.

✉ Calle Felipe Serrate, 48013 Bilbao ☎ 944 24 08 77 🖐 €25–€65 🚌 26, 56, 62 🚇 San Mamés

BARRAINKUA CULTURAL CENTRE
One of the main venues of the International Puppet Festival in November. Puppeteers from around the world use stick, glove, shadow and string marionettes to entertain adults and children.

✉ Calle Barrainkua 5, 48009 Bilbao ☎ 944 24 59 02 🖐 From €6 🚇 Abando Interchange

BILBOROCK
www.bilbao.net/bilborock
This 17th-century baroque church was acquired by the city council in the 1990s and has been converted into a wonderful multifunctional venue. Theatre performances, festivals, film screenings, and music concerts of all genres are regularly staged. The acoustics are excellent, and it's perfectly located in the old quarter, the heart of the city's buzzing nightlife.

✉ Muelle de la Merced 1, 48003 Bilbao ☎ 944 15 13 06 🕐 Opening times and admission prices vary according to the performance, but the tourist office can provide full details

COTTON CLUB
www.cottonclubbilbao.com
Funky DJs and live jazz, blues and rock bands. A mixed crowd is attracted by the unpretentious atmosphere and great cocktails.

✉ Calle Gregorio de la Revilla 25 (entrance on Calle Simon Bolivar), 48005 Bilbao ☎ 944 10 49 51 🕐 Sun–Thu 6.30pm–3am, Fri–Sat 6.30pm–6am. Closed Aug 🖐 Free 🚇 Abando Interchange 🚇 Indautxu

KAFE ANTZOKIA
www.kafeantzokia.com
In 1995 this former theatre was overhauled and became a cultural venue with a focus on promoting exciting live music. Basque rock bands play frequently, as do national reggae and pop groups. Each Sunday there is a children's show. The venue is tured into a restaurant every lunchtime.

✉ Calle San Vicente 2, 48001 Bilbao ☎ 944 24 46 25 🖐 Some events are free; concerts from €6 🚇 Abando Interchange

Opposite Walk among the sharks at Aquarium Donostia

KARTELL-ONN
Just in front of the Guggenheim Museum, this sleek shop is the Spanish outlet of the famed Italian interiors and homewares firm. The smaller items from local and international designers are very tempting.
✉ Alameda Mazarredo 67, 48001 Bilbao ☎ 944 17 10 30 ⏰ Mon–Fri 10.30–2, 4.30–8, Sat 10.30–2 🚇 Moyúa

LIBRERÍA ANTICUARIA ASTARLOA
www.libreriastarloa.com
Lovers of old books, codices, facsimiles and other gems will appreciate this antiquarian bookshop. Vintage texts, yellowing maps and ancient books line the dusty shelves inside this old *librería*. Weighty tomes describe the history of Bilbao and the region, many in Basque. Several old English-language travel books make intriguing reading.
✉ Calle Astarloa 4, 48001 Bilbao ☎ 944 23 16 07 ⏰ Mon–Fri 10–2, 4–8, Sat 10–2 🚇 Abando Interchange 🚇 Moyúa

LOEWE
www.loewe.com
Reassuringly expensive unisex fashion in central Bilbao. Loewe is heaven for those who wish to splash their cash on hats, gloves, dresses and scarves.
✉ Gran Vía 39, 48009 Bilbao ☎ 944 79 06 40 ⏰ Mon–Fri 9.30–8, Sat 9.30–1 🚇 Abando Interchange 🚇 Moyúa

MUSEO GUGGENHEIM
www.guggenheim-bilbao.es
The Guggenheim Museum's store should not to be missed by lovers of modern art books. More than 2,000 titles are on display in a range of languages. The museum shop also stocks its own selection of purses, leather diaries, gloves and cutting-edge jewellery.
✉ Avenida Abandoibarra s/n, 48001 Bilbao ☎ 944 35 90 85 ⏰ Tue–Sun 10–8 (also Jul–Aug Mon) 🚇 Abando Interchange

PALACIO EUSKALDUNA JAUREGIA (PALACIO DE CONGRESOS Y DE LA MÚSICA)
www.euskalduna.net
Since its opening in 1999 this wackily designed wood, steel and glass playhouse in Bilbao's old shipyard district has hosted music, drama, dance and conference events. Some performances are in Basque.
✉ Avenida Abandoibarra 4, 48011 Bilbao ☎ 944 03 50 00/902 54 05 39 💶 €10–€45 🚌 26, 56, 62

SOMBREROS GOROSTIAGA
Hats for every age and occasion are sold in this establishment. Most have a traditional feel, such as the range of top hats and boaters. You can also buy an authentic Basque beret.
✉ Calle Víctor 9, 48005 Bilbao ☎ 944 16 12 76 ⏰ Mon–Sat 10–1.30, 4–8. Closed Sat pm Jul–Sep 🚇 Abando Interchange 🚇 Plaza Unamuno

TEATRO BARAKALDO ANTZOKIA
www.teatrobarakaldo.com
This is Bilbao's other great theatre, with a distinctive concave and convex modern facade. Drama and dance, rather than concert performances, dominate the playlist here. The frequency of shows really hots up during the summer months and the theatre is also used as a cinema.
✉ Calle Juan Sebastián Elcano 4, 48901 Barakaldo, near Bilbao ☎ 944 78 06 00 💶 From €12 🚇 Barakaldo

LA VAJILLA
This brimming store sells everything for the kitchen, from the elegant to the ergonomic. Spanish coffee cups, sets of tumblers and stainless-steel stovetop coffee-makers make fine gifts to take home.
✉ Gran Vía 24, 48001 Bilbao ☎ 944 23 08 32 ⏰ Mon–Sat 10–1.30, 4.30–8. Closed Sat in Jul–Aug; Sat pm in Jun, Sep, Oct 🚇 Abando Interchange 🚇 Diputación

DONOSTIA
AQUARIUM DONOSTIA
www.aquariumss.com
More than 5,000 fish, plus a handful of sharks, entertain visitors to Donostia's waterfront aquarium. The tanks are set up with different habitats, including an Atlantic section, tropical lake section and one devoted to rays. For the best view, walk through the glass tunnel under the main tank.
✉ Plaza Carlos Blasco de Imaz, 20003 Donostia ☎ 943 44 00 99 ⏰ Jul–Aug daily 10–9; Easter–Jun, Sep daily 10–8; Oct–Easter Mon–Fri 10–7, Sat–Sun and holidays 10–8. Closed 1 Jan, 25 Dec 💶 Adult €12, child (4–12) €6, under 4 free

BARRENETXE
www.barrenetxe.net
The best pastry shop and bakery in town (and one of the most prestigious *pastelerías* in the region), Barrenetxe has a café attached to the shop if you'd like to sit down to enjoy your purchases. Choose from the fine selection of delicious cakes (the house specialties, *txintxorros*, made with almonds and orange, are fabulous), or something savoury, such as a toasted sandwich made with the bakery's own bread. The prettily wrapped chocolates make excellent gifts.
✉ Plaza Gipuzkoa 9, 20004 Donostia ☎ 943 42 44 82 ⏰ Mon–Sat 9–8, Sun 9–1 🚇 RENFE station on Puente Maria Cristina

BATAPLÁN
www.bataplandisco.com
Bataplán is a great indoor and outdoor dance venue, overlooking the long Playa de la Concha. Although not quite as exclusive as it was in days gone by, Bataplán still expects its visitors to dress to impress. Dance to music spun by pop and rock DJs until the early hours of the morning.
✉ Paseo de la Concha s/n, 20007 Donostia ☎ 943 47 36 01 ⏰ Fri–Sat 10–late 💶 €14 🚇 RENFE station on Puente María Cristina

EZEIZA VINOS
An excellent and highly recommended wine shop, this is conveniently located near the cathedral. There's a wide selection of local and national wines including

a particularly good selection of Riojas; it also offers some fine French wines. There are regular tastings and other events. The helpful staff will be pleased to make recommendations.
✉ Calle General Prim 16, 2004 Donostia ☎ 943 46 68 14 🕐 Mon–Sat 10–1.30, 5–8 🚉 RENFE station on Puente Maria Cristina

LOREAK MENDIAN
www.loreakmendian.com
Donostia supports a lively surf culture and their preferred clobber comes from this local label. In this shop near the old town, its distinctive daisy motif is found on T-shirts, bags, jeans and women's wear in natural fabrics that are both cool and wearable.
✉ Calle Hernani 27, 20003 Donostia ☎ 943 43 41 76 🕐 Mon–Sat 10–8

PALACIO DE CONGRESOS KURSAAL
www.kursaal.org
Several live music and theatre events formerly held at the Teatro Victoria Eugenia take place at this large auditorium. Everything from rock music to opera is on the year-round schedule.
✉ Avenida de la Zurriola 1, 20002 Donostia ☎ 943 00 30 00 🕐 Varies 🚉 RENFE station on Puente María Cristina

PARQUE DE ATRACCIONES MONTE IGUELDO
www.monteigueldo.es
A fun, child-oriented theme park near the Monte Igueldo hotel. Parents can take in the stunning Atlantic views from the clifftop location while their children play. Rides include dodgem cars, a funicular train, trampolines,

toboggans, river rapids and a small zoo. No facilities for babies on site.
✉ Paseo del Faro, 20008 Donostia ☎ 943 21 35 25 🕐 Jun–Sep daily 10–9; Apr–May, Oct 11–8; Oct–Mar Mon–Fri 11–6, Sat–Sun 11–8 🚏 Around €2 per ride 🚉 Donostia Central 🚌 Buses marked 'Igueldo'

PLAYA DE LA CONCHA
Enjoy free year-round fun on one of northern Spain's finest beaches, 1.2km (0.75 mile) long. The beach continues for another 500m (550 yards) around the Palacio de Miramar where it becomes known as the Playa de Ondarreta. Swimming is possible from June until September, although a few brave souls take dips a couple of months either side of those dates! Behind the beach there are snack bars, toilets and a few shops.
✉ Playa de la Concha, 20003 Donostia 🚏 Free

PONSOL
Straw hats, top hats and bowlers line the shelves, but most visitors want to get their hands on a traditional Basque beret. Here they are made with distinction using fine felt and leather inner strips.
✉ Calle Narika 4, 20003 Donostia ☎ 943 42 08 76 🕐 Mon–Sat 10–1.30, 4–8 🚉 RENFE station on Puente María Cristina

TEATRO PRINCIPAL
Drama and dance rule behind the red facade of the Teatro Principal. The 1930s building features huge interior balconies from which you can watch cutting-edge Basque- and Spanish-language performances. This old town playhouse also hosts an annual festival in November dedicated to

horror films. There is a small bar, but it is not always open.
✉ Calle Mayor 1, 20003 Donostia ☎ 943 48 19 70 🚏 Around €15 🚉 RENFE station on Puente María Cristina 🚌 5, 8, 9, 13, 16, 25, 26

HONDARRIBIA
REAL GOLF CLUB DE SAN SEBASTIÁN
www.golfsansebastian.com
This fine 18-hole golf course is very long, and slopes, rather than water and sand, are the main hazards. All are welcome at the on-site clubhouse.
✉ Carretera from Donostia to Hondarribia, Urb. Jaizkibel, 20280 Hondarribia ☎ 943 61 68 45 🕐 Daily 9–8 🚏 €80 per round in summer; €110 in winter 🚌 The Valle de Jaizubia is 14km (9 miles) northeast of Donostia. To get there, take the A-8 autoroute towards Irún, then get off at Exit 4 for Jaizkibel

PAMPLONA
CUCHILLERÍA GÓMEZ
www.cuchilleriagomez.com
This shop was founded in 1943 in an ancient building at the top end of Calle Estafeta. It stocks knives, gifts, images of bulls and typical monuments from Pamplona, with prices ranging from €8 to €1,800.
✉ Calle Estafeta 15, 31001 Pamplona ☎ 948 22 34 32 🕐 Mon–Sat 9.30–1.30, 4.30–8

ELIZONDO
Although this cake shop-cum-deli is famous for its housebrand chocolate, you will also find tempting local cheeses such as the smoked Idiazábal and creamy Roncal, bottles

of cider and *patxarán* (a sweet but very strong aperitif), pâtés and other local Navarran delights.

✉ Calle Curia, 1, 31001, Pamplona ☎ 948 21 11 25 🕐 Daily 7–2, 5–8.30

KUKUXUMUSU

www.kukuxumusu.com

Kukuxumusu creates cartoons and adapts them for different media, selling them internationally. This shop is now something of a city landmark.

✉ Calle Estafeta 76, 31001 Pamplona ☎ 948 22 73 94 🕐 Mon–Sat 10–8.30

TEATRO GAYARRE

www.teatrogayarre.com

Teatro Gayarre is a meeting point for locals who enjoy dance, classical music and similar performances. The theatre's name is a tribute to the famous tenor from the Roncal, Julian Gayarre.

✉ Calle Carlos III 1–3, 31002 Pamplona ☎ 948 22 23 33 🖐 Varies according to performance

TERUEL

DINÓPOLIS

www.dinopolis.com

You can step into the land of the dinosaurs in some of Aragón's wildest countryside. Wander around the giant park, where life-size models of these giant reptiles work, eat and play. An educational history of the various species, as well as several palaeontology clubs, makes this a great, well-rounded day out.

✉ Poligono Los Planos, 44002 Teruel ☎ 902 44 80 00 🕐 Jul to mid-Sep, Easter, Christmas daily; May–Jun Wed–Sun; mid-Sep to Apr Sat–Sun. Closed 14 Jan, Feb 🖐 Adult €22, child €17

ZARAGOZA

PARQUE DE ATRACCIONES DE ZARAGOZA

www.atraczara.com

This giant theme park has a host of activities for children. They can ride on a mini roller-coaster, picnic in the beautiful grounds or get behind

JANUARY

FESTIVIDAD DE SAN SEBASTIÁN

www.donostiasansebastian.com/tamborrada

A 24-hour fife and drum festival with bands of marching chefs in the streets for 24 hours celebrating the city's patron saint's day.

✉ Donostia 🕐 19–20 January

FEBRUARY–MARCH

CARNAVAL

Carnival celebrations.

✉ Bilbao and other towns

MARCH–APRIL

LA TAMBORRADA

Rhythmic drumming through the streets during Holy Week.

✉ Calanda, near Alcañiz

JUNE–JULY

CONCURSO DE RECORTADORES

www.recortadores.com

For those who prefer a contest in which the bull remains intact and unharmed and man and bull face each other on equal terms, the *recortadores* contest is a hair-raising exhibition of agility and courage.

✉ Pamplona 🕐 During San Fermín

JULY

FIESTA DE SAN FERMÍN

www.sanfermin.com

▷ 183.

✉ Pamplona

INTERNATIONAL JAZZ FESTIVAL

www.jazzvitoria.com

Important jazz festival, attracting bands and combos from all over

Europe and farther afield.

✉ Vitoria-Gasteiz

VAQUILLA DEL ANGEL

www.fiestasdelangel.com

Ten-day festival with parades, music, dance and more.

✉ Teruel 🕐 Early July

JULY–AUGUST

INTERNATIONAL FOLKLORE FESTIVAL OF THE PYRENEES

Traditional music and dance.

✉ Jaca 🕐 Late July–early August, odd-numbered years

AUGUST

FIESTA DE LA VIRGEN BLANCA

Week-long fiesta with bullfights, fireworks and giant figures.

✉ Vitoria-Gasteiz 🕐 3–9 August

INTERNATIONAL FIREWORKS COMPETITION

Attracts exhibitors of displays from all over the world.

✉ Donostia

SEMANA GRANDE

Huge celebration with Basque races, games, music and dance.

✉ Bilbao

SEPTEMBER

INTERNATIONAL FILM FESTIVAL

www.sansebastianfestival.com

Big festival with premieres.

✉ Donostia

OCTOBER

VIRGEN DEL PILAR

Major festival in the name of the Virgin, with floats, bullfights and *jota* dancing.

✉ Zaragoza 🕐 Around 12 Oct

the wheel of an electric car. There is also a huge swimming pool with slide. Cafés, restaurants and baby-changing rooms.

✉ Paseo Duque de Alba s/n, Pinares de Venecia, 50007 Zaragoza ☎ 902 37 80

00 🕐 Jun to mid-Sep Sat–Sun noon–10, Mon–Fri 5–10; mid-Sep to May Sat–Sun noon–10 🖐 To use all attractions, adult €15 (€17 on Sat), children under 110cm (3.5ft) €11.50

Opposite *Early evening on the fashionable La Concha beach at Donostia (San Sebastián)*

EATING

PRICES AND SYMBOLS

The restaurants are listed alphabetically (excluding Le, La and Les). The prices given are the average for a two-course lunch (L) and a three-course dinner (D) for one person, without drinks. The wine price is for the least expensive bottle.

For a key to the symbols, ▷ 2.

AGOITZ/AOIZ

BETI-JAI

www.beti-jai.com

This rural hotel restaurant prides itself on the excellence of its cuisine. It is considered one of the finest in Navarra, and offers a selection of regional recipes. The *canelón de txangurro* (spider crab canelone) is prepared with a piquant black pasta flavoured with squid ink; simpler specialties include steaks and fresh fish. The desserts are exquisite. You can dine informally on tapas and light meals at the adjoining café-bar.

✉ Calle Santa Agueda 4, 31430 Agoitz ☎ 948 33 60 52 🕒 Daily 2–3.30, 8.30–10.30. Closed 2 weeks in Aug 🖐 L €25, D €45, Wine €14

BILBAO (BILBO)

ASADOR ARANDA

www.asadordearanda.com

Fine Castilian food is dished up at this friendly, locally recommended eatery. The house specialty is roast lamb cooked in a clay oven—and is highly recommended.

✉ Calle Egaña 27, 48010 Bilbao ☎ 944 43 06 64 🕒 Mon–Sat 1–4, 9–12, Sun 1–4 🖐 L €27, D €48, Wine €12 🚇 Abando Interchange 🚇 Indautxu

BAITA GAMINIZ

www.gaminiz.com

A modern restaurant with an emphasis on cod and fresh seafood. There's an excellent gourmet shop (daily 10–8). In summer, dine on the riverside terrace.

✉ Alameda de Mazarredo 20, 48001 Bilbao ☎ 944 24 22 67 🕒 Daily 1.30–3.30, Tue–Sat 9–11.15 🖐 L €45, D €65, Wine €17 🚇 Abando Interchange 🚇 Moyúa

GUGGENHEIM RESTAURANT

www.restaurantguggenheim.com

This world-food restaurant is in the Museo Guggenheim. You may be able to get a table if you chat to the museum staff, but if you are making the trip specifically to eat then it's wise to reserve a table. It's under the direction of renowned Basque chef and TV personality, Martin Berasategui.

✉ Avenida Abandoibarra 2, 48001 Bilbao ☎ 944 23 93 33 🕒 Tue–Sun 1.30–3, Wed–Sat 9–10.30. Closed 6–20 Jan 🖐 L €20, D €50, Wine €16 🚇 Abando Interchange 🚇 Moyúa

EL MARAKAY CAMPUZANO

Basque-style tapas are available at low prices at this warm, friendly bar-cum-restaurant. Unusually for Spain, it's a fully non-smoking establishment.

✉ Plaza Emilio Campuzano 26, 48001 Bilbao ☎ 944 41 50 66 🕒 Daily 9am–11pm 🖐 Tapas from €2, Wine €9 🚇 Abando Interchange 🚇 Indautxu

EL PERRO CHICO

El Perro Chico has become one of the coolest places to dine in Bilbao. It serves fine Basque classics. Reserving a table is essential.

✉ Calle Arechaga 2, 48010 Bilbao ☎ 944 15 05 19 🕒 Tue–Sat 12.30–3, 9–11.30. Closed 25 Jul–15 Aug 🖐 L €35, D €50, Wine €14 🚇 Abando Interchange

SUA

www.sua.es

Stylish and colourful, this fashionable restaurant is a good place to try affordable Basque cuisine. (Set price menus on weekdays (€15–€20) make it an even cheaper lunchtime option.) The gimmick here is to display the dishes on offer under the temperatures at which they are served, but the cuisine doesn't need such tricks. The dishes, which mix Basque favourites with plenty of international influences, do very nicely on their own—the chef is an erstwhile Spanish champion. Try the scallops in *provolone* broth, and don't miss the fabulous desserts. In true Basque tradition, the restaurant also boasts an excellent *pintxo* bar, laden with these delicious Basque treats (French bread with a variety of original toppings).

✉ Calle Marqués del Puerto 4, 48009 Bilbao ⏰ Mon–Sat 1.30–4, 8–midnight 🍴 L €18, D €35, Wine €10

VÍCTOR MONTES

www.restaurantevictor.com

Bilbao has legions of fine restaurants, but traditional and old-fashioned Víctor Montes is still extremely hard to beat in the fine food stakes. There is also a good tapas bar.

✉ Plaza Nueva 2, 48005 Bilbao ☎ 944 15 16 78 ⏰ Mon–Sat 12.30–3, 9–11 🍴 L €35, D €50, Wine €14 🚇 Abando Interchange

YANDIOLA

www.yandiola.com

Chef Ricardo Pérez's new location in La Alhóndiga, Bilbao's splendid new multidisciplinary cultural and wellness centre, is an ideal place to showcase his extraordinary talents. Original touches distinguish traditional ingredients and recipes such as cod prepared *sobre risotto* (on risotto), *a la vizcaina* (Basque salt cod), *al pil-pil* (hot peppers) and *al ajo arriero* (oil, garlic and peppers).

✉ Alameda Rekalde 27, 48001 Bilbao ☎ 944 13 36 36 ⏰ Tue–Sat 1–3.30, 8–11.30, Mon 1–3.30. Closed Easter week 🍴 L €45, D €60, Wine €16

ZORTZIKO

www.zortziko.es

Original fare is served at this cool Bilbao eatery which has been awarded one Michelin star. It's the best spot in the city to sample traditional Basque ingredients cooked with an interesting twist. Reserve your table.

✉ Alameda de Mazarredo 17, 48001 Bilbao ☎ 944 23 97 43 ⏰ Tue–Sun 1–3.30, 9–11.30, Mon 1–3.30 🍴 L €75, D €105, *Menú de degustación* (tasting menu) €115, Wine €22 🚇 Abando Interchange

CALATAYUD
MESÓN DE LA DOLORES

www.mesonladolores.com

A 15th-century palace on one of Calatuyud's most emblematic squares contains this delightful hotel-restaurant. Rustic, traditional and welcoming, it serves classic Aragonese cuisine with modern touches. The roast lamb is a favourite, but Mesón de la Dolores also serves some tasty seafood. The desserts are not to be missed—especially if made with chocolate.

✉ Plaça Mesones 4, 50300 Calatayud ☎ 976 88 90 55 ⏰ Daily 1.30–3.30, 8.30–10.30 🍴 L €20, D €30, Wine €14

DONOSTIA (SAN SEBASTIÁN)
AKELARRE

www.akelarre.net

Pedro Subijana is one of the finest chefs in Spain, with a starry reputation and innumerable awards. The setting is almost as dazzling as the cuisine, with a beautiful glassy dining area looking out over the Cantabrian Sea from the heights of Monte Igueldo. The special tasting menu *(menu de degustación)* is highly recommended, and offers a selection of the chef's most celebrated recipes and most daring new inventions. For a special treat, this offers one of the most memorable dining experiences in the country.

✉ Paseo del Padre Orcolaga 56, 20008 Donostia ☎ 943 31 12 09 ⏰ Jan–Jun Wed–Sat 2–3.30, 9–11, Sun 2–3.30; Jul–Dec Tue–Sat 2–3.30, 9–11 🍴 L €85, D €115, Wine €26

ARZAK

www.arzak.es

The restaurant's name is synonymous with a remoulding of the Basque cuisine into a new, groundbreaking style. This place has three Michelin stars, so reserve a table.

✉ Avenida Alcalde José Elosegui

273, 20015 Donostia ☎ 943 28 55 93 ⏰ Jan–14 Jun Wed–Sat 1–4, 9–11, Sun 1–4; 2 Jul–Dec Tue–Sat 1–4, 9–11, Sun 1–4. Closed 15 Jun–1 Jul, 2–26 Nov 🍴 L €95, D €125, Wine €24 🚇 RENFE station on Puente María Cristina

ELCIEGO
MARQUÉS DE RISCAL GASTRONOMIC RESTAURANT

www.luxurycollection.com/marquesderiscal

This restaurant is part of the spectacular 'City of Wine', a characteristically sculptural titanium creation from Frank Gehry. As well as the vineyards and bodega, it also incorporates a very luxurious hotel. The Marqués de Riscal is the smarter of the two restaurants within the complex, and offers refined regional cuisine under the helm of renowned local chef, Francis Paniego, a Michelin-star chef at his restaurant El Portal in Ezcaray in La Rioja's Sierra de la Demanda highlands. The cuisine is paired (of course) with a superlative wine selection.

✉ Calle Torea 1, 01340 Elciego ☎ 945 18 08 80 ⏰ Tue–Sat 1.30–4, 8.30–11 🍴 L €45, D €65, Wine €18

GETARIA
KAIA

www.kaia-kaipe.com

Food doesn't come much fresher or more authentic than at this combination of restaurant and brasserie. The upstairs restaurant windows look out over the old fishing port of Getaria, where fresh fish is brought in every day. The best is found on the menu here—most delicious served simply grilled. Start with the velvety anchovies, now a delicacy but once a local staple, which have been carefully prepared according to age-old recipes. The brasserie downstairs offers a slightly simpler menu, but fresh fish is still the highlight—it is prepared barbecue-style in a fish-shaped grill.

✉ General Arnau 4, 20808 Getaria ☎ 943 14 05 00 ⏰ Daily 2–4, 9–11 🍴 L €35, D €55, Wine €12 (brasserie less expensive)

Opposite *Marqués de Riscal Gastronomic Restaurant, Elciego*

HONDARRIBIA (FUENTERRABÍA)

ALAMEDA
www.restalameda.com
The Txapartegi brothers, Kepa and Gorka, cook seafood as well as anyone else in the Basque country. Light combinations of fish and citric fruits balance upland delicacies such as game in season at this Michelin-starred standout.
✉ Minasoroeta 1, 20280 Hondarriba ☎ 943 64 27 89 ⏰ Wed–Sat 1–3.30, 8–11.30, Sun, Tue 1–3.30. Closed Christmas, 8–14 June, 5–11 Oct. 🍴 L €65, D €85, Wine €16

SEBASTIÁN
www.sebastianhondarribia.com
A delightfully old-fashioned restaurant in the historic heart of Hondarribia, this is located in a former grocery store and preserves much of its appealing original facade. The intimate dining rooms are softly lit and decorated with traditional paintings and mirrors, with crisp white linen and fresh flowers on the tables. The classic Basque cuisine is prepared with original, modern touches and includes rice broth with clams and prawns, and steak with delicately smoked Idiazabal cheese. The home-made desserts are fabulous—try the praline cake.
✉ Calle Mayor 11, 20280 Hondarribia ☎ 943 64 01 67 ⏰ Tue–Sat 1.30–3.45, 8.45–10.30, Sun 1.30–3.45 🍴 L €45, D €60, Wine €16

HUESCA

LILLAS PASTIA
www.lillaspastia.es
One of Spain's most extraordinary young chefs, Carmelo Bosque, is at the helm at this excellent restaurant which has been awarded a Michelin star. Located under the casino in a Modernista building dating from 1909, this restaurant has become a mecca for gourmets. Try delectable delights such as the almond, lychee and cucumber soup with a sardine crust—the perfect marriage of flavours and textures—or the roast venison with chestnut purée and foie gras. The desserts are unmissable.

✉ Plaza de Navarra 4, 22002 Huesca ☎ 974 21 16 91 ⏰ Mon, Wed–Sat 2–4, 9–11, Sun 2–4. Closed all day Sun in summer and 2 weeks in Nov 🍴 L €65, D €85, Wine €22

LAGUARDIA

MARIXA-RIOJA
www.hotelmarixa.com
A very popular local favourite since 1954, this restaurant is especially famous for its roast meats and game (in season). The vegetables, for which La Rioja is celebrated throughout Spain, are also delicious, and the extensive dessert list is superb. There are three dining rooms, but the Salón de Cristal with its huge picture windows offers the best views of the Ebro valley. It's part of a charming rural hotel, a good base for wine tourism. Reservations are essential, particularly at weekends.
✉ Calle Sancho Abarca 8, 01300 Laguardia ☎ 945 60 01 65 ⏰ Daily 1–3, 8.30–11 🍴 L €25, D €40, Wine €14

PAMPLONA (IRUÑA)

ALT WIEN
An immensely agreeable spot for tea, coffee and home-made cakes. It's a pretty kiosk-café, in Pamploma's elegantly manicured public gardens.
✉ Parque de la Taconera s/n, 31001 Pamplona ☎ 948 21 19 12 ⏰ Daily 9am–11pm

EL BURGALÉS
El Burgalés is 70 years old and still going strong. It offers a massive selection of freshly made *pintxos* (Basque style tapas consisting of small discs of bread with toppings), sandwiches and local Rioja and Navarrese wines.
✉ Calle Comedias 5, 31001 Pamplona ☎ 948 22 51 58 ⏰ Daily 10am–3pm, 6pm–11pm 🍴 L €16, D €25, Wine €12

RESTAURANTE CASA OTANO
www.casaotano.com
Casa Otano has been a bar, restaurant and guesthouse since the 1920s. The upper floor serves Navarrese cuisine, while the bar is famous for its fried dishes, such as pepper and spinach croquette.

✉ Calle de San Nicolás 5, Casco Antiguo, 31001 Pamplona ☎ 948 22 50 95 ⏰ Mon–Sat 1–6, 9–1, Sun 1–4. Closed 15–31 Jul 🍴 L €25, D €35, Wine €12. Tapas from €2

RESTAURANTE RODERO
www.restauranterodero.com
This elegant restaurant is close to the bullring and Club Taurino. The chef, Koldo Rodero, is known for highly individual, creative adaptations of traditional dishes using seasonal produce. It's wise to reserve a table.
✉ Calle de Emilio Arrieta 3, 31002 Pamplona ☎ 948 22 80 35 ⏰ Daily 1–4, 9–11.30. Closed Sun and Mon evenings 🍴 L €65, D €85, Special menus €54–€90, Wine €18

SARVISÉ

CASA FRAUCA
www.casafrauca.com
This wonderful little rural hotel and restaurant sits on the fringes of the stunning National Park of Ordesa and Monte Perdido in the Aragonese Pyrenees. The rustically decorated restaurant, with stone walls and solid wooden furnishings, is perfectly suited to the sturdy country cuisine. Warm up with hearty stews—perhaps *adobo de cerdo*, pork stew with artichokes, or something unusual like rice with rabbit and snails, a local delicacy.
✉ Carretera Ordesa, 22374 Sarvisé ☎ 974 48 63 53 ⏰ Mon–Sat 2–4, 9–10.30, Sun 2–4. Closed Mon in low season, Jan and Feb 🍴 L €22, D €30, Wine €12

TERUEL

LA MENTA
One of the most elegant restaurants in Teruel, this is a good option for trying out local cuisine prepared with the finest market produce. Expect to find classic recipes like oven-baked hake with local asparagus and bacon, or steak with a cheese, tomato and balsamic vinegar compote. The dining rooms are charmingly decorated for a special experience. Those who are looking for a lighter meal can fill up at the bar, which offers a range of tapas and *raciones*.
✉ Calle Bartolomé Esteban 10, 44001

REGIONS · EUSKADI, NAVARRA AND ARAGÓN · EATING

Teruel ☎ 978 60 75 32 ⏱ Tue–Sat 2–4,
8.45–10.30. Closed 3 weeks in Jan and 2
weeks in Jul ♿ L €25, D €35, Wine €14

LA TIERRETA
www.latierreta.com

This elegant modern restaurant in the
centre of Teruel is crisply decorated
in shades of cream and blue. The
cuisine is based on traditional local
recipes, prepared with the best
seasonal ingredients and served with
a contemporary twist. The classic
Spanish dish *rabo de toro* (ox tail)
is served here in an aromatic red
wine stew, and accompanied with
cardamom potatoes. Or you could
try wild boar with black olives and
tomatoes. In March, the restaurant
hosts a special gourmet celebration
of the black truffle, a local delicacy.
✉ Calle Francisco Piquer 6, 44001 Teruel
⏱ Mon–Sat 1.30–4, 9–11. Closed 2 weeks
in Jul ♿ L €25, D €40, Wine €16

VITORIA-GASTEIZ
CUBE
www.cubeartium.com

In the glossy Artium Museum is
an equally glossy café/restaurant.
Among the contemporary dishes
on the menu is a salad of scallops,
hazelnuts and gorgonzola, and cod
with a cardamom, shitake mushroom
and asparagus sauce. There's a
'tasting' menu at €40, as well as an
à la carte option. A cafeteria serves
fresh breakfasts and light meals.
✉ Calle Francia 24 (Museo Artium), 01002
Vitoria-Gasteiz ☎ 945 20 37 28 ⏱ Tue–Sat
10am–11pm, Sun 10–2 ♿ L €32, D €40,
Wine €10

ZARAGOZA
CASA JUANICO

This mythical tapas bar started out in
1924 and little has changed since. It
is very close to the Pilar cathedral, in
the heart of Zaragoza's old town, and
is always heaving with people. The
combination of good, home-cooked
food at great prices is hard to beat.
There is a daily fixed price menu
during the week and a wide selection
of tapas and *pinchos*. Reservations
are recommended for the dining
area, which fills up quickly.
✉ Plaza de Santa Cruz 21, 50003 Zaragoza
☎ 976 39 72 52 ⏱ Tue–Sat 11–midnight,
Sun 11–4 ♿ L €20, D €25, Wine €10

LA RINCONADA DE LORENZO
www.larinconadadelorenzo.com

A long-established local favourite,
La Rinconada de Lorenzo specializes
in classic Aragonese fare. Now run
by Lorenzo's sons, it retains its old-
fashioned charm, with pretty, painted
tiles decorating the walls. The kitchen
produces stalwarts of the region's
cuisine, including wonderful *migas*
(a popular Spanish country dish,
prepared here with ham, chunks
of fried bread, peppers and garlic),
sturdy bean stews flavoured with
chorizo, fresh fish, and simple home-
made desserts. Service is friendly.
✉ Calle La Salle 3, 50006 Zaragoza ☎ 976
55 51 08 ⏱ Mon–Sat 2–4, 9–11, Sun 2–4.
Closed Mon in Jul and Aug ♿ L €20, D €30,
Wine €12

ZUMAIA
BEDUA
www.bedua.es

Bedua is on the banks of River Urola
in a Basque stone farmhouse which
dates back to the Middle Ages.
A popular *asador* (roast house), it
specializes in succulent local meat
and fresh fish, grilled over hot
coals or roasted in a brick oven in
traditional style. Basque delicacies
like baby eels are on the menu in
season. Finish your meal with home-
made rice pudding. It's an informal
spot, which welcomes families.
✉ Carretera Zumaia-Meagas Km 2, 20750
Zumaia ☎ 943 86 05 51 ⏱ Daily 1.30–4,
8–12 ♿ L €25, D €34, Wine €10

Below *Table set for alfresco dining*

STAYING

PRICES AND SYMBOLS

The prices are for a double room for one night including breakfast, unless otherwise stated. All the hotels listed accept credit cards unless otherwise stated. Note that rates can vary widely throughout the year.

For a key to the symbols, ▷ 2.

BILBAO (BILBO)

CARLTON
www.hotelcarlton.es
The interior of this Victorian-era white mansion positively brims with 21st-century features. The spacious guest rooms have satellite TV and WiFi. The restaurant serves Basque cuisine.
✉ Plaza Federico Moyúa 2, 48009 Bilbao ☎ 944 16 22 00 🛏 €115–€275 excluding breakfast (€20) ① 142 (40 non-smoking) 🅿 📶 🚇 Abando Interchange 🚇 Moyúa

CONDE DUQUE
www.hotelcondeduque.com
The guest rooms in this modern, comfortable, central, three-star hotel all have 20-channel satellite TV, broadband internet access, safe-box and minibar. The private bathrooms have modern touches, such as a waterproof radio, magnifying mirror and telephone.
✉ Campo de Volantin 22, 48007 Bilbao

☎ 944 45 60 00 🛏 €90–€130, weekend offers available ① 67 (48 non-smoking) 🅿 🚇 Abando Interchange

GRAN HOTEL DOMINE BILBAO
www.granhoteldominebilbao.com
A contemporary hotel with an incomparable setting opposite the Guggenheim museum, Gran Hotel Domine has become the haunt of celebrities and the fashion pack. The interior was designed by Javier Mariscal, and boasts spectacular rooms set around a lofty central atrium. The cool, retro-themed bar, Splash and Crash, and the sleek restaurant Beltz the Black are both popular. The teak-paved rooftop terrace looks over the museum and the river.
✉ Alameda de Mazarredo 61, 48009 Bilbao ☎ 944 25 33 00 🛏 €140–€295 ① 145 🅿 📶

PETIT PALACE ARANA
www.petitpalacearana.com
Rooms have hydro-massage showers, interactive TV and modem point. Bicycle rental is available.
✉ Calle de Bidebarrieta 2, 48005 Bilbao ☎ 944 15 64 11 🛏 €65–€215 excluding breakfast, check for special offers on their website ① 64 (50 non-smoking) 🅿 🚇 Abando Interchange 🚇 Casco Viejo

RIPA
www.hotel-ripa.com
The basic amenities give this hotel a one-star rating, but it does have a telephone, TV and private bathroom in most of the rooms. Reserve if possible. Parking costs €8 per night.
✉ Muelle Ripa 3, 48001 Bilbao ☎ 944 23 96 77 🛏 €60–€75 ① 15 🚇 Abando Interchange 🚇 Casco Viejo

DONOSTIA (SAN SEBASTIÁN)

HOTEL PARMA
www.hotelparma.com
A pleasant, family-run hotel. All rooms have private bathroom and satellite TV.
✉ Paseo de Salamanca 10, 20003 Donóstia ☎ 943 42 88 93 🛏 €90–€150 excluding breakfast (€10) ① 27 🅿

DE LONDRES Y DE INGLATERRA
www.hlondres.com
An elegant belle-époque hotel on Playa de la Concha, with sea views.
✉ Calle de Zubieta 2, 20007 Donostia ☎ 943 44 07 70 🛏 €135–€285 per room excluding breakfast (€18) ① 148 (20 non-smoking) 🅿 🚇 5, 16, 26 🚆 RENFE station on Puente María Cristina

Above *The exciting city of Bilbao has a range of accommodations to choose from*

MONTE IGUELDO

www.monteigueldo.com

The rooms are very modern in this quiet hotel overlooking the city from on high.

✉ Paseo del Faro 134, 20008 Donostia ☎ 943 21 02 11 🖐 €145–€205 including breakfast ⓘ 125 🆔 🏊 Outdoor 🚌 Buses marked 'Igueldo' 🚉 Donostia Central

HONDARRIBIA (FUENTERRABÍA)
PARADOR DE HONDARRIBIA

www.parador.es

Some rooms in this small *parador* have terraces with extensive views. It's located in a 10th-century castle.

✉ Plaza de Armas 14, 20280 Hondarribia ☎ 943 64 55 00 🖐 €225–€265 per room ⓘ 36 rooms (11 non-smoking)

PAMPLONA (IRUÑA)
GRAN HOTEL LA PERLA

www.granhotellaperla.com

One of the city's most historic hotels, where past guests include Ernest Hemingway, Orson Welles, and the celebrated matador Manolete, La Perla was dramatically renovated in 2007 as a luxurious, five-star boutique hotel. The interior has been exquisitely remodelled, but the furnishings remain elegant and traditional, with antiques and pretty prints. Its rooms are highly sought after during the San Fermín festival, because they overlook Calle Estafeta, a hotspot for the bull running action. Reserve months in advance—and be prepared to pay up to four times the official rate during this period.

✉ Plaza del Castillo 1, 31001 Pamplona ☎ 948 22 30 00 🖐 €245–€475 (at least triple this during San Fermín) ⓘ 44 🆔

HOSTAL ARRIAZU

www.hostalarriazu.com

This is a three-star hostel that looks more like a hotel. The rooms are soundproofed. All rooms have TV, minibar and safe.

✉ Calle Comedias 14, Casco Antiguo, 31001 Pamplona ☎ 948 21 02 02 🖐 €75–€85 excluding breakfast (€9). During San Fermín €275 excluding breakfast ⓘ 11 rooms, 3 suites (11 non-smoking) 🆔

IRUÑA PALACE HOTEL TRES REYES

www.hotel3reyes.com

This four-star hotel has all the modern amenities, including satellite TV, sauna, spa baths, squash court, sun lounge and even a hairdresser.

✉ Jardines de la Taconera s/n, Casco Antiguo, 31001 Pamplona ☎ 948 22 66 00 🖐 €220–€275 excluding breakfast. During San Fermín €650 ⓘ 112 classic rooms, 40 executive rooms and 8 suites (100 non-smoking) 🆔 🏊 Outdoor 📺 🍽 3, 4, 15

MAISONNAVE

www.hotelmaisonnave.es

All rooms in this central three-star hotel have a satellite TV, desk, safe and minibar. The rooms have been soundproofed.

✉ Calle Nueva 20, Casco Antiguo, 31001 Pamplona ☎ 948 22 26 00 🖐 €75–€175 excluding breakfast (€12). During San Fermín €415 ⓘ 138 🆔

PUENTE LA REINA/GARES
EL PEREGRINO

www.hotelelperegrino.com

Puente la Reina is a village along the Camino de Santiago, which boasts beautiful Romanesque churches. This hotel is named after the pilgrims, and is located in a restored medieval mansion. It's part of the prestigious Relais et Châteaux group. The lush gardens are shaded with palms. Each of the rooms is individually decorated with a stylish mixture of antique and contemporary furnishings, and superb sculptures and paintings by renowned artists such as Eduardo Chillida can be found in every corner. There's an excellent restaurant, one of the very best in the region, for enjoying some refined local cuisine.

✉ Carretera N-111 Pamplona-Logroño km 23, 31100 Puente La Reina/Gares ☎ 948 34 00 75 🆔 €165–€275 ⓘ 13 🆔 🏊 Outdoor

SALLENT DE GÁLLEGO
BOCALÉ

www.bocale.com

A pretty, chalet-style hotel high in the prettiest part of the Aragonese Pyrenees, this is perfect for a rural escape. In winter, you can ski or

snowboard at nearby Formigal, and in summer activities include hiking and horse-riding. The rooms, with their wooden beamed ceilings and individual balconies, are cosy. Best of all is the basement pool, decorated to resemble Roman baths (the waters are said to be curative and the town boasts six thermal treatment spas).

✉ Avenida de Francia s/n, 22640 Sallent de Gállego ☎ 974 48 85 55 🖐 €105–€175 ⓘ 21

SOS DEL REY CATÓLICO
PARADOR DE SOS DEL REY CATÓLICO

www.parador.es

This *parador* lies 2km (1 mile) out of town on the Zaragoza road. The spacious, elegant rooms have views.

✉ Calle Arquitecto Sainz de Vicuña 1, 50680 Sos del Rey Católico ☎ 948 88 80 11 🖐 €135–€165 per room, excluding breakfast (€14). Discounts available for over 60s ⓘ 66 rooms 🆔

VITORIA-GASTEIZ
PALACIO DE ELORRIAGA

www.hotelpalacioelorriaga.com

A handsomely converted *casa solariega* (noble mansion) from the 16th and 17th centuries, this is now a tranquil and idyllic hotel. The mellow brick and stone, exposed beams, and beautiful garden complete with pond make it a restful retreat from the hubbub of the city. The centre of Vitoria is just a kilometre down the road, but feels a world away. The interior is warm and welcoming, with simply furnished but spacious rooms. There's a good country restaurant serving delicious local specialties.

✉ Calle Elorriaga 15, 01192 Vitoria-Gasteiz ☎ 945 26 36 16 🖐 €95–€135 ⓘ 21 🆔 📺

ZARAGOZA
GRAN HOTEL

www.nh-hoteles.es

This hotel in central Zaragoza is perfectly located for exploring the city on foot.

✉ Calle de Joaquín Costa 5, 50001 Zaragoza ☎ 976 22 19 01 🖐 €95–€210 per room excluding breakfast (€18) ⓘ 133 rooms 📺 🆔

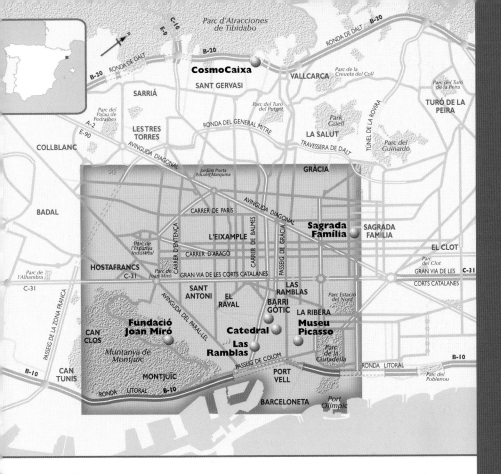

BARCELONA

Glossy, glamorous Barcelona is one of the most stylish cities on the Mediterranean. At its heart is an alluring Gothic Quarter, one of the largest and most complete medieval kernels in Europe. Overlooked by the jagged spires of a vast cathedral, it is a fascinating warren of shadowy stone passages and crooked alleys. Spreading northwest of the old city is the Eixample, the city's 19th-century expansion, an elegant grid of broad boulevards lined with handsome *modernista* mansions and apartment buildings. The most famous of these were created by Antoni Gaudí, an eccentric and immensely gifted architect and artist whose fairytale visions took concrete form all across Barcelona. His buildings sway and undulate, mosaic tiles shimmer and dazzle, and roof terraces are built to resemble dragons and knights. His most famous monument, the great temple of the Sagrada Família, remains unfinished, but its enormous, tubular towers are perhaps the city's most recognizable emblem.

A visit to the Park Güell, Gaudí's green and colourful hillside park, which offers splendid views of the city below, is unmissable. But Barcelona is no museum town: the Gothic Quarter is packed with great shops, bars and restaurants, and the Eixample is home to some of the city's most stylish boutiques and plushest hotels. There is a year-round buzz on the streets, particularly on the famous Rambla, a mile-long promenade which links the city centre with the seaside.

Barcelona reclaimed its seafront for the 1992 Olympics, building new beaches, marinas and opening up the city to the sea. The sandy beaches and long seafront promenade remain among Barcelona's biggest attractions, particularly during the searing summer heat. The city's reputation for fantastic nightlife also comes into its own during the summer, when the beachfront clubs, bars and restaurants bring the party outside.

Blau Grana

FC Barcelona Camp Nou

Museu del FC Barcelona

Casa Provincial de Maternitat

Museu Monestir de Pedralbes, Palau Reial de Pedralbes

L'Illa Diagonal

LES CORTS

TRAVESSERA

PLAÇA DE FRANCESC MACIÀ

MADRID

Universitat Industrial

ESTACIÓ BARCELONA CENTRAL-SANTS

Museu P Cirac

SANTS

Parc de l'Espanya Industrial

Presó Model

HOSTAFRANCS

LA BORDETA

MAGORIA

Parc de Joan Miró

SANT ANTONI

Plaça de Toros les Arenes

GRAN VIA DE LES CORTS CATALANES

Espanya

PLAÇA D'ESPANYA

Magòria La Campana

Parc de la Font Florida

EL POLVORÍ

Poble Espanyol

Miles van der Rohe Pavelló d'Alemanya

Caixa Forum

Palau de la Metal·lúrgia

Palau Fira de Mostres

Palau del Cinquantenari

Font Màgica

Palau de Victòria Eugènia

Palau de Congressos

LA FRANÇA

Palaus Alfons XIII

Palau Municipal d'Esports

Poble Sec

Jardí Botànic

Institut Nacional d'Educació Física de Catalunya (INEFC)

Palau Nacional

Museu Nacional d'Art de Catalunya

Museu Etnològic

Teatre Mercat de les Flors

Inst del Teatre

Santa Madrona

Parc de Montjuïc

Piscines Bernat Picornell

CAN CLOS

Palau Albéniz

Museu Arqueològic

Fundació Joan Miró

POBLE SEC

Anella Olímpica

Auditorio sot del Migdia

Palau Sant Jordi

Estadi Olímpic de Lluís Companys

Estadi d'Hoquei Pau Negre

MONTJUÏC

Jardins Mossèn Cinto Verdaguer

MIRAMAR

Avinguda de Miramar

Jardins de Miramar

Cementiri del Sud Oest

CANTUNIS

Castell de Montjuïc

Museu Militar

Jardins del Josep Costa i Llobera

BARCELONA

300 m

300 yds

GRÀCIA

L'EIXAMPLE

LAS RAMBLAS

BARRI GÒTIC

CASC ANTIC

RIBERA

EL FORT PIUS

ANTIGA ESTACIÓ DEL NORD

BARCELONETA

CosmoCaixa, Tibidabo

Park Güell

Museu Ceràmica

Hospital de la Santa Creu i Sant Pau

Casa Fuster

Casa Comalat

Palau Robert

Museu de Música

Casa de les Punxes

Casa Milà (La Pedrera)

L'EIXAMPLE

Casa Thomas

Centre Català d'Art

Museu Egipci

Fundació Antoni Tàpies

Museu del Perfum

Manzana de la Discòrdia

Museu Diocesà

Universitat Central

Casa Calvet

Sagrada Família

El Monumental

Auditori Municipal y Museu de la Música

Centre de Cultura Contemporània de Barcelona

Museu d'Art Contemporani

Casa Municipal de Misericòrdia

Palau de la Música Catalunia

Arc de Triomf

Arc del Triomf

Parc de l'Estació del Nord

Parc de la Ciutadella

Museu de Zoologia

Museu de Geologia

Museu Picasso

Museu Barbier-Mueller d'Art Precolombi

Universitat Pompeu Fabra

Parlament de Catalunya

Parc Zoològic

Esglèsia de Betlem

Palau Antic Hospital Santa Creu

Palau de la Virreina

La Boqueria

Santa Maria del Pi

Gran Teatre del Liceu

Museu del Calçat

Catedral

Palau de la Generalitat

Museu Diocesà

Museu Frederic Marès

Museu d'Història de la Ciutat

Mercat Santa Caterina

Museu de Xocolata

Ajuntament

Museu Textil i d'Indumentària

Antic Mercat del Born

Palau Güell

Plaça Reial

Santa Maria del Mar

La Llotja

Esglèsia de la Mercè

Museu de Cera

Correus i Telègrafs

Estació Barcelona de França

Drassanes

Monument a Cristòfol Colom

Palau de Mar

Museu d'Història de Catalunya

Dàrsena Nacional

Dàrsena del Comerç

Reial Club Marítim

Port Vell

L'Aquàrium de Barcelona

BARCELONETA

Poliesportiu Marítim

Platja de la Barceloneta

Port Olímpic

Torre Mapfre

Estació Marítima

World Trade Center

Torre de Jaume I

D · E · F

211

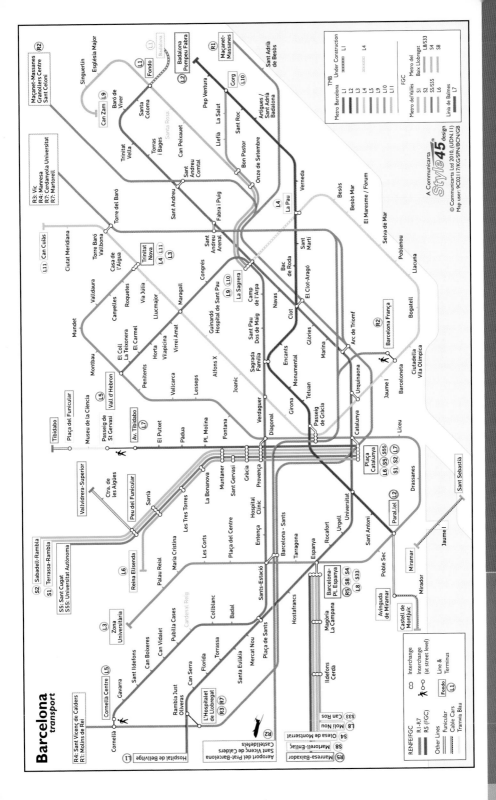

Barcelona transport

REGIONS BARCELONA • CITY MAPS

213

AQUÀRIUM DE BARCELONA
www.aquariumbcn.com

Barcelona's state-of-the-art aquarium is one of the finest in Europe, with 21 tanks housing creatures that include poisonous and tropical fish and less exotic varieties. The first section focuses on the Mediterranean; here you will find communities of eels and octopuses. The next section, devoted to the Red Sea and other tropical waters, is more vibrant. Here, reef sharks and bright yellow butterfly fish are on display among native vegetation. The biggest crowd-pleaser is the close encounter with the grey sharks, guitarfish, and eagle and marble rays in the Oceanarium. A wide glass tunnel lets you see these sleek creatures from all angles as you are moved along by a conveyor belt. Upstairs, the Explora! section has 50 interactive games and activities to entertain the children.

✚ 211 D5 ✉ Moll d'Espanya del Port Vell s/n, 08039 Barcelona ☎ 932 21 74 74 🕐 Jul–Aug Mon–Fri 9.30–9, Sat–Sun 9.30–11; Jun, Sep Mon–Fri 9.30–9, Sat–Sun 9.30–9.30; Oct–May daily 9.30–9 ✋ Adult €17.50, child (4–12) €12.50, under 4 free 🚇 Drassanes, Barceloneta 🚌 14, 17, 19, 36, 38, 40, 45, 57, 59, 64, 91, 157

BARCELONETA
www.barcelonaturisme.com

Barceloneta (Little Barcelona) is a working-class (blue collar) *barri* (quarter) by the sea with a strong maritime history, and is now the city's popular playground. The Plaça de la Barceloneta is a focal point in the area, a picturesque square with a central fountain, a couple of *café-terrazas* and the Iglesia de Sant Miquel del Port, built in 1755.

The main boulevard is the Passeig Joan de Borbó, which stretches out alongside the harbour all the way down to the sea. It's easy to dismiss the street as a tourist trap, but enjoying a paella in the sea air of Barceloneta on Sunday is as traditional as eating *monas* (a type of cake) at Easter, and is another culinary experience to add to your list. However, get there either before or after the Catalán lunch hour (1.30–

3.30) or you will be in for a wait.

✚ 211 E5 ℹ️ Ciutat 2, Plaça Sant Jaume, 08002 Barcelona ☎ 932 85 38 34 🚇 Barceloneta

BARRI GÒTIC
▷ 216–217.

CASA MILÀ
www.lapedreraeducacio.org

Known locally as La Pedrera (The Quarry) and completed in 1910, Casa Milà is one of the most poetic and memorable works created by Antoni Gaudí (1852–1926). Reflecting the Catalán architect's obsessions and inspirations, the exterior is rich in symbolism, and the folds of wave-like creamy limestone rear up over the street like a misplaced sea cliff.

The building is now owned by one of Catalonia's major banking institutions, and most apartments are in private hands, but three parts of the edifice are open to the public. The museum, Espai Gaudí, is in the fabulous attic, a serene labyrinth of redbrick parabolic arches. An apartment with a recreated early 20th-century interior and a wonderfully organic shape is the setting for fabulous period pieces. But the building's tour de force is its roof, whose undulating lines mirror the arches of the attic below. The centurion-like chimney-stacks, composed of *trencadís* (broken ceramics) and smooth concrete, are now a symbol of the city.

During July and August, jazz and flamenco performances are held on the rooftop. The entrance fee usually includes a glass of cool *cava* (sparkling wine).

✚ 211 E2 ✉ Passeig de Gràcia 92, 08027 Barcelona ☎ 902 40 09 73 🕐 Mar–Oct daily 9–8; Nov–Feb 9–6.30; box office closes 7.30 ✋ Adult €10, under 12 free 🚇 Diagonal 🚌 7, 16, 17, 22, 24, 28 📞 By arrangement, tel 902 40 09 73. Audiotours in English, French, Catalán, Spanish, Italian and German included in admission fee 📖 Excellent value guidebook €12 🏪 One on ground floor: books and objects by local designers inspired by Gaudí; one in apartment: books, accessories and reproduction period toys

CATEDRAL
▷ 218.

COSMOCAIXA
▷ 219.

L'EIXAMPLE
www.barcelonaturisme.com

The expansion district's symmetrical blocks, designed in 1859 by Ildefons Cerdà (1815–76), contain the world's highest concentration of *modernista* architecture. The main boulevard, Passeig de Gràcia, is home to the Manzana de la Discòrdia (▷ 221).

The Quadrat d'Or (Golden Square) consists of a hundred or so blocks edged by carrers del Bruc and d'Aragó, the Passeig de Gràcia and the Diagonal. The region has been described as the greatest living museum of late 19th-century architecture, and includes such buildings as the Casa Terrades by Puig i Cadafalch (1876–1956), more commonly known as the Casa de les Punxes (House of Spikes) for its spires and weathervanes.

✚ 211 E2 ℹ️ Plaça de Catalunya, 17 soterrani, 08002 Barcelona ☎ 932 85 38 32 🕐 Daily 9–9 🚇 Passeig de Gràcia, Diagonal 🚌 16, 17, 20, 22, 24, 28, 39, 44, 45 (to the Quadrat d'Or)

FUNDACIÓ JOAN MIRÓ
▷ 220.

Opposite Barcelona Head *by Roy Lichtenstein (1992) in Barceloneta*
Below *Casa Milà, Gaudí's other-worldly apartment block*

INFORMATION

www.barcelonaturisme.com
➕ 211 D4 ℹ Ciutat 2, 08002 Barcelona
☎ 932 85 38 34 🕐 Mon–Fri 9–2
🚇 Jaume I, Liceu

INTRODUCTION

Next to modernism, the Gothic period had the greatest influence on Barcelona's architecture. An afternoon's stroll around the ensemble of 13th- to 15th-century buildings, grand plazas and narrow streets of the city's Barri Gòtic is a must.

The Barri Gòtic dates principally from the 14th and 15th centuries, the zenith of Barcelona's maritime and mercantile power. The area was originally almost entirely enclosed by fourth-century Roman walls, traces of which are still visible along the Via Laietana to the northeast; the southern limits are bounded by the thoroughfares of Las Ramblas (▷ 226). In this tiny nucleus, the machinery of medieval government and commerce functioned in purpose-built palaces and halls, while a series of squares served as public gathering places—functions they still fulfil today.

WHAT TO SEE

PLAÇA DEL REI

This small, well-preserved, medieval paved square lies in the heart of the Barri Gòtic and once rang with the comings and goings of official visitors and buyers and sellers of flour and hay. It is flanked by the 13th- to 16th-century structures of the Palau Reial (Royal Palace), and the Conjunt Monumental de la Plaça del Rei.

The Mirador del Rei, on the square's western side, was used as a watchtower, and the Palau de Loctinent, on the left of the *mirador* (balcony), was the official home of the viceroy after Catalonia (Catalunya) lost its independence in the 16th century.

PLAÇA DE SANT JAUME

The Plaça de Sant Jaume has been the city's political and social hub since Roman times. The spacious square is flanked on one side by the Casa de la Ciutat, or Ajuntament, and on the other by the Palau de la Generalitat (▷ 217), and acts as a backdrop for many spontaneous public events. The Barça soccer team greets ecstatic crowds from the Ajuntament's balcony after major wins, and the two great Catalán folk traditions of *castellers* (human towers) and the *sardana* (a group dance) are played out here on public holidays.

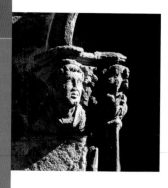

Above *Sunlight strikes a carving on one of the quarter's Gothic buildings*
Top *The facade of the Ajuntament looks out over Plaça de Sant Jaume*

PALAU DE LA GENERALITAT

The Generalitat is the name of both Catalonia's autonomous government and the building from which it governs. So far, 115 presidents of Catalonia have ruled from its 15th-century Gothic interior, making it one of the few medieval buildings still in continuous use for its original purpose. When Generalitat presidents are in town they stay next door at the 14th-century Casa dels Canonges, on Carrer del Bisbe. The hanging enclosed walkway joining the two buildings dates from the 1920s and was styled on Venice's Bridge of Sighs.

✉ Plaça de Sant Jaume ☎ 933 18 65 96 🕐 2nd and 4th Sun of each month 10.30–1.30 🚇 Jaume I, Liceu 🚌 14, 16, 17, 19, 38, 40, 45, 59 👆 Free 🎧 No tours, visits by prior application on Sat and Sun, non-solicited visits on 2nd and 4th Sun of every month

CASA DE LA CIUTAT (AJUNTAMENT)

The Ajuntament started out as the seat of the Consell de Cent, one of the world's first democratic representative councils, made up of 100 guild leaders and ordinary citizens. Although the Ajuntament is not as spectacular as the Generalitat, its classic early 1900s facade hides a Gothic interior. The highlight is the Saló de Croniques, with murals dating from 1928 by painter Josep Maria Sert, who went on to decorate New York's Rockefeller Center.

✉ Plaça de Sant Jaume 1 ☎ 934 02 73 64 🕐 Sun 10–2 🚇 Jaume I 🚌 16, 17, 19, 45 👆 Free 🎧 No tours available; advance booking for large groups

PLAÇA DE SANT FELIP NERI

The pretty square of Sant Felip Neri is entered from the Baixada de Santa Eulàlia, the street where Barcelona's patron saint met her grisly death. The square itself is peaceful, with a central fountain and baroque church, but it has a dark past. The shrapnel holes you see on the church next to the infant school are the evidence of a massacre of 20 children by a bomb dropped by Fascist aviation in 1938.

The Plaça del Pi, with its Gothic masterpiece, the Església Santa María del Pi, is a good place to take a break. The foundations of nearby Carrer de Petrixol were laid in 1465 and the street now houses some of the most famous of Barcelona's *granjes* (pastry and hot chocolate cafés).

MORE TO SEE

CARRER D'AVINYÓ

Once full of inexpensive hostels and a notorious stamping ground for the city's ladies of the night, Carrer d'Avinyó is now full of hip clothing stores and contemporary galleries.

Below left *Tile detail on Casa de l'Arcadia in Barri Gòtic*
Below *A shop in one of the medieval buildings on Plaça del Rei*

REGIONS | BARCELONA • SIGHTS

INFORMATION

www.website.es/catedralbcn

✚ 211 E4 ✉ Plaça de la Seu 3, 08002 Barcelona ☎ 933 15 15 54 🕐 Daily 8–1.15, 5.15–7.30 💵 Free; special (less crowded) midday visits (1.30–4.30) €5, under 8 free 🔲 Guided visits available Fri and Sat by prior arrangement, tel 933 15 22 13 Ⓜ Liceu 🚌 16, 17, 19, 45 📖 Various available at €2, €3 and €9 🏪 Two shops

Below *Barcelona's La Seu Cathedral was begun in early Catalán Gothic in 1298 and completed with a neo-Gothic facade in 1913*

CATEDRAL

The plans for the interior of the cathedral were first laid down in 1298, and for the next 150 years four different architects worked on the edifice and produced cloisters and chapels that show Catalán Gothic architecture at its best.

THE CLOISTER

The most pleasing part of the cathedral is undoubtedly the cloister, and a few minutes spent among its orange and medlar trees and its shady palms are an effective battery-charger. The pond serves as home to a gaggle of white geese, which are said to represent the purity of Santa Eulàlia, Barcelona's patron saint. Its mossy, central fountain once provided fresh water for the clergy.

THE INTERIOR

The crypt houses Santa Eulàlia's marble tomb, dating from the ninth century. The central choir, with its beautifully carved 14th-century stalls, is worth lingering in. The coats of arms represent members of the chapter of the Order of the Golden Fleece. Peek under the misericords (choir seats) to see the sculptures of hunting scenes, games and other pastimes.

Another highlight is the Capella del Santíssim Sagrament, a small chapel immediately to the right of the main entrance. The chapel's vaulted roof soars to more than 20m (66ft), but its treasure is the 16th-century figurine *Christ of Lepanto*. The figure famously curves to one side—this, according to legend, happened while dodging an Ottoman cannonball during the famous Battle of Lepanto in 1571.

On the opposite side of the cathedral's entrance is the baptistery, with a plaque bearing the names of six South American natives said to have been brought back by Christopher Columbus in 1493 and christened in the cathedral. Finally, take the lift (elevator) up to the roof for panoramas over the city and close-ups of the 19th-century spires.

The altar has two large sixth-century Visigoth capitals (crowning features on the columns) in one of the small chapels off the ambulatory (behind the main altar) and an altarpiece with a superb painting of the *Transfiguration* by Bernat Martorell (1400–52).

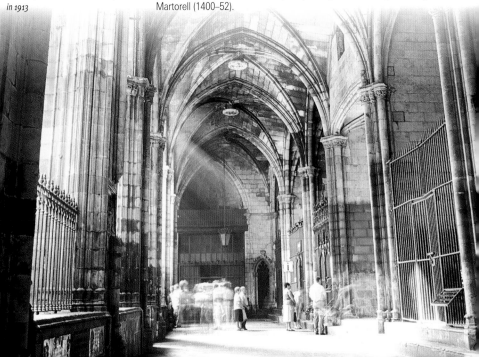

COSMOCAIXA

When the old Science Museum was reopened on its original outer Barcelona site at the end of 2004, it was renamed CosmoCaixa. And indeed this high-tech nuance is more fitting for this multimedia extravaganza covering all the scientific disciplines. Located at the foothills of Tibidabo, the site includes ample landscaped outdoor areas for relaxing and taking a break.

The exhibition spaces are enclosed underground in a daring five-floor structure by local architects Esteve and Robert Terrades. After descending the spiral staircase, you arrive at the Sala de la Matèria, the museum's permanent collection. The fundamental laws of material, energy, waves and light and the origins of the earth and civilization are explained through 64 interactive models and games, divided into four sections (Live, Intelligent, Civilized and Inert Material). Exhibits include an enormous Foucault's Pendulum, an extensive collection of fossils, and plenty of bugs and insects behind glass. The museum has even managed to make rocks look sexy with an awesome 'Geology Wall'. Occupying an entire side of the hall, enormous examples of chalk, marble, volcanic and glacial rocks and stone are mounted from a dramatic height.

At the opposite end of the hall is the exotic 'Sunken Forest': an Amazonian rain forest with more than 80 species of plant and tree and 50 species of animal life. The lower level features close encounters with the fish that dwell in the artificial pond, and lizards, frogs, turtles and other creatures.

THE PLANETARIUM
Under a futuristic dome experience: 'Genesis' (the history of the universe), 'Far-Off Galaxies' and 'The Blind Man with Stars in his Eyes' (or astronomy for kids).

¡TOCA, TOCA!
¡Toca, Toca! (or Touch, Touch!) allows infants to come into (supervised) contact with baby tortoises, lizards and even snakes in their natural habitat.

CLICK I FLASH
The Click section allows children aged three to six to investigate light, force, balance and perceptions of speed through experiments such as bubble blowing in different shapes. The Flash section contains touchy-feely contraptions, which allow youngsters to change the flow of a river, perform simple electronic experiments and play with microscopes and other instruments.

INFORMATION
www.cosmocaixa.com

✚ Off map 211 D1 ✉ Carrer Teodor Roviralta 47–51, 08022 Barcelona ☎ 932 12 60 50 ⏰ Tue–Sun 10–8 💳 Adults and students €3, children under 8 free. Planetarium and supervised activities: Adults €3, students €2; activities €2
🚋 Avinguda del Tibidabo 🚌 17, 22, 58, 73, 75, 60 🎧 Guided tours of permanent collection: Tue–Fri 11am, Sat and Sun 4pm 💳 €3. No audiotours

TIPS
» All exhibits have explanations and instructions in English.
» The exhibits continue outside the main building in the huge esplanade of Plaça de la Ciència. Take time to examine the Sun Dial, the 'Litofones' (musical rocks) and the 'Telescope of Sound': two parabolic discs that allow two people to 'whisper' to each other from 40m (130ft) away.

Above *CosmoCaixa is one of the city's most innovative and exciting museums*

REGIONS • BARCELONA • SIGHTS

INFORMATION

www.bcn.fjmiro.cat

🔲 210 B4 ✉ Parc de Montjuïc, 08038
Barcelona ☎ 934 43 94 70 🕐 Jul–Sep
Tue–Sat 10–8; Oct–Jun Tue–Sat 10–7
(Thu until 9.30); Sun and holidays
10–2.30 💷 Adult €8.50, under 14 free.
Temporary exhibitions only: adult €5
🚇 Paral.lel then Funicular de Montjuïc
🚌 50, 55 🎧 Audiotour €5. Free tours
in Catalán and Spanish only: Sun 11.30
📖 Guidebook €12 🍴 🛒 🏛 Two
shops

TIP

» Have a wander through the small
sculpture garden next to the Fundació.
There are wonderful views, as well as
some interesting sculptures.

FUNDACIÓ JOAN MIRÓ

Set in a modernist building dating from the mid-1970s, the Joan Miró Foundation
enjoys a hilltop position on Montjuïc, with panoramic glimpses of the Barcelona
skyline visible throughout the gallery.

THE MAN AND HIS ART

Joan Miró (1893–1983) was one of the most prolific Catalán artists of the 20th
century. He also worked in sculpture and tapestry throughout his life, but rarely
deviated from a bright palette of blue, red, yellow and green.

TAPESTRY AND EARLY INFLUENCES

The collections are spread over 10 *salas* (rooms), the first stop being the Tapestry
Room. The most spectacular piece here is the *Foundation Tapestry*, which was
designed especially for the gallery in 1979. Before you enter the next galleries,
don't miss *Mercury*, a fascinating fountain-sculpture created for the Spanish
Pavilion at the 1937 Paris World's Fair by American avant-garde artist Alexander
Calder (1898–1976).

The Joan Prats Gallery shows Miró's early works and development. Miró was
inspired by Van Gogh and Cézanne; Van Gogh's influence is clearly visible in the
charming *Portrait of a Young Girl* (1919). In the 1920s Miró moved to Paris, where
he abandoned realism for imagination; the 1925 *A Music Hall Usher* is a key work
of this stage. Part of a series known as *The Dream Paintings*, this is one of the
100 works Miró produced between 1924 and 1928.

PILAR JUNCOSA GALLERY

Many of Miró's later works are in the Pilar Juncosa Gallery. A particularly poetic
example of this time is *The Gold of the Azure* (1967). In some cases Miró's
paintings became mere gestures, as can be seen in the last room, which
contains three extraordinary, large-scale triptychs. The most powerful of these
is *Cell for a Solitary Man I, II and III* (1968), a trio of irregular black lines on a
white background evoking the despair and solitude of a condemned man in
his cell.

The spectacular sculpture garden on the rooftop terrace is unmissable. *The
Caress of a Bird* is one of the quirky works here: a 1967 piece showing how Miró
began to introduce bright colours to his bronze sculptures.

famous meeting spot is the Plaça del Sol, a relaxed venue for coffee by day and a lively social spot at night.
⊞ 211 E1 🛈 Plaça de Catalunya, 17 soterrani, 08002 Barcelona ☎ 932 85 38 32 🌐 Daily 9–9 🚇 Diagonal, Fontana 🚌 16, 17, 22, 24, 25, 27, 28

HOSPITAL DE LA SANTA CREU I SANT PAU

www.hspau.com
www.rutadelmodernisme.com
This work by *modernista* architect Lluís Domènech i Montaner (1850–1923) is the largest of his buildings—beautiful, detail-rich and still a working hospital. The complex consists of 48 mosaic-covered pavilions, which serve as hospital wards. Heavy with symbolism, the hospital is almost a metaphor for the *modernista* creed itself: Catalán nationalism, exuberant use of new materials and an abundance of references to mother nature. The hospital is not strictly open to the public except on a guided tour, but nobody seems to mind if you take a discreet walk around the gardens to view the pavilions from the outside.
⊞ Off map 211 F1 ✉ Carrer de Sant Antoní María Claret 167–171, 08025 Barcelona ☎ 934 88 20 78 🌐 Sat–Sun 10–2, by guided tour every half-hour in Spanish, French, English 👣 Tour: adult €6.50. Free for grounds only 🚌 15, 19, 20, 25, 35, 45, 47, 50, 51

MANZANA DE LA DISCÒRDIA (ILLA DE LA DISCÒRDIA)

www.rutadelmodernisme.com
These emblematic buildings stand side by side on Passeig de Gràcia and were built by Modernisme's three undisputed masters when the style was at its zenith. At No. 35 is Casa Lleó i Morera, adapted from an existing building in 1905 by Montaner. It features rounded corner balconies, female figures holding up innovations of the period and a wedding-cake dome on the roof.

Casa Amatller, at No. 41, by Puig i Cadafalch (1867–1956), was built in 1900. It has northern European architectural influences and Gothic details. The facade is dotted with

eccentric stone carvings of animals blowing glass, pouring chocolate and taking photographs, references to the Amatller family's chocolate fortune and hobbies.

The most famous of the trio is Casa Batlló, at No. 43, by Antoni Gaudí (1852–1926). The rippling effect of the facade is achieved through his trademark technique of *trencadís*, the art of covering surfaces with pieces of broken ceramic. On a sunny day it glitters like a giant jewel. The building is said to represent St. George and the dragon: The upper facade is the dragon's back and the tiles represent its scales.

Except for the ground floor of the Casa Amatller, only Casa Batlló is open to the public (daily 9–8 €16.50, free under 6), but the exteriors alone are mesmerizing.
⊞ 211 D3 🛈 Centre de Modernisme booth, Plaça de Catalunya, Sotterani, 08002 Barcelona, ☎ 933 17 76 52 🚇 Passeig de Gràcia 🚌 7, 16, 17, 22, 24, 28

MONESTIR DE PEDRALBES

This 14th-century Gothic monastery is in the leafy suburb of Pedralbes. Elisenda de Montcada, wife of Jaume II, founded the monastery in 1326 for the nuns of the Order of St. Clare. There is an exhibit depicting monastic life, but the monastery's real gem is its three-tiered Gothic cloister. The intricately carved alabaster tomb of Queen Elisenda lies off the cloister, as does the Cappella de Sant Miquel, frescoed by Catalán painter Ferrer Bassa in 1346.
⊞ Off map 210 B1 ✉ Baixada del Monestir 9, 08034 Barcelona ☎ 932 03 92 82 🌐 Tue–Sun 10–2 👣 Adult €5, under 16 free (includes admission to Museu d'Història de la Ciutat, Museu-Casa Verdagner and Park Güell Interpretation Centre). Free 1st Sun of every month 🚌 22, 63, 64, 78 🚆 FGC Reina Elisenda (Line U6) 👣 Tours in Spanish and Catalán 1st Sun of each month; in Catalán only all other Sun. No audiotour 🏪 Small shop

Above *The chapel-like entrance of Hospital de la Santa Creu i Sant Pau*
Opposite *Fundació Joan Miró (top); detail of Miró's Foundation Tapestry (bottom)*

GRÀCIA

www.barcelonaturisme.com
Once an outlying village of Barcelona, Gràcia is now one of the city's most pleasant suburbs, yet signs of its earlier existence are still visible in the form of narrow streets, plazas and workshops. It dates back to 1626, when a group of Carmelite nuns founded the Nostra Senyora de Gràcia convent here. The village was annexed to the main city following the construction of the Passeig de Gràcia in 1897. The district's most

MONTJUÏC

www.barcelonaturisme.com

Montjuïc is the city's lungs. This steep, landscaped, rocky bluff jutting out into the Mediterranean is covered in woodland and is home to some of the city's top museums. The main events of the Olympics were held here in 1992. At the top of the hill, and reached by the Telefèric de Montjuïc cable-car, is an 18th-century fortress—Castell de Montjuïc—now housing the Museu Militar (Military Museum; closed Mon), with a collection of arms and armoury. The huge upper terrace gives sweeping views. Below the museum, the Jardines de Miquel Costa i Llobera cactus garden offers views of the port. The southern side of the mountain is reached from Plaça d'Espanya and Avinguda de la Reina Maria Cristina. The Museu Nacional d'Art de Catalunya (▷ 224), the Mies van der Rohe Pavilion (built for the 1929 World's Fair), CaixaForum art gallery and the Fundació Joan Miró (▷ 220) are here, and the rest of Montjuïc can be navigated from here via a series of escalators.

✚ 210 B5 🚇 Espanya then No. 50 or PM bus, or Paral.lel then Funicular de Montjuïc 🚌 50, PM, 193 (weekends and public holidays only); pick up cable-car (Telefèric de Montjuïc) from the Avinguda de Miramar, which is where the funicular drops you off

MUSEU DEL FC BARCELONA

www.fcbarcelona.es

Barça is the world's largest football (soccer) club and Spain's fifth-largest company. Camp Nou is the largest stadium in Europe. A visit to the museum, the second most visited in the city after the Museu Picasso, allows access to the empty stadium.

✚ 210 A1 ✉ Avinguda Aristides Maillol, entrance 7 or 9, 08028 Barcelona ☎ 934 96 36 09 🕐 2 Apr–28 Oct Mon–Sat 10–8, Sun 10–2.30; 29 Oct–1 Apr Mon–Sat 10–6.30, Sun 10–2.30; restricted hours on match days 💷 Museum and Stadium: adult €17, child (under 13) €14 📷 Guided tours of stadium during museum hours (tours until 1 hour before museum closes) 🚇 Collblanc 🚌 15, 52, 53, 54, 56, 57, 75

MUSEU D'HISTÒRIA DE CATALUNYA

www.mhcat.net

The Palau de Mar houses the Museu d'Història de Catalunya: Catalonia's history from the Iberians to the post-Fascist period. The museum sprawls over four floors, the upper two are for the main exhibition. The exhibits consist of re-created environments, historical sound recordings and footage, and interactive gadgets. Some rely on verbal rather than visual communication, and as the majority of the written texts are in Catalán you might have to make do with the handbook you are given at the entrance. On the third level, a cinema shows a propaganda film of Franco and his family.

✚ 210 B4 ✉ Plaça de Pau Vila 3, 08003 Barcelona ☎ 932 25 47 00 🕐 Tue and Thu–Sat 10–7, Wed 10–8, Sun 10–2.30 💷 Adult €4, child (7–18) €3, under 7 free. Also free 1st Sun of every month, 23 Apr, 18 May, 11 Sep and 24 Sep 🚇 Barceloneta 🚌 14, 17, 39, 40, 45, 57, 59, 64 ☕ Café-terrace

MUSEU D'HISTÒRIA DE LA CIUTAT

www.museuhistoria.bcn.es

Your ticket to the 15th-century Palau de Clariana-Padellàs also gives access to other buildings on Plaça del Rei and the Roman city beneath its foundations, the most extensive remains of their type in Europe. The ruins are cleverly lit and viewed from an intricate series of walkways. Many exhibits have only Catalán and Spanish (Castilian) explanations. The museum continues in the 16th-century Capilla Reial de Santa Agata and the Saló de Tinell (a banqueting chamber), which has six semicircular stone arches that are the largest of their kind ever to have been erected in Europe.

✚ 211 E4 ✉ Plaça del Rei s/n, 08002 Barcelona ☎ 932 56 21 22 🕐 Jun–Sep Tue–Sat 10–8, Sun and holidays 10–3; Oct–May Tue–Sat 10–2, 4–8, Sun and holidays 10–4 💷 Adult €6, family with more than 3 children €2, free 1st Sat of every month after 4pm. Ticket allows free entry to Monestir de Pedralbes (▷ 221), Casa-Museu Verdaguer, and the Interpretation Centre at Park Güell 🚇 Jaume I 🚌 16, 17, 19, 40, 45 📷 Tours in Catalán or Spanish: Sun 11.30; Jul–Aug Wed at 6.30pm. Tours in English by appointment. No audiotours 📖 Guidebook at ticket office and gift shop €25 🏛

MUSEU PICASSO

The most popular museum in Barcelona is dedicated to Pablo Picasso (1881–1973), and covers the artist's formative years in the city, his famous Blue Period (1901–04) and his variations on the Velázquez masterpiece *Las Meninas*. The permanent collection is on the top two floors.

EARLY WORKS

The oils that line the walls of the first section are from Picasso's adolescence. They are mainly portraits, such as the famous *Man with Hat* (1895). Other works include *Carrer de La Riera de Sant Joan* (1900), a view from the artist's studio window, and *Passeig de Colom* (1917), another view-inspired painting. The next rooms deal with the artist's social impressions of his first trip to Paris, and include what must surely be one of the most passionate paintings of all time, *The Embrace* (1900). His ground-breaking Blue and Rose periods are possibly the least represented in the museum, although the space devoted to them does contain *The Madman* (1904), in which Picasso conveys human suffering with unprecedented skill.

THE 'LAS MENINAS' PAINTINGS

The Between the Wars rooms illustrate the artist's first venture into what would become known as Cubism in *Figure with Fruit Bowl* (1917). But much of this work acts as a mere interlude to the 'Las Meninas' series of paintings. From the early 1950s Picasso started looking towards the great artists, such as El Greco, Manet and Courbet, but his prime obsession was with Velázquez. The result was a series of canvases on the common theme of the Spanish painter's masterpiece *Las Meninas* (dated 1656, on show in the Prado — ▷ 74–75).

FINAL YEARS

The final section, The Last Years, shows Picasso's need to increase his output. He worked around the clock, producing a spontaneous, almost naïve and infantile style. He also dabbled in ceramic work and collage work; examples of both are in the final room.

INFORMATION

www.museupicasso.bcn.es

✚ 211 E4 ✉ Carrer Montcada 15–23, 08003 Barcelona ☎ 932 56 30 00 ⏰ Tue–Sun 10–8 💶 Adult €9, under 16 free. Also free first Sun of every month. Entrance to temporary exhibitions €5. Combined museums ticket €22 ❓ Group bookings must be made before 2pm the day prior to visit; tel: 933 19 63 10 🚇 Jaume 1, Arc de Triomf 🚌 16, 17, 19, 39, 40, 45, 51, 59 📖 Guidebook available in all major European languages and Japanese €9.50 ☕ Elegant café, run by the chic Hotel Arts 🎁 Two gift shops

Opposite left *Telefèric cable-cars ascending Montjüic*
Opposite right *The museu d'Història de Catalunya in the Palau de Mar*
Below *Feathery plants cascade over the arched galleries in Museu Picasso*

MUSEU MARÍTIM

www.museumaritimbarcelona.com

The Maritime Museum is housed in the former Royal Shipyards (Drassanes Reials), the only complete example of its kind in the world; the huge 13th-century Gothic vaults and soaring arches are stunning. The arched facade is under renovation, as are some parts of the interior, but this does nothing to detract from the sheer grandeur.

Inside, the emphasis of the collection is on the Catalán nautical history, and in particular its conquest of parts of the Mediterranean. The museum's star feature is *La Galera Reial*, a 60m-long (195ft) replica of the royal galley built by John of Austria. Extensive documentation on the original vessel made it possible for this model to be built in 1971 to celebrate the fourth centenary of *La Reial's* finest hour.

A visit to the *Santa Eulàlia* is also included in the entry price. Anchored across the road in the port itself, this 19th-century tall ship was bought by the Museu Marítim in 1997.

➕ 211 D5 ✉ Avinguda de les Drassanes s/n, 08001 Barcelona ☎ 933 42 99 20 🕐 Daily 10–8 ✋ Adult €7, child (7–16) €3.50. Also free 1st Sat of every month after 3pm. The *Santa Eulàlia:* adult €2.50, child €1.20. Temporary exhibitions: adult €2.50, child €1.20. planetarium €3 🚇 Drassanes 🚌 14, 18, 36, 38, 57, 59, 64, 91 🎧 Audiotours included in admission 📖 Guidebook €8 ♿

MUSEU NACIONAL D'ART DE CATALUNYA (MNAC)

www.mnac.es

The museum has an outstanding collection of Romanesque and Gothic religious works, and covers Catalonia's major artistic movements. It is in the Palau Nacional, a reproduction baroque palace that dominates the Plaça d'Espanya and has views over the city and Tibidabo. The Romanesque (11th- to 13th-century) frescoes were gathered from around the region in the 1920s in a campaign to save Catalonia's heritage. One of the most stunning examples is the *Apse of Santa Maria de Taüll*, a vivid portrait of Christ and five of the apostles (Àmbit or Area VII). The Gothic collection starts with a room of decorative elements rescued from the mansions of Barcelona. Gallery XII contains many pieces by Jaume Huguet (*c*1415–92), the most prominent painter of the Catalán school in the late 15th century.

The Collección Cambó, of the Renaissance and baroque periods, has its own gallery and the entire collection of 20th-century art from the Museu d'Art Modern has moved here, as well as the Thyssen-Bornemisza Collection, an exquisite collection of Old Masters, including Fra Angelico, Titian and Velázquez.

➕ 210 B4 ✉ Palau Nacional, Parc de Montjuïc, 08038 Barcelona ☎ 936 22 03 75 🕐 Tue–Sat 10–7, Sun and holidays 10–2.30 ✋ Adult €8.50 (free 1st Sun every month). Entrance to temporary exhibitions is extra. Combined admission to Poble Espanyol available €12 🚇 Plaça d'Espanya 🚌 9, 13, 27, 30, 37, 50, 55, 56, 57, 71, 75, 80, 91, 95, PM 📷 Free guided tours Sat, Sun at 12.30 in Spanish, English, French, German and Japanese. No audiotours 📖 Guidebook €18

MUSEU PICASSO

▷ 223.

PALAU DE LA MÚSICA CATALÁNA

www.palaumusica.org

Designated a UNESCO World Heritage Site in 1997, this concert hall was designed by architect Lluís Domènech i Montaner (1850–1923) at the beginning of the 1900s. It is one of the few fin de siècle buildings in Europe that continues to fulfil the function for which it was intended.

Unless you have tickets to a concert, visits are by guided tour only. An excellent 20-minute film takes you through the building's history and the artists who have graced its stage over the past 100 years. You are then led into the concert hall itself. Be prepared for an assault on your senses, as it takes a while to absorb the riot of sublime details. Your eyes are logically drawn to the stage area, with its 18 ceramic and terracotta figures. The prime focus, however, and the hall's main light source, is the extraordinary multihued-glass inverted dome, surrounded by 40 female heads. One of the most spectacular pieces of secular glasswork of all time, the dome rises out of an ornate ceiling dotted with hundreds of ceramic rose heads.

➕ 211 E4 ✉ Carrer Sant Francesc de Paula 2, 08003 Barcelona ☎ 902 47 54 85 🕐 Mon–Sun 10–3.30 ✋ Adult €8, under 12 free 🚇 Urquinaona 🚌 16, 17, 19, 40, 45 and all routes to Plaça d' Urquinaona 📷 Guided tours lasting 50 min every half-hour in Catalán, Spanish and English. Tickets from the Les Muses del Palau gift shop or online. Tours may be cancelled at short notice owing to rehearsals in the concert hall 📖 Small pocket guidebooks €10, larger book on the concert hall €30 ♿

PALAU REIAL DE PEDRALBES

www.museuceramica.bcn.es
www.museuartsdecoratives.bcn.es
This stately palace, with landscaped gardens, was built in 1924 as a residence for the royal family when they visited Barcelona, although they never stayed here. Architect Antoni Gaudí (1852–1926) left his mark in the form of a parabolic arch that tops the Umbracle, a covered pavilion set among the shrubbery. The palace is now home to two museums, the Museu de Ceràmica and the Museu de les Arts Decoratives. The Museu de Ceràmica's collection spans the period from the 11th century to the present day, while the smaller Museu de les Arts Decoratives covers industrial, furniture and object design from the Middle Ages.
➕ Off map 210 B1 ✉ Avinguda Diagonal 686, 08034 Barcelona ☎ Museu de Ceràmica: 932 80 50 24. Museu de les Arts Decoratives: 932 80 50 24 🕐 Tue–Sat 10–6, Sun 10–3 🖐 Entry to both museums and Museu Textil I d'Indumentària: adult €5; free 1st Sun of every month 🚇 Palau Reial 🚌 7, 33, 63, 67, 68, 74, 75, 78, 113

PARC DE LA CIUTADELLA

www.bcn.cat/parcsijardins
This is the largest and greenest park in the city. It also contains the zoo, various museums, the Parlament de Catalunya (Catalán Parliament), a hothouse and one of the prettiest cafés in the city. The park was used as the setting for the Universal Exhibition of 1888, for which the grandiose Arc de Triomf, at the northern end, served as the main entrance point.

The park is also noted for its sculpture, in particular Roig i Soler's *Lady with the Parasol* (1885; alias Pepita), which has become a symbol of the city. Activities for children include play areas, the fish-filled boating lake and bicycles for rent.
➕ 211 F4 ✉ Passeig Picasso 15, 08003 Barcelona 🚇 Arc de Triomf, Ciutadella-Vila Olímpic 🚌 14, 17, 36, 39, 40, 41, 42, 45, 51, 57, 59, 64

PARK GÜELL

www.casamuseugaudi.org
This site of 17ha (42 acres) is one of the most magical works by architect Antoni Gaudí (1853–1926). The project was commissioned in 1900 by industrialist Eusebi Güell, who intended to use the land to build a large élite residential estate of some 60 houses. Unfortunately only two buyers ever signed up.

Two gatehouses with roofs coated in rich shimmering *trencadís* (broken pottery) flank the main entrance. From here steps are dominated by a grotto-like fountain sporting a Catalán flag. Farther up is the park's icon and most popular photo opportunity, a brightly decorated salamander. At the top of the stairs lies what was intended to be a covered marketplace, the Sala Hipóstila. Eighty-six columns connected by shallow vaults support the elevated square above and are again covered in *trencadís*. The main square itself offers sweeping views of the city from a sinuous, lizard-like bench. The 1906 Casa-Museu Gaudí showcases some of the furniture Gaudí designed for the Casa Batlló and Casa Milà (▷ 221 and 215 respectively), and for Palau Güell.

➕ Off map 211 F1 ✉ Carrer d'Olot s/n and Carretera del Carmel s/n, 08014 Barcelona ☎ Casa-Museu Gaudí: 932 19 38 11 🕐 Park: daily 10–dusk. Casa-Museu Gaudí: daily 10–6 (until 8pm in summer). Last ticket sold 15 min before closing 🖐 Park: free. Casa-Museu Gaudí: adult €5, under 11 free; combined admission to Casa-Museu Gaudi and Sagrada Família available €9 🚇 Lesseps 🚌 24, 25, 28, 31, 32, 74; 24 is the only bus going directly to the gate. The others stop 10–15 min walk away 📖 Guidebook in variety of languages €10 🍴 Café-bar overlooking main square 🍽 Basic café at entrance 🏬 Shop at main entrance

PLAÇA REIAL

www.barcelonaturisme.com
The bars and *terrazas* that line the Plaça Reial's generous diameter are a magnet for locals and visitors on balmy summer evenings. During the day, the *plaça* is much quieter and some of its architectural features can be more easily appreciated. The square's lampposts, a homage to Hermes, the Catalán patron god of business, were designed by a promising young architect named Antoni Gaudí. Note that the Plaça Reial also has a bad reputation for pickpockets, so be careful, especially in the surrounding narrow streets.
➕ 211 E4 ℹ Ciutat 2, Plaça de Sant Jaume, 08002 Barcelona, ☎ 932 85 38 34 🚇 Liceu, Jaume I 🚌 14, 17, 19, 38, 40, 45, 59, 91

Above *Palau Reial de Pedralbes (left);*
Gaudí's salamander at Park Güell (right)
Opposite *Replica of the 16th-century La*
Galera Reial at Museu Marítim

INFORMATION

www.barcelonaturisme.com

➕ 211 D4 ℹ️ Plaça de Catalunya, 17 soterrani, 08002 Barcelona ☎ 932 85 38 34 Ⓜ️ Catalunya, Liceu, Drassanes 🚌 14, 18, 38, 57, 59, 64 and all routes to Plaça de Catalunya or the Plaça Portal de la Pau

LAS RAMBLAS

Las Ramblas was described by writer Somerset Maugham as 'the most beautiful street in the world' and is without doubt the very heart of the city. It is, however, actually several streets in one, hence the plural, and leads down to the port. There is a constant flow of tourists and locals ambling down Las Ramblas, stopping to buy newspapers or flowers at the pretty kiosks, or enjoying the constant theatre provided by mime artists, dancers, acrobats, puppeteers and more. Just remember to keep a sharp eye on your bags—this is prime pickpocketing territory.

Rambla de Canaletes is the top section just below Plaça de Catalunya, named for the 19th-century Canaletes fountain said to possess powers of enchantment condemning all who drink from it to fall in love with the city and ineluctably return to Barcelona. This is followed by the Rambla dels Estudis, named after the university that stood here. It is also known as the Rambla dels Ocells (of the birds), after the hawkers who sell caged birds. The Rambla dels Flors (of the flowers) is probably the prettiest part of the route, with flower stalls and street performers.

HALFWAY POINT

The giant pavement mural designed by Catalán artist Joan Miró in 1976 marks the halfway point of Las Ramblas. It is overlooked by a whimsical *modernista* umbrella shop (now a bank), adorned with twirling parasols and a giant dragon holding a lamp and a furled umbrella. Some 50m (55 yards) back up the Rambla is the entrance to La Boqueria, the city's fabulous produce market, which also has some excellent cafés and tapas bars. Here, the street's name changes again, this time to the Rambla dels Caputxins, after a now-demolished convent. The opera house, the Teatre del Liceu, is on your right, and the Café de la Opera is opposite, still serving its famous *xocolate amb xurros* (hot chocolate and fritters).

TOWARDS THE PORT

The next stretch, the Rambla de Santa Mònica, has always been the threshold of Barcelona's port, and there are dozens of portrait artists here. The Rambla de Mar wooden walkway, the final stretch, was opened in 1994.

POBLE ESPANYOL

www.poble-espanyol.com

This collection of 115 examples of Spanish architecture lies at the foot of Montjuïc and was constructed for the 1929 World's Fair. Once you enter through the reproduction of the walled city of Ávila's grand gateway and its huge Plaza Major, dozens of tiny streets are laid out before you, their architecture ranging from whitewashed Andalucían abodes to the high-Gothic style of Burgos.

The village also has its own working community of artisans, and at night the place buzzes with bars, cabaret-restaurants and clubs.

🔒 210 A3 ✉ Avinguda Marquès de Comillas s/n, 08038 Barcelona ☎ 935 08 63 00 🕐 Mon 9–8, Tue–Thu 9am–2am, Fri–Sat 9am–4am, Sun 9am–midnight 🖐 Adult €9 child (7–12) €6; under 7 free; combined entry with MNAC available €12. Free Sun 8pm–midnight 🚇 Espanya 🚌 9, 13, 27, 38, 50, 55, 57, 91 and all routes to Plaça d'Espanya

PORT VELL

Barcelona's modern port and marina is the perfect place for a stroll, and is especially popular with Barcelonins at weekends, when bicyclists, dog-walkers and strolling families are all out and about. The area is also known for two famous pieces of public art. The first is *Barcelona Head*, by American artist Roy Lichtenstein (1923–97), which stands at the entrance to the marina. The second is a full-scale replica of the world's first steam-powered submarine, which was invented in 1862 by the Catalán Narcís Monturiol (1819–85).

🔒 211 D5 🏛 Ciutat 2, Plaça de Sant Jaume, 08002 Barcelona 🚇 Barceloneta/Drassanes 🚌 14, 17, 19, 20, 36, 39, 40, 45, 51, 57, 59, 64

LAS RAMBLAS
▷ 226.

LA SAGRADA FAMÍLIA
▷ 228–229.

SANTA MARÍA DEL MAR

Owing to its relatively short construction period, the 14th-century Santa María del Mar is the most complete example of Catalán Gothic architecture, and is set in a pretty square from which you can relax and enjoy the view.

Named Saint Mary of the Sea for King Jaume I's ex-voto promise to build a great church to protect the Catalán fleet, Santa Maria del Mar is the seafarers' talisman.

Its central nave, 32m (105ft) high and the widest in Europe, is flanked on either side by two aisles and supporting columns. They soar up to a series of fan vaults, with a further set of eight at the far end of the church set in a semicircle to define the presbytery.

The church also has glorious examples of 15th- to 18th-century stained-glass windows.

🔒 211 E4 ✉ Passeig del Born I, 08003 Barcelona ☎ 933 10 23 90 🕐 Mon–Sat 9–1.30, 4.30–8, Sun 10–1.30, 4.30–8 🖐 Free 🚇 Jaume I 🚌 16, 17, 19, 22, 39, 40, 45, 51, 59 📖 Small leaflet/book €3

TIBIDABO

www.tibidabo.es

Tibidabo is the highest mountain of the Collserola hills. At 512m (1,680ft), its peak dominates the city.

At night the monumental church, the Sagrat Cor (Sacred Heart), and the statue of Christ by Frederic Marès (1893–1991) are lit up and can be seen for miles around. Most people make the steep ascent for more earthly pleasures.

The Parc d'Atraccions was inaugurated in 1899 and some of its fun rides date back to the early days of the 20th century. There is also a small museum here dedicated to period automata.

Getting to the park is a ride in itself. The more than 100-year-old, wooden-seated Tramvia Blau (Blue Tram) rattles passengers up from the train station to just below the summit, from where you make the rest of the trip in a high-speed funicular railway that runs directly to the park entrance.

🔒 Off map 211 D1 ✉ Plaça del Tibidabo, 08035 Barcelona ☎ 932 11 79 42 🕐 Jul–Aug Mon–Thu noon–10, Fri–Sun noon–11; Jun, Sep Mon–Fri noon–8, Sat–Sun noon–9; Mar–May, Oct Sat–Sun noon–7; Nov–Feb Sat–Sun noon–6 🖐 Adult €25, child under 1.2m (3.6ft) in height €9 🚌 17, 60, 73, T2 🚆 FGC to Pie de Funicular, then funicular; or bus or FGC to Avinguda Tibidabo, then Tramvia Blau and funicular

Opposite top *The facade of the Teatre del Liceu, Barcelona's famous opera house*
Opposite bottom *Bust on the facade of the old Teatre Principal on Rambla de Santa Monica*
Below *The Ferris wheel and other rides at Tibidabo's Parc d'Atraccions*

INFORMATION

www.sagradafamilia.org

✚ 211 F2 ✉ Carrer de Mallorca 401, 08013 Barcelona ☎ 932 07 30 31

🕐 Mar–Sep daily 9–8; Oct–Feb daily 9–6; 25–26 Dec, 1 and 6 Jan 9–2

✋ Adult €12, child under 10 free; elevator €3 🚇 Sagrada Família 🚌 19, 33, 34, 43, 44, 50, 51 🎧 Audiotours €4 in English, French, German, Italian, Spanish or Catalán. Guided tours €16, child (10–18) €7, child (6–10) €5, held daily but language alternates, phone for details. English: 11am, 1pm, 3pm, 5.30pm

📖 Large selection available in gift shop

🍴 Food and snack machines only

🛍 Shop selling books on the church and Gaudí, plus gift items

TIPS

» Before you go in, take a walk around the exterior of the building and cross Carrer de la Marina to reach Plaça Gaudí, as the best views of the Nativity Facade are from this small park and lake.

» Take a five-minute walk up the Avenida de Gaudí, towards the Hospital de Sant Pau, to get a better view of the overall dimensions of the church.

» If you decide to use the audioguides, you will be asked to leave some identification (passport, driver's licence, etc) as a deposit. If you don't have these with you, you may be asked for a credit card.

INTRODUCTION

Love it or loathe it, you cannot ignore La Sagrada Família, or Temple Expiatori de la Sagrada Família (Expiatory Temple to the Holy Family), to give it its full name. Its towers and cranes are visible from all over Barcelona and it is the one must-see item on every visitor's itinerary. Work on La Sagrada Família is progressing continually and what you see will depend on when you go. Entry to the interior is at the Passion Facade on Carrer de Sardenya. After passing the gift shop on your left and the lift (elevator) to the towers on your right, you reach the central nave. The whole area resembles a building site, but the sheer scale of the work will take your breath away.

It is one of the great ironies of Barcelona that a building widely perceived as a triumph of modernism should have been conceived as a way of atoning for the sins of the modern city. The original idea came from Josep Bocabella, a bookseller and conservative Catholic.

The first architect, Francesc de Villar, envisaged a conventional Gothic-style church, but when Gaudí took over the project at the age of 31 in 1883 he was given free rein and his fantasies were let loose. It is not always realized that Gaudí, despite the playfulness of his architecture, was a deeply religious man. In his later years he devoted himself totally to La Sagrada Família, living like a recluse in a hut on the site, refusing to draw a salary, wearing simple clothes, eating little food and begging passers-by and rich businessmen for money to allow work on the church to continue.

In 1936, 10 years after Gaudí's death, his plans for La Sagrada Família were destroyed in an anarchist riot, so it is impossible to be certain what the finished building would have looked like. Nevertheless, despite widespread opposition, work on the church resumed in 1952 and it has now taken on an unstoppable momentum, driven by massive worldwide interest and financed by public subscription and the money from entrance fees. There was a public outcry in 2007, when the local government announced that a tunnel to accommodate the new high-speed AVE train would be built beneath the future Glory facade. The furore rumbles on. Despite this, the current plan is to complete the temple by 2026, in time for the centenary of Gaudí's death.

WHAT TO SEE

NATIVITY FACADE

This is the sculptural high point of the church, begun in 1891 and completed during the lifetime of the architect Antoni Gaudí (1852–1926). The stone carvings

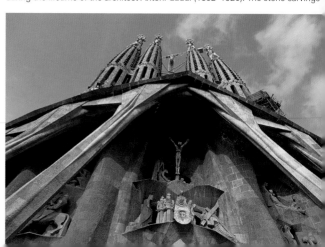

Opposite *Josep Maria Subirachs' Passion Facade sculpture*

Right *The once controversial nude crucifixion by Subirachs*

A CHANGING CHURCH

It is envisaged that the nave will have five aisles, divided by a forest of pillars. Work has already begun on four massive stone columns designed to support the central spire, which will be 170m (558ft) high and topped by a cross, making La Sagrada Família once again the tallest building in Barcelona. Around the spire will be four more towers, dedicated to the evangelists and topped with the symbols of an angel, an ox, an eagle and a lion. As you stand in the nave, look left to see Gaudí's altar canopy and the neo-Gothic wall of the apse; to the right, work has begun on the Glory Facade (which will eventually be the church's main entrance), together with four more towers. Straight ahead, across the transept, a doorway leads outside for a close-up look at the Nativity Facade. The entire church will one day be surrounded by an ambulatory, or external cloister. Despite all the construction work, the completed church seems a long way off, but as Gaudí himself said: 'My client is in no hurry.'

on the facade drip with detail, so that at times it resembles a fairy grotto, a hermit's cave or a jumble of molten wax. The theme is the joy of creation at the birth of Jesus, and it deliberately faces east to receive the first rays of the rising sun. At the heart is the nativity scene, featuring Joseph, Mary and Jesus; above them angels play trumpets and sing to celebrate the birth. Three doorways, dedicated to Faith, Hope and Charity, depict other biblical scenes, from the marriage of Mary and Joseph to the presentation of Jesus in the temple.

At least 30 species of plants which are native to both Catalonia and the Holy Land have been identified in the facade, echoing the theme that all creation worships Jesus. This theme reaches its climax in the Tree of Life, a ceramic green cypress tree swarming with doves that tops the facade, between the tall towers.

PASSION FACADE

In contrast to the richness of the Nativity Facade, the figures on the Passion Facade are harsh and angular, evoking the pain and humiliation of Christ's crucifixion and death. The Catalán sculptor Josep Subirachs (b1927), who completed these figures in 1990 and still has a workshop on the site, has come in for much criticism, but Gaudí always intended that this should be a bleak and barren counterpart to the joyful scenes of the Nativity.

Six huge, leaning columns support a portico containing a series of sculptural groups beginning with the Last Supper and ending with the naked Christ on the cross. The figures of Roman centurions are clearly influenced by Gaudí's chimneys on the roof of Casa Milà (▷ 215).

Look for the *Kiss of Death*, a sculpture showing Jesus' betrayal at the hands of Judas, complete with a biblical reference in stone (Mark 14:45) and a 'magic square' whose rows, columns, diagonals and corners all add up to 33, Christ's age at the time of his death.

THE TOWERS

By the time of Gaudí's death in 1926, only one bell tower had been completed, but there are now four towers above each of the Nativity and Passion facades. The final plans show a total of 18 towers, dedicated to the 12 apostles, the 4 evangelists (or Gospel writers), Christ and the Virgin Mary. The dramatic spires, which are up to 112m (367ft) tall, are covered in ceramic mosaics. Gaudí maintained that by looking at the towers, your gaze would be drawn upwards to heaven, transmitting the words of the prayer *Sanctus, Sanctus, Sanctus, Hosanna in Excelsis* (Holy, Holy, Holy, Glory to God in the Highest) that is spelled out in broken ceramic tiles at the top.

Spiral staircases give access to the towers, and there is also a lift (elevator) at each end of the building that takes you most of the way. Climbing the towers gives close-up views of the spires and also allows you to look down over the central nave. Another good vantage point is the footbridge linking two towers above the Nativity Facade.

THE CRYPT

The cathedral's original architect, Francesc de Villar, designed the crypt in neo-Gothic style; it is reached by an entrance to the right of the Passion Facade and now contains a museum. Among the items on display are some of Gaudí's scale models and drawings (although most were destroyed during the Civil War), and sketches and casts for the Passion Facade by Josep Subirachs. There is also a confessional box and a tenebrarium (a candle-holder used during Holy Week), both designed by Gaudí. You can look into the workshop where artists are at work preparing plaster casts for the Glory Facade.

One of the chapels, dedicated to Our Lady of Carmen, contains Gaudí's simple stone tomb, with the Latin inscription *Antonius Gaudí Cornet, Reusensis*, a reference to his home town of Reus.

Opposite *Detail of two of the magnificent towers of La Sagrada Família*

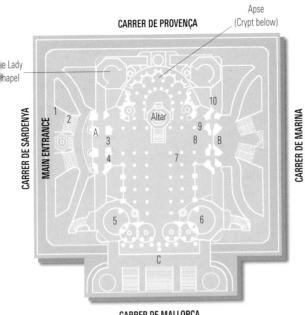

CARRER DE PROVENÇA

Apse
(Crypt below)

e Lady
hapel

Altar

10

9

8

A

B

1

2

3

4

7

5

6

C

CARRER DE SARDENYA

MAIN ENTRANCE

CARRER DE MARINA

CARRER DE MALLORCA

KEY

1 Main entrance
2 Information
3 Shop
4 Lift (elevator) 1
5 Baptistery
6 Chapel of the Sacrament
7 Models
8 Lift (elevator) 2
9 Stairs
10 Portal of the Rosary
A Passion Facade
B Nativity Facade
C Glory Facade

WALK

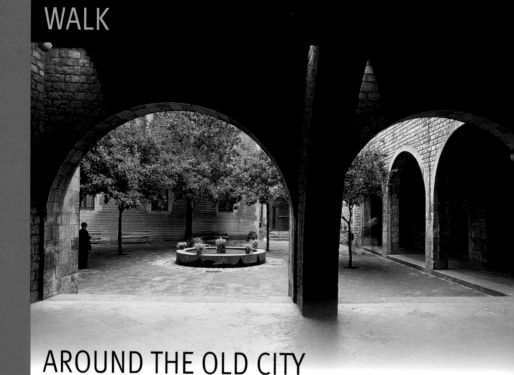

AROUND THE OLD CITY

Barcelona's captivating Gothic Quarter is a maze of narrow stone streets encircling an enormous cathedral with theatrical spires. This walk begins at the prestigious opera house, the Liceu, and winds through tiny alleys and charming squares to culminate in a perfect Gothic time-capsule, the little Plaça Sant Just.

THE WALK

Distance: 1.3km (0.8 miles)
Allow: 2 hours, including visits to monuments
Start at: Teatre Liceu (Las Ramblas), map 211 D4
End at: Plaça Sant Just, map 211 E4

HOW TO GET THERE

Nearest Metro: Liceu.

★ Begin the walk in front of the prestigious Opera House, a copy of the opulent 19th-century original which burned down in 1994.

Cross the street to find Carrer Cardenal Casanyes, which will bring you to Plaça del Pi, dominated by the austere stone bulk of the Gothic church of Santa María del Pí.

❶ The Plaça del Pi, and the adjoining Plaça Sant Josep Oriol, are pretty squares, with a clutch of popular terrace cafés. Just left of the Taller de Tapas, a good tapas bar and restaurant, is the tiny passage Carrer de l'Ave Maria, which leads into Carrer Banys Nous.

Turn left and then immediately right into another narrow passage, the Baixada de Santa Eulàlia. This steep street is named after the city's first patron saint, a fourth-century martyr who was rolled down this hill in a barrel, one of 13 ordeals designed to persuade her to renounce her faith.

Continue up the street until you see a passage on the left, just before the chic Hotel Neri. This leads to the lovely Plaça de Sant Felip Neri.

❷ A baroque church flanked by historic mansions occupies this square. A large stone fountain stands in the centre. On weekday mornings, you might share the square with the smocked infants attending the nursery school. The Hotel Neri has a stylish little terrace on the square.

Leave the square by the archway to your right, and follow the street until you emerge near the cathedral (▷ 218).

❸ Enter the cathedral cloister, shaded with palms and home to a dozen honking white geese (an ancient tradition which some believe has its roots in an homage to the purity of Santa Eulàlia). You can access the cathedral through the side door from here, and admire the martyr's alabaster coffin under the main altar.

Emerge from the cathedral by the main entrance, which will take you out onto Pla de la Seu. Turn right, and right again onto Carrer Comtes. A little farther on the left is the entrance to the Museu Frederic Marès.

❹ The museum contains everything from Romanesque sculpture to 19th-century dolls. It is located in a beautiful Gothic mansion with a stone courtyard dotted with orange trees. There is a delightful outdoor café here (open Easter to October).

When you exit the museum, turn left, and continue along Carrer Comtes for about 50m (55 yards). Turn into the central patio of the Palau del Lloctinent (also known as the Arxiu de la Corona de Aragó) with its pond and fountain and emerge on the other side onto Plaça del Rei, the city's most beautiful Gothic square.

❺ You can visit the main buildings of this ensemble — the sober Gothic throne room and the royal chapel — as part of a visit to Museu d'Història de la Ciutat (▷ 222; entrance on Carrer Veguer). This museum is built over the ruins of Roman Barcino (partly visible through a pavement-level window on Carrer Veguer).

Continue down Carrer Veguer, go right on Llibreteria, next left into Carrer Dagueria, cross Carrer Sant Jaume and continue up Carrer Dagueria. This emerges onto the charming Gothic square of Sant Just, named after the church which overlooks the square. There are good cafés here with terraces, the perfect place to end this walk.

WHEN TO GO

This walk is suitable all year round. If you want to visit museums, avoid Mondays when many are closed.

WHERE TO EAT
CAFÉ BLISS

A genuine charmer, with outdoor tables on a Gothic square. Light meals, drinks and snacks.
✉ Plaça Sant Just 4 ☎ 932 68 10 22 🕐 Daily 9am–midnight (until 1am Fri and Sat)

CAFÈ DE L'ACADÈMIA

Excellent Catalán cuisine, with a great value lunchtime fixed-price menu, and tables on the square.
✉ Carrer Lledó 1 (corner with Plaça Sant Just) ☎ 933 19 82 53 🕐 Mon–Fri 1.30–4, 8.30–midnight. Closed weekends and 3 weeks in Aug

CAFÈ D'ESTIU

www.textilcafe.com
A tranquil, enchanting place for coffee and cakes under orange trees.
✉ Plaça Sant Iu 5–6 (next to Museu Frederic Marés) ☎ 933 10 30 14 🕐 Easter–Oct Tue–Sun 10–10

TALLER DE TAPAS

www.tallerdetapas.com
Freshly prepared tapas in a stylish eatery, with a terrace.
✉ Plaça Sant Josep Oriol 9 ☎ 933 01 80 20 🕐 Daily 10am–midnight

PLACE TO VISIT
MUSEUM FREDERIC MARÈS

www.museumares.bcn.cat
✉ Plaça Sant Iu 5 ☎ 932 56 35 00 🕐 Tue–Sat 10–7, Sun 10–3 👜 €5, free first Sun of the month and Wed pm 🚌 17, 19, 40, 45 🚇 Jaume I

Above *Geese in the cathedral cloister*
Opposite *Loggia of Museu Frederic Marès*

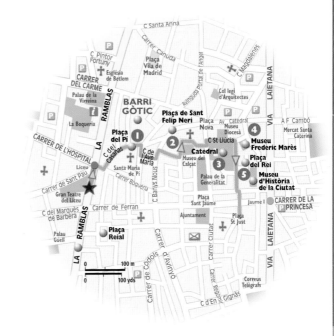

AROUND MODERNISTA BARCELONA

The fairytale buildings created by Antoni Gaudí are among Barcelona's most beautiful and emblematic sights. This walk ambles through the Eixample, the city's opulent 19th-century extension, which is home to the greatest concentration of *modernista* monuments in the world.

THE WALK

Distance: 1km (0.5 miles)
Allow: 2 hours, including visits to monuments
Start at: Casa Batlló, map 211 D3
End at: Casa Fuster, map 211 E2

HOW TO GET THERE

Nearest Metro: Passeig de Gràcia.

★ Begin in front of Gaudí's glorious Casa Batlló (▷ 221), which appears like a vision on the city's most exclusive boulevard, the Passeig de Gràcia. It looks like something from a child's story book, with its swirling walls, glinting tiles and undulating roof (said to resemble a dragon). Next door is the Casa Amatller, with a stepped roof apparently studded with chocolate buttons, and on the corner of the block is a creamy mansion with icing-sugar flourishes. These three mansions were each created by one of the leading architects

of the Modernisme movement: Antoní Gaudí, Puig i Cadafalch, and Domènech i Muntaner. Modernisme, the Catalán version of art nouveau, was being developed at about the same time as the Eixample, this 19th-century district of Barcelona, was being laid out, and it has left its playful imprint everywhere.

Continue along Passeig de Gràcia, keeping the Casa Batlló on your left, and turn left onto Carrer d'Aragó.

❶ On the right, you can't miss the Fundació Tàpies, topped with a wire cloud, a sculpture, *Núvol i cadira (Cloud and Chair),* by Antoni Tàpies. The building, by Muntaner, was one of the earliest works of Modernisme.

Continue along Carrer d'Aragó, then turn right into Rambla de Catalunya, an attractive tree-lined boulevard with lots of terrace cafés and shops. There

are numerous *modernista* mansions along this street, mostly by minor architects, but delightful nonetheless.

❷ Walk up one block of the Rambla de Catalunya to find the Farmàcia Bolos (at No.77), with charming turn-of-the-20th-century stained glass. The Eixample is dotted with plenty of examples of Modernisme, from pharmacies to bakeries, and this is one of the prettiest.

Continue strolling along Rambla de Catalunya for another two blocks until you see the entrance to the Passatge de la Concepció on the right (just after Carrer Provença).

❸ This is a charming, narrow street lined with villas, built at the end of the 19th century. There are good restaurants here now. The Passatge de la Concepció leads back to the Passeig de Gràcia.

Across the street, you can't miss Gaudí's extraordinary apartment building, La Pedrera (▷ 215).

❹ Also known as Casa Milá, it looks as though it was made of whipped cream. Go inside to see a period apartment, and the fine roof terrace.

When you leave, turn right and continue up Passeig de Gràcia. Just before you cross busy Avinguda Diagonal, glance to the right.

❺ The fairy-tale Nordic castle with conical towers and spires 300m (330 yards) down the Diagonal on the left is the Casa de les Punxes (House of the Needles) built by Puig i Cadafalch in 1905. Closer on the right is Palau Quadras, now the Casa Asia cultural centre, also by Puig i Cadafalch.

Cross Avinguda Diagonal and continue on Passeig de Gràcia towards the splendid *modernista* building which you will see directly in front of you. The Casa Fuster, now a luxury hotel, was one of Domenèch i Muntaner's last projects. (Muntaner is best known for the gorgeously over-the-top Palau de la Musica.) The lounge bar and restaurant are open to the public, and combine original details with sleek contemporary design.

WHEN TO GO
Any time is a good time. Come on a weekday if you want to avoid the shopping crowds which throng this neighbourhood on Saturdays.

WHERE TO EAT
BAR MUT
Trendy café-tapas bar in a beautifully restored 1930s venue.
✉ Carrer Pau Claris 192, 08037 Barcelona ☎ 932 17 43 38 ⏰ Daily 8am–midnight

CASA CALVET
www.casacalvet.es
A fine restaurant in an elegant building designed by Gaudí.
✉ Carrer de Casp 48 ☎ 934 12 40 21 ⏰ Mon–Sat 1.30–3.30, 8–11. Closed Easter week, 2 weeks in Aug

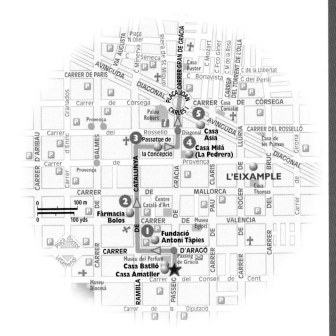

EL TRAGALUZ
A bar/restaurant located on a charming street.
✉ Passatge de la Concepcieo 5 ☎ 934 87 01 96

MAURI
Celebrated tearoom and *pastelería* (cake shop).
✉ Rambla de Catalunya 102 ☎ 932 15 81 46 ⏰ Mon–Sat 9–2, 4–9

PLACE TO VISIT
FUNDACIÓ TÀPIES
www.fundaciotapies.org
✉ Carrer Aragó 255 ☎ 934 87 03 15 ⏰ Tue–Sat 10–8 💷 Adult €7, under 16 free 🚌 7, 16, 17, 20, 22, 24, 28, 39, 43, 44, 45, 47, 63, 67, 68 🚇 Passeig de Gràcia

Opposite Cloud and Chair *sculpture on Fundació Tàpies*
Below *Rooftop view from La Pedrera*

MÍNGUEZ
www.adolfodominguez.com
This top Spanish designer's cool linen suits were responsible for a fundamental shift in men's fashion in Spain. This is the main branch of a popular chain selling ladies' wear and sportswear too.
✉ Passeig de Gràcia 32, 08007 Barcelona ☎ 934 87 41 70 ⏱ Mon–Sat 10–8.30 Ⓜ Passeig de Gràcia

AGATHA
Agatha jewellery is well known beyond Spain and this shop has a sizeable collection of pieces. The makers are famous for their cultured pearl necklaces. You'll also find gloves, handbags (purses) and sunglasses, as well as perfumes in beautiful bottles.
✉ Rambla de Catalunya 112, 08008 Barcelona ☎ 934 15 59 98 ⏱ Mon–Sat 10.30–8.30 Ⓜ Diagonal

ARMAND BASI
www.armandbasi.com
The pleasant flagship store of this ultra-hip Spanish designer, it's the only place in town where you can view his complete men's and women's collections. Items include soft leather jackets, timeless suits, classic knitwear, evening dresses and accessories.
✉ Passeig de Gràcia 49, 08007 Barcelona ☎ 932 15 14 21 ⏱ Mon–Sat 10–8.30 Ⓜ Passeig de Gràcia

BULEVARD ROSA
www.bulevardrosa.com
This Barcelona shopping area has a twin; the first to open was this one in Passeig de Gràcia, and the second sprang up on Avinguda Diagonal. Both offer a mix of well-known designer boutiques and outlets, plus a handful of small local shops. Bulevard Rosa is famous for good clothes and quality shoes.
✉ Passeig de Gràcia 55–57, 08007 Barcelona ☎ 932 15 83 31 ⏱ Mon–Sat 10am–11pm Ⓜ Passeig de Gràcia

CAMPER
www.camper.es
The informal style of the Camper shops reflects the concept of the label itself. This family business sells comfortable, stylishly quirky shoes, made from durable, high-quality leather.
✉ Carrer de València 249, 08007 Barcelona ☎ 932 15 63 90 ⏱ Mon–Sat 10–9 Ⓜ Diagonal

CASAS
All the most prominent labels are here under one roof: Dr. Martens and Caterpillar, and seriously trendy Début, Pura López, Mare, Rodolfo Zengarini and Robert Clergerie. Look for the house collection by Camilla Casas.
✉ Avinguda del Portal de l'Àngel 40, 08002 Barcelona ☎ 933 02 11 32 ⏱ Mon–Sat 10–9 Ⓜ Catalunya

D BARCELONA
Unusual, trendy design pieces are displayed here. There are items for the home, imaginatively designed fashion accessories and playful gifts. Look for Storm watches, Mathmos lava lamps, household utensils by Koziol and Pylones, and painted cows by Cow Parade.
✉ Carrer del Rec 61, 08003 Barcelona ☎ 933 15 07 70 ⏱ Mon–Sat 11–9 Ⓜ Barceloneta

Opposite *Mercat de la Boquería*

DIAGONAL MAR
www.diagonalmarcentre.es
Diagonal Mar is a shopping mall in part of a major regeneration project. A host of shops sell books, fashion, shoes, household items, groceries and more.
✉ Avinguda Diagonal Mar 3, 08019 Barcelona ☎ 902 53 03 00 🕙 Mon–Sat 10–10 🚇 Selva de Mar

EL BULEVARD DELS ANTIQUARIS
www.bulevarddelsantiquaris.com
The Bulevard has the most comprehensive selection of antiques in Barcelona—furniture, jewellery, gift items, china and more—with a guarantee of authenticity.
✉ Passeig de Gràcia 55–57, 08007 Barcelona ☎ 932 15 44 99 🕙 Mon–Sat 10.30–2, 5–8.30 🚇 Passeig de Gràcia

EL CORTE INGLÉS
www.elcorteingles.es
This is Spain's most prominent and popular department store, and quite simply a classic. Its superior wares include clothes, food, shoes, electrical appliances, sports gear and more. Perfect if you don't have time for specialist shops.
✉ Plaça de Catalunya 14, 08002 Barcelona ☎ 933 06 38 00 🕙 Mon–Sat 10–10 🚇 Catalunya

ELS ENCANTS
www.encantsbcn.com
One of the most characteristic of Barcelona's markets. There's an inexhaustible supply of reminders of the past: old toys, fading photographs of people, old-fashioned wedding gowns and hats, and antiquated kitchen accessories.
✉ Plaça de les Glòries, 08013 Barcelona ☎ 932 46 30 30 🕙 Mon, Wed, Fri–Sat 9–2 🚇 Glòries

EL TRIANGLE
www.eltriangle.es
In this busy central shopping mall, you'll find branches of all the main-street chains here, including FNAC, Habitat and Sephora.

✉ Plaça de Catalunya, 08002 Barcelona ☎ 933 18 01 08 🕙 Mon–Sat 10–10 🚇 Catalunya

ESCRIBÀ
www.escriba.es
Arguably the most divine chocolates and pastries in the city. Owner Antoni Escriba is a multiple Champion Patisser of Barcelona who specializes in *rambla*, a combination of biscuit (cookie), truffle and chocolate.
✉ Avinguda de Gran Vía 546, 08011 Barcelona ☎ 933 01 60 27 🕙 Daily 8.30am–9pm 🚇 Urgell

FNAC
www.fnac.es
There are three branches of this store: at El Triangle, Diagonal Mar and L'Illa. Choose from music, books, hi-fi systems, video and photographic supplies, and IT-related products.
✉ Plaça de Catalunya 4, 08002 Barcelona ☎ 933 44 18 00 🕙 Mon–Sat 10–10 🚇 Catalunya

GOTHAM
www.gotham-bcn.com
Gotham stocks a fabulous selection of accessories, furniture and design pieces dating from the 1950s, 1960s and 1970s, alongside some reproductions of 20th-century interior design classics.
✉ Carrer de Cervantes 7, 08002 Barcelona ☎ 934 12 46 47 🕙 Mon–Sat 10.30–2, 5–8.30 🚇 Liceu

L'ILLA
www.lilla.com
This is the city's most upmarket mall. The main focus here is on fashion and accessories. Famous labels include Corte Fiel, FNAC, Decathlon, Benetton, Massimo Dutti, Caprabo, Mandarina Duck, Bang & Olufsen and Zara and for a taste of fresh seafood: Lluís Genaro's Fishhh!
✉ Avinguda Diagonal 545–557, 08029 Barcelona ☎ 934 44 00 00 🕙 Mon–Sat 10–9.30 🚇 María Cristina

JEAN-PIERRE BUA
www.jeanpierrebua.com
This chic boutique on the swish Diagonal Avenue was the first to

import big Parisian names to the city. The owner is a personal friend of Jean-Paul Gaultier's, and his range features, as do those of Comme des Garçons, the Belgian designer Dries Van Noten, John Galliano and Dolce and Gabbana.
✉ Avinguda Diagonal 469, 08036 Barcelona ☎ 934 39 71 00 🕙 Mon–Sat 10–2, 4.30–8.30 🚇 Hospital Clinic

LOEWE
www.loewe.es
Loewe has always been the ultimate Spanish luxury fashion label, with its classic top-quality leather goods, clothes and accessories.
✉ Passeig de Gràcia 35, 08007 Barcelona ☎ 932 16 04 00 🕙 Mon–Sat 10–8.30 🚇 Passeig de Gràcia

LA MANUAL ALPARGATERA
www.lamanualalpargatera.com
La Manual Alpargatera specializes in handmade espadrilles and sandals. At the open workshop at the Barri Gòtic store you can view the skilled craftspeople at work. In addition, there's a good collection of walking sticks and hats.
✉ Carrer d'Avinyó 7, 08002 Barcelona ☎ 933 01 01 72 🕙 Mon–Sat 9.30–1.30, 4.30–8 🚇 Jaume I

MERCAT DE LA BOQUERÍA
www.boqueria.info
Of Barcelona's markets, La Boquería is easily the best, and most popular with tourists and locals alike. Located right in the heart of the city, just off Las Ramblas, the market offers a superb range of fresh produce. Once you've done your shopping, you can stop at one of the bars and soak up the bustling atmosphere.
✉ La Rambla 91, 08002 Barcelona ☎ 933 18 25 84 🕙 Mon–Sat 8am–8.30pm 🚇 Liceu

MUXART
www.muxart.com
Hermenegildo Muxart started his own accessories business in 1989, and his collections have enjoyed international recognition ever since. He caters mainly for women and sells fine leather shoes and handbags

(purses). Men have their own collection, Mister X, and children are not forgotten.

✉ Carrer Roselló 230, 08008 Barcelona ☎ 934 88 10 64 🚇 Diagonal

PEPA PAPER
www.pepapaper.com
This fashionable stationery shop stands out for its letterhead designs and wide range of fun items, including funky pencils and paper, and original presents. There is also a personalized card service.

✉ Carrer de París 167, 08036 Barcelona ☎ 934 94 84 20 🕐 Mon–Fri 10–8.30, Sat 10–2, 5–8.30 🚇 Hospital Clínic

VILA VINITECA
www.vilavinatéca.com
Vila Viniteca carries about 4,500 different wines and spirits, many of which are exclusive to the shop. All Spain's wine regions are represented, alongside a solid selection sourced from the world's most significant wine-producing countries.

✉ Carrer Agullers 7 and 9, 08003 Barcelona ☎ 932 68 32 27 🕐 Mon–Sat 8.30–2.30, 4.30–8.30; Aug 8.30–2.30 🚇 Jaume I

VINÇON
www.vincon.com
Modern European design in an enormous old palatial setting. Stock includes small items such as Filofaxes and smart kitchenware as well as the city's best selection of contemporary furniture and lighting and the most impressive and elaborate art-nouveau fireplaces.

✉ Passeig de Gràcia 96, 08008 Barcelona ☎ 932 15 60 50 🕐 Mon–Sat 10–8.30 🚇 Diagonal

ENTERTAINMENT AND NIGHTLIFE

L'ANTIC TEATRE
www.lanticteatre.com
This theatre in a charmingly run-down 18th-century mansion near the Palau de la Música (▷ 224) puts on a mixed bag of performances, from dance to documentary screenings, music to mime. The quality is consistently high, and there is a lovely terrace bar where you can chill

out after the show. Performances are mainly at weekends only. Check the door (or their website) for details. Credit cards are not accepted.

✉ Carrer Verdaguer i Callís 12, 08003 Barcelona ☎ 933 15 23 54 🖐 From €5 🚇 Urquinaona

L'AUDITORI
www.auditori.cat
L'Auditori, designed by the Spanish architect Rafael Moneo, is the venue for jazz, folk classical and contemporary music concerts.

✉ Carrer de Lepant 150, 08013 Barcelona ☎ 932 47 93 00 🖐 From €12 🚇 Glòries

BCN ROUGE
BCN Rouge's rooms are on the small side, with dark velvet walls bathed in candlelight. It's the perfect place for a romantic date.

✉ Carrer Poeta Cabanyes 21, 08004 Barcelona ☎ 934 42 49 85 🕐 Thu 11pm–3am, Fri–Sat 11pm–4.30am 🖐 Free 🚇 Paral.lel

BENIDORM
With its perceptive 1960s decor, Benidorm gives a new lease of life to the term kitsch. The interesting interior design theme extends to the smaller details, with retro gadgets placed throughout the bar. It is a light-hearted place for a drink to start off the evening.

✉ Carrer Joaquín Costa 39, 08001 Barcelona ☎ 933 17 80 52 🕐 Mon–Thu 7pm–2am, Fri–Sat 7pm–3am 🖐 Free 🚇 San Antoni

BIKINI
www.bikinibcn.com
Bikini is a classic in Barcelona when it comes to nightlife and the music scene. Its three halls stage many different styles of music such as Latin jazz, pop and rock, as well as DJ sessions. Snacks are available.

✉ Carrer de Deu i Mata 105, 08029 Barcelona ☎ 933 22 08 00 🖐 From €12 🚇 Les Corts

CAFÉ DE L'ÒPERA
This fin de siècle café is popular among intellectuals and opera

enthusiasts alike. The *chocolate con churros* is a must. The terrace out on Las Ramblas is a prime people-watching and purse-snatching point.

✉ La Rambla 74, 08002 Barcelona ☎ 933 17 75 85 🕐 Daily 8.30am–2.30am 🖐 Free 🚇 Liceu

CATWALK
www.clubcatwalk.net
This club has two halls with elaborate furnishings and is a place for trendsetters in cutting-edge designer wear. Upstairs the DJs play hip hop music, while downstairs it's house and techno. Theme nights are held.

✉ Carrer de Ramón Trias Fargas s/n, Marina Village, 08005 Barcelona ☎ 932 21 61 61 🕐 Thu–Sun midnight–6am 🖐 €15 (includes one drink) 🚇 Ciutadella-Vila Olímpica

CAFÉ DIETRICH
House music fills the dance floor. One of the two large bars looks out on to a garden. There's also a stage, popular with drag queens.

✉ Carrer del Consell de Cent 255, 08011 Barcelona ☎ 934 51 77 07 🕐 Daily 10.30pm–3am 🖐 Free 🚇 Urgell

ESPAI JOAN BROSSA
www.espaibrossa.com
Shows here include flamenco, contemporary ballet, magic, poetry and a handful of daring productions. The team also performs street entertainment on Sunday.

✉ Carrer Allada Vermell 13, 08003 Barcelona ☎ 933 10 13 64 🖐 From €9 🚇 Arc de Triomf

HARLEM JAZZ CLUB
www.harlemjazzclub.es
Live music is a way of life for the regulars who come for the tango, flamenco, Celtic music, bossa nova and, of course, the jazz. The crowd is mixed and spans all ages.

✉ Carrer Comtessa de Sobradiel 8, 08002 Barcelona ☎ 933 10 07 55 🕐 Tue–Thu 8pm–4am, Fri–Sat 8pm–5am 🖐 Free 🚇 Drassanes

JAMBOREE
www.masimas.com
One of the busiest jazz clubs in town,

and popular with visitors. There is live jazz and blues; the later the evening, the funkier the music.

✉ Plaça Reial 17, 08002 Barcelona ☎ 933 01 75 64 ⏱ Daily 8.30pm–5am ✋ From €8 🚇 Liceu

LUZ DE GAS

www.luzdegas.com

This old music hall is a prime concert venue. The 30-something crowd consists of regulars as well as visitors. Enjoy some great live music. Arrive early to avoid a long wait.

✉ Carrer de Muntaner 246, 08021 Barcelona ☎ 932 09 77 11 ✋ From €12 🚇 Diagonal

MARSELLA

This Toulouse Lautrec-style bar dates back to the beginning of the 19th century, and even serves absinthe (liqueur made from wormwood).

✉ Carrer de Sant Pau 65, 08001 Barcelona ☎ 934 42 72 63 ⏱ Mon–Thu 10pm–2.30am, Fri–Sat 10pm–3.30am ✋ Free 🚇 Liceu

METRO

www.metrodiscobcn.com

One of the largest gay discos in the city, this place has two dance floors, one playing Spanish music, the other international house.

✉ Carrer de Sepúlveda 185, 08001 Barcelona ☎ 933 23 52 27 ⏱ Sun–Thu midnight–5am, Fri–Sat midnight–6am ✋ From €6 🚇 Universitat

MOOG

www.masimas.com

Moog stages some of the city's best DJ sets. There are two spaces, and although the music varies the crowd is the same — electronic-music fans who dance until the early hours.

✉ Carrer de l'Arc del Teatre 3, 08002 Barcelona ☎ 933 01 72 82 ⏱ Daily 11.30pm–5am ✋ From €8 🚇 Drassanes

PALAU DE LA MÚSICA CATALÁNA

www.palaumusica.org

Attending a concert in this flamboyant art nouveau hall is an unforgettable experience. The interior is like a large garden. The building

is around 100 years old and was conceived and realized by architect Domènech i Muntaner.

✉ Carrer Sant Francesc de Paula 2, 08003 Barcelona ☎ 902 44 28 82 ✋ From €12 🚇 Urquinaona

RAZZMATAZZ

www.salarazzmatazz.com

This former steel factory has three different halls hosting music events of all kinds. The largest is a venue for live music concerts, lounge, techno, pop and Brazilian nights. The other two are set up for DJ use.

✉ Carrer del Almogàvers 122, 08018 Barcelona ☎ 933 20 82 00 ⏱ Thu–Sat 1am–6am. Times vary for live concerts ✋ From €16 🚇 Marina

RENOIR FLORIDABLANCA

www.cinesrenoir.com

This arty venue screens seven original-language films at once, all subtitled in Spanish. Very central — close to the old town and Raval area.

✉ Carrer de Floridablanca 135, 08011 Barcelona ☎ 934 26 33 37 ✋ From €8 🚇 Sant Antoni

SALA APOLO

www.sala-apolo.com

This 1940s music hall has played host to some of the hippest acts in the world. Just about everyone who is anyone on the international music scene has played here.

✉ Carrer Nou de la Rambla 113, 08004 Barcelona ☎ 934 41 40 01 ✋ From €12 🚇 Paral-lel

SWEET CAFÉ

http://sweetcafebcn.blogspot.com

A gently lit, minimalist club playing house music to a less minimalist, mainly gay crowd. Mellow early on in the evening, it gets packed out with a fashionable crowd from midnight onwards.

✉ Carrer de Casanova 75, 08011 Barcelona ⏱ Tue–Sat 10pm–3am, Sun 8pm–2.30am ✋ Free 🚇 Urgell

LOS TARANTOS

www.masimas.com/tarantos

Although Barcelona is not particularly known for its flamenco, this *tablao* (flamenco bar) is a taste of Seville in the heart of the Barri Gòtic. It is transformed into a nightclub at midnight, featuring hip hop, R'n'B and funky sounds.

✉ Plaça Reial 17, 08002 Barcelona ☎ 933 18 30 67 ⏱ Shows daily 8.30, 9.30, 10.30 ✋ From €8 🚇 Liceu

TEATRE BORRÁS

Drama by British playwrights is a feature here, with Catalán versions of works by Noël Coward, Shakespeare and Oscar Wilde.

✉ Plaça Urquinaona 9, 08010 Barcelona ☎ 934 12 15 82 ✋ From €10 🚇 Urquinaona

TEATRE DEL LICEU

www.liceubarcelona.com

One of the most prestigious opera houses in Europe, the Liceu has

Below *El Corte Inglés department store*

undergone a comprehensive restoration following a fire in 1992. Opera is first class; classical music concerts and ballet productions are also performed.

✉ La Rambla 51–59, 08002 Barcelona ☎ 934 85 99 00 ✋ €12–€180 Ⓜ Liceu

TEATRE LLIURE
www.teatrelliure.com

In Catalonia's most prestigious theatre two halls are the settings for diverse plays, music events, dance performances and other shows. There is also a good restaurant and café.

✉ Passeig de Santa Madrona 3, 08034 Barcelona ☎ 932 89 27 70 ✋ From €12 Ⓜ Espanya

TEATRE NACIONAL DE CATALUNYA
www.tnc.es

This is Catalonia's official public theatre. A mixture of Spanish and international productions are staged here.

✉ Plaça de les Arts 1, 08013 Barcelona ☎ 933 06 57 00 ✋ From €16 Ⓜ Glòries

TEATRO TÍVOLI
www.teatral.net/tivoli

Commercial theatre is performed here, and the famous Catalán theatre company, La Cubana, is a regular.

✉ Carrer de Casp 8, 08010 Barcelona ☎ 934 12 20 63 ✋ From €14 Ⓜ Urquinaona

LA TERRRAZZA
www.laterrrazza.com

When the warm weather arrives, the party moves outside. At La Terrrazza, you can dance under the stars in a stunning outdoor venue. There are top international DJs and a glossy crowd.

✉ Avinguda Marqués de Comillas s/n, Poble Espanyol, 08004 Barcelona ☎ 932 72 49 80 Ⓒ May–Sep Fri–Sat midnight–6am ✋ €16 Ⓜ Espanya

TINTA ROJA
www.tintaroja.net

It is worth making your way to humble, but increasingly fashionable, Poble Sec to experience this unusual

nightspot, which mixes a new-world Buenos Aires bohemian vibe with cabaret, tango acts and even a spot of trapeze, to go with your drinks.

✉ Carrer Creu dels Molers 17, 08004 Barcelona ☎ 934 43 32 43 Ⓒ Tue–Sat 9.30pm–2.30am Ⓜ Poble Sec

VERDI
www.cines-verdi.com

Non-commercial, original-language films are subtitled in Spanish here. The sister cinema, Verdi Park, is at Carrer Torrijos 49.

✉ Carrer Verdi 32, 08012 Barcelona ☎ 932 38 78 00 ✋ From €8 Ⓜ Fontana

YELMO CINEPLEX ICARIA
www.yelmocineplex.com

This multiplex has 15 screens, all showing subtitled original-language films.

✉ Carrer de Salvador Espriu 61, 08005 ☎ 932 21 75 85 ✋ €8 Ⓜ Ciutadella-Villa Olímpica

SPORTS AND ACTIVITIES
BERNAT PICORNELL
www.picornell.cat

This swimming pool is one of the city's popular leisure complexes. It also has a public gymnasium with a complete range of sports facilities.

✉ Avinguda de l'Estadi 30–40, 08038 Barcelona ☎ 934 23 40 41 Ⓒ Mon–Fri 7am–midnight, Sat 7am–9pm, Sun 7.30–8 (Oct–May until 4) ✋ Adult €9, child €7 Ⓜ Espanya

BICICLOT
www.biciclot.com
www.bikinginbarcelona.com

This bicycle club has a high profile in promoting cycling around Barcelona and organizing rides within the city. It also runs workshops

throughout the region. You can rent bicycles here and find everything you'll need for your ride.

✉ Passeig Maritim de al Barceloneta 33, 08003 ☎ 932 21 97 78 Ⓒ Summer daily 10–3, 4–8; winter Fri–Sun 10–3, 4–6 ✋ €18 one day, €6 one hour Ⓜ Ciutadella-Vila Olímpica

CAMP NOU (FC BARCELONA)
www.fcbarcelona.com

A great atmosphere is guaranteed here whether you attend a national or Champions League game.

✉ Avinguda de Aristides Maillol s/n, 08028 Barcelona ☎ 934 96 36 00 Ⓒ Guided tours available (phone for details) ✋ From €25 Ⓜ María Cristina

PALAU SANT JORDI
www.agendabcn.com

This steel-and-glass stadium was built for the 1992 Olympic games. The hall is now used for all kinds of events, including sports fixtures.

✉ Passeig Olímpic 5–7, 08038 Barcelona ☎ 934 26 20 89 Ⓒ Sat–Sun 10–6 if no competiton ✋ Free when no events on Ⓜ Espanya

POLIESPORTIU MUNICIPAL EUROPOLIS
www.europolis.es

A fitness complex located under the Europa soccer arena, with a gym, squash courts, swimming pool, restaurant, bar and shop. Medically trained staff are on hand, and those who prefer not to break into a sweat can simply reserve a beauty treatment. (Other branches are listed on their website.)

✉ Carrer de Sardenya 553, 08024 Barcelona ☎ 932 10 07 66 Ⓒ Mon–Fri 7am–11pm, Sat 8–8, Sun 9–3 ✋ €12.50 Ⓜ Alfons 📅

HEALTH AND BEAUTY

INSTITUTO FRANCIS

www.institutofrancis.com

This salon offers basic beauty treatments: body and face peeling, waxing, massage and more. Stays open at midday when most others close. Appointments recommended.

✉ Ronda de Sant Pere 18, 08010 Barcelona ☎ 933 17 78 08 🕐 Mon–Fri 9.30–8, Sat 9–2 👋 Face peeling €35. Depilation from €24 🚇 Urquinaona

KORÉ

www.kore.es

Treatments include reflexology, chiropody, chiropractic therapy, kinesiology and aromatherapy.

✉ Gran Vía 433, Principal 1, 08015 Barcelona ☎ 934 25 44 40 🕐 Mon–Fri 10–2, 4–6 👋 Reflexology from €50. Massage from €35 🚇 Rocafort

MANITAS

Specializes in manicure treatments. Also has conventional beauty treatments, such as body- and face-peeling. Appointments are advisable.

✉ Carrer de Calabria 272, 08029 Barcelona ☎ 934 10 56 04 🕐 Mon–Fri 10–8 👋 Manicure from €12. Face peeling from €35 🚇 Entença

FOR CHILDREN

IMAX

www.imaxportvell.com

One of the few IMAX cinemas with three projection systems—IMAX, OMNIMAX and 3D—shown on the 27m-high (90ft) screen of this complex in the Maremagnum mall.

✉ Moll d'Espanya s/n, 08039 Barcelona ☎ 932 25 11 11 🕐 Varies 👋 €13 🚇 Drassanes

JOVE TEATRE REGINA

www.jtregina.com

The stories performed here are popular with children and are delivered in many languages. Also has puppetry (hand and string).

✉ Carrer Sèneca 22, 08006 Barcelona ☎ 932 18 15 12 🕐 Weekends. Closed Aug and Sep 👋 From €10 🚇 Diagonal

Opposite *The stadium of Barcelona's Camp Nou football club*

FESTIVALS AND EVENTS

JANUARY
CAVALCADA DELS REIS
Procession of the three Magi.

FEBRUARY
CARNESTOLTES
Carnival with processions and parades, dancing, concerts, fancy dress and the ritual Enterrament de la Sardina (Interment of the Sardine).

MARCH–APRIL
SETMANA SANTA
Easter processions in Barcelona are few and far between.

APRIL
FERIA DE ABRIL
Andalucían festival with flamenco, dance and song.

SANT JORDI
Barcelona's Lovers Day, 23 April Sant Jordi, patron saint of Catalonia. Men give roses, women give books to commemorate the 23 April, 1616 deaths of Miguel de Cervantes and William Shakespeare.

APRIL–MAY
FESTIVAL DE MÚSICA ANTIGA
International festival of early music.

JUNE
FESTIVAL DEL GREC
Major performing arts festival.
🕐 Throughout June

SANT JOAN
Festival of fire celebrating St. John and Midsummer's Eve, with huge bonfires and fireworks on the days surrounding the feast and all-night partying.

JUNE–JULY
CLASSICS ALS PARCS
Classical concerts in various venues, mainly open air.

SEPTEMBER
DIADA NACIONAL DE CATALUNYA
Catalán National Day 11 September commemorating Barcelona's defeat ending the War of the Spanish Succession in 1714.

FESTA MAJOR DEL LA BARCELONETA
Three-day festival with dancing on the beach, feasting and fireworks.

FESTES DE LA MERCÈ
Week-long fiesta with parades, giants, *correfoc* (fire-running, when a parade of *dracs* or dragons runs through the streets spitting fire), dancing and firework displays.

OCTOBER–DECEMBER
FESTIVAL INTERNACIONAL DE JAZZ DE BARCELONA
The oldest jazz festival in Spain.

PARC D'ATTRACIONS TIBIDABO
www.tibidabo.es

This theme park is one of the world's oldest. The high-speed Tibidabo funicular takes visitors to the top of the hill—a great way to start the fun. Attractions here fit in with the fin-de-siècle atmosphere, and there are excellent views over the city.

✉ Plaça del Tibidabo, 08035 Barcelona ☎ 932 11 79 42 🕐 Changes regularly 👋 Adult €26, child (under 1.20m/4ft) €10, (under 90cm/3ft) free 🚠 Funicular Tibidabo

ZOO BARCELONA
www.zoobarcelona.com

The zoological park lies at the heart of historic Parc de la Ciutadella. Care has been taken to design the animals' space in harmony with their natural environments. The dolphins are one of the most popular attractions.

✉ Parc de la Ciutadella, 08003 Barcelona ☎ 932 25 67 80 🕐 Jun–Sep 10–7; 16 Mar–May, 1–25 Oct 10–6; 26 Oct–15 Mar 10–5 👋 Adult €17, child (3–12) €10 🚇 Ciutadella-Vila Olímpica

PRICES AND SYMBOLS

The restaurants are listed alphabetically (excluding Le, La and Les). The prices given are the average for a two-course lunch (L) and a three-course dinner (D) for one person, without drinks. The wine price is for the least expensive bottle.

For a key to the symbols, ▷ 2.

AGUA

www.aguadeltragaluz.com
Agua is so close to the beach that when you are at your table you can even get sand in your shoes. Owing to the location, Sunday lunchtime is busy, with people stopping for a beer and a bite to eat.
✉ Passeig Marítim de la Barceloneta 30, 08005 Barcelona ☎ 932 25 12 72 ⏱ Mon–Thu 1.30–4, 8.30–midnight, Fri 1.30–4, 8.30–1, Sat 1.30–5, 8.30–1, Sun 1.30–5 🖐 L €30, D €45, Wine €16 🚇 Ciutadella-Vila Olímpica

AGUT

Agut builds its menu on Catalán food, served in a welcoming atmosphere. The Agut family, owners and managers of the restaurant for the last three generations, offer a menu reflecting seasonal availability as well as some popular perennials.
✉ Carrer d'En Gignàs 16, 08002 Barcelona

☎ 933 15 17 09 ⏱ Tue–Sat 1.30–4, 8.30–11, Sun 1–4. Closed Aug 🖐 L €20, D €40, Wine €12 🚇 Jaume I

EL ASADOR DE ARANDA

www.asadoraranda.com
This amazing building is a prime example of modernist Catalán architecture. Inside, the huge dining room's decor is medieval Castilian in style. The *asador* (grill house) is best known for its delicious baby lamb, served simply roasted in a wood-burning oven.
✉ Avinguda del Tibidabo 31, 08022 Barcelona ☎ 934 17 01 15 ⏱ Mon–Sat 1–5, 9–12, Sun 1–5 🖐 L €40, D €55, Wine €16 🚇 Avinguda del Tibidado

BAR JAI CA

This is a rowdy, friendly neighbourhood bar tucked down a tiny back street in Barceloneta. The bar groans with all kinds of delicious morsels, from stuffed mussels with spicy tomato sauce, to fried artichokes. Popular with locals, it's often hard to get a table, particularly out on the tiny pavement terrace, so arrive early to ensure a seat.
✉ Carrer Ginebra 13, 08003 Barcelona ☎ 933 19 50 02 ⏱ Daily 7pm–late 🖐 Tapas from €4, Wine €10 🚇 Barceloneta

BAR RA

Bar Ra is a trendy, colourful restaurant with an enormously popular terrace just behind the famous Boquería market. A young, boho-chic crowd of visitors and locals come for the varied breakfasts—muesli, muffins, bagels and more, as well as the exotic fusion cuisine served at lunch and dinner. The menu spans the world, with Argentine steaks, Indian curries and fresh Mediterranean dishes. Service is young, and there's usually live music or DJ sessions in the evenings. In winter, tables are inside in a curious interior passage, but the upbeat vibe remains.
✉ Plaça de la Gardunya ☎ 933 01 41 63 ⏱ Mon–Sat 10–12.30 (breakfast), 1.30–4, 9–midnight (also Sun in summer) 🖐 L €25, D €40, Wine €12 🚇 Liceu

LA BOMBETA

A very popular old fishermen's bar in La Barceloneta, this is perfect for those on a budget who love fresh seafood. You can either settle at a table or stand at the bar and dig into some of the generous tapas. Choose from steamed mussels, *esqueixada*

Above *One of the tempting dishes served at Casa Calvet*

(cold cod with vegetables) or fried squid and *patatas bravas* (spicy potatoes) to name but a few. No credit cards.

✉ Carrer de La Maquinista 3, 08003 Barcelona ☎ 933 19 94 45 🕐 Thu–Tue 10am–midnight. Closed Sep and last 2 weeks in Feb 🖐 L €15, D €25, Wine €10 🚇 Barceloneta

BOTAFUMEIRO

A classic restaurant in Barcelona that has built its reputation on *arroz caldoso* (casseroled rice) and the house lamb. Diners are attracted first and foremost by the delicious shellfish. The service is faultless and you'll be served a great selection of cold meats and shellfish, with some very good wines. Open late, so it's ideal for a post-performance or soccer match bite to eat. The restaurant has a no-smoking section.

✉ Gran de Gràcia 81, 08012 Barcelona ☎ 932 17 96 42 🕐 Daily 1.30pm–1am 🖐 L €75, D €110, Wine €18 🚇 Fontana

CAFÈ DE L'ACADÈMIA

The lovely Plaça Sant Just, one of the best preserved Gothic squares in the city, is the setting for this charming restaurant. On the menu, you'll find expertly prepared Catalán cuisine with a contemporary twist: Try *bacallà* (cod) with tomato confit and garlic mousse, and don't miss out on the wonderful desserts. In summer, a candle-lit terrace opens on the square itself. Curiously, the restaurant is closed at weekends.

✉ Carrer Lledó 1, 08002 Barcelona ☎ 933 19 82 53 🕐 Mon–Fri 1.30–4, 9–11.30. Closed 2 weeks in Aug 🖐 L €25, D €35, Wine €12 🚇 Jaume I

CA L'ISIDRE

www.calisidre.com
Over the last 25 years this charming family-owned restaurant in El Raval has perfected a dynamic, varied menu. Its specials fall into two main groups: market cuisine and confectionery. The menu can change on a daily basis according to the seasonal availability of ingredients, so your duck liver might be served with plums, chestnuts, puréed grapes

or Chinese mandarins. The owner's daughter is the driving force behind the desserts, such as chocolate soufflé with coconut ice-cream. There is a no-smoking section.

✉ Carrer de les Flors 120, 08002 Barcelona ☎ 934 41 11 39 🕐 Mon–Sat 1.30–3.30, 8.30–10.30. Closed holidays and 1–18 Aug 🖐 L €75, D €90, Wine €22 🚇 Paral.lel

CASA CALVET

www.casacalvet.es
Casa Calvet, art nouveau in style, is in the first house built by Antoni Gaudí in central Barcelona in the 19th century. The building has now been converted into an apartment block with the restaurant on the ground level. Miquel Alija offers a modern take on Mediterranean cuisine; his menu includes vegetables with Iberian ham, prawns (shrimp) cooked in rosemary oil and duck liver with Seville oranges.

✉ Carrer de Casp 48, 08010 Barcelona ☎ 934 12 40 12 🕐 Mon–Sat 1–3.30, 8.30–11. Closed holidays and Aug 🖐 L €45, D €75, Wine €15 🚇 Urquinaona

CASA LEOPOLDO

www.casaleopoldo.com
An outstanding culinary hotspot in the old town, this is close to the Teatre del Liceu, Barcelona's famous opera house. Casa Leopoldo is a cross between an Andalucían tavern, a French bistro and an Italian trattoria. A well-known classic in Barcelona, it opened in 1929, the year of the World's Fair, and serves traditional Catalán dishes such as fried fresh fish and oxtail stew.

✉ Carrer de Sant Rafael 24, 08001 Barcelona ☎ 934 41 30 14 🕐 Tue–Sat 1.30–4, 9–11.30, Sun 1–4.30. Closed Easter and Aug 🖐 L €35, D €45, Wine €14 🚇 Liceu

CAN MAJÓ

www.canmajo.es
Right in the heart of La Barceloneta, the city's former fishing quarter, this restaurant serves excellent Mediterranean cuisine. Fresh fish and shellfish are used to enrich the tastes of such popular dishes as lobster casserole, sautéed Norwegian lobster

and baked hake. As it's right on the waterfront, this is an idyllic place in summer.

✉ Carrer de l'Almirall Aixada 23, 08003 Barcelona ☎ 932 21 54 55 🕐 Tue–Sat 1–4.30, 8–11.30, Sun 1–4.30 🖐 L €40, D €50, Wine €14 🚇 Barceloneta

CINC SENTITS

www.cincsentits.com
Chef Jordi Artal and family have developed into a Barcelona mainstay at the very highest level serving consistently exquisite contemporary interpretations of local products based on local recipes. Look for innovative yet never over-the-top bizarro cooking and wine surprises you will want to write down (though you won't have to, as a printout of dishes and wine pairings comes with the bill).

✉ Carrer d'Aribau 58, 08011 Barcelona ☎ 933 23 94 90 🕐 Tue–Sat 1.30–3.30, 8.30–11.30 Closed Aug 🖐 L €45, D €95, Wine €16 🚇 Passeig De Gràcia

COMERÇ 24

www.projectes24.com
Carles Abellan is another supremely talented chef trained by Ferran Adrià at the mythical El Bulli restaurant in Roses (▷ 282). Bold, adventurous and innovative cuisine awaits, delivered in a series of *platillos* — little plates — each bearing an extraordinary delicacy in which smell, form and texture are as important as taste. These gourmet tapas take their influence from around the world, and might include anything from Japanese-style tuna, to intricate mini-towers of smoked and pickled fish, or an elaborately deconstructed Catalán onion soup. Even the macadamia nuts have been given gold leaf jackets. Choose from one of two menus, the Festival and Gran Festival, and be warned that you won't go home with much change from €100 per head. The memories, however, will linger a lifetime.

✉ Carrer Comerç 24, 08003 Barcelona ☎ 933 19 21 02 🕐 Tue–Sat 1.30–3.30, 8.30–midnight. Closed 2 weeks Aug, Christmas week, Easter week 🖐 L €60, D €75, Wine €22 🚇 Barceloneta or Jaume I

D9

Reserve a table early at D9 (pronounced 'dee-now', Catalán for 19), where creative Mediterranean cuisine, modest prices and an intimate setting ensure there's also a crowd. The restaurant is in a side street, just off Carrer Ample, and has simple wooden furnishings. Specials are marked up on a board and include a soup, meat, fish and vegetarian dish. These might include parmesan puffs with tomato chutney, grilled hake with sautéed baby squid and vegetables, or steak with a gorgonzola and walnut sauce. Service is delightful.

✉ Carrer Carrabassa 19, 08002 Barcelona ☎ 933 02 01 02 🕓 Mon 1–3.30, Tue–Fri 1–3.30, 8.30–11.30, Sat 1–4 ,8.30–11.30. Closed lunch in Aug 🖐 L €12, D €30, Wine €10 🚇 Drassanes

HOFMANN

www.hofmann-bcn.com

One of the most prestigious restaurants in the city, with an acclaimed cookery school, this has recently moved to new premises. Mey Hofmann is regarded as one of the best chefs in Spain; she gained her first Michelin star in 2004. The menu tempts guests with exquisite dishes such as sardine pie with tomato and onion, and mushroom-stuffed turbot dressed with a pine vinaigrette. This establishment excels at desserts: Try the house ice-cream or the cheese board with a complementary wine. The restaurant has a no-smoking section.

✉ Carrer la Granada del Penedès 14–16, 08006 Barcelona ☎ 932 18 71 65 🕓 Mon–Fri 1.30–3.15, 9–11.30. Closed Aug 🖐 L €60, D €75, Wine €14 🚇 Jaume I

L'ILLA DE GRÀCIA

www.illadegracia.cat

This is the place to come for healthy food at very reasonable prices. The garlic soup, stewed apples, and vegetable and potato pies are just a few of the menu's highlights. The setting is simple, shunning design fads and glitz. The food is nutritious and very generously portioned, making L'Illa de Gràcia one to remember for a quiet, inexpensive evening out. No credit cards.

✉ Carrer de Sant Domènec 19, 08012 Barcelona ☎ 932 38 02 29 🕓 Tue–Sun 1.30–4, 9–12 🖐 L €18, D €36, Wine €10 🚇 Fontana

INÒPIA

www.barinopia.com

Albert Adrià, brother to Ferran (the legendary chef behind the restaurant El Bullí, ▷ 282), opened this bright, modern tapas bar a couple of years ago. His concept is simple: Choose the most traditional and best-loved Spanish tapas and prepare them with top quality ingredients. The results are outstanding. A simple salad of tuna and tomato melts divinely in the mouth when prepared with succulent, flavourful Montserrat tomatoes. A marinated artichoke wrapped around an anchovy is the perfect marriage of textures and flavours when prepared with ingredients of this calibre. It's a neighbourhood favourite, well off the beaten track, and unmissable.

✉ Carrer Tamarit 104, 08015 Barcelona ☎ 934 24 52 31 🕓 Tue–Fri 7–11, Sat 1–3.30, 7–11 🖐 L €25, D €45, Wine €12 🚇 Poble Sec

EL JARDÍ

www.eljardibarcelona.es

The medieval hospital, now the national library, overlooks a fine Gothic courtyard in the heart of the Raval district. An outdoor café occupies a pretty corner of the square, and offers alfresco dining all year round. The menu is short and light—sandwiches, crêpes, tapas and salads—but there is always a lunchtime dish of the day. It's a wonderful place to retreat, and linger over coffee and pastries during the day, or a cocktail in the evenings. Occasional live music performances, perhaps jazz or Brazilian music.

✉ Carrer Hospital (Antic Hospital de Santa Creu), 08001 Barcelona 🕓 Tue–Sun 10–10 🖐 L €20, D €25, Wine €10 🚇 Liceu

KAIKU

It's easy to miss this unassuming restaurant, despite its beachfront location, and yet it serves some of the freshest and most imaginative cuisine in the city. Try the outstanding *arròs del xef*, a sublime paella-style concoction with lightly smoked rice, prawns, mussels, chunky wild mushrooms and artichokes. The starters might include an astonishingly light sea anenome in *tempura*, or ultra-fresh clams from the Galician *rías*.

✉ Plaça del Mar 1, 08003 Barcelona ☎ 932 21 90 82 🕓 Tue–Sun 1–4 🖐 L €35, Wine €12 🚇 Barceloneta

LLUÇANÈS

www.restaurantllucanes.com

This long-established restaurant has recently moved from its former home in a small Catalán town to the spectacular new market complex in Barceloneta. Owner-chef Àngel Pascual has already garnered a Michelin star for his superb reinventions of classic Catalán and Mediterranean cuisine: for example, a robust and flavoursome hare and lobster terrine reflects the traditional Catalán delight in fusing the flavours of *mar i terra* (sea and mountain).

✉ Plaça Font s/n, 08003 Barcelona ☎ 932 24 25 25 🕓 Tue–Sat 1.30–3.30, 8.30–11.30, Sun 1.30–3.30 🖐 L €45, D €85, Wine €18 🚇 Barceloneta

MAMA CAFÉ

www.mamacaferestaurant.com

Mama Café was designed in harmony with the philosophy of feng shui, which could explain its fresh and relaxing atmosphere. The restaurant is very spacious, with the kitchen set in the middle and painted bright shades of red, blue, yellow and orange. The salads are made to be enjoyed, and the vegetable soups, turkey with mustard and grilled cuttlefish with basmati rice are all good. Mama Café operates as a café in the afternoon.

✉ Carrer Doctor Dou 10, 08001 Barcelona ☎ 933 01 29 40 🕓 Mon–Sat 1–1 🖐 L €16, D €35, Wine €14 🚇 Catalunya

MESOPOTAMIA

This Middle Eastern restaurant in Gràcia was established by Pius

Hermés, a university professor of Semitic languages. It's a warm and comfortable spot where the taste of the food is intense. A variety of meats, seasoned with herbs and spices, feature on the menu. The leg of lamb and the aubergines (eggplants) marinated in yoghurt sauce are simply amazing. During weekends guests can request a narguilé, a waterpipe for smoking tobacco, fruits and honey. There are two sittings every evening, so reserve a table.

✉ Carrer de Verdi 65, 08012 Barcelona
☎ 932 37 15 63 🕐 Tue–Sat 8.30pm–1am. Closed 23 Dec–8 Jan 🍴 D €35, Wine €14
Ⓜ Fontana

MOO

www.hotelomm.es
Located inside the achingly fashionable Hotel Omm, the Moo restaurant is the brainchild of the Roca brothers of the famed El Cellar de Roca near Girona. Their second restaurant is a cutting-edge affair, serving up fashionista food. Leave room for the exquisite perfume-infused desserts.

✉ Carrer de Roselló 265, 08008 Barcelona
☎ 934 45 40 00 🕐 Daily 1.30–3.30, 8.30–10.30 🍴 L €45, D €120, Tasting menu (with wine pairing) €120, Wine €24
Ⓜ Diagonal

NERVIÓN

Spain's Basque country is famous for one of the best food traditions in the country. Ingredients at this Eixample restaurant are renowned for being fresh, especially the fish and the meat, and its creative chefs have an excellent reputation. Nervión specializes in meat dishes; chef Juan Sáiz sources the best cuts from the local market. It also has an excellent selection of wines.

✉ Carrer de Còrsega 232, 08036 Barcelona
☎ 932 18 06 27 🕐 Mon–Sat 1–4, 9–11.30. Closed Easter, Christmas and Aug 🍴 L €45, D €50, Wine €22 Ⓜ Diagonal

NONELL

www.nonell.es
In a wonderful location in the heart of the Gothic Quarter, this elegant restaurant combines tradition and modernity in both the decor and the menu. Pretty original tiles in striking orange and black are on the floor, while the tables and settings are bright and contemporary. In summer you can dine out on an expansive terrace, shaded by orange umbrellas, just around the corner from the theatrical spikes of the Gothic cathedral. There's a wide range of creative Mediterranean and fusion dishes to choose from, with a menu which changes constantly according

to what's in season. Traditional roast suckling pig served with a cherry confit, and risotto with shellfish and calamari (squid) are among the offerings at Nonell.

✉ Carrer Sagristans 3 (Plaça Isidre Nonell), 08002 Barcelona ☎ 933 01 13 78 🕐 Daily 1–4, 8–midnight 🍴 L €35, D €45, Wine €14
Ⓜ Jaume I or Urquinaona

NOU CAN TIPA

In La Barceloneta's main street, this noisy bar is a local classic. It serves steamed mussels, fresh fish and shellfish, in addition to the delicious tapas. The house special is cod. As the name indicates, portions are generous (estar tip) means 'to be full' in Catalán). Reserving is advisable.

✉ Passeig de Joan de Borbó 6, 08003 Barcelona ☎ 933 10 13 62 🕐 Tue–Sun 1pm–11.30pm 🍴 L €14, D €25, Wine €12
Ⓜ Barceloneta

ORGANIC

www.antoniaorganickitchen.com
This old warehouse, in the heart of El Raval, has been transformed into a relaxed vegetarian shop and restaurant. Customers can drop by to pick up good organic produce or stay

Above La Bombeta (▷ 242–243) serves up delicious seafood in Barceloneta, a district popular for its nightlife

a little longer to enjoy an affordable lunch in the restaurant. There is a no-smoking section.

✉ Carrer de la Junta de Comerç 11, 08001 ☎ 933 01 09 02 🕔 Daily 12.30pm–midnight; shop open from 9.30am 🍽 L €10, D €15, Wine €9 🚇 Liceu

OUT OF CHINA
www.outofchinabarcelona.com
Generally speaking, Chinese restaurants in Barcelona are not much chop. One bright spark is this restaurant that aims to serve 'home-made' Chinese food. Amid an enticing setting of bright, black and Shanghai kitsch, you can order a pretty good dim sum and other east Asian dishes.

✉ Carrer Muntaner 100, 08036 Barcelona ☎ 934 51 55 55 🕔 Mon–Sun 1–4, 8.30–12 🍽 L €16, D €30, Wine €10 🚇 Diagonal

ELS PESCADORS
www.elspescadors.com
Els Pescadors' roots as a typical fishermen's tavern are still obvious — contemporary fashion and design are of little significance here. Its reputation is built on excellent fish and rice dishes, and on seasonal stews with mushrooms. The wine is exclusively Spanish and the desserts are made with seasonal fruits. In summer, try to get a table on the terrace.

✉ Plaça de Prim 1, 08005 Barcelona ☎ 932 25 20 18 🕔 Daily 1–3.45, 8–12. Closed Easter 🍽 L €45, D €55, Wine €14 🚇 Poble Nou

PITARRA
www.restaurantpitarra.cat
Pitarra, a traditional Catalán restaurant in the Barri Gòtic, looks back on over a century of history and has no shortage of character. It was named after Serafí Pitarra, a famous Catalán actor and former resident of the building, and the rooms are decorated with his personal effects, such as books and clocks. The cuisine is excellent, particularly the *canelone*, the Valencian paella and seasonal highlights, notably the mushroom-based dishes. The service is attentive but not intrusive.

✉ Carrer d'Avinyó 56, 08002 Barcelona ☎ 933 01 16 47 🕔 Mon–Sat 1–4, 8.30–11. Closed Aug 🍽 L €35, D €45, Wine €14 🚇 Drassanes

ELS QUATRE GATS
www.4gats.com
It's not just the food that draws people to visit this legendary restaurant, although it is renowned for its traditional Catalán dishes. It was here that well-known avant-garde artists of the early 19th century such as Pablo Picasso and his contemporaries, used to hold their intellectual gatherings.

✉ Carrer de Montsió 3 bis, 08002 Barcelona ☎ 933 02 41 40 🕔 Daily 1–1 🍽 L €24, D €50, Wine €16 🚇 Catalunya

QUO VADIS
www.restaurantquovadis.com
This restaurant dates back to the 1950s. Its location near the Teatre del Liceu has always made it a popular option for a post-opera dinner. The choice of dishes is wide and features examples of Spanish and French cuisine with a modern slant, as well as typical Catalán fare. Excellent wine and cava list.

✉ Carrer del Carme 7, 08001 Barcelona ☎ 933 02 40 72 🕔 Mon–Sat 1–4, 8.30–11.30. Closed Aug 🍽 L €40, D €65, Wine €22 🚇 Liceu

RITA BLUE
www.ritablue.com
This is a restaurant, pub and club rolled into one, split over two spacious, diverse floors. Rita Blue is a trendy and bustling place where rubbing shoulders with the stars isn't out of the question. The restaurant

Below *Silenus Restaurant is a haunt for artists and serves suitably creative dishes*

serves Mediterranean, Greek, Moroccan and Lebanese cuisine, including fried fish and couscous.
✉ Plaça Sant Agustí 3, 08001 Barcelona ☎ 934 12 40 86 🕐 Mon–Wed 7pm–2am, Thu–Sat 7pm–3am ✋ D €25, Wine €12 🚇 Liceu

SALAMANCA
www.gruposilvestre.com
Silvestre and his staff take care of every detail to ensure the perfect dining experience. This restaurant features outstanding seafood, such as prawns (shrimp) from Huelva, oysters and clams. Eat alfresco on the terrace to enjoy the view.
✉ Carrer de l'Almirall Cervera 34, 08003 Barcelona ☎ 932 21 50 33 🕐 Daily 8am–1am ✋ L €25, D €45, Wine €12 🚇 Barceloneta

SET PORTES
www.7puertas.com
Established in 1836, this restaurant (its name means seven doors) has always served generous portions of high-quality, traditional cuisine using fresh ingredients from the local market. Rice dishes are the main attraction, so don't miss the famous mixed fish and meat paella, or the *arròs negre* (rice cooked in squid ink). A no-reservations policy, and its popularity mean you should either arrive early or be prepared to wait. Sunday evenings are very busy.
✉ Passeig de Isabel II 14, 08003 Barcelona ☎ 933 19 30 33 🕐 Daily 1pm–1am ✋ L €40, D €55, Wine €14 🚇 Barceloneta

SILENUS
www.restaurantsilenus.com
In keeping with the fact that it is next to one of the city's most outstanding contemporary art museums, the Museu d'Art Contemporàni de Barcelona, Silenus is the meeting point for young artists. It is modern through and through, so much so that hanging a clock was thought to be too conventional and instead the time is projected on to an interior wall. The food is a creative mix of Spanish and Catalán. Monthly art shows are also held here. There is a no-smoking section.

✉ Carrer dels Àngels 8, 08001 Barcelona ☎ 933 02 26 80 🕐 Mon–Thu 1.30–4, 8.30–11.30; Fri–Sat 1.30–4, 8.30–12 ✋ L €18, D €45, Wine €14 🚇 Liceu

TALAIA
www.talaia-mar.es
Talaia offers a fantastic view of the port and beach. The menu features Mediterranean dishes, all well presented. Choose from such dishes as liver terrine with apple nougat, pine nuts and a Modena sauce, minted beans and roasted squid pasta. If you aren't very hungry, try a *pica pica*, a perfect compromise between a snack and lunch. The restaurant has a no-smoking area.
✉ Carrer de la Marina 16, 08005 Barcelona ☎ 932 21 90 90 🕐 Tue–Sun 1–4, 8–12 ✋ L €40, D €65, Wine €16 🚇 Ciutadella-Vila Olímpica

TAPIOLES 53
www.tapioles53.com
A 'gastronomic club' (you'll be asked to sign up—membership free), Tapioles 53 is run by Australian Sarah Stothart, whose dishes may include a mascarpone cheese and porcini mushroom tart or a selection of antipasti, followed by spinach gnocchi or a beef bourguignon. Desserts include a pavlova or marinated figs. The food is impeccable and the wine list intelligently contrived. Choose from set menus, with either three or five courses. Reservations only.
✉ Carrer de Tapioles 53, 08004 Barcelona ☎ 933 29 22 38 🕐 Tue–Sat 9pm–11.30 ✋ 3-course menu €40, 5-course menu €60, Wine included 🚇 Paral-lel

EL TRAGALUZ
www.grupotragaluz.com
A huge, glass ceiling looks down on this restaurant. The space is split over three floors: On the upper floor, an à la carte menu is served, while guests on the ground level can order tapas. The food is essentially the same but portions vary in size—a great idea if you want to sample before you commit to a sit-down meal. Try the salad with ginger, and cod with roasted pepper and garlic.

✉ Passeig de la Concepció 5, 08007 Barcelona ☎ 934 87 01 96 🕐 Tue–Sun 1.30–4, 8.30–midnight ✋ L €35, D €55, Wine €16 🚇 Diagonal

LA VENTA
www.restaurantelaventa.com
La Venta is set in garden terraces at the foot of Tibidabo mountain, with views over the city. This is a great place to eat if you have spent your day on the mountain. It serves traditional Catalán cuisine, such as sea urchin sprinkled with cheese. Reserving a table is advisable.
✉ Plaça Doctor Andreu s/n, 08035 Barcelona ☎ 932 12 64 55 🕐 Mon–Sat 1–3.30, 9–11 ✋ L €35, D €55, Wine €16 🚌 Tramviá Blau

VÍA VENETO
www.viaveneto.com
This classic restaurant combines luxury, good taste and creativity. Josep Monje's professionalism is reflected in his dishes, which include Montserrat tomatoes with meatballs, warm scallops with Romesco mousse, monkfish tail with sesame seeds, and seasonal dishes such as mushrooms and white truffles. Leave some room for the superb desserts.
✉ Carrer de Ganduxer 10, 08021 Barcelona ☎ 932 00 72 44 🕐 Mon–Fri 1–4, 8.45–11.30, Sat 8.45–11.30. Closed Aug ✋ L €50, D €75, Wine €22 🚇 María Cristina

WU SHU
www.wushu-restaurant.com
Give your palate a jolt at Wu Shu, where Australian chef Brad Ainsworth prepares the best hot and spicy Thai food in the city. The *Laksa*, a piquant noodle broth packed with plump succulent giant prawns, is recommended, but you can also choose from wok dishes, Thai curries, summer rolls and more. Vegetarian dishes can be prepared on request. The setting is small, sleek and welcoming. There's an excellent daily set price lunch for €12.
✉ Avenida Marqués d'Argentera 1, 08003 Barcelona ☎ 933 10 73 13 🕐 Tue–Sat 1–midnight, Sun 1–5 ✋ L €20, D €35, Wine €12 🚇 Barceloneta

PRICES AND SYMBOLS

The prices are for a double room for one night including breakfast, unless otherwise stated. All the hotels listed accept credit cards unless otherwise stated. Note that rates can vary widely throughout the year..

For a key to the symbols, ▷ 2.

1898

www.nnhotels.es

A splendid late 19th-century building, which once housed the Phillipines Tobacco Company, has been converted into a luxurious four-star hotel. The location, right on the Rambles, can't be beaten and the interior combines classic elegance with contemporary style. The suites and bedrooms are handsomely decorated in a strikingly modern interpretation of colonial style, and all rooms are equipped with stylish plasma TVs and all the latest amenities, including WiFi. There is a wonderful rooftop terrace with plunge pool (great in the summer), an indoor pool, gym and a stylish restaurant, serving an excellent menu, and a bar. Meeting rooms serve business travellers.

✉ La Rambla 109, 08002 Barcelona ☎ 935 52 95 52 💵 €180–€320 🛏 169 🛗 🏊 Indoor and outdoor 🚇 Catalunya

987 BARCELONA

www.987hotels.com

One of the newest of the glossy designer hotels which have become so popular in Barcelona, 987 Barcelona is well located in the chic Eixample district. The elegant and restrained exterior of the building belies the 21st-century opulence within its walls. Rooms and public spaces boast striking interior decoration, with a colourful palate which mixes minimalist black and white with bold splashes of purple, violet, sky blue and apple green. While most rooms are resolutely contemporary, some of them have retained their original architectural details such as delicate painted ceilings and stuccowork. The lounge bar recalls the hip hotel bars of New York, and is a favourite with the fashion pack. The restaurant, with its huge black-and-white murals, serves wonderful modern Mediterranean cuisine.

✉ Carrer Mallorca 288, 08037 Barcelona ☎ 934 76 33 96 💵 €135–€345 🛏 88 🚇 Diagonal or Verdaguer

ARTS BARCELONA

www.hotelartsbarcelona.com

The Arts hotel is fabulously situated, right next to the beach, in one of the towers of the Puerto Olímpico. All the rooms command spectacular views of the coast and across to Tibidabo, in the north of the city. The lavishly decorated rooms range from Japanese suites and apartments to luxury executive suites and a 350sq m (3,770sq ft) royal suite. The spa is the best and most luxurious in the city.

✉ Carrer de la Marina 19–21, 08005 Barcelona ☎ 932 21 10 00 💵 €315–€640 🛏 482 (241 non-smoking) 🛗 🏊 Outdoor 🍴 🚇 Ciutadella-Vila Olímpica

CHIC & BASIC

www.chicandbasic.com

A 19th-century townhouse in the fashionable neighbourhood of La Ribera has been transformed into one of the city's sleekest budget hotels. It's a favourite with the young and hip, who come for the minimalist all-white decor and funky coloured lighting and the trendy White Bar. Chic & Basic has the perfect location—around the corner from some of the city's best shopping and sightseeing. They also run a great budget hostal in the El Raval neighbourhood.

✉ Carrer Princesa 50, 08003 Barcelona ☎ 932 95 46 52 💵 €95–€145 🛏 31 🛗 🚇 Jaume I

CLARIS

www.derbyhotels.es

Home to an important collection of Egyptian art, and only minutes away from some of the most outstanding art-nouveau buildings in town, the sumptuous Claris offers impeccable service in the luxurious setting of a 19th-century palace. It's just 50m (55 yards) away from the exclusive Passeig de Gràcia, within walking distance of the thriving central area, with its shops, restaurants, bars and clubs. Amenities include 24-hour room service, a sauna and Japanese garden.

✉ Carrer de Pau Claris 150, 08009 Barcelona ☎ 934 87 62 62 🖐 €210–€480 ⓘ 124 🅢 🏊 Outdoor 📶 🚇 Passeig de Gràcia

COLÓN

www.hotelcolon.es

Facing the Gothic cathedral in the heart of the city, this hotel is minutes away from Portaferrisa and Portal de l'Àngel shopping areas, as well as historical squares such as Sant Jaume and El Rei. Rooms are equipped with music, TV, safe and minibar, and some have balconies overlooking the cathedral. The front rooms have the best views, but are also noisy because of the bells. Although it's quieter at the back, sit is less interesting. There's an on-site restaurant and piano bar. Parking is available.

✉ Avinguda Catedral 7, 08002 Barcelona ☎ 933 01 14 04 🖐 €140–€265 excluding breakfast (€10) ⓘ 145 🅢 🚇 Jaume I

CONTINENTAL PALACETE

www.hotelpalacete.com

There is excellent service at this 19th-century palace, in the heart of town, north of Plaça de Catalunya. You can dine under the glittering chandelier, surrounded by sumptuous white and gold decor. Traditional elegance is combined with fully equipped, modern rooms, some overlooking Rambla de Catalunya. Room and laundry service, bar, internet access and fax facility, car rental, money exchange and free 24-hour light buffet are all provided.

✉ Rambla de Catalunya 30, 08007 Barcelona ☎ 934 45 76 57 🖐 €140–€225 ⓘ 19 🅢 🚇 Passeig de Gràcia

DUQUESA DE CARDONA

www.hduquesadecardona.com

This charming hotel occupies an elegant 17th-century palace, rebuilt in the 19th century, and recently tastefully transformed into a quiet oasis in the heart of the Gothic Quarter. The hotel prides itself on the quality of its service, and has a special concierge service, called 'Ask Me', to assist guests during their stay. The rooftop terrace has a small plunge pool and an outdoor café-bar, and offers spectacular views over the yachts bobbing in the port below.

✉ Passeig Colom 12, 08002 Barcelona ☎ 932 68 90 90 🖐 €165–€295 ⓘ 44 🏊 Outdoor 🅢 🚇 Drassanes

GALLERY HOTEL

www.galleryhotel.com

This hotel belongs to the Design Hotel Association—not a chain as the name might suggest, but a worldwide association for hotels that care about contemporary design. All the modern and spacious rooms are fully equipped with TV, soundproofed windows and minibar. The excellent restaurant serves first-rate Mediterranean food and haute cuisine. For the business traveller, conference halls and business rooms are also available.

✉ Carrer de Rosselló 249, 08008 Barcelona ☎ 934 15 99 11 🖐 €140–€325 ⓘ 115 (22 non-smoking) 🅢 📶 🚇 Diagonal

GRANADOS 83

www.derbyhotels.es

Located on one of the prettiest and quietest streets of the chic Eixample district, this hotel belongs to the prestigious Derby Group. The contemporary rooms (some of which boast private balconies) are fitted out with luxurious African zebrawood and leather furnishings, but the highlight is the original Buddhist and Hindu works of art which decorate the public areas and the bedrooms. There's a fashionable terrace bar

next to the rooftop pool and a chic restaurant for fine dining.

✉ Carrer Enric Granados 83, 08008 Barcelona ☎ 934 92 96 70 🖐 €165–€415 ⓘ 77 🏊 Outdoor 🅢 🚇 Passeig de Gràcia

GRAND HOTEL CENTRAL

www.grandhotelcentral.com

This large, elegant hotel sits on the edge of the fashionable shopping and dining neighbourhood of the Born. The spacious rooms are plush and luxurious, decorated with a muted palette of cream and beige tones, and well equipped with state-of-the-art amenities. Bathrooms are well-stocked with a selection of Molten Brown goodies. But the real draw of the Grand Hotel is its stunning rooftop swimming pool, which measures a glorious 10m (33ft) by 5m (16ft)—a far cry from the tiny splash pools found in most other Barcelona city-centre hotels. From the water, or from the adjoining sun terrace, you can enjoy some incomparable views across the ancient rooftops of the old part of the city.

✉ Via Laietana 30, La Ribera, 08003 ☎ 932 95 79 00 🖐 €215–€640 ⓘ 137 🅢 🏊 Outdoor 📶 🚇 Jaime I

GRAN VIA

www.nnhotels.es

This 19th-century palace next to Passeig de Gràcia still has a grandiose air, with furniture and works of art from the period, old-world gilt and chandeliers; the wide, sweeping *modernista* staircase with its elegant banister is the finishing touch. It has three meeting rooms, a business centre and an outdoor terrace garden. The spacious, if rather faded, guest rooms all have a safe, minibar, satellite TV and internet access. There is a pleasant roof terrace, and parking is available.

✉ Gran Vía de les Cortes Catalánes 642, 08007 Barcelona ☎ 933 18 19 00 🖐 €120–€175 excluding breakfast (€8) ⓘ 53 🅢 🚇 Urquianona

Opposite *The rooftop plunge pool and terrace area at Hotel 1898*

HOSTAL OLIVA

www.hostaloliva.com

A beautiful, well-kept hostel—one of the few to be found in the Passeig de Gràcia, near Plaça de Catalunya. Built in 1931, it has an old-fashioned lift (elevator), marbled floors and mirrors, which all create a wonderful atmosphere. There are only 16 guest rooms, all of which have a TV. Some have bathrooms and a few overlook the art nouveau buildings nearby. This is a great place if you're on your own as the area is very safe; the only downside is the noise level, due in part to the wooden floorboards. ✉ Passeig de Gràcia 32, 4°, 08007 Barcelona ☎ 934 88 01 62 🖐 €75–€90 excluding breakfast ❶ 16 🚇 Catalunya

HOSTAL PALACIOS

www.hostalpalacios.com

This is a very pretty hostal in a fine old *modernista* mansion. Many of the original details, including the sumptuous carved doors and the beautiful tiled floors, have been preserved. The rooms have been simply but stylishly furnished with modern fabrics and the bathrooms are all bright and contemporary. There is an internet terminal and a lounge area with piano. Walls are thin, so bring some ear plugs. ✉ Rambla de Catalunya 27, 08007 Barcelona ☎ 933 01 30 79 🖐 €88–€130 ❶ 11 🚇 Passeig de Gràcia

HOTEL 54 BARCELONETA

Barceloneta once had a curious lack of accommodation, considering its prime seaside location, but this situation is slowly changing. The newest kid on the block is the chic, boutique-style Hotel 54, which is housed in the former Fishermen's Guild but has been dramatically transformed. Bold colours define the interior design, which even features special multicoloured lighting in the bedrooms. There's a popular restaurant, run by one of the city's best-loved restaurateurs, and a trendy bar-cum-nightclub. ✉ Passeig Joan de Borbó 54, 08003 ☎ 932 25 00 54 🖐 €120–€175 ❶ 28 🚇 Barceloneta

HOTEL AB SKIPPER

www.hotelabskipper.com

A striking and ultra-modern five-star hotel, the enormous AB Skipper recently opened right on the seafront in Barceloneta. It has a long list of amenities, including two outdoor pools (one surrounded by gardens, the other with sea views), two excellent restaurants, four café-bars, a spa and wellness centre, and even a jogging circuit. The best rooms have terraces and splendid sea views, but all are immaculately furnished and well equipped. ✉ Avinguda Litoral 10, Barceloneta 08005 ☎ 932 21 65 65 🖐 €235–€375 excluding breakfast (€23) ❶ 241 🚇 Outdoor 🏊 🚇 Barceloneta

HOTEL CIUTAT VELLA

www.hotelciutatvella.com

A new three-star hotel (opened in 2007) in the heart of the old city, this is a good choice for style-conscious travellers with a limited budget. Unusually for a three-star hotel, it offers a wide range of accommodation, from standard double and individual rooms to triples and dorm-style quadruple rooms which feature two sets of bunk beds. The striking black, white and scarlet decor extends to the lobby, where there's an internet café. There are numerous cafés close by for breakfast, so give the expensive hotel buffet a miss. ✉ Carrer Tallers 66, El Raval 08001 ☎ 934 81 37 99 🖐 €90–€180 excluding breakfast ❶ 40 rooms 🚇 Universitat

HOTEL VILLA EMILIA BARCELONA

www.hotelvillaemilia.com

A modern, glassy, elegant boutique hotel, this is set a little way from the centre, but is still only a few blocks from all the main sights of the Passeig de Gràcia. The comfortable rooms are soothingly decorated with pale wood furnishings and cool shades of cream and dove grey. At the entrance is the Zinc Bar, with striking black and white decor, a huge faux-baroque chandelier, and low sofas. The roof terrace has rattan

sofas with plump white cushions—perfect for a romantic cocktail. There's no restaurant, but there are numerous dining options nearby. The service is outstanding: personal, friendly and very welcoming. ✉ Carrer Calàbria 115–117, 08015 Barcelona ☎ 932 52 52 85 🖐 €125–€340 ❶ 53 🚇 Rocafort

MAJESTIC

www.hotelmajestic.es

This charming hotel has a long history and lives up to its name in every way. Run by the Soldevila Casals family for the past three generations, it's the epitome of quality service and traditional hospitality. There's a restaurant, buffet and two bars. Every room has been carefully designed and decorated. Each contains a minibar, safe, cable TV and internet access. You can also enjoy a massage or relax in the spa and steam room. ✉ Passeig de Gràcia 68, 08007 Barcelona ☎ 934 88 17 17 🖐 €195–€370 excluding breakfast (€21) ❶ 233 (175 non-smoking) 🚇 Outdoor 🏊 🚇 Passeig de Gràcia

MARKET HOTEL

www.markethotel.com.es

This chic little hotel is set above a restaurant, part of a very popular chain which has recently begun applying its winning formula of stylish decor and modest prices to the hotel business. The rooms are decorated in black and white, with splashes of red to add warmth. It's located in wonderful, traditional neighbourhood, close to the *modernista* Mercat de Sant Antoni. The hotel is a great bargain, and therefore you'll need to reserve well in advance. ✉ Passatge Sant Antoni Abad 10 (Carrer Comte Borrell 6), 08015 ☎ 933 25 12 05 🖐 €95–€140 ❶ 30 🚇 Sant Antoni

PALACE HOTEL

www.hotelpalacebarcelona.com

Founded in 1919, this classic grand hotel, formerly the Ritz, on a pleasant tree-lined boulevard in the heart of the city is the ultimate in luxury and elegance. The interior is sumptuous, and some of the suites have tiled Roman baths that you step down into. The service is exceptional and the staff are multilingual. Famous patrons have included surrealist Salvador Dalí. There's a sauna, beauty salon and hairdressers on site. In 2009 the hotel underwent a large restoration, which added rooms with contemporary decor, and refreshed the public areas.

✉ Gran Vía de les Corts Catalánes 668, 08010 Barcelona ☎ 935 10 11 30 ✋ €250–€490 🛏 120 (60 non-smoking) ♿ 🅿 Ⓜ Passeig de Gràcia

PENINSULAR
www.hotelpeninsular.net
The Peninsular is an oasis in the vibrant and central El Raval district of Barcelona. The Peninsular was built at the end of the 19th century, and has the typical features of an art nouveau house, such as the impressive high ceiling found in the dining room. The guest rooms are basic, but spacious and clean; most have a bathroom, telephone and safety deposit box,

and most overlook bustling family apartments. There is a beautiful tiled inner courtyard surrounded by attractive hanging plants.

✉ Carrer de Sant Pau 34, 08001 Barcelona ☎ 933 02 31 38 ✋ €80–€140 🛏 80 ♿ Ⓜ Liceu

SANT AGUSTÍ
www.hotelsa.com
Constructed in the first half of the 19th century in the old Convent of St. Augustine, this hotel claims to be the oldest in the city, and has been run by the Tura-Monistrol family for over a century. It's in El Raval district so is convenient for those wanting to explore the old part of Barcelona, which has now been turned into a trendy, cosmopolitan area, full of art galleries, bars and restaurants. The rooms are comfortable, of a reasonable size and fully equipped; those at the top have great views. Unfortunately, the pretty square in front of the hotel has become a magnet for the city's homeless.

✉ Plaça Sant Agustí 3, 08001 Barcelona

☎ 933 18 16 58 ✋ €120–€180 🛏 75 ♿ Ⓜ Liceu

W BARCELONA
www.w-barcelona.com
Ricardo Bofill's striking sail-shaped skyscraper at the southern end of the Barceloneta beach is the city's new waterfront skyline and, along with the Jean Nouvel Torre Agbar across town, one of the two bookends of Barcelona's avant-garde architecture. This glass-and-steel monolith reflects the sunrise, the sunset, and any other natural phenomenon in this corner of the Mediterranean. The bright, technologically replete rooms all have panoramic views and the restaurants, terraces, cafés, and nightclubs are first rate, with Carles Abellán's restaurant, Bravo, in pride of place.

✉ Plaça Rosa dels Vents 1, Barceloneta 08039 ☎ 932 952 800 ✋ €210–€315 excluding breakfast 🏊 Indoor/outdoor Ⓜ Barceloneta

Below *The terrace bar at Granados 83*

CATALONIA, VALENCIA AND MURCIA

Spain's luminous eastern coast follows the curve of the Mediterranean, but the landscape varies enormously from north to south. The rocky coves of the Costa Brava in northern Catalonia are almost within sight of the verdant Pyrenees—a far cry from the arid, desert-like interior of Murcia in the far south of the region. There, the beaches of the Mar Menor enjoy year-round sunshine, making them a magnet for holidaymakers. In the middle of the Mediterranean coast are the glorious sandy beaches of the Costa Blanca, the lively city and port of Valencia, and a string of cheerful seaside resorts in all shapes and sizes.

Catalonia, in the northeastern corner of Spain, has its own language and a unique history and culture. There are splendid Romanesque churches and monasteries, stunning natural parks, splendid mountains, and expansive wetlands, home to myriad varieties of birdlife. Catalán cuisine enjoys a stellar reputation, with more award-winning restaurants and celebrity chefs than almost anywhere else in Spain, and the region has become a gourmet mecca.

Valencia, south of Catalonia, is known as 'the orchard of Spain'. The Arabs introduced the irrigation techniques still in use today, which ensure that the famous Valenciano oranges, along with all kinds of other fruit and vegetables, grow plump and sweet. The region's capital, also called Valencia, is a vibrant and alluring city. The tiny old quarter, overlooked by the lofty belltower which has become the city's symbol, retains its ancient charm, but this is contrasted with the futuristic appeal of the fabulous City of Arts and Sciences and the new marina.

Besides the popular resorts of the Mar Menor, Murcia is surprisingly little visited. But its capital is an engaging, friendly city with a fantastic tapas tradition and a wealth of pretty squares. The region boasts one of the last unspoilt corners of the Mediterranean in Calblanque natural park and some delightful hill towns.

CATALONIA, VALENCIA AND MURCIA • SIGHTS

ALACANT (ALICANTE)

www.comunitatvalencia.com
www.alicanteturismo.com

With its long, white-sand beaches, wealthy yachting marina and lively centre, Alicante is an unexpectedly stylish stopping point along the Mediterranean coast. Valencia's second city, named Lucentum (City of Light) by the Romans, is a charming blend of ancient and modern. It is a bustling place, fashioned with elegant walkways (including the sea-skirting Explanada de España), lush gardens and tiled *paseos* adorned with the distinctive Alicante red marble.

The Mercado Central (Mon–Sat 8–2), on Avenida Alfonso X el Sabio, is based within an impressive *modernista* building and is bustling market life at its best. Old city walls still stand, and crowning the settlement is an imposing hilltop fortress, the Carthaginian Castillo de Santa Bárbara (Apr–Sep daily 10–8; Oct–Mar 9–7), which is accessible via a lift (elevator) cut through the mountainside.

Looking up from Postiguet beach towards the castle on the Bencantil rock, you can make out the likeness of a Moorish profile, one of Alicante's best-known symbols.

✚ 475 L8 🛈 Rambla Méndez Núñez 23, 03002 Alicante ☎ 965 20 00 00 🚊 Alacant: Estación Madrid (RENFE) or Estación de Murcia (FGV)

ANDORRA

www.andorra.ad

The promise of inexpensive goods, great skiing and a relaxing spa bath is more than enough to tempt many visitors to Spain across the border into tiny Andorra.

Nestling between Spain and France, this Catalán-speaking principality measures more more than 468sq km (180sq miles) yet has the largest ski area in the Pyrenees. Its four resorts—Ordino-Arcallis, Pal-Arinsal, Pas de la Casa-Grau-Roig and Soldeu-El Tarter—share 281km (175 miles) of slopes (for more informationon visit the website www.skiandorra.ac). Andorra also claims to have the largest thermal spa in Europe, Caldea, which is in Les Escaldes. The mirrored building, resembling a modern cathedral, houses a beautifully constant 32°C (90°F) indoor lagoon.

Many popular duty-free shops line the nearby streets; their electronic and sports goods are the best bargains to be had. But to enjoy some unspoiled aspects of Andorran life, and to get away from the hypermarkets and congested roads (there are no planes or trains), head for the mountains for some walking, trekking, mountain-bicycling or horseback riding.

✚ 467 M2 🛈 Oficina d'Informació i Turisme del Comú d'Andorra la Vella, Plaça de la Rotonda, Andorra la Vella ☎ 376 82 71 17

BESALÚ

www.besalu.cat

At the meeting point of the Fluvià and Capadella rivers, and close to the Parc Natural de la Garrotxa (▷ 264) and the French border, is the small town of Besalú, which makes an interesting stop-off.

Hints of a medieval and Roman past can be seen in the town's steep streets and attractively arcaded main square (Plaça Libertat), and in the churches of Sant Pere and San Vincenç. The Pont Fortificat, the bridge spanning the Fluvià, with a gatehouse portcullis, was built in the 12th century using rocks from the riverbed and is a reminder of the town's former strategic importance during battles involving Visigoths and Moors.

Besalú is also the site of the Miqwé (guided tours from tourism office 10.30, 12, 1.30, 4.30, 6), one of Spain's most important Jewish ritual baths, which can be found on a wander through the town's old Jewish quarter.

If you don't feel like walking, you can pick up the Aerotren instead, a brightly decorated tourist train that takes you on three routes past the town's main sights.

✚ 467 P3 🛈 Plaça Llibertat, 17850 Besalú ☎ 972 59 12 40

Opposite *A fortified Romanesque bridge spans the River Fluvia at Besalú*
Below left *Colour-coordinated flower tubs decorate houses in an Alicante street*
Below *The Castillo de Santa Bárbara, on a rocky hillside, overlooks Alicante*

CADAQUÉS

www.cadaques.org

Hidden away at the end of a deep inlet in the southern part of the Cap de Creus peninsula is this coastal gem of a fishing town. Whitewashed houses with brightly painted shutters line the bedrock streets, which twist down to the main pebble bay.

Along the scenic promenade is a row of outdoor cafés. Cadaqués was an inspirational artists' enclave, popularized by Salvador Dalí and frequented by Pablo Picasso, American photographer Man Ray and film director Luis Buñuel.

Dalí's home at nearby Port lligat continues to attract a crowd (15 Mar–6 Jan; advance reservations required, tel 972 25 10 15 or online at www.salvador-dali.org). Note that if you are driving you should use the designated parking area signed as you enter the town—the narrow streets make this no place for cars.

🞢 467 P3 🛈 Carrer Cotxe 2-A, 17488 Cadaqués ☎ 972 25 83 15 🚌 Figueres, then bus to Cadaqués (six per day, Jul–Sep; three per day, Oct–Jun)

CARTAGENA

www.ayto-cartagena.es

The Roman ruins and maritime history may draw you to this naval town, some 57km (35 miles) southeast of Murcia. It was originally founded by the Carthaginians in 223BC (hence its name) and is now the base of the Spanish

Mediterranean fleet. The walls of its arsenal house the Museo Naval (Tue–Sun 10–1.30), with model ships and maps, and on the impressive seafront walkway is the world's first submarine, launched by naval officer Isaac Peral in 1888.

There is a splendid Roman theatre, with a superb museum designed by Rafael Moneo which opened in spring 2008 and the city's long and exciting history is recounted in the modern Centro de Interpretación located high above the city in the remnants of a castle (Jul–Sep daily 10–2, 4–7; mid-Mar to Jun Tue–Sun 10–2.30, 4.30–7; Oct to mid-Mar daily 10–5.30). For the best views of the city and distinguished port, head to Parque Torres, within the walls of Castillo de la Concepción.

🞢 474 K9 🛈 Plaza Almirante Bastarreche s/n, 30202 Cartagena ☎ 968 50 64 83 🚌 Cartagena

LA CERDANYA

www.cerdanya.net

Straddling the French–Spanish border in the eastern Pyrenees (Pirineos) is La Cerdanya (called Cerdagne in France), a wide, fertile basin skirted by mountain ranges, including the Serra del Cadí to the south. While there are no towns of any great note, this is a gorgeous natural environment to explore. With Puigcerdà as its capital, the basin's cooler climate attracts many coastal city-dwellers in the heat of summer.

In winter, skiers head to the resorts near La Molina and Masella.

Llívia, 6km (4 miles) across the border in France, is a quirk of history, a Spanish town completely surrounded by French territory. The 1659 Treaty of the Pyrenees saw Spain hand over 33 villages to France as the border was redrawn, but it refused to surrender Llívia as it officially had city status.

🞢 467 N3 🛈 Carrer Querol 1, 17520 Puigcerdà ☎ 972 88 05 42 🚌 Puigcerdà

COSTA BLANCA

www.costablanca.org

Costa Blanca, the 'white coast', offers everything from beaches and natural parks to high-rise resorts and lively fishing ports. In the north, headlands give way to pleasant villa territory and the tourism of Benidorm and its crowded beaches.

The coast's southern extreme, meanwhile, is more desert-like, with some dense apartment developments. Best known for its beaches, this 160km (100-mile) coastline is also interspersed with rugged shores and pretty coves.

From the picturesque town of Pilar de la Horadada, with its 15th-century watchtower, the Costa Blanca stretches north to Dénia, where some of the most beautiful beaches can be found.

In between lie the natural parks of the La Mata salt flats at Torrevieja and Penyal d'Ifac (Peñon de Ifach) at Calp (Calpe). A path can be climbed in about an hour to the top of the latter, a mighty rock that forms a distinct feature on the coastline, and which has been transformed into a nature park to protect its unique vegetation and 300-plus species of animals.

From busy Alicante (▷ 255), tours run to Isla de Tarbarca, a designated marine reserve.

🞢 475 L9 🛈 Servei Municipal de Turisme, Plaza de Canalejas 1, 03501 Benidorm ☎ 966 81 54 63

Left *The town of Cartagena has a long maritime history and is now Spain's major naval base*

COSTA BRAVA

The Costa Brava runs south of the Spanish–French border from Portbou to Blanes. Here, a series of mountain ranges plunges into the sea, interspersed with small, pine-edged coves and long, sandy beaches, around which the coast's famous resorts have developed.

NORTHERN SIGHTS

Starting in the north, the Pyrenees give way to the largely uninhabited Cap de Creus peninsula. El Port de La Selva is a fishing town with a lively wharf and marina, and is the gateway to the Sant Pere de Rodes monastery (▷ 265). Also on the peninsula is Cadaqués (▷ 256), the haunt of artists since the 18th century.

Farther south, the sweeping Badia de Roses stretches for 15km (9 miles). The Parc Natural dels Aiguamolls (▷ 263) forms a large part of this section, with Roses (▷ 265) to the north and Empúries (▷ 258) to the south. Beyond Empúries is the fishing port of L'Escala, renowned for its anchovies. Opposite Torroella de Montgrí (▷ 266) are the Illes Medes, a small archipelago and fascinating marine reserve that you can visit by glass-bottom boat operated from nearby L'Estartit. Pals is a pretty town, slightly inland from Platja de Pals, between L'Estartit and Begur.

SOUTHERN RESORTS

Rolling slopes characterize the coastline south of here, where sheer cliffs and tiny coves contrast with the packed resorts of Palamós and Platja d'Aro. Farther south still is Sant Feliu de Guíxols, with its waterfront and ruined 10th-century monastery. Begur, another medieval seaside town, lies in the shadow of a 17th-century castle with five keeps.

The southernmost sections of the Costa Brava contain its busiest resorts. Tossa de Mar, set around a semicircular bay, was established by the Romans and has an attractive old town. Farther south is brash Lloret de Mar, the largest of the southern resorts, and over-developed Blanes marks the end of the Costa Brava.

Blanes has two botanical gardens: Mar i Murtra, on Passeig Karl Faust, with fine sea views; and Pinya de Rosa, between Blanes and Lloret de Mar, with a collection of tropical plants.

INFORMATION

www.infotossa.com
www.blanes.net

➕ 467 P3 ℹ️ Passeig Catalunya 2, 17300 Blanes ☎ 972 33 03 48

ℹ️ Avinguda del Pelegrí 25, 17320 Tossa de Mar ☎ 972 34 01 08

TIP

» To avoid the busy package resorts, head for the quieter northern end of the coast.

Above *The home of Salvador Dalí (now a museum) overlooks the pretty village of Port Lligat*
Below *The beach of the S'Agaro villa development on the southern Costa Brava*

ELX (ELCHE)

www.turismedelx.com

Elx has the most extensive plantation system in Europe, a swaying sea of 200,000 date palms, many reaching a height of 25m (82ft). Originally planted by the Moors, the groves form a bizarre and yet strangely mesmerizing sight. The Hort del Cura (summer daily 9–8.30; winter daily 9–6) is the most popular grove with visitors and is also one of the best places to view the palms.

To further intrigue you, this beguiling 5,000-year-old city also stages the Misteri d'Elx (mystery plays). The plays are live performances of religious theatre that have been given here since the 15th century (▷ 448). To learn more about the plays visit the Museu de La Festa, which has a stimulating virtual display (Jun–Sep Tue–Sat 10–1.30, 5–8.30, Sun and festivals 10–1.30; Oct–May Mon–Fri 10–1.30, 4.30–8, Sun and holidays 10–1).

These two jewels in Elx's crown have earned it UNESCO World Heritage Site status. Iberian history has also left a remarkable seal upon the town. The world-famous, fifth-century BC La Dama d'Elx sculpture, a masterpiece of this period and now on display in Madrid, was found here. But these are not Elx's only claims to fame: Almost half the country's shoes are produced here, so there are plenty of shopping opportunities for those in search of new footwear.

✚ 474 K8 ⓘ Parque Municipal s/n, 03202 Elx ☎ 965 45 27 47 ▣ Elche

Above A Classical robed statue rises from the ruins of Empúries
Above left The gardens of the Hort del Cura (Priest's Orchard) in Elx

EMPÚRIES

www.mac.es

The fascinating ruins of Empúries, one of Catalonia's most important archaeological sites, overlook the Mediterranean against a backdrop of green pines. Among the knee-high walls are the remains of a Graeco-Roman coastal town that was founded between the seventh and third centuries BC. Greek traders first landed on a nearby island, now joined to the mainland and home to the village of Sant Martí d'Empúries. They soon formed an inland colony, then known as Emporian, which was seized by the Romans in the third century BC. The conquerors renamed the town Emporiae, and proceeded to build fine mansions with impressive mosaics, an amphitheatre and a marketplace.

Take the time to walk down to the shoreline, where you can still make out the remains of the Greek breakwater that was built to protect the port.

✚ 467 P3 ✉ Ruinas d'Empúries, 17130 Empúries, L'Escala ☎ 972 77 02 08 ⓒ Jun–Sep and Semana Santa daily 10–8; Oct–May daily 10–6 🖐 Adult €3, child €1.50

FIGUERES

▷ 259.

GIRONA (GERONA)

▷ 260.

LLEIDA (LÉRIDA)

http://turisme.paeria.es

A ruined fortress with a cathedral built within its walls is the undoubted highlight of a visit to the Catalán provincial capital.

Set high above the Río Segre, the town is dominated by the Seu Vella (Old Cathedral), which is surrounded by the remains of La Zuda, a Moorish castle. The Seu Vella has towering Gothic cloisters, and was once used as a military mess.

The Plaça de Sant Joan, a central square in the old town below the Seu Vella, is the site of the 18th-century Seu Nova (New Cathedral) and some manorial buildings, which include the rebuilt 13th-century town hall, the Paeria. If you can't face the walk between the cathedrals, take the lift (elevator) from the square. There are great views from the city walls.

The Museu de Lleida (Jun–Sep Tue–Sat 10–8, Sun 10–2; Oct–May Tue–Sat 10–7, Sun 10–2), which opened in 2007, describes the history of the city from prehistoric times through to today by means of engaging, modern displays.

✚ 466 M4 ⓘ Carrer Ajor 31, 25002 Lleida ☎ 902 25 00 50 ▣ Lleida

FIGUERES

TEATRO-MUSEU SALVADOR DALÍ

There is really only one reason to visit Figueres: To learn more about Salvador Dalí (1904–89), the town's most famous son, and his legacy, the Teatro-Museu Salvador Dalí (Jul–Sep daily 9–8; Mar–Jun, Oct Tue–Sun 9.30–6; Nov–Apr Tue–Sun 10.30–6; last admission 45 min before closing time). The structure of this former theatre is as bizarre and eccentric as the artist himself, and is now crowned with golden eggs and a latticed glass dome. Flanked by a tower of televisions and with a facade adorned with statues brandishing baguettes, the building is now considered the largest Surrealist object in the world.

The interior is just as unconventional. On show is a whole spectrum of Dalí creations, from his earliest pieces to his later works, forming an artistic statement of his Cubist, Impressionist, Futurist and Surrealist ideals. One of the most spectacular images is entitled *Gala Nude Looking at the Sea, Which, at a Distance of Twenty Metres, is Transformed into a Portrait of Abraham Lincoln* (*c*1975). It makes use of double images to recreate the distinctive face of the American president.

Dalí also produced a number of pieces expressly for the museum, including the Mae West Room, which portrays the face of the famous actress using paintings and furniture, including a sofa in the shape of lips. And in the upstairs Palau del Vent (Palace of the Wind), Dalí and his wife Gala are portrayed in a ceiling mural.

FIGUERES TOWN

A trip around Figueres town itself is very worthwhile. La Rambla is an attractive central avenue around which cafés and bars spill out on to the street. Just off it is the Museu del Joguet (Jun–Sep Mon–Sat 10–7, Sun and holidays 11–6; Oct–May Tue–Sat 10–6, Sun and holidays 11–2), Catalonia's Toy Museum, with around 4,000 interesting items. Castell de Sant Ferran, on a hill at the end of Pujada del Castell 1km (0.5 mile) northwest of town, is a massive military fortification built in the 18th century (Jul–Sep daily 9–7; Jan–Jun Tue–Sat 10.30–2).

The Dalí-Joies collection at the Casa-Museu Salvador Dalí is a staggering display of 39 jewels which includes the artist's original designs, undertaken between 1932 and 1970.

INFORMATION

www.figueresciutat.com
467 P3 Plaça del Sol s/n, 17600 Figueres 972 50 31 55 Jul–Sep Mon–Sat 8.30–8.30, Sun 9–3; Oct–Jun Mon–Sat 8.30–3 Figueres

TIP

» The Teatro-Museu Salvador Dalí has an optional signposted tour which you can follow, but to avoid the crowds it is best to choose your own route.

Below *The stage area of the Teatro-Museu Salvador Dalí*

REGIONS CATALONIA, VALENCIA AND MURCIA • SIGHTS

INFORMATION

www.ajuntament.gi

🕂 467 P3 ℹ️ Rambla de la Llibertat 1,
17004 Girona ☎ 972 22 65 75 🚉 Girona

TIPS

» In the heart of the commercial area
is the Rambla de la Llibertat, one of the
city's liveliest spots and the setting for its
market in medieval times.
» To reach the walls of the city, head
for the Passeig Arqueològic and the
Museu Arqueològic (Jun–Sep Tue–Sat
10.30–1.30, 4–7, Sun 10–2; Oct–May
Tue–Sat 10–2, 4–6, Sun 10–2).

GIRONA (GERONA)

This city is full of medieval charm. The shadowy alleyways and stairs of its old
quarter occupy a fortified hill overlooking the riverside, and the brightly restored
houses along the Río Onyar provide great views. Arab-influenced narrow streets
and the best-preserved Jewish quarter in Spain give some clues as to Girona's
mixed history and inhabitants, but it was in the Middle Ages that some of the
most outstanding historical buildings were constructed.

EL CALL AND THE CATHEDRAL

El Call, Girona's Jewish Quarter, is a cool, stone warren of narrow passageways
and meandering streets. In the Middle Ages, this was home to one of the largest
and most influential Jewish communities in Spain. Its history is recounted in the
absorbing Centre Bonastruc Ça Porta on Carrer Força (Jun–Oct Mon–Sat 10–8,
Sun 10–3; Nov–May Mon–Sat 10–6, Sun 10–3; €3.50).

The city's impressive and newly restored cathedral (Apr–Oct 10–8, Nov–Mar
10–7) stands at the top of a sweeping flight of stairs. The baroque facade was
a later addition: the interior is pure Catalán Gothic, at its most austere and
tremendous. The nave boasts the widest single-span Gothic arch in Europe.

OTHER SIGHTS

Near the cathedral are two enjoyable museums: the Museu d'Historia de la
Ciutat (City History Museum, Tue–Sat 10–2, 5–9, Sun 10–2), in an historic
townhouse, and the Museu d'Art (Art Museum, Tue–Sat 10–2, 5–9, Sun 10–2)
with a particularly good collection of medieval and Gothic art. The Banys Àrabs,
or Arab Baths (Apr–Sep Tue–Sat 10–7, Sun 10–2; Oct–Mar Tue–Sun 10–2), in a
12th-century Romanesque building, are among the best kept in the country.

Above The River Onyar runs through
Girona separating old town from new

MONTSERRAT

Montserrat is many things: a mountain, a shrine, a monastery and a defining symbol of Catalán identity and spirituality. The complex is made up of the monastery, a museum and a lunar landscape that was declared a national park in 1987.

THE LEGEND OF LA MORENETA

The lofty position of the ninth-century Benedictine monastery makes it an arresting sight, perched high against a bedrock of fluted buttresses. Here the legend surrounding La Moreneta ('the little dark one'), the venerated smoke-blackened statue of the Virgin, continues to attract thousands of visitors annually. According to legend the statue, supposedly brought to Barcelona by St. Peter in AD50 and hidden in a cave, was found in this area in AD880. When it was discovered by shepherds, they tried to take it to the nearby town of Manresa. However, on reaching the site where the monastery now stands, they could get no farther, and a chapel was built in the Virgin's name. This subsequently developed into the monastery.

MONASTIC SIGHTS

The Plaça de la Creu is the main entry point to the monastery. It was named after a huge cross designed by the sculptor Josep Subirachs (b1927), and bears the question 'Who is God?' engraved in various languages. Plaça de Santa María, a long esplanade designed by Puig i Cadafalch (1876–1956), is the huge focal point of the complex and leads you to the threshold of the monastery.

Today around 80 Benedictine monks live here. The legendary Virgin is now housed inside the basilica. Built in the 16th century and restored in the 19th century, it is approached through a splendid courtyard. Inside, the statue is enthroned in a silver altarpiece in the 'holy room', which can be reached up a staircase above the high altar.

Montserrat is also a great place to walk around, with various chapels, 13 hermitages and some giddy views of the valley below.

The famous boys' choir, L'Escolania, is one of the oldest in Europe. Every day at 1pm (noon on Sun, except Jul) the choristers sing the Salve and the *Virolai*, a hymn to the Virgin.

INFORMATION

www.abadiamontserrat.net

✚ 467 N4 🏠 08199 Montserrat 🕿 938 77 77 77 ⊕ Basilica: Mon–Fri 7.30–7.30, Sat–Sun 7.30–8.30. Shrine: daily 8.30–10.30, 12–6.15 (also Jul–Sep 7.30pm–8.30pm). Museum: Mon–Fri 10–6, Sat–Sun 9.30–6.30 👋 Museum: adult €7, child (8–16) €4 🚌 9am from Plaça dels Països Catalans, Barcelona, returns 6pm summer, 5pm winter 🚡 Aeri de Montserrat, cable-car, every 15 min, except 1.45–2.20. Cremallera (railway) approx. every 20 min 7.48am–9.08pm. Sant Joan funicular: from monastery's cable-car station to top of mountains, near Sant Joan hermitage, every 20 min. Santa Cova funicular: from monastery's cable-car station to Holy Cave every 20 min 📖 💻 🎟

TIPS

» The Tot Montserrat card is a good deal—it includes round-trip train fares from Barcelona, Cremallera (rack-and-pinion railway), both funiculars, museum entrance, audiovisual exhibition and meal. Adult €39.

» The Trans Montserrat offers the same package minus audiovisual exhibition and meal for €23.50.

Below *Montserrat has been sculpted by wind and rain*

MONESTIR DE POBLET
www.poblet.cat

Poblet's 12th-century fortified monastery is a stunning sight, beautifully set in wine-growing country, and easily merits a visit for its architectural glories and excesses. This home to a small community of Cistercian monks has towering gateways, an elaborate facade and an intricate belfry, all grouped together on their site among the Muntanyes de Prades.

Founded by Ramón Berenguer IV in 1150 in thanks to God for the regaining of Catalonia from the Moors, this triple-walled monastery was once the most important in Catalonia, where the kings of the region chose to be buried. It also became a popular stopping place during royal journeys. However, mob violence in the 19th century largely destroyed it. Thankfully, much of the sculpted stonework survived and this grand building has since been carefully restored. The monks returned here in 1940.

Inside the monastery, noteworthy features include the Royal Pantheon, begun in 1359; the Romanesque cloisters, with a pavilion-covered fountain; and the adjacent chapterhouse, which contains the sunken tombs of the abbots.

✚ 466 M4 ✉ Monestir de Poblet 43448 Poblet, Vimbodí ☎ 977 87 00 89 ⊕ 15 Jun–14 Sep Mon–Fri 10–12.45, 3–6, Sun 10–12.30, 3–6; 16 Mar–13 Jun, 15 Sep–12 Oct Mon–Fri 10–12.45, 3–6, Sun 10–12.30, 3–5.30; 13 Oct–15 Mar Mon–Fri 10–12.45, 3–5.30, Sun 10–12.30, 3–5.30 💺 Adult €6, under 18 €4; combined admission to the three museums of the Cistercian Route (Poblet, Santes Creus and Vallbona) €10 🚉 L'Espluga de Francolí RENFE station, then 3km (2-mile) walk 🎧 Compulsory 1-hour guided tour departs every half-hour

MONTBLANC
www.montblancmedieval.org

Set beside the Río Francolí and still housed within sturdy medieval walls, Montblanc gives a tranquil taste of small-town Spanish life.

Its main gateway is the stone Torre-portal de Boue, although it is another gateway—the Torre-portal de Sant Jordi—that commemorates the local legend that St. George slew his dragon here. Every spring, on the feast day of Catalonia's patron saint, the town celebrates the legend by having a large festival.

Montblanc's complex of tight, narrow, cobbled streets and a collection of impressive Roman and Gothic buildings make for interesting exploration. The Gothic church of Santa María, begun in the 14th century and never fully completed, is a special find, with an elaborate facade featuring climbing cherubs and an ornately paved outer courtyard entrance. And don't miss the *montblanquins*, sweet toasted almonds that are a special delicacy of the town and which you can buy from local cake shops.

As Montblanc lies only 8km (5 miles) east of Poblet (see left), you can combine a trip here with a visit to the monastery in the course of a day.

✚ 467 M4 ℹ Antiga Església de Sant Francesc, 43400 Montblanc ☎ 977 86 17 33 🚉 Montblanc

MONTSERRAT
▷ 261.

MORELLA
www.morella.net

The commanding sight of Morella's towering medieval fortress rising out of the hilly Els Ports landscape is dramatic enough to entice you closer. You can enter the inner city through any of its grand gateways, but Portal Sant Miquel is an especially formidable sight. These gateways were once connected by 2.5km (1.5 miles) of walled battlements, parts of which you can still walk, and beyond them is a labyrinth of streets leading up towards the fortress. Most notable of these streets is Carrer Blasco de Alagón, which has timbered walkways. From the fortress you are rewarded with a bird's-eye view of the town and countryside.

✚ 471 L5 ℹ Plaça Sant Miquel s/n, 12300 Morella ☎ 964 17 30 32

Above *Iglesia de Santa María, Montblanc*
Opposite *Carved window detail, Murcia (top); Parc Nacional d'Aigüestortes (bottom)*
Below *Monestir de Poblet*

MURCIA

www.murciaciudad.com

Its tree-lined streets, architectural contrasts and lack of overt tourist development make Murcia a city apart. It was founded in AD825, and its old quarter, city walls and present-day system of irrigation bear testament to this ancestry. Rising high above the city is the cathedral (daily 10–1, 5–7), with a Renaissance tower and 23 different chapels. Having taken four centuries to complete, it embraces a mixture of rival styles. Most impressive is the grand baroque west front.

In the nearby, narrow, bustling Calle de Trapería is a casino and gentleman's club (daily 9–9), with Mudéjar walls, a ballroom and a ladies' powder room with a neo-baroque ceiling.

➕ 474 K9 ℹ️ Plaza del Cardenal Belluga s/n, 30004 Murcia ☎ 968 35 87 49 🚆 Murcia

OLOT

http://areadepromocio.olot.org

Olot is a town of real architectural charm and repays a little leisurely exploration. It calls itself the 'city of volcanoes' and is an ideal starting point for a tour of the surrounding Parc Natural de la Garrotxa (▷ 264). No fewer than four volcanoes can be found in the city itself. A trail leads to Volcà de Montsacope and the botanical gardens, a high point with fantastic views over the surrounding area.

The town is also famous for its 19th-century school of landscape painting, many examples of which can be seen in the Museu de la Garrotxa (Jul–Sep Tue–Sat 11–2, 4–7; Oct–Jun Tue–Fri 10–1, 3–6, Sat 11–2, 4–7, Sun 11–2).

➕ 467 N3 ℹ️ Carrer Hospici 8, 17800 Olot ☎ 972 26 01 41

ORIHUELA

www.orihuela.com

A lush landscape of citrus, almond and olive trees, plus the second-largest palm plantation in Europe, add a delicious charm to this bustling provincial capital. The fertility and richness of its lands have made Orihuela, focal point of the Vega Baja district, a coveted place throughout history. Romans, Visigoths, Moors, Christians and Catalonian-Aragónese have all fought over its lands.

The old quarter has a number of fine buildings, including the Gothic Catalán cathedral and 16th-century Colegio de Santo Domingo, which was originally a monastery before being converted to a university. The Palacio Rubalcava, one of the best of the town's noble houses, is now the visitor information office.

➕ 474 K9 ℹ️ Calle de Francisco Die 25 (Palacio Rubalcava), 03300 Orihuela ☎ 965 30 27 47 🚆 Orihuela

PARC NACIONAL D'AIGÜESTORTES I ESTANY DE SANT MAURICI

www.parcsdecatalunya.net

This national park has an area of impressive proportions and offers great trekking opportunities. Officially established in 1955, it covers 10,230ha (25,268 acres) and contains more than 200 lakes, dense forest and mountain peaks towering to heights of 3,000m (9,800ft).

The higher peaks are popular with mountaineers and climbers, but there are easier, marked trails at the lower levels. These link mountain refuges that allow you to take longer journeys (camping is not allowed).

Access to the park is through entry points at Boí (to the west) and Espot (to the east). Jeeps and taxis ferry visitors to the park's fringes. No private vehicles are allowed access.

➕ 466 M2 ℹ️ Carrer de les Graieres 2, 25528 Boí ☎ 973 69 61 89 ℹ️ Calle Prat de la Guarda 4, 25597 Espot ☎ 973 62 40 36 🚆 La Pobla de Segur 🚢 Visit the park information offices for guided tours, walking trips and activities

PARC NATURAL DELS AIGUAMOLLS

www.parcsdecatalunya.net

This 4,783ha (11,814-acre) wetland area, at the heart of the Costa Brava, is the second most important habitat of its kind in Catalonia, after the Delta de L'Ebre. Before the advent of extensive agriculture and commercial development the marshland was even bigger, occupying the whole of the alluvial plain. Now it is a pleasant, peaceful place and has a good selection of clearly marked paths.

Since the park's foundation in 1983 more than 323 different species of bird have been spotted here, including resident flamingos, avocets, purple herons and egrets, as well as occasional visitors such as lapwings, oystercatchers and terns.

The observatory tower, which is shaped rather like a large grain store, provides prime views of the marshes and nearby Badia de Roses, and the walk out to it should give you plenty of opportunity to enjoy the natural surroundings.

➕ 467 P3 ℹ️ Parc Oficina, El Cortalet, 17486 Castelló d'Empúries ☎ 972 45 42 22

REGIONS CATALONIA, VALENCIA AND MURCIA • SIGHTS

PARC NATURAL DEL DELTA DE L'EBRE

www.parcsdecatalunya.net

This designated natural park is a unique area of wetland, the second largest in Spain (after the Parque Nacional de Doñana ▷ 368–369) and an uncommercialized, tranquil spot that is distinctly different from anywhere else in the country. Spread over 320sq km (124sq miles) and bisected by the Río Ebro (L'Ebre in Catalán), it is best explored by boat or bicycle. The *transbordadors* are simple ferries that cross the river and connect the towns of Deltebre and Sant Jaume d'Enveja.

The coastal stretches of the park, such as Salines de la Trinitat, provide a habitat for an array of waterbirds, as well as a winter breeding ground for such species as the marsh harrier and the purple heron. Inland, the delta's flat lands support a patchwork of rice fields.

✚ 471 M5 ℹ Ecomuseu, Centre d'informació, Carrer Martí Buera 22, 43580 Deltebre ☎ 977 48 96 79 ▮ L'Aldea, Amposta, Camarles, L'Ampolla

PARC NATURAL DE LA GARROTXA

www.parcsdecatalunya.net

Grand views of crater rims and volcanic cones punctuating a rolling, wooded landscape make this park a memorable touring area, particularly via the GI-524 road between Olot (around which the park is based

▷ 263) and Banyoles. But don't expect bubbling lava and steaming craters, as the volcanoes last erupted about 10,000 years ago.

Instead, the Baixa Garrotxa region offers panoramas of fertile valleys and now-dormant cones. There are well-marked trails for those who want to explore on foot, and the Natural de La Fageda d'en Jordà reserve offers tranquil walking through a beautiful beech forest.

The Volcà del Croscat trail near the Lava Campsite takes you to a dramatic, part-forested and part-mined volcano. You can also rent a horse-drawn carriage or take a short train tour from the Lava Campsite.

✚ 467 N3 ℹ Centres d'Informació del Parc Natural, Casal dels Volcans, Avenida Santa Coloma s/n, 17800 Olot ☎ 972 26 62 02

PEÑÍSCOLA

www.peniscola.es

Calling itself the 'city by the sea', Peñíscola, a rocky promontory jutting out into the sea, blends a lively visitor resort with its quieter, historic old quarter. Dominating the town is the Castell del Papa Luna (Oct–Palm Sunday daily 10.30–5.30; rest of year daily 9.30–9.30), a fortress built by the crusader Knights Templar, which rises high on a craggy outcrop that juts into the Mediterranean. The castle's name comes from one of its chief residents, Pedro de Luna, or Benedicto XIII, who moved in

here in 1411 and who is famous for refusing to give up his title of anti-pope (a role set up in opposition to the elected pope).

A web of winding cobbled streets leads towards the 14th-century stronghold, whose thickset, fortified walls (built on the remains of an Arab citadel) reflect its former strategic purpose. The castle's ramparts have views over the bay and busy fishing port below. You can take a stroll down to the sea and along the palm-lined Passeig Marítim.

✚ 471 L5 ℹ Passeig Marítim, 12598 Peñíscola ☎ 964 48 02 08

RIPOLL

www.ajripoll.org

Set within a scenic valley, the rather shabby-looking town of Ripoll has one of Catalonia's most important monuments. Known as the 'cradle of the nation', the Monestir de Santa María (Jun–Aug daily 10–1, 3–7; Sep–Jun 10–1, 3–6) is a Benedictine establishment that was founded by Wilfred the Hairy in the ninth century.

Of particular note is the grand Romanesque West Portal, a superb example of early Christian art. This doorway, with its array of religious carvings—including scenes from the Apocalypse—survived a fire in 1855 that all but ruined the rest of the monastery. The portal is now housed behind a glass conservatory.

The church's interior is a 19th-century copy of the original, early 11th-century version. Its very simplicity evokes the solemn piety of the original monastic community.

The beautiful two-tiered cloisters, which were not as badly damaged by the fire as the main monastery building, are also accessible.

✚ 467 N3 ℹ Plaça Abat Oliba s/n, 17500 Ripoll ☎ 972 70 23 51 ▮ Ripoll

Left *A tiny hermitage sits in the centre of the Santa Margarida volcanic crater in Parc Natural de la Garrotxa*

Opposite top *Houses cluster around the Monestir de Sant Joan de les Abadesses*

Opposite bottom *Monestir de Sant Pere de Rodes, above Llançà*

ROSES
www.roses.cat

A distinctive white-sand beach sweeping around an arcing bay is what brings most visitors to Roses, and a stroll along the Passeig Marítim promenade is the best way to enjoy the scene. Apartments and hotels line the waterfront of this ancient town, which was first inhabited by trading Greeks 3,000 years ago. Apart from the ruined citadel, which contains remains of the original settlement of Rhode, the Castell de La Trinitat (above the lighthouse) and a megalithic park with three standing stones are the only scant reminders of this historic past. Now Roses is a busy package-holiday resort, and when the crowds descend it can feel overdeveloped.

🚩 467 P3 ℹ️ Avinguda de Rhode 101, 17480 Roses ☎ 902 10 36 36 🚆 Figueres, then bus to Roses (departs every half-hour in summer, every hour in winter)

SAGUNT (SAGUNTO)
www.sagunt.com/turismo

Set on a mountainside, Sagunt's first-century BC Teatro Romano (May–Sep Tue–Sat 10–8, Sun 10–2; Oct–Apr Tue–Sat 10–6, Sun 10–2) has undergone a number of restoration projects and is now open for live summer performances. From its seats there are wonderful views over the terracotta patchwork of roof tiles

in the old town, to the ramshackle Moorish castle above and the medieval church spires below. The walls of the ruined fortress, perched high on a rocky promontory, are nearly 1km (0.6 mile) long.

While the amphitheatre and the environs of the old town are attractive, modern Sagunt is very industrialized.

🚩 471 L6 ℹ️ Plaça Cronista Chabret s/n, 46500 Sagunt ☎ 962 65 58 59 🚆 Sagunt

SANT JOAN DE LES ABADESSES
www.santjoandelesabadesses.com

This small, pleasant country town, overlooking the Serra Cavallera and just 10km (6 miles) from Ripoll's Monestir de Santa María (see left), is home to another great Benedictine foundation, the Monestir de Sant Joan de les Abadasses. This monastery (Mar–Oct daily 10–2, 4–7; Nov–Feb Mon–Fri 10–2, Sat–Sun 10–2, 4–6) was also established in the late ninth century by Wilfred the Hairy, as a gift for his daughter, Emma, whom he appointed the first abbess. Of particular interest inside are the Romanesque church, the Gothic cloisters and sculptures, including the 13th-century Santíssim Misteri, a group that represents the lowering of the cross.

Down in the main town, the arcaded baroque Plaça Mayor is

worth seeing, as is the Pont Vell. This 12th-century bridge, with a distinct Gothic arch, was destroyed first by an earthquake in 1438 and then again during the Spanish Civil War. It was restored in 1976.

🚩 467 N3 ℹ️ Plaça Abadia 9, 17860 Sant Joan de les Abadesses ☎ 972 72 05 99 🚆 Ripoll

SANT PERE DE RODES

Negotiate the steep climb up to this Benedictine monastery and you will be rewarded with impressive Romanesque architecture and coastal views. The monastery stands in an imposing situation, 500m (1,400ft) up a scrub-forested mountainside, and is reached either by road from the outskirts of El Port de la Selva or via a marked walking track through Vall de Santa Creu.

Built mostly between the 10th and 12th centuries, it became one of the most important and powerful monasteries along the Costa Brava after gaining independence in AD934. Its cathedral still has some of its original stonework and is flanked by the impressive Torre de Sant Miquel. The two-tiered cloisters are a good spot to contemplate the splendid isolation of this former monastic community. The best time to visit is in the morning, when the sun lights up the hillside. It can be gloomy in the afternoons.

🚩 467 P3 ✉️ Monestir Sant Pere de Rodes, 17489 Port de la Selva, Girona ☎ 972 38 75 59 🕐 Jun–Sep Tue–Sun 10–8; Oct–May 10–5 💶 Adult €5, child (7–21) €3, under 7 free

SITGES

www.sitgestour.com

This former artistic retreat, consisting of 17 beaches clustered around a small hill, ranks as one of the best and most fashionable of the Mediterranean seaside towns. Sitges does a good job of blending its busy beach resort with its cultural scene, and has a fine selection of restaurants, a few private galleries and several museums.

While there isn't actually much to do here, it is a pleasant place to wander around, although a thriving club scene means it can get busy in summer.

On the north side of this now-popular gay and family destination, the beaches of San Sebastián and Dels Balmins give way to Port Esportiu Aiguadolç, one of the town's three marinas. To the south, white sands are divided by break-waters and backed by the palm-lined Marítim Passeig. A baroque parish church crowns this much-painted beachside view. Behind it is the original old town, which has some fine mansions, whitewashed houses and narrow streets.

La Ruta dels Americanos leads past the town's grand houses. These were built by residents who had made their fortunes in Cuba in the 1930s (a free map of the self-guided walking tour is available from the visitor information office).

The Museu del Cau Ferrat (mid-Jun to Sep Tue–Sun 10–2, 5–9; Oct to mid-Jun 9.30–2, 3.30–6.30, Sun and holidays 10–3), former home of the eccentric artist Santiago Rusiñol (1861–1931), gives an insight into the Catalán school of Modernisme, which thrived in the town. Exhibits include ceramics, woodwork and paintings.

➕ 467 N4 ℹ Carrer Sínia Morera 1, 08870 Sitges ☎ 938 94 43 05 🚉 Sitges

TARRAGONA

▷ 267.

TORROELLA DE MONTGRÍ

www.torroella.org

Best known for its classical music festival, held in July and August, this small town of winding streets has a distinct medieval appeal. It is set on the Río El Ter, 30km (18 miles) from Girona, and was built beneath a 13th-century castle, now ruined. The former medieval port has an attractive arcaded main square and a Gothic church, and is the main point of access to L'Estartit, the premier scuba-diving base on the Costa Brava. From here you can take a boat trip out to the protected Reserva Marina Illes Medes, an archipelago that was once a shelter for smugglers, coral fishermen and pirates.

Back in Torroella, the Museu del Mediterrània (Mon–Sat 10–2, 5–8,

Sun and holidays 11–2), housed in a splendid mansion, contains exhibits on the marine reserve and local history.

➕ 467 P3 ℹ Passeig Marítim s/n, PO Box 33, 17258 L'Estartit ☎ 972 75 19 10

VAL D'ARÁN

www.aran.org

The high valley of Val d'Arán is almost entirely surrounded by towering peaks that are snow-clad in winter and luxuriously green in summer. Not only does its Atlantic-facing position set this area apart, but so too does its commonly spoken language, Aranese, which is derived from aspects of Catalán, Gascon and Basque. Some 30 different settlements are spread along the Río Garona, which flows northwards to France (where it is called the Garonne) and forms the valley's only natural route out. Driving into the Val d'Arán at its eastern gateway from Port de la Bonaigua is not for the fainthearted. The hairpin of roads and vertiginous drops makes the route a little nerve-racking at times, but it does have some particularly stunning scenery.

➕ 466 M2 ℹ Carrer Sarriulèra 10, 25530 Vielha ☎ 973 64 01 10 🚉 Lleida, then bus

Above *The pleasant little seaside town of Sitges, whose excellent sandy beach is lined with palm trees and overlooked by a Romanesque church*

TARRAGONA

Tarragona's hilltop location has served it well throughout a troubled past of attacks. Within its walls, Roman ruins—including parts of a chariot racetrack and a seaside amphitheatre—pay testament to a city that was once held to be the most elegant in all imperial Spain. The earliest documented evidence of the city dates back to the sixth or seventh century BC, although it was established as the imperial Roman stronghold of Tarraco in 218BC. The first century of the Christian era saw the construction of temples, mansions, a forum, a circus, an amphitheatre, aqueducts and thermal baths. But the invasion of the Visigoth army in AD476 marked the end of Roman influence.

ORIENTATION

The city divides into two distinct areas: the upper section, which leads into the old medieval walled quarter; and a more modern area below. Rambla Nova, a tree-lined walkway surrounded by café-bars and restaurants, is at the heart of the upper town. It leads to the Balcó del Mediterrani, a lookout point facing the sea.

From the adjoining Passeig de Les Palmeres you can see the Roman amphitheatre (Easter–Sep Tue–Sat 9–9, Sun 9–3; Oct–Easter Tue–Sat 9–5, Sun 9–3), with original second-century AD terraces that back on to the Mediterranean. At the opposite end of Rambla Nova is a monument dedicated to Catalonia's castellers, who build human pyramids.

THE OLD TOWN

Parallel to Rambla Nova is Rambla Vella, from which you can explore the tightly woven streets of the old town as they climb to the cathedral (Mon–Sat). On the edge of the old quarter, at Plaça del Rei, is the Museu Nacional Arqueològic (Jun–Sep Tue–Sat 9.30–8.30, Sun 10–2; Oct–May Tue–Sat 9.30–1.30, 3.30–7, Sun 10–2), with a well-preserved section of the Roman walls. Nearby, the remains of the Circ Roma chariot stadium give an insight into the city's past. From the walls, the city's greatest defence, walk along the Passeig Arqueològic (Apr–Sep Tue–Sat 9–9, Sun 9–3; Oct–Mar Tue–Sat 9–5, Sun 10–3) for an excellent overall view of the city.

Across town, about 1.5km (1 mile) to the northwest, is the ancient Roman necropolis (Jun–Sep Tue–Sat 10–1.30, 4–8, Sun 10–2; Oct–May Tue–Sat 9.30–1.30, 4–7, Sun 10–2).

INFORMATION

www.tarragonaturisme.cat

✚ 467 M4 🛈 Carrer Major 39, 43003 Tarragona ☎ 977 25 07 95 🕐 Jul–Sep Mon–Fri 9–9, Sat 9–2, 4–9; Oct–Jun Mon–Fri 10–2, 4.30–7, Sat–Sun 10–2

🚉 Tarragona

TIP

» When Mass is held, access to the cathedral and its Museu Diocesà (Jun–Sep 10–5; Oct–Feb 10–2; Mar–May 10–1, 4–7) is through the cloisters, signposted down what appears to be a back alley. If you stand with the facade in front of you, the signpost points to the left.

Below *The Passeig Arqueològic, a Roman aqueduct near Tarragona*

INFORMATION

www.comunitatvalencia.com
www.turisvalencia.es

✚ 471 L7 ℹ️ Poeta Querol s/n, Bajos
Teatro Principal, 46002 Valencia
☎ 963 51 49 07 🚉 Valencia

TIPS

» Once gritty and louche, Valencia's port is now very popular for eating out and partying. The brand new marina offers numerous entertainment options, and the beaches which spread north of the port have been cleaned up to offer an endless stretch of golden sand dotted with beach umbrellas.

» There are more beaches south of the city (hop on a bus); these are generally quieter but have fewer facilities.

VALENCIA

An alluring Mediterranean city, shaded with palm trees and scented with orange blossom, Valencia attracted surprisingly few international visitors until just a few years ago. Then, the stunning Ciutat de les Arts i les Ciències, a spectacular arts and entertainment complex designed by celebrity architect, Santiago Calatrava, put Valencia on the map. The city's place on the international stage was cemented in 2007 when it hosted the Louis Vuitton America's Cup. In preparation for the event, Valencia was thoroughly cleaned up and modernized. The Metro line was expanded, and the port area (formerly run-down and seedy), has been completely transformed into a vibrant new sports, dining and nightlife zone. Locals speak Valencià, and street signs and menus are usually in Valencian and Castilian Spanish.

CIUTAT VELLA (OLD CITY)

The Ciutat Vella (Old City) is set a couple of miles inland from the port area and beaches. It is tucked behind the remnants of the medieval walls, still studded with sturdy towers, and contains a tiny cluster of Gothic churches and monuments linked by narrow streets and elegant squares. The Ciutat Vella is easy to get around on foot, with all the sights within an easy stroll of each other.

The cathedral sits at the heart of the old city, its Gothic bulk hidden behind a baroque facade. You can climb the belltower, known as El Micalet (Mon–Sat 10–6, Sun 2–5.30) to enjoy spectacular views. The Lonja (Silk Exchange) is one of the finest civil Gothic buildings in Europe, with elaborate stone carvings and a forest of twisted columns in the main hall. Valencia grew rich on oranges at the end of the 19th century, and the city is embellished with several *modernista* (a local strand of the art-nouveau movement) monuments, including the delightful Mercat Central (market) and the train station, which still retains its beautifully carved ticket booths.

The trendy Barri del Carme neighbourhood is full of boutiques and art galleries, as well as the city's excellent and enormous contemporary art museum IVAM (Institut Valencià d'Art Modern, Tue–Sun 10–8).

CIUTAT DE LES ARTS I LES CIÈNCIES

www.cac.es

The unmissable City of Arts and Sciences occupies a futuristic, white complex designed by Santiago Calatrava. It comprises a superb Museu de les Ciènces (Science Museum), with interactive exhibits; L'Hemisphèric (planetarium); the L'Oceanogràfic, one of the largest aquariums in Europe, and L'Umbracle, a sleek contemporary garden. The Palau de les Arts hosts opera, ballet, theatre and music performances by local and international artists. For details of opening and prices, check the comprehensive and multilingual website.

Below *The ornate (Churrigueresque) alabaster portal of the 18th-century Palacio del Marques de Dos Aguas, which now houses the National Ceramics Museum*

VIC

www.victurisme.cat

The main reason to visit the medieval town of Vic is for its bustling market. Held on Tuesday and Saturday mornings in the enormous Plaça Major, this event alone shows off the town's rich commercial heritage.

The Plaça Major is the centre of town life every day of the week: it's a magnificent medieval set-piece, laid out when the city was the seat of a powerful bishopric. Neat arcades run down each side, dotted with shops, cafés, and butchers selling Vic's celebrated *embotits* (cured sausages). Look for surviving Gothic and Renaissance mansions, including Casa Moixó and Casa Beuló, all clearly signposted. The helpful tourist office is just off the Plaça Major.

Vic was occupied by the Romans before its establishment as a medieval marketplace. A few scant ruins remain from this time, including parts of a second-century AD Roman temple within the castle walls.

Opposite the 18th-century neoclassical cathedral, with its elaborate Romanesque tower, is Catalonia's leading episcopal museum, the Museu Episcopal (Apr–Sep Tue–Sat 10–7, Sun and festivals 10–2; Oct–Mar Tue–Fri 10–1, 3–6, Sat 10–7, Sun and festivals 10–2), housing a wealth of Romanesque art.

✚ 467 N3 🛈 Carrer de la Ciutat 4, 08500 Vic ☎ 938 86 20 91 🚊 Vic

Left to right Xàtiva's castle ramparts; boats gather in the lively port at Xàbia

XÀBIA (JÁVEA)

www.xabia.org

With its old quarter, busy fishing port and lively beach area, Xàbia is a town of three attractive parts.

The old town is set farthest inland, and is characterized by the use of golden Tosca stone, carved locally. Here, too, is the 'pink house', the striking *modernista* residence of Senyoreta Josefina Bolufer, built from a fortune she and her family made from the export of raisins to America. The fortified Gothic Església de Sant Bertomeu reveals its medieval past in the form of arrow holes and openings for the use of mortars. Simple whitewashed fishermen's houses with cane awnings mark the fishing quarter close to the port of Duanes del Mar, and the golden stretch of El Arenal beach is backed by café-bars. Besides the stretch of sand at El Arenal, the rest of the beach is largely pebbly. The town has grown considerably, with numerous new villa developments and apartment blocks filling in the bay between the old town and the port. Just inland, the Natural Park of Montgó offers walking paths, a profusion of wild flowers (particularly in spring), and glorious views out across the limpid waters of the bay.

✚ 471 L8 🛈 Plaza de La Iglesia 4, 03730 Xàbia ☎ 965 79 43 56

XÀTIVA

www.xativa.es

This ancient settlement, site of one of Spain's greatest Moorish fortresses, is now a refreshing mountain town retreat.

The castle itself (May–Sep Tue–Sun 10.30–7; Oct–Apr 10.30–6), a fusion of Iberian and Roman strongholds that was later strengthened by the Moors, looms large on the hillside. Here, the surrounding *huerta* (agricultural land) meets the Sierra Vernissa, and a palpable mountain coolness adds to the calm air of this former papal city. Xàtiva's old town, featuring some impressive facades and ornate doorways, is ideal if you would like to wander in the shade. The grand Renaissance Colegiata Basilica (daily 10.30–1) is in the middle of town, as are numerous stately mansions, most now in private hands.

For a more unusual sight, you may like to visit the Museu de l'Almodí (15 Jun–15 Sep Tue–Fri 9.30–2.30, Sat–Sun 10–2; 16 Sep–14 Jun Tue–Fri 10–2, 4–6, Sat–Sun 10–2). The museum's portrait of Felipe V is hung upside-down, which has been the tradition in this town after he set fire to it in 1707 during the War of Succession.

✚ 471 K7 🛈 Alameda Jaume I 50, 46800 Xàtiva ☎ 962 27 33 46 🚊 Xàtiva

CAMÍ DEL FORT

This spectacular there-and-back walk takes you from the popular waterfalls of Les Fonts d'Algar up through the Serra de Bèrnia to the ruins of the Renaissance Fort d'Bèrnia. Each twist of this route, the PR-V48 Camí del Fort (Fort Trail), reveals new outlooks—limitless views of the Mediterranean, lush orange and *nispero* (medlar) orchards in the Algar valley, and the jagged peaks of the Serra d'Aitana range. Originally used as a wine-, corn- and raisin-trading route between La Marina Alta and Callosa d'En Sarrià, the track later became a supply route to the 16th-century Fort de Bèrnia, built to repel Ottoman pirate attacks. The trail is waymarked with yellow and white stripes.

THE WALK

Distance: 10km (6 miles)
Allow: 4–5 hours return
Total ascent: 670m (2,200ft)
Start/end at: El Algar
Maps and guides: The information booths in Callosa d'En Sarrià and Polop have a leaflet on the Camí del Fort route. You can also download a route map from the town website www.callosa.es
Parking: There are numerous small parking areas in El Algar or you can park at the camping area up the (extremely steep) hill out of the village. Each restaurant in the village also has parking for customers.

HOW TO GET THERE

El Algar is 3km (2 miles) along the CV-7531 road from Callosa d'En Sarrià.

★ The village of El Algar makes an unapologetic play for the busy tourist trade. It is full of restaurants and feeds off the demand for the waterfalls and springs of Les Fonts d'Algar. There are short, easy trail walks around the various waterfalls (about 45 minutes return).

From the entrance booth to Les Fonts d'Algar, next to Les Fonts restaurant, walk up the extremely steep paved road out of the village. After 150m (165 yards) you pass another entrance booth to Les Fonts before the hill briefly flattens and you reach an intersection. Turn left, signed for Fort d'Bèrnia PR-V48 (a detour right goes to the Zona de Acampada and

Jardí Botanic). Continue uphill on a paved road through vast, mesh-covered *nispero* orchards (the fruit is a cross between a nectarine and an apricot). There are views from here right to Benidorm and the Mediterranean.

At an unsigned fork in the road, take the left fork that continues uphill along a rougher road (the right fork immediately drops right). The road becomes an intermittent concrete and gravel track, moving into more natural rocky terrain with pine trees.

At a concrete section on a sharp left-hand corner, look for a small wooden trail sign, marked 'PR-V48

Fort de Bèrnia', off the right side of the track in front of an earth bank. The footpath starts here.

The path zigzags up the slope before climbing more directly through pine trees to a stone outcrop with a yellow and white waymarker. Soon the trail enters more open country, with impressive views to Callosa d'En Sarrià and Serra d'Aitana. The trail, at times less distinct but regularly waymarked, continues to zigzag up the slope. Beyond a 4m-high (13ft) rock outcrop, the path climbs left and you glimpse Serra de Bèrnia's serrated ridgeline. Just past one of several waymarked boulders is a trail information board on the Camí del Fort (Fort Route).

❶ The Moors built many agricultural terraces here before they were finally forced out in 1609, and the 18th century saw further terrace expansion to accommodate vineyards. A 20th-century outbreak of phylloxera disease wiped out the vines and the mountain population began an exodus to the coast.

The path now zigzags uphill, with a pyramidal peak on the left. The slope eases off as you head first towards the peak, then veer round to the right below it until you reach Cueva del Bardalet (Bardalet Cave).

❷ This stone-walled *cester* (derived from the verb *cestajar*, meaning 'to siesta') is used by shepherds for keeping livestock out of the midday sun. It's deep, so take care if you walk around its overgrown walls.

Beyond the *cester*, you reach a T-junction with a wooden trail sign indicating the PR-V48 to Fort de Bèrnia off to the right. The trail climbs gently and then meanders over towards the Serra de Bèrnia ridgeline, passing through thicker vegetation dotted with eucalyptus bushes. You eventually reach an opening and Bancal Roig.

❸ At the ruined house of Bancal Roig the animal pen is used by shepherds to store livestock over winter. The building is split into two and has a *triador* area, where sheep or goats were mated. Red roof tiles and the remains of the rudimentary rooms lie scattered around.

From Bancal Roig, pass a dry mountain lake along a wider track. As you follow the mountain contours, you get fine sea views. Beyond a short section of trees you enter a clearing. The much smaller path you need goes off the main track on the left side of the clearing, indicated by a wooden trail sign marked 'Fort de Bèrnia'. The path climbs up through trees, becoming steeper on a broad open ridge with scrub. Go right at a small Y-fork in the track and above you will see trail signs near the fort.

Follow the 'Fort' sign uphill to an information board and continue past another sign, with a profile of the surrounding mountain ranges, to the fort entrance.

❹ Built in 1562, Fort de Bèrnia was designed by renowned Renaissance architect Joan Baptista Antonelli. It has a four-pointed star shape and Felipe II hoped that its high position overlooking the Mediterranean would help foil Ottoman pirate attacks. Ultimately, however, its location proved its undoing, for it was simply too far from the coast to provide an effective defence. The fort was abandoned after just 50 years and destroyed to prevent the enemy from using it.

The return route is an exact reversal of the way up—except that it is all downhill. An additional route option takes you from the fort around the Serra de Bèrnia. It is a more serious undertaking and adds around three hours to the route time—see the Camí del Fort route leaflet for more details.

WHEN TO GO
The route can be walked year round, but it offers little shelter from the sun. Outside the summer period it is easier to avoid the crowds that visit the Algar waterfalls.

WHERE TO EAT
El Algar is the only place for provisions en route and has a range of restaurants and bars. These establishments are generally open only during daylight hours.

Above left *The Algar valley is renowned for its clementine and orange groves*
Above right *A tumbling waterfall at Les Fonts d'Algar*
Opposite *The ruins of the Fort de Bèrnia look out over the Mediterranean*

FROM THE COSTA BLANCA TO THE SERRA D'AITANA

The heartland of La Marina, the area spanning the mid-coastal region of the Costa Blanca and the high mountains of its interior, features on this drive. It is a landscape of mountain backdrops, plunging valleys and craggy outcrops. Fertile agricultural terraces, orange orchards and olive and almond groves lead upwards to the dramatic slopes of the Serra d'Aitana.

THE DRIVE
Distance: 125km (78 miles)
Allow: 1 day
Start at: Alicante, map 475 L8
End at: Finestrat, map 471 L8

★ Begin your drive from the main marina in Alicante (▷ 255). With the 16th-century Castillo de Santa Bárbara to your left, head northwards on the N-332 to Valencia. Bear right shortly after, then take the right turn signed 'Valencia/Madrid/Murcia E-15/AP-7'. Bear right on to the N-340 signed to Valencia, right again onto the N-332, also signed to Valencia, then immediately right and left. Stay on the N-332 and continue through Villajoyosa, to Benidorm.

Bypass Benidorm and bear right towards Callosa d'En Sarrià. At

the first roundabout, turn right on to the CV-70 signed to La Nucia. Through the following series of nine roundabouts, follow signs for La Nucia until you reach this former Moorish stronghold. Continue towards Polop, where respite from the hot sun can be found in the cool spring waters that pour from the 221 spouts of the *chorros* (jet) fountain. At the next roundabout, take the CV-715 towards Callosa d'En Sarrià.

❶ On the slopes of Almedia mountain and protected from the winds by the surrounding Aitana, Bèrnia and Aixortà ranges, Callosa d'En Sarrià has an average annual temperature of 17°C (62°F). The narrow streets and old quarter of this former Moorish farming community are best explored on

foot. The neoclassical Iglesia de San Juan Bautista, in the Plaça Mayor, is renowned for its baroque organ, dating from 1754.

Leave town on the C-3313 signed for Guadalest.

❷ Built on a sheer rock pinnacle, the walled town and fortress of Guadalest are Spain's second most visited spot. Stone steps lead to an impressive portal that was carved out of the rock over 1,000 years ago. From the ramparts of the Castillo de San José, reached via the 18th-century Casa Orduña mansion,

Above *The high town of Benimantell is surrounded by fertile agricultural terraces and orchards*

he views of the teetering belfry
f the town's church give way to a
ackdrop of agricultural terracing and
ountain vistas. Reflections of the
astle can be seen in the dammed
eservoir below, which supplies
enidorm's water.

ollow the signs to nearby
enimantell.

Benimantell is one of the Costa
lanca's highest towns.

he high pass known as the Puerto
e Confrides (966m/3,169ft) follows
hortly after you leave Benimantell;
nen you descend towards the
illage of Ares.

ontinue until Alcoleja is signed
ft at a crossroads. At the next
tersection, an optional left turn
ill take you into this pretty village's
arrow streets. Otherwise, turn right
n the A-164 in the direction of
'enàguila.

4 The ancient settlement of
Penàguila is renowned for the beauty
of its Jardín de Santos.

Continue on the CV-785, signed
for Villajoyosa and Aitana. The road
condition deteriorates slightly. Turn
left, signed for Base d'Aitana, to
reach the Puerto de Tudons pass at
1,027m (3,369ft).

Shortly afterwards, turn right towards
Sella. As you descend, there are
views to the coast and Benidorm.
Bear left towards Sella.

5 Nestled beneath Puig Campana,
the second-highest mountain in the
province (1,406m/4,613ft), is the
lovely town of Sella, a good base
for walks. Its whitewashed houses
and narrow, twisting streets reveal a
tranquil, untouched, rural Spain.

Leave town and continue your
descent, then take the CV-758 signed
to Finestrat.

WHEN TO GO
Avoid weekends, as many
restaurants along the route close on
Saturday, and on Sunday virtually the
whole of Spain takes to the roads.
The drive is particularly lovely in early
spring, when the almond orchards
are swathed in pink blossom.

WHERE TO EAT
BAR MORA
Friendly café-bar.
✉ Calle Sol 1, 03517 Guadalest ☎ 965 88
58 87 🕔 Sun–Fri 10–7

CAFÉ PLAÇA
Local bar offering a range of tapas.
✉ Plaza de España 15, 03510 Callosa
d'En Sarrià ☎ 965 88 02 50 🕔 Mon–Fri
7.30am–10.30pm, Sat 7.30am–1am

CA L'ANGELES
Classic local dishes, including
seafood and hearty stews (olla de
trigo) in winter.
✉ Calle Gabriel Miro 12, 03520 Polop de la
Marina ☎ 965 87 02 26

EL RIU
Family-run restaurant with a home-
produce craft stand next door.
✉ Carretera Callosa-Guadalest Km 7,
03517 ☎ 965 88 05 07 🕔 8 Jul–23 Jun
Sun–Fri 12–5

VENTA LA MANTAÑA
Chargrilled meats, and home-made
desserts at this traditional restaurant.
✉ Carretera de Alloi 9, Benimantell ☎ 965
88 51 41

PLACES TO VISIT
CASTILLO DE SAN JOSÉ AND CASA
ORDUÑA
✉ Calle Iglesia 2, 03517 Guadalest ☎ 965
88 53 93 🕔 Easter–Oct daily 10.15–1.45,
3.15–8; Nov–Easter 10.15–1.45, 3.15–6
👆 Adult €4, child (4–10) €1.50

IGLESIA DE SAN JUAN BAUTISTA
✉ Plaça Mayor, 03510 Callosa d'En Sarrià
🕔 Open only for Mass, daily

JARDÍN DE SANTOS
✉ 03815 Penàguila ☎ 965 10 09 09
🕔 Wed–Fri 11–7, Sat–Sun 11–9 👆 Free

MONTSENY NATURAL PARK

This drive winds through the glorious green hills and mountains of the Montseny Natural Park. It's very scenic, and offers numerous options for hiking, including the popular path to the top of the highest peak, Turo de l'Home.

THE DRIVE
Distance: 90km (56 miles)
Allow: 4 hours, not including stops
Start/end at: Vic, map 467 N3

★ Vic is an attractive and prosperous market town, with a handsome, arcaded main square, the Plaça Major. This is where a colourful market is held on Tuesdays and Saturdays, with all kinds of stalls selling everything from fresh country produce, to the famous local *fuet* (a cured sausage), as well as clothes and kitchen items.

From the centre of Vic, follow signs for Barcelona and take the C17 south for 7km (4.5 miles). At Tona, take the turning signposted for Seva and the Parc Natural Montseny. The little road, the BV-5303, which soon becomes the BV-5301, winds gently into the forested hills of the natural

park, one of Catalunya's loveliest hidden corners.

❶ After about 5km (3 miles) you will arrive at El Brull, a tiny village with the remnants of a ruined castle and a charming Romanesque church.

Continue south along the BV-5301.

❷ The road winds up for another few miles, reaching the Collformic pass, where a viewing point offers magnificent views over the hills and the confluence of three beautiful valleys. There's a welcoming inn for lunch or a snack, and there are some walking paths which strike off from here.

The road begins to level off, but continues its sinuous journey through the wooded hills. Just after a sharp loop, you'll see a small signpost

(quite easy to miss) for the friendly Hotel Sant Bernat on the hilltop— have a drink on the lawn, which offers unforgettable views over most of the natural park.

❸ The BV-5301 heads towards Montseny, the little village which has given the park its name. It's a relaxed, tranquil spot, with a beautiful backdrop of hazy peaks. This is the main tourism centre of the region, with a few campsites, a couple of hotels and restaurants.

As the BV-5301 heads south, the landscape begins to level out. There are several wonderful, rural restaurants on the side roads: one of the best is the charming Can Barrina which is also a small hotel.

❹ Little Sant Esteve de Palautordera a peaceful village, is the next stop, with a simple church, a horse-riding centre (Hípica Can Vila) and an adventure-tourism company (Montseny Adventure) which can arrange everything from balloon rides to guided hikes.

When you reach the main road, the C-35, turn left and make for Sant Celoni. Avoid the town centre, and follow signs for Campins and Santa Fé de Montseny. A narrow but well-paved road, the BV-5114 wiggles through pine forest, stopping first at Càmpins.

❺ This tiny village is clustered on the southern peaks of Montseny, and was home to Frederic Pitarra, a famous 19th-century Catalán playwright.

On the left, as the road begins its twisting ascent northwards, you'll see a signpost for the Turó de l'Home.

❻ At 1,706m (5,597ft), Turó de l'Home is the highest peak in the natural park. There are several great hiking routes up to the peak.

Returning to the BV-5114, drive northwards until you see the signs for the Hotel Sant Marçal. The hotel is set next to a lovely Romansque chapel, a popular spot for weddings. More hikes splinter off from here, including a fairly easy ascent up the Turo de l'Home.

❼ The BV-5114 meets the G-I520, where you should turn left and make for Viladrau. This pretty little town is set around a tiny square on the banks of a river, and is famous for its mineral water.

From Viladrau, turn left on the G-I520, following signs for Seva. Then you can rejoin the BV-5303, and return to Vic.

WHEN TO GO
This drive is best in spring and autumn: In spring, the rivers are full and the hills are green and lush, and in autumn the changing colours of the leaves are very beautiful. Avoid Sundays, when Catalán families come day-tripping. Reserve your table at restaurants in advance, particularly at weekends.

WHERE TO EAT
COLLFORMIC
www.collformic.net
This inn serves good home cooking, and the house specialty is local meat grilled over charcoal.
✉ Carretera de Santa Maria de Palautordera a Seva Km 26,400, 08553 El Brull ☎ 938 84 10 89 🕐 Wed–Fri 9–6, Sat–Sun 9–8. Closed last 2 weeks of Jul, 1st week of Aug

HOTEL SANT BERNAT
www.santbernat.com
A delightful hotel set in gardens on top of the hill. The restaurant serves refined Catalán cuisine, but simpler fare, including sandwiches, is also available. It's very child-friendly, with a play area and three gorgeous Saint Bernard dogs.
✉ Carretera Santa Maria Palautordera a Seva Km 20,8, 08460 Montseny ☎ 938 47 30 11 🕐 Daily 1.30–3.30, 8.30–10.30

HOTEL SANT MARÇAL
www.hotelhusasantmarcal.com
A charming hotel, run by a delightful family, which may be part of the Husa chain but doesn't feel like it. Excellent, contemporary Catalán and Mediterranean cuisine in the restaurant.
✉ Carretera GIV-5201 de Viladrau a Santa Fe del Montseny Km 0 ☎ 938 47 30 43 🕐 Daily 1.30–3.30, 8.30–10.30

CAN BARRINA
www.canbarrina.com
A fabulous restaurant, serving elegant Catalán cuisine, in a 17th-century *masia* (farmhouse) They also have a handful of antique-filled rooms.
✉ Carretera de Palautordera al Montseny Km 12,670, 08460 Montseny 🕐 Daily 1.30–3.30, 9–11

Opposite *Detail of a sgraffito-decorated building in Vic*

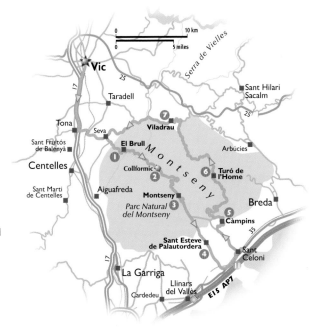

AGOST
AGOST
www.dip-alicante.es/agost
A number of shops and a museum give you an idea of the quality of pottery from Alicante. Most shops sell traditional, handmade pieces.
✉ 03698 Agost ☎ 965 69 10 43, 965 69 14 79 (city hall, tourism)

ALICANTE
AULA CULTURA CAM
Classical music and jazz concerts and theatrical performances are put on here. Movies in their original language are also screened, and puppet shows for younger audiences are staged.
✉ Avenida Doctor Gadea 1, 03003 Alicante ☎ 965 90 56 39 🕐 Closed Aug 👆 Varies considerably 🚇 1, 2, 20, 27

ENOTECA BERNARDINO
A good wine shop (with bar/restaurant attached), claiming to have more than 2,500 different wines from all over Spain. The service is attentive and the staff knowledgeable; there is a broad range of prices.
✉ Calle de Foglietti 34–36, 03007 Alicante ☎ 965 28 08 73 🕐 Shop: Mon–Sat 9–2, 5–8.45

Above Jazz is a part of the Alicante arts scene

HESPERIA ALICANTE GOLF AND SPA HOTEL
www.hesperia.es (hotel)
www.spa-hesperiaalicante.com
Relax in the sauna or Turkish bath after a swim in the indoor or outdoor pool at this 5-star hotel. Reflexology, facials and full body massages are available. In addition to the golf course, the hotel is close to a beach.
✉ Avenida de las Naciones, Playa de San Juan, 03540 Alicante ☎ 965 23 50 00 🕐 Daily 8–10 👆 Basic programme: massage, facial and exfoliation bath €148.75. All treatments include complimentary use of baths and saunas 🚍 From Alicante, follow the coast road north to the beach at Albufera San Juan. Head past the middle of town, then in the direction of Campello Playa

TEATRO PRINCIPAL
www.teatroprincipaldealicante.com
This 19th-century theatre is the pride of Alicante, and puts on concerts, ballet, opera and theatre. It proudly claims that all the most important Spanish performers of the last 200 years have played here.
✉ Plaza Ruperto Chapí s/n, 03001 Alicante ☎ 965 20 31 00 👆 From €9

V. PASCUAL
A wonderful little gift shop that stocks a huge variety of herbs

(used medicinally by the Spanish), a very good collection of Valencian-style pottery and ceramics, and a selection of traditional handcrafted pieces, including coffee pots and full breakfast sets.
✉ Avenida Alfonso X El Sabio 15, 03001 Alicante ☎ 965 14 01 39 🕐 Mon–Fri 10–2, 5.30–8.30, Sat 10–2

ALTEA
ALBIR MARINA
www.albirmarina.com
Albir Marina runs boat trips in the Balearic Islands. The marina also rents out boats, holds courses for beginners and arranges long-term expeditions.
✉ Avenida del Puerto 22, 3° Piso, 03590 Altea ☎ 965 84 51 75 👆 Boat rental from €80 for a half-day

BENIDORM
AQUALANDIA
www.aqualandia.net
Benidorm's finest water park has giant slides and rapids, swimming pools and watersports. The complex is outdoors, so bring water-resistant sunblock. There are bars, shops, restaurants and baby-changing facilities on site.
✉ Sierra Helada, Rincon de Loix, 03500 Benidorm ☎ 965 86 40 06 🕐 Early

May–early Oct daily 10am–dusk. Closed mid-Oct to early May ♿ Adult €27, child (3–12) €20 🚗 Take the Benidorm exit from the A-7 between Alicante and Valencia; the park is signposted from Benidorm's ring road. Alternatively, from central Benidorm head along Avenida Europa, then follow Avenida del Mediterraneo and Avenida de Penetracion

MUNDOMAR
www.mundomar.es
Several different outdoor habitats have been built to house rare birds, jungle reptiles and desert species here, but the real attractions are the dolphins, seals and killer whales. Baby-changing rooms and plenty of fast-food options.
✉ Sierra Helada, Rincon de Loix, 03500 Benidorm ☎ 965 86 01 00 🕐 Jul–Aug daily 10–8; May–Jun daily 10–7; Sep–Apr daily 10–6; ♿ Adult €25, child €20 🚗 See Aqualandia (▷ 276)

TERRA MITICA
www.terramiticapark.com
A great, family-fun theme park with more than 15 rides dedicated to children under the age of 12. Head down the Falls of the Nile water ride, sit on the runaway train or take off on the Flight of the Phoenix. Several family-oriented shows are staged daily including a pirate battle and a Roman horse display. Baby-changing rooms on site.
✉ Sierra Helada, Rincon de Loix, 03500 Benidorm ☎ 902 02 02 20 🕐 Late Mar to mid-Jul; mid-Ju to end Jul 10.30am–11pm; Aug 10.30am–2am; Sep 10–1am (attractions open until 10pm); mid-Sep to Oct weekends only. Check website as times can change ♿ Adult €35, child €26.50 🚗 Take exit 65A from the main A-7, or the N-300, N-332 or N-340 to reach the Benidorm-based park

GIRONA
ART GIRONA
www.art-girona.com
Art Girona makes and sells thousands of tin soldiers, grouped together in historical or geographical series. It's opposite the town council in a pedestrian precinct at the entrance of the old town.
✉ Plaça del Vi, 8 Baixos, 17004 Girona

☎ 972 20 41 34 🕐 May–Aug Mon–Fri 9.30–1.30, 4–8; Sep–Apr Mon–Sat 9.30–1.30, 4–8

DECATHLON
A huge store which stocks lots of sports equipment, including golf and swimming, and at good prices. Parking available.
✉ Polígono Industrial Mas Gri s/n, 17003 Girona ☎ 972 41 76 63 🕐 Mon–Sat 10–10 🚗 South of Girona. Take the N-2

VINOS ROVIRA TURAN
A wide choice of Catalán wines, sold by the litre, that can be taken away in a demijohn, a wineskin or a glass bottle. The most popular choices are red and rosé wines from Empordá, and reds, whites and rosés from Tarragona. Also Spanish liqueurs, including muscatel, garnacha, cognac and anisette. Very close to the Iglesia de San Pau.
✉ Carrer de Sant Isidre 52, 17003 Girona ☎ 972 20 36 30 🕐 Mon–Sat 9–2, 4.30–8.30

MANISES
MANISES
www.manises.com
Manises is a small town with an important tradition of ceramics and pottery production dating back to the 14th century. The local Museo de Cerámica highlights the golden periods of the industry—look for the interesting blue and the multi-hued shapes. Some factories and workshops sell beautiful kitchenware.
✉ 46940 Manises ☎ 961 52 56 09 (tourist office) 🕐 Museum: Tue–Sat 10–1, 4–7, Sun 11–2

OLIVA
OLIVA NOVA HOTEL
www.olivanova.com
The Health Beauty Spa Centre at this hotel has two saunas, a Turkish bath, a whirlpool and a fitness complex. All are free to use after you have paid the inexpensive day fee. Also an outdoor pool, tennis courts, kids' club and a golf course.
✉ Urbanización Oliva, Nova Golf, 46780 Oliva ☎ 962 85 76 00 🕐 Mon–Sun 10–9 ♿ Day use of sauna, Turkish bath, gym

and fitness centre €30 🚗 Follow coast road for 70km (43 miles) west from Valencia. The Oliva Nova Hotel is on the beach between Denia and Oliva

ROSES
AQUA BRAVA WATER PARK
www.aquabrava.com
Aquabrava has Europe's largest wave pool as well as several adrenalin-pumping slides among its 20 different water-based activities. More sedate fun for younger children includes floating down the tranquil rapids. The park also has two bars, an information office, a shop and baby-changing facilities. Free buses bring visitors in from the area around the park (see website).
✉ Carretera de Cadaqués, 17480 Roses ☎ 972 25 43 44 🕐 Jun–Sep daily 10–7 ♿ Adult €23, child €13 🚗 Aquabrava is 1km (0.5 mile) from Roses along Cadaqués road

TARRAGONA
ARSIS DISCOS
This shop lies near the Teatro Metropol (see below) and Ateneu de Tarragona. It sells an eclectic range of music and has a particularly wide selection of Spanish and Latin music. It also sells accessories for videos, CDs and DVDs.
✉ Carrer Fortuny 10, 43001 Tarragona ☎ 977 22 52 23 🕐 Mon–Sat 10–2, 5–9

TEATRO METROPOL
Non-Catalán speakers can enjoy the best national dance and musical performances at this theatre. The auditorium seats 500.
✉ Carrer Rambla Nova 46, 43004 Tarragona ☎ 977 24 47 95 🕐 Closed Jul, Aug ♿ €12–€22

VENTURA
Ventura is a traditional ceramics shop and workshop in Miravet, an outlying area of Tarragona. Prices suit every budget. The attractive handpainted Miravet ceramics are famous across the region. The shop also sells ceramic utensils.
✉ Carrer Raval 74, Miravet, 43747 Tarragona ☎ 977 40 75 87 🕐 Mon–Fri 8–1, 3–7.30, Sat 7–6

TORDERA

MEDIEVAL MAGIQUE
www.castellmedieval.com
This light and sound show lasts about three hours and can include dinner. Watch the historical re-enactment of a jousting match between two counts on horseback in the medieval castle of the Counts of Valltordera. After the main show there is flamenco, and the chance to dance.
✉ Carrer San Jaume 58, 08490 Tordera ☎ 937 64 11 11 🕐 Phone for confirmation ✋ Adults €45, child (5–10) €23; under 5 free

VALENCIA

ARTESANÍA HUERTA DE SAN VICENTE
www.huertadesanvicente.es
This craft shop stocks a wide variety of goods made from wood, iron and ceramics, as well as contemporary-looking souvenirs and reproductions of traditional objects. It also sells rustic furniture. Unlike those sold in most nearby areas, Valencian ceramics can often be found at reasonable prices.
✉ Calle San Vicente 41, 46005 Valencia ☎ 963 51 48 61 🕐 Mon–Fri 10–2, 5–8, Sat 10.30–2, 5.30–8 🚇 Plaza de Espanya

GRAN CAFÉ
A long-standing local favourite, which is a quiet spot for a drink during the week, but hots up with cabaret acts and DJs at weekends. Great house music and drinks, including the local

Agua de Valencia cocktail (cava, orange juice and Cointreau).
✉ Gran Vía Marqués del Turia 76, 46005 Valencia ☎ 963 34 26 40 🕐 Mon–Sun 6pm–2.30am ✋ Free

LA INDIANA
www.laindiana.com
A huge, glossy club which famously features a shark-filled aquarium and attracts a faithful crowd of local fashionistas. There are two floors, with resident and guest DJs playing the latest dance music, with a different theme each night: Thursdays for hip hop and R 'n' B; Fridays for funk and Latin. Dress to impress or the bouncers won't let you in.
✉ Calle San Vicente 97 ☎ 963 82 0891 🕐 Thu, Fri, Sat midnight–late ✋ €20–€22 (includes drink, reduction with flyer)

KALAHARI EXPEDICIONES Y AVENTURAS
www.kalahariaventuras.com
Kalahari runs one-day and weekend expeditions for non-professionals into the area around Valencia. Rafting, mountain climbing, canyoning and hydro-speeding available.
✉ Calle Mar 47, Bajo Izda, 46003 Valencia ☎ 963 77 44 44/606 41 49 85 ✋ Expeditions from €38

LINDA VUELA A RÍO
www.lindavuelaario.com
You'll find clothes and accessories for the young and stylish here. Spanish urban fashion emerged

during the 1990s, and this shop has selected some of its most celebrated designers, including Locking Shocking, Miriam Ocariz, Mireya Ruiz, Spastor, Ion Fiz and Alianto.
✉ Gran Vía Marqués del Turia 31, 46005 Valencia ☎ 963 51 77 46 🕐 Mon–Sat 10–2, 5–8.30 🚇 Colón

LLADRÓ
www.lladro.com
World-renowned, high-quality local porcelain producers, with the finest and probably most expensive collections in Spain. Mostly handmade figures, from classical to contemporary themes. Limited editions and exclusive reproductions.
✉ Calle Poeta Querol 9, 46002 Valencia ☎ 963 51 16 25 🕐 Mon–Sat 10–2, 4–8 🚇 Colón

MERCAT CENTRAL
Beautiful, *modernista* market with stalls selling fresh food, preserves and local wine. This is a good opportunity to try—and buy— regional produce such as delicious cheeses, finely seasoned sausages, airtight-packaged seafood and wines. Don't miss the famous Valencian oranges. It's also a good place to purchase those authentic paella pans.
✉ Plaça del Mercado s/n, 46001 Valencia 🕐 Mon–Sat 8–3, some stalls open later. No fish market on Mon

MINICINES ALBATROS
www.cinesalbatrosbabel.com
Fifteen screens mostly showing subtitled European films.
✉ Calle Fray Luis Colomer 4, 46001 Valencia ☎ 963 93 26 77 🕐 Mon–Sun 5.30–11 ✋ €8

L'OCEANOGRAFIC AQUARIUM
www.cac.es/oceanografic
Using the very latest technology, the park has recreated arctic, tropical, jungle and river habitats to house a wide range of mammals, fish, crustaceans and undersea vegetation. The Dolphinarium and Sea Lion Island should appeal to younger children. Baby-changing facilities are available.

Avenida Autopista de el Saler, 46013
Valencia ☎ 902 10 00 31 🕐 Mid-Sep
to May daily 10–8; Jun to mid-Sep
10am–midnight 🖐 Adult €25, child €18

PALAU DE LES ARTS
www.lesarts.com
Santiago Calatrava's spectacular
edifice evokes a giant eye, or perhaps
an enormous ship in full sail. Part
of the celebrated City of Arts and
Sciences, it opened to the public
in 2007. The programme features
everything from opera and theatre to
jazz and flamenco.
Autopista del Saler 1 ☎ 961 97 55 00
🖐 From €8

PALAU DE LA MÚSICA
www.palaudevalencia.com
This was one of the leading examples
of Valencian architecture—until
Santiago Calatrava stole the plaudits
with his monumental Ciudad de
las Artes y las Ciencias (City of Arts
and Sciences), next door. The venue
stages concerts from classical to
modern and holds exhibitions.
Paseo de la Alameda 30, 46023 Valencia
☎ 963 37 50 20 🕐 Mon–Sun 10.30–1.30,
5.30–9 🖐 From €20 concerts (exhibitions
are free)

ROPA FRANCIS MONTESINOS
www.francismontesinos.com
Francis Montesinos is one of
Valencia's most important fashion
designers, and always closes
the Barcelona Fashion Week.
His creations have featured in
magazines all over the world and he
runs a prosperous chain of shops
throughout Spain. Classic women's
clothes are his primary interest.
Everthing is very expensive.
Conde Salvatierra 25, 46004 Valencia
☎ 963 94 06 12 🕐 Mon–Sat 10–2, 4.30–9

SUEÑOS Y AVENTURAS
www.suaventura.com
This place offers both mountain
and aquatic activities, including
mountain-bicycling, canoeing, quad-
bicycling and rafting. If this sounds
too energetic, try hot-air ballooning
or horseback-riding as new ways of
seeing the area.

Rubén Vela 37, Pta. 5, 46006 Valencia
☎ 963 34 25 35 🕐 Daily 9–2, 4–7
🖐 From €35

TEATRO PRINCIPAL
Valencia's most important theatre
occupies a beautiful building in the
Barrio Antiguo. It features dramas,
musicals and dance productions,
as well as promoting and hosting
a few cultural festivals throughout
the year.
Barcas 15, 46002 Valencia ☎ 963 53
92 00 (information) 🕐 Closed Mon
🖐 €8–€20

FESTIVALS AND EVENTS

FEBRUARY
CARNAVAL
Catalonia's biggest and most
bizarre *rua* takes place in Sitges,
but Barcelona's procession is also
respectably raucous and ribald.
Sitges

MARCH
LAS FALLAS DE SAN JOSÉ
Valencia's 19 March celebration
of San José is the city's main
yearly event, with three weeks
of celebrations, fireworks, and
bullfights (▷ 448).
Valencia

MARCH–APRIL
SEMANA SANTA
Major Easter processions and floats.
Cartagena, Lorca, Orihuela, Moncada,
Valencia

MAY–JUNE
MOROS Y CRISTIANOS
Re-enactment of Christian-Moorish
battles throughout Valencia and
Murcia.
Costa Blanca

JUNE
DÍA DE SAN JUAN
Hogueras (bonfires), processions
and fireworks on the beach.
San Juan de Alicante

JULY
FERIA DE JULIO
Music, superb fireworks and Battle of
the Flowers.
Valencia

AUGUST
MISTERI D'ELX
▷ 448. Music and fireworks.
Elx

LA TOMATINA
The world's biggest food fight—with
tomatoes.
Buñol

SEPTEMBER
FESTES DE LA MERCÉ
Barcelona's patron saint, Our lady of
Mercy, popularly known as La Mercé
involves concerts, street dances,
processions of *gegants* (giants), *caps
grossos* (big heads), fire-breathing
dragons, and spark-spewing devils.
Barcelona 🕐 Around 24 September

SANTA TECLA FESTIVAL
This major street festival sees the
streets fill with characters such as
cabezudos (giants with enormous
heads), *diables* (devils) and medieval
beasts. The acrobatic feats of the
famous *castellers* (human towers) are
worth seeing.
Tarragona 🕐 14–24 September

L'UMBRACLE
www.cac.es
The Umbracle, part of Santiago
Calatrava's daring City of Arts and
Sciences, incorporates a garden and
a panoramic walkway. The structure
is formed by a 'tunnel' of sweeping
arches, which frame beautiful views
of the surrounding complex.
Avenida Autopista de el Saler, 46013
Valencia ☎ 902 10 00 31 🕐 Open 24
hours 🖐 Free

Opposite *Artesanía Huerta de San Vicente
sells Valencian ceramics*

PRICES AND SYMBOLS

The restaurants are listed alphabetically (excluding Le, La and Les). The prices given are the average for a two-course lunch (L) and a three-course dinner (D) for one person, without drinks. The wine price is for the least expensive bottle.

For a key to the symbols, ▷ 2.

ALACANT (ALICANTE)
DÁRSENA

www.darsena.com

This popular restaurant has a privileged view of the port. The cuisine is well known in town and the decor elegantly combines maritime themes. Dársena is proud of its enormous variety of rice options (over 70 in a menu of 140 dishes). ✉ Muelle del Levante 6, Marina Deportiva, 03001 Alicante ☎ 965 20 75 89 🕔 Daily 1.30–4.30, 9.30–11.30 🖐 L €35, D €50, Wine €12

MONASTRELL

www.monastrell.com

Chef María José San Román's restaurant is a triumph, from the vanguard architecture to the progressive menu offering an eclectic mix of local products. The dessert menu features rich offerings, plus a range of cheeses.

✉ Calle San Fernando 10, 03002 Alicante. ☎ 965 20 03 63 🕔 Tue–Sat 1–4, 8–midnight 🖐 L €35, D €60, Tasting Menu €75, Wine €22

NOU MANOLÍN

www.noumanolin.com

Nou Manolín is a prestigious restaurant operated by the Catelló family. It attracts food experts from all over the world and locals alike, and serves delicious high-quality produce, fabulous seafood and amazing rice dishes, with no detail left to chance. Downstairs is a popular tapas bar, with a wonderful range of gourmet treats. ✉ Calle Villegas 3, 03001 Alicante ☎ 965 20 03 68 🕔 Mon–Sun 1.30–4, 8–12 🖐 L €35, D €50, Wine €14

PIRIPI

www.piripi.com

This is an exceptionally popular restaurant, so make sure you reserve a table. The chef uses fresh seasonal ingredients, and the cuisine is slanted towards the Mediterranean, with excellent rice, fish and seafood. They serve great tapas too. ✉ Avenida Óscar de Esplá 30, 03003 Alicante ☎ 965 22 79 40 🕔 Mon–Sun 1.30–4, 8–12. Closed 24 Dec 🖐 L €34, D €48, Wine €14

RACÓ DEL PLA

www.racodelpla.com

Reserve early for a table at this welcoming, family-run restaurant, where the rustic decoration is complemented by crisp white tablecloths, where you can tuck into some great local specialities like baby broad beans prepared with ham and foie gras, *fritura de la casa* (a platter piled high with ham croquettes, calamari, prawns and small local fish in batter), or *olleta Alicantina,* an aromatic stew with lentils and rice. They also offer a wide range of shellfish (such as razor clams, oysters, mussels). ✉ Calle Doctor Nieto 42, 03013 Alicante ☎ 965 21 93 73 🕔 Mon, Wed–Sun 2–4, 8.30–10.30. Closed 2 weeks in Aug 🖐 L €25, D €35, Wine €12

LA TABERNA DEL GOURMET

www.latabernadelgourmet.com

A fashionable, chrome-and-wood bar, which serves excellent gourmet tapas as well as more substantial dishes. For tapas, try the delicious fried artichokes and asparagus, or smoked tuna carpaccio. The rice dishes, a specialty of this stretch of coast, are particularly good. The *arros a la banda,* prepared with tiny prawns and baby octopus is scrumptious.

Fresh fish and shellfish arrive daily: ask your waiter what's good. The wine list is excellent and includes numerous local wines, along with at least one good choice from virtually every Spanish wine region.

✉ Calle San Fernando 10, 03002 Alicante ☎ 965 20 42 33 🕐 Daily noon–midnight ✋ L €25, D €35, Wine €12

CALP
LOS ZAPATOS
www.loszapatos.com
This restaurant may be small, but it's got a huge reputation. Chef Egon Abb is a globetrotter and his elegant contemporary cuisine takes its influence from around the world. The menu changes regularly, depending on what's freshest at the market, but might include such delights as *Olleta de Calpe* — a sumptuous fish stew packed with local fish and prawns with a bubbling cheese crust. The wine list is surprisingly adventurous, with a good selection of both classic and new. They also offer a simple menu for children.

✉ Calle la Santa María 7, 03710 Calp ☎ 965 83 15 07 🕐 Summer daily 1.30–3.30, 9–11; rest of year Mon, Thu–Sun 1.30–3.30, 9–11 ✋ L €30, D €35, Wine €14

DÉNIA
EL POBLET
www.elpoblet.com
Quique Dacosta is one of the most talked-about young chefs in Spain and counts two Michelin stars among his many awards. His restaurant, just outside the popular seaside resort of Dénia, is a gastronomic temple, and visitors are advised to reserve tables well in advance. Choose from one of several wonderful tasting menus *(menu de degustació)* or go à la carte. Among the specialties are extraordinary dishes like *El Bosque Animado* which powerfully evokes the taste and smells of the forest, as well as contemporary variations of Mediterranean rice dishes and the famously succulent local red prawns *(gamba roja de Dénia)*. The villa boasts a glassy dining area, and an attractive terrace for alfresco dining in summer.

✉ Carretera Las Marinas Km 2.5, Dénia ☎ 965 78 41 79 🕐 Tue–Sat 2–4, 9–11, Sun 2–4 ✋ L €75, D €85, Wine €26

GIRONA (GERONA)
BOIRA
The main dining room here is up a stairway leading from the handsome, arcaded Plaça Independencia. A simpler café, serving tapas and light meals, is on the ground floor and boasts a terrace on the square. Upstairs, modern Mediterranean and Catalán cuisine is on the menu, and there is an excellent fixed price menu at lunchtimes on weekdays. There is a no-smoking section.

✉ Plaça Independencia 17, 17001 Girona ☎ 972 20 30 96 🕐 Daily 1.30–4, 9–11 (restaurant), 10am–midnight (café-bar) ✋ Tapas from €2.50, L €20, D €30, Wine €10

LOS PADULES
Close to the town hall and Plaça de Bell-Lloc, this is a convenient place to try some local tapas in a Catalán house. No credit cards.

✉ Calle Nou del Teatre 10 bajo, 17004 Girona ☎ 972 20 30 54 🕐 Daily 1–5, 7–2 ✋ One tapas dish €3, Wine €8

LLOFRIU
SALA GRAN
www.salagran.com
The perfect place to taste traditional Catalán food on the Costa Brava, in a typical stone house. The restaurant is air-conditioned. Reservations are advisable because it's a very popular location for wedding banquets.

✉ Calle Barceloneta 44, 17124 Llofriu ☎ 972 30 16 38 🕐 Mid-Jul to Aug Tue–Sun 1–4, 8–11; Sep to mid-Jul Wed–Sun 1–4, 8–11, Mon 1–4. Closed 10 Jan–10 Feb ✋ L €35, D €45, Wine €10

MONTSENY
CAN BARRINA
www.canbarrina.com
Beautifully located in a mellow, country house overlooking the rolling hills of Montseny, this charming rural restaurant has a fine reputation. The rustically decorated dining rooms with their thick stone walls are cosy in winter and cool in summer.

The chef prepares elegant, Catalán cuisine, with traditional dishes and more innovative creations sitting side by side on the menu. The ovenbaked monkfish or the local venison from Montseny is recommended. Finish with artisanal cheeses — superb. There are also 14 delightful antiques-furnished bedrooms.

✉ Carretera Palautorda a Montseny Km 12,670, 08460 Montseny ☎ 938 47 30 65 🕐 Daily 1.30–3.30, 8.30–10.45 ✋ L €40, D €50, Wine €10

MURCIA
COMEDOR DE CASINO
www.casinomurcia.com
Murcia's extravagant, Mozarabic Casino was built at the end of the 19th century as a meeting place, rather than a place to gamble. Its splendid, if rather over-the-top, architecture has everything from a faux-Moorish entrance hall, to a glassy pavilion with with classical statues. The Casino contains a restaurant, open to visitors, which serves a very good value fixed-price lunch menu on weekdays (€10). It's popular with local workers, who come for the good home-cooked food and the extravagant setting.

✉ Calle Trapería 18, 30001 Murcia ☎ 968 22 06 58 🕐 Tue–Sat 1–5, 8–midnight, Sun 1–5 ✋ L €20, D €25, Wine €12

LA TAPA
www.latapa.org
Murcia is famous for its tapas, and the *tapeo* (a bar crawl from tapas bar to tapas bar) is a local institution. La Tapa overlooks the Plaza de las Flores, long famous for its wide range of eating options and packed with locals every night. It is a classic, brightly lit, rather basically furnished Spanish bar, one of the best known in the city, with traditional favourites like *patatas bravas, croquetas,* anchovies, and all kinds of delicious tidbits. Like most of the bars on this square, this is child-friendly, with a terrace.

✉ Plaza de las Flores 13, 30004 Murcia ☎ 968 21 13 17 🕐 Daily 11–midnight ✋ L €20, D €25, Wine €10

Opposite *Torrijos restaurant in Valencia*

PINOSO
PACO GANDÍA

This restaurant specializes in paella, and is also known for its *arroz con conejo y caracoles* (rice with rabbit and snails), a popular Spanish classic.
✉ Calle San Francisco 2, 03650 Pinoso ☎ 965 47 80 23 🕓 Daily 1.30–3.30. Closed Sun Jun–Jul and Aug 🖐 L €40, Wine €14

PLATJA D'ARO
LA GOLA

www.hostallagola.com
In an attractive, whitewashed seaside hotel, the restaurant serves tasty local specialties including baby eels *(angulas)*. There is a terrace, a parking area and wheelchair access. Reservations are advisable for the weekends when it gets very busy.
✉ Playa de La Gola, 17257 Platja d'Aro ☎ 972 75 92 43 🕓 Daily 1–4, 8–11 🖐 L €36, D €52, Wine €12

ROSES
EL BULLI

www.elbulli.com
This is the most celebrated restaurant in Spain—and one of the most highly acclaimed in the world. Chef Ferran Adrià spends six months in his 'laboratory' creating the extraordinary culinary masterpieces that will feature on the restaurant's unique tasting menu. Diners are presented with around 30 tasting dishes—edible cling film, parmesan ice cream, and tangerine bon bons with curry have all featured. Reserve months in advance, but be prepared for disappointment. Scheduled to close forever in December of 2012, the scramble for tables is impossible.
✉ Cala Montjoi, Apartado 30, 17480 Roses ☎ 972 15 04 57 🕓 Wed–Sat 7.30–9.30, Sun 1.30–3. Also occasionally Mon, Tue and a few days in early Oct; check website or phone for times 🖐 D €250 (only taster menu available), Wine €25

EL SALER
CASA CARMINA

Escape from the big city of Valencia to this comfortable, family-run restaurant, which continues the tradition of exquisite local food.
✉ Calle Embarcadero 4, 46012 El Saler ☎ 961 83 02 54 🕓 Tue–Sat noon–4, 8–11 🖐 L €24, D €35, Wine €9 🚗 18km (11 miles) south of Valencia along the coast road

SANT POL
SANT PAU

www.ruscalleda.com
Not only is this one of Catalonia's top restaurants, with three Michelin stars, but chef-de-cuisine Carme Ruscalleda is one of Spain's most important chefs. The menu changes regularly but may include dishes like crystallized tomato and vegetable bouquets with pine nuts and basil; and sea bass steamed in fig leaves and served with fig chutney. The tasting menu is highly recommended.
✉ Calle Nou 10, 08395 Sant Pol de Mar ☎ 937 60 06 62 🕓 Wed, Fri–Sun 1.30–3.30, 9–11; Thu 9–11. Closed 3 weeks in May and 3 weeks in Nov 🖐 L €40, D €55, Tasting menu €150, Wine €26

TARRAGONA
AL NATURAL

www.alnatural.biz
The buffet focuses on vegetarian food, although there are some meat options. The wines are organic. There is a no-smoking section.
✉ Calle Arquitecte Rovira 3, 43001 Tarragona ☎ 977 21 64 54 🕓 Mon–Sat 1–4 🖐 L €22 (fixed price including glass of wine), D €30, Wine €9

LA CANTONADA

This is one of the oldest cafés in Tarragona. Don't miss the *llesca*, Catalán bread smothered in a wide variety of toppings.
✉ Calle de Fortuny 23, 43001 Tarragona ☎ 977 21 35 24 🕓 Daily 9am–1am 🖐 L €16, D €28, Wine €8

FORTI DE LA REINA

www.fortidelareina.com
Set in an elegantly restored 18th-century bastion at the end of the Platja Llarga, this place offers views over the Mediterranean and back to the city of Tarragona. The menu features refined fish and seafood recipes, including excellent rice cooked in squid ink with lobster, as

well as some regional meat dishes. The lengthy wine list includes the finest Catalán and Spanish wines.
✉ Platja del Miracle s/n, 43007 Tarragona ☎ 977 24 48 77 🕓 Tue, Sun 1.30–4, Wed–Sat 1.30–4, 9–11 🖐 L €40, D €50, Wine €16

TOSSA DE MAR
VÍCTOR

A modest but welcoming restaurant serving excellent local specialties including traditional rice dishes and beautifully fresh fish. There are one or two surprisingly adventurous treats on the menu, including lobster croquettes. The restaurant is simple, but service is warm and friendly.
✉ Avenida La Palma 17, 17320 Tossa de Mar 🕓 Daily 2–4, 8.30–10.30. Closed Mon Oct–Jun, Feb 🖐 L €35, D €45, Wine €12

VALENCIA
A FUEGO LENTO

www.afuegolento.com
Excellent ingredients, all beautifully presented, are used in a range of wonderful tapas, fresh Valencian vegetables and red meats, grilled and *a la piedra* (seared on hot stones). There are enticing chocolate desserts, especially the mousse. The service is attentive. It is in the heart of the Old City's nightlife hub, the Barri Carme.
✉ Calle Caballeros 47, 46001 Valencia ☎ 963 92 18 27 🕓 Mon–Fri 1–4.30, 9–12, Sat 9–12 🖐 L €30, D €40, Wine €14 🚇 Plaza del Ayuntamiento/Alameda

CASA MONTAÑA

www.emilianobodega.com
This is an old and popular *tasca* (café-restaurant), founded in 1836. It is usually crowded, so reserving a table is advisable. It serves good seafood tapas and claims one of the longest wine lists in Valencia.
✉ José Benlliure 69, 46011 Valencia ☎ 963 67 23 14 🕓 Tue–Sat 12.30–3.30, 7.30–11, Sun 10–3.30. Closed 15–30 Aug, also Sun Jul–Aug 🖐 Tapas €2–€4, Wine €10 🚇 Amargarosa 🚌 1, 2

CA'SENTO

www.casento.net
This is one of the city's finest restaurants. Chef Raúl Alexandre,

alumnus of El Bulli, see left) has won international plaudits for his creative Mediterranean cuisine. The wine cellar has more than 300 references. ✉ Calle Méndez Núñez 17, 46024 Valencia ☎ 963 30 17 75 ✪ Tue–Sat 2–4, 9–11, Mon 2–4. Closed Easter week and Aug ✋ L €40, D €50, Tasting menu €75, Wine €24

CIVERA
www.marisqueriascivera.com
Traditional dishes are served here, most of them containing delicious seafood. Try the specials: *caldeta de langosta* (lobster) and *arroz meloso de pollo y conejo* (rice with chicken and rabbit). Most of the waiters understand English, and there are also English menus.
✉ Calle Lérida 11, 46009 Valencia ☎ 963 37 59 17 ✪ Daily 1–4, 8–12. Closed Easter, last week in Aug, 1st week in Sep ✋ L €40, D €55, Wine €10

LA SUCURSAL
www.ivam.es
This modern restaurant in the glossy, minimalist Museum of Contemporary Art is run by the well-known Salvador family. It has a cool, laid-back

atmosphere, with a correspondingly innovative menu.
✉ Calle Guillem de Castro 118, 46003 Valencia ☎ 963 74 66 65 ✪ Mon–Fri 1.30–3.30, 8.30–11.30, Sat 9–11.30 ✋ L €35, D €45, Wine €12 🚌 5

TORRIJOS
www.restaurantetorrijos.com
This is one of Valencia's top restaurants, serving creative rice dishes as well as fish and seafood. Exceptional dishes include *arroz con pintada y alcachofas* (rice with guinea fowl and artichokes), and warm salad with wild mushrooms and scallops.
✉ Calle Doctor Sumsi 4, 46005 Valencia ☎ 963 73 29 49 ✪ Mon–Sat 1.30–3.30, 9–1.30 ✋ L €50, D €95, Wine €22 🚌 19, 22, 89

VIC
CARDONA 7
Celebrated chef Jordi Parramón won all kinds of awards at his previous, eponymous restaurant but has swapped the pressures of haute cuisine for a simpler, bar-style environment. Cardona 7 is a gourmet tapas bar, serving delicious small portions *(mitges racions)* of original

and exquisite cuisine. There are some Catalán classics on the menu, such as the salad of pigs' trotters with Mallorcan *sobrassada,* but you'll also find some international dishes with Asian and international influences, including, sometimes, a selection of sushi. The desserts are excellent.
✉ Carrer Cardona 7, 08500 Vic ☎ 938 86 38 15 ✪ Tue–Sat 1.30–4, 8–12, Sun 1.30–4 ✋ L €30, D €45, Wine €10

XATIVA
CASA LA ABUELA
www.casalaabuela.es
A classic restaurant in the old quarter, this has been a favourite for over five decades. The name means 'Grandmother's House', but the restaurant serves assured, contemporary Mediterranean cuisine, prepared with the freshest seasonal produce. The oven-baked sea bass with garlic is very tasty, and the more adventurous might consider the stewed hare in red wine.
✉ Carrer Reina 21, 46800 Xativa ☎ 962 27 05 25 ✪ Tue–Sat 8–11 ✋ L €35, D €40, Wine €12

Below *La Sucursal restaurant in Valencia*

PRICES AND SYMBOLS

The prices are for a double room for one night including breakfast, unless otherwise stated. All the hotels listed accept credit cards unless otherwise stated. Note that rates can vary widely throughout the year.

For a key to the symbols, ▷ 2.

ALACANT (ALICANTE)
HOSTAL LES MONGES PALACE
www.lesmonges.net

A cozy, central budget hotel in a restored 18th-century building. Each room is different in style and quality, so it's a good idea to look at a few before checking in. Amenities include private bathroom and satellite TV and one room has a Jacuzzi.

✉ Calle San Agustín 4, 03002 Alicante ☎ 965 21 50 46 🛏 €50–€65 excluding breakfast (€6) 🛈 22 🕓

CALABARDINA
HOTEL AL SUR
www.halsur.com

A lovely whitewashed villa, with cobalt blue shutters and doors, this is located at the southernmost tip of Murcia near the wild and beautiful headland of the Cabo Cope. There's a North African feel to the decoration, with its gleaming white walls and arches, and small palm-shaded garden. Rooms are individually decorated in soothing shades of cream, lavender, dove grey and pale green. Breakfast is served on a terrace offering stunning sea views, and evening meals can be prepared with advance notice. The lounge area has a small library and board games.

✉ Torre de Cope 24, 30889 Calabardina ☎ 968 41 94 66 🛏 €98–€110 🛈 8

CARAVACA DE LA CRUZ
EL MOLINO DEL RIO
www.molinodelrio.com

Caravaca de la Cruz is one of the most authentic and attractive towns in the Murcian interior. Set in rolling hills about 10km (6 miles) from the town, this 16th-century mill has been converted into tranquil self-catering apartments, overlooking shady gardens and a pool. There are plenty of activities in the area, including hiking and birding. It's a great option for families.

✉ Camino Viejo s/n, 30400 Caravaca de la Cruz ☎ 968 70 84 58 🛏 €120–€135 🛈 6 apartments, plus one double room

GIRONA (GERONA)
HOTEL CARLEMANY
www.carlemany.es

This is a modern, four-star hotel, full of sculptures and works of art. It has wheelchair access, an internet centre, babysitting services and a piano bar. The soundproofed, air-conditioned bedrooms have TV and VCR. Pets are allowed on request.

✉ Placa Miquel Santalo 1, 17002 Girona ☎ 972 21 12 12 🛏 €135–€155 excluding breakfast (€12) 🛈 89 (2 non-smoking) 🕓

JAVEA (XABIA)
HOTEL EL RODAT
www.elrodat.com

In the hills above the popular seaside resort of Javea, this elegant and luxurious small hotel is set in lush gardens. The rooms and suites are classically decorated with pastel prints and traditional furnishings, and are all extremely comfortable. There are also eight garden villas available, with between two and four bedrooms as well as fully equipped kitchens. Numerous activities can be arranged, from hiking in the nearby

Above *The Lauria in Tarragona*

Montgó natural park, to horse-riding or bicycling. The hotel's spa offers a whole host of beauty treatments.

✉ Calle de la Murciana 9. Carretera Cabo de la Nao s/n 03730 Javea ☎ 966 47 07 10 ✋ €155–€330, garden villa €295–€375 🛏 42, 8 villas 🅂 🏊 Indoor and outdoor 🍴

LLORET DE MAR
SANTA MARTA
www.hstamarta.com
All rooms have a balcony, bath, safe and minibar. Some also have a refrigerator and telephone with free local calls. The hotel has tennis courts, and pets are allowed for a daily supplement of €12. The hotel is located on a small beach.

✉ Playa Santa Cristina, 17310 Lloret de Mar ☎ 972 36 49 04 🅲 Closed 16 Dec–31 Jan ✋ €185–€292 excluding breakfast (€18) 🛏 76 🅂 🏊 Outdoor

PLATJA D'ARO
XALOC
www.ghthotels.com
The hotel has a bar and gardens. The guest rooms are equipped with a safe, balcony, bathroom, hairdryer and satellite and cable TV. Dogs (up to 5kg/11lb) are allowed.

✉ Cala Rovira 9, 17250 Platja d'Aro ☎ 972 32 11 40 🅲 Closed 30 Sep–29 Apr ✋ €98–€196 🛏 47 🅂 🏊 Outdoor

S'AGARO
HOSTAL DE LA GAVINA
www.lagavina.com
This opulent hotel is surrounded by peaceful gardens. The rooms have TV, minibar, safe, hairdryer and telephone. The hotel has a gift shop and internet access. There's 24-hour room service.

✉ Plaza Rosalera s/n, 17248 S'Agaro ☎ 972 32 11 00 🅲 Closed Nov–Feb ✋ €190–€410 excluding breakfast (€25) 🛏 74 🅂 🏊 Outdoor 🍴

EL SALER
PARADOR DE EL SALER
www.parador.es
ts 18-hole golf course and soccer pitch make this modern hotel ideal for sports-lovers. Guest rooms are arge and brightly decorated.

✉ Avenida de los Pinares 151, 46012 El Saler ☎ 961 61 11 86 ✋ €155–€245 excluding breakfast (€16) 🛏 58 🅂

🏊 Outdoor 🍴 🚌 18km (11 miles) south of Valencia along the coast road

TARRAGONA
CIUTAT DE TARRAGONA
www.hotelciutatdetarragona.com
This four-star hotel's soundproofed rooms are equipped with minibar, satellite TV, telephone, safe and hairdryer. There's also an ice machine on each floor, 24-hour room service, a fitness centre and a shopping gallery. The café-bar serves breakfasts, snacks and cocktails. The hotel offers airport transfer and wheelchair-friendly rooms. Pets are allowed on request.

✉ Plaça Imperial Terraco 5, 43005 Tarragona ☎ 977 25 09 99 ✋ €85–€165 excluding breakfast (€14) 🛏 168 (4 non-smoking and wheelchair-friendly rooms available) 🅂 🏊 Outdoor 🍴

LAURIA
www.hlauria.com
This three-star establishment is small, comfortable, and a good budget choice. Rooms are equipped with bath or shower, TV, telephone, safe and hairdryer. Amenities include a restaurant-café, bar, nightclub, pool, room service, laundry, dry cleaning and babysitting. Pets are allowed on request.

✉ Rambla Nova 20, 43004 Tarragona ☎ 977 23 67 12 ✋ €75–€90 excluding breakfast (€10) 🛏 72 🅂 🏊 Outdoor

TOSSA DE MAR
HOTEL DIANA
www.diana-hotel.com
This huge Catalán-style building has an inner courtyard with fountains, palms and flowers. Features include a conference room, coffee shop and room service. Rooms are equipped with a TV with English-language channels and a mini refrigerator, and some have balconies facing the beach and some have a terrace. This is a child-friendly hotel.

✉ Plaça de España 6, 17320 Tossa de Mar ☎ 972 34 18 86 🅲 Closed 1 Dec–1 Mar ✋ €85–€135 🛏 21 🅂

VALENCIA
AD HOC
www.adhochoteles.com
This comfortable old hotel is a splendid early 20th-century mansion run by an antiques-lover. It offers free wireless access and the service is as sophisticated as the decor.

✉ Calle Boix 4, 46003 Valencia ☎ 963 91 91 40 ✋ €85–€230 excluding breakfast (€13) 🛏 28 (20 non-smoking) 🅂 🚇 Colón 🚌 2, 95

HOTEL SILKEN PUERTA VALENCIA
www.hoteles-silken.com
An ultra-modern hotel near the stunning City of Arts and Sciences and the new marina in Valencia, this is part of a chain but boasts all kinds of original details. Not least of these is the vibrant mural across the glassy exterior, designed by local boy and international celebrity Javier Mariscal. Rack prices are high, but internet deals regularly bring the price of a stylish double room down to just €60—making this one of the best bargains in the city. You might want to splash out on a suite with a private terrace. There are amenities for business visitors, including WiFi.

✉ Avenida Cardenal Benlloch 28, 46021 Valencia ☎ 963 93 63 95 ✋ €88–€275 🛏 157 🅂 🍴

VILARDIDA
HOTEL LES VINYES
www.lesvinyes.com
Tucked away in a tiny village surrounded by vineyards, this lovely ochre-coloured hotel is an enchanting rural retreat. It's perfectly located for wine tourism in the Penedés and Priorat regions, and just a 30-minute drive to the beaches of the Costa Daurada or the monumental city of Tarragona. The hotel has its own little spa and even a small stables. The stylish interior is decorated in warm colours and there's an excellent restaurant, open to guests daily and to non-residents on Friday and Saturday nights.

✉ Calle Vilardida 13, 43812 Vilardida ☎ 977 63 91 93 ✋ €145–€160, suites €190–€240 🛏 7 🅂 🏊 Outdoor 🍴

CASTILE-LEÓN AND LA RIOJA

Castile-León is the historic heart of Spain, formed by two ancient and powerful kingdoms. This region encompasses the northern swathe of the great *meseta,* a high plain, at the centre of Spain. Castles still crown almost every town, just as they did in the Middle Ages, and palaces, cathedrals and pantheons still attest to the wealth and influence of the early monarchs. Much of the region is agricultural, with endless fields of grain stretching into the distance, pocked here and there with small market towns. But the cities are extraordinary: Salamanca, a magnificent Renaissance ensemble with an ancient university; Burgos, with its spectacular cathedral and splendid royal convents; and León, home to the breathtaking Romanesque pantheon of the kings as well as one of the finest cathedrals in Europe. To the west are secret valleys and mountains, where few tourists penetrate, and where ancient traditions and dialects are still preserved. To the north, León is divided from Asturias and Cantabria by the stunning mountain range of the Picos de Europa, now a national park.

Neighbouring La Rioja is the second-smallest of Spain's 17 autonomous communities, a lush region criss-crossed with rivers. It has become synonymous with the production of Spain's most celebrated wines. In recent years, numerous celebrity architects—among them Frank Gehry, Santiago Calatrava and Zaha Hadid—have designed glamorous new bodegas for some of the most high-profile labels. This has brought the region plenty of very welcome attention, and a slew of designer accommodation and restaurants in its wake. But this fertile region cultivates plenty more besides grapes: Its abundant fresh produce, including mouthwatering asparagus and artichokes, is famous throughout Spain, and forms a large part of this region's delicious local gastronomy. Not as rich in historical monuments as Castile-León, La Rioja does boast the beautiful cathedral at Santo Domingo de la Calzada, a stopping point on the Camino de Santiago which cuts across this entire region.

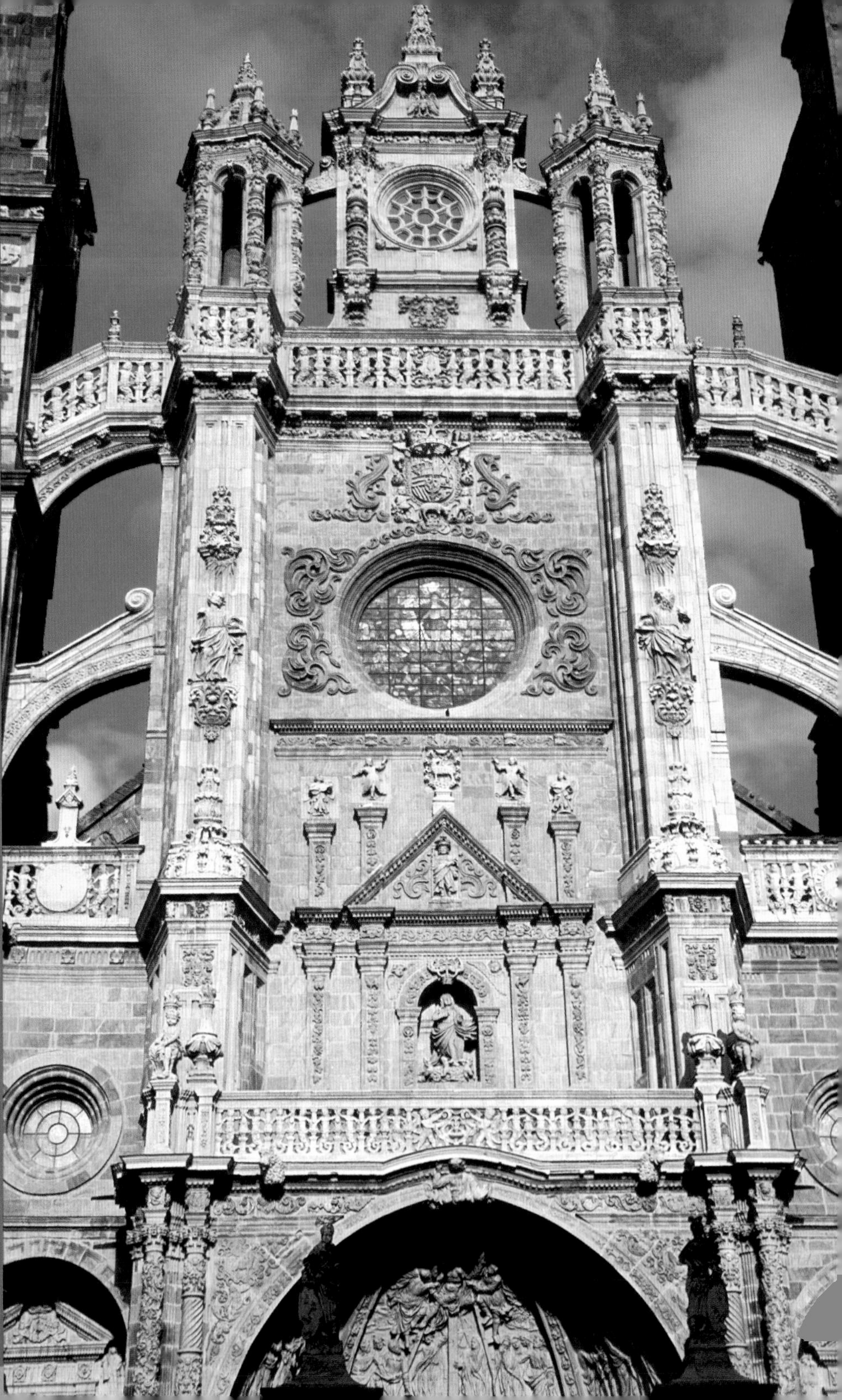

AGUILAR DE CAMPOÓ

www.turwl.com/aguilar

www.aguilardecampoo.com

Originally inhabited by the Iberians, Romans and Visigoths, this isolated town in the broad Pisuerga valley has a rich religious legacy. The imposing Romanesque Monasterio de Santa María la Real (daily 9–2, 4–6; closed Mon) has been heavily restored, but still has a charming cloister. Legend has it that soldier-mercenary El Cid (1026–99) took refuge in the monastery during his campaigns.

The 14th-century Colegiata de San Miguel Arcángel (Jun–Sep daily 10–1.30, 5–7.30; Oct–May 12–1 only by guided tour; reservations tel 600 09 55 15), overlooking the main plaza, retains its Romanesque portal and a fine Renaissance retablo (altarpiece). Around town are numerous stylish mansions, including the 16th-century Palacio de los Manrique, with its two-floored, arched facade.

🞠 464 F2 🛈 Plaza España 15, 34800 Aguilar de Campoó ☎ 979 12 36 41 🚉 Aguilar de Campoó

ASTORGA

www.ayuntamientodeastorga.com

The small, bustling provincial capital of Astorga is a modern town with an eccentric, fairytale-looking Gaudí palace, with soaring granite towers, and a cathedral, which can be seen for some distance across the surrounding flatlands.

The Palacio Episcopal (Tue–Sat 10–2, 4–8, Sun and holidays 10–2), designed by Antoni Gaudí (1852–1926), is a strange addition. Commissioned by Bishop Grau in 1887 after a fire destroyed his original residence, it was finally completed several years later by diocesan architect Ricardo García Guereta, who eventually took over from Gaudí in 1906. Inside the palace is the Museo de los Caminos, with interesting displays on the famous pilgrimage to Santiago de

Compostela (▷ 144–146). Opposite and in complete contrast is the sandstone Gothic-baroque cathedral, originally built in the 15th century and with an intricately sculptured south-facing facade. At night it is superbly lit.

The Museo del Chocolate, for those with a sweet tooth, describes all about the history of Astorga's chocolate industry.

🞠 463 E3 🛈 Plaza Eduardo de Castro 5, 24700 Astorga ☎ 987 61 82 22 🚉 Astorga

BÉJAR

Dramatically perched on a narrow promontory, Béjar is an ideal base for hiking in the adjacent sierra, where several established trails wind between giant boulders and past lakes. The town is a mix of appealing old buildings and dour modern architecture, so it's best to stick to the old town's streets.

In the Plaza Mayor is the fortified 16th-century Palacio Ducal, once home to the dukes of Béjar and now a school, plus an arched arcade and the 13th-century Iglesia de El Salvador. Inside the church are three striking stained-glass windows.

During Corpus Christi festivities, just after Easter, the bizarre Hombres del Musgo (Moss Men) procession commemorates the time when Christian forces retook Béjar from the Arabs by camouflaging themselves with moss. If you miss Corpus Christi, take a drive past the Hombres del Musgo statue on the corner of Calle 20 de Agosto, opposite the Parque de la Antigua

at the westernmost point of the old town. The most spectacular view of the town's precarious location over the Río Cuerpo de Hombre is from the narrow, twisting SA220 road to Ciudad Rodrigo.

🞠 468 E6 🛈 Paseo de Cervantes 6, 37700 Béjar ☎ 923 40 30 05

EL BURGO DE OSMA

www.burgosma.es

Quiet, medieval streets and an enduring monumental legacy make this walled town on the Río Ucero a delightful stop-off. It was first settled in pre-Roman times, when it was called Uxama, and is now best entered via La Puerta de San Miguel, a stone gateway through which the towering cathedral (Jun–Sep Tue–Sun 10–1, 4–7; Oct–May Tue–Sun 10.30–1, 4.30–6) is reached. The cathedral is a mix of Romanesque, Gothic and baroque styles, with an elaborate retablo (altarpiece) and flamboyant cloister, and overlooks the idyllic wooden porticoes and stone fountain of Plaza de San Pedro. Along the cobbled, colonnaded Calle Mayor lies the spacious Plaza Mayor, edged by the 1694 Hospital de San Agustín (Tue–Sun 12–2, 5–8) and the 18th-century ayuntamiento (town hall).

El Burgo de Osma's Roman history, preserved in the form of aqueducts and underground cisterns, can be glimpsed at the Uxama ruin site, 2km (1 mile) southwest of the town along the N-122 road towards Valladolid.

🞠 464 H4 🛈 Plaza Mayor 9, 42300 El Burgo de Osma ☎ 975 36 01 16

Opposite *The richly decorated south facade of Astorga's cathedral*

Right *The fortified walled town of Béjar is set against the backdrop of the Sierra Béjar*

INFORMATION

www.turismoburgos.es

✚ 464 G3 🚉 Burgos ℹ️ Bajos Teatro Principal, Paseo del Espolón s/n, 09003 Burgos ☎ 947 28 88 74 🕐 Jun–Sep Mon–Sat 10–2, 5–8, Sun 10–2; Oct–May Mon–Sat 10–2, 4.30–7.30, Sun 10–2

Above *The cathedral spires and Plaza Mayor at dusk*

Opposite top *El Cid Campeador statue in Plaza del Cid*

Opposite bottom *Arco de Santa María was the main gateway to the city*

INTRODUCTION

Ornate, inspired monuments, a venerable history, refreshing open spaces and a healthy community spirit make Burgos a pleasure to visit. The city is spread along and split in two by the placid, tree-lined Río Arlanzón. Its older, more attractive part lies on the northern side. There, the audacious towers of the Gothic cathedral, a world-renowned example of this most flamboyant period, dominate the skyline. Tucked in among a warren of fashionable shopping streets, such as Calle Vitoria, is a string of other impressive buildings, including Arco de Santa María and Casa del Cordon. For a breath of fresh air, take a stroll along the Paseo del Espolón or climb up the Castillo for great city views.

Originally inhabited by the Romans and by Visigoth tribes, Burgos proper was founded with the construction of a castle for Alfonso III in the late ninth century. By the mid-10th century, Fernán González ruled here as Count of Castile. Legendary warrior Rodrigo Díaz de Vivar—better known as El Cid Campeador— was born at nearby Vivar del Cid, and he and his wife, Doña Jimena, are buried in Burgos Cathedral. Fernando I made the city the capital of Castilla y León in the 11th century, and Alfonso VI made it the episcopal seat by building the original cathedral, subsequently replaced by Fernando III's Gothic masterpiece. In the 15th and 16th centuries the city enjoyed a period of immense success that saw the construction of many of its monuments, but by the mid-18th century its fortunes were waning. Badly hit by Napoleon's forces in the early 19th-century War of Independence and used by Franco as his base during the Spanish Civil War, Burgos only really regained its prosperity in the late 20th century.

WHAT TO SEE

CATEDRAL

www.catedraldeburgos.es

Burgos' main draw, both for pilgrims on the Camino and visitors, is its great Gothic cathedral, a UNESCO World Heritage monument, whose construction, started in the 13th century, continued for 500 years. It overlooks both the Plaza de Santa María, with its exquisite fountain and traditional inns, and the Plaza del

Rey San Fernando, lined with cafés and Castile's typical glass-balconied houses. Justifiably claiming to be one of the world's most beautiful Gothic structures, the cathedral has a towering facade, with two latticed, pinnacled spires soaring towards the heavens.

The first impression of the interior is of over-bearing richness and complexity; it's better to concentrate on the individual side chapels and their works of art. The Capilla de los Condestables, at the opposite end to the main entrance, is the most striking, with a star-shaped vault and triple retablo (altarpiece), including work by the brothers Gil and Diego de Siloé. In the north transept is the extraordinary Escalera Dorada, a double stairway built by Diego de Siloé in 1519 to make up for the difference in levels between the cathedral floor and the upper street.

More star vaulting covers the Capilla de la Consolación and rises to the central dome, a fitting background for the simple stone slab beneath that marks the burial place of El Cid (see Introduction opposite). The choir stalls, museum and 14th-century cloister, reached via four other chapels, are all well worth seeing.

✉ Plaza del Rey San Fernando ☎ 947 20 47 12 🕐 Mid-Mar to Oct 9.30–7; Nov to mid-Mar 10–6 ✋ Adult €5, child (7–14) €1, under 7 free 🎧 Audioguide €4

TIP
» The modern CAB (Centro de Arte Contemporáneo; www.cabdeburgos.com) is a sleek new museum featuring exciting new art.

ARCO DE SANTA MARÍA
The main medieval city access gate was the substantial Arco de Santa María, leading to the Puente Santa María (one of eight bridges in the city) from Plaza del Rey San Fernando. Built in the 14th century and redesigned in the 16th century in the name of Charles V, its exuberant facade, all turrets and battlements, is decorated with chunky statues which include El Cid and Charles V himself. Inside the tower is an interesting art museum and the Museo de Farmacia, lined from floor to ceiling with porcelain medicine jars.

✉ Plaza del Rey San Fernando ☎ Art museum and Museo de Farmacia: 947 22 88 68 🕐 Art museum and Museo de Farmacia: Tue–Sat 11–2, 5–9, Sun 11–2 ✋ Art museum and Museo de Farmacia: free

MONASTERIO DE SANTA MARÍA LA REAL DE HUELGAS
This outwardly austere and militaristic-looking monastery, noted for its Mudéjar craftsmanship, lies on the city's western outskirts, about 1km (0.6 mile) from central Burgos. It was founded in 1187, and such was its power and standing that many Castilian rulers were buried here, including Fernando III and Alfonso XI. The main church, with its opulent Churrigueresque (Spanish baroque) retablo (alterpiece), contains the tombs of 16 monarchs, including Henry II of England's daughter, Eleanor, and her husband and monastery co-founder, Alfonso VIII. Other tombs of note are those of Los Infantes de la Cerda and Doña Berenguela (mother of Fernando III). In the Sala Capitular, off the superb Romanesque cloister with its Mudéjar decoration, you can see the standard captured by Christian forces when they decisively defeated the Moors at the Battle of Navas de Tolosa in 1212. The Museo de las Ricas Telas has an outstanding collection of textiles, jewels and weapons found in the tombs.

✉ Compases de Huelgas s/n ☎ 947 20 16 30 🕐 Monastery and museum: Tue–Sat 10–1.15, 3.45–5.45, Sun and holidays 10.30–2.15 ✋ Monastery and museum: €5.50

CARTUJA DE MIRAFLORES
Some 4km (2.5 miles) to the east of the city, in secluded woodland, is the still active Carthusian monastery of Cartuja de Miraflores. In front of the high altar is Gil de Siloé's sensational, star-shaped, alabaster tomb of the parents of Catholic Monarch Isabel I, Juan II of Castile and Isabel of Portugal. Siloé was also responsible for the magnificent altarpiece, gilded with the first gold to arrive from the Americas, and the tomb of the Infante Alfonso, who died in 1468, leaving Isabel to succeed to the throne of Castile.

🕐 Mon–Sat 10–3, 4–6, Sun and festivals 11.20–12.30, 1–3, 4–6 ✋ Free

INFORMATION

www.castillodecoca.com

➕ 464 F4 ✉ Castillo de Coca, 40480 Coca ☎ 617 57 35 54 🌐 Apr–Sep daily 10.30–1, 4.30–7; Oct–Mar Mon–Fri 10.30–1, 4.30–6, Sat–Sun 11–1, 4–6. Closed 1st Tue of every month 👆 €3.50 👆 All visits by guided tour 🏛

CASTILLO DE COCA

The multi-towered Castillo de Coca, a rich blend of Gothic and Mudéjar styles, soars above the treetops in the otherwise unremarkable town of Coca. This castle, more than any other in Spain, fulfils every storybook notion of what a castle should look like, with its double layer of crenellated walls and bristling towers. The decorative use of brick, attributed to Mudéjar craftsmen, is what sets the castle apart from others of the era. The bricks provide elegant ornamental stripes along the facades and adorn the archways. The castle was constructed from 1453 onwards, and was finally completed around the end of the century, but was attacked soon after in 1521. However, the damage inflicted then was nothing compared with that suffered in 1808, when Napoleon stationed his troops here during the War of Independence. The French sacked and burned the town, destroying valuable municipal archives, and left the castle in ruins. In 1931 the castle was declared a national monument.

THE EXTERIOR

Visible from far away, the castle's most striking features are its restored Mudéjar walls, among the best examples of this military style in Spain. The castle is built around a deep, dry moat from alternate rose and grey limestone bricks, with bold turrets and towers and fine geometric decorative detail. Of its four towers, the biggest is La Torre del Homenaje, 25m (80ft) high; from the top there are sweeping views over the town and surrounding pine forests. The gardens around the moat are well maintained, with flowers year round.

THE INTERIOR

Inside the castle there is a series of rooms and a chapel set around the Patio de las Armas, a reconstruction of the original. The Capilla (chapel) has two Flemish panels showing the Annunciation and Crucifixion, and a scallop-shaped font that was taken from the town's old Iglesia de Santiago. On display in the Sala de Armas, patterned with red, white and blue Moorish tiles, are suits of armour, a Moorish chair and historical documents, including the agreement between the archbishop of Seville and Juan II of Castile to build the fortress. The adjoining museum has Roman and Celtiberian archaeological objects, ceramics and five marble pillars.

The Sala de los Jarros (Jug Room), inside the Torre Pedro Mata, has such superb acoustics that your whispered voice will bounce back at you from different directions. You can climb out on to the rooftops of the inner courtyard for more splendid views, and a look at the cold dungeons rounds off the visit.

Opposite left *The donkey is still a popular form of transportation in Covarrubias*
Opposite right *The cloister of Ciudad Rodrigo's Gothic cathedral*
Below *Castillo de Coca*

CASTILLO DE LA MOTA

To see a fairytale castle, visit this candy-pink fortress overlooking Medina del Campo. Built in Mudéjar style from a bewildering number of bricks in the 15th century, its walls bear multiple cannonball scars. Stroll around the outer wall for great views over Medina and the surrounding area. Isabel I lived here for several years until her death and it once served as a state prison. Inside, only the sparse lower floor is open to visitors. There is a small chapel, a salon with an odd collection of old chairs, a 1912 Austrian piano and, on the wall, a painted world map.

✚ 464 F4 ✉ Castillo de la Mota, 47400 Medina del Campo ☎ 983 80 10 24 ◐ Mon–Sat 11–2, 4–7 (Oct–Mar 4–6), Sun 11–2 🖐 Free 🚉 Medina del Campo

CIUDAD RODRIGO

www.turismociudadrodrigo.com

Thanks to its strategic location in the Río Águeda valley near the Portuguese border, this fortified town is awash with military history. French troops ransacked it during the War of Independence and the Duke of Wellington retook the city in 1812, earning him the title Duke of Ciudad Rodrigo. Fernando II of León built the jagged city wall in the 12th century and also constructed the substantial cathedral (daily 12–2, 4–6), primarily Romanesque-Gothic in style, with three naves and a cannonball-pocked facade.

The uninspiring 16th-century castle is now an ivy-draped *parador*, and the Plaza Mayor is graced by the elegant arches of the Casa Consistorial government building, also built in the 16th century. A good way to get a feel for the whole city is to walk the walls. This 2.2km (1.4-mile) stroll offers superb views of the narrow streets, with their Renaissance houses and palaces, and of the *meseta* (plateau) landscape. Signs indicate notable spots en route, such as where Wellington's troops breached the defences, and sporadic access points allow shorter walk options.

✚ 468 D5 ⛊ Plaza Mayor 7, 37500 Ciudad Rodrigo ☎ 923 49 84 00 🚉 Ciudad Rodrigo

COVARRUBIAS

www.ecovarrubias.com

Few places can match the medieval feel of Covarrubias, with its half-timbered houses, peaceful atmosphere and impressive religious monuments. Although popular with visitors, especially during weekends, it retains its character. An arched portal in the fortified walls leads to the cobbled streets, which have just a few café-bars and local shops.

The splendid 10th-century Colegiata (Wed–Mon 10.30–2, 4–7) contains numerous tombs, including those of Princess Kristina of Norway, who married Don Felipe, brother of Alfonso X of Castile, and Fernán

González, founder and hero of Castile (*d* AD970). Its 16th-century Gothic cloisters, Flemish triptych by Gil de Siloé (active 1467–1505) and church organ also stand out.

✚ 464 G3 ⛊ Monseñor Vargas Blanco s/n, 09346 Covarrubias ☎ 947 40 64 61

CUEVAS DE VALPORQUERO

These extraordinary karst caves lie at an altitude of 1,309m (4,295ft) in the Los Argüellos mountains. Water power has shaped a convoluted network of chambers through the limestone rock, including Pequeñas Maravillas, with its beautiful, illuminated lake, and the Virgen con Niño, a famous formation resembling Mary holding the baby Jesus.

Gran Rotonda is the largest accessible cavern, measuring 5,600sq m (60,300sq ft) in area and with a ceiling 20m (66ft) high, while the Cementerio Estalactitico is awe-inspiring. The 2km (1.2-mile) tour is reached via a constructed stairway and path, and is undertaken in constant year-round conditions of 7°C (45°F) temperature and 90 per cent humidity.

Except in the summer months, the Cascada de Hadas emerges from the rocks 15m (50ft) up in the Hadas chamber.

✚ 463 E2 ✉ Cuevas de Valporquero, Diputación Provincial de León, Plaza de Regla s/n, 24071 León ☎ 987 57 64 08 ◐ 18 May–Sep daily 10–2, 3.30–7; 16 Mar–17 May, Oct–15 Dec Fri–Sun and festivals 10–5. Closed 16 Dec–15 Mar 🖐 Adult €7, child (6–14) €5.50; under 6 free ⛏ Visit by guided tour only

INFORMATION

www.leon.es
✚ 463 e2 🚉 León 🛈 Plaza de Regla 3, 24003 León ☎ 987 23 70 82, also 902 20 30 30 ⚙ Jun–Sep daily 9–8; Oct–May 9–2, 4–6

INTRODUCTION

León is best explored on foot. In addition to its three architectural master-pieces, stylish León has several refined squares, such as Plaza de San Marcos; a pedestrian-only old quarter, known as Barrio Húmedo; and attractive walkways, including those just off the Avenida de la Facultad de Veterinaria, which follows the Río Bernesga. Gardens dotted with cafés and the odd market stall provide popular *paseos* (promenades) and add to the city's overall appeal.

Founded by the Romans, the city of León owes its name to the legion of Legio VII Gemina Pia Felix, which first quartered here. Rome later established a permanent settlement and Legio became León. In around the third century León became the chief city of the Christian advance across the northern mountains. It was totally destroyed in AD998, when a Moorish raid tore down the Roman walls, but was reconquered in 999. Alfonso V of León was crowned king here in the same year, initiating an era of grandeur that saw the kingdoms of León and Castile united in 1230 under Fernando I and a surge in the number of pilgrims en route to Santiago de Compostela (▷ 144–146). For the next 700 years León suffered from a gradual decline, until its fortunes recovered at the end of the 19th century. In 1934 the poorer workers of the city joined the miners of Asturias in the October Revolt, an attempt to resist the spread of fascism. It failed; around 2,000 miners lost their lives and their villages were ransacked in the precursor to the Spanish Civil War.

WHAT TO SEE

CATEDRAL

www.catedraldeleon.org
The focal point of Plaza de Regla is the 13th-century Gothic cathedral, with an enormous yet delicately beautiful rose window. Above the flying buttresses and pinnacles two soaring towers stand free of the main west facade. Beneath

are some of the best examples of Spanish Gothic sculpture, in the Puerta de la Virgen Blanca, the central doorway, including the figure of Santa María la Blanca on the central shaft and scenes of the Last Judgement above. Inside, the many stained-glass windows create a magical spectrum of lights, with blues, reds, greens, purples and golds. The 16th-century two-tiered retrochoir (the space behind the altar) is considered the most important in Spain. The excellent Museo Catedralicio-Diocesano, in the cloisters, contains a wide-ranging collection of works, including a series of wooden statues of the Virgin Mary dating from Roman times.

✉ Plaza de Regla 4 ☎ 987 87 57 70 🕓 Cathedral: summer Mon–Sat 8.30–1.30, 4–8, Sun 8.30–2.30, 5–8; rest of year until 7pm. Museum: Jul–Sep Mon–Fri 9.30–2, 4–7.30, Sat 9.30–2, 4–7; Jun Mon–Sat 9.30–1.30, 4–7; Oct–May Mon–Fri 9.30–1.30, 4–7, Sat 9.30–1.30 ✋ Cathedral: free. Museum: €5, cloister only €1.

PANTEÓN REAL

The Panteón Real (Royal Pantheon) of the early kings of Castile and León and the adjoining Basílica de San Isidoro together form one of Europe's most significant monuments. Built to house the relics of St. Isidore, the largely Romanesque basilica was completed in 1149 by Petrus de Ustambem. Inside, more than 200 capitals crown the columns, depicting myriad religious scenes, including the Last Supper. Outside, the main facade is dominated by the Puerta del Cordero (Doorway of the Lamb) and Puerta del Perdón (Doorway of Pardon). Next door is the Panteón Real, whose two sunken vaults contain the tombs of 23 kings and queens and 12 royal children. The ceilings of the chambers are decorated with some of the finest frescoes of Romanesque art. Scenes include images of winged bulls, angels and Jesus, painted in terracotta reds and eggshell blues.

✉ Plaza de San Isidoro 4

HOSTAL DE SAN MARCOS

www.parador.es

Originally built by the Knights of Santiago, the Hostal de San Marcos is an extraordinary spectacle of lavish ornamentation, with a massive facade measuring 100m (330ft) long. It is a double-decker arrangement of medallions, columns and niches in the plateresque style. The building, once a hospital and hospice, and even a prison, is now a plush *parador*. It consists of three main parts: the luxury hotel, with a café-bar open to non-residents; Renaissance cloisters; and a church behind a grand doorway heavily decorated with scallop shells, at the far right of the facade. The cloisters, also accessible to non-guests, are lined with religious statues and headstones. Visitors can ask to venture farther into the *parador*, up the grand stairway to the upper floor of the cloister.

✉ Plaza de San Marcos 7 ☎ 987 23 73 00

BARRIO HÚMEDO

The network of small backstreets that makes up the Barrio Húmedo, or 'wet quarter', so-dubbed for its numerous watering holes and taverns, lies south of the cathedral and north of Plaza Mayor. It is the heart of León's social life, with tapas bars, cafés and restaurants. Each evening the area buzzes with activity as people move from bar to bar before dinner.

MORE TO SEE

MUSEO DE ARTE CONTEMPORÀNEO DE CASTILLA Y LEÓN

www.musac.es

One of the most dramatic contemporary buildings in the city contains this stimulating new museum of contemporary art. MUSAC also offers a varied programme of activities, from films to music.

✉ Avenida de los Reyes Leoneses, 24008 León ☎ 978 09 00 00 🕓 Tue–Sun 10–3, 4–9 ✋ Free

Opposite top *The rose window and towers of the cathedral*
Opposite bottom *Passing the time of day and catching up on the gossip*
Below *Detail from the Gothic cathedral*

REGIONS CASTILE-LEÓN AND LA RIOJA • SIGHTS

HARO

www.haro.org

Wine and more wine, exquisite houses and a charming plaza characterize this 10th-century hilltop town at the heart of La Rioja wine region overlooking the Río Tirón and Río Ebro. Haro's long-held reputation for wine was further enhanced by a group of Bordeaux viniculturalists who set up business here around 1880 after their own region suffered from the *phylloxera* vine blight.

The Plaza de La Paz has porticoed walkways and fine glass-balconied apartments, although cars are prevalent too. Along the narrow street leading to the late-Gothic Iglesia Santo Tomás are numerous bodegas (wineries) and bars that offer deals to lure Rioja wine-lovers in their direction.

Considering that Haro is surrounded by bodegas, surprisingly few offer tours. However, La Muga, in the Barrio de Bodegas, has one of the best (Jun–Sep Mon–Fri 10 (English), 11 and 12 (Spanish); Oct–May 11 and 4.30, Spanish only; visits must be reserved in advance, tel 941 30 60 60). The Museo del Vino (Mon–Sat 10–2, 4–8, Sun 10–2) has interesting, if text-heavy (Spanish only), displays explaining the entire wine process, and can be found on three floors opposite the Estación Enológica on Avenida Bretón de los Hererros.

✚ 465 H3 ℹ Plaza Monseñor Florentino Rodríguez s/n, 26200 Haro ☎ 941 30 33 66

LERMA

www.citlerma.com

A grandiose palace, a vast plaza and an eclectic huddle of churches and monasteries give hilltop Lerma more interest than its harsh *meseta* (plateau) surroundings may imply. The town provides a brief and absorbing insight into the sense of greatness that suffused the population of Spain during the golden days of the 17th century.

Lerma was founded in the Middle Ages, but it was the appointment in 1598 of Felipe III's ostentatious ally, Don Francisco Gómez, as Duke of Lerma that heralded the construction of both the overwhelming Palacio Ducal, now a *parador* (state-run hotel) with its impressive courtyards, and the adjacent, immense Plaza Mayor.

Among several other buildings dating from the Duke's time is the Iglesia Colegial de San Pedro (guided tours daily; reserve in the information office), with a statue of his archbishop uncle.

Next to the information office is an arched passageway that links up with the ex-Convento de Santa Teresa overlooking the Río Arlanza.

Beyond the old town's stone gateway, the Arco de la Cárcel (prison arch), are the steep, cobbled streets that surround Calle del General Mola.

✚ 464 G3 ℹ Calle Audiencia 6 bajo, 09340 Lerma ☎ 947 17 70 02 🚉 Lerma

LEÓN

▷ 294–295.

LOGROÑO

www.logroturismo.org

La Rioja's engaging and vibrant capital is a mix of notable churches, spacious parks and modern practicality, with plenty going on for culture vultures and tapas-lovers.

For centuries the Puente de Piedra bridge spanning the Río Ebro demarcated the kingdoms of Castile and Navarra. Nowadays pilgrims cross it to reach the cobbled Rúa Vieja, leading to the Iglesia de Santiago, and then leave Logróno via Puerta de Revellín, a pretty archway through the old town wall.

A regal sculpture of 19th-century war hero General Espartero, mounted on horseback, presides over the beautiful Paseo de Espolón park at the heart of the city.

The Catedral de la Redonda (Mon–Sat 8–1, 6.30–8.45, Sun 9–2, 6.30–8.45) was built between the 12th and 18th centuries, and its imposing towers dominate every view of the city. Inside are three naves separated by grand columns and a majestic organ.

Every September the Fiesta de San Mateo explodes on to the streets and into the bars of Logroño. This is a great time to visit, with fireworks, drinking, music, feasts and parades.

✚ 465 H3 ℹ Calle Portales 29 bis, 26001 Lograño ☎ 941 27 33 53

Below left *Arcaded shopping on the Plaza Mayor in Lerma*

Below *A cobbled pathway leads to the Iglesia Colegial de San Pedro in Lerma*

Above *Hardware shop in Palencia, the provincial capital*
Left *The red rock formations of Las Médulas, in the wild Bierzo mountains of León*

LAS MÉDULAS

www.fundacionlasmedulas.com

Las Médulas is like a miniature Grand Canyon. Orange rock spires, vast caves and a broad, wooded canyon setting make its mines an extraordinary sight. The Romans came here in the first century AD looking for gold and developed innovative open-cast mining techniques. They constructed vast stretches of canals around the mountains (several of which can be explored today) and forced water through tunnels to undermine the mountainside. They then sifted the debris for gold.

Las Médulas, a UNESCO World Heritage Site, is crossed by a network of footpaths that leads visitors through the great basin, where the mouths of truncated tunnels can still be seen in the cliff faces. The Mirador de Orellán gives a breathtaking panoramic view of the area, and the chance to see how natural and human history—albeit a very destructive mining operation—can meld together with time. The superb countryside here also has enjoyable walks. Entrance tickets can be bought at the visitor office and tours leave from here; there is also a fascinating exhibition with interactive computer displays charting the history of the mines.

➕ 464 D3 ✉ Instituto de Estudios Bercianos, Aula Arqueológica de Las Médulas, 24442 Las Médulas ☎ 987 42 28 48 🕐 Visitor office: Apr–Sep daily 10–1.30, 3.30–6 (Sun 10–2); Oct–Mar Sat 10–1.30, 3.30–6, Sun 10–2. Mine site: open at all times ✋ Adult €2, under 8 free ☕ Hourly; €2.50; must be reserved in advance, tel 619 25 83 55

MONASTERIO DE SANTA MARÍA LA REAL

www.najera.es

Nájera is most famous for being on the Camino de Santiago pilgrimage route (▷ 144–146) and has only one thing to detain you: The spectacular 11th-century Monasterio de Santa María la Real is one of five on La Rioja's Ruta de los Monasterios (Route of the Monasteries). It was founded in 1032 by García Sánchez III after he discovered an image of the Virgin here, and features the majestic Claustro de los Caballeros, Gothic-style cloisters with plateresque windows. The Gothic wooden choir stalls, El Coro, were built in 1495 and are among the best in Spain. In the Panteón de los Reyes are tombs and sarcophagi of Castile-León and La Rioja nobility and founding kings. At the heart of the monastery is the cave where García found the Virgin image.

➕ 465 H3 ✉ 26300 Nájera ☎ 941 36 10 83 🕐 Tue–Sat 10–1, 4–5.30, Sun and holidays 10–12.30, 4–5.30 ✋ €3 ☕ Guided visits (in Spanish) available if reserved in advance: adult €4, under 12 €1

PALENCIA

www.turismocastillayleon.com

Sprouting out of the vast Tierra del Campo flatlands is the town of Palencia, whose main attractions cluster around the Gothic cathedral. Dominating the Plaza de Inmaculada Concepción, the cathedral was erected between the 14th and 16th centuries. In the Capilla Mayor is an outstanding plateresque retablo (altarpiece) by Juan de Flandes, and below it is a Visigothic crypt with sturdy arches. In 1208 Alfonso VIII set up Spain's first university in Palencia.

Of the several museums in the town, the Museo Catedralicio (mid-May to Sep Mon–Sat 8.45–1.30, 4.30–7.30, Sun 11.15–1; Oct to mid-May Mon–Sat 8.45–1.30, 4–6.30, Sun 11.15–1), with paintings by El Greco and Zurbarán, stands out.

➕ 464 F3 ℹ Calle Mayor 105, 34001 Palencia ☎ 979 74 00 68 🚉 Palencia

PARQUE NATURAL RÍO LOBOS

www.turismocastillayleon.com

With its high cliffs, eagles and caves, the Parque Natural Río Lobos, near Ucero, is a little-known treasure for walkers and nature-lovers. The most popular attraction in the 25km (15-mile) canyon is the 12th-century Ermita de San Bartolomé, part of a Cistercian monastery overlooked by a giant cave.

Carved out by the Río Lobos, the verdant canyon is also home to vultures, wild boar, otters and wild cats. The Puente de los Siete Ojos is an impressive bridge, lying halfway up the canyon, between Ucero and Hontoria del Pinar. It is best reached via a 12km (7.5-mile) trail but can also be seen from the SO-960 minor road from San Leonardo de Yagüe. Several other well-marked trails allow short strolls or full-day walks.
✚ 464 H4 ℹ Centro de Visitantes del Parque, Antigua Piscifactoría, 42317 Ucero ☎ 975 36 35 64 🚫 Closed 15 Dec–15 Mar

PEÑAFIEL

www.turismopenafiel.com

Peñafiel's main landmark, a white-stone castle set on a high ridge, is visible from a long way off and conjures up images of a stranded battleship. Originally built in the 10th century, its walls and central tower were reconstructed in 1466 by Juan II. Occupying the castle's interior is the excellent Museo Provincial del Vino, which reveals the wine-making process through interactive displays, videos and audio tours.

Walking the ramparts of the castle gives outstanding views over the Río Duero and the old town. Look for the antiquated, wooden Plaza del Coso which hosts bullfights in August.
✚ 464 G4 ℹ Plaza del Coso 2, 47300 Peñafiel ☎ 983 88 15 26

PEÑARANDA DE DUERO

www.penarandadeduero.com

Peace and quiet and an unspoiled medieval heart make this town an ideal interlude en route through the Duero valley. The town is dominated by its 15th-century hilltop castle (closed), and its Plaza de Condes de Miranda is overlooked by the 16th-century Palacio Avellanada and the 17th-century La Colegiata de Santa Ana (both closed Mon). Around the plaza, medieval wooden-beamed houses supported on stone-pillared arcades look out on to the Gothic roll of justice monument, where justice was once meted out to criminals.
✚ 464 G4 ℹ Calle Trinquete 7, 09410 Peñaranda de Duero ☎ 947 55 20 63

Above *Detail of Christ as a pilgrim in Santo Domingo de Silos*
Below *Roofscape of Peñaranda de Duero*

SALAMANCA

▷ 300–303.

SAN MIGUEL DE ESCALADA

Hidden away on the right bank of the Río Esla among rolling hills is this curious church, regarded as one of the province's architectural jewels. A journey through pleasant farmlands and tiny hamlets leads to the small, restored building, the only remaining part of a monastery that was built here over an earlier, Visigothic chapel in AD913 by monks from Córdoba. Pilgrims en route to León detoured to see its distinct Mozarabic style, with marble columns supporting three horseshoe naves, and the splendid twelve-arched porch.

✚ 464 E3 ✉ Carretera Mansilla de las Mulas, 24166 Escalada ☎ 987 33 31 53 (town hall) 🕐 May–Oct Tue 10.15–2, Wed–Sun 10.15–2, 4.30–8; Nov–Apr Tue–Sat 10–2, 4–6, Sun 10–2 💲 Free

SANTO DOMINGO DE LA CALZADA

www.santodomingodelacalzada.org

A legendary miracle of resurrected fowl, atmospheric old streets and a pilgrim heritage make this town one of the region's most popular attractions. It was founded by Santo Domingo in the 11th century, when he built his own hermitage here following rejection by nearby monasteries, and protrudes from the plains around the Río Oja.

Inside the grand cathedral, a live cockerel and hen are kept on display to mark Santo Domingo's miraculous resurrection of a pilgrim after he was killed for rebuffing the advances of an innkeeper's daughter. When the *corregidor* (local ruler) heard the pilgrim still lived, he declared in disbelief that he was as alive as the cooked cock and hen on his dinner plate; at this point, it is claimed, the birds promptly got up and flew off.

The Convento de San Francisco, on the town's ring road, has beautiful cloisters inside and the interesting Monumento al Peregrino (Pilgrim's Monument) outside.

✚ 464 H3 ⓘ Calle Mayor 70, 26250 Santo Domingo de la Calzada ☎ 941 34 12 30

Above *Plaza Mayor and Torre Exenta, Santo Domingo de la Calzada*

SANTO DOMINGO DE SILOS

www.abadiadesilos.es

Set among gentle *meseta* (plateau) hills, the town of Santo Domingo de Silos has just one major highlight, an active Benedictine monastery (tel 947 39 00 49, Tue–Sat 10–1, 4.30–6, Sun, Mon and festivals 4.30–6), although it warrants any length of detour.

When the monk Domingo Manso (his saintly status was bestowed at his death) arrived in Silos in 1041, he rebuilt its monastery, which had previously been destroyed by Moorish attacks. Only in the 13th century was it renamed the Monasterio de Santo Domingo in tribute to his work.

With a hulking, unadorned exterior looking down on the village's red-tiled roofs, the monastery's delicate and richly decorated interior comes as a surprise. In addition, there is a fine two-floored Roman cloister which has columns with interesting capitals and reliefs depicting Christ as a pilgrim, the Ascension and the doubting of St. Thomas. Look up in the lower cloister and admire the brightly decorated and artistic wooden panels of the Mudéjar ceiling.

Just 3km (2 miles) from Silos is the narrow and deep Cañon de Yecla. This dramatic natural feature can be safely explored along a pathway built on to the rock face.

✚ 464 G3 ⓘ Calle Audiencia 6 bajo, 09340 Lerma ☎ 947 17 70 02

SIERRA DE GREDOS

www.gredos.net

With many peaks soaring to more than 2,000m (6,500ft) and its network of winding, quiet roads, the Sierra de Gredos is a popular destination for hikers and drivers alike. This impressive, rugged range, hemmed in by the Río Tormes to the north and Río Tiétar in the south, rises up from the valleys to its high point of Pico Almanzor, at 2,592m (8,504ft).

A network of trails criss-crosses the range, including the popular route from La Plataforma up to the aptly named Laguna Grande, a striking, high mountain lake below Almanzor. Other walking hotspots are reached from El Hornillo (the start point for hikes along the main Circo de Gredos route) and El Arenal, both of which lie above Arenas de San Pedro.

Wildlife-lovers who spend any length of time in the mountains are likely to see, among other animals, mountain goats, eagles, red kites and goshawks.

Of the surrounding towns and villages, El Barco de Ávila, with a Gothic church and 14th-century castle, and Arenas de San Pedro, with its 14th-century Castillo de la Triste Condesa (Castle of the Sad Countess), are worth a brief visit in themselves.

✚ 469 E6 ⓘ Plaza Mayor 2, 05600 El Barco de Ávila ☎ 920 34 08 88 ⓘ Ávila

INTRODUCTION

Salamanca has an old district largely built from sandstone quarried at nearby Villamayor. It is compact and easily explored on foot, with its main sites grouped together between the central Plaza Mayor and the Río Tormes. The network of narrow and winding streets that branches out from this square is full of superbly constructed buildings.

Salamanca was besieged by Hannibal in 217BC and acted as an important cross-country staging post for silver shipments when under Roman occupation. The city then changed hands between Moorish and Christian armies several times during the medieval battle for Spain. However, it was only the founding of its university in the early 13th century and the subsequent establishment of numerous monasteries, convents and churches that put Salamanca on the international map. Felipe II married his first wife, María of Portugal, here in 1543. After a slow decline in fortunes from the 17th century onwards, the city suffered particularly badly during the War of Independence (1808–14), when many of its finest buildings were destroyed. Franco used it as his headquarters during the Spanish Civil War. Today the city is particularly popular with foreign-language students and has retained enough of its medieval glory to have been designated a World Heritage Site by UNESCO in 1988 and European City of Culture in 2002, for which it styled itself 'a town of thoughts, meetings and knowledge'.

WHAT TO SEE

UNIVERSIDAD DE SALAMANCA

www.usal.es

Founded in 1218, Salamanca's university was a powerhouse of European thought and at least the equal of rivals at Oxford, Paris and Bologna. Its Escuelas Mayores still has a remarkable sandstone facade dating from 1534 at its entrance, featuring popes, the busts of monarchs Fernando V and Isabel I (who paid for all the work), a battle between Venus and Hercules, and a small frog that is reputed to bring good luck to those who spot it. In the square in front of the university is a statue of Fray Luis de León (1527–91), a leading academic who was imprisoned by the Inquisition, and who returned to the lecture room several years later to begin with his habitual and now famous words: 'As we were saying yesterday…'. Although you can't enter it, the upstairs library has a fine wooden ceiling, but it is also possible to see Fray Luis's lecture room — virtually unchanged since the 16th century. Opposite the Escuelas Mayores is

INFORMATION

www.salamanca.es

✚ 468 E5 🚆 Salamanca ℹ️ Plaza Mayor 32, 37000 Salamanca ☎ 923 21 83 42 🕐 Mon–Sat 9–2, 4.30–8, Sun 9–2, 4.30–6.30 ❓ A smaller branch is at the Casa de las Conchas (▷ 303)

Opposite *Convento de las Dueñas, with the cathedral in the background*
Below left *Relaxing in Plaza Mayor*
Below *Detail on a building in Plaza Mayor*

TIPS

» The main fiestas are held on 12 June and 8 September, but the city is just as pleasant in winter and has fewer visitors and students at this time.

» Try the local meal of *chanfaina*, a pork and rice dish that sometimes also includes tripe.

the Museo Universitario, almost hidden among cloister arches. It has a beautiful ceiling depicting the zodiac painted by Fernando Gallego in 1490, once in the university's library.

✚ 303 A2 ✉ Patio de las Escuelas 1 (off Calle de los Libreros) ☎ 923 29 44 00 🕐 University and Museum: Mon–Fri 9.30–1.30, 4–7, Sat 9.30–1.30, 4–6.30, Sun 10–2 💲 University and Museum: €5, under 12 free (free Mon 9.30–1.30)

PLAZA MAYOR

This is simply the loveliest square in Spain. It was built between 1729 and 1755 under the orders of Felipe V in thanks for the city's support during the War of the Spanish Succession earlier that century. The plaza was designed by Alberto Churriguera (1676–1750), who along with his two brothers gave his name to an ornate form of baroque architecture (Churrigueresque) and who was responsible for many of the city's finest buildings. The plaza is arcaded with iron balconies and plaques that commemorate Spanish monarchs from Alfonso XI right up to the current Juan Carlos, and take in Franco and various noblemen and explorers. It is also home to the impressive Pabellón Real (Royal Pavilion) and *ayuntamiento* (town hall). Bullfights were held in the square until the 19th century, but now it is the hub of the city's social life and is a good spot to wander around, shop or people-watch over an expensive cup of coffee (preferably at sunset, when the light on the sandstone is at its prettiest).

✚ 303 A1

CATEDRAL NUEVA AND CATEDRAL VIEJA

www.catedralsalamanca.org

Construction work on the Catedral Nueva started in 1513, but it took 200 years to finish. Apart from enormously high naves, it features elaborate baroque choir stalls, bas-relief columns that look like palm trees and magnificent Renaissance doorways, including the 17th-century baroque entrance that was restored to include an astronaut. The finest chapels are the Capilla Dorada, Todos los Santos and Nuestra Señora de la Soledad. Outside, the west front is famous for its intricate stonework. Work on the adjoining older, smaller and less gaudy Romanesque Catedral Vieja began in the mid-12th century and was completed in the early 13th century. Its Byzantine dome is known as the Torre del Gallo (Cockerel Tower) and can be seen from almost anywhere in the city. Inside, there are 13th-century murals by Antón Sánchez de Segovia and a stately 15th-century altarpiece by Nicholas of Florence. The latter features Salamanca's patron saint, La Virgen de la Vega, and 53 panels depicting incidents from the lives of Christ and the Virgin Mary. Also worth investigating is the enclosed cloister, with its Gothic tombs; the chapterhouse; the Capilla de San Martín, with frescoes dating from 1242; and the Capilla de Santa Catalina, with its interesting gargoyles. Ente the Catedral Vieja from the Catedral Nueva.

✚ 303 A2 ✉ Plaza Juan XXIII ☎ 923 21 74 76 🕐 Jul–Aug daily 9–8; Jun, Sep 10–1.30, 4–5.30; Sep–Jun 10–12.30, 4–5.30 💲 Catedral Vieja: €5

Below *The main entrance of the Catedral Nueva is adorned with plateresque relief carvings*

CONVENTO DE SAN ESTEBAN

The city is full of stunning religious buildings but the pick of them is this 16th-century convent, with an especially beautiful facade in the plateresque style featuring the Crucifixion and the stoning of St. Stephen (San Esteban in Spanish) by Juan Antonio Ceroni (1610). Inside is an ornate 1693 altarpiece by Alberto Churriguera, a collection of paintings, shrines, silver and gold objects, and the score of a 10th-century Gregorian chant. Opposite, and almost as fine, is the Convento de las Dueñas, a former Mudéjar palace with 16th-century pentagonal cloisters and, in the upstairs gallery, carvings depicting several characters from Dante's *Divine Comedy*.

✚ 303 B2 ✉ Plaza del Concilio de Trento s/n ☎ 923 21 50 00 🕐 Jun–Sep daily 9–1, 4–8; Oct–May 9–1, 4–7 💲 €2

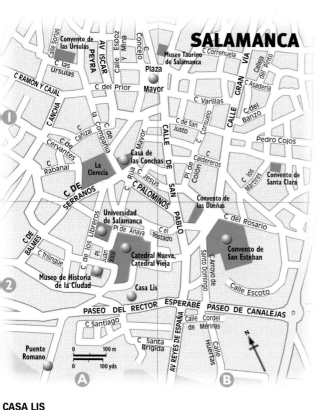

SALAMANCA

Above *The old and new cathedrals tower over the surrounding buildings and the Río Tormes*

CASA LIS
www.museocasalis.org

This is a museum of art nouveau and art deco in an art nouveau structure, partly constructed from painted glass. The Museo de Art Nouveau y Art Decó contains more than 1,600 late 19th- and early 20th-century items, including Emile Gallé glasswork, a superb collection of Lalique scent bottles, porcelain dolls and Fabergé jewels, as well as paintings and sculptures.

➕ 303 A2 ✉ Calle El Expolio 14 ☎ 923 12 14 25 🕐 Apr–15 Oct Tue–Fri 11–2, 5–9, Sat–Sun 11–9; 16 Oct–Mar Tue–Fri 11–2, 4–7, Sat–Sun 11–8 (also Aug Mon 11–2) 👋 €4

CASA DE LAS CONCHAS

The house of shells is named after the 400 scallop shells (the symbol of pilgrims on their route to Santiago de Compostela ▷ 144–146) that are carved across its outside walls. Inside is a visitor information office.

➕ 303 A1 ✉ Calle de la Compañía 2 ☎ 923 26 93 17 🕐 Mon–Fri 9–9, Sat–Sun 9–2, 4–7

MORE TO SEE
PUENTE ROMANO

Built by the Romans in the first century AD across the Río Tormes, the bridge still has 15 of its original 26 arches and gives an excellent view of the city.

➕ 303 A2 ✉ Carretera de la Fregeneda s/n

MUSEO DE HISTORIA DE LA CIUDAD

A swift coverage of Salamanca's history can be found here, focusing on the 18th and 19th centuries.

➕ 303 A2 ✉ Plaza Juan XXIII 15–17 ☎ 923 21 41 80 🕐 Tue–Sat 10–2, 4–7, Sun 10–2
👋 Free

SIERRA DE LA PEÑA DE FRANCIA

A drive along the winding, narrow roads of the Sierra de la Peña de Francia unveils a beguiling cluster of villages and a landscape that together form a living medieval museum. The mountains stretch from the village of Miranda del Castañar in the east towards Hoyos in the west, and are named after the French settlers who came here following the Reconquest. The range rises abruptly to 1,723m (5,651ft) at the summit of Peña de Francia, which is reached via a precipitous road and topped by the Monasterio de Peña de Francia (hospederiapenadefrancia.com), where you can stay or eat. For a taste of medieval life, head to La Alberca, a village frozen in time,

where pigs roam cobbled streets and houses are built from wood, mud and pebbles. A precipitous drive from La Alberca takes you into the forested, wilderness valley of Valle de las Batuecas.

✚ 468 D5 ℹ Paseo de Cervantes 6, 37700 Béjar ☎ 923 40 30 05 🚉 Béjar

SORIA

www.ayto-soria.org

Amassed alongside the Río Duero is the modern provincial capital of Soria, whose stark outer appearance hides a few monumental gems, spacious parks and a rich poetic heritage. The grand, 16th-century Palacio de los Condes de Gomara, now a courthouse, with its rows of arched windows, stands out, as does the Romanesque Iglesia de San Juan de la Rabanera. The 13th-century Monasterio de San Juan de Duero (closed Mon), across the river on the eastern outskirts, has a superb Mudéjar cloister. All around the town are poetic links, particularly to Sevillian poet Antonio Machado (1875–1939), who once lived here. The Parque Alameda de Cervantes, right in central Soria, is a lovely garden park.

✚ 465 H4 ℹ Calle Medinaceli 2, 42003 Soria ☎ 975 21 20 52 🚉 Soria

TORDESILLAS

www.tordesillas.net

This town, set on the north bank of the Río Duero, holds a special place in world history and contains the outstanding Monasterio de Santa Clara. Reached via a stone, arched medieval bridge are the Casas del Tratado (closed Mon), the location in 1494 of the signing of the Treaty of Tordesillas, which divided up the non-Christian world between Spain, which got South America except Brazil, and Portugal, which got (uncharted territory in) Africa and India. Later, the building became the prison of Juana la Loca (Joanna the Mad), daughter of Fernando V and Isabel I, who was locked up here (▷ 35).

Excellent guided tours will take you around the Monasterio de Santa Clara (closed Mon), a mid-14th-century monastery, whose church has a stunning gold roof.

✚ 464 F4 ℹ Casas del Tratado, Calle Tratado, 47100 Tordesillas ☎ 983 77 10 67

TORO

www.toroayto.es

The old fortified town of Toro is strung out along the exposed edge of a high moor overlooking the fertile valley of the Río Duero. Visitors flock here to see its notable churches and monasteries.

Leading the way is the 12th-century Romanesque Iglesia Colegiata de Santa María la Mayor, whose Portada de la Majestad has a facade depicting the Last Judgement and the life of Mary. Inside is the outstanding *Virgen de la Mosca* painting, attributed to the Dutch artist Gerard David (c1460–1523).

The Real Monasterio de Sancti Spiritu (guided tours only Tue–Sun 10.30, 11.15, 12, 5.30, 6.15 and 7, to reserve tours tel 980 10 81 07); founded in the 14th century by the Portuguese, is a complex of Mudéjar buildings housing some remarkable Flemish tapestries.

➕ 463 E4 ℹ Plaza Mayor 6, 49800 Toro ☎ 980 69 47 47

VALLADOLID

www.asomateavalladolid.org

Proud, lively and full of monumental buildings, Valladolid manages to break through its otherwise industrial facade to prove well worthy of a visit. Officially founded in the 11th century by Count Ancúrez (although settlements were established here much earlier), it has witnessed the coronation of Fernando III and his mother Berenguela in 1217 and the death of Christopher Columbus in 1506, and was Spain's capital during the reigns of Felipe II and Felipe III.

The austere 16th-century cathedral and the flamboyant Iglesia de San Pablo, with its elaborate facade, are highlights. The 15th-century Colegio de San Gregorio, next door, has a pretty courtyard and is currently used for temporary exhibitions. Its permanent art collection has been moved to Palacio de Villena, the building just in front of San Gregorio.

Inside the main chapel of the cathedral is an inspired retablo (altarpiece), carved by Spanish sculptor Juan de Juni (1506–77) in 1572; the Museo Diocesano y Catedralicio (Tue–Fri 10–1.30, 4.30–7, Sat–Sun and festivals 10–2), reached from the cathedral, features wonderful sculptures, tombs and religious silverware.

➕ 464 F4 ℹ Pabellón de Cristal, Acera de Recoletos, 47001 Valladolid ☎ 983 21 93 10/983 21 94 38 🚉 Valladolid

VALLE DE LAS BATUECAS

The drive to this valley is likely to have you holding on to your car seats: It involves a dizzy descent along a series of mountain switchbacks into wild, forested lands. There are a few small stopping places on the way, so

you can pull over and peer down into the valley below. Reached via the SA-201 back road and the 1,240m-high (4,067ft) Puerto de Portillo pass from La Alberca, the valley floor—650m (2,130ft) lower than the pass—is the setting for the Carmelite Monasterio de San José de las Batuecas. The monastery was founded in 1597, and today encourages only visitors with a genuine interest. A footpath to the left of the entrance follows the enchanting Valle de Batuecas along a marked trail to a set of three prehistoric caves. The neolithic paintings here are rather disappointing but the walk is great.

➕ 468 D5 ℹ Paseo de Cervantes 6, 37700 Béjar ☎ 923 40 30 05

VILLAFRANCA DEL BIERZO

www.villafrancadelbierzo.org

This charismatic village lies in the lush Valle de Burbia. Repopulated by the French in the 11th century, Villafranca commands a natural defensive position that is reflected in its imposing 16th-century castle, now privately owned.

The town itself is replete with slate-roofed houses and flowered balconies. Pilgrims on their way to Santiago de Compostela (▷ 144–146) come here to rest and eat before the steep climb ahead. According to tradition, injured pilgrims arriving at the Puerta del Perdón's Iglesia del Santiago who were unable to continue over the 1,100m-high (3,600ft) Pedrafita pass could receive their forgiveness here instead. The

Iglesia de San Francisco, founded in the 13th century, is another of the town's interesting churches, and has pleasant views over the valley.

➕ 463 D2 ℹ Avenida Bernardo Díez Ovelar 10, 24500 Villafranca del Bierzo ☎ 987 54 00 28

ZAMORA

www.ayto-zamora.org

Fortified Zamora has an idyllic setting above the Río Duero that makes it one of the most attractive and relaxing places in the region. The town is reached along a Romanesque stone bridge and is dominated by its 12th-century cathedral, with a Byzantine roof dome of 16 panels. Inside, a museum has a display of finely crafted Flemish tapestries, one of the best collections in Spain. Opposite is the town's castle, now an art college. The 12th-century Iglesia de San Juan has a beautiful rose window and a statue of Merlin outside, used in the town's *Semana Santa* (Holy Week) processions. The nearby Iglesia de Santiago del Burgo, dating from the 11th and 12th centuries, is yet another interesting church.

Calle Balborraz, sloping gently downwards from the Plaza Mayor, is a charming, cobbled street lined with shops and cafés.

➕ 463 E4 ℹ Plaza de Arias Gonzalo 6, 49004 Zamora ☎ 980 53 36 94 🚉 Zamora

Opposite *Río Duero (top) and Monasterio de Santa Clara (bottom) in Tordesillas*
Below *Calle Balborraz in Zamora*

RIOJA WINE COUNTRY

The small province of La Rioja, bordering Castile-León to the east, is one of Spain's most important wine-growing regions. It is famous for its smooth and velvety red wines, as well as its excellent peppers.

THE DRIVE
Distance: 144km (89 miles)
Allow: 4–6 hours
Start at: Alfaro, map 465 J3
End at: Santo Domingo de la Calzada, map 464 H3

★ Alfaro is one of the main wine-producing centres in La Rioja. There are several bodegas here, open for purchases, but not generally for tastings and tours, unless by special arrangement. Alfaro is at the confluence of the rivers Alhama and Ebro, and its most prized monument is the 16th- to 17th-century Iglesia-Colegiata de San Miguel, with its interesting facade with a triumphal arch and, inside, 15 *retablos* (altarpieces).

With the red-and-white bullring on your right and Bodega Palacios Remondo on your left, take the N-232 towards Logroño. This is quite a busy road, as it is used by northbound trucks opting to avoid the highway

tolls. It passes through open country, dotted with vineyards, and alongside the rail line for much of the journey to Calahorra.

❶ Calahorra, on a 385m (1,263ft) hill at the confluence of the rivers Cidacos and Ebro, was conquered by Romans and Moors before coming under the control of the kingdom of Navarra in 1045. It is a pretty town with a Gothic cathedral, 16th- to 18th-century Palacio Episcopal and interesting churches, including the Iglesia de San Francisco, with a lovely baroque facade.

From the town take the N-232 northwards, signed to Logroño, passing under the AP-68 highway. Continue through sumptuous, open vine country and past the village of El Villar de Arnedo. The road eventually crosses back over the AP-68 before passing closer to the Río Ebro and heading into the town of Logroño. Follow signs for *centro urbano*.

❷ Logroño (▷ 296) lies on the banks of the Río Ebro and is the capital of La Rioja region. This lively city has plenty to see. The imposing 15th- to 18th-century Catedral de la Redonda is top of the list, along with the Paseo de Espolón park. Pilgrims pass along Logroño's Rua Vieja before leaving via the Puerta de Revellín.

Take the N-232 out of Logroño, passing the Palacio del Vino bodega on your right on the outskirts. Continue on the N-232, signed for Santander, to reach Fuenmayor.

❸ Surrounded by vineyards and with wine stores along its main street, the pleasant country town of Fuenmayor has an excellent restaurant, Mesón Alameda, opposite the church.

Out of town, turn right on to the N-232, signed to Vitoria-Gasteiz. The road passes through rolling hills covered with vineyards and offers

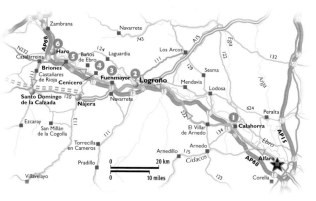

sweeping views over the Ebro valley. After about 6.5km (4 miles), you can take a detour right to Cenicero.

4 The sleepy town of Cenicero has bodegas that offer door sales. Its 16th-century Iglesia de San Martín is also worth a visit.

Return to the N-232 and turn right. Near Baños de Ebro, a black bull silhouette dominates the skyline as you pass through drier, more desert-like country. Soon you will see Briones perched on a hill on the right.

5 Precarious-looking Briones is home to the magnificent 16th-century Iglesia de Santa María, at the top of the village. It has high vaulted ceilings, a grand, blue organ over an arch in the entrance and a beautiful side chapel. Walk up behind the church to reach a promenade with bird's-eye views over the verdant valley.

Return to the N-232 and turn right, signed towards Santander. The route winds through open country with distant ranges of hills ahead. At the N-232/N-124 junction, stay on the N-124, signed to Haro and Vitoria; you soon see Haro ahead. Turn right towards Haro, signed AP-68, and then left at a roundabout to reach the town (the N-124 goes straight on to Vitoria). Follow the signs for *centro urbano*.

6 Haro (▷ 296) is a modern town with an elegant Plaza Mayor, plenty of wine-buying outlets and the impressive Iglesia de Santo Tomás. Don't miss a trip to La Muga winery.

Leave Haro for Santo Domingo de la Calzada on the LR-111/N-126—it is the road at the bottom of the hill

below the Plaza Mayor. As you turn left on to the road there are great views of the mountains and the agricultural valley. Continue straight over the N-232, through Castañares de Rioja in the middle of a big flat plain. Pass under the N-120 Burgos road and continue along a gorgeous tree-lined approach road to Santo Domingo de la Calzada (▷ 299).

WHEN TO GO
This drive is possible at any time of year, and even when the grapes are not being harvested there is plenty to see on the wine trail.

WHERE TO EAT
MESÓN ALAMEDA
Has great fish dishes and is more stylish than other rural restaurants.
✉ Plaza Felix Azpilicueta 1, 26360 Fuenmayor ☎ 941 45 00 44 🕐 Sep–Jul Tue–Sat 1–3.30, 8–10.30, Sun 1–3.30

TABERNA DE LA CUARTA ESQUINA
A local classic, with reasonably priced traditional cuisine.
✉ Calle Cuatro Esquinas 16, 26500 Calahorra ☎ 941 13 43 55

PLACE TO VISIT
LA MUGA WINERY
www.bodegasmuga.com
✉ Barrio de la Estación, 26200 Haro ☎ 941 31 18 25 🚌 Tours Jun–Sep Mon–Fri: 10 (English), 11, 12 (Spanish); Oct–May 11 and 4.30 (Spanish only); €4

Opposite *View over the wine-growing lands of the Rioja valleys*
Below *Grapes growing in Haro (left); the 16th-century church in Briones (right)*

VALLE DEL SILENCIO

A thousand years ago, monks came to this remote corner of the mountainous El Bierzo region to find solitude and peace. Some established monasteries, while others hid themselves away in isolated caves. The region is known as the Valle del Silencio (the Valley of Silence) but also as the 'Terciada Berciana', after the region of ancient Egypt where monks once lived and devoted themselves to God. This circular walk takes in spectacular mountain scenery and some charming traditional villages. Note that walkers need to be moderately fit. The walk is well signposted.

THE WALK

Distance: 15km (9 miles)

Allow: 6–7 hours

Ascent: Maximum altitude is around 1,300m (4,265ft)

Start/end at: San Clemente de Valdueza

HOW TO GET THERE

To reach San Clemente de Valdueza, take the LE161, following signs for San Esteban de Valdueza and then for Peñalba de Santiago. You will need your own car as the local bus service is limited.

★ Begin in the pretty mountain village of San Clemente de Valdueza, which sits at a modest 685m (2,247ft) but enjoys a splendid mountainous backdrop. Near the church, a cement path leads towards an old mill. From here, the main route—called the Camino de la Ramosa—begins. Follow this signposted route, keeping the River Oza on your left. Cross the stream, heading through groves of chestnut and walnut trees, and descend the Pumares valley. You will pass the Pumares fountain just before reaching the main road. Follow the signposts and continue along the road for about 0.5km (0.25 miles). The pretty riverbank is lined with trees, including alder, poplar and ash. Continue walking, keeping the river on your left, until you reach a crossroads. Take the left turn down towards the river, and, beyond the ruined house, turn left (look for the turning near a sign reading 'Coto de Caza' nailed to a tree). The path winds steadily upwards, towards the peak of Alto de Valdelaviña (920m/3,018ft). A spectacular panorama unfolds as you climb.

❶ At the summit, the path traces the route of one of the two Roman canals built to convey gold from the mines of Las Médulas (▷ 297). This level section continues for about 2.5km (1.5 miles) before arriving at a spectacular viewing point. From here you can gaze out at the grey-slate village of Peñalba de Santiago, silhouetted against the mountains.

From the viewing point, the path begins the ascent to the village of Montes.

❷ The winsome Ermita de la Santa Cruz is on the left near the entrance to the village. It was built 200 years ago, but vestiges of a much earlier Visigothic structure have been incorporated into the doorway.

Turn right, keeping the peak of Aquiana and the spiky crags known as the 'Twelve Apostles' in front of you. A small street leads to the Romanesque monastery of San Pedro de Montes, now sadly neglected, which dates back to the 12th century. In front of the monastery, take the street leading to the right, and follow the road which leads to the Montes stream. Cross the stream and continue through the woods to the Castro Rupiano viewing platform (1,090m/3,576ft). From there, the path turns left and levels out into a beautiful meadow, especially lovely in springtime. Just after crossing a small stream, the path divides and you should head downhill.

❸ The path ascends again after crossing another stream, and

reaches the top of Chano Callao (1,315m/4,314ft), the highest point of this walk, which affords magnificent views. Peñalba is a beautiful sight, traditional grey-slate buildings huddled around the church.

The path drops down, through oak forest, into meadow. Take the right fork and head towards Peñalba.

❹ Take a moment to wander around this atmospheric mountain village, with its exquisite Mozerabic church—all that survives of the 10th-century monastery founded by San Genadio.

The route continues down the asphalted road for about 1km (0.5 miles), passing a mirador (viewing point) and a fountain. At El Jardonal (signposted), turn right. The path climbs gently, and you should continue walking until you reach the ruins of the little hermitage of San Mateo. Then follow the route past an irrigation channel, over another stream, and into a shady oak forest.

❺ The path emerges at a natural stone balcony, called 'La Previsa', from where you can enjoy more sublime mountain views.

The path begins its descent here, winding down (note that the pathway can be slippery in wet weather) to reach the river at the bottom of the valley. A municipal water plant sits on the river bank, and you have to walk through it to cross the river and reach the main road. Continue along the road for about 0.5km (0.25 miles) towards San Juan del Tejo, and then cross to the right bank of the river. The path wends through forest, past a recreation area, and over a stream, still heading in the direction of San Juan del Tejo. At San Juan del Tejo, the path joins the road which will take you back to San Clemente.

WHEN TO GO
This walk is suitable from spring until autumn. In winter, snow and severe weather make it difficult.

WHERE TO EAT
There are no restaurants along this route, so bring a picnic. The nearest big town is Ponferrada (21km/ 13 miles) with numerous restaurants, tapas bars and cafés. It is also the best place to find picnic supplies.

MESÓN EL NOGALEDO
An old-fashioned inn, in a pretty village midway between Ponferrada and San Clemente, this serves hearty local cuisine at very reasonable prices.
✉ Calle El Conde s/n, 24415 San Estebán de Valdueza ☎ 987 45 28 79

WHERE TO STAY
Most accommodation options in the region are in casas rurales (self-catering properties). There are several hotels in Ponferrada.

HOTEL BIERZO PLAZA
A 17th-century townhouse now contains this welcoming small hotel, which enjoys a fine location on Ponferrada's main square. Rooms are spacious and simply furnished. The restaurant, Taberna los Arcos, offers a good fixed-price lunch menu, local specialties and tapas.
✉ Plaza del Ayuntamiento 4, 24400 Ponferrada ☎ 987 45 62 27 🖳 €75–€110

CASA TURPESA
http://casaturpesa.blogspot.com/ Self-catering accommodation in a beautifully restored slate house, typical of the region, with two bedrooms (a double and a single). It's in the centre of one of the loveliest villages in the Valle del Silencio.
✉ Peñalba de Santiago ☎ 987 42 55 66, 615 45 45 89 🖳 From €180 for a weekend

INFORMATION
The Ponferrada tourist office has a leaflet outlining this circular route, which is called Sendero Circular de la Tebaida Berciana. There is a short description and a map at www.ponferrada.org.

Opposite Las Médulas

AROUND SALAMANCA

Stroll around Salamanca's magnificent old quarter, a golden city of resplendent monuments and elegant squares. This walk takes in the city's most important sights, from the stunning Plaza Mayor to the opulent baroque church of La Clerecía and the superb and ancient university buildings.

THE WALK

Distance: 2km (1.25 miles)
Allow: 5 hours, including sightseeing
Start/end at: Plaza Mayor, map 303 A1

★ Begin your walk in the heart of Salamanca, the impressive Plaza Mayor. This showcase square, a refined, 18th-century baroque ensemble built of golden stone, is full of cafés and bars, perfect for breakfast or a coffee break.

Leave the square by the passage next to the 12th-century Romanesque church of San Martín, which overlooks the little Plaza del Corrilla and leads to Rúa Mayor.

Walk down bustling Rúa Mayor, one of the main arteries of the medieval city, until you reach the junction with Rúa Antigua, which curves to the right. Here, you'll find two of Salamanca's most emblematic buildings: the Casa de las Conchas

(House of Shells): and the frothy, baroque spires of La Clerecía, one of the most distinctive churches in the city.

❶ The Renaissance palace known as the Casa de las Conchas (▷ 303) was built for newly weds Don Rodrigo Arias and Maldonado and Doña María de Pimental between 1493 and 1503. The facade is covered with the symbols of the two families—the fleur de lis, and the shells *(conchas)* for which the palace is named.

Opposite, the exuberantly baroque church of la Clerecía is considered one of the most important examples of the style in Spain.

Continue down Rúa Antigua and turn left onto Calle de los Libreros where you will soon arrive in front of the magnificent plateresque facade of Salamanca's university (▷ 301).

❷ According to tradition, visitors must try to find *La Rana* (the frog) among the menagerie of stone creatures carved into the facade (good luck and a quick marriage reward the keen-eyed). Visit the atmospheric lecture rooms and old library, then cross the street into the Patio de las Escuelas. Head through the passage at the back to find the University Museum, with an exquisite 18th-century zodiacal ceiling.

Return to Calle de los Libreros, turn left, and then immediately left onto Calle Calderón de la Barca. This emerges near the monumental Plaza Anaya, dominated by the enormous Catedral Nueva (▷ 302).

❸ The New Cathedral was begun in 1513, and was one of the last Spanish cathedrals to be built in the Gothic style. On the other side of the Catedral Nueva is the 12th- to 13th-century Catedral Viejo (▷ 302), a mixture of late Romanesque and early Gothic architecture. Look for the Torre del Gallo (Cock's Tower), named after the weather vane in the form of a cockerel which sits atop the curious, Byzantine-style dome.

④ Just behind the Catedral Viejo, on Calle El Expolio, is the Museo Art Deco y Art Nouveau, housed in a winsome art nouveau mansion, the Casa Lis. Beyond it, you can gaze at the remarkable, 400m (437-yard) Puente Romano (Roman Bridge).

Take the Patio Chico, a small passage behind the Casa Lis, which snakes via the Plaza de Carvajal towards the Convento de San Esteban (▷ 302).

⑤ This is another plateresque masterpiece, with a beautiful church and cloisters. The cloisters of the Convento de las Dueñas (▷ 302), directly across the street, are even lovelier, with more exquisite stonework and a wealth of fabulous creatures adorning the capitals.

Leave the convent and turn left onto Calle Juan de la Fuente, and then right when it meets Calle San Pablo to return to the gorgeous, golden Plaza Mayor.

WHEN TO GO
This walk can be undertaken at any time of the year, but don't forget that most sights and monuments close for two to three hours at lunchtime.

WHERE TO EAT
LA POSADA
www.laposada.net
A traditional inn serving regional favourites at reasonable prices.
✉ Calle Aire y Azucena 1, 37001 Salamanca
☎ 923 21 72 51 🕐 Mon–Sat 1–4, 7–11, Sun 1–5

LA VIGA
Cheap and cheerful, this is a favourite for the local specialty—*jeta,* fried or roasted pig snout. Order a portion with a draught beer.
✉ Calle del Consuelo, 37001 Salamanca
☎ 923 21 09 04 🕐 Daily noon–midnight

MESÓN CERVANTES
One of the most reliable of the taverns on Salamanca's beautiful main square, with a good range of tapas.
✉ Plaza Mayor 15, 37002 Salamanca
☎ 923 21 72 13 🕐 Daily 8am–1am

PLACE TO VISIT
IGLESIA DE LA CLERECÍA
✉ Calle Compañia 5, 37002 Salamanca

☎ 923 26 46 60 🕐 Tue–Fri 10.30–12.45, 5–6.45, Sat and public hols 10–1.15, 5–7.15, Sun 10–1.15 💶 €3 ⎘ Guided visits Tue–Fri 10.30, 11.15, 12.00, 12.45, 5, 5.45 and 6.45pm, Sat and public hols 10, 10.50, 11.40, 12.30, 13.15, 5, 5.45, 6.30 and 7.15pm

Above *Detail of the plateresque facade of the university*
Opposite *Convento de las Dueñas below the Catedral Nueva and Catedral Vieja*

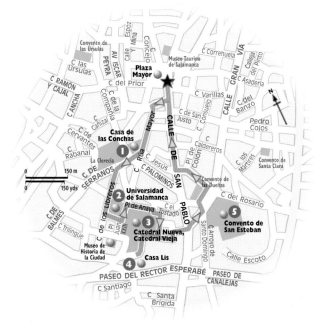

ATAPUERCA
SIERRAACTIVA
www.visitasatapuerca.com

The SierraActiva complex was established in 1995 to research the prehistoric sites around Atapuerca, 15km (9 miles) northeast of Burgos. The tour of the excavations is especially interesting.

✉ Parque Arqueológico, 09199 Atapuerca ☎ 902 02 42 46 🕐 Jul–mid Sep daily; Apr–Jun weekends and holidays only; mid-Sep to Oct weekends only; phone for times 🖐 €12 (for park, archaeological site, and museum)

BURGOS
AMBIGÚ
www.ambiguburgos.com

A classic in the popular nightlife zone of Bernardillas, this lively bar offers a little of everything from morning coffee to tapas during the day. In the evenings, the atmosphere heats up, with occasional live gigs (often on Thursday, but phone to check) and guest DJs at weekends.

✉ Plaza Roma 11 ☎ 947 221 962 🕐 Daily from 8am–late 🖐 Free

ARTESANÍA LOS CACHARROS
Pottery and handcrafted products with both traditional and contemporary designs are sold here.

✉ Calle de Puebla 15, 09001 Burgos ☎ 947 27 73 29 🕐 Mon–Fri 10–2, 5.30–8.30, Sat 10–2

CASA QUINTANILLAS
The place to come for *queso de Burgos*, a local white cheese. There's a wide variety of other cheeses for sale, but those made with sheep's milk are the best.

✉ Calle Paloma 13, 09001 Burgos ☎ 947 20 25 35 🕐 Mon–Sat 10–8.30, Sun 10.30–3

CLOSE TO ME
This nightclub attracts trendy young things who come to drink and dance to the Latin jazz or electronic beats.

✉ Plaza Llanas de Afuera 19, 09003 Burgos ☎ 947 26 18 62 🕐 Sun–Wed 6pm–3am, Thu–Sat 6pm–5am 🖐 Free

HERMANOS DOMINGO
www.laboteria.es

It is an old Spanish tradition to carry a *bota de vino*, or soft leather wine bag, while out walking, and to drink the wine directly from the *bota*. Hermanos Domingo's workshop is the place to learn more about this custom and to buy the best *botas*.

✉ Calle San Cosme 15, 09004 Burgos ☎ 947 47 19 09 🕐 Mon–Fri 9–2, 4–8

LIBRERÍAS HIJOS DE SANTIAGO RODRIGUEZ
www.librerias-hsr.es

HSR, in the old city, claims to be the oldest bookstore in Spain. The service is excellent and there is a considerable stock in several languages.

✉ Plaza Mayor 22, 09003 Burgos ☎ 947 20 14 43 🕐 Mon–Fri 10–2, 5–8, Sat 10–2

QUINTA AVENIDA
www.quintavenida.com

Quinta Avenida plays blues, jazz and soul, and is one of the most interesting venues in town. Enjoy a light meal, and choose from a wide variety of creative drinks while you take in the band. Live concerts on Thursday.

✉ Paseo de la Quinta s/n, 09002 Burgos ☎ 947 20 00 19 🖐 Entrance free; drinks €6

TEATRO CLUNIA
This theatre has a schedule of carefully selected 20th-century plays and contemporary Spanish works, from well-known companies and touring productions.

✉ Santa Agueda s/n, 09003 Burgos ☎ 947 20 30 40 🖐 From €8

Opposite Taste the local wines on a winery tour or buy them in Haro

TEATRO PRINCIPAL DE BURGOS

A traditional theatre in the old city. It promotes young theatre companies that perform works by up-and-coming playwrights and also stages classic Spanish plays, all at quite reasonable prices. For those who like clowns, there are performances throughout the year.

✉ Paseo de Espolón s/n, 09003 Burgos ☎ 947 28 88 73 🖐 From €6

VIEJA CASTILLA

www.laviejacastilla.com
A small but well-stocked deli, its cheese selection is interesting, and includes the highly recommended *queso de arenillas de Ripisuerga* (dried cheese from Ripisuerga) and *queso de Burgos*. While you're here, try the renowned Castilian honey.

✉ Calle Paloma 21, 09002 Burgos ☎ 947 20 73 67 🕐 Mon–Sat 10–2.15, 5.30–9.30, Sun 11–3

VINACOTECA EL LAGAR

www.el-lagar.org
They take wine culture very seriously here, with its huge cellar and tasting bar, and regular expert sessions. A specialist in wines from the Ribera del Duero and Rioja regions.

✉ Calle San Lesmes 14 bajos, 09004 Burgos ☎ 947 20 62 89 🕐 Mon–Sat 11–2, 6–9.30

LEÓN

AUDITORIO CIUDAD DE LEÓN

www.auditoriociudaddeleon.net
A classical music, opera and concert venue, in a modern, 1,200-seat building near the cathedral. There is a restaurant and a café on site, and jazz bands perform live at weekends.

✉ Avenida Reyes Leoneses 4, 24008 León ☎ 987 24 46 63 🖐 €15–€30 🚌 11

CAFÉ EKOLE

http://lajouja.es/ekole/
Ekole is a beautiful café near the cathedral that brings the outside inside with an indoor patio. Occasional concerts are put on by local groups, and art and photography exhibitions as well as poetry readings are also staged.

✉ Calle Fernado González Regeral 1, 24003 León ☎ 987 22 57 02 🖐 Free 🚌 2, 3, 4, 5, 8, 10, 12

CLUB ADEMAR-LEÓN

www.ademar.com
This prestigious handball team plays in the Spanish Honour Division and participates in European competitions. A store at the stadium sells team T-shirts, key rings and more.

✉ Avenida Saenz de Miera s/n, Estadio Antonio Amilivia, 24009 León ☎ 987 26 31 71 🕐 Times vary 🖐 €8–€20 🚌 1, 2

CUESTA CASTAÑÓN

Try-as-you-buy at this Spanish-style deli stocking everything from charcuterie and cheese to sweetmeats and candies. They also have a good selection of wine and herbal digestives. It's perfect for stocking up on gifts for food-loving friends.

✉ Calle Castañones 2, 24003 León. ☎ No phone 🕐 Mon–Sat 10–2, 5–9

EL ESPÍRITU DE LA ESQUINA

This craft and gifts store is a specialist in accessories for men and women, selling bags, belts and wallets, as well as beautiful ceramics, jewellery, leather goods, toys and stationery. A good place to find an original gift, and good value.

✉ Cervantes 11, 24003 León ☎ 987 24 65 52 🕐 Mon–Fri 11–2, 5.30–9, Sat 11–2 🚌 2, 3, 4, 5

GRAN CAFÉ

This elegant and long-established bar is in León's Barrio Húmedo, a very lively nightlife zone. Quieter and more relaxed than many of its neighbours, it has an upstairs salon for candle-lit dinners and cabaret acts.

✉ Calle Cervantes 9, 24003 León ☎ 987 27 23 01 🖐 Usually free, small cover charge for concerts 🚌 2, 3, 4, 5

HADOCK CAFÉ

www.hadock.com
Popular café/bar where you can sit all afternoon or dance all night.

You can also surf the web using the high-speed internet connection, or play pool or darts. A range of music is played.

✉ Calle Santisteban y Osorio 9, 24004 León ☎ 987 20 92 56 🕐 Daily 5pm–4am, Fri–Sat until 5am 🖐 Free 🚌 2, 9

ISAMAR

www.catering-isamar.com
Isamar is a food and wine shop selling all kinds of traditional regional products, including smoked meats, chorizo (Spanish sausage), blood sausage, El Bierzo peppers and wines. In addition there are pastries, fruit and vegetables, and a coffee shop. In the San Marcelo area of the city.

✉ Calle Alférez Provisional 2, 24002 León ☎ 987 22 24 12 🕐 Mon–Fri 9.30–2.30, 6–9, Sat 9.30–2.30, Sun 10.30–2 🚌 4, 5

EL LEÓN ANTIGUO

By day this place serves a good selection of beers and tapas; by night it transforms into a lively bar. Small but great for a drink, with a variety of music. Popular with a mid-30s crowd.

✉ Plaza El Cid 18, 24003 León ☎ 987 22 69 56 🕐 Mon–Wed 10–2, 7–midnight, Thu–Sat 10–2, 7–4 🖐 Free 🚌 2, 3, 4

LEÓN TÍPICO

This souvenir store is the shop to visit if you're looking for authentic regional produce and crafts. Local specialties include El Bierzo peppers, *botillo* (mixed pork meat) and *nicanores de Boñar* (puff pastry), and a selection of wines. As for crafts, the shop stocks earthenware and ceramics.

✉ Plaza de Regla s/n, 24001 León ☎ 987 22 67 93 🕐 Jun–Aug Mon–Sat 9.15am–9.30pm; Sep–May 10–2, 4–8 🚌 2, 3, 4, 5, 8, 10, 12

LIBRERÍA PASTOR

www.libreriapastor.com
A classical bookshop with several branches around the city; this is one of the best. It has a large stock of books on a wide range of subjects. There's also a good selection of travel guides and maps.

✉ Plaza Santo Domingo 4, 24001 León
☎ 987 22 59 50 ⏰ Mon–Fri 10–1.30,
4.15–8, Sat 10–1.45 🚌 2, 3, 4, 5, 8, 10, 12

MUSEU DE ARTE CONTEMPORÁNEO DE CASTILLA Y LEÓN
www.musac.es
León's stunning new art museum, MUSAC offers much more than the artworks in its galleries. There are workshops every weekend; themes have included a breakdance workshop for teenagers), film screenings, photography classes and much more. There is also an excellent programme of activities for children.
✉ Avenida de los Reyes Leoneses 24, 24008 León ☎ 987 09 00 00 ⏰ Tue–Sun 10–3, 4–9 💵 Free

EL RASTRO
This street market by the river, sells antiques, art, crafts, jewellery, clothes, books, coins, CDs and a lot more. Prices are negotiable, but you need to get here early for the best bargains. There's a food market Wednesday and Saturday mornings in the Plaza Mayor.

✉ Paseo Papalaguinda, 24001 León
⏰ Sun 9–2.30 🚌 2, 3, 4, 5

RIALTO
You can find a great selection of pieces of jewellery and watches here by such top makers as Tag Heuer, Longines, Maurice Lacroix and Breitling. Glass and silver items (picture frames, vases and the like), porcelain figures and stationery are also sold.
✉ Avenida República Argentina 28, 24004 León ☎ 987 20 96 23 ⏰ Mon–Fri 10.15–2, 5–8.30, Sat 10.15–2 🚌 5

MATAPOZUELOS
VALWO WILDLIFE PARK
Valwo is a nature park where you can wander along paths through beautiful countryside with all sorts of fascinating flora and fauna. Animals—from exotic birds to deer, hippos and big cats—can be seen in the meadows and grasslands of the park. There is a restaurant, a café and baby-changing rooms; and visitors can stay overnight in a log cabin.
✉ Carretera Mojados–Matapozuelos, 47230 Matapozuelos ☎ 983 83 27 59

⏰ Apr–Sep daily 11–7; Easter and Oct weekends 💵 Adult €16, child €12 🚗 35km (22 miles) south of Valladolid along the N-601

OLMEDA
PARQUE TEMÁTICO DEL MUDÉJAR THEME PARK
www.pasionmudejar.com
A country theme park, with a focus on young children, just south of Olmedo on the N-60. Stroll or take the mini-train around the park's grasslands, historical monuments, lakes and geysers. Hundreds of different types of plants and animals give the place a real outdoor feel. There is a restaurant on site.
✉ Arco San Francisco s/n, 47410 Olmedo ☎ 983 62 32 22 ⏰ Easter–Sep daily 10–2, 4–9; Oct–Easter Wed–Sun 10–2, 4–7 💵 Adult €4.50, child €3.50

SALAMANCA
BOUTIQUE DEL TORERO
www.boutiquedeltorero.net
The owner of this kitsch shop takes his souvenirs very seriously, even though the scenes depicted on the iron, plastic, leather and ceramic pieces are usually far from accurate. As well as souvenirs, it offers a wide range of flamenco dresses and bullfighting costumes.
✉ Plaza del Mercado 4, 37001 Salamanca ☎ 923 12 15 11 ⏰ Mon–Fri 10–2, 4.30–8.30, Sat 10–2

FILMOTECA DE CASTILLA Y LEÓN
Cult films, retrospectives, festivals and more, at the regional Filmoteca (film institute). It is housed in the 17th-century Casa de la Caridad (Charity Hospital), now attractively renovated. Films are usually shown undubbed (v.o.—versión original).
✉ Calle Doña Gonzala Santana 1 ☎ 923 21 25 16 ⏰ Mon–Fri 11–2, 5–8, Sat 11–2. Performance times vary 💵 From €5, entrance to building free

HERNANDEZ GUTIERREZ
Close to Gran Vía, this family-run butcher has an excellent selection

Left A treat for art nouveau and art deco fans in Salamanca

of cooked meats and is great for regional-food aficionados. The choice of hams is huge, and the expensive *cerdo de la sierra salmantina*, a local classic, can be enjoyed at a far lower price than in most restaurants.

✉ Calle Correhuela 13–19, 37001 Salamanca ☎ 923 26 99 85 🕐 Mon–Fri 8–2, 5–8, Sat 8–2

LUÍS MÉNDEZ
www.luismendez.net
For some truly original and exquisite jewellery, visit the gallery of this prestigious designer. Regarded as one of the finest designers in Spain, Luís Méndez specializes in exquisite and intricate filigree work, creating extraordinarily detailed pieces in gold and silver. There are two lines: the Classic is more traditional than the Design.

✉ Calle Felipe Espino 2, 37002 Salamanca ☎ 923 26 07 25 🕐 Tue–Sat 11–1, 5–8

LA MADRILEÑA
A traditional Salamancan delicatessen, La Madrileña offers a range of delicious confectionery, among other items. Included in the range are *rosquillas, bollos* and *chochos* (all local breads). The *hornazo* is the best of a huge pastry selection. Good sweets and home-made jams also for sale.

✉ Plaza Mayor 7, 37002 Salamanca ☎ 923 21 36 15 🕐 Daily 10.30–12.15, 5–9

MUSEO ART NOUVEAU Y ART DECO
www.museocasalis.org
A surprisingly child-friendly museum dedicated to art nouveau and art deco. The facade is a giant stained-glass window. Exhibits are a mix of funky designs, cool lights and early 20th-century style.

✉ El Expolio 14, 37008 Salamanca ☎ 923 12 14 25 🕐 Tue–Fri 11–2, 5–9, Sat–Sun 11–9 🍴 Adult €4, child €3, under 14 free 🚌 Plaza Mayor stop, then walk down Rua Mayor for 500m (550 yards) to Calle Gibraltar

NEW PARK
This huge games parlour in a shopping centre is a great way

FESTIVALS AND EVENTS

JANUARY
SAN ANTON
Celebrates the blessing of animals with long processions of creatures past the church of San Anton.
✉ Salamanca, Burgos, Logroño, Valladolid, Zamora 🕐 17 January

MARCH–APRIL
SEMANA SANTA
Impressive penitential processions celebrating Holy Week.
✉ León, Salamanca, Valladolid, Zamora

JUNE
EL COLACHO
Corpus Christi celebrations with a figure disguised as the Devil who runs through the streets jumping over babies born during the year.
✉ Castrillo de Murcia

DÍA DE SAN JUAN
Bullfights and dance.
✉ León

to entertain children while adults indulge in retail therapy. Attractions range from the high-tech to *futbolín* (soccer tables), and there is plenty for toddlers. Although it sounds highly commercial, New Park is a successful concept all over Spain and a chance for your children to mix with local ones.

✉ Centro Comercial El Tormes, Avenida Salamanca, s/n., 37900 Salamanca ☎ 923 13 13 15 🕐 Mon–Thu noon–11, Fri, Sun noon–midnight, Sat noon–2am 🍴 Average price per game: €1.50

TEATRO LICEO
This 19th-century theatre and concert hall is the preferred venue of top Spanish musicians when they're in town. All genres appear on the schedule, from pop and rock to jazz and world music. Well-known plays by local groups, usually amateurs, are also staged.
✉ Plaza del Liceo s/n, 37002 Salamanca ☎ 923 28 17 16 🍴 €8

JUNE–JULY
DÍA DE SAN PEDRO
Start of two-week festival with parades, music, dancing, bullfights and feasting.
✉ Burgos 🕐 29 June

SEPTEMBER
DÍA DE SAN MATEO
Fiesta to celebrate the wine harvest.
✉ Logroño

FIESTA DE SALAMANCA
Two weeks of processions, music, feasting and fireworks.
✉ Salamanca

OCTOBER
INTERNATIONAL FILM FESTIVAL
The Semana Internacional de Cine de Valladolid began as a religious film festival in 1956 and has developed into Spain's most important forum for art cinema.
✉ Valladolid 🕐 First week of Cotober

SPORT WELL
www.gimnasiosportwell.es
This gym has a wide range of activities, including aerobics, salsa classes and t'ai chi. For a relaxing visit, try one of the spa treatments: massage, hydrotherapy and sauna.
✉ Calle Rodríguez Fabrés 15, 37005 Salamanca ☎ 923 24 54 25 🕐 Mon–Fri 8am–10.30pm, Sat 11–2.30, Sun 12–2.30 🍴 One-day pass €12. One-hour massage €25 🚌 6, 9

VALDELATEJA
BALNEARIOS DE VALDELATEJA
www.relaistermal.com
The friendly hotel specializes in muscular treatment, using a variety of methods including bubble baths and massage. Staff are also on hand to offer beauty care, and the hotel has inexpensive rooms.
✉ Km 55–56, Carretera Burgos–Santander (N-623), 09145 Valdelateja ☎ 947 15 02 20 🕐 Mon–Fri 10–1.30, 4–7, Sat 9.30–1.30, Sun 9.30–2 🍴 20-min massage €30

PRICES AND SYMBOLS

The restaurants are listed alphabetically (excluding Le, La and Les). The prices given are the average for a two-course lunch (L) and a three-course dinner (D) for one person, without drinks. The wine price is for the least expensive bottle.

For a key to the symbols, ▷ 2.

ARANDA DE DUERO

MESÓN EL PASTOR

www.meson-elpastor.com
The roast lamb from Aranda is famous throughout Spain, and there's nowhere better to try it than this classic, old-fashioned tavern. With clusters of heavy wooden tables set around a huge brick oven, it has three dining rooms. The succulent suckling lamb so beloved of central Spain is the highlight of the menu, slowly roasted for two hours to preserve its juices, but there are also some excellent seafood options. The desserts are home-made and include a classic cream puff *(hojaldre relleno)* and rice pudding. The famous local Ribera de Duero wines provide an excellent accompaniment.
✉ Plaza de la Virgencilla 11, 09400 Aranda de Duero ☎ 947 50 04 28 🕐 Mon, Wed–Sat 1.30–4, 8.30–11, Tue 1.30–4 🍴 L €28, D €34, Wine €12

BURGOS

CASA AVELINO

www.casaavelino.com
This venerable restaurant has been going for more than a century, and prides itself on its classic local dishes, prepared to traditional Castillian recipes. Try the roast lamb, or the rich hare stew. Game and wild mushrooms are offered in season (late autumn).
✉ Calle Emperador 58, 09003 Burgos ☎ 947 20 61 92 🕐 Mon–Tue, Wed–Sat 1–4, 9–midnight 🍴 L €22, D €25, Wine €10

CASA OJEDA

This perennially popular lunch and dinner spot specializes in meat and fish. It has been going strong for almost a century.
✉ Calle de Victoria 5, 09004 Burgos ☎ 947 20 90 52 🕐 Mon–Sat 1–4, 9–11.30, Sun 1–5 🍴 L €32, D €48, Wine €14

FÁBULA

www.restaurantefabula.com
Fábula is a big hit with locals in Burgos, who like the combination of fresh, contemporary cuisine, a fine wine list—and modest prices.
✉ Calle La Puebla 18, 09004 Burgos ☎ 947 26 30 92 🕐 Tue–Sat 1.30–4, 9–12, Sun 1.30–4 🍴 L €28, D €42, Wine €14

LANDA PALACE

www.landahotel.com
Excellent regional dishes are served in this beautifully decorated restaurant in a superb five-star hotel (▷ 320). Reservations are essential.
✉ Km 235, Carretera Madrid–Irún, 09001 Burgos, A1 ☎ 947 25 77 77 🕐 Daily 1–4, 9–11.30 🍴 L €40, D €45, Wine €14

MESÓN DEL CID

www.mesondelcid.es
Built into a palace in the very heart of this old city, Mesón del Cid certainly has a majestic atmosphere. The service is excellent and the food (sturdy local Castilian fare—roast meats predominate) first rate.
✉ Plaza Santa María 8, 09003 Burgos ☎ 947 20 87 15 🕐 Mon–Sat 12.30–3.30, 8–11.30, Sun 12.30–3.30 🍴 L €34, D €48, Wine €15

RINCÓN DE LA MERCED

www.nh-hoteles.es
The menu here is innovative, balancing regional produce with international dishes.

Calle La Merced 3, 09007 Burgos
947 47 99 00 Mon–Sat 1–4,
8.30–11.30, Sun 1–4 L €30, D €46,
Wine €12

TAPELIA
www.tapelia.com
Tapelia offers lighter versions of the
heavy cuisine of Castile. Vegetarians
will be pleased to find some options
and there are meat and fish dishes.
Part of a popluar chain of (currently)
29 restaurants, this specializes in rice
dishes from Alicante.
Plaza Rey San Fernando s/n, 09003
Burgos 947 27 80 00 Daily 1–4, 8–12
L €20, D €26, Wine €10

CALAHORRA
TABERNA DE LA QUARTA ESQUINA
This old-fashioned stone tavern, with
bright flowers in the window-boxes,
is found in the centre of the pretty
Riojano village of Calahorra. There are
three charming dining rooms, all with
wooden beams, rustic furnishings
and old prints on the walls. Friendly
and family-run, it has gained a big
reputation locally for the quality of its
food: the freshest regional vegetables
(famous throughout Spain), delicious
fish from the Bay of Cantabria, and
local meat. Typical recipes include
cod with peppers and excellent game
(in season).
Calle Cuatro Esquinas 16, 26500
Calahorra 941 13 43 55 Thu–Mon
1.30–3.30, 8.30–11, Tue 1.30–3.30. Closed 3
weeks in Jul L €30, D €46, Wine €14

CASTRILLO DE LOS POLVAZARES
CUCA LA VAINA
www.cucalavaina.com
This little village, 5km (3 miles)
outside Astorga, is home to a
charming rural hotel with a good
restaurant. This region is famously
the home of the Maragatos, a
distinct ethnic group with their
own traditions, and this is one of
the loveliest Maragato villages. The
restaurant serves local favourite,
cocido Maragato, which, like all
cocidos (stews), is served in stages,
but, unlike the classic Castillian stew,

is served meat first (and there are
nine diffferent meats in the dish),
rather than broth first. There is a
small terrace for summer dining.
Calle Jardin s/n, 24718 Castrillo de los
Polvazares 987 69 10 78 Tue–Sat
1.30–4, 8.30–10.30, Sun 1.30–4 L €24,
D €32, Wine €12

COVARRUBIAS
DE GALO
www.degalo.com
The lovely, medieval town of
Covarrubias contains numerous
good eateries, but this handsome
old inn stands out. Come here for
hearty, Castillian fare: potatoes with
wild boar, chargrilled steaks and olla
podrida. The latter, a sturdy stew
of beans, chorizo, black sausage,
pork and vegetables, literally means
'rotten pot', but tastes much better
than it sounds. It was apparently
invented in the village of Covarrubias
in the 18th century and is the most
famous local dish. Roast meats,
including local lamb, are cooked in
the traditional brick oven.
Calle Monseñor Vargas 10, 09436
Covarrubias 947 40 63 93 Mon–Tue,
Thu–Sun 2–4, 9–11. Closed Feb L €28,
D €36, Wine €12

EZCARAY
ECHAURREN
www.echaurren.com
A handsome rural hotel in a
converted post house, Echaurren
enjoys a beautiful location in one of
La Rioja's most picturesque mountain
villages. The main hotel restaurant
has a fine reputation, with veteran
chef Marisa Sánchez preparing
time-honoured family recipes such
as chickpea stew with monkfish
and clams, or the classic mountain
dish, local red beans flavoured with
pungent chorizo. The hotel also
runs El Portal, a Michelin-starred,
contemporary restaurant featuring
innovative cuisine created by
dynamic young chef Francis Paniego.
The imaginative tasting menu (€85) is
worth the expense. Reservations
are essential at both restaurants.
Calle Heroes de Alacázar 2, 26280
Ezcaray 941 35 40 47 Echaurren:

Mon–Sat 1.30–4, 8.30–11, Sun 1.30–4
(also Sun 8.30–11 in Jul and Aug);
El Portal: Jan–Jun Wed–Sat 1.30–4,
8.30–11, Sun 1.30–4; Jul–Dec Tue–Sat
1.30–4, 8.30–11, Sun 1.30–4

FRÓMISTA
HOSTERÍA DE LOS PALMEROS
www.hosteriadelospalmeros.com
This welcoming establishment, in a
charming little town full of beautiful
Romanesque monuments, is one
of the best places to try hearty
local cuisine like estofados (stews),
and oven-baked fish with wild
mushrooms. Service is friendly
and attentive, and the setting is
delightfully old-fashioned. Dine
outside on the terrace in summer.
For dessert, try the rich, creamy
tocinillo de cielo, made with egg yolks
and cream.
Plaza de San Temlo, 34440 Frómista
979 81 00 67 Mon, Wed–Sat
1.30–3.30, 8.30–10.30 (also Tue in summer).
Closed 3 weeks in Jan L €40 D €44,
Wine €14

HARO
BEETHOVEN I
www.restaurantebeethoven.com
One of three Beethoven restaurants
in Haro, this is a big, welcoming,
traditional eaterie, with country-style
decoration, including dark wooden
beams and furnishings, and pretty
painted tiles. The original owner,
who started the restaurant in 1941,
shared a birthday with the composer,
and gave it its unusual name. Like
many of La Rioja's best restaurants,
Beethoven is proud of the region's
famously tasty vegetables and fresh
produce, which take pride of place on
the seasonal menu. Don't miss the
fabulous wild mushrooms, which are
served in autumn. The roast meats,
particularly the lamb, are excellent
and it's worth leaving room for the
wonderful home-made desserts. You
can also dine well (and inexpensively)
on a wide range of tapas, available at
the long—and perpetually crowded—
bar downstairs.
Calle Santo Tomás 10, 26200 Haro
941 31 00 18 Daily 11–midnight
L €24, D €32, Wine €12

LEÓN

ADONÍAS

This restaurant, in front of the public library, is one of the best in the city. Traditional dishes are prepared with some modern touches.
✉ Calle de Santa Nonia 16, 24003 León ☎ 987 20 67 68 🕐 Mon–Sat 1–4, 8–12. Closed 2 weeks in summer 🖐 L €30, D €50, Wine €14 🚌 2, 6, 7, 8

BODEGA REGIA

www.regialeon.com
An attractive rustic restaurant, on the edge of the Barrio Húmedo, known as the place for tapas.
✉ Calle Regidores 9–11, 24003 León ☎ 987 21 31 73 🕐 Mon–Sat 1–4, 8.30–12 🖐 L €25, D €35, Wine €12 🚌 2, 3, 4, 5, 8, 10

CASA POZO

Casa Pozo is a well-known restaurant that has been in business since 1936. In summer the outdoor terrace is a charming place to sit and dine afresco.
✉ Plaza San Marcelo 15, 24003 León ☎ 987 22 30 39 🕐 Mon–Sat 1–4, 8–11.45, Sun 1–4 🖐 L €24, D €38, Wine €13 🚌 2, 3, 4, 5, 8

CATEDRAL

www.argored.com/catedral
Regional dishes served here include roast suckling lamb, León-style tripe and a delicious potato stew with prawns (shrimp).
✉ Calle Mariano Domínguez Berrueta 17, 24003 León ☎ 987 21 59 18 🕐 Daily 10am–midnight 🖐 L €20, D €34, Wine €10 🚌 2, 3, 4, 5, 8, 10, 12 (Plaza de Santo Domingo nearest stop)

EL MOLÍN DE JAVIER EMPERADOR

Occupying a 19th-century brick mill, this restaurant has Roman foundations and serves traditional Leónese cuisine with some creative touches. The restaurant has a no-smoking section.
✉ Carretera Villaquilambre–Robledo 11, 24008 León ☎ 987 28 35 60 🕐 Tue–Sat 2–5, 8–1, Sun 2–5 🖐 L €24, D €34, Wine €10 🚊 Villaquilambre Cercanias stop near the restaurant 🚌 Villaquilambre

RESTAURANTE VIVALDI

www.restaurantevivaldi.com
Vivaldi is generally considered to be the finest dining option in León. You may choose to order à la carte, but its two, five-course, set-menu options make for much better value.
✉ Calle Platerias 4, 24003 León ☎ 987 26 07 60 🕐 Tue–Sat 1–3.30, 9–11.30 🖐 Set menus from €65, Wine €18

LOGROÑO

KABANOVA COMEDOR

www.kabanova.com
A chic, sleek, steely restaurant, with ultramodern decor, this is an excellent dining option in the wine capital of Logroño. The cuisine is refined without relying on excessive frills; try artichokes with truffles, or pigs' trotters stuffed with foie gras, baby squid with wild mushrooms, or excellent desserts. The *menú del día* (available Tuesday to Saturday) offers a five-course meal with a glass of Rioja wine for a very reasonable €20. There is also an excellent *menú de degustación* (tasting menu, €34). The wine list is well chosen, with about 50 options, mostly from the famous La Rioja region.
✉ Calle Guardia Civil 9, 26005 Logroño ☎ 941 21 29 95 🕐 Tue–Sat 1.45–3.45, 8.45–11 🖐 L €24, D €36, Wine €12

MÉSON EGÜÉS

www.mesonegues.com
Méson Egüés is a classic *asador* (roast house) which has enjoyed an excellent reputation throughout the city since it opened two decades ago. The lamb chops, roasted in the traditional style over charcoal, are lip-smackingly delicious, especially when paired with a fine Rioja wine. Besides the famous roast meat and fish, you'll also find delicious local grilled vegetables—including local plump, white asparagus, and juicy peppers. Finish with traditional desserts, including a scrumptious cheesecake with tangy *membrillo* (quince jelly).
✉ Calle Campa 3, 26005 Logroño ☎ 941 22 86 03 🕐 Mon–Sat 2–4, 8.30–10.30. Closed Easter week 🖐 L €25, D €34, Wine €12

MEDINA DEL CAMPO

CONTINENTAL 1904

A traditional building in the heart of the historic town of Medina del Campo, this family-run restaurant serves up plentiful portions of home-cooked food. Sturdy, old-fashioned recipes predominate, including *morcilla con pasas y piñones* (black sausage with raisins and pine nuts) and grilled meats, which are prepared over charcoal. On Mondays and Saturdays, they prepare their famous *cocido,* a Castillian stew, made with pork and vegetables. Desserts are also traditional, with classics such as *leche frita* (a kind of cooked custard) featuring on the menu. At weekends, it's hard to find a free table, so reserve well in advance. There is also a tapas bar near the entrance, where guests can fill up on a wide range of delicious snacks.
✉ Plaza Mayor 15, 47400 Medina del Campo ☎ 983 80 10 14 🕐 Mon, Wed–Sun 1–4, 8–11. Closed last 2 weeks in Oct 🖐 L €22, D €30, Wine €12

PALENCIA

LA TRASERILLA

www.la-traserilla.es
Palencia, a sleepy little provincial capital, often gets overlooked by visitors in a rush to reach the big nearby cities of Burgos, León or Valladolid. But besides its beautiful cathedral, it can also boast this delightful restaurant, a charming fusion of old and new in terms of both its architecture and its cuisine. In the kitchen, Miguel Sánchez whips up sublime dishes such as sardine fillets with apple compote and tomato vinaigrette, or suckling lamb with wild mushrooms and cider. The weekday, fixed-price lunch menu is excellent value at under €22. The desserts are excellent—the chocolate terrine with chestnuts and ginger is highly recommended. The setting is warm and inviting, with modern furnishings contrasting elegantly with the original fittings of the 19th-century building. There is also a tapas bar, with a wide range of *pinchos* (canapés).

Calle San Marcos 12, 34001 Palencia ☎ 979 74 54 21 🕙 Daily 1–4, 8–11 👜 L €24, D €34, Wine €12

PEÑARANDA DE DUERO
LA POSADA DUCAL
www.laposadaducal.com
For those enjoying a gentle meander through the great wine country of the Ribera de Duero region, La Posada del Ducal makes a delightful stopover. An elegant and historic inn on the main square of this beautiful little town, it contains an excellent restaurant serving classic local dishes. The handsome dining rooms, with their wooden beams and low ceilings, are cosy and welcoming. Topping the menu is roast suckling lamb, the regional classic, with other popular dishes such as *revuelto* (scrambled eggs) with wild mushrooms, and a pastry filled with hazelnut and pine-nut cream to finish. The wine list is, perhaps unsurprisingly, strong on local wines.
✉ Calle La Cava 1, 09410 Peñaranda de Duero ☎ 947 55 23 47 🕙 Daily 1.30–4, 8.30–10.30 👜 L €24, D €28, Wine €12

SALAMANCA
EL CLAVEL
The draws here, apart from the meticulous service, are the warm decor, intimate atmosphere and creative cuisine.
✉ Calle Clavel 6, 37001 Salamanca ☎ 923 21 61 75 🕙 Mon–Sat 1.30–4, 9–12 👜 L €24, D €30, Wine €10

LA POSADA
www.laposada.net
The menu at La Posada consists of dishes based upon traditional meat and vegetables. There's an excellent mixed vegetable stew, but the highlight is definitely the escalopes in port.
✉ Calle Aire y Azucena 1, 37001 Salamanca ☎ 923 21 72 51 🕙 Mon–Sat 1–4, 7–11, Sun 1–5 👜 L €26, D €38, Wine €10

LE SABLON
www.restaurantesablon.com
Refined and creative French and Belgian cuisine is the main focus at this elegant and intimate restaurant, but you'll also find sophisticated regional dishes. They also serve especially good game in season (October to February). The wood-panelled restaurant is full of paintings by Alicantino artist Miguel Alías, and is conveniently located close to the Plaza Mayor. The desserts are magnificent and beautifully presented, and the wine list, unusually, primarily features French wines.
✉ Calle de Espoz y Mina 20, 37002 Salamanca ☎ 923 26 29 52 🕙 Mon 1.30–3.30, Wed–Sat 1.30–3.30, 9–11.15. Closed Jul 👜 L €45, D €45, Wine €12

SANTO DOMINGO DE LA CALZADA
EL RINCÓN DE EMILIO
www.rincondeemilio.com
A welcoming restaurant, with a series of dining areas, this is a local favourite. It's a great lunch option if you have been to see the cathedral. It is proud of its celebrated local produce: flavoursome vegetables, fish brought daily from the Bay of Cantabria, and local meats. Highlights on the menu include the classic Riojana dish, *manitas de cerdo* (pigs' trotters) served with a piquant sauce of delicious local peppers and chorizo; and *lechal asado* (roast suckling lamb). In summer, the garden area with an outdoor barbecue is great for families.
✉ Plaza de Bonifacio Gil 7, 26250 Santo Domingo de la Calzada ☎ 941 34 09 90 🕙 Mon, Wed–Sat 2–4, 9–11, Tue 2–4 👜 L €24, D €30, Wine €12

PRICES AND SYMBOLS

The prices are for a double room for one night including breakfast, unless otherwise stated. All the hotels listed accept credit cards unless otherwise stated. Note that rates can vary widely throughout the year.

For a key to the symbols, ▷ 2.

BURGO DE OSMA
POSADA DEL CANÓNIGO

http://posadadelcanonigo.es/
A 17th-century mansion, built for one of the religious dignitaries attached to the cathedral, has been attractively converted into a charmingly old-fashioned country hotel. It's located on the main square, in the heart of the walled old quarter, and has retained many of its original details, including the heavy wooden beamed walls and ceilings. Rooms are comfortable and traditional, with antique furniture and floral prints. There's an excellent restaurant, serving regional dishes.
✉ Calle San Pedro de Osma, 43200 Burgo de Osma ☎ 975 36 03 62 💶 €75–€100 🛈 11

BURGOS
ABBA BURGOS HOTEL

www.abbaburgoshotel.com
This friendly and functional four-star hotel offers spacious rooms and bathrooms and modern amenities.

✉ Calle Fernán Gonzalez 72, 09003 Burgos ☎ 947 00 11 00 💶 €80–€155 excluding breakfast (€15) 🛈 99 (60 non-smoking)

FERNÁN GONZÁLEZ

www.hotelfernangonzalez.com
This 18th-century building has been given a modern facade, but walk inside and you're met with baroque chairs, wooden statues and Gothic pillars. The lobby is rather eclectic, but the bedrooms are much simpler and more habitable.
✉ Calle de Calera 17, 09002 Burgos ☎ 947 20 94 41 💶 €80–€150 🛈 74 (50 non-smoking)

HOTEL LA PUEBLA

www.hotellapuebla.com
For style on a budget, there's nowhere better than this sleek little hotel in the historic heart of Burgos. Each room is individually decorated in a plush modern style, with bold wallpaper and silk cushions, and all are equipped with contemporary amenities from satellite TV and DVD players to internet connection. Services normally found only in luxury hotels, such as a pillow selection and even a water menu, are offered. Bicycles to tour the town are also on offer.
✉ Calle la Puebla 20, 09004 Burgos ☎ 947 20 00 11 💶 €75–€110 🛈 19

LANDA PALACE

www.landahotel.com
A luxurious, five-star retreat with ornate rooms—some with four-poster beds and attentive service. The mellow stone building is modern, but looks medieval. The restaurant serves seasonal regional food and excellent rice dishes (▷ 316).
✉ Km 235, Carretera Madrid–Irún (AI), 09001 Burgos ☎ 947 25 77 77 💶 €175–€210 excluding breakfast (€18) 🛈 39 🛏 Indoor and outdoor

LAS VEGAS

www.hotelasvegas.com
A good, inexpensive option with WiFi and a restaurant.
✉ Km 245, Carretera Madrid–Irún, 09007 Burgos ☎ 947 48 44 53 🕐 Closed 22 Dec–8 Jan 💶 €70–€80 excluding breakfast (€8) 🛈 78

NH PALACIO DE LA MERCED

www.nh-hotels.com
This hotel is a 17th-century landmark building built around a stunning cloister opposite the cathedral. There is a good on-site restaurant.
✉ Calle de la Merced 13, 09002 Burgos ☎ 947 47 99 00 💶 €95–€250 excluding breakfast (€16) 🛈 110 (14 non-smoking)

Above *A room in the luxurious Landa Palace in Burgos*

EZCARAY

CASA MASIP
www.casamasip.com

A traditional, mellow stone house in the wine-producing town of Ezcaray, this has wooden beams and cool stone walls. Bedrooms are cosy and comfortable, combining original details with modern furnishings in bright colours. Guests can enjoy the pretty little garden, enclosed by stone walls and full of flowers. There's a good restaurant and tapas bar, and bicycles can be rented.

✉ Avenida Academia Militar 6, 26280 Ezcaray ☎ 941 35 43 27 💶 €75–€125 🛏 12

LEÓN

HOSTAL OREJAS
www.hostal-orejas.es

A good option for a budget stay in León. Amenities include free internet access.

✉ Calle Villafranca 8, 2° y República Argentina 28, 24001 León ☎ 987 25 29 09 💶 €65 excluding breakfast (€5) 🛏 49 🛏 5, 7

AC HOTEL SAN ANTONIO
www.ac-hoteles.com

Facilities at this modern hotel include internet access and a sauna.

✉ Calle Velázquez 12, 24005 León ☎ 987 21 84 44 💶 €85–€175 excluding breakfast (€14) 🛏 84 (6 non-smoking) 🛏 2, 9

PARÍS
www.hotelparisleon.com

This hotel has classical decor with comfortable rooms, all equipped with private bathroom, hairdryer, telephone, satellite TV and minibar. The hotel has recently added a small spa, with sauna, Jacuzzi, pool and beauty treatments.

✉ Calle Ancha 18, 24003 León ☎ 987 23 86 00 💶 €85–€105 excluding breakfast (€5) 🛏 53 (10 non-smoking) On one floor 2, 3, 4, 5, 8, 11

SAN MARCOS
www.parador.es

Treat yourself to a stay at this historic Gothic building. All rooms have minibar, safe deposit box and satellite TV. Facilities include money exchange, a bar, a garden and a shop.

✉ Plaza San Marcos 7, 24001 León ☎ 987 23 73 00 💶 €195–€250 excluding breakfast (€22). Discounts available for people over 60 🛏 225 🛏 10, 12

SILKEN LUIS DE LEÓN
www.hotelluisdeleon.com

All rooms have a private bathroom, hairdryer, telephone, modem connection, interactive TV, minibar, safe deposit box and room service.

✉ Calle Fray Luis de León 26, 24005 León ☎ 987 21 88 20 💶 €85–€145 excluding buffet breakfast (€12) 🛏 113 (15 non-smoking) 🛏 2, 4

SALAMANCA

AC PALACIO SAN ESTEBAN
www.ac-hoteles.com

AC Palacio San Esteban is a five-star hotel in a restored convent. All rooms have windows looking out onto the inner patio.

✉ Arroyo de Santo Domingo 3, 37001 Salamanca ☎ 923 26 22 96 💶 €115–€215 excluding breakfast (€16) 🛏 51 (1 floor non-smoking) 🛏

PETIT PALACE LAS TORRES
www.hthotels.com

This hotel has modern, well-equipped rooms. There are six superb, luxurious suites with PCs and high tech wireless access.

✉ Plaza Mayor 26 (entrance on Calle Consejo 4), 37002 Salamanca ☎ 923 21 21 00 💶 €85–€210 excluding breakfast (€10) 🛏 53 (38 non smoking)

RECTOR
www.hotelrector.com

This hotel is warm and comfortable, with art-nouveau decoration and wooden furniture. Advance reservations are advised.

✉ Paseo Rector Esperabé 10, 37008 Salamanca ☎ 923 21 84 82 💶 €145–€195 excluding breakfast (€14) 🛏 13

SAN POLO
www.hotelsanpolo.com

A three-star family-run hotel in the heart of town. Rooms are clean and functional with internet access.

✉ Arroyo de Santo Domingo 2–4, 37008 Salamanca ☎ 923 21 11 77 💶 €55–€150 excluding breakfast 🛏 36 🛏 1, 4, 5, 6, 8, 10

SORZANO

CASA JOSEPHINE
www.casajosephine.com

For something different, consider renting this exquisite *casa rural* which occupies an elegant 19th-century mansion. Filled with beautiful objects and tasteful furnishings, it offers all kinds of luxurious amenities including daily cleaning service, 24-hour room service, WiFi and you can even ask for a private chef to cater for you. The house is rented in its entirety and has five double bedrooms, which can accommodate between 10 and 12 people. The minimum rental is for two nights.

✉ Calle Concejo 8, 26191 Sorzano ☎ 941 44 71 66 💶 €520 per night for the whole house 🛏 5

TORO

JUAN II
www.hoteljuanii.com

A very good value hotel in central Toro the Juan II has basic rooms and public areas, with the bonus of beautiful views over the Río Duero. There is a restaurant.

✉ Paseo del Espolón I, 49800 Toro ☎ 980 69 03 00 💶 €85–€90 🛏 42 🚍 Outdoor From Zamora take N-122 30km (18 miles) east to Toro

VILLANUSUR RÍO DE OCA

VALLE DE OCA

A gorgeous rural hotel and restaurant in a handsome country town, this is set in a mansion which dates back to 1810. The interior is spectacular, with a fabulous fusion of contemporary and modern fittings—twirling faux-baroque chandeliers and velvet chaise longues are offset with bold zebra prints, for example. There are just eight exquisite rooms with hand-painted wallpaper and delightful original details. The restaurant serves creative Spanish cuisine and is equally chic inside.

✉ Calle La Plaza 8, 09258 Villanusur Río de Oca ☎ 947 59 46 02 💶 €110–€145 🛏 9

CASTILE-LA MANCHA AND EXTREMADURA

Castile-La Mancha and Extremadura are two of Spain's most neglected regions—sparsely populated and historically poor. Yet few regions can offer such insight into the Spanish heartland, a glimpse at a part of Spain that few tourists ever penetrate. There are stretches of unspoilt wilderness, and a clutch of old-fashioned towns and villages where tourism is still a new concept.

The vast, flat plains of Castile-La Mancha have a particular, haunting beauty. It was here that Don Quixote courted the fair (if imaginary) Dulcinea and tilted at windmills. The windmills survive, along with a string of sturdy castles—more reminders of the age of knights, when this region was on the frontier between Christian and Moslem kingdoms. To the south are the extensive vineyards of Valdepeñas, a comfortable little wine town, once best known for its affordable table wine, but which is increasingly gaining a reputation for excellence and innovation. Come in autumn to join in with one of the many local wine festivals, celebrated as the grape harvest is completed.

Extremadura, on the western borders of Spain, feels distinctly Portuguese in places—a consequence of the shifting frontier. It remains one of the poorest regions in Spain, although things have improved considerably since Luís Buñuel filmed his 1932 classic *Tierra Sin Pan* (Land Without Bread) here. In the 15th and 16th centuries, young men fled the poverty by sailing to the Americas, newly discovered by Europeans, in order to make their fortunes. Those who returned with their pockets full of coins built mansions and churches: golden cities like Trujillo and Cáceres survive intact from the age of the conquistadores, beautiful time-capsules that rank among the loveliest—yet least visited—sights in all Spain. Extremadura also boasts some verdant natural parks, perfect for birding and hiking.

ALCALÁ DEL JÚCAR

www.alcaladeljucar.net

The real appeal of Alcalá del Júcar is its impressive location, on a tight bend of the Río Júcar. The whitewashed, red-tiled buildings of this tiny township cling to the steep cliffs that rise high above the river. Great viewpoints are found on the winding back road to the west of town, and on the main CM-3201, approaching from the south.

The town's castle, perched precipitously on the apex of the bend, is its most obvious landmark and was built by the Moors in the 12th century. Today only its tower and some short sections of wall remain, but other medieval buildings abound in the town and the rippled rocks of the cliffs are every bit as dramatic as the man-made attractions.

Also worth a visit is the Iglesia de San Andrés, built between the 15th and 18th centuries, and, just to the south, a Roman bridge.

➕ 470 J7 ℹ Avenida de los Robles 1, 02210 Alcalá del Júcar ☎ 967 47 30 90

ALCÁNTARA

www.alcantara.es

Alcántara is a pleasant medieval town on the banks of the mighty Tajo (Tagus) river, and the six-arched Roman bridge (AD105), just to the northwest, is a masterpiece of engineering. The name Alcántara comes from the Arabic *al kantara*, meaning 'bridge'. The structure rises almost 70m (230ft) above the river and, even allowing for the fact that it was restored in the late 19th century, it is remarkable. The bridge still bears the main road north across the river. The town itself has some interesting sights, including the 16th-century Convento de San Benito, complete with a half-finished cathedral and a Gothic cloister.

➕ 468 D6 ℹ Avenida de Mérida 21, 10980 Alcántara ☎ 927 39 08 63

LA ALCARRIA

www.alcarria.org

La Alcarria is the area to the east and southeast of Guadalajara (▷ 110), made famous by Camilo José Cela in his 1949 book *Viaje a La Alcarria* (Journey to Alcarria). Today its real attraction lies in the historic towns that are dotted around the area, including Torija and Pastrana.

Torija, about 25km (15 miles) northeast of Guadalajara on the A-2, is known as the gateway to La Alcarria. Its beautifully restored castle houses a museum to Cela's work (Fri 5–8, Sat–Sun 12–8).

Pastrana, 45km (28 miles) southeast of Guadalajara, between the Tajo (Tagus) and the Tajuña, is the highlight of the area, thanks to its impressive 15th-century Palacio Ducal (owned by Alcala University, and currently undergoing remodelling) and La Colegiata e Iglesia de Nuestra Señora de la Asunción (Mon–Fri 10–2, Sat–Sun all day, but not during Mass). It was built between the 14th and 16th centuries, creating a blend of Gothic and Renaissance styles, and the church has a three-storey, gold altarpiece.

➕ 469 H5 ℹ Plaza de los Caídos 6, 19001 Guadalajara ☎ 949 21 16 26

ALMAGRO

www.ciudad-almagro.com

Almagro owes its present-day appearance to the well-heeled bankers and traders who settled here during the reign of Carlos I.

It's a tidy little town, superbly preserved and full of life. The focal point of the settlement is the wood-beamed Plaza Mayor, with an original medieval colonnade.

The square is also home to the 17th-century Corral de Comedias playhouse (Jul–Aug Tue–Fri 10–2, 6–9, Sat 10–2, 6–8, Sun 11–2, 6–8; Apr–Jun, Sep Tue–Fri 10–2, 5–8, Sat 10–2, 5–7, Sun 11–2, 5–7; Oct–Mar Tue–Fri 10–2, 4–7, Sat 10–2, 4–6, Sun 11–2, 4–6), something you are unlikely to see anywhere else in Spain. Made of wood throughout and not unlike a Shakespearean theatre in appearance, it features a cobbled courtyard with a retractable cloth roof and a balcony around three sides. The best way to experience the theatre is to see a play here — these are put on at weekends all year round and during the annual Festival Internacional de Teatro Clásico in July.

Other sites include the impressive Parroquia de San Bartolomé (only for Mass: Mon–Sat 7.30pm, Sun 12), with its white and gold neo-rococo nave and central rotunda, and the much more restrained Iglesia de Madre de Dios, dating from the 14th century. A statue of a seamstress on a small roundabout to the east of the Plaza Mayor is testimony to the town's lacework industry, and fine examples of the craft are sold in many artisan shops on and around the Plaza Mayor.

➕ 469 G8 ℹ Plaza Mayor 1, 13270 Almagro ☎ 926 86 07 17

Opposite *A Roman six-arched bridge spans the Tajo at Alcántara*
Below *Lace-making is a traditional craft in Almagro*

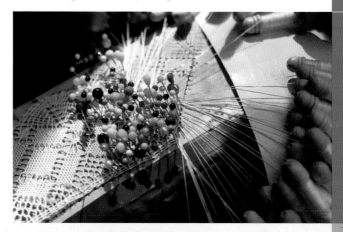

BELMONTE

The village of Belmonte itself has little to offer, but the 15th-century Castillo del Belmonte (Jun–Sep Tue–Sun 10–1.30, 4.30–7.30; Oct–May Tue–Sun 10–1.30, 3.30–5.30) is one of the biggest and most unusual medieval fortresses in Spain, with a highly original layout. Designed as both a home and a castle, it was built around a triangle. Its most impressive feature, apart from its sheer size, are the elaborate Mudéjar doorways and ceilings that can be found throughout. The castle was abandoned in the 18th century and wasn't occupied again until Eugénie de Montijo, better known as the wife of Napoléon III, came to live here after her husband's death in 1873. Many of the rooms are now suffering from years of neglect.

✛ 470 H7 ℹ Calle Lucas Parra 20, 16640 Belmonte ☎ 967 17 07 41 ⓒ Closed Mon

CÁCERES

▷ 327.

CALATRAVA LA NUEVA

www.turismocastillalamancha.com
The 13th-century convent-castle complex at Calatrava (Tue–Sun 10–2, 5.30–8) is among the most impressive in Castile-La Mancha and has a long and turbulent history. Wrapped around a rocky outcrop and with fabulous views out across the Sierra de Calatrava, the dark, foreboding walls of the castle create a striking silhouette and loom large and ominous over a pass leading into La Mancha. The fortress played an important part in the seesawing fortunes of Muslim and Christian forces. During the first Muslim invasion, when the resident Knights Templar conceded that they could no longer hold their fortress, the abbott of Fitero, in Navarra, mounted a heroic defence. As a result, the Order of the Knights of Calatrava was founded here in 1158. The fortress was rebuilt to form the vast convent-castle that dominates the site today.

✛ 469 G8 ℹ Plaza Mayor 1, 13001 Ciudad Real ☎ 926 21 10 44 ⓒ Closed Sun

CHINCHILLA DE MONTE-ARAGÓN

Chinchilla, known for its ceramics and its whitewashed cave dwellings, is a little village packed with history and arts and crafts. This is all overseen by a ruined medieval castle, which was the fortress stronghold of the Knights of Santiago and their grand master, the Marquis de Villena (1384–1434), in the 15th century. The village, lying in the castle's shadow, is rather run down, but it is compact and has a pleasant main square. Of particular interest are the cave dwellings in the northern corner, which were built outside the walls of the old city in the 16th century to house Muslim families that had emigrated from Granada and Guadix.

✛ 470 J8 ℹ Calle Fernando Núñez de Robres 4, 2520 Chinchilla de Monte-Aragón ☎ 967 26 00 01

CIUDAD REAL

www.ciudadreal.es
Ciudad Real is an inviting and immaculately kept city with a long history. It is not as well situated or as scenic as its northern cousin, Toledo, and it does have a much more modern feel, but what it lacks in medieval architecture it more than makes up for in amenities.

Ciudad Real was founded by Alfonso X in 1255 to provide an administrative focus for the region's three military orders (Calatrava, San Juan and Santiago), and to allow the Castilian kings to keep their immense power in check.

Only a few medieval buildings remain. Chief among these are the Puerta de Toledo, with its Moorish-inspired archway; the Catedral Basílica de las Órdenes Militares or Catedral de Santa María del Prado, built from the 16th to the 19th centuries; the Iglesia de San Pedro; and the 13th-century Iglesia de Santiago (open for Mass only), with Mudéjar decoration, built for the Knights of Santiago.

The Museo Municipal López Villaseñor (Jul–Aug Tue–Sun 9–2; Apr–Jun Tue–Sun 10–2, 5–8; Sep–Mar Tue–Sun 10–2), just opposite the cathedral, has a permanent exhibition of paintings by the locally born artist (1924–96).

Fans of author Miguel de Cervantes (1547–1616) can visit the Museo del Quijote (Jul–Aug daily 9–2; Apr–Jun 10–2, 6–9, Sep–Mar 10–2), housed in a modern structure next to the Parque de Gasset.

✛ 469 G7 ℹ Plaza Mayor 1, 13001 Ciudad Real ☎ 926 21 10 44 ⓒ Closed Sun

CÁCERES

Cáceres gained UNESCO World Heritage status for its many historic monuments, including Roman foundations, Moorish walls and numerous magnificent Renaissance buildings. It is a large town, but is surprisingly easy to negotiate, thanks partly to the fact that most points of interest can be found within a small area. In the 16th and 17th centuries, many impoverished Extremadurans sailed for the Americas in order to make their fortunes. Those who returned, with their pockets full of south American silver, built churches and mansions to show off their newfound riches.

The old town, or Ciudad Monumental, of Cáceres benefited from this influx of wealth and is now a breathtakingly beautiful ensemble, apparently frozen in time, still encircled by medieval walls. The old town dominates the northeastern corner of Cáceres and adjoins the long, avenue-like Plaza Mayor, which in summer is the social heart of the city. This was used as a meeting place for the town's elders as long ago as the Reconquest, and is still dominated by Moorish walls and the massive Torre de Bujaco, both of which date from the 12th century. The life, sights and sounds of the Plaza Mayor and old town are unforgettable by night.

THE CATHEDRAL AND OTHER CHURCHES

Access to the old town is up a grand flight of stairs through the Arco de Estrella. The highlight here is the 15th-century Concatedral de Santa María (Mon–Sat 10–1, 6–7.30, Sun and festivals 9.30–2, 5–7.30), late Romanesque and early Gothic in style, and with an exquisitely carved cedar altarpiece.

Another church worth mentioning is the Iglesia de Santiago (daily 9–12, 6–8), where the knightly order of the same name was founded. Beyond these churches, much of the charm of the town lies in walking its narrow, cobbled alleys and unexpectedly coming up on squares with elaborately decorated palaces, of which there are literally dozens.

If you'd like to know more about the heritage of the town as well as see a few works by El Greco (c1541–1614), among others, check out the Museo de Cáceres (Tue–Sat 10–2, 5.30–8.30, Sun 10–2), which sits over an original 12th-century Arabic well.

INFORMATION

www.turismocaceres.org

✚ 468 D7 ℹ Plaza Mayor 3, 10003 Cáceres ☎ 927 01 08 34 🕐 May–Sep Mon–Fri 9–2, 5–7, Sat–Sun 9.45–2; Oct–Apr Mon–Fri 9–2, 4–6, Sat–Sun 9.45–2

Above *Casa Toledo Montezuma in Cáceres*
Opposite left *The church of San Pedro in Ciudad Real*
Opposite right *The 15th-century Castillo del Belmonte*

INFORMATION

www.cuenca.org

⊞ 470 J6 ⓘ Calle Alfonso VIII 2, 16001 Cuenca ☎ 969 24 10 51 ⏰ Mon–Fri 9.30–2, 4–7, Sat–Sun 9.30–2, 4–6.30 🚆 Cuenca

TIP

» As with many of the region's hilltop towns (including Toledo and Segovia), Cuenca is best seen from afar in the evening light. A good vantage point at any time is the road leading up to the *parador* and the Puente de San Pablo, high above the gorge. The latter also provides pedestrian access to the old town.

Above *Mansions built by* conquistadores *line Calle Alfonso VIII*
Below *Cuenca's Puente de San Pablo walkway spans the gorge*

CUENCA

Cuenca's old town is squeezed skywards by the steep gorges of the Júcar and Huécar rivers. It is packed with museums, churches and fine medieval monuments, the most famous of which are the wood-beamed Casas Colgadas (Hanging Houses), which are cantilevered out over the cliffs to make the best use of available living space. Little is known about the town before the eighth century, when Muslim invaders fortified a settlement here, establishing the town's textile industry by producing carpets.

OLD TOWN

At the heart of the upper city is the Plaza Mayor and the heavily restored Catedral de Nuestra Señora de Gracia. Much of it dates from the 12th and 13th centuries, making it the earliest example of Gothic architecture in Spain, although the main facade was rebuilt in 1902. Other highlights include the Torre del Ángel (Tower of the Angel), a superb baroque altarpiece in marble, jasper and gilded bronze. The restored Casas Colgadas are best enjoyed from the Puente de San Pablo. One of these Hanging Houses—to the left as you look towards the cliff—contains the Museo de Arte Abstracto Español (Jul–Sep Tue–Fri 11–2, 5–7, Sat 11–2, 4–8; Oct–Jun Tue–Fri 11–2, 4–6, Sat 11–2, 4–8, Sun 11–2.30), which has a big collection of weird and wonderful works of art.

LA CIUDAD ENCANTADA

About 30km (19 miles) north of Cuenca, high in the Serranía de Cuenca, is the Enchanted City. Here the karst limestone has been weathered and sculpted into wild shapes, the most distinctive of which have been given names.

SCIENCE MUSEUM

The Museo de la Ciencia (tel 969 24 03 20; mid-May to mid-Sep Tue–Sat 10–2, 4–8, Sun 10–2; rest of year Tue–Sat 10–2, 4–7, Sun 10–2) has an ingeniously eccentric clock, state-of-the-art displays and a planetarium (all in Spanish).

VENTANO DEL DIABLO

The Window of the Devil is a natural double archway and balcony sculpted high into the side of the Júcar gorge, best experienced at sunset on the drive back from the Ciudad Encantada.

CONSUEGRA

www.aytoconsuegra.es
www.consuegra.es

Consuegra, or rather the small hill just to the south of it, is home to some of the most famous windmills in Castile-La Mancha, if not the world. The windmills throughout this region were immortalized by Miguel de Cervantes (1547–1616) in his epic novel *Don Quixote*. Perhaps the most memorable story is an episode in which Don Quixote, a self-appointed knight errant and doer of good deeds, attacks a line of windmills in the mistaken belief that they are giants. Although the windmills are not named, those at Consuegra have become synonymous with the tale, thanks to their dramatic location.

The ramshackle town litters the foot of a hill topped by a brooding 13th-century castle (Mon–Fri 9.15–1.45, 3.45–5.45, Sat–Sun 10.45–1.45, 3.45–5.45) that has been restored to give visitors an idea of what it must have looked like when it was home to the Knights of Malta. However, the real stars of this lofty little perch are the dozen windmills marching along the ridge behind the castle. The first one you reach on the way up the hill has been converted into a visitor office, and upstairs you can see the working cogs of the mill; the second one is a refreshment shop. But what really makes these windmills more spectacular than any others in the region is their location, with tremendous views out over classic Castile-La Mancha country.

✚ 469 G7 ℹ Cerro Calderico, Molino Bolero s/n, 45700 Consuegra ☎ 925 47 57 31

CORIA

http://turismo.coria.org

This town lays claim to Europe's most perfectly preserved Roman walls, as well as to a high concentration of fine buildings. The dominant feature is the castle tower, built into the northwestern corner of the original Roman walls in the 15th or 16th century. The walls, built between the third and fourth centuries AD, are no less monumental than the castle tower and are well preserved.

In the heart of the old town is the cathedral (daily 10–1, 5–7.30; museum: Tue–Sat 10–1, 5–7.30, Sun 10–1), high on the cliffs overlooking the Alagón valley. Inside the building, the primarily Gothic stonework is austere, providing a stark contrast to the gaudy high-baroque altarpiece. Below is the Puente Viejo, or Puente Sin Río (Bridge Without a River), which was left high and dry when the river changed its course at the end of the 17th century.

✚ 468 D6 ℹ Avenida de Extremadura 39, 10800 Coria ☎ 927 50 13 51

CUENCA

▷ 328.

GUADALUPE

▷ 330.

LAS HURDES

www.todohurdes.com

Beyond the Valle del Jerte and Sierra de Tormantos lie the stark, sparsely populated Hurdes mountains, in the northwestern corner of Castile-La Mancha. Las Hurdes have long been associated with poverty in the region, due in part to a 1932 film by Luis Buñel called *Las Hurdes—Land Without Bread*. Now it's considered a haven for wildlife and outdoor enthusiasts, although it is a harsh place in which to scrape a living.

Begin a foray into the mountains at the visitor information office in Camínomorisco, which can advise on trekking routes and other activities such as fishing, hunting and watersports. Among the highlights are Chorro de los Ángeles, a waterfall 300m (1,000ft) high, near the ruins of the 13th-century Convento de Nuestra Señora de los Ángeles, and the waterfalls and volcano just a short walk from El Gasco village.

✚ 468 D6 ℹ Avenida de les Hurdes, 10620 Caminomorisco ☎ 927 43 53 29

Below left *Musicians in the village of Nuñomoral, a good base for excursions to Las Hurdes*
Below *Windmills at Consuegra: Don Quixote's 'giants' are a prominent landscape feature*

INFORMATION

www.monasterioguadalupe.com

✚ 468 E7 ✉ Real Monasterio de Santa María de Guadalupe, 10140 Guadalupe ☎ 927 36 70 00 🕐 Monastery and museums: daily 9.30–1, 3.30–6.30 ✋ Adult €5, child (7–14) €2, under 7 free; entry to main chapel free to all 🚻 Admission by guided tour only (included in admission price); Spanish only 🈺

TIPS

» The visitor office (opposite the monastery on Plaza Mayor) produces a map and leaflet detailing some excellent walks in the area. The best lasts about two hours, taking in a number of hermitages and springs as it winds along easy tracks through the nearby hills.

» If you want to visit during *Semana Santa* (Holy Week, from Palm Sunday to Easter Sunday), reserve a room months, maybe years, ahead.

Below *Guadalupe monastery dominates this small Extremaduran town*

GUADALUPE

Guadalupe's monastery is one of the most important pilgrimage sites in Spain, not to mention one of the best surviving examples of Gothic Mudéjar architecture in the world. Its secluded mountain setting and charming Plaza Mayor add to its appeal.

Legend has it that a shepherd discovered a dark-faced statue of the Virgin on this site in the 13th century. The Hieronymite monastery subsequently built here came under the patronage of Alfonso XI and was often visited by the royals. It soon gained a reputation as one of Spain's holiest sights, so much so that Christopher Columbus named a Caribbean island after it. The Latin American connection continues in Mexico, which adopted the Virgin of Guadalupe as its patron saint. The present-day monastery dates from the 14th and 15th centuries.

THE MONASTERY

The Monasterio de Guadalupe rises from the rugged Sierra de Villuercas above a little town of well-kept cobbled streets and jutting, wood-beamed balconies. The main facade overlooks the Plaza Mayor, its sheer scale and magnificence out of all proportion to anything else in the vicinity. Up close, the facade is an intricate tableau of swirling Gothic Mudéjar tracery.

A tour of the working monastery includes what is arguably the finest Mudéjar cloister in Spain. The Museo de Bordados (Embroidery Museum) is an extraordinary display of ecclesiastical wealth and decadence, with its gold-thread vestments and altar drapes, some adorned with images of skulls and grim reapers. The Museo de Libros Miniados (Manuscript Room) has books a metre (3ft) high of musical scores dating from a time when all books were handwritten.

Paintings by Zurbarán (1598–1664) hang in the sacristy, allegedly the only such series in Spain still in its original setting. The small but splendid *Confession in Prison* by Francisco de Goya (1746–1828) hangs in the Museo de Pintura y Escultura. Behind the altar, visitors are shown the small statue of the Virgin of Guadalupe and are invited to touch or kiss an image.

The monastery also runs its own hostel (more like a luxury monastic hotel), which is based around the second Gothic cloister.

JEREZ DE LOS CABALLEROS

The little village of Jerez was built up through conquistador wealth, and the result is an astonishingly rich collection of churches, convents and mansions.

Apparently miles from anywhere in the middle of dry, empty hill country, Jerez de los Caballeros existed as long ago as Roman times, but it was the foundation of the town's castle by the Knights Templar that established it as a base of strategic importance. In the 16th century conquistadors brought their gold here, allowing the town to flourish, and in 1525 it was declared a city by Charles V. Churches worth visiting include Santa María de la Encarnación (free guided tours only through the tourist office), next to the castle and thought to have been built over an original Visigothic basilica; and San Bartolomé (free guided tours as above) and San Miguel (free guided tours as above), both begun in the 15th century in the Gothic style and with later baroque additions.

➕ 472 D8 ℹ Plaza de la Constitución 4, 06380 Jerez de los Caballeros ☎ 924 73 03 72

MÉRIDA
▷ 332.

MONASTERIO DE YUSTE

www.yustedigital.com

Charles V (1500–58) chose to spend his final years in this impressive, if austere, complex of buildings on wooded slopes high above the village of the same name. The monastery was badly damaged by fire during the Spanish War of Independence (1808–13), but has since been restored.

This is still a working monastery, and the king's palace next door has been turned into a museum. Guided tours, in Spanish only, take in the king's somewhat spartan rooms, complete with grand fireplaces, rustic stonework and heavy wooden ceilings.

➕ 468 E6 ✉ Monasterio de Yuste, 10430 Cuacos de Yuste ☎ 927 17 21 30 🕐 Monastery and museum: Mon–Sat 9.30–

12.30, 3.30–5.30, Sun 9.30–11.30, 3.30–5.30
🖐 Adult €3, child (5–16) €2, under 4 free
🎫 1-hour tour, available in Spanish only

MONTES DE TOLEDO

www.montesdetoledo.org

The Montes de Toledo range, within easy striking distance of Toledo, is one of the most wild and sparsely populated areas in the region, if not Spain. The walking here is excellent, and the area is also renowned for its hunting.

To the southwest of Toledo is the tiny foothill town of San Pablo de Los Montes; farther south, across a spectacular mountain pass in the direction of Robledillo, are some natural springs. These are tapped by the Balneario de Robledillo (tel 925 41 53 00), a hotel-cum-restaurant that will fill baths with the allegedly curative waters for a few euros.

A little to the south of Robledillo, and still within the Montes de Toledo, is the Parque Nacional de Cabañeros, stretching across a vast open plain at the foot of the mountains.

Park information is available from the interpretation office to the west of Bullaque (daily 9–2, 3–6).

➕ 469 F7 ℹ Plaza de la Merced 4, 45002 Toledo ☎ 925 25 93 55 🕐 Closed Mon pm

OLIVENZA

www.ayuntamientodeolivenza.com

In addition to its 15th-century castle and a number of important religious and secular buildings, Olivenza's appeal lies in its heritage, which is typified by whitewashed houses and distinctly Portuguese designwork throughout the town.

Olivenza was originally founded by the Knights Templar in the 13th century as a border outpost and, as with so many towns along the Río Guadiana, ownership has veered back and forth between Spain and Portugal ever since. It became Spanish for good only in 1801.

The defensive walls and castle (May–Sep Tue–Sun 11–2, 5–8; Oct–Apr Tue–Sun 11–2, 4–7), with its magnificent Torre del Homenaje, were built by Juan II of Portugal, and the 16th-century churches

Above *Magdalena church in Olivenza*
Below *Statue of Charles V at the Monasterio de Yuste*

of Magdalena (daily 9–2) and Santa María del Castillo (daily 9–1, 5–8) were built in the Portuguese Manueline style, characterized by whitewashed walls.

Many of the town's historic houses are similarly designed, including the Palacio de los Duques de Cadaval (now the town hall) and the Panadería del Rey, home to an excellent ethnographic museum (May–Sep Tue–Fri 11–2, 5–8, Sat 10–2, 5–8, Sun 10–2; Oct–Apr Tue–Fri 11–2, 4–7, Sat 10–2, 4–7, Sun 10–2).

There are some fantastic viewpoints of the town from the 2101 road across the Río Guadiana, 10km (6 miles) to the west of the town of Olivenza.

➕ 468 C8 ℹ Plaza de España s/n, 06100 Olivenza ☎ 924 49 01 51

INFORMATION

www.consorciomerida.org
www.ciudadesdepatrimonio.org
✚ 468 D8 ℹ Avenida José Álvarez Sáez
de Buruaga s/n, 06800 Mérida ☎ 924
00 97 30 🕓 Jun–Sep Mon–Fri 9–1.45,
5–7.15, Sat–Sun and public holidays
9.30–1.45; Oct–May Mon–Fri 9–1.45,
4–6.15, Sat–Sun and public holidays
9.30–1.45 🚉 Mérida

MÉRIDA

Modern Mérida, the capital of Extremadura, is still only half the size of its
precursor, the Roman city of Augusta Emerita, established in 25BC.It contains
more Roman ruins than anywhere else in Spain and has been awarded
UNESCO World Heritage status. The city was ceded first to the Visigoths and
then the Muslims, before Alfonso IX retook the city in 1230. Mérida later became
a vital outpost on the Portuguese frontier, but suffered damage during the
Spanish War of Independence against the French at the beginning of the 19th
century. It was only in the 20th century that it once more became a commercial
hub with clout.

LAYOUT AND SIGHTS

Mérida is built on the banks of the Río Guadiana. The heart of the city is to the
east of the river, which is crossed by the 60-arch Puente Romano, a miracle
of engineering still used by pedestrians today despite being 2,000 years old.
Opposite the Puente Romano is the Alcazaba, a fortress founded by the Moors in
AD835, the first of its kind to be built by Muslims in Spain.

 The social focus is the Plaza España and the roads leading off it, but the best
place to start your city tour is the visitor information office. This is outside the
gate of the impressive Roman ruins (Jun–Sep daily 9.30–1.45, 5–7.15; Oct–May
9.30–1.45, 4–6.15), which include the Anfiteatro Romano, once the scene of
gladiatorial contests, and the Teatro, with its restored backdrop of two-tiered
columns. The theatre hosts a celebrated classical theatre festival every summer.
Over the street is the Museo de Arte Romano, which houses a collection of
relics, frescoes and mosaics. The Templo de Diana is hidden in the backstreets,
as are the Arco de Trojan and the Casa del Mitreo, the latter containing yet
more fine frescoes and mosaics. The massive wall of the Embalse de Prosperina
(Prosperina Reservoir), 425m (1,395ft) long and 21m (69ft) high, dates from
Roman times and is 8km (5 miles) north of town.

Above *Ruins of the Teatro Romano*
in Mérida

PARQUE NATURAL LAGUNAS DE RUIDERA

www.lagunasderuidera.net

This natural park is an oasis of life in an otherwise dry and barren landscape, and in the summer it's a popular spot for camping and picnicking, plus swimming and other watersports. The park consists of a series of long, thin lakes stretching about 25km (16 miles) from north to south. The landscape features groves of holm oak, together with junipers, elms and poplars, and birdlife abounds in the form of ducks, coots and bustards.

The best place to begin a visit is at the visitor office in Ruidera. The Cascada del Hundimiento waterfall, a short walk from the village, is highly recommended by the visitor office, but is rather disappointing and not really worth the effort.

Marginally more impressive is the Cueva de Montesinos, at the southern end of the park. The cave is much deeper than it looks, and there are steps leading down into its bowels (take a torch). The remains of the Castillo de Rochafrida are nearby. ✚ 469 H7 🛈 Centro de Recepción de Visitantes, Avenida Castilla La Mancha s/n, 13249 Ruidera, Ciudad Real ☎ 926 52 81 16 🕓 Closed Mon–Tue

Below *The Parque Natural de Monfragüe (right) is popular with hikers (below)*

PARQUE NATURAL DE MONFRAGÜE

www.monfrague.com

About 25km (16 miles) south of Plasencia is the Parque Natural de Monfragüe, which supports the largest population of birds of prey in Spain, not to mention the largest colonies of black vultures and imperial eagles in the world. While this may not sound all that exciting to non-ornithologists, the combination of craggy, mountainous scenery and superb views makes the park one of the highlights of the region, and the birds are undeniably impressive.

You could begin your visit at the information office in the village of Villarreal de San Carlos, signed from the main road. (A short distance farther down the road is another visitor office, but information here is in Spanish only.) To see the birds, you can cross the bridge over the Tajo (Tagus) river and follow the road round to a parking area at the Salto del Gitano rock pillar. Opposite you will see a huge crag that is home to most of the park's colonies and, at the right time of year, up to 250 breeding pairs of black vultures.

The best time to see the birds is during the spring and summer, but even in the middle of winter you can still be sure of a good display.

If you want to explore the park there are numerous well-signed walks—the best starts at the southern end of the bridge and climbs to a ruined ninth-century castle at the top of the hill. ✚ 468 E6 🛈 10695 Villarreal de San Carlos ☎ 927 19 91 34

PLASENCIA

www.aytoplasencia.es

The town of Plasencia, at the foot of the Sierra de Tormantos in a tight bend of the Río Jerte, is packed full of noble mansions, medieval walls and old Gothic churches. It has a lively atmosphere that belies its comparatively compact size.

Plasencia has been a thriving commercial town since it was founded by Alfonso VIII in 1186. Subsequent centuries saw it rise to prosperity under the patronage of Extremaduran nobles, who left a rich artistic legacy.

The cathedral—actually two cathedrals—probably represents the pinnacle of this golden age. The Catedral Vieja (Old Cathedral) was built in the 13th and 14th centuries, then in the 16th century the Catedral Nueva (New Cathedral) was tacked on to it. Of note are the fine plateresque south and west facades and, inside, the flamboyant walnut choir stalls (1520) by woodworker Rodrigo Alemán.

The interpretation office (Jun–Sep Tue–Sat 10–2, 5–7, Sun 9–1; Oct–May Tue–Sat 10–2, 4–6, Sun 9–1), which houses a second visitor office (the main one is opposite the south facade of the cathedral), is a short walk from the heart of the town, but is well worth the effort.

Plasencia also provides the perfect base for jaunts along the high mountain roads that pass through Extremadura's most impressive scenery. ✚ 468 D6 🛈 Calle Torre Lucià, 10600 Plasencia ☎ 927 42 38 43

SEGÓBRIGA

www.turismocastillalamancha.com
The Roman ruins at Segóbriga are among the most impressive in Spain, and the site has an excellent museum. Its secluded location is in a gentle landscape, the hills between Aranjuez and Cuenca.

The monuments seen today were built in the first century AD, but the town remained a commercial site until the third century. In the fifth and sixth centuries Visigoths added the basilicas and vast necropolis, the ruins of which also remain. Here you will find an impressively preserved theatre and amphitheatre, plus the ruins of the basilica, thermal baths and numerous walls and squares.

✚ 470 H6 ✉ Parque Arqueológico de Segóbriga, Carretera de Saelices a Villamayor de Santiago s/n, 16430 Saelices ☎ 629 75 22 57 🅳 Tue–Sun 10–9 👋 Adult €5, under 11 €3 🔲 Small, outdoor bar 🏛 Museum shop

SIGÜENZA

www.siguenza.es
This town of red-tiled buildings and church spires is piled high on a hill above Río Henares. It was a commercial outpost from Roman times, becoming more important during the Moorish invasion of the eighth century.

The cathedral (guided tours Tue–Sat 11, 12, 4.30, 5.30, Sun 12, 5.30) was begun in 1130, and attained its monumental size and feel during four centuries of building. The result is a mixture of Romanesque, Gothic, Mudéjar, Renaissance and high baroque styles. The interior is exquisitely decorated, with marble striped columns and sublime stained-glass windows, particularly the rose window of the west facade. Among the artworks is an *Anunciación* by El Greco (c1541–1614). The Plaza Mayor, opposite the cathedral, is a Renaissance gem, with graceful arcaded 15th-century palaces.

✚ 470 H5 ℹ Ermita de Humilladero, 19250 Sigüenza ☎ 949 34 70 07 🅳 Closed Mon in winter

TALAVERA DE LA REINA

www.talavera.org
The main reason to visit Talavera is for its centuries-old ceramics industry, which still thrives in huge commercial showrooms, smaller craft shops and a ceramics museum. The Museo Ruiz de Luna (Tue–Sat 10–2, 4–6.30, Sun 10–2), in a restored medieval building inside the old city, has an extensive collection of local ceramic masterpieces dating from as early as the 16th century.

✚ 469 F6 ℹ Palenque 2, 45600 Talavera de la Reina ☎ 925 72 14 54

TRUJILLO

▷ 335.

VALDEPEÑAS

www.valdepenas.es
Valdepeñas has been a wine-making town for centuries, and many of the vineyards still maintain traditional bodegas, where visitors can sample and buy the wine. This region produces about half of Spain's wine; the best is bottled in Valdepeñas. All bottles carry the *denominación de origen* label (only the *denominación de origen calificada* is higher), which indicates that the wine has met strict standards. The best place to start any visit is at the Museo del Vino (Tue–Sat 10–2, 5–7, Sun and festivals 12–2). This has a state-of-the-art exhibition about wine-making in the region. The visitor office, in Windmill Gregorio Prieto at the north end of town, has a list of vineyards.

For the natural option, Dionisos, near the visitor office, specializes in organic wines. The Bodegas Real occupies an impressive vineyard and château 10km (6 miles) southeast of town on the Cózar road.

✚ 469 G8 ℹ Plaza de España s/n, 13300 Valdepeñas ☎ 926 31 25 52 🅳 Closed Mon

ZAFRA

www.zafra.es
The little town of Zafra is full of arcaded squares and narrow cobbled streets. It is overlooked by a 15th-century castle where Hernán Cortés (1485–1547) is said to have stayed prior to sailing to Mexico in the early 16th century.

There are fine churches, convents and secular buildings that exude medieval grandeur. The nine-towered castle, now a luxury *parador* (state-run hotel) was built in 1437 by the second Duke of Feria during the Christian Reconquest of the region. The grand Renaissance patio was added in the 16th century. The layout of the rest of the town is medieval.

The most impressive religious building is the 16th-century Colegiata de la Candelaria (Jun–Sep Mon–Tue, Thu–Sat 10.30–1, 6.30–8.30, Sun and festivals 10.30–1; Oct–May Mon–Tue, Thu–Sat 10.30–1, 5.30–7.30, Sun and festivals 10.30–1) and its Remedios chapel, which has 10 paintings by Francisco de Zurbarán (1598–1664). Also of interest are the wooden Mudéjar ceiling and dome of the Convento de Santa Catalina.

✚ 468 D8 ℹ Plaza de España 8, 06300 Zafra ☎ 924 55 10 36

TRUJILLO

Trujillo is a delight, redolent with the riches of the 16th-century *conquistadors* and has fine views from its walls. The castle is still visited daily by devout locals, who come to pray to the much-venerated statue of Our Lady of Victory, Trujillo's patron saint. Development at the foot of the old town has threatened to spoil it, but essentially little has changed here in the last 500 years. This is the birthplace of Francisco Pizarro (*c*1475–1541), the man responsible for the rout of the vast Inca Empire. Long before Pizarro's day, the Muslims had built a splendid castle on the hill with 360-degree views across the surrounding plain.

HISTORIC TRUJILLO

The old part of town is dominated by the castle, which, although empty now, has fine views from its walls. Down the hill is the Iglesia de Santa María la Mayor, founded in the 13th century. It has a fine three-level altarpiece and a tall bell tower with sweeping panoramas. Also nearby is the Casa-Museo de Pizarro daily 10–2, 4–7), decorated and furnished as a 16th-century house.

The social and spiritual hub of the town is the wide Plaza Mayor. Apart from the statue of Pizarro, its most important monument is the Palacio del Marqués de la Conquista (Mon–Fri 10–1, 4–6, Sat–Sun 11–2, 4.30–7), with a coat of arms on one corner containing the busts of Pizarro and his wife, Inés. The Gothic Puerta de las Limas, to the north, is named after the fruit carved into its mouldings. The visitors' book is a roll-call of Spanish royalty, and includes the names of Charles V, Felipe II and Felipe V. Just off the eastern corner of the Plaza Mayor, the Palacio de los Duques de San Carlos is now occupied by Hieronymite nuns who are famous for their sweet treats. Pull the bell to gain entry and place your order—and linger a while to take a look at the magnificent patio adorned with the double-headed eagle of the Habsburg coat-of-arms.

OSBORNE BULLS

Approaching town from the south, you can't miss the vast bulls' silhouettes on the horizon just off the main road. These bulls advertise Osborne sherry and brandy. There are 91 Toros de Osborne standing by roadsides in Spain.

INFORMATION

www.trujillo.es
www.turismoextremadura.com
🚩 468 E7 🚩 Plaza Major s/n, 10200 Trujillo ☎ 927 32 26 77 🕓 Daily 10–2, 4.30–7

Opposite *Decorative tiled sign at Bodegas Senorio de los Llanos in Valdepeñas, capital of one of Spain's most important wine regions*
Below *A statue of Francisco Pizarro stands on the Plaza Mayor*

REGIONS CASTILE-LA MANCHA AND EXTREMADURA • SIGHTS

THE MOUNTAINS AND WINDMILLS OF LA MANCHA

Castile-La Mancha is often seen as a harsh, unforgiving place with little to offer the casual visitor, but beyond the barren, sun-parched plains lies a fascinating region just waiting to be explored. Medieval monuments, Castilian castles and traditional towns abound, but the region is most famous for its windmills, immortalized in Miguel de Cervantes' epic novel *Don Quixote*. This drive explores the highlights of the province's vast and varied landscape, and includes the most famous windmills in Spain.

THE DRIVE

Distance: 210km (130 miles)
Allow: 1 day
Start/end at: Toledo, map 469 G6

★ Toledo (▷ 114–115) is one of Spain's finest jewels, rich in art and treasure.

From Toledo, take the CM-401 towards Navahermosa. As you crest the brow of the first hill, your reward is an expansive view of the landscape ahead. Pass through Polán to reach a gently rolling landscape of low hills; the first small pass brings you out on a ruler-straight road pointing towards the wall of mountains on the horizon. At the CM-403, turn left and then right after 9km (5.5 miles), following signs to San Pablo de los

Montes, which lies at the foot of the mountains proper. At the first roundabout in San Pablo turn right, following signs to Las Navillas. Skirt the western edge of the town to a turn-off on the left with the small sign 'Baños de Robledillo'.

Take this narrow, winding road to the top (the views are superb, and from here well-marked trails strike off into the hills, so if you need to stretch your legs, this is the perfect place).

Return to and continue down the long, sweeping hairpins on the far side of the hill and at the bottom you'll find yourself in Robledillo, home to the Balneario de los Baños (the hotel on the right just as you enter the village).

❶ The highlight of Robledillo is bathing in the area's curative spring water. The water is artificially heated, but if the ceramic plaque on the hotel's dining room wall is anything to go by, it's still beneficial to a host of rheumatic, renal and urinary disorders.

To continue your drive, stay on the same road to a T-junction, and then head right for 1.5km (1 mile) to reach the CM-4017. Turn left for 10km (6 miles) to reach a crossroads with a fuel station on the left. Alternatively, turn right on reaching the CM-4017 if you want to visit the Parque Nacional de Cabañeros. Continue straight on, skirting the base of the mountains all the way to Los Yébenes.

② The hillside town of Los Yébenes is famous for its olive oil, but in the 19th century it was a renowned centre of banditry. It has two fine medieval churches and windmills that are mentioned by name in Cervantes' *Don Quixote*.

From Los Yébenes, take the N-401 south, following signs to Ciudad Real. After 18km (11 miles) turn left on to the CM-4116.

③ As you breeze through workaday Urda, the splendid windmills of Consuegra, stone built and painted white, each with four great latticed sails, heave into view. They stand above the town, gaunt against the sky on the summit of an incongruous hill. Soon after, turn right to Consuegra (▷ 329); the industrial

suburbs are uninspiring, but as you enter the town proper, turn right to follow the sign to the castle and windmills.

Carry on through town until you see Toledo signed to the left. Follow this turning and at a roundabout head straight over a small bridge, before bearing right again to follow signs towards Madridejos (this can be confusing, but you should end up going north eventually!). At the CM-4025, turn left; the road hardly kinks for 15km (9 miles), after which it weaves in and out of rolling hills. Turn left just beyond these to reach Orgaz.

④ The charming medieval village of Orgaz has a wood-beamed Plaza Mayor, an 18th-century church, a 15th-century castle and the bizarrely

named Puente de los Cinco Ojos (Bridge of the Five Eyes).

Follow signs back to Toledo.

WHEN TO GO
Toledo can be unbearably busy in July and August, but once you're out in the countryside things are considerably quieter at any time of year. That said, the desert-like heat of July and August is best avoided. If you want Toledo to yourself, or if you want to experience the mountains and plains in more dramatic, windswept weather, autumn is a good alternative—just don't expect much in the way of atmosphere.

WHERE TO EAT
BALNEARIO DE ROBLEDILLO
The café-restaurant at this hotel specializes in home cooking.
✉ Paraje de los Baños del Robledillo, 45120 San Pablo de los Montes ☎ 925 41 53 00
🕐 Daily, all day. Phone to reserve

PLACE TO VISIT
BALNEARIO DE ROBLEDILLO
For details, ▷ Where to Eat above.

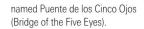

Above left The mountains of La Mancha are home to a wide variety of birds
Above right Rooftops of Toledo
Opposite Consuegra's windmills

SIERRA DE GREDOS AND BEYOND

This drive takes in the majestic Valle del Jerte as well as some of Extremadura's more isolated gems, and because it's relatively compact, it should provide a good day's outing. After a misty morning tour of the Monasterio de Yuste, have a mid-morning coffee at the top of the Sierra de Tormantos to steel your nerves for the descent. Lunch in Plasencia can then be followed by an afternoon spent walking or birding in the Parque Natural de Monfragüe, before easing south to medieval Trujillo as the sun sets over the plains.

THE DRIVE
Distance: 135km (84 miles)
Allow: 1 day
Start at: Monasterio de Yuste, map 468 E6
End at: Trujillo, map 468 E7

★ Monasterio de Yuste (▷ 331) is where Charles V retired in 1556 after his abdication. He died here two years later.

From the monastery follow signs to Garganta la Olla. This basic, occasionally potholed road winds through a rocky, boulder-strewn landscape with good views of the Valle de la Vera.

❶ The slopes around pretty, terracotta-tiled Garganta are heavily terraced (crops grown here include

paprika and asparagus). There is a fine viewpoint overlooking the town.

At an intersection in the village, turn right and follow the road for 150m (165 yards), then turn right again, following signs to Piornal. This is a narrow road with several blind hairpins, but it has great views of the interlacing valleys ahead, where waterfalls appear as white smudges cascading down the mountainsides.

❷ The views from Puerto de Piornal (1,269m/4,162ft) are breathtaking in clear weather (in other words, most of the year).

Just beyond the pass you come to Hospedería La Serrana (see Where to Eat opposite). Continue straight

through Piornal (ignoring the sharp left turnoff to Pasarón de la Vera) as the road zigzags down into the vast Valle del Jerte, which runs the length of the Sierra de Gredos and Sierra de Tormantos. After 7km (4 miles), where this road bends sharply back on itself to the left, a small *camino rural* (country road) heads right. Follow this for 500m (550 yards) to the parking area at the Garganta de Bonal. A short footpath leads up to the stunning Cascada El Caozo.

After visiting the waterfall, head back to continue down through the cherry-tree terraces of Valdastillas (spring is the best time to see the trees, when they are covered in white blossoms). Soon after, the road joins the main N-110 at the bottom of the Valle del Jerte. Turn left here towards Plasencia. This fast, straight road makes a nice change from the tortuous hairpins of the hills.

As you near Plasencia, look out for pylons topped with storks' nests, and for the occasional sign that says *Vía Pecuaria*, sometimes with an outline of a bull—this marks ancient livestock migration routes across Spain. At the roundabout on the outskirts of Plasencia, head right across the Río Jerte to reach the centre of town.

❸ The town of Plasencia (▷ 333) is full of noble mansions, ancient towers and hidden churches.

From Plasencia, follow signs to Trujillo on the EX-208. Just after the 5km (3-mile) marker you come to a confusing roundabout junction; keep straight here, following Trujillo signs. This stretch offers little in the way of scenery, but you're certain to see occasional birds of prey along this road, a tantalizing taste of what's to come in the Parque Natural de Monfragüe.

❹ Monfragüe (▷ 333) is a vast area of towering rugged peaks, deep gorges and forests rich in flora and fauna.

A line of wooded hills ahead signals the edge of the park, and soon the road starts to wind up and over a small pass before bearing you to Villarreal de San Carlos. Continue to follow the road around, over the Tajo and past the vast, bird-covered outcrop at Salto del Gitano (▷ 333). The road is quite rough, but the landscape is impressive as it twists and turns through the intimate gorge of Arroyo de la Vid. Pass straight through the ramshackle little town of Torrejón el Rubio to reach Trujillo (▷ 335).

❺ At dusk, Trujillo's medieval monuments are at their most magical. The views of this impressive, fortified outpost as you approach from Monfragüe are simply dazzling.

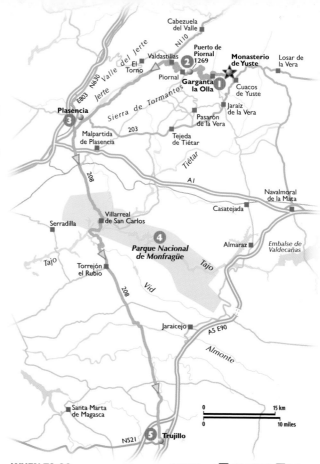

WHEN TO GO

Much of Extremadura's plains landscape can be unbearably hot in high summer (July and August). The months either side are best for warm, dry weather. In winter, all of the towns highlighted on the route go into hibernation, although many of the places of interest stay open.

WHERE TO EAT
BAR/RESTAURANT LA VICTORIA

This popular restaurant and bar is ideal for a drink and a bite to eat at the end of the drive.
✉ Plaza Mayor 26, 10200 Trujillo
☎ 927 32 10 06 ◷ Daily 8am–midnight

HOSPEDERÍA LA SERRANA

Located on top of the Sierra de Tormantos, La Serrana is a simple hotel with a good café and restaurant serving snacks and main meals.
✉ Carretera Garganta la Olla Km1.5,

10615 Piornal ☎ 927 47 60 34 ◷ Daily 8am–11.30pm

PLACE TO VISIT
MONASTERIO DE YUSTE

✉ 10430 Cuacos de Yuste ☎ 927 17 21 30 ◷ Tue–Fri 10.30–1.30, 3–5.15, Sat–Sun 10.30–5.15 💶 Adult €3, child (5–16) €2, under 4 free

Opposite *A street in the old town of Plasencia*
Below *Bulls grazing on the flat landscape near Trujillo*

CASCADING POOLS IN THE SIERRA DE TORMANTOS

Tucked into a narrow, steep-sided valley in the heart of the Sierra de Tormantos are Los Pilones (The Pools) of the Garganta del Infierno (Gorge of Hell), one of the natural highlights of the region. Beyond the pools, the river and its valley are no less remarkable, and the circuit described here takes in the very best scenery the region has to offer. The waypoints in the directions refer to numbered marker posts along the route.

THE WALK

Distance: 10km (6 miles)
Allow: 2.5 hours
Ascent: Approximately 450m (1,500ft)
Start/end at: Trailhead behind interpretation centre
Parking: Ample parking at interpretation centre

HOW TO GET THERE

The interpretation centre is signposted just off the N-110, about halfway between Cabezuela del Valle and Jerte.

★ From the start point behind the interpretation centre (Waypoint 1), follow the sign to Los Pilones up a steep track; you'll soon glimpse the cascading river ahead and to your right. Follow the painted white and yellow markers up the trail (they should be fairly frequent—if you can't see them for a while, you may have taken a wrong turning) for 250m (275 yards) to an intersection on the path. Turn left at the intersection (Waypoint 2, signed to Los Pilones) along a wide, level track and after just 20m (22 yards) turn right up another narrow trail (also signed). Follow the markers up this trail for 250m (275 yards) to another intersection. Turn right along the wide, level, sandy track here and follow it for 100m (110 yards) or so to an obvious fork (Waypoint 3). Head left at the fork up a stony trail for 200m (220 yards) to a viewpoint (signed Vista Panorámica).

Continue along the trail for another 200m (220 yards) or so to an intersection. Turn right here down a sandy (subsequently paved) track to a picnic site by the river (Waypoint 4). Continue along the path, heading upstream, until you come to another picnic spot near the river. Soon after, a wooden footbridge (Waypoint 5) crosses the river.

❶ The footbridge offers fine views of Los Pilones upstream and is a great spot for taking photographs.

After crossing, continue upstream along a cabled path. When this runs out, bear right, away from the river, until you come to a wider track (it's not easy to find, but as long as you stay near the river and head upstream, you'll cross it sooner or later). Continue upstream along an easier, grassy trail for about 1km (0.6 mile) to a footbridge. Staying on the opposite side of the river to the refuge (Waypoint 6), continue upstream for about 200m (220 yards) until you reach the Garganta del Collado de las Yeguas. Follow the markers to the shallowest point (Waypoint 7). After days of heavy rain this part of the route may be impassable, but it's usually just a matter of using the stones to step across the shallows. After crossing the stream bear left, following the bluff round to continue up the path high above the Garganta del Infierno. Follow the path and the markers up and along the side of the valley for a little over 1km (0.6 mile) as far as the splendid Puente Nuevo (Waypoint 8).

② Despite its name the stone Puente Nuevo is anything but new. It was in fact built by the Romans.

Cross the bridge and follow the path downstream and away from the river. Take a moment here to gaze upstream and across to the Fuente Roblehermoso waterfall on the far side of the valley.

Continue to follow the markers (now white, yellow and red) along a well-paved path for about 1km (0.6 mile) as far as a T-junction with a wide sandy track. Turn left here and soon after you come to a major

intersection of wide tracks (Waypoint 9). Continue left, descending along a wide, sandy track. The markers seem to run out, but stay on this track for almost 2km (1.2 miles), ignoring paths that branch off to the left and right, until you have a bird's-eye view of Los Pilones below.

③ Los Pilones are essentially a series of bowl-shaped pools carved into the granite bedrock of the river by a corresponding sequence of idyllic waterfalls. In the summer, this entire section of river is like a natural water park, perfect for swimming in the deep, crystal-clear pools and picnicking on the sun-baked granite.

Continue to follow the track around a

long, sweeping bend to the right, in the direction of Jerte, until you reach an obvious hairpin bend (Waypoint 10), with a narrower trail heading straight on. Follow the hairpin around to descend to the interpretation centre at the start.

WHEN TO GO
The best time to visit Los Pilones is in the early summer, when the water is low enough (and warm enough) to swim in the pools. Weekdays are likely to be less busy than weekends.

WHERE TO EAT
LOS PILONES BAR
✉ Opposite the park turnoff on the N-110, Km 370, 29569 Los Pilones ☎ 927 47 02 04 🕐 Daily 8am–midnight

Opposite and below right *Los Pilones make a fun natural swimming pool in the summer*
Below left *A bee eater in flight*

CÁCERES

AUDITORIO DE CÁCERES

Contemporary plays and concerts (pop, Spanish, flamenco, classical and ethnic) and other events are hosted here. The brown marble, square building accommodates up to 1,150 people.

✉ Avenida Isabel de Moctezuma s/n, 10005 Cáceres ☎ 927 23 72 36 ✪ Closed Jul–Aug 🖐 From €12 🚌 2

CONVENTUAL DE SAN PABLO

The convent of San Pablo was founded in the late 15th century, and is known throughout Spain for its flamboyant baroque retablo (altarpiece).

The convent also has a well-deserved fine reputation for the delicious biscuits and cakes made by the nuns. Try the *perrunillas,* if they're available: these delicious, lemon-scented crumbly almond biscuits are a local specialty.

✉ Plaza de San Mateo s/n ☎ 927 24 70 37 ✪ Varies; check with the tourist office, or ring the bell

GRAN TEATRO

www.granteatrocc.com

Theatre performances—both classic and contemporary—and music concerts from pop and rock to folk and local traditional sounds feature here at the Gran Teatro. Festivals include classic and children's theatre, Festival Flamenco, Otoño Musical (Autumn Musical), Envideo for young filmmakers, and Poelia, for poetry. There is also a cafeteria for refreshments.

✉ Calle San Antón s/n, 10003 Cáceres ☎ 927 01 08 84, 927 01 08 85, 927 01 08 86 (information); 927 21 10 81 (box office) 🖐 From €10 🚌 1, 2, 6

LOS IBÉRICOS

A shrine to top-quality local produce, especially all things porcine. Ham, chorizo, *morcilla (*black pudding/blood sausage)—you name it, Los Ibéricos has got the best of it. It's perfect for buying souvenirs, thanks to the shop's try-before-you-buy tasting policy. It also sells local cheeses, honey, pastries, wines and liqueurs. Shipping is possible throughout Europe.

✉ Calle Paneras 14, 10003 Cáceres ☎ 927 22 07 20 ✪ Mon–Sat 10–2, 5.30–8.30, Sun 11–2 🚌 1, 2, 6

RUTA DE LA PLATA

www.centrocomercialrutadelaplata.com

This shopping mall is the biggest in the region, with a good range of stores to suit a wide range of tastes. The clothes shops include Cortefiel, Zara and Springfield. You will also find shoes, crafts, household goods and even furs. The mall complex includes bars, restaurants, a multi-screen cinema and a hypermarket. Parking is free.

✉ Calle Londres s/n, 10005 Cáceres ☎ 927 23 20 81 ✪ Mon–Fri 10–10, Sat 10–10, Sun 12–12, but all stores closed 🚌 5, 7

CUENCA

ARTESANÍA RAMÓN DEL CASTILLO

A popular shop specializing in pottery. The craftspeople here make

and use age-old tools. There's a wide range of prices depending on exclusivity and quality.
✉ Plaza Mayor 11, 16001 Cuenca ☎ 969 21 12 63 🕐 Mon–Sat 10–9

CERAMICA ADRIÁN NAVARRO
In the heart of the shopping area, in front of the cathedral, this shop stands out because of its pitchers from Mota del Cuervo. It also sells pottery and souvenirs of the city, including interesting tableware. Some items are expensive.
✉ Calle Severo Catalina, 16001 Cuenca ☎ 969 21 28 28 🕐 Jun–Sep daily 11–2, 4.30–9.30; Oct–May 11–2, 4–8

MULTICINES CUENCA
www.elmulticine.com
Cuenca's only cinema has five screens featuring standard European and American movies, translated into Spanish. It is never crowded.
✉ Calle Tarancón s/n, 16025 Cuenca ☎ 969 24 12 20 ✋ €5, Mon €3

TEATRO AUDITORIO DE CUENCA
www.auditoriodecuenca.es
A conservative theatre that features classical Spanish plays by Calderón de la Barca, Miguel de Cervantes and, sometimes, Carlo Goldoni and Shakespeare. They put on the occasional contemporary play. There is also opera, dance and classical music.
✉ Paseo de Huécar s/n, 16004 Cuenca ☎ 969 23 27 97; 902 40 59 02 (ticket sales) ✋ €6

TRUJILLO
LA ALMAZARA
www.etrujillo.com
This small, charming shop with vaulted ceilings sells an excellent range of foods. The shop's main product—exquisite Iberian acorn ham—hangs on the walls. There are also Iberian sausages, local wines, olive oils, regional honey and cheeses such as Ibores and Torta del Casar. The products from the shop are exported all over Spain.

MARCH–APRIL
PASCUA
Major Easter festival with processions.
✉ Trujillo

SEMANA SANTA
Processions of peñas (clubs or societies) dressed as penitents and carrying floats bearing religious icons through the streets.
✉ Trujillo, Mérida, Cáceres, Cuenca, Albacete

APRIL
SAN JORGE
Riotous celebration of the feast of St. George.
✉ Cáceres

✉ Plaza Mayor 3, 10200 Trujillo ☎ 927 32 24 05 🕐 Mon–Sat 10–2, 5.30–8.30

LA CARBONERA
Singer-songwriters and pop, rock and ethnic bands play concerts at this venue, a popular bar in a street full of similar drinking holes. One room is reserved for quiet drinking and chatting.
✉ Calle García de Paredes 18, 10200 Trujillo ☎ 927 32 24 07 🕐 Fri 10pm–4.30am, Sat 10pm–6.30am ✋ Free

EL CASTILLO DE TRUJILLO
www.trujillo.es
You will find crafts made in Trujillo and the surrounding countryside in the old chapel of this ninth-century Arab castle (La Hermita de San Pablo), in the upper part of the city. Baskets, wrought-iron work, glassware, earthenware and wooden objects are displayed alongside paintings by local artists. There are spectacular views of the city and its surroundings from the castle. The courtyard is particularly fine, with its eight magnificent towers. The Albaraca, a 13th-century dairy farm, also has towers where local crafts are exhibited.

MAY
WOMAD FESTIVAL
Huge World of Music and Dance festival, featuring international bands.
✉ Cáceres

JULY–AUGUST
DRAMA FESTIVAL
Festival concentrating on classical themes, with performances of Greek plays and Shakespeare's Roman tragedies.
✉ Mérida

SEPTEMBER
VENDIMIA
Grape harvest festival.
✉ Valdepeñas

✉ Cerro Cabeza de Zorro, 10200 Trujillo ☎ 927 32 26 77 (tourist information office) 🕐 Crafts: daily 10–2, 5–8.30; castle: daily 10–2, 4–7 (until 8pm in summer) ✋ Castle €2

CONVENTO SANTA CLARA
Trujillo has a long tradition of pastry-making. The nuns at the Santa Clara convent produce a wonderful selection of treats, such as toasted cream and sweet rolls. The ingredients are always of the highest quality.
✉ Calle de Santa Clara s/n, 10200 Trujillo ☎ 927 32 06 38 🕐 Mon–Sat 9.30–1, 5–7, Sun 9.30–11.30, 5–7

TEATRO JUAN PIZARRO DE ARAGÓN
Plays, comedies, classical and contemporary dramas, clown shows and entertainment for children are staged at this converted 17th-century palace, with some occasional flamenco and classical music concerts.
✉ Plazuela de Aragón s/n, 10200 Trujillo ☎ 927 32 10 50 🕐 Oct–Feb ✋ €12–€18

Opposite Mountain-cured hams are Spain's caviar

PRICES AND SYMBOLS

The restaurants are listed alphabetically (excluding Le, La and Les). The prices given are the average for a two-course lunch (L) and a three-course dinner (D) for one person, without drinks. The wine price is for the least expensive bottle.

For a key to the symbols, ▷ 2.

ALMAGRO

CALATRAVA

www.restaurantecalatrava.com

A long-established favourite in the pretty and historic town of Almagro, this offers classic Castilian cuisine, from *revueltos* (scrambled egg with fresh asparagus, wild mushrooms or whatever is in season) to oven-baked lamb. You could also try game in season (autumn and winter), and leave room for old-fashioned desserts like *pan de calatrava* (a delicious lemon-and-cinnamon flavoured cross between bread-and-butter pudding and charlotte).

✉ Calle Bolaños 3, 13270 Almagro ☎ 926 86 13 53 🕔 Tue–Thu, Sat–Sun 1.30–4, 8.30–10.30, Fri 1.30–4 🍴 L €24, D €34, Wine €12

CÁCERES

ATRIO

www.restauranteatrio.com

With two Michelin stars, this is the most distinguished restaurant in town and one of the finest in Spain. It's located just north of central Cáceres. The cuisine is sophisticated, with dishes such as roast clams with truffle purée, lamb stuffed with mushrooms and prawns, and leeks with a fruit sauce. The wine list specializes in the Ribera del Duero and Rioja regions.

✉ Avenida de España 30, Bloque 4, 10002 Cáceres ☎ 927 24 29 28 🕔 Mon–Sun 2–5, 9–12 🍴 L €75, D €105, Sampler menu €115, Wine €26

CORREGIDOR

This is a deeply traditional and long-standing restaurant with a rustically decorated dining room. The menu includes Spanish specialties from across the country, including paella, meat and fresh fish dishes, but it prides itself particularly on its authentic Extremaduran cuisine. Try the traditional *migas*, a simple local dish prepared with breadcrumbs, vegetables and chunks of sausage, or the game in season.

✉ Calle Moret 7, 10003 Cáceres ☎ 927 21 61 09 🕔 Tue–Sat 2–4, 8.30–10.30, Sun 2–4. Closed mid-July to mid-Aug 🍴 L €22, D €32, Wine €12

EL PUCHERO

www.restauranteelpuchero.com

El Puchero has a terrace on the lovely square. The specials at El Puchero include traditional local dishes and game prepared with fresh regional produce. Try their *migas*.

✉ Plaza Mayor 7, 10003 Cáceres ☎ 927 24 54 97 🕔 Daily 1–4, 9–11 🍴 L €24, D €32, Wine €10

TORRE DE SANDE

www.torredesande.com

The chef at Torre de Sande specializes in incorporating the best local products—such as Iberian pork, *retinto* (a kind of veal), game and wild mushrooms—into his artistic creations. It's beautifully set in a 15th-century palace which has a garden terrace, open in summer.

✉ Los Condes 3, 10003 Cáceres ☎ 927 21 11 47 🕔 Tue–Sat 2–4, 9–11, Sun 2–4 🍴 L €65, D €75, Wine €18

CUENCA

BANZO

www.restaurantebanzo.es

This is a very popular new establishment in Cuenca, which may be a small provincial town but has plenty of buzz thanks to its big student population. At Banzo, they specialize in 'grandmother's cooking' *(la cocina de la abuela),* but give a modern twist to traditional recipes. Adventurous palates will enjoy the wild boar carpaccio, or the confit of suckling pig. The bar area offers more traditional fare, as well as a good value *menu del dia* on weekday lunchtimes.

✉ Calle Mateo Miguel Ayllón 8, 16002 Cuenca ☎ 969 23 01 79 🕔 Wed–Sat 2–4, 8.30–11, Sun–Mon 2–4, bar open all day 🍴 L €18, D €38, Wine €10

EL FIGÓN DE PEDRO
www.figondepedro.com
El Figón de Pedro offers delectable *migas ruleras de pastor* (a local dish containing fried breadcrumbs, garlic and sausage) and a superb *besugo al horno* (oven-roasted sea bream). The service is particularly professional, with well-informed staff, and the atmosphere is great. It has only 13 tables, so make sure you make a reservation.
✉ Cervantes 13, 16004 Cuenca ☎ 969 22 68 21 🅲 Mon–Sat 1.30–4, 9–11.30, Sun 1.30–4 ✋ L €26, D €38, Wine €16

MESÓN CASAS COLGADAS
www.mesoncasascolgadas.com
In a town famed for its river crabs, trout and game, sampling local fare is a must. Casas Colgadas is as traditional as they come and was the venue of choice for Prince Felipe and Leticia's first post-wedding supper. Romantic without being cloying, regional dishes include crab-stuffed aubergines (eggplants), loin of deer with chestnuts and rice pudding with cinnamon ice cream. Located in the famous hanging houses, the restaurant offers unforgettable views over the gorge.
✉ Canónigos s/n, 16001 Cuenca ☎ 969 22 35 09 🅲 Mon 1.30–4, Wed–Sun 1.30–4, 9–12 ✋ L €26, D €42, Wine €14

PLAZA MAYOR
This restaurant is in the heart of the old city, and serves excellent regional cuisine, specializing in meat dishes. The wine list is long and varied.
✉ Plaza Mayor 5, 16001 Cuenca ☎ 969 21 14 96 🅲 Jun–Aug Tue–Sat 9am–1am, Sun 10–6; Sep–May Tue–Sat 11–11, Sun 11–5 ✋ L €24, D €36, Wine €12

TOGAR
An inexpensive and intimate venue that is a popular spot with locals. The traditional *cordero asado* (roast lamb) is simply presented and delicious. The desserts (all made on the premises) should definitely be tasted—the pineapple mousse is a must. There's an extensive and prestigious wine list. The service is

occasionally rather slow. The menu of the day costs €14.
✉ Avenida República Argentina 1, 16002 Cuenca ☎ 969 22 01 62 🅲 Daily 1–4, 8–11 ✋ L €12, D €25, Wine €9

OLIVENZA
DOSCA
www.hoteldosca.com
A handsome, whitewashed 19th-century mansion in the delightful border town of Olivenza, this is now an attractive little hotel with a fine restaurant and café. The restaurant serves tasty regional and Spanish dishes, prepared with a light touch. These include the classic Extremaduran peasant dish, *migas*, and a wonderful lamb stew. There are tasty home-made desserts to follow. In summer, you can dine out on the terrace.
✉ Plaza de la Constitución 15, 16100 Olivenza ☎ 924 49 10 65 🅲 Daily 1.30–3.30, 8.30–10.30 ✋ L €18, D €26, Wine €10

PLASENCIA
VIÑA LA MAZUELA
www.restaurantelamazuela.es
Choose between the simple café-bar with the heaped plates of tapas and *raciones,* or the pretty restaurant area for a full menu featuring excellent modern Spanish cuisine. The best seasonal produce is used in sumptuous dishes such as local lamb stuffed with wild mushrooms and rosemary, or sautéed scallops with foie gras. Desserts include a white chocolate 'crunch' with local cherries and cinnamon cream.
✉ Avenida Las Acacias 1, 10600 Plasencia ☎ 927 42 57 52 🅲 Daily 1.30–3.30, 9–11, bar open all day. Closed Sun in summer and Wed in winter ✋ L €22, D €32, Wine €12

TRUJILLO
BIZCOCHO PLAZA
www.restaurantebizcochotrujillo.com
A pretty restaurant enclosed by arches in the middle of the town's plaza, it is a great place for representational home cooking. All the produce used is local and carefully presented.
✉ Plaza Mayor 8, 10200 Trujillo ☎ 927 32

20 17 🅲 Daily 1–4.30, 8–11.30 ✋ L €20, D €28, Wine €14

EL DORADO
www.parador.es
This old refectory of a 16th-century convent, now the Parador de Trujillo (▷ 347), showcases a mural and glazed tiles from Talavera, plus Castilian furniture. The restaurant offers regional and national dishes, with an emphasis on *retinto* (a kind of veal), ham and Iberian sausages. There is a daily fixed-price menu and an ample cellar.
✉ Calle Santa Beatriz de Silva 1, 10200 Trujillo ☎ 927 32 13 50 🅲 Sun–Thu 1.30–4, 8.30–10.30, Fri–Sat 1.30–4, 8.30–11 ✋ L €28, D €44, Wine €12

MESÓN LA TROYA
A very popular restaurant in a 16th-century palace, well known for its generous portions, reasonable prices and friendly service. For a starter, try a Spanish potato omelette, salad or *embutidos* (various kinds of sausages). The main dishes are excellent, and include white beans, lamb stew and pork. The two atmospheric, vaulted dining rooms are decorated with ceramic plates and photographs of famous people.
✉ Plaza Mayor 10, 10200 Trujillo ☎ 927 32 13 64 🅲 Daily 1–4.30, 8.30–11.30 ✋ L €18, D €28, Wine €9

PIZARRO
The restaurant has won many awards for its simple, regional cooking. Facing on to the Plaza Mayor are five balconies where diners can eat al fresco. The house specials include truffled chicken, Manuela-style potatoes and tomato soup with prickly pears. Partridge stew and roast lamb are other delightful main dishes. The wine list has a wide regional and national selection. Reservations are recommended.
✉ Plaza Mayor 13, 10200 Trujillo ☎ 927 32 02 55 🅲 Wed–Mon 1.30–4, 8.30–11 ✋ L €26, D €36, Wine €8

Opposite *Choose from many regional dishes*

PRICES AND SYMBOLS

The prices are for a double room for one night including breakfast, unless otherwise stated. All the hotels listed accept credit cards unless otherwise stated. Note that rates can vary widely throughout the year.

For a key to the symbols, ▷ 2.

CÁCERES
NH PALACIO DE OQUENDO

www.nh-hoteles.es
In this luxury hotel in a renovated 16th-century palace in the old town, the rooms have a lovely feeling of space and light. There are an on-site restaurant and bar, and meeting rooms for business visitors. Hotel guests are entitled to a discount in the public parking area.
✉ Plaza de San Juan 1, 10003 Cáceres ☎ 927 21 58 00 ✋ €85–€160 excluding breakfast buffet (€15) ⓘ 86 (45 non-smoking) ⑤

PARADOR DE CÁCERES

www.parador.es
Cáceres' *parador*, in a 14th-century palace, has a wonderful medieval atmosphere and very professional service. The decor sets the scene perfectly, incorporating plenty of armour, natural materials, arches and columns. The guest rooms are spacious and comfortable. All have telephone, satellite TV, minibar and safe; some have views of the attractive inner patio. The *parador* also has a laundry service and a restaurant serving fine local cuisine.
✉ Ancha 6, 10003 Cáceres ☎ 927 21 17 59 ✋ €159–€165 excluding breakfast (€17) ⓘ 33 ⑤

CUACOS DE YUSTE
LA CASONA DEL VALFRÍO

www.lacasonadevalfrio.com
A wonderful base for exploring the forests and hills of northern Extremadura, this enchanting rural hotel is lost in the countryside on the outskirts of Cuacos de Yuste. Charles V (Carlos I of Spain) chose to retire to the monastery nearby, and the utter peace and tranquillity remain lasting enticements. An old granary has been handsomely restored to house this rural retreat, retaining the wooden beams and other attractive original details. Each of the rooms is individually and rustically decorated and named after a famous historical character. It's set in extensive gardens, with mature trees and an outdoor pool.
✉ Carretera Cuacos-Valfrío km 4, 10430 Cuacos de Yuste ☎ 927 19 42 22 ✋ €105–€210 ⓘ 6 🏊 Outdoor

CUENCA
CUEVA DEL FRAILE

www.hotelcuevadelfraile.com
A restored 16th-century convent with a magnificent inner patio has well-equipped rooms with Castilian-style decor. You will find original features dotted throughout. There are also plenty of modern comforts and extensive gardens. Numerous activities can be arranged for you.
✉ Km 7, Carretera Cuenca–Buenache, 16001 Cuenca ☎ 969 21 15 71 ✋ €115–€130 excluding breakfast (€12) ⓘ 75 rooms ⑤

LEONOR DE AQUITANIA

www.hotelleonordeaquitania.com
Right in the old city, the Leonor de Aquitania is an unusual three-star hotel. This typical example of a Cuenca 'hanging house' was built in the 18th century but has been restored several times since. The last time, artists Eduardo Chillida and Gerardo Rueda were responsible for the renovations and have chosen wooden furniture and elegant lamps. Rooms are decorated in light shades.
✉ San Pedro 60, 16001 Cuenca ☎ 969 23 10 00 ✋ €110–€132 excluding breakfast (€12) ⓘ 48 ⑤

Above *The restored Cueva del Fraile*

PARADOR DE CUENCA

www.parador.es

Like so many of Spain's *paradores*, this 16th-century convent building has been transformed into a modern and comfortable hotel, with traditional and contemporary elements in the decoration. The guest rooms are comfortable and spacious. The restaurant is stunning.

✉ Subida a San Pablo s/n, 16001 Cuenca ☎ 969 23 23 20 🖐 €155–€165 excluding breakfast (€18) ⓘ 63 🅿 🏊 Outdoor ⛽

POSADA DE SAN JOSÉ

www.posadasanjose.com

This rambling 18th-century, six-floor building, once home to the artist Velázquez's daughter-in-law, is in Cuenca's historic heart. It was once a choir school and is now a very charming and tranquil place to stay, adorned with ancient beams and uneven floors and filled with antiques. The rooms are simple—none has a TV or telephone—but prettily decorated in crisp white, and all have a bathroom and some have balconies or small terraces. There is no restaurant but the bar is open for breakfast (fantastic) and dinner. Reserve well in advance.

✉ Julián Romero 4, 16001 Cuenca ☎ 969 21 13 00 🖐 €45–€160 excluding breakfast (€9) ⓘ 22

GUADALUPE

HOSPEDERÍA DEL REAL MONASTERIO

www.monasterioguadalupe.com

Stay in the peaceful setting of a 13th-century monastery, incorporating Gothic, Renaissance and baroque architectural styles. Part of the building is still used by Franciscan monks, who also run the *hospedería*. The simple but comfortable rooms surround a three-floor Gothic cloister. There is also a restaurant that serves local food. Reservations for weekends are required at least two months in advance.

✉ Plaza de Juan Carlos 1, 10140 Guadalupe ☎ 927 36 70 00 ⊘ Closed 4 weeks in Jan–Feb 🖐 €70–€85 excluding breakfast (€8) ⓘ 47 🅿

JARANDILLA DE LA VERA

PARADOR DE JARANDILLA

www.parador.es

This was where Charles V (Carlos I of Spain) chose to stay while the monastery at Yuste was being prepared for his retinue. A splendid castle-palace, it is set in some of the loveliest countryside in Extremadura—short hikes will lead you to waterfalls, natural pools and wonderful picnic spots. Activities can be arranged, including bicycling, horse-riding, tennis and hiking. The thick stone walls ensure that the summer heat doesn't penetrate, and there are antique furnishings. You can count on good regional cuisine at a reasonable price.

✉ Avenida García Prieto s/n, 10450 Jarandilla de la Vera ☎ 927 56 01 17 🖐 €125–€150 ⓘ 53 🅿 🏊 Outdoor (summer only)

PLASENCIA

PARADOR DE PLASENCIA

www.parador.es

A very special accommodation option, Plasencia's *parador* is housed in a 15th-century convent of golden stone. Perfectly located in the historic centre, it offers enormous rooms furnished with antique, or antique-style furnishings including four-poster beds, a fine restaurant serving excellent regional cuisine (set menu €32) in the exquisitely tiled former refectory, gardens and a small outdoor pool—essential during the burning Extremaduran summers.

✉ Plaza San Vicente Ferrer s/n, 1600 Plasencia ☎ 927 42 58 70 🖐 €165–€180 ⓘ 66 🅿 🏊 Outdoor (summer only)

TRUJILLO

LAS CIGÜEÑAS

www.hotelasciguenas.com

An elegant hotel with comfortable rooms decorated in a simple style, containing old-fashioned furniture. Guest rooms have a telephone, satellite TV with movie channels and a minibar. Services include laundry service, bar and meeting rooms.

✉ Avenida de Madrid s/n, 10200 Trujillo ☎ 927 32 12 50 🖐 €65–€98 excluding breakfast (€8) ⓘ 78 🅿

HOSTAL TRUJILLO

www.hostaltrujillo.com

A small hotel in the old Hospital de Espíritu Santo, a lovely 16th-century building. Inside, the brick vaults and chapel are spectacular, and the spacious bedrooms have simple decor and classical furniture; each comes with satellite TV. The restaurant serves regional dishes. Other features include meeting rooms, a laundry service and a beautiful garden terrace with views.

✉ Calle Francisco Pizarro 4–6, 10200 Trujillo ☎ 927 32 22 74 🖐 €65–€80 excluding breakfast (€15) ⓘ 19 🅿

PARADOR DE TRUJILLO

www.parador.es

This quiet *parador* in Trujillo's historic quarter is set in the converted 16th-century Convento de Santa Clara. The interiors are spacious and well lit, and most of the rooms in the old, galleried cloisters have good views. The decor is spartan, with a few rustic details as well as modern amenities. The restaurant, El Dorado (▷ 345), serves regional dishes such as wild boar.

✉ Calle Santa Beatriz de Silva 1, 10200 Trujillo ☎ 927 32 13 50 🖐 €148–€170 excluding breakfast (€14) ⓘ 47 🅿 🏊 Outdoor ⛽

ZAFRA

CASA PALACIO CONDE DE LA CORTE

www.condedelacorte.com

An elegant aristocratic palace, built in the 19th century, now houses a chic hotel. The interior is replete with antiques, floral prints and lavish chandeliers. The former owner of the palace raised bulls for bullfighting, and the *torero* connection has been retained, not just in the illustrious client list which includes some of the most celebrated bullfighters of the 20th century, but also with old black-and-white photographs and the rather macabre collection of bulls' skulls. Choose between standard double rooms or luxurious suites.

✉ Plaza del Pilar Redondo 2, 06300 Zafra ☎ 924 56 33 11 🖐 €110–€225 ⓘ 14, plus 1 suite 🅿 🏊 Outdoor

ANDALUCÍA

Andalucía is home to almost all the most famous Spanish clichés from flamenco to bullfighting, and yet this huge region resists all easy definitions. It encompasses a vast swathe of the Iberian peninsula, bounded to the south by the Atlantic and to the east by the Mediterranean, and its geography includes everything from snowy peaks to arid desert. It contains some of Spain's highest mountains in the Sierra Nevada, its most important wetlands in the magnificent Coto Doñana National Park, and some of the greatest monuments of Al-Andalus, including the world-renowned Alhambra in Granada and the Mezquita in Córdoba.

The last Muslim kingdom in Spain (Granada) fell in 1492, but their legacy lives on throughout Andalucía. From the gleaming white villages which dot the hillsides, to the saffron and spices which feature in local cuisine, even the syncopated rhythms of flamenco, there are constant reminders of the North African cultures which once ruled this region. The three great cities of Al-Andalus—Sevilla, Córdoba and Granada—are still among the most captivating cities in Spain and essential stops on any visitor's itinerary.

For some, Andalucía means sun, sea and sand, whether the built-up coast of the Costa del Sol, with its glossy marinas and villa complexes, or the quieter and less glitzy charms of the Costa de la Luz, or the family-friendly conurbations of the Costa Tropical round Almería. A short drive inland will reveal a different world, slower, quieter and more traditional than the beachfront hubbub. Some of the region's least explored and most beautiful corners include the Sierra de Cazorla, near Jaén, an extensive natural park encompassing hills, forests and rivers, and the Sierra Morena north of Sevilla, where wild boar still snuffle through the forest of Mediterranean oak and eagles wheel overhead.

ALMERÍA
www.almeria-turismo.org
Towering above this city is the Alcazaba, a 10th-century Moorish fortress (Apr–Oct Tue–Sun 9–8.30; Nov–Mar 9–6.30) that could house an army of 20,000. Apart from the Alcazaba, most of Almería's Moorish monuments have been lost. The cathedral, begun in 1524 and built like a fortress to protect it from pirates, stands on the site of a ruined mosque. Highlights of its gloomy Gothic interior are the exquisitely carved choir stalls and the red and black jasper altar. Plaza Vieja, a beautiful 17th-century pedestrian square with palm trees, is to the north of the cathedral.

The city's cultural attractions include CAMA (Centro de Arte Museo de Almería), with a collection of largely contemporary paintings (Mon 6–9, Tue–Sat 11–2, 6–8, Sun 11–2), and the Centro Andaluz de la Fotografía, Andalucía's first photographic museum (Tue–Sun 9–6.30, until 8.30 in summer).
🞡 474 H11 🛈 Parque Nicolás Salmerón, corner of Calle Martínez Campos, 04002 Almería ☎ 950 27 43 55 🚉 Almería

LAS ALPUJARRAS
The hills and deep valleys of the Alpujarras are backed by the peaks of the Sierra Nevada. Villages here have whitewashed houses, a legacy of the Moors who settled here after the Christian Reconquest.

The three villages of the Poqueira gorge are particularly worth seeing: Pampaneira, with craft shops; Bubión, with an excellent museum of Alpujarran life, the Casa Tradicional Alpujarreña (Wed–Mon 11–2, Fri–Sat, 5–7), and the Taller del Telar, a

Clockwise from left to right *Iglesia de San Pedro, Arcos de la Frontera; the interior of the Cuevas Menga, neolithic dolmens in Antequera; rooftops and houses of Aracena*

weaver's workshop (daily 11–12.30, 5–8.30); and Capileira, the highest and most picturesque of the three. To the east of the gorge via another scenic road is Trevélez, the highest village in Spain, which is famous for its superb cured ham.
🞡 473 H10 🛈 Avenida de Madrid s/n, 18420 Lanjarón ☎ 958 77 04 62

ARACENA
www.aracena.es
Aracena is an attractive agricultural town, with steep cobbled streets, mainly visited for the spectacular Cueva de las Maravillas (Cave of Marvels; daily 10.30–1.30, 3–6; ticket office on Calle Pozo de la Nieve; adult €7.70, child 6–17 €5.50), the largest cave in Spain, with amazing galleries and natural formations.

Paved walkways and staircases lead past small lakes into this ethereal underground world. The passageways and galleries are full of fantastical stalactites, stalagmites and other wonders, and many of them have been enhanced with lights and music. Guides point out the highlights on the tour, which ends in the Sala de los Culos (Room of the Backsides), where the natural sculptures resemble parts of the human anatomy.

Back in town, busy Plaza Marqués de Aracena is lined with 19th-century buildings. From the quiet

Plaza Alta, which was the central square of old Aracena, you can climb up to the medieval castle ruins and the adjacent priory church of Nuestra Señora de los Dolores. This has an ornamental Mudéjar tower that was built by the Knights Templar in the late 13th century. Aracena is also known for its excellent *jamón serrano* (ham).
🞡 472 D9 🛈 Plaza San Pedro s/n, 21200 Aracena ☎ 959 12 82 06

ARCOS DE LA FRONTERA
www.ayuntamientoarcos.org
Arcos de la Frontera sits on a limestone crag high above the plain. It is the westernmost example of Andalucía's famous *pueblos blancos* (white towns), and has one of the most beautiful old town centres in the country. Many fine churches and public buildings surround the Plaza del Cabildo, including the 15th-century Gothic-Mudéjar Iglesia de Santa María de la Asunción, which dominates the square. The *mirador* (viewing point) looks out over the river gorge with stunning views.

The Iglesia de San Pedro, built over a former Moorish fortress, at the edge of the cliff, is mainly visited for its imposing bell tower. It also has a fine 16th-century altarpiece and other paintings.
🞡 472 E11 🛈 Plaza del Cabildo s/n, 11630 Arcos de la Frontera ☎ 956 70 22 64

Above *Playa de la Caleta in the old town, the most attractive of the beaches in Cádiz*

BAEZA

www.baeza.net

Set on a hillside overlooking wheat fields and olive groves, this town of traditional whitewashed houses and tiled roofs has a timeless air and a quiet pace, ideal for exploring the beautiful plazas, Renaissance palaces and ornate churches. Plaza del Pópulo, a superb Renaissance square, is also called the Plaza de los Leones after its central fountain, which is adorned with ancient stone lions thought to be Roman in origin. Palacio de Jabalquinto, now a seminary, is the finest of Baeza's old palaces, with a flamboyant Gothic front studded with diamond-shaped bosses (Mon–Fri 9–2; closed Sat–Sun). Visit the Catedral de Santa María for its altarpiece, painted *rejas* (screens) and silver monstrance hidden behind a painting of St. Peter (Jun–Sep daily 10.30–1, 5–7; Oct–May 10.30–1, 4–6).

✚ 473 G9 🛈 Plaza del Pópulo s/n, 23440 Baeza ☎ 953 74 04 44

CADIZ

▷ 353.

CARMONA

www.turismo.carmona.org

Carmona is one of the oldest and most interesting walled towns in Andalucía. It stands on a hill 250m (800ft) high, and consequently its viewpoints and bell towers provide wide-ranging views of the surrounding countryside.

The town's impressive Roman gateways, the Puerta de Sevilla and the Puerta de Córdoba, are well preserved, but the highlight is the Roman necropolis, where more than 900 family tombs in deep chambers were carved out of the rock between the second century BC and fourth century AD (Tue–Fri 9–6, Sat–Sun 9.30–2.30). Two of the most striking tombs are the Tumba de Servilia, with a huge colonnaded courtyard and covered chambers and galleries, and the Tumba del Elefante, with a stone sculpture of an elephant. The optional guided tour points out many other interesting features.

The ruins of two fortresses, as well as the town's whitewashed houses, are reminders of the Moorish era, as is the Patio de los Naranjos (Orange Tree Patio) beside the Iglesia de Santa María, and the window arches and tiles of the Casa de Cabildo, the old town hall.

Outstanding Gothic and Renaissance architecture can be seen in the churches of Santa María (Mon–Fri 10–2, 5–7, Sat 10–2), San Felipe (closed except for special events) and San Pedro (Mon, Thu 11–2, 4.30–6.30, Tue–Wed, Fri–Sat 11–2), and in the *ayuntamiento* (town hall). The Museo de la Ciudad, in the mansion of the Marqués de las Torres, has displays on the city's history (daily 11–2, also Tue–Fri 6.30–8.30).

✚ 472 E10 🛈 Alcázar de la Puerta de Sevilla, 41410 Carmona ☎ 954 19 09 55

CÓRDOBA

▷ 354–357.

COSTA DE LA LUZ

The Coast of Light is Andalucía's Atlantic coast, stretching 300km (190 miles) from the Straits of Gibraltar to the Portuguese border. The beaches are fabulous—long, wide stretches of sand, backed by generally low-key development.

At its eastern end is Tarifa, a windsurfing capital and Spain's southernmost mainland town. From here you can gaze at the Rif mountains of Morocco rising in the distance across the Straits of Gibraltar or make the 90-minute ferry trip to Tangier.

There are good beaches at Conil de la Frontera, Zahara de los Atunes and Los Caños de Meca (the last is surrounded by a natural park with pine groves). Nearby is Cape Trafalgar, where British Admiral Nelson fell in battle against the French in 1805. Just inland lies the Moorish-style hilltop town of Vejer de la Frontera, with whitewashed houses and a tiled central square.

Beyond Cádiz (see opposite) are the popular resorts of Rota and Chipiona, and the coastal sherry towns of El Puerto de Santa María and Sanlúcar de Barrameda. The Roman ruins of Baelo Claudia (Jun–Sep Tue–Sat 9–8; Mar–May, Oct Tue–Sat 9–7; Nov–Feb Tue–Sat 9–6; Sun and festivals 9–2) overlook the sea at Bolonia.

✚ 472 C10–D11 🛈 Paseo de la Alameda, 11380 Tarifa ☎ 956 68 09 93 🛈 Avenida de los Remedios 2, 11150, Vejer de la Frontera ☎ 956 45 17 36 🛈 Carretera el Punto, 11140 Conil de la Frontera ☎ 956 44 05 01 🛇 Cádiz

CÁDIZ

Cádiz is the oldest, continually inhabited city in western Europe. Known to the Phoenicians as Gadir and the Romans as Gades, the citizens are still called Gaditanos and are famous for their attractive, but almost impenetrable, local accent. Piled up at the tip of a narrow isthmus jutting towards Africa, the old town of Cádiz is a maze of narrow streets, full of shops and houses with wrought-iron balconies, and leading to small squares and broad plazas (▷ 380–381). The city borders the sea, and the salt air has weathered the buildings to give the place an evocative atmosphere of genteel decay. It also has the bustle of everyday Spanish life, yet is relaxed and unspoiled by tourism.

Modern Cádiz is a rather anonymous grid-like sprawl, but it does enjoy some wonderful beaches. The most popular of these is the Playa de la Victoria, a 3km (2-mile) stretch of golden sand. The prettiest beach is the Playa de la Caleta, in the old town, which is tucked picturesquely between two castles. Cádiz is famous throughout Spain for its spectacular carnival, a three week-long fiesta with costumes, processions and satirical song competitions.

HISTORIC CÁDIZ

In the 18th century Cádiz was a great seaport, and the wealth reaped from the gold and silver trade with the Americas was used to endow it with magnificent churches and public buildings. You can climb the Torre Tavira (Jun–Sep 10–8; Oct–May 10–6), one of the city's ancient watchtowers, for a sweeping view over the city and out to sea, plus a camera obscura.

Several churches worth visiting include the historic Oratorio de San Felipe Neri (Mon–Sat 10–1), with an *Immaculate Conception* (1680) by Bartolomé Murillo (1617–82) above the high altar, and the *capilla* (chapel) in the Hospital de Mujeres (Mon–Fri 10–1), with a glorious baroque interior and *Ecstasy of St. Francis* by El Greco (1541–1614). And don't miss the baroque cathedral, with its magnificent neoclassical facade, vast interior and golden dome (daily 10–1, Tue–Fri also 4–7).

The Museo de Cádiz (Tue 2.30–8 groups morning only; Wed–Sat 9–8.30, Sun 9–2.30) has a fine display of Phoenician, Greek and Roman objects and, upstairs, an excellent fine arts collection that includes works by Zurbarán, Murillo, Rubens and the Sevillaño artist Alonso Cano. The museum overlooks the Plaza de Mina, the most elegant square in old Cádiz, with manicured flower gardens and neat ranks of neoclassical townhouses.

INFORMATION

✚ 472 D11 🛈 Avenida Ramon de Carranza s/n, 11005 ☎ 956 20 31 91 🕓 Mon–Fri only 🚉 Cádiz

Above *Seafood vendors in the busy port of Cádiz*
Below *The facade of the baroque cathedral*

REGIONS ANDALUCÍA • SIGHTS

INTRODUCTION

Córdoba is smaller and less frenetic than Seville, and has a number of fine churches, monuments and museums. A less obvious Moorish legacy, and a highlight of the city, are the brightly tiled and flower-filled patios of the houses, which can be glimpsed through wrought-iron grilles. Juxtaposed with the rich history of the old quarters are the stylish shops and restaurants of the modern city, which give this university town a lively air. But without doubt Córdoba's principal attraction is La Mezquita.

Córdoba was founded by the Romans around 152BC and was conquered by the Moors in the eighth century. The city became the capital of Moorish Spain for the next three centuries, and was the most cultivated city in Europe in the 10th century, with some 1,000 mosques and 600 public baths, and even street lighting. In 1236 the Christians, led by Fernando III, recaptured Córdoba, marking a long period of decline. It was not until the 20th century that Córdoba flourished once again, this time through agriculture, light industry and tourism.

WHAT TO SEE

LA MEZQUITA-CATEDRAL

www.mezquitadecordoba.org

This is one of the most beautiful Arabic monuments in the world. Construction was started by Emir Abd al-Rahman I in AD785, and further enlarged and embellished over the next two centuries. Only the massive size of the exterior walls gives a clue to the splendour within, as Moorish architectural style does not focus on exterior decoration.

You enter through the Patio de los Naranjos (Courtyard of the Orange Trees), where worshippers washed before praying. Pass through the Puerta del Perdón, to the magnificent interior. There are 19 naves, divided by more than 1,000 columns holding up two levels of arches. The columns are marble, jasper and onyx, and the arches are decorated in alternating stripes of red brick and white stone. At the far end is the *mihrab*, a prayer niche indicating the direction of Mecca, although for some unexplained reason it faces south rather than east.

In 1523 Charles V installed a cathedral in the middle of the mosque, to 'Christianize' the building, though he later chided his architects: 'To build something ordinary, you have destroyed something unique in the world.'

INFORMATION

www.turismodecordoba.org

➕ 473 F9 ℹ️ Palacio de Congresos, Calle Torrijos 10, 14003 Córdoba ☎ 957 47 12 35 ℹ️ Calle Caballerizas Reales 1, 14004 Córdoba ☎ 902 20 17 74 or 957 20 17 74 🚃 Córdoba

Opposite *The famous clustered arches inside the Mezquita*
Below left *Córdoba is rich in the flamenco tradition*
Below *View from the courtyard of the Mezquita*

REGIONS ANDALUCÍA • SIGHTS

355

Although the cathedral has some exquisitely carved choir stalls and other fine features, the earlier Mudéjar Capilla Real and Capilla de Villaviciosa are far more fitting to this monumental house of worship.

✚ 357 B3 ✉ Calle Cardenal Herrero ☎ 957 47 05 12 🕔 Apr–Jun Mon–Sat 10–7, Jul–Oct, Mar 10–6.30, Nov, Feb 10–5.30, Dec–Jan Mon–Sat 10–5, Sun 9–10.15, 2–7 ✋ Adult €8, child (9–12) €4, under 9 free; free Mon–Sat 8.30–10am

LA JUDERÍA

Between La Mezquita and the Plaza de las Tendillas is La Judería, the labyrinth of narrow streets and squares that comprised the old Jewish quarter. The Jewish population was ejected from Spain by the Catholic Monarchs, Fernando V and Isabel I, in 1492. A 14th-century Sinagoga (synagogue) in Calle Judíos is the sole surviving Jewish building in the area.

At the end of this street is the Puerta de Almodóvar, a 14th-century city gate. Look for the Calleja de las Flores, a flower-bedecked cul-de-sac whose walls frame the belfry of La Mezquita in what has become a classic Córdoba scene and sought-after photographic subject. In Plaza Maimónides is the Museo Municipal Taurino (Museum of Bullfighting; closed for restoration until at least 2011).

✚ 357 A2

Museo Municipal Taurino ✉ Plaza de Maimónides s/n ☎ 957 20 10 56 🕔 Tue–Sat 10–2, 4.30–6.30 ✋ Adult €4, free on Fri.

Sinagoga ✉ Calle Judíos ☎ 957 20 29 28 🕔 Tue–Sat 9.30–2, 3.30–5.30, Sun and festivals 9.30–1.30 ✋ Free to EU citizens, otherwise €0.30

ALCÁZAR DE LOS REYES CRISTIANOS

The Palace of the Christian Kings was built in the late 13th century by the Christian conquerors to replace the Moor's Alcázar, or fortress, which stood next to La Mezquita. It served as a palace for the Catholic Monarchs, was the headquarters of the Inquisition and a 19th-century prison. The highlight is the magnificent Moorish gardens, a series of terraced ponds in a former orchard.

✚ 357 A3 ✉ Calle Campo Santo de los Mártires s/n ☎ 957 42 01 51 🕔 Jul–Aug Tue–Sat 8.30–2.30; May–Jun, Sep–15 Oct Tue–Sat 10–2, 5.30–7.30; 16 Oct–Apr Tue–Sat 10–2, 4.30–6.30; all year Sun, public holidays 9.30–2.30 ✋ Adult €5, free on Fri

Above *The 13th-century Alcázar de los Reyes Cristianos has been both a palace and a prison*

MUSEO ARQUEOLÓGICO PROVINCIAL

Córdoba's archaeological museum is in the Renaissance Palacio de los Páez, north of La Judería. The arcaded entrance patio is a traditional Córdoban feature, and the building has coffered ceilings and elegant staircases. Córdoba's history is detailed in the fine exhibits of prehistoric, Roman and Moorish art and objects.

⊹ 357 B2 ⊠ Plaza de Don Jerónimo Páez 7 ☎ 957 35 55 17 🕐 Tue 2.30–8.30, Wed–Sat 9–8.30; Sun and holidays 9–2.30. Closed Mon 🎫 €2.50; free to EU citizens with ID

PALACIO DE VIANA

www.palacioviana.com

This restrained and austerely beautiful palace, the historic home of the Marqueses of Viana, dates back to the 14th century. Enlarged and expanded over time, it is elegantly arranged around 12 exquisite patios. Córdoba is famous for its fragrant, flower-filled patios, and hosts a celebrated contest every year, but few compare with the beauty of those in the Palacio de Viana—lush, green, tranquil, with just the sound of birdsong and trickling fountains.

   The elegant interior can also be visited (by guided tour only), when visitors can admire the impressive Mudéjar ceilings, Flemish tapestries, frescoes, and displays of armour and weaponry. The period furnishings are mostly original, and there are also some fine ceramics and a large painting collection.

⊹ 357 B1 ⊠ Plaza Don Gome 2, 24001 Córdoba ☎ 957 49 67 41 🕐 16 Jun–Sep Mon–Sat 9–2; Oct–May Mon–Fri 10–1, 4–6, Sat 10–1. Closed Sun and 1–15 Jun 🎫 Adult €7, under 10 free; patios only €4

Above *A shop selling decorative plates*
Below *The fortress walls of the Alcázar*

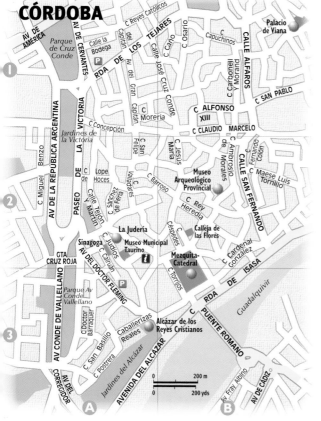

COSTA DEL SOL

www.visitacostadelsol.com

This is one of the most famous resort destinations in the world, and runs roughly from Nerja in the east to Sotogrande in the west. With 325 days of sunshine a year and an average water temperature of 18°C (64°F), it attracts visitors year round. If you've come for the sun, the sandy (although often crowded) beaches, the golf or the nightlife, you can have a good time on almost any budget. However, there is not much in the way of sightseeing or Spanish culture here—for that you will have to head inland to the more traditional mountain villages. The city of Málaga gives access to the Costa del Sol and has several attractions (▷ 366–367). Torremolinos is the most developed and most visited resort, and is crowded in high season, but on the plus side it has a long beachside promenade, the Paseo Marítimo. Fuengirola is another large resort, although the high-rise hotels crowding the seafront here make it less attractive. The best of the resorts include Estepona (right), Marbella (▷ 367) and Nerja (▷ 368).

✚ 473 F11 ℹ Plaza Blas Infante 1, 29620 Torremolinos ☎ 952 37 95 12 ℹ Avenida Jesús Santos Rein 6, 29640 Fuengirola ☎ 952 46 74 57. Multilingual information 952 12 62 79 🚇 Torremolinos and Fuengirola

CUEVA DE LA PILETA

www.cuevadelapileta.org

Some 26km (16 miles) southwest of Ronda is a series of caverns filled with palaeolithic wall paintings (guided tours daily Jun–Sep 10–1, 4–6; Oct–May 10–1, 4–5; adult €8, child 5–11 €5). The paintings date from 25,000BC, and were executed in red and yellow ochre and charcoal. There are some interesting natural formations here, including the Sala del Castillo (Castle Chamber), with stalagmites that resemble castle architecture, and the water-filled Salón del Lago (Lake Chamber).

✚ 472 E11 ℹ Plaza de España 9, 29400 Ronda ☎ 952 16 73 43 🚇 Benaoján-Montejaque, 6km (4 miles) from the cave

ÉCIJA

www.ecija.es
www.turismoecija.es

Écija, set beside the Río Genil, has an extraordinary skyline. Its 11 churches, with baroque towers adorned with steeples, domes and tiles, make a memorable impact and have earned the town its sobriquet, Ciudad de las Torres (City of Towers). One of the most remarkable towers is that of the Iglesia de Santa María. Ornate mansions reflect the town's prosperous history, including the Palacio de Peñaflor on Calle Castellar (interior closed for restoration. Reopening dates will be announced

when restoration plans are finalized: the palace may be converted into a hotel), with an elegantly curved facade decorated with frescoes, and the Palacio de Benamejí, which houses the Museo Histórico Municipal (Jun–Sep Tue–Fri 10–2.30, Sat 10–2, 8–10, Sun and holidays 10–3; Oct–May Tue–Fri 10–1.30, 4.30–6.30, Sat 10–2 and 5.30–8, Sun and holidays 10–3).

✚ 473 E9 ℹ Palacio de Benamejí, Plaza de la Constitucion 1, 41400 Écija ☎ 954 83 04 31

ESTEPONA

www.estepona.es

This resort on the western end of the Costa del Sol is one of the more appealing along this stretch. Although hotels and apartment blocks line the waterfront here, there has been sensible planning and landscaping, and it has the bonus of an attractive old town behind it. There is a fine beach backed by a broad promenade lined with flower-beds, shrubs and palms. The pleasant old town retains some cobbled streets and pretty houses, and at its heart is the charming Plaza de las Flores, with jasmine and orange trees.

At the western end is the fishing port and yacht marina and an old lighthouse.

✚ 472 E11 ℹ Avenida San Lorenzo 1, 29680 Estepona ☎ 952 80 20 02

Opposite *The Rock of Gibraltar*
Left *Looking across the town of Estepona*
Below *Golfers on the course at Torremolinos, Costa del Sol*

GIBRALTAR
www.gibraltar.gov.gi
Gibraltar is an overseas territory of the UK. From the end of Main Street you can take a cable-car (daily 9.30–5.45; closed Oct–Apr Sun) to the Upper Rock, the towering mass that dominates the skyline, where you can visit the Apes' Den (daily 9.30–7). This is the home of the famous Barbary apes, a breed of tailless monkey. Tradition says that if the apes leave the Rock, Gibraltar will cease to be British.

Also here is St. Michael's Cave (daily 9.30–7), a huge natural cavern sometimes used as a concert venue, and the Upper Galleries, or Great Siege Tunnels (daily 9.30–7), excavated in the 18th century for military defence. In town the Gibraltar Museum has Moorish baths (Mon–Fri 10–6, Sat 10–2).

🚩 472 E11 ℹ️ Duke of Kent House, Cathedral Square (main office), and Casemates Square ☎ 45000 or 74950

GRANADA
▷ 360–365.

GUADIX
www.guadix.es
Guadix is often covered in red dust that blows in from the surrounding hills, and is remarkable for its modern cave dwellings outside the walled old quarter. Carved out of the soft rock of the hills, the caves were a refuge for dispossessed Moors in the 16th century. Today they have modern amenities, and their whitewashed facades create a contrast to the brown hills. The town's focal point is the magnificent red-sandstone cathedral (Mon–Sat 11–1, 4–6; museum: Mon–Sat 10.30–1, 4–7, Sun 9.30–1). It adjoins a handsome Renaissance square, Plaza de la Constitución (also called Plaza Mayor), from where cobbled alleyways lead to more Renaissance buildings in the upper town. The Cueva Museo (Cave Museum; Jul–Sep Mon–Sat 10–2, 5–7, Sun 10–2; Oct–Jun 10–2, 4–6, Sun 10–2) has re-created a cave dwelling.

🚩 473 H10 ℹ️ Avenida Mariana Pineda s/n, 18500 Guadix ☎ 958 66 26 65 🚉 Guadix

HUELVA
www.turismohuelva.org
Set beside a wide estuary, Huelva was once a great maritime city and the departure point for Christopher Columbus (Cristóbal Colón in Spanish) on his first voyage to the Americas in 1492.

Most of the main sights lie near the palm-fringed main square, Plaza de las Monjas, in the heart of the city. These include the Catedral de La Merced, with a white baroque interior (Mon–Sat Mass only 7pm, Sun and festivals 11–7), and the churches of San Pedro (Mon–Sat Mass only 8pm, Sun and festivals 10.30–7.30) and La Concepción (closed for restoration). The Museo Provincial has a huge Roman waterwheel, a reconstructed Celtic house and objects from Huelva's mining history (Tue–Sat 9–8, Sun, holidays 9–3). North of the museum is the Barrio Reina Victoria, with English-style houses for workers of Río Tinto mining company.

🚩 473 H10 ℹ️ Plaza Alcalde Coto Mora 2, 21001 Huelva ☎ 959 25 74 03 🚉 Huelva

ITÁLICA
www.museosdeandalucia.es
Founded by General Scipio in 205BC, Itálica (9km/6 miles north of Seville) was one of the most important cities of the Roman Empire and the birthplace of the emperors Trajan (cAD52) and Hadrian (AD76). It was a busy port, until the river changed course and the city was abandoned. You can still see the Roman foundations of streets and villas, and remains of the huge amphitheatre. This was one of the largest in the Roman Empire, capable of holding 25,000 spectators, and despite its dilapidated state you can make out the rows of seats and animal pens.

Other highlights are the Neptune mosaic in the Casa de Neptuno, and the bird mosaic depicting 33 avian species in the Casa de los Pájaros. There are also Roman baths. Part of the ancient town lies unexcavated beneath Santiponce, where you can also see a Roman theatre.

🚩 472 D10 ✉️ Avenida de Extremadura 2, 41970 Santiponce ☎ 955 62 22 66 76 🕐 Apr–Sep Tue–Sat 8.30–8.30, Sun and holidays 9–3; Oct–Mar Tue–Sat 9–5.30, Sun and holidays 10–4 💶 €2; free to EU citizens with ID ❓ Site map available at ticket office

INTRODUCTION

Granada has both a prosperous new city and a historic older core, the latter arguably Spain's finest treasure. The city is set at the foot of Spain's highest mountain range, the Sierra Nevada, and surrounded by a fertile plain. It rambles over two hills (one of which is home to the spectacular Alhambra) that lie about 670m (2,200ft) above sea level. The many green areas and fountains, and the two rivers, the Genil and Darro, make it a pleasant city to roam around. Although the new city is growing fast, Granada is easy to explore on foot. However, some sections can be a bit hilly—such as the lovely walk through the Albaicín and up to the old gypsy quarter on Sacromonte hill.

First settled by native tribes from the fifth century BC, Granada was later colonized by the Romans, who called it Illibris, a name it retained until it fell to the invading Moors in AD711, who called it Granada. By the 13th century it had become one of Europe's richest and largest cities, with a vibrant cultural scene and expertise in trading. The Moorish rulers established their power base, the Alhambra, on a hilltop above the city, the complex of palaces, fortress and garden that we see today. It was built mainly under the Muslim Nazrid dynasty in the 14th century and fell to the Christian kings, along with the city, in 1492. Ferdinand and Isabella started a building expansion scheme which continued until 1526, when Charles V commissioned his vast Renaissance palace.

By the 18th century, the population of the city had declined and Granada became sidelined from national events. In the Napoleonic Wars, French troops occupied the Alhambra, blowing up some of the towers. In 1832 international attention was drawn to Granada by the publication of Washington Irving's book *Tales from the Alhambra*, and artists began to live and work in the city. Foreign visitors followed, and in 1870 the Alhambra was declared a national monument, marking the start of the ongoing restoration. Granada itself endured a bloody time during the Spanish Civil War, when Nationalists ran riot through the city. Among their victims was the poet and playwright Federico García Lorca.

WHAT TO SEE

ALBAICÍN

You could easily spend a day exploring the narrow streets of this old Moorish quarter. Many of the whitewashed houses here have delightful secluded interior gardens. Although little remains of the dozens of mosques that once filled

INFORMATION

www.turismogranada.org
www.granadatur.com
✚ 473 G10 🛈 Calle Virgen Blanca 9, 18009 Granada ☎ 902 40 50 45
🕙 Mon–Fri 9–7, Sat 10–2 🛈 There is a smaller office in the Alhambra
🚉 Granada

Opposite *Jardines del Portal, Alhambra*
Below left *Detail of decoration on the Palacio de los Nazaríes, Alhambra*
Below *A house in the old quarter of Albaicín*

REGIONS ANDALUCÍA • SIGHTS

361

Opposite *The magnificent Muslim palace of the Alhambra*
Below left *Decoration on the facade of Palacios de los Nazaíes*
Below right *Palacio de Carlos V*

Albaicín's streets, the area has largely avoided modern developments. It is increasingly becoming home once again to immigrants from North Africa, and their influence is notable in the number of *teterías* (tea shops) and restaurants.

To explore the Albaicín, simply wander up the pleasant Carrera de Darro, many of whose buildings have notable facades (look in particular for the Real Cancilleria at the bottom and the Museo Arqueológico at the top). About halfway along is El Bañuelo (Tue–Sat 10–2), Spain's finest Moorish baths, once part of the Mezquita del Nogal (Mosque of the Walnut Tree), which previously stood here. The baths were constructed in the 11th century using earlier ruined Visigothic and Roman building materials—these are most noticeable in the columns' capitals. Right at the top of Albaicín is the Mirador de San Nicolás, a lookout point with great views to the Colegiata del San Salvador, which stands on what was once Albaicín's largest mosque, and the Iglesia de San Juan de los Reyes, still retaining its original 13th-century minaret.
➕ 365 B2

CATEDRAL AND CAPILLA REAL
www.capillarealgranada.com
Taken together, these Christian buildings are almost as impressive as the Alhambra. The very ornate five-nave Renaissance cathedral has a spectacular altar and an enormous central dome, as well as a beautiful facade. Inside are many works by artist Alonso Cano (1601–67), including the west font.
As with many Christian buildings in Granada, the cathedral was built on the site of a former mosque. Construction began in 1518 under Diego de Siloé (1495–1563) but did not finish for another 186 years. Next door, and with a separate entrance, is the late-Gothic Capilla Real (Royal Chapel), which was built as a resting place for the Catholic Monarchs Fernando V and Isabel I. Their small, simple, lead coffins are in the crypt with various other members of their close family, including their daughter, Juana la Loca (Joanna the Mad); the tombs themselves are built of much more impressive Carrara marble. The museum in the chapel's sacristy houses Isabel's art collection, including works by Botticelli, her sceptre and crown and Fernando's sword.
➕ 365 A2 ✉ Plaza de la Lonja, Gran Vía de Colón 5 ☎ 958 22 29 59 🕐 Apr–Oct Mon–Sat 10.30–1.30, 4–8, Sun 4–8; Nov–Mar Mon–Sat 10.30–1.30, 4–7, Sun 4–7 🖐 Cathedral: €3.50, Capilla Real: €3.50

MONASTERIO DE LA CARTUJA
This early 16th-century Carthusian monastery on the northern edge of the city is one of Spain's gaudiest baroque buildings. Many other styles were also incorporated during its 300 years of construction. In addition to a wonderful

frescoed cupola, the monastery's sanctuary and Churrigueresque sacristy are spectacular, decorated with twisting marble columns and statues and paintings. Informal guided tours with a resident monk are occasionally available.

✚ 365 off A2 ✉ Paseo de la Cartuja s/n ☎ 958 16 19 32 ◉ Apr–Oct Mon–Sat 10–1, 4–8, Sun 10–12; Nov–Mar Mon–Sat 10–1, 3.30–6, Sun 10–12 ✋ €3.50

CASA MUSEO DE FEDERICO GARCÍA LORCA

www.garcia-lorca.org

This was the airy summer home of the family of poet and playwright Federico García Lorca (1899–1936). He was born here and wrote much of his work in the house. Lorca had something of a love-hate relationship with Granada, but spent much of his free time here and was fascinated by its gypsy population. The house is decorated prettily on the outside—a refreshing contrast to the city's other major sites. Inside, there is plenty of Lorca memorabilia, including manuscripts, furniture, pictures, costumes from Lorca productions, and the great man's bed and ink-stained writing desk. There is another museum dedicated to Lorca near the airport in the Fuente Vaqueros area, which he described as 'this most pleasant, modern, earthy and liberal of villages'.

✚ 365 off A1 ✉ Calle Poeta García Lorca 4, 18340 Fuente Vaqueros ☎ 958 51 64 53 ◉ Jul–Aug Tue–Sun 10.30–2.30; Apr–Jun, Sep Tue–Sun 10–12.30, 5–8, Oct–Mar Tue–Sun 10–12.30, 4–6.30 ✋ Adult €3.50, child (12–14) €1.50

SACROMONTE

www.sacromontegranada.com

The network of caves carved out of the clay rock on Sacromonte hill has been home to generations of gypsies, although heavy rain in 1962 forced many to move. The caves are close to the Albaicín and offer popular (although not always high-quality) performances of flamenco: Each cave was known by the name of the artists who lived and performed there. Equally interesting are the caves themselves, many of which have electricity, telephones, plumbing and interiors decorated with copperware and ceramics. There is also a Benedictine monastery on top of the hill, where the ashes of Granada's patron saint, St. Cecilio, are kept.

✚ 365 C1

TIPS

» Although the city is busy around Easter, the *Semana Santa* (Holy Week) celebrations here are spectacular.

» There are many street beggars (especiallly those carrying sprigs of rosemary near the cathedral and the Alhambra). A firm refusal is usually effective, but be extremely careful with your bags and never bring out wallets.

» A small *tapa* or *pincho* comes free with each drink in many bars.

» An interpretation centre at Sacromonte (Centro de Interpretación de Sacromonte; Apr–Oct Tue–Fri 10–2, 5–9, Sat–Sun 10–9; Nov–Mar Tue–Fri 10–2, 4–7, Sat–Sun 10–7; museum €5, *mirador* viewing platform €1), contains exhibits on local culture, flora and fauna.

LA ALHAMBRA

Visitors to the Alhambra can enjoy three main areas—the Palacio Nazaríes, the Alcazaba and the Generalife—as well as what is probably Spain's loveliest *parador* (advance reservation absolutely essential). Throughout, the combination of running water as decoration, evocative trees such as cypresses and artwork of the highest standard makes for a unique and relaxing visit.

✚ 365 C2 ✉ Main access via Cuesta de Gomérez ◉ Mar–Oct daily 8.30–8 (also Tue–Sat 10pm–11.30pm); Nov–Feb daily 8.30–6 (also Tue–Sat 10pm–11.30pm) ✋ Adult €12, under 8 free; €12 for night visit, children under 12 free

Alcazaba

This fortress is the oldest part of the Alhambra, reconstructed over the ruins of a castle in the ninth century and now little more than a shell containing ramparts and towers. The most elaborate interiors are those of the Torre de las Armas and the tall Torre de la Vela. During fiestas, young women keen to avoid becoming old maids ring the bell in the latter, from where the views across the surrounding countryside are fantastic. Towards the southern edge of the Alcazaba is the delightful Jardín de los Ardaves.

Palacios de los Nazaríes

The star of the Alhambra is the Palacios de los Nazaríes (Nazrid Palaces), also called the Casa Real (Royal House) and packed with superb Moorish craftsmanship throughout its various rooms and courtyards. There are Arabic inscriptions in the stuccowork everywhere, as well as decorative tiling and intricate wooden carving, and majestic columns and ceilings, so remember to look up. Simply wandering around is rewarding, although there are some must-sees here. In particular, look out for the Salón de los Embajadores (Hall of the

Below *A beautifully decorated courtyard in the Palacios de los Nazaríes*

Ambassadors), where all official diplomatic business was conducted; the Patio de los Arrayanes (Myrtle Court), with its beautiful pool and myrtle hedges; and the Sala de la Barca (Boat Room), with an inverted boat-shaped wooden ceiling. The most famous area is the Patio de los Leones (Court of Lions), an open arcaded space surrounded by 124 slender columns and with a central fountain featuring 12 stone lions. Off here are several important rooms, including the Sala de los Abencerrajes, where the noble Abencerraje family was murdered as a result of sexual and political intrigue. The highlight here is the tall, domed ceiling with geometric vaulting. Opposite is the Sala de las Dos Hermanas (Room of the Two Sisters, which refers to two marble floor slabs), similarly decorated with a honeycomb dome, where the Sultan's preferred wife lived.

Generalife

Finally, there is the Generalife, a serene collection of walkways, patios and geometric pools, with beautiful hedges and careful planting. It was begun in the 13th century but was renovated constantly over the centuries (the upper gardens were once olive groves). Built as a retreat from the daily business of the sultan's life, the Generalife is now the venue for the city's annual music and dance festival in June. The Patio de la Acequia (Court of the Long Pond) is the complex's famous focal point, with a long, slender pool over which arch jets of water; look for the Patio de los Cipreses (Cypress Court).

Above *The cathedral is regarded as one of the most outstanding examples of its kind in Spain*

MORE TO SEE

CASA DE LOS PISAS (MUSEO DE SAN JUAN DE DIOS)

www.museosanjuandedios.es

This renaissance mansion holds a collection dedicated to San Juan who, legend has it, died on this spot. The collection consists of painting, sculpture and treasures in precious metals. The real treat is the edifice itself, with forged metal details, wood panelling and a fountain surrounded by gardens.

🕀 365 B2 ✉ Calle Convalecencia 1 ☎ 958 22 21 44 🕓 Mon–Sat 10–1, Tue–Thu 5–8 💷 €3

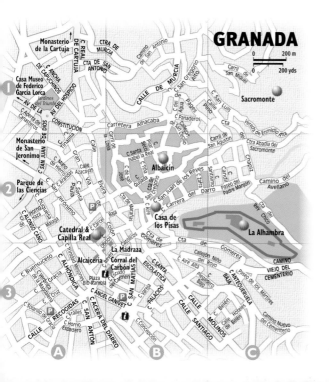

JAÉN

www.aytojaen.es

Jaén is a large, hilly town, set below a hilltop castle and surrounded by olive groves. It is less Andalucían in character than other settlements in the area, resembling instead the cities of central and northern Spain.

Although it is not a top destination, the provincial town has an attractive old centre and several fine monuments, particularly its cathedral on Plaza de Santa María (cathedral museum: Tue–Sat 8.30–1.30, 5–7). Begun in the mid-16th century, it took more than 250 years to build, and has a magnificent west facade with twin towers 60m (200ft) high, and elegant Corinthian columns and statuary. Highlights in the interior are more Corinthian columns, the exquisitely carved 16th-century choir stalls and the Santo Rostro (Holy Face), claimed to be the cloth with which St. Veronica wiped Christ's brow on his way to the crucifixion.

Also of interest in the town are the splendid Baños Árabes (Arab Baths), with splendid brickwork ceilings, star-shaped windows and Moorish columns and arches (Tue–Fri 9–8, Sat–Sun 9.30–2.30). They lie below the Palacio de Villadompardo, a 16th-century palace that now houses two museums, the Museo Internacional de Arte Naïf and the Museo de Artes y Costumbres Populares (both same times as Arab Baths). The old Moorish quarters of La Magdalena and San Juan are worth exploring, as are the city's many churches and palaces, which display a variety of styles. The Museo Provincial, near the train station, contains some outstanding Iberian stone sculptures from the fifth century BC (Tue 3–8, Wed–Sat 9–8, Sun 9–2.30).

There is a magnificent view over the city and surrounding countryside from the Castillo de Santa Catalina, now a *parador* (state-run hotel).
✚ 473 G9 🛈 Calle Maestra 13, 23007 Jaén ☎ 953 24 26 24 🚌 Jaén

JEREZ DE LA FRONTERA

www.turismojerez.com

Jerez is the capital of the 'sherry triangle', where Spain's famous fortified wines are produced. Tours of the bodegas, or cellars, are an enjoyable way to learn about the different types of sherry. Many are located in town—check with the visitor information office for details. Jerez's other great attraction is the Real Escuela Andaluza del Arte Ecuestre (Royal Andalucían School of Equestrian Art), where you can watch choreographed shows of horsemanship featuring the elegant, locally bred Cartujano horses (Aug Tue, Thu, Fri noon; Jan, Feb, late Dec Thu noon; rest of year Tue, Thu noon).

Other places worth visiting include the Moorish Alcázar (May–15 Sep Mon–Sat 10–8, Sun 10–3; rest of year daily 10–6), which has a camera obscura, and the Centro Andaluz de Flamenco, a flamenco centre in the heart of the old gypsy quarter (Mon–Fri 9–2).
✚ 472 D11 🛈 Alameda Cristina, next to the Claustros de Santo Domingo ☎ 956 32 47 47 🚌 Jerez de la Frontera

LANJARÓN

There are beautiful walks in the countryside around Lanjarón and up into the southern slopes of the Sierra Nevada. This largely modern town, with a ruined Moorish castle where Islamic forces made their last stand in 1500, is known for its spa waters. The Balneario spa baths are open from March to December, and bottled Lanjarón water is sold throughout Spain.
✚ 473 G10 🛈 Avenida de la Alpujarra, 18420 Lanjarón ☎ 958 77 04 62 🚌 Several buses daily from Granada and Motril

MÁLAGA

www.malaga.eu

A bustling provincial capital, Málaga is Andalucía's second-largest city and gateway to the Costa del Sol. Its historic old town has narrow streets, squares, churches and lively bars. Among the highlights is the cathedral, begun in the 16th century and known as La Manquita (meaning 'one-armed old woman') because of its solitary tower (Mon–Sat 10–6.45). Inside are some intricately carved mahogany and cedar choir stalls. The adjoining church, the Iglesia del Sagrario, has a Renaissance doorway and a stunning high altar (daily 9–12.30, 6–7.30).

The Alcazaba, a ninth-century Moorish fortress (Jun–Sep Tue–Sun 9.30–8; Oct–May 8.30–6), climbs above the town, its buildings linked by cobbled ramps and archways, with shady terraces and gardens on the various levels. In the upper section of the fortress is the former 11th-century Moorish palace. There are views from the ramparts, but higher still is the renovated 14th-century hilltop Castillo de Gibralfaro (Tue–Sun 9–6).

Pablo Picasso was born in Málaga in 1881, and his birthplace, the Casa Natal Picasso, is now the headquarters of the Picasso Foundation and displays mementos of the artist (Casa Natal Picasso: Mon–Sat 10–8). The Museo Picasso Málaga opened in the Palacio de los Condes de Buenavista in 2003, and exhibits 186 works from the artist's private collection (Tue–Thu and Sun 10–8, Fri–Sat 10–9).

The city's newest museum, the Museo del Patrimonio Municipal de Málaga (Apr–Sep Tue–Sun 11–9; rest of year Tue–Sun 10–8; free) opened in 2007 in a sleek, purpose-built contemporary building. Plans, paintings, sculpture and much more document the city's history over the last 500 years. There are also plans to build a new museum to hold part of the Thyssen collection ▷ 78–79). The modern CAC (Centro de Arte Contemporaneo) contains an excellent display of contemporary art. The Museo Provincial de Arqueológia (Archaeological Museum; Avenida Europa 49; daily 9–2) contains displays on Málaga's history since Phoenician times and a collection of Moorish ceramics.

The Paseo del Parque is a palm-lined promenade where people take their evening *paseo* (stroll).
✚ 473 F11 ℹ Pasaje de Chinitas 4, 29105 Málaga ☎ 952 21 34 45 ℹ Avenida de Cervantes 1, Paseo del Parque, 29106 Málaga ☎ 952 13 47 30 (municipal office) 🚂 Málaga

MARBELLA
www.marbella.es
This is the Costa del Sol's most glamorous resort, 56km (35 miles) west of Málaga, and is popular with the international yachting set. It is a large town with fine beaches, a charming old town of narrow streets and traditional houses and churches, and, along the coast to the west, luxury hotels, villas and golf courses. The focus of the old town, the Casco Antiguo, is the pretty square of Plaza de los Naranjos, lined with orange trees. The Paseo Marítimo promenade stretches along the coast to either side of town. To the west are wealthy enclaves, including the plush Guadalmina development and the marina at Puerto Banús.
✚ 473 F11 ℹ Plaza de los Naranjos, 29600 Marbella ☎ 952 82 35 50

MOJÁCAR
www.mojacar.es
Mojácar Playa is the main resort on the Costa de Almería and has an excellent beach with clear water. The old town of Mojácar lies 2km (1 mile) inland and is known as Mojácar Pueblo.

Beyond the souvenir shops that serve the crowds of summer visitors, the town is a charming place to wander around, and its narrow, sunlit streets and squares are decked with flowers. Its strong Moorish influence lasted well into the 20th century, and just 40 years ago some of the women of the town still wore veils. Look for the restored main fountain, built by the Moors, the 15th-century Iglesia de Santa María (open for Mass), and the central Plaza Nueva, with a *mirador* overlooking the surrounding countryside.

You may also spot *indalos*, matchstick figures painted on many doorways to ward off evil, a prehistoric symbol derived from regional cave drawings.
✚ 474 J10 ℹ Calle Glorieta 1, 04638 (Plaza Nueva) Mojácar Pueblo ☎ 950 47 51 62 ℹ Avenida de Andalucía, 04638 Mojácar Playa ☎ 950 61 50 25

Opposite left *Olive groves near Jaén*
Opposite right *Lanjarón is known for its mineral water*
Below *Holiday-makers at Málaga*

MONTEFRÍO

www.montefrio.org

The scenic village of Montefrío lies between two crags, each topped by a church, and is surrounded by olive-growing country. The neoclassical domed Iglesia de la Encarnación is at the heart of the village (Mon–Sat 11–1.30, Sun noon–1.30, afternoons for Mass only, winter 7.30, summer 8.30). Look for the swallows' nests around its eaves. From here you can climb uphill to the Iglesia de la Villa, the best of the two hilltop churches, which is surrounded by the ruins of a Moorish fortress and has grand views over the town (summer Tue–Sun noon–2; Sun 5–7pm, winter 4–6). It was designed by Diego de Siloé (c1495–1563) and has superb vaulting. There are many prehistoric and Roman sites in the area, notably Las Peñas de los Gitanos, which has neolithic stone tombs. It lies 8km (5 miles) away on the road to Illora (open at all times).

✠ 473 G10 🛈 Plaza de España 7 (adjacent to Iglesia de la Encarnación), 18270 Montefrío ☎ 958 33 60 04

MONTORO

www.cordobaturismo.org

Montoro stands on a spur by the Río Guadalquivir and is a relaxed, friendly town with rambling streets and old buildings. On the central Plaza de España stands the Iglesia de San Bartolomé, with a three-tiered tower. Inside, its coffered ceiling is inlaid with mother-of-pearl. Opposite the church is the 16th-century town hall.

In the old town, attractions include a small archaeological museum (Sat–Sun 11–1), housed in the Iglesia de Santa María de la Mota, and at Calle Grajas 17, the Casa de las Conchas, decorated with sea shells inside and out (daily; private house—knock on the door). The river is spanned by the 15th-century bridge of Las Doñadas, paid for by local women.

✠ 473 F9 🛈 Plaza de España 8, 14600 Montoro ☎ 957 16 00 89

NERJA

www.nerja.org

Although Nerja is a popular resort, it has escaped the overdevelopment that blights most other parts of the Costa del Sol. The largest of its small but attractive beaches is at Burriana, east of town.

The old, whitewashed town is set amid cliffs, and overlooks beaches and rocky coves. The Balcón de Europa is the most famous feature, a palm-lined promenade that runs along the cliff top, with views of the sea and mountains.

The Cuevas de Nerja are limestone caves, 4km (2.5 miles) east of town, with stalactites, stalagmites and grottoes (15 Jun–15 Sep daily 10–2, 4–8; rest of year 10–2, 4–6.30; adult €8.50, child 6–12 €4.50).

✠ 473 G11 🛈 Calle Puerta del Mar 2 (by the Balcón de Europa), 29780 Nerja ☎ 952 52 15 31

OSUNA

www.osuna.es

This former ducal village has some of the finest Renaissance mansions in the region, whose facades can be admired in the course of a leisurely stroll. A particularly good collection can be found to the north of the shady Plaza Mayor, including Palacio de los Cepadas, Palacio de Puente Hermoso, Palacio del Cabildo Colegial and Palacio de los Marqueses de la Gomera (now a hotel and restaurant, www.hotelpalaciodelmarques.com). Also of interest are the buildings of the old university and the splendid Renaissance Colegiata church, with its gilded altarpiece, fine paintings and atmospheric crypt (May–Sep Tue–Sun 10–1.30, 4–7; Oct–Apr 10–1.30, 3.30–6.30). Nearby is the Convent de la Encarnación, with *azulejos* tiling (May–Sep Tue–Sun 10–1.30, 4–7; Oct–Apr 10–1.30, 3.30–6.30).

✠ 472 E10 🛈 Calle Carrera 82 (Antiguo Hospital), 41640 Osuna, ☎ 955 81 57 32 🚊 Osuna

PARQUE NACIONAL DE DOÑANA

www.mma.es

This is Spain's largest national park, and is one of the most important ecological reserves and wetland sites in the world. From the 13th century the area was used as a vast hunting ground for Spanish royalty, and it later formed part of the lands of the dukes of Medina Sidonia. The park takes its title from Doña Ana, the

Duchess of Medina Sidonia, after whom the hunting lodge was named in 1595. Concern for preserving the special environment led to the creation of the national park in 1969, and in 1994 it was designated a UNESCO World Heritage Site.

The national park occupies 50,720ha (125,278 acres) around the delta of the Río Guadalquivir, incorporating beach habitat, shifting dunes and stable sands (known as *cotos*), as well as a vast wilderness of pools and marshes (known as *marismas*). Depending on the season, it is an excellent place to see migrating birds, and for some species—including the greylag goose—it is their main wintering ground. Other species—such as the purple heron, crested coot and endangered imperial eagle—have their homes here. Among the 33 species of mammals are the Iberian lynx, red deer and wild boar.

Access to the park is strictly controlled to reduce human impact; visits are conducted from three visitor offices reached via the road between El Rocío and the resort of Matalascañas. The main base lies about halfway along the road at El Acebuche, and has an exhibition and audiovisual show, footpaths and birdwatching hides. La Rocina visitor office, near El Rocío, has similar facilities. A third office, Palacio del Acebrón (21760 El Rocío), 7km (4.5 miles) west of La Rocina on a minor road has exhibits and a footpath that circles a lake and forest. Two other centres can be found in Sanlúcar de Barrameda and to the north of the park near Villemanrique de la Condesa. Trips in all-terrain vehicles can be booked at the El Acebuche visitor centre. You can also visit the park on a boat trip up the Río Guadalquivir from Sanlúcar de Barrameda.

🗺 472 D10 🛈 El Acebuche (main tourist office) ☎ 959 44 87 11, 959 44 87 39 🚍 Jeep tours into the park's interior (privately operated) can be reserved at the tourist information office. Sanlúcar de Barrameda boat trip and guided walks: phone 956 36 38 13. Reservations essential

Above *View from the Balcón de Europa at Nerja*
Opposite left *Sierra de Segura, part of a vast protected area, with outstanding scenery*
Opposite right *The tower and dome of the Iglesia de la Incarnación at Montefrío*

PARQUE NATURAL CABO DE GATA-NÍJAR

www.degata.com
The Cabo de Gata, the southeastern corner of Spain, is thought to be the driest and hottest place in Europe. Some 37,513ha (92,657 acres) along this coast have been designated an area of special protection. This is a prime wetland for breeding birds and migrants, particularly the salt marshes behind San Miguel de Cabo de Gata, where you can see flamingos, avocets, storks and egrets. Europe's only indigenous palm, the dwarf fan palm, grows here.

🗺 475 J10 🛈 Centro de Interpretación Las Amoladeras, 04150 Carretera Retamar-Pujaire Km 7 ☎ 950 16 04 35

PARQUE NATURAL CAZORLA, SEGURA, VILLAS

www.cazorla.es
Spain's largest natural reserve receives high winter rainfall and has thick forests of evergreen oaks and pines, and native elder, maple and juniper. Andalucía's longest river, the Río Guadalquivir, rises in the south of the park and flows north to the Embalse del Tranco (Tranco Reservoir). You may see Spanish ibex (mountain goat) here, plus wild boar, red deer, golden eagles, griffon vultures and peregrine falcons.

Tiny hilltop villages are scattered throughout the region, but the gateway to the park is Cazorla, at its southwestern edge. This village of whitewashed houses stands below La Yedra, the tower of a ruined Moorish castle (Tue 3–8, Wed–Sat 9–8, Sun and festivals 9–2), with the looming cliffs of the Peña de los Halcones as its backdrop. Also of interest is the ruined Renaissance Iglesia de Santa María. The park entrance is east of Cazorla, beyond Iruela, home to a Moorish castle. The interpretation office at Torre del Vinagre is 34km (21 miles) northeast through the mountains and has excellent displays on the park's ecology (Jul–Sep daily 10–2, 5–9.30; Apr–Jun daily 11–2, 4–7; Oct–Mar daily 10–2, 4–6).

Two other villages lie northeast of the Tranco Reservoir: Hornos, perched on a rock outcrop below a ruined Moorish castle; and Segura de la Sierra, spectacularly set below a restored hilltop castle (which now contains an interpretation centre, Apr–Oct Tue–Sun 11–2, 5–8; Nov–Mar Wed–Sun 11–2, 4–7), and with a labyrinth of narrow streets, fine Arab baths and a Renaissance fountain. There are good roads through the park and some short walks near Cazorla, but only a few waymarked paths lead into the mountains. You can reserve day walks, horse-riding, bicycling and four-wheel-drive trips into the remote regions of the park through companies in Cazorla.

🗺 474 H9 🛈 Park visitor information office, Calle Martínez Falero 11, 23470 Cazorla ☎ 953 72 01 25 🛈 Visitor information office, Paseo de Santo Cristo 17, 23470 Cazorla ☎ 953 71 01 02

PARQUE NATURAL DEL TORCAL DE ANTEQUERA

The name Torcal is derived from the Spanish word meaning 'twist', an apt description for the limestone pinnacles and cliffs that make up this bizarre landscape, formed over millions of years by geographical faults and erosion. The park covers 1,171ha (2,892 acres) and its maze of narrow gullies, towering reefs and ravines supports a surprising number of plants, birds and other wildlife, including the ocellated lizard, the largest lizard in Europe. This is also good walking territory; one route starts at the visitor office, taking you on a circuit past some of the park's most striking natural sculptures.

473 F10 Plaza de San Sebastián 7, 29200 Antequera 952 70 25 05 Antequera

PRIEGO DE CÓRDOBA

www.aytopriegodecordoba.es
www.turismodepriego.com

This provincial town is graced by baroque churches and an elaborate fountain, and is set below the highest mountain in the province, the 1,570m (5,150ft) La Tiñosa. The Barrio de la Villa, with its white walls and carefully arranged flower baskets, is the old Moorish quarter. Among the town's churches is Iglesia de la Asunción (hours change frequently). Its plain, whitewashed facade conceals a glorious interior housing two

treasures: the sacristy, which looks like a froth of white stucco, with scrolls and cornices, emblems and statues, all topped by a cupola; and an exquisitely carved altarpiece. The Iglesia de San Pedro (daily Mon–Sat 10–1), La Aurora (daily 11–1) and Iglesia de San Franciso (hours change frequently) are worth a visit.

In a quiet square at the western end of town are the 16th-century fountains Fuente de la Salud and the early 19th-century the Fuente del Rey, with statues of Neptune and Amphitrite at its heart, and dozens of mask-shaped spouts pouring water into stepped basins.

473 F10 Calle del Río 33, 14800 Priego de Córdoba 957 70 06 25

EL ROCIO

www.rocio.com

Its location on the border of the Parque Nacional de Doñana (▷ 368–369) makes El Rocio an ideal base for birding. The town itself has wide, sandy, unpaved streets and broad, unsurfaced squares. The two-storey wooden buildings here have railed verandas so that local farmers riding into town can tie up their horses. A pilgrimage and pentecostal celebration, the Romería del Rocío, takes place here each Whitsun. The revered image of Nuestra Señora del Rocío (Our Lady of the Dew), a 13th-century carved wooden statue, is kept in the church.

472 D10 Avenida de la Canaliega s/n, 21750 El Rocio 959 44 38 08

RONDA

www.turismoderonda.es

Ronda is dramatically perched on the ridge of the deep rocky gorge of El Tajo. Its whitewashed houses cling to the ledge either side of the Puente Nuevo, a massive 18th-century arched bridge that spans the gorge. Thanks to this defensive situation, Ronda has been settled since early Celtic times. The Romans made it a military outpost, and under the Moors it became a provincial capital, adorned with palaces and mosques. It remained independent until finally falling to the forces of the Catholic Monarchs in 1485. Later, its impregnable position made it a stronghold for the 19th-century bandits who ruled the surrounding mountains. Their story is told in the Museo del Bandolero (Bandit Museum) in the old town (Jun–Oct daily 10.30–8.30; Nov–May 10.30–7).

The Puente Nuevo spans the narrowest part of the gorge, standing 96m (315ft) above its floor, and connects the old town and new. The central part of the bridge was once used as a prison, and from here there are views of the gorge walls and countryside.

The *mirador*, another viewpoint, can be reached via a walkway that runs along the gorge, behind the parador to the gardens of the Paseo Blas Infante.

The old Moorish town, called the Ciudad, is on the south side of the gorge and is the most atmospheric part of Ronda. There are beautiful Renaissance palaces here, and steep, narrow lanes leading down to the old Baños Árabes (Arab Baths: Mon–Fri 10–6, Sat, Sun, public holidays 10–3). The shady Plaza Duquesa de Parcent is the focal point, laid out in front of the Iglesia de Santa María Mayor. Nearby is the 14th-century Palacio de Mondragón, a former Moorish palace and now the Museo Municipal (Jun–Oct Mon–Fri 10–6; Nov–May Mon–Fri 10–6, Sat, Sun and festivals 10–3).

On the north side of the gorge is the Mercadillo, the commercial new town. Ronda's main square, Plaza de España, is on this side next to the Puente Nuevo. Nearby is an elegant bullring, the Plaza de Toros, the second oldest in Spain (1785) and one of the country's largest. The famous matador Pedro Romero (1754–1839) established the rules of bullfighting here. You can visit the bullring and its small museum (daily 10–6).

➕ 472 E11 ℹ️ Plaza de España 9, 29400 Ronda ☎ 952 87 12 72 ℹ️ Paseo de Blas Infante s/n, 29400 Ronda ☎ 952 18 71 19 🚉 Ronda

SEVILLA (SEVILLE)
▷ 372–375.

SIERRA NEVADA
www.sierranevada.es
This range of snowcapped mountains contains the highest peaks in Spain—Mulhacén, at 3,478m (11,411ft), and Pico Veleta, at 3,398m (11,148ft)—and part of it has been designated a natural park. From Granada you can drive to the ski resort Solynieve (meaning 'sun and snow'), but access beyond it into the park is on foot or by bicycle

Opposite Puente Nuevo spans El Tajo gorge linking the old and new town at Ronda
Right The spectacular snow-capped mountains of the Sierra Nevada

only. From Solynieve you can climb Veleta, which will take two to three hours. Otherwise, access to the Sierra Nevada is to the south via Las Alpujarras (▷ 351).
➕ 473 H10 ℹ️ El Dornajo, 18160 Guejar-Sierra ☎ 958 34 06 25 ℹ️ Lanjar de Andarax, 04470 Lanjar de Andarax ☎ 950 51 35 48

ÚBEDA
www.ubedainteresa.com
Some of the finest Renaissance buildings in Spain are found at Úbeda. The most renowned of these surround the Plaza de Vázquez de Molina, including the Capilla del Salvador, a private burial chapel dating from the 16th century (Mon–Sat 10–2, 5–7, Sun 10.45–2, 4.30–7). Its facade is decorated in an elaborate style resembling the intricate work of medieval silversmiths, and its interior is also beautiful. The Palacio de las Cadenas (Palace of the Chains), now the town hall, and the Iglesia de Santa María de los Reales Alcázares (closed for restoration) are also on the Plaza de Vázquez de Molina. Úbeda is known for its green-glazed pottery, examples of which are on display in many shops around town. Other churches and buildings can be seen in the Plaza San Pedro and the Plaza del Primero de Mayo.
➕ 473 G9 ℹ️ Palacio del Marqués del Contadero, Calle Bajada del Marqués, 23400 Úbeda ☎ 953 75 08 97

ZAHARA DE LA SIERRA
www.zaharadelasierra.es
One of Andalucía's most remarkable white towns clings to a rocky hillside beneath a hilltop Moorish castle (open at all times). The small village square lies in front of the baroque Iglesia de Santa María de la Mesa (open for Mass). A viewing balcony overlooks the Embalse de Zahara reservoir below. At the other end of this short main street is the Iglesia de San Juan (daily 9.30–8). Climb to the castle for some magnificent views.
➕ 472 E10 ℹ️ Plaza de San Juan, 11688 Zahara ☎ 956 12 31 14

ZUHEROS
www.zuheros.es
Zuheros is a village of narrow streets and whitewashed houses, set high on a hillside in the Sierra Subbética range southeast of Córdoba. Overlooking the main square are the handsome parish church, the Iglesia de la Virgen de los Remedios, and the museum, with objects from prehistoric, Roman and Moorish times (Tue and Thu groups only, tel 957 69 45 14; Jun–Sep Sat–Sun and festivals 12.30–2.30, 6.30–8.30; Oct–May 12.30–2.30, 4.30–6.30). Remains of a Moorish castle are built into rocks above the town. The Cueva del Cerro de los Murciélagos (Cave of the Bats), has prehistoric paintings and rock formations.
➕ 473 F9 ℹ️ Carretera Zuheros-Baena, Km 1.5, 14870 Zuheros ☎ 957 09 00 30

INTRODUCTION

s the city's main attractions lie close together and its network of streets
particularly alluring, walking in Sevilla (Seville in English) is both sensible
nd a pleasure. But to see the city's true character you should visit when its
esidents are celebrating, perhaps during the processions of *Semana Santa* (Holy
Veek—Palm Sunday to Easter Sunday) or the debauchery of the Feria de Abril,
mmediately afterwards.

Seville was an important port city under the Romans (when it was called
ispalis) and a cultural focus when ruled by the Visigoths. During Muslim rule
when it was called Ishbiliya), it was a powerful state that, at its height in the 11th
entury, stretched from Murcia to Portugal. The city returned to Christian hands
fter a two-year siege in 1248, when Fernando III of Castile resettled around
5,000 Castilians in the city to create a genuinely tri-cultural mix of Christians,
ews and Muslims.

Seville became Spain's most important city in 1503, when it won a monopoly
n Spanish trade with the Americas. Its population tripled and it played an
mportant part in Spain's Golden Age as home to such artists as Zurbarán and
Murillo. Plague halved the population in 1649, and as the Río Guadalquivir silted
p, the city's fortunes suffered.

Mid-19th-century industrialization and the establishment of an exotic
tereotype—compiled of images of Carmen, bullfighting and gypsies—attracted
isitors and helped Seville regain some of its former glory. This was further aided
y its first great international fair, the Exposición Iberoamericana, in 1929. The
uge Expo World's Fair of 1992 also helped, although the city still faces many
roblems, not least unemployment.

WHAT TO SEE

ALCÁZAR (REALES ALCÁZARES)

ww.patronato-alcazardesevilla.es
lthough nominally a fortress dating back to the 10th century, the highlight
f the Alcázar is the Palacio de Don Pedro. Built in the 14th century by Pedro
he Cruel, this spectacular Mudéjar palace is still used by the Spanish royal
amily when visiting and for royal wedding feasts. It is reminiscent of Granada's
lhambra (▷ 364–365), thanks to its combination of water features, gardens
nd intricate Islamic detail, including Mudéjar plasterwork, arches and tiling
hroughout.

Look for the Patio de las Doncellas (Court of the Maidens), Camara Regia
Royal Chamber), Patio del Yeso (Gypsum Court) and Salón de Embajadores (Hall
f Ambassadors), the last topped by a dome representing the universe. There are
lso gardens that make a good retreat from the busy city, especially in summer.
374 B2 ☒ Patio de Banderas s/n ☎ 954 50 23 24 ⊙ Apr–Sep Tue–Sat 9.30–7, Sun
.30–6; Oct–Mar Tue–Sat 9.30–7, Sun 9.30–2.30 ✋ €7.50

BARRIO DE SANTA CRUZ

ww.barriosantacruz.com
his area near the Alcázar was once the city's Jewish quarter. Little of this period
f its history remains, although one of its former synagogues still stands in the
orm of the Iglesia de Santa María la Blanca. Inside the church is *The Last Supper*
(640) by Bartolomé Murillo (1617–82), who lived in Barrio de Santa Cruz. You
ould spend an afternoon just wandering around the *barrio*'s alleyways among
he orange trees, looking at the wrought ironwork and the whitewashed houses,
nd stopping for coffee at one of the many cafés or shops.
374 B2

INFORMATION

www.turismo.sevilla.org
✚ 472 D10 ▮ Avenida de la
Constitución 21B ☎ 954 22 14 04
⊙ Mon–Sat 9–7, Sun 10–2 🚉 Estación
de Santa Justa, 1km (0.5 mile) from
central Seville

Below *Exquisite tiling in Plaza de España*
Opposite *The Giralda minaret is all that
remains of the 12th-century mosque on
which the cathedral now stands*

ANDALUCÍA • SIGHTS

REGIONS

TIPS

» Seville is allegedly the birthplace of tapas; its bars have a bewildering choice.
» Avoid the city during July and August, when it becomes swelteringly hot.
» Look after your valuables: Seville has one of the worst reputations for petty thievery in Spain.

CASA DE PILATOS

www.fundacionmedinaceli.org/monumentos/casapilatos

This 16th-century palace belonging to the Dukes of Medinaceli (the current duke still lives in part of it) is a surprisingly successful mixture of Mudéjar (ceilings and tiles), plateresque (portal), Moorish (arches) and Gothic (balustrade) elements. It was built by the first Marquis of Tarifa, styled on the House of Pontius Pilate in Jerusalem. In the main courtyard are three Roman statues dating from the fifth century BC and a fountain imported from Genoa. Around the rooms is a collection of paintings, including works by Italian artist Sebastiano del Piombo (1485–1547) and by Francisco de Goya (1746–1828). The palace is slightly off the main tourist trail, so is less hectic than other sights and even more pleasurable.

✚ 374 B2 ✉ Plaza Pilatos 1 ☎ 954 22 52 98 🕐 Mar–Sep daily 9–7; Oct–Feb daily 9–6 ✋ Museum: €9. Patio and gardens: €6; free to EU citizens with ID Tue 1–5 ❓ First level: guided tour only

CATEDRAL

www.catedraldesevilla.es

Depending on the criteria you use, this is the largest church in the world. Built on the site of a 12th-century mosque between 1401 and 1507, the Gothic cathedral claims to hold the remains of Christopher Columbus (c1451–1506). The overpowering sensation inside the cathedral is of its vastness—it has five naves and enormous side chapels, all built simply but impressively. There is plenty to see, including the 15th-century stained-glass windows, elaborate 15th-century choir stalls, and works by Goya, Murillo and Zurbarán in the treasury. The imposing Capilla Mayor contains an enormous Gothic retablo (altarpiece) with 45 scenes from the life of Christ, probably the finest altarpiece in the world. Next door, and accessible from the cathedral, is the famous Giralda. This 12th-century minaret is all that remains of the original mosque on which the cathedral stands, and can be climbed via a series of ramps for views over Seville.

✚ 374 B2 ✉ Plaza Virgen de los Reyes, Avenida de la Constitución ☎ 954 21 49 71 🕐 Mon–Sat 11–5, Sun and festivals 2.30–6 ✋ €8 (also entry to La Giralda), free on Sun

PLAZA DE TOROS DE LA MAESTRANZA

www.plazadetorosdelamaestranza.com

This historic bullring is possibly Spain's most attractive and is its most venerable, at almost 250 years old. Bullfighting is central to life in Seville and Andalucía and a visit here, even if not to an actual *corrida*, gives some idea of its role. A small bullfighting museum has displays of matador costumes and *corrida*-related art.

➕ 374 A2 ✉ Paseo Cristóbal Colón 22 ☎ 954 22 45 77 🕐 Daily 9.30–7; on bullfight and concert days 9.30–3. Bullfights: mostly Sun, Apr–Sep ✋ €5

MORE TO SEE

ARCHIVO DE INDIAS

Here a fabulous collection of maps and documents dates back to 1492, including correspondence between Isabel and Columbus. Displays change.

➕ 374 B2 ✉ Avenida de la Constitución 3 ☎ 954 21 12 34 🕐 Mon–Sat 10–4 ✋ Free

CALLE SIERPES

This is the best street for one-stop Spanish shopping, whatever you want. There are plenty of cafés where you can take a break.

➕ 374 B1

Above *Orange trees are a familiar sight in Seville*
Below *Plaza de España is a popular place for a stroll*

HOSPITAL DE LA CARIDAD

This hospital has been caring for the poor and sick since the 17th century. It contains works by Bartolomé Murillo (1618–82) and Juan de Valdés-Leal (1622–90), plus courtyards and a baroque chapel.

➕ 374 B2 ✉ Calle Temprado 3 ☎ 954 22 32 32 🕐 Mon–Sat 9–1.30, 3.30–7.30, Sun and festivals 9–1 ✋ €4

MUSEO DE BELLAS ARTES

www.juntadeandalucia.es

The former Convento de la Merced is now one of the country's most important art museums, with a particular bias towards the Seville school of artists. There are works by El Greco and Zurbarán, but of particular note are the religious paintings of local artist Bartolomé Murillo and the unsettling canvases by Juan de Valdés-Leal. The early 17th-century building itself has three pleasant patios decorated with flowers and *azulejos* (ceramic tiles).

➕ 374 A1 ✉ Plaza del Museo 9 ☎ 954 22 18 29, 954 22 07 90 🕐 Tue 3–8, Wed–Sat 9–8, Sun 9–2 ✋ €1.50

TORRE DEL ORO

A defensive lookout since the early 13th century, the 12-sided Tower of Gold was once covered in ornamental tiles. It is now a maritime museum.

➕ 374 B2 ✉ Paseo de Cristóbal Colón s/n ☎ 954 22 24 19 🕐 Tue–Fri 10–2, Sat–Sun 11–2 ✋ €1.50, free on Tue

SIERRA DE GRAZALEMA

The famous *pueblos blancos*, or white towns, of Andalucía's Málaga and Cádiz provinces are villages of whitewashed houses that lie among the mountains of the Parque Natural Sierra de Grazalema. This tour takes you to some of the finest.

THE DRIVE
Distance: 80km (50 miles)
Allow: 4–5 hours (extra time for detour to Garganta Verde)
Start/end at: Grazalema, map 472 E10

★ Start at Grazalema, which lies in the shadow of the mountain of Peñón Grande. From here, take the Ronda road and go straight on at a junction, signed for Ronda and Ubrique. The road winds uphill beneath huge cliffs. At a junction, go straight on along the A-372, which becomes the A-2302, signed to Ubrique. Follow this as it runs under the peaks of the Sierra del Caillo and passes Villaluenga del Rosario, the highest village in Cádiz province.

Continue through the valley known as La Manga (The Sleeve), where rocky slopes rise up and stone walls follow the base of the cliffs. The road bends sharply right just beyond a picnic spot and viewpoint; shortly after this, turn right at a junction to reach Benaocaz. There is parking for a few cars in Plaza de Vista Hermosa on the outskirts.

❶ The settlement of Benaocaz was founded by the Moors in the eighth century and is a typical *pueblo blanco*, with whitewashed houses set on a hillside backed by limestone crags and wooded slopes. The main square, Plaza de las Libertades, is encircled with pillars that are decorated with small ceramic tiles depicting local sights.

From Plaza de Vista Hermosa, keep left down Calle Laverado and head on through Plaza de las Libertades. Turn left down Calle San Blas, then right at the main road and follow the A-2302 for Ubrique.

❷ The moderately large town of Ubrique, renowned for its leatherwork, lies below the dramatic cliffs of Cruz de Tajo.

Continue along the wider and faster A-373 towards Villamartín for about 8km (5 miles). Look for signs to El Bosque and for a turning on the right on to the A-372 signed for Benamahoma, Ronda and Grazalema. Beyond this the road climbs towards the Sierra del Pinar, passing above Benamahoma.

❸ The attractive *pueblo blanco* of Benamahoma celebrates its Moorish

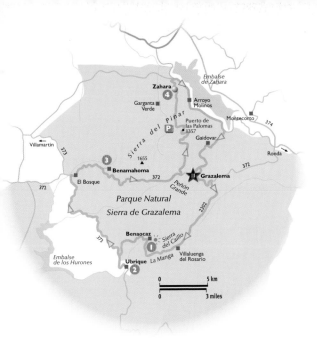

heritage with a lively fiesta on the first Sunday of August, featuring mock battles between Moors and Christians.

Continue along the A-372, which enjoys magnificent views of limestone crags to the right. After about 8km (5 miles) turn left, signed for Zahara. You now enter a beautiful mountain area that is cloaked in woods of cork and holm oak and pinsapo pine, a conifer that held on here after the last Ice Age and is now flourishing in the Parque Natural Sierra de Grazalema.

The road climbs slowly through a series of S-bends to reach the Puerto de Las Palomas (Pass of the Doves) at 1,357m (4,452ft), from where it descends through more S-bends.

About 5km (3 miles) below the pass, there is a car parking area on the left from where a path heads off for several kilometres to the impressive Garganta Verde canyon. It takes about two to three hours to reach the canyon, and you must get a permit to walk there in advance — this can be obtained from the information office in Avenida de la Disputación in El Bosque or Plaza de España in Grazalema. Continue towards Zahara and you will soon pass an olive-oil production centre, Almazara El Vínculo.

Almazara is open for visits during normal working hours (see Place to Visit, right). There are sometimes tastings here, but don't sip too much if you are not used to it.

❹ The village of Zahara lies just beyond the hotel. To enter it, turn left up a steep dirt road. You can park on the right at the bottom of the hill, or if there is no room here you will need to continue up to the new concrete parking area on the left. From the parking area walk straight on, past the castle above, and into the main square. Zahara perches on a rocky hill topped by the ruins of a 12th-century castle. It is one of the most attractive *pueblos blancos* and was declared a national monument in the 1980s (▷ 371).

Leave Zahara the way you came in. Turn left, then immediately right, following signs for Arroyo Molinos. When you reach the main road, turn right towards Grazalema, and at the next junction turn left on to a road signed for Arroyo Molinos. At the next intersection, turn right, again signed for Arroyo Molinos, and follow the road above the reservoir. Just beyond the end of the reservoir, turn right towards Grazalema and continue through wooded mountains till the road meets another. Turn right here to return to Grazalema.

WHEN TO GO
Any time from spring to autumn, though you may hit bad weather in the high pass during winter.

WHERE TO EAT
RESTAURANT LAS VEGAS
Great views out over the Sierra de Cádiz.
✉ Plaza de las Libertades 5, 11612 Benaocaz ☎ 956 12 55 02 🕐 Summer 8–5, 7–12; winter 8am–midnight. Closed Mon

PLACE TO VISIT
ALMAZARA EL VINCULO ALOJAMIENTO RURAL
www.molinoelvinculo.com
Small rural hotel, attached to an olive mill; wine and olive tastings.
✉ Carretera de Zahara-Grazalema Km 1, 11688 Zahara ☎ 956 12 30 02

Right *The hills around the sierra are cloaked in cork trees*
Opposite *Climb up to Zahara's Moorish castle for fantastic views*

ALMERÍA TO COWBOY COUNTRY

From Almería this drive heads first to the pottery village of Níjar, and then continues through remote mountains and desert canyons. This is where several of the so-called Spaghetti Westerns were filmed, including *A Fistful of Dollars*, and where the Wild West lives on in theme parks today.

THE DRIVE

Distance: 100km (62 miles)
Allow: 3 hours (longer if time is spent at Níjar and Mini Hollywood)
Start/end at: Almería, map 474 H10

★ Drive east out of Almería from the big roundabout at the bottom of the Rambla de Belén. Follow signs for Murcia and Mojácar. In 17km (10.5 miles) join the A-7/ E-15.

Beyond Almería's outskirts and airport, you enter the strange world of *plasticultura*, where fruit and vegetables are produced intensively inside *invernaderos* (greenhouses).

Acting as a backdrop to the Campo de Níjar sea of plastic are the Sierra de Alhamilla mountains. After about 30km (19 miles) turn left, signed for Níjar; a little farther on is the town itself. Enter Níjar by its long main street, Avenida García Lorca, where there is plenty of parking.

❶ Níjar's pottery industry was established by the Moors. Today there are many shops selling ceramics along Avenida García Lorca and the adjoining Barrio Alfarero. While in Níjar, stop at Plaza la Glorieta, the main square of the upper town, which is reached by heading uphill from the top of

Avenida García Lorca. The 16th-century Iglesia de Santa María de la Anunciación here has a fine Mudéjar coffered ceiling above the nave.

Leave Níjar by heading back down Avenida García Lorca, then at the intersection turn left towards Campohermoso and Murcia. At the next intersection turn left on to the AL-102, signed for Lucainena de las Torres, and drive uphill. Stop at the next junction before turning right, again signed for Lucainena (the signpost is on the opposite corner but may be obscured by a tree). Continue into the Sierra de Alhamilla, a dry mountain landscape dotted with oak trees and low scrub. High above Níjar you get a view of the plain below. The road becomes rougher here and about 16km (10 miles) beyond Níjar it descends to Lucainena de las Torres.

❷ The pretty church and whitewashed houses of Lucainena are overlooked by the towering peaks of the Peñón de las Turrillas.

Continue for 9km (5.5 miles), finally descending along a straight stretch of road lined with eucalyptus trees to a junction with the N-340. Turn right to visit the village of Sorbas.

❸ Sorbas has a dramatic location on the edge of a rugged gorge. Like Níjar, it has a tradition of ceramics, although the pottery produced here is more functional and less decorative. The limestone cave complex of Cuevas de Sorbas is 2km (1.2 miles) southeast of the village.

Back on the main route, turn right at the junction with the N-340 back towards Almería. Continue through the increasingly desert-like countryside, its grey-brown

sandstone hills bare of vegetation and sculpted into bizarre shapes by the wind. The road bypasses the town of Tabernas, which is overlooked by a Moorish castle that may appear impressive, but is in fact disappointingly decrepit.

❹ You are now in the celluloid version of the Wild West, whose landscapes stood in for those of America's cowboy country in numerous films made during the mid-20th century. Today, the area is home to three Wild West theme parks that pay homage to this legacy. The first is Texas Hollywood, reached by a dirt track and complete with a dusty cowboy town, cavalry fort and Native American tepee village. As at the other Western attractions, mock gunfights are staged and you can rent horses and dress up in cowboy gear. The best (and most expensive) of the theme parks is Mini Hollywood, about 6km (4 miles) southwest of Tabernas.

Just beyond Mini Hollywood, the N-342 joins the Granada–Almería highway—the A-92. Turn right to reach the approach track to the third

cowboy theme park. Named Western Leone after Sergio Leone, the maker of *A Fistful of Dollars* and *The Good, the Bad and the Ugly*, this is the least expensive of the Western attractions. It has the most authentic setting, above a dry gulch.

Return to Almería south along the highway.

WHEN TO GO
In the middle of summer this region gets uncomfortably hot, so spring and autumn are the best times.

WHERE TO EAT
There are limited facilities for eating and drinking along this route. All the theme parks have simple snack bar-cafés. You could also try:

RESTAURANTE LAS ERAS
Local dishes in rustic surroundings, ✉ Carretera Murcia s/n, Tabernas ☎ 950 36 52 69

PLACES TO VISIT
CUEVAS DE SORBAS
www.cuevasdesorbas.com
✉ 2km (1.2 miles) southeast of Sorbas (04270) ☎ 950 36 47 04 (reservations advised) ✋ Call for reservations 🎫 Three different levels of tours available: 1 hour €13, 3 hour €27.50, 5 hour €45 (includes rapelling, gear provided)

MINI HOLLYWOOD
✉ Carretera Nacional 340, 04200 Tabernas ☎ 950 36 52 36 🕐 Easter–Oct daily 10–9; Nov–Easter Sat–Sun 10–6 🎫 Adult €19, child (4–12) €9

TEXAS HOLLYWOOD
✉ Carretera Nacional 340, 04200 Tabernas ☎ 950 16 54 58 🕐 Mar–Oct daily 10–9; Nov–Feb Sat–Sun 10–6 🎫 Adult €14, child €8

WESTERN LEONE
✉ Intersection N-340/A-92, towards Guadix (18500) ☎ 950 16 54 05 🕐 Apr–Oct daily 10–9; Nov–Mar daily 10–5 🎫 Adult €11, child €6

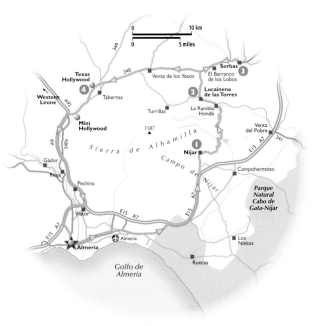

Opposite *The legacy of countless Spaghetti Westerns at Mini Hollywood*

A STROLL THROUGH OLD CÁDIZ

This walk meanders along the narrow streets of the old town of Cádiz, taking in museums and one of the city's most interesting churches en route.

THE WALK

Distance: 2.5km (1.5 miles)
Allow: 3 hours, with visits to museums and churches
Start/end at: Plaza San Juan de Dios, map 472 D11
Parking: Underground garage opposite the visitor office at the start of the walk

HOW TO GET THERE

Cádiz sits on Andalucía's Costa de la Luz. Plaza San Juan de Dios, the main square, is right in the heart of the city.

★ Start in the Plaza San Juan de Dios. Both the regional and municipal tourist information offices are located at either end of this square. On one side is the *ayuntamiento* (town hall), crowned with a blue cupola. From the south corner by the town hall, head down Calle Pelota to reach the Plaza de la Catedral.

❶ This lovely square is shaded by palm trees and lined with attractive old buildings that complement the baroque cathedral. The Iglesia de Santiago, at one end of the plaza, has an interesting bell tower.

Exit the square along Calle Compañía, alongside the bell tower. The buildings lining this cobbled street feature pretty balconies that overhang the clothes and shoe shops below. It leads to the busy square of Plaza de la Flores.

❷ The flower market and fountain here are surrounded by fine buildings, including the art-nouveau post office. To the left of the post office is the market square, Plaza Libertad; the covered market located here in the square is liveliest in the morning.

Leave the market square along Calle Hospital de Mujeres, passing the hospital itself on your left.

❸ With its ornate facade, the

Hospital de Mujeres is one of the finest baroque buildings in Cádiz. Peek into the vestibule to see the shrine dedicated to the Virgin and the pretty tiled courtyard. The chapel here opens mornings to allow visitors to view the painting *Ecstasy of St. Francis*, by El Greco (1541–1614), which depicts the saint experiencing a vision.

Turn right along Calle Sagasta and then left along Calle Santa Inés. This route passes the Museo de las Cortes de Cádiz, home to an incredible scale model of the late 18th-century city, carved in wood and ivory.

❹ Next door is the Oratorio de San Felipe Neri, which also opens its doors to visitors each morning; here, above the altar, is the *Immaculate Conception*, by Bartolomé Murillo (1617–82).

From the church head down Calle San José, crossing Calle Benjumeda and Calle Cervantes, then turn left along Calle Junquera to reach Plaza de San Antonio.

❺ This vast square is edged with seats that make a pleasant place to relax in the sunshine. Take time to admire its grand buildings, and the pastel facade of the Iglesia de San Antonio.

Leave the plaza on the same side as you entered, but turn down Calle Ancha instead. From here go left along Calle San José to Plaza de Mina and the Museo de Bellas Artes y Arqueológico.

❻ This museum is the pride of Cádiz and one of the best in Spain. The ground-level collection of historical objects (especially the Roman displays) is outstanding; the next floor has the city's art treasures, including work by Murillo, Rubens and Zurbarán.

For a grand view out to sea, follow Calle General Menacho or Calle Santiago Terry from here to the sea wall. Then return to the museum and turn left on Calle Tinte to reach Plaza San Francisco. From the square's opposite corner, follow Calle San

Francisco through Plaza de San Agustín and along Calle Nueva back to Plaza San Juan de Dios.

WHEN TO GO
Any time of year is good, but for a real feel of Cádiz come during its Carnival, February to March, when the whole city participates in the music, fun and frivolities.

WHERE TO EAT
PASAJE ANDALUZ
A good place for lunch.
✉ Plaza San Juan de Dios 9, 11005 Cádiz
☎ 956 28 52 54 ◉ Jan–Nov Sat–Thu 10–5, 8–midnight

PLACES TO VISIT
MUSEO DE CÁDIZ
✉ Plaza de Mina 5, 11004 Cádiz
☎ 956 21 22 81 ◉ Tue 2.30–8, Wed–Sat 9–8.30, Sun 9.30–2.30 🖐 €1.50, EU citizens free

MUSEO DE LAS CORTES DE CÁDIZ
✉ Calle Santa Inés 9, 11003 Cádiz
☎ 956 22 17 88 ◉ Tue–Fri 9–1, 4–7, Sat–Sun 9–1 🖐 Free

Opposite *The old town of Cádiz*
Left *The facade of the cathedral*
Below *Statue of the Virgin in San Felipe Neri*

REGIONS | ANDALUCÍA • WALK

381

ALMERÍA

AUDITORIO MUNICIPAL MAESTRO PADILLA

This is the main theatre in town, staging plays, exhibitions and all kinds of music and dance.

✉ Plaza Alfredo Kraus s/n, 04007 ☎ 950 27 30 02 🖐 Up to €30 🚌 11, 18 from Paseo de Almería

LA CLÁSICA

A popular bar/nightclub which features pop music every night, this place is spacious and modern, with three bars. There are live music or other performances once a month.

✉ Calle Poeta Villaespesa 4, 04003 Almería ☎ 950 26 02 52 🕐 Tue–Sat 3pm–7am 🖐 Free

COPPELIA

A dance shop in the Galerías Comerciales, Coppelia specializes in clothes and shoes for ballet, Spanish classical dance and flamenco. It also sells fashion clothing.

✉ Paseo de Almería 45, 04001 Almería ☎ 950 24 12 49 🕐 Mon–Fri 10–1, 5.30–8, Sat 10–1

MUSEO DEL ACEITE DE OLIVA

Lovers of Mediterranean cuisine should not miss the Olive Oil Museum. There is a comprehensive selection here, as well as wine and other regional products. Guided walks through the city's historic district are offered, plus sampling at the museum at the end of the tour.

✉ Calle Real 15 Bajo, 04001 Almería ☎ 950 62 00 02 🕐 Mon–Fri 10–1, 5.30–8, Sat 10–1 🖐 €4

TEATRO CERVANTES

Although occasionally used for minor live performances, this theatre is primarily a cinema.

✉ Calle Poeta Villaespesa 1, 04001 Almería ☎ 950 23 70 93 🖐 €5

TEATRO MUNICIPAL APOLO

This theatre is used by small companies to stage everything from plays to concerts and dance. Most shows are free. It is often used for puppet shows, school plays and experimental theatre.

✉ Rambla del Obispo Orberá 25, 04001 Almería ☎ 950 26 92 68 🕐 Two to three

performances weekly at 9pm and 10pm 🖐 Up to €25

ALMUÑÉCAR

PARQUE DEL MAJUELO, ALMUÑÉCAR

These ornithological gardens are occupied by more than 200 species of tropical bird. A family of ostriches roams around the park. In addition, there is a fascinating cactus park. You can drive down to the sea for a swim after your visit.

✉ Plaza de San Cristobal, 18690 Almuñécar ☎ 958 63 11 25 🕐 Apr–Sep 11–2, 6–9, Oct–Mar 10–2, 4–6 🖐 Free 🚗 Almuñécar is on the coast, 40km (25 miles) from Granada, between Nerja and Motril

CASARES (MÁLAGA)

ADVENTURE BUG

www.adventurebug.com

This adventure tour company organizes trips throughout Andalucía, from the mountains of the Alpujarras to the rural whitewashed *pueblos*, and local seaside strolls. A multitude

Above *Olive oil comes in a variety of flavours*

of activities are available, including trekking, bicycling, surfing, skiing, snowboarding, flamenco dancing, ceramics and more, with English-speaking staff.

✉ Calle Juan Ceron 20, 29690 Casare, Málaga ☎ 952 89 43 08 or 635 81 78 19 ✋ All tours begin at Málaga airport (shuttle van to pick you up). Prices vary depending on type of tour. Tours start at €30–€50 (half day) and can last up to a week. Weeklong tours range around €800–€1,200 and include accommodations and most meals.

CÓRDOBA

BIANCO
This fashionable café-bar near the lively Ciudad Jardín nightlife zone is furnished with minimalist designer fittings. In the afternoons, it is a relaxed place to enjoy a coffee and a chat, but things heat up in the evenings. There are theme nights every Thursday, and DJs keep things lively on Fridays and Saturdays. There is a small stage, and occasionally the bar hosts live gigs by local groups.

✉ Calle Damasco 22, 14004 Córdoba ☎ 957 23 87 91 🕒 Daily 4pm–2am

BISTROT
This friendly bar recreates the atmosphere of Parisian bars at the turn of the 20th century in its pretty interior, but it draws a crowd for the terrace on one of Córdoba's most emblematic squares. Linger over a coffee or a cocktail and watch the world go by. It attracts a younger crowd in the evenings, but there's an eclectic mix during the day. Snacks are served.

✉ Plaza Corredera 5, Córdoba 🕒 Mon–Sat 12–4, 8pm–2am, Sun noon–4pm

EL CORTE INGLÉS
www.elcorteingles.es
You can buy anything from furniture to food, and goods are of excellent quality. The fashion department stocks extensive clothing ranges by Spanish and international designers. Not to be missed during the sales!

✉ Calle Ronda de los Tejares 30, 14008 Córdoba ☎ 957 22 28 81 🕒 Mon–Sat 10–10

ECO-PARQUE AVENTURA
www.noerescapaz.es
Just a 20-minute drive from the city centre, this adventure park is the perfect place to bring the children. The setting, by a river in the hills of the Sierra de Córdoba, is beautiful, and the Eco-Parque offers activities to suit all ages and abilities. The main circuit includes an adventure course through the treetops, but there are other activities on offer, from mountain-bicycling and paint-balling to river fishing.

✉ Carretera de Villaviciosa km12, Las Solanes del Pilar, Córdoba ☎ 687 52 26 00 🕒 Sat–Sun 10–7, later in summer ✋ Park free; additional charge for activities

GRAN TEATRO DE CÓRDOBA
www.teatrocordoba.com
This venue hosts the best artists in town. As well as classical theatre productions, it stages opera and ballet and symphony orchestras, chamber and contemporary music. It has a bar.

✉ Avenida de Gran Capitán 3, 14008 Córdoba ☎ 957 48 06 44; advance tickets 902 36 02 95 ✋ Varies according to the show

GRIFOS OK
During the day this is just another tapas bar, but at night it is the perfect place for a drink while listening to the latest rock and pop sounds on the spacious terrace. The bar has an extensive range of beers on offer.

✉ Camino de los Sastres s/n, Ciudad Jardín, 14004 Córdoba ☎ 957 45 47 00 🕒 Sun–Thu 11am–midnight, Fri–Sat 11am–2.30am ✋ Free

MERYAN
www.meryancor.com
Meryan has been handcrafting leather for many years, using techniques in accordance with old traditions. The shop sells ready-made items, although most of the work is custom made. Jewellery and cigarette boxes make excellent presents or souvenirs.

✉ Calleja de Las Flores 2, 14003 Córdoba ☎ 957 47 59 02 🕒 Mon–Fri 9–8, Sat 9–2

TABLAO FLAMENCO EL CARDENAL
www.tablaocardenal.com
A flamenco club, probably the most popular in Córdoba. It features first-class performances by guitarists and dancers, and promises an excellent Andalucían night out.

✉ Calle Torrijos 10, 14003 Córdoba ☎ 957 48 31 12 🕒 Shows Mon–Sat at 10.30pm. Closed for a few days in Jan (phone for details) ✋ €25 (includes one drink)

ZOCO ARTESANAL
www.artesaniadecordoba.com
Zoco Artesanal is a conglomerate of crafts workshops where the biggest association of craftspeople in the province works and markets its products. It offers metal and leatherwork, ceramics in Mozarabic style, and avant-garde designs and crafts in many other media.

✉ Calle Judíos s/n, 14004 Córdoba ☎ 957 20 40 33 🕒 Mar–Dec daily 10–8; Jan–Feb Mon–Fri 10–7, Sat 10–1

DESIERTO DE TABERNAS

MINI HOLLYWOOD
More than 100 Spaghetti Westerns were made at this Wild West town. The entrance fee allows access to a Texan ranch (five minutes' drive away), with a Mexican bar, restaurant and Wild West fort. Several shows take place at Mini Hollywood every hour or so, including a shootout. There are few sites dedicated to the very young.

✉ Carretera N-340, 04200 Desierto de Tabernas ☎ 950 36 52 36 🕒 Easter–Oct daily 10–9; Nov–Easter Sat–Sun 10–6 ✋ Adult €19, child €9 🚌 25km (15 miles) along the N-340 from Almería towards Tabernas

GRANADA

AUDITORIO MANUEL DE FALLA
www.orquestaciudadgranada.es
This modern concert hall, home to Granada's symphony orchestra, stages a variety of symphony music and hosts visiting orchestras.

✉ Paseo de los Mártires s/n, 18009 Granada ☎ 958 22 00 22, 958 22 11 44 (tickets) ✋ €5–€25 🚌 30, 32

EL CAMBORIO

El Camborio is in a real cave in the Sacromonte hillside district with a varied selection of music, from techno to flamenco. It's popular with a young, studenty crowd. There are stunning views of the Alhambra from the garden.

✉ Camino del Sacromonte 47, 18010 Granada ☎ 958 22 12 15 ⏱ Daily midnight–7am 🖐 €7 🚌 31, 32. Free bus from Plaza Nueva on Thu

LA CHUMBERA

www.carmendelascuevas.com

This fabulously authentic *peña* (flamenco folk club) in the heart of the *gitano* (gypsy) district is a must for those seeking the spirit of flamenco. Lessons are available from the nearby Escuela Carmen de las Cuevas.

✉ Camino del Sacromonte s/n, 18008 Granada ☎ 958 21 56 47 ⏱ Daily 9.30pm–late (check for concert times) 🖐 Entry from €7

EL CORTE INGLÉS

www.elcorteingles.es

Sells everything except household goods. Slightly more expensive than elsewhere, but the quality is consistently higher, and there is superior customer service and all-day opening. Good café next to the supermarket in the basement and a restaurant on the second floor.

✉ Carrera del Genil 20–22, 18005 Granada ☎ 958 22 32 40 ⏱ Mon–Sat 10–10 🚌 7, 10, 11, 13, 33

DISCOS OJEDA

Although you'll find music from all genres in this music store, it specializes in flamenco. Ask for recommendations: The staff are very helpful. It's also a good place to find out about upcoming flamenco related events, or to hear about the off-the-beaten track places where local musicians like to gather.

✉ Gran Via de Colón 21, Granada ☎ 958 27 76 52 ⏱ Mon–Sat 10–1.30, 5–8.30

ESHAVIRA

This is an authentic music club and bar that's been going for years. Live jazz and flamenco are performed at least three nights a week. It's the haunt of local musicians, artists and intellectuals, and is tucked down a tiny alley off Calle Elvira, so can be a little hard to find.

✉ Calle Postigo de la Luna 2, 18010 Granada ☎ 958 29 08 29 ⏱ Daily 10pm–5am 🖐 Live performances €6–€10; some free 🚌 11, 23, 32

GRANADA 10

Granada 10 fills up with a cosmopolitan mix of people of all ages—singles, couples and groups—for great cocktails and a standard selection of contemporary and classic pop music. Located in an old cinema, it still shows cult classics during the afternoons.

✉ Calle de la Carcel Baja 10, 18010 Granada ☎ 958 22 40 01 ⏱ Daily midnight–8am 🖐 €10 (one free drink) 🚌 11, 13, 23, 32

GUITARRERÍA BELLIDO Y GIL DE AVALLE

www.granadaguitar.com

The best place for handcrafted guitars, although factory-made ones are also sold. Stocks handmade cellos, violins and double basses, as well as antique string instruments and accessories like books, music scores and CDs.

✉ Plaza Realejo 15, 18009 Granada ☎ 958 22 16 10 ⏱ Jul–Aug Mon–Fri 10–1.30, 6–9; Sep–Jun Mon–Fri 10–1.30, 5–8, Sat 10–1.30 🚌 6

HAMMAM BAÑOS ARABES

www.hammamspain.com

These Arab baths offer a 90-minute session that alternates between the hot and cold pools. Enjoy the Eastern music, Moorish-style decoration and exotic aromas, then complete the experience with a 15-minute massage (reservations essential). Sessions are mixed. Reserve in advance and take swim gear (towels and lockers are provided). There's also a tea room upstairs and a restaurant serving local-style food with a Moorish influence.

✉ Calle Santa Ana 6, 18009 Granada ☎ 958 22 99 78 ⏱ Mon–Fri 10am–11pm, Sat–Sun 10am–midnight 🖐 Baths €21, baths and massage €30; special low-season prices available 🚌 30, 31, 32

METRO

This specialist language bookshop has a range of dictionaries, grammar books and learning materials. It also offers the best selection of English-language fiction, guidebooks and books on Spanish history and culture. The owner speaks English.

✉ Calle Gracia 31, 18002 Granada ☎ 958 26 15 65 ⏱ Mon–Fri 10–2, 5–8.30, Sat 11–2 🚌 4, 6

LA OLIVA

www.laolivagourmet.com

La Oliva specializes in extra-virgin olive oils from Andalucía. Also sells fine wines and an excellent range of the best local produce, including organic foodstuffs such as honey, preserves, cheeses, nuts, cakes, herbs and spices. The owner invites you to taste before buying. Search the side streets around Plaza Mariana Pineda to find it.

✉ Calle Rosario 9, 18009 Granada ☎ 958 22 57 54 ⏱ Mon–Fri 11–2.30, 5–8.30 (7–10pm in summer), Sat 11–3. Closed Sat Jul–Aug 🚌 23 (Fuente de las Batallas stop)

PARQUE DE LAS CIENCIAS

www.parqueciencias.com

A hands-on, interactive science park in a state-of-the-art building and grounds housing a planetarium, an observatory, a Foucault pendulum and a butterfly farm. There's a café and a shop.

✉ Avenida del Mediterráneo s/n, 18006 Granada ☎ 958 13 19 00 ⏱ Tue–Sat 10–7, Sun and holidays 10–3. Closed Mon, 1 Jan, 1 May, 17–28 Sep, 24–25 Dec 🖐 Museum €6, planetarium €2.50 🚌 4, 5, 10, 11

PEÑA FLAMENCA LA PLATERÍA

www.laplateria.org.es

This authentic flamenco music and dance venue hosts some of Spain's top performers (the performances are on Saturday and Thursday). It attracts real enthusiasts, who help to create a lively atmosphere. It is in an alley in the old Moorish quarter of the Albaicín. Snacks and drinks are served.

✉ Placeta Toqueros 7, 18010 Granada 🕿 958 22 77 12 🕐 Daily 12–3, 8–1. Performances at 11pm ✋ €7 🚌 31, 32

SHERPA

www.sherpagranada.com

This shop stocks clothing and equipment for adventure sports enthusiasts, especially walkers, climbers, cavers and skiers. In Sherpa you can try out the specialist climbing gear on the in-house climbing wall before buying. A small noticeboard in the shop gives details of trips, courses and second-hand items for sale.

✉ Calle Paz 20, 18002 Granada 🕿 958 52 33 61 🕐 Mon–Fri 10–1.30, 5–8.30, Sat 10–2

SIERRA NEVADA SKIFIELD

www.cetursa.es

Spain's biggest ski resort is just 25 minutes away from Granada. It has 52 lifts and 60km (40 miles) of slopes. The resort is ugly and modern, but the skiing is varied and challenging. Its southern location means there are lots of sunny days, a long season,

and mountain-bicycling, horseback-riding and trekking in summer months. There are several good bars and cafés in the resort.

✉ Cetursa-Sierra Nevada S.A., Plaza de Andalucía, Edificio Cetursa C.P., 18196 Granada 🕿 958 24 91 00, 902 70 80 90 (information line), 958 20 40 00 (customer services) 🕐 Mid-Dec to late Apr ✋ Low season: 1-day pass €34; 6-day pass €170. High season: 1-day pass €41; 6-day pass €222. Concessions for under 12s and over 65s. (Photo required for the 5- and 6-day passes) 🚌 Take the N-420 direct from Granada's ringroad, then follow the signs for the Sierra Nevada

TEATRO ISABEL LA CATÓLICA

This grand theatre stages events including classical drama, comedy, opera, Spanish light opera, jazz and pop concerts.

✉ Calle Almona del Campillo 2, 18005 Granada 🕿 958 22 15 14 or 958 22 29 07 (ticket sales) ✋ €15 🚌 11, 13

MARBELLA
INCOSOL SPA AND HOTEL

www.incosol.com

Beauty care and massage are practised to perfection here. Treatments include body wraps,

underwater massage and exfoliation. Relax afterwards in one of the quiet pools or saunas. There is also an 18-hole golf course on site.

✉ Urbanizacion Golf Rio Real, 29600 Marbella 🕿 952 86 09 09 🕐 Daily 8–8 ✋ One-day Relax package: lunch, massage and three treatments €140 🚌 Five min west of Marbella, towards Puerto Banús. Take exit to Rio Real

MIJAS COSTA
GRAN HOTEL GUADALPIN THALASSOTHERAPY SPA

www.granhotelguadalpin.com

The spa facilities here are absolutely fabulous. You can swim in one of the many ornately tiled pools, take a steam or whirlpool bath, or use the high-pressure showers. A range of body massage options is available, but it's wise to telephone ahead to reserve your place. The spa specializes in thalassotherapy (sea-water treatments), and there are also a number of beauty treatments. There are a number of golf courses near by.

✉ Mijas Golf, 29650 Mijas Costa 🕿 952 47 30 50 🕐 Mon–Sat 9–1, 4–8 ✋ Half-hour massage €58 🚌 Take the Coín road from Fuengirola, turning off towards the Gran Hotel Guadalpin Byblos

Above *La Oliva in Granada offers a range of delicious produce, which makes for perfect souvenirs or gifts*

MOJÁCAR
MERCADILLO DE MOJÁCAR
Popular Sunday market selling all sorts of antiques and second-hand goods. It also welcomes artists and craftspeople selling paintings, handmade musical instruments and South American crafts. There are more than 20 stands.

✉ Centro de Artesanía, junction of road to Turre, 04638 Mojácar ⏰ Sun 9–2

SEVILLE
AIRE DE SEVILLA
www.airedesevilla.com
This modern-day *hammam* (Arab bathhouse) offers a salt bath, hydro-massage bath, sauna and other water-based therapies, as well as massage. Try its mud and seaweed wrap treatments. Towel and footwear are supplied, but bring your bathing suit—facilities are mixed.

✉ Calle Aire 15, 41004 Seville ☎ 955 01 00 25 💶 Bath only €21, bath and massage €32; reservation required 🚌 C3, C4, 21, 23

AQUÓPOLIS SEVILLA
www.aquopolis.es
At this small, family-oriented water park east of Seville, the rides vary from giant water pools and long, winding tubes to steep, multi-person slides. There are on-site baby-changing facilities.

✉ Avenida del Deporte s/n, 41020 Seville ☎ 954 40 66 22 ⏰ Jul–Aug daily 12–8; late May, Jun, Sep daily 12–7 💶 Adult €18, child €13.50 🚌 55, 22

EL ARENAL
www.tablaoelarenal.com
An Andalucían *tablao* (flamenco bar), El Arenal features prize-winning flamenco performers.

✉ Calle Rodo 7, 41001 Seville ☎ 954 21 64 92 ⏰ Shows daily 8, 10. 💶 €37 (includes one drink). Dinner with show from €72; show with tapas €55 🚌 C4

CAFÉ BAR ABADES
A trendy meeting place serving cocktails, this café hosts classical music ensembles and small theatre companies occasionally.

✉ Calle Los Abades 13, 41004 Seville ☎ 954 22 56 22 ⏰ Mon–Sat 4pm–2.30am, Sun 4–9 💶 Free 🚌 21, 23, 40, 41, 42

LA CARBONERÍA
This place is popular with locals for its eclectic mix of music. There's no sign outside, so look for a red door and people waiting at around 11pm. Simple meals and tapas are available.

✉ Calle Levíes 18, 41004 Seville ☎ 954 21 44 60 ⏰ Daily 9pm–3am 💶 Free 🚌 C3, C4, 21, 23

CASA DE LA MEMORIA DE AL-ANDALUZ
www.casadelamemoria.es
Showcased in a beautiful courtyard, this spectacular venue features skilled flamenco performers. Classes can also be arranged in this meeting spot and cultural centre for fans for the *cante jondo*.

✉ Calle Ximenez de Enciso 28, 41004 Seville ☎ 954 56 06 70 ⏰ Daily 10–2, 6–11; shows daily 9pm 💶 From €15 🚌 C3, C4, 21, 23

LA CAVA DE BETIS
This humidified cellar on the banks of the Río Guadalquivir sells all things tobacco related, including imported hand-rolled cigars. Also humidifiers, cutters and cases. Renowned as one of the best stores for cigars in southern Spain.

✉ Calle Betis 36, 41010 Seville ☎ 954 27 81 85 ⏰ Mon–Fri 10–2, 5.30–8.30, Sat 10–2 🚌 C3, 40

EL CORTE INGLÉS
www.elcorteingles.es
This is the largest of four central city branches of Spain's most prestigious department store chain. There is a cafeteria and good-quality restaurant on the top floor. A gourmet food shop and extensive wine cellar are located on the ground level.

✉ Plaza del Duque de la Victoria 8, 41002 Seville ☎ 954 597 000 ⏰ Mon–Sat 10–10 🚌 13, 14

ISLA MAGICA
www.islamagica.es
Isla Magica has a range of activities, although the roller-coasters, gardens and outdoor walking areas are the big attractions. There are trains and mini-rides for those aged under 10 and baby-changing facilities.

✉ Pabellón de España, Isla de la Cartuja, 41092 Seville ☎ 902 16 17 16 ⏰ Jul to mid-Sep Sun–Fri 11–11, Sat 11am–midnight; Apr–Jun Sat–Sun 11–8; Oct–Nov Sat–Sun 11–9 💶 High season: adult (over 13) €28, under 13 €20; low-season: adult €20, child €18. Half-day passes available

LIBRERÍA VÉRTICE
www.libreriavertice.com
A bookstore specializing in hard-to-find publications, but also stocking best sellers. It has Spanish, French, English, German and Italian books, and other languages.

✉ Calle San Fernando 33–35, 41004 Seville ☎ 954 21 16 54 ⏰ Mon–Sat 10–1.30, 4.30–8.30 🚌 C3, C4, 5, 25, 26, 30, 31, 33, 34, 35

MARÍA ROSA
www.mariarosa-sevilla.com
Sharp suits, frilly frocks and flouncy shawls for men, women and children

are sold here. Staff will help you pinpoint your own style. There is also a selection of flamenco shoes.

✉ Calle Cuna 13, 41004 Seville ☎ 954 22 21 43 🕐 Mon–Fri 10–1.30, 5–8.30, Sat 10–1.30 (Dec–May also 5–8.30pm) 🚌 10, 11, 12, 15, 20, 24, 27, 32

PLAZA DE TOROS DE LA MAESTRANZA
www.plazadetorosdelamaestranza.com
At one of Spain's most notable bullrings, tours are available.

✉ Paseo de Colón 12, 41004 Seville ☎ 954 50 13 82 🕐 Bullfights usually Sun evenings, Apr–Oct 🎟 From €6 to €4,150 🚌 C4, B2, 43 🍴

PUERTO DE CUBA
www.puertadecubasevilla.com
This swanky café-bar sits at the end of the famous Calle Betis, the bar-lined street which overlooks the river. From its terrace, you can enjoy splendid views out across the water to the Torre de Oro and the Giralda (both illuminated at night). It gets crammed on weekend evenings, when service can be incredibly slow.

✉ Plaza de Cuba, 41010 Sevilla 🕐 Daily noon–2am

SOPA DE GANSO
Tapas is served during the day in an informal dance café in the lively Plaza Alfalfa. Sopa de Ganso is popular with young and energetic locals. Definitely one of the 'in' bars.

✉ Calle Pérez Galdós 8, 41004 Seville ☎ 954 21 25 26 🕐 Daily 1pm–3am 🎟 Free 🚌 10, 11, 12, 15, 20, 24, 27, 32

TEATRO LOPE DE VEGA
www.teatrolopedevega.org
This traditional Italian-style theatre seats a total of 750 in a multi-level auditorium rich with gold leaf and red velvet. It stages some of the top national theatre events.

✉ Avenida María Luisa s/n, 41013 Seville ☎ 954 59 08 55 or 954 59 08 67 (ticket sales) 🎟 From €5 🚌 C1, C3, C4, 21, 25, 26, 30, 31, 33, 34, 35 🚇 Calle Enramadilla

TEATRO DE LA MAESTRANZA
www.teatromaestranza.com
A modern and spacious venue where

FESTIVALS AND EVENTS

FEBRUARY–MARCH
CARNAVAL
Parades, flamenco, dancing and feasting.
✉ All over

MARCH–APRIL
SEMANA SANTA
Most dramatic Holy Week processions in Spain.
✉ All over

APRIL
FERIA DE ABRIL
▷ 448.
✉ Seville

MAY
CRUCES DE MAYO
Fiesta which includes 'prettiest patio' competition.
✉ Córdoba

ROMERÍA DEL ROCIO
▷ 448.
✉ Rocio 🕐 Whitsun

MAY–JUNE
CORPUS CHRISTI
Processions and bullfights.
✉ Granada, Seville, Ronda, Vejer de la Fronterar and Zahara del la Sierra

JUNE
FERIA DE SAN BERNABÉ
Spectacular fiesta with parades.
✉ Marbella

excellent acoustics complement some of the most prestigious operas in the world. There is a café and bar.
✉ Paseo de Cristóbal Cólon 22, 41001 Seville ☎ 954 22 65 73 🎟 From €12 to €75 🚌 C4, B2, 43

VERA COSTA
PARQUE AQUATICO AQUAVERA
www.aquavera.com
At this mammoth water park that gets busy in summer, rides are gigantic, although there is a

INTERNATIONAL FESTIVAL OF MUSIC AND DANCE
Flamenco and chamber music.
✉ Alhambra and Generalife, Granada

JULY
INTERNATIONAL GUITAR FESTIVAL
Classical, flamenco and Latin American music festival.
✉ Córdoba

VIRGEN DEL MAR
Parades, equestrian events, concerts and partying.
✉ Almería

AUGUST
FERIA DE MÁLAGA
Drinking and dancing, parades and fireworks.
✉ Málaga

SEPTEMBER
BIENNIAL FLAMENCO FESTIVAL
Years ending in even numbers.
✉ Seville

CORRIDA GOYESCA
Flamenco and bullfights in 18th-century dress.
✉ Ronda

OCTOBER
FERIA DE SAN LUCAS
Old-established festival with parades, music and revelry.
✉ Jaén

children's pool for the little ones. Older kids can hurtle down the Black Hole, Kamikaze or a number of fearsome-looking slides. You can also float around the park on large yellow inflatable tubes. There's a self-service restaurant.
✉ Carretera de Vera a Garrucha-Villaricos, 04620 Vera Costa ☎ 950 46 73 37 🕐 Mid-May to mid-Aug daily 10.30–7.30; early May and Sep daily 11–6 🎟 Adult €18, child €13, under 4 free; half-day pass: adult €10.80, child €7.80

PRICES AND SYMBOLS

The restaurants are listed alphabetically (excluding Le, La and Les). The prices given are the average for a two-course lunch (L) and a three-course dinner (D) for one person, without drinks. The wine price is for the least expensive bottle.

For a key to the symbols, ▷ 2.

ALMERÍA
RINCÓN DE JUAN PEDRO

Both traditional local cuisine and international fare are on the menu here. The meat and fish dishes are all of excellent quality and the daily specials menu features delicious Almerían delicacies. The restaurant has been family-run since 1966 and continues to attract locals as well as visitors. It's an excellent place to try local tapas and *raciones*, too.

✉ Calle Federico de Castro 2, 04003 Almería ☎ 950 23 58 19 🕔 Tue–Sat 12–4, 8–11.30, Sun–Mon 12–4 ✋ L €12, D €28, Wine €8

CÁDIZ
EL BALANDRO

www.restaurantebalandro.com
A good choice for reasonably priced fish and seafood (it also has an island-shaped tapas bar for cheaper snacking), El Balandro has one of the most extensive and innovative menus in Cádiz.

✉ Alameda de Apodaca 22, Cádiz ☎ 956 22 09 92 🕔 Tue–Sat 1–4, 8–11 ✋ L €15, D €32, Wine €14

CÓRDOBA
ALMUDAINA

www.restaurantealmudaina.com
Housed in a beautiful 16th-century mansion that originally belonged to Bishop Don Leopoldo de Austria, this well-known, reputable restaurant opposite the Alcázar has seven inviting dining rooms and serves traditional Córdoban cuisine. House dishes are *salmorejo* (a thick *gazpacho* with ham and egg), *rabo de toro* (oxtail) and sea bass with asparagus sauce. There's a *menú del día* for €25.

✉ Jardines de los Santos Mártires 1, 14004 Córdoba ☎ 957 47 43 42 🕔 Mon–Sat 12–4, 8.30–12, Sun 12–4 ✋ L €35, D €46, Wine €14

BODEGAS CAMPOS

www.bodegascampos.com
At this *taberna*, established in 1908, you can sample the house's own montilla sherry and a selection of quality wines accompanied by a selection of tapas. There is also a prestigious restaurant with five dining rooms, serving traditional local cuisine with modern influences. There are areas for non-smokers. Parking is available.

✉ Calle Lineros 32, 14002 Córdoba ☎ 957 49 75 00 🕔 Mon–Sat 1.30–4, 8–12, Sun 12.30–4. Closed 24, 31 Dec ✋ L €35, D €55 (cheaper at the bar), Wine €12

Above *Salads in Andalucía are huge and made with the freshest ingredients*

EL CABALLO ROJO

www.elcaballorojo.com

This is one of Córdoba's best-known eateries, with a menu focusing on regional, Sephardic and Mozarabic cuisine. Dishes include lamb in honey, Mozarabic-style monkfish, and there are delicious desserts. A rooftop patio overlooks the Mezquita. Reservations recommended.

Calle Cardenal Herrero 28, 14003 Córdoba ☎ 957 47 53 75 🖐 Daily 1–4, 8–11. Closed 24 Dec 🖐 L €26, D €44, Wine €14

EL CHURRASCO

www.elchurrasco.com

El Churrasco is one of the best restaurants in the city, specializing in traditional Andalucían cuisine. It is most renowned for its *churrasco* (grilled pork with pepper sauce). The extensive menu (there's even a Braille version) includes fish and meat dishes. Don't miss a peek at the bodega: the wine selection is phenomenal. Reservations are recommended.

Calle Romero 16, 14003 Córdoba ☎ 957 29 08 19 🖐 Daily 1–4, 8–12. Closed Aug 🖐 L €32, D €48, Wine €14

PIC-NIC

An interesting restaurant that takes a healthy approach to fine dining. Instead of overloading its visitors with rich sauces and heavy combinations, chef Antonio Canals uses only the freshest, prime ingredients.

Calle Ronda de los Tejares 16, 14008 Córdoba ☎ 957 48 22 33 🖐 L €23, D €34, Wine €13 🖐 Tue–Sat 1.30–4, 9–12, Mon 1.30–4. Closed Easter week and Aug

RESTAURANTE FEDERACIÓN DE PEÑAS (KIKO)

www.federaciondepenas.com

Generous portions, delicious cooking and reasonable prices are Kiko's main attractions. Most dishes can be shared, unless you opt for *gazpacho* or another soup, or *revuelto* (scrambled eggs).

Calle Conde y Luque 8, 14003 Córdoba ☎ 957 47 54 27 🖐 Thu–Tue 12–4, 7.30–11. Closed 15 Jan–15 Feb 🖐 L €22, D €34, Wine €9

TABERNA RESTAURANTE PUERTA SEVILLA

www.puertasevilla.com

This *taberna*, set around a typical *Cordobesa* patio filled with flowers, is in the old Alcázar area, which takes its name from the western entrance to the district. It is a well-known establishment with a growing reputation for good food. The menu is traditional Córdoban and Mediterranean, with modern Spanish dishes. They also serve *raciones* for a lighter meal. There is wheelchair access and parking.

Calle Postrera 51, 14004 Córdoba ☎ 957 29 73 80 🖐 Daily 1–5, 8.30–12 🖐 L €28, D €40, Wine €12

FRIGILIANA
LA BODEGUILLA

http://labodeguillafrigiliana.com/

Rosaria and her four daughters will treat you like one of the family at this delightful little village restaurant. The mountain town of Frigiliana is one of the prettiest in Andalucía. The home-made cuisine is based on time-honoured recipes prepared with the best local ingredients: Try the grilled pork chops served with *papas a lo pobre* (potatoes with onions and peppers) and fried eggs. The restaurant also has simple rooms to rent, and can arrange self-catering accommodation in the village.

Calle Chorruelo 7, 29788 Frigiliana ☎ 952 53 41 16 🖐 Easter–Oct daily 2–4, 8.30–10.30; winter weekends only 🖐 L €28, D €38, Wine €10

GRANADA
CAFÉ FÚTBOL

www.cafefutbol.com

The Café Fútbol has a terrace under sycamore trees in a quiet, central square, ideal in summer for home-made ice-creams and *horchata*, a refreshing almond milk drink. Thick hot chocolate and fried doughnuts (*chocolate y churros*) are served all day in winter. No credit cards.

Plaza Mariana Pineda 6, 18009 Granada ☎ 958 22 66 62 🖐 Daily 6am–3am 🖐 Coffee €1.50, chocolate €1.80, *churros* €1.70, *horchata* €2.50, ice-creams €1.50–€5.50 🖐 23

CASA JULIO

A classic in Granada, this unmodernized bar is tucked away in an alley close to Plaza Nueva and Calle Elvira. The few tables outside get snapped up quickly. The *fritura de pescado* is an immense platter of Andaluz-style, deep fried fish, considered among the best in the city. The grilled prawns are excellent.

Calle Hermosa 5, 19010 Granada 🖐 Daily noon–1am 🖐 L €18, D €22, Wine €10

CUNINI

www.marisqueriacunini.com

The best Mediterranean fish and fresh shellfish from northern Spain are delivered daily to Cunini and cooked to perfection. There's a large terrace overlooking the pretty square for alfresco dining but it's probably best known for its wonderful tapas bar (always packed).

Plaza de la Pescadería 14, 18001 Granada ☎ 958 25 07 77 🖐 Daily 12–4, 8–12 🖐 L €20, D €45, Wine €13 🖐 5, 11

OCAÑA

An established, traditional restaurant that offers tasty local dishes at reasonable prices, the patio and cave entice visitors. It specializes in sherry—refreshing on a hot day. It has four different sections—bustling bar, rustic restaurant, Andalucían patio and private dining room.

Plaza del Realejo 1, 18009 Granada ☎ 958 25 64 70 🖐 Daily 7am–midnight 🖐 Three-course set lunch €12 per person, D €28, Wine €12 🖐 23

PILAR DEL TORO

www.hotelcasadelpilar.com

This 17th-century townhouse has been converted into a classy bar and restaurant. Drinks are served on a patio adorned with a fountain and plants. The restaurant serves regional dishes, and there is a list of fine wines. You can sit outdoors in summer. There is a hotel here, too.

Calle Hospital de Santa Ana 12, 18010 Granada ☎ 958 22 38 47 🖐 Bar: Mon–Sat 9am–2am. Restaurant: Mon–Sat 1.30–4, 8.30–12 🖐 L €25, D €40, Wine €12 🖐 31, 32

REGIONS ANDALUCÍA • EATING

LA HERRADURA

HOTEL LA TARTANA

www.hotellatartana.com

Dine out on the terrace, romantically candle-lit at night, at the Hotel La Tartana. This 18th-century mansion, converted into a simple but delightful little hotel with a beautiful interior patio and lush mature gardens, boasts one of the most unusual restaurants on the Costa Tropical. The American and Pan-Asian menu is perfect if you've had a surfeit of local dishes and want something different. There are steaks, stir-fries, delicious fresh fish and plenty more.

✉ Urbanización San Nicolás, 18697 La Herradura ☎ 958 64 05 35 🕓 Daily 2–4, 9–1 🖐 L €28, D €35, Wine €12

MÁLAGA

BAR LO GÜENO

www.logueno.es

With more than 75 tantalizing dishes on offer, such as sautéed oyster mushrooms (setas) with garlic, parsley and goat's cheese, you are spoiled for choice here. The L-shaped bar is always busy, but there are tables outside. There is also an excellent range of Rioja wines.

✉ Calle Marín García 9, 29005 Málaga ☎ 952 22 30 48 🕓 Daily 1–5, 8–1am 🖐 L €15, D €30, Wine €10

CASA PEDRO

www.casapedro.es

This long-established, family-run fish restaurant overlooks the sea, and the seafood served here is some of the freshest you will taste. The sardines and the paella are recommended.

✉ Calle Quitapeñas 121, El Palo, 29018 Málaga ☎ 952 29 00 13 🕓 Daily 1–4.15, 8.30–12. Closed Mon eve 🖐 L €18, D €28, Wine €12

MOJÁCAR

MESÓN CASA EGEA

The cuisine here uses all sorts of meats and the freshest of fish—bought in daily from the local fishermen. Traditional dishes (on offer at lunchtime only) include trigo cocido (meat stew), migas (fried breadcrumbs) and gurullo con conejo (a stew made with chick peas, rabbit, potatoes, sautéed onions and peppers, garlic and wheat pasta). Air-conditioning is a bonus, as is the terrace with sea views.

✉ Playa Mojácar, Paseo Mediterráneo 127, 04638 Mojácar ☎ 950 47 21 90 🕓 Tue–Sun 11–4.30, 7.30–11.30 (Jul–Aug daily). Closed Nov 🖐 L €28, D €38, Wine €10

PARQUE NATURAL CABO DE GATA

MESÓN EL TEMPRANILLO

With a perfect harbour-side location, El Tempranillo has a good reputation. The chef's signature dish is fresh paella, made to order with locally caught fish. There's a terrace and air-conditioned dining room.

✉ Puerto Deportivo de San José, 04118 San José (Nijar) ☎ 950 38 02 06 🕓 Tue–Sun 11–5, 7–11 (12–12 Jun–Sep) 🖐 L €27, D €38, Wine €10

RESTAURANTE LA PALMERA

www.hostalrestaurantelapalmera.com

An attractive family hotel and restaurant right by the beach. As you might expect, it specializes in fresh fish—grilled, baked and fried. The menu also includes spaghetti, paella, all kinds of Spanish rice dishes and fried calamari.

✉ Calle Aguada 7, 04149 Agua Amarga (Nijar) ☎ 950 13 82 08 🕓 Jul–Aug daily 9am–2am; Sep–Jun 9am–11.30pm 🖐 L €32, D €38, Wine €10

SEVILLE

LA ALBAHACA

www.andalunet.com/la-albahaca

Refined dining in an elegant and antiques-laden 18th-century mansion. A tree-shaded terrace extends on to one of the quietest and prettiest squares in Seville, and there are four dining rooms decked out with stunning azulejo tiles, where you can enjoy traditional Andalucían dishes. Previous famous patrons include the late Charlton Heston. Reservations are advisable during Easter, La Feria (April) and in summer.

✉ Plaza de Santa Cruz 12, 41001 Seville ☎ 954 22 07 14 🕓 Mon–Sat noon–4, 8–12 🖐 L €34, D €42, Wine €14 🚌 1, 21, 22, 23, C3, C4

CERVECERIA GIRALDA

Very popular with tourists, this atmospheric tapas bar is located in an old Arab bathhouse. The selection of tapas is enormous and the jamón ibérico (cured, acorn-fed ham) is in high demand. Excellent views of the Giralda add to the moment.

✉ Calle Mateos Gago 1, 41004 Seville ☎ 954 22 74 35 🖐 L €16, D €28, Wine €8 🕓 Daily 1pm–midnight

CORRAL DEL AGUA

www.andalunet.com/corral-agua
www.corraldelagua.es

The Corral del Agua is under the same ownership as La Albahaca (see left). Come here for alfresco dining under the citrus trees of the secluded garden (interior seating is also available). Specials include sea bass in dry sherry and leg of lamb with spinach and pine nuts.

✉ Callejón del Agua 6, 41004 Seville ☎ 954 22 07 14, 954 22 48 41 🕓 Mon–Sat 12–4, 8–12 🖐 L €34, D €44, Wine €14 🚌 1, 21, 22, 23, C3, C4

DOÑA ELVIRA

www.barriosantacruz.com

A patio terrace extends from a Sevillan house into a small tree-lined square. The tasty combination of Spanish and Mediterranean dishes includes gazpacho, Andalucían paella, fried seafood and oxtail. A fixed-price lunch menu is available for less than €16.

✉ Plaza de Doña Elvira 6, 41004 Seville ☎ 954 21 54 83 🕓 Daily 12–12. Closed 24 Dec and 1 Jan 🖐 L €18, D €40, Wine €15 🚌 1, 21, 22, 23, C3, C4

HABANITA BAR

www.habanita.es

This cute little restaurant is tucked into an alley near the bustling shopping district of Alfalfa. Their specialty is Cuban fare, but they also feature typical Spanish tapas and delicious salads. Try the exotic pork loin with dates, or the Cuban sampler platter. Vegetarian and vegan choices are on offer as well. Warm Caribbean decor, refreshing mojitos and Cuban music set the mood.

✉ Calle Golfo 3, Seville ☎ 606 71 64 56

⊙ Mon–Sat 1–4, 8–12. Closed Aug
✋ L €12, D €27, Wine €10

KIOSKO DE LAS FLORES
www.kioscodelasflores.com
Enjoy a riverside repast on the banks of the Río Guadalquivir, with a good view across to the Seville skyline. There is both indoor and alfresco seating. A specialist in seafood since 1930, the restaurant serves a good selection of fried and grilled fish dishes, including *boquerones* (anchovies) and a mammoth combination platter. It's frequented mainly by tourists.
✉ Betis s/n, 41010 Seville ☎ 954 27 45 76
⊙ Mon–Sat 11–4, 7–12 ✋ L €24, D €35, Wine €12 🚌 C3, 40

RESTAURANTE SAN MARCO
www.restaurantesanmarco.com
This is one of three San Marco restaurants in Seville, but is definitely the one with the most interesting layout. It is built within the stables of an elegant, 17th-century *sevillano* townhouse, and serves Italian cuisine with a touch of Moorish influence. Pizzas and pasta sit side by side with fresh fish and meat dishes. Save room for the wonderful desserts.
✉ Calle Cuna 6, 41004 Seville
☎ 954 21 24 40 ⊙ Tue–Sun 1.30–4, 8.30–midnight ✋ L €30, D €40, Wine €12
🚌 1, 21, 22, 23, C3, C4

EL RINCONCILLO
www.elrinconcillo.es
Tapas were reputedly born here, in one of the oldest and most atmospheric bars in Seville, dating back to 1670. Beamed ceilings, colourfully tiled walls and wooden barrels decorate the small room. Most people choose to stand, drinking wine tapped from barrels and ordering small platefuls of tapas through a hatch in the wood panelling. However, a small seating area at the back can accommodate four or five tables of diners. El Rinconcillo is extremely popular with the locals.
✉ Calle Gerona 40, 41003 Seville
☎ 954 22 31 83 ⊙ Tue–Sun 1pm–1.30am.

Closed 15 Jul–1 Aug ✋ Tapas around €3
🚌 10, 11, 12, 15, 20, 24, 27, 32

TREVÉLEZ
MESÓN LA FRAGUA
www.hotellafragua.com
This Alpujarras restaurant claims to be the highest such place in Spain's highest village. It's a small, family-run place with an extensive wine list, friendly service, attractive rustic decor and mountain views. The food is hearty local fare at good prices. The local delicacy is a dish of cured ham, spicy sausage, black pudding (blood sausage), fried egg and fried potatoes. It is essential to reserve a table, during weekends in particular.
✉ Calle San Antonio 4, Barrio Medio, Trevélez ☎ 958 85 85 73 ⊙ Daily 1–4.30, 8–11 ✋ L €15, D €28, Wine €8 🚌 Take the A4 from Granada south towards Motril, turning off for the Alpujarras along the A348 through Lanjarón. The Trevélez turn-off is the A4132 just before Órgiva

Below *Even the pizzas are created with a Moorish influence*

PRICES AND SYMBOLS

The prices are for a double room for one night including breakfast, unless otherwise stated. All the hotels listed accept credit cards unless otherwise stated. Note that rates can vary widely throughout the year..

For a key to the symbols, ▷ 2.

ALMERÍA
HOTEL SEVILLA

Rooms are simple and basic in the pleasant, modern environment at the Sevilla. The efficient staff dispense a friendly service. All the rooms have a private bathroom, TV and telephone and some have a terrace. Free WiFi is available. However, there is no cafeteria or restaurant on the premises. You will find breakfast in nearby cafés.

✉ Calle Granada 25, 04003 Almería ☎ 950 23 00 09 💶 €42–€65 excluding breakfast 🛏 37 ❖

CÁDIZ
ATLÁNTICO

www.parador.es

The Atlántico is a spacious, modern hotel with babysitting and spa facilities. All the rooms in this *parador* have views of the Atlantic, cable TV and a telephone.

✉ Avenida Duque de Nájera 9, 11002 Cádiz ☎ 956 22 69 05 💶 €132–€145 excluding breakfast (€16) 🛏 149 rooms (95 non-smoking) ❖ 🏊 Outdoor 🚼

CARMONA
PARADOR DE CARMONA

www.parador.es

This modern structure was built within the walls of a 14th-century fortress that once belonged to Pedro I of Castile (Pedro the Cruel). The rooms are spacious. The medieval refectory makes an impressive dining room.

✉ Calle Alcázar s/n, 41410 Carmona ☎ 954 14 10 10 💶 €165–€175 🛏 63 rooms ❖ 🏊 Outdoor

CÓRDOBA
ALBUCASIS

www.hotelalbucasis.com

Within this hotel's ivy-covered courtyard walls is an eclectic decor comprising old pistols and modern furniture, and there's a comfortable public lounge. The rooms all have private bathrooms, telephones, and some have televisions.

✉ Calle Buen Pastor 11, 14003 Córdoba ☎ 957 47 86 25 🕐 Closed 6 Jan–5 Feb 💶 €65–€95 excluding breakfast (€8) 🛏 10 ❖

GONZÁLEZ

www.hotel-gonzalez.com

This 16th-century townhouse used to be a Moorish palace. All rooms have private bathrooms; some have balconies overlooking the central courtyard. Breakfast, lunch and dinner are available and can all be

Above *Courtyard in the Parador de Carmona*

taken alfresco. Amenities include a cafeteria (open only for breakfast) and satellite TV.

✉ Calle Manríquez 3, 14003 Córdoba C957 47 98 19 💶 €65–€75 excluding breakfast (€5) 🛏 31 ❖

HOTEL MAIMÓNIDES

www.eurostarshotels.com

Situated right opposite the Mezquita, few places are better located for getting to know the history of this city. Its top feature is a pretty courtyard with a fountain (where breakfast and dinner are served), and it has pleasant bedrooms and a friendly atmosphere.

✉ Calle Torrijos 4, Córdoba ☎ 957 47 15 00 💶 From €60–€145 excluding breakfast (€15) 🛏 82 (52 non-smoking) ❖

PARADOR DE LA ARRUZAFA

www.parador.es

There are stunning panoramic views over Córdoba from this opulent four-star hotel. The guest rooms are large, bright and well decorated, and each comes equipped with a TV, minibar and telephone. Other facilities include a tennis court, bar, lift (elevator), gift shop, garden and playground.

✉ Avenida de la Arruzafa s/n, 14012 Córdoba ☎ 957 27 59 00 💶 €150–€165 excluding breakfast (€16) 🛏 94 ❖ 🏊 Outdoor 🚌 13 every half-hour from Córdoba centre bus terminal ⛌ 5km (3 miles) north of Córdoba. From Avenida del Brillante, drive 2km (1 mile) towards Avenida de la Arruzafa. From the junction, continue down the avenue for 500m (550 yards)

GRANADA
AMÉRICA
www.hotelamericagranada.com
Stay in the grounds of the Alhambra palace complex. All bedrooms have private bathrooms, TV and telephone. Parking is at a discounted rate in the nearby public parking area. Reserve in advance.
✉ Calle Real de la Alahambra 53, 18009 Granada ☎ 958 22 74 71 🕐 Closed 1 Dec–28 Feb ✋ €120–€145 excluding continental breakfast (€10) 🛏 16, plus 1 suite 🚭 🚌 30, 32

CASA DE FEDERICO
www.casadefederico.com
This enchanting hotel is located in a tastefully restored historic townhouse, which retains the original wooden beams and features exposed brick walls. The rooms are elegantly decorated with a perfect fusion of old and new: Crisp, modern furnishings and contemporary amenities are offset with charming original details. Most rooms boast small balconies. It's handily located in the centre, close to the cathedral.
✉ Calle Horno Marina 13, 18001 Granada ☎ 958 20 85 34 ✋ €120–€145 🛏 14 🚭

CASA MORISCA
www.hotelcasamorisca.com
Some of the rooms in this Moorish mansion have magnificent views of the Alhambra. Buffet breakfast is available, in the vaulted cellar, and drinks are served on the patio.
✉ Cuesta de la Victoria 9, 18010 Granada ☎ 958 22 11 00 ✋ €125–€225 excluding buffet breakfast (€12) 🛏 12, plus 1 suite and 1 tower room with special views 🚭 🚌 31, 32

PALACIO DE SANTA INÉS
www.palaciosantaines.com
A sophisticated hotel is housed in two 16th-century palaces. The special Alhambra suite offers superb views of the Alhambra. All rooms have

cable TV. Breakfast is the only meal served in the hotel.
✉ Cuesta de Santa Inés 9, 18010 Granada ☎ 958 22 23 62 ✋ €120–€180 excluding buffet breakfast (€12) 🛏 33 🚭 🚌 31, 32

MÁLAGA
LARIOS
www.room-malehotels.com
This art-deco-style hotel in the city's most fashionable shopping street has a rooftop terrace with bar. All rooms have satellite TV, minibar and telephone as well as chic, fashionable furnishings.
✉ Calle Marqués de Larios 2, 29005 Málaga ☎ 952 22 22 00 ✋ €110–€235 excluding breakfast (€15) 🛏 41, 6 junior suites (3 non-smoking) 🚭

MOJÁCAR
PARADOR DE MOJÁCAR
www.parador.es
In this luxurious, roomy, modern four-star hotel, right on the beach, the restaurant offers fresh fish every day. The hotel facilities include a conference room, a bar, satellite TV, tennis and watersports.
✉ Playa de Mojácar, 04638 Mojácar ☎ 950 47 82 50 ✋ €135–€142 excluding breakfast (€15) 🛏 98 🚭 🚰 Outdoor

PARQUE NATURAL CABO DE GATA
MIKASA
www.mikasasuites.com
Mikasa combines modern style with traditional local elements in an intriguing way and has appeared in interior design magazines. Reception is closed between 3 and 6 in the afternoon to allow guests an undisturbed siesta. Facilities include a heated swimming pool, tennis court, spa and beauty treatments.
✉ Carretera de Carboneras s/n, 04149 Agua Amarga ☎ 950 13 80 73 🕐 Closed Jan–15 Mar ✋ €122–€285 🛏 15 rooms, 5 suites 🚭 🚰 Outdoor 📺

SEVILLE
ALFONSO XIII
www.westin.com
This palatial Mudéjar-style monument was built in 1928 as Europe's most luxurious hotel. Moorish opulence is

paired with Andalucían flamboyance, and vaulted ceilings and marble columns surround a large central courtyard. Facilities include two restaurants (the one in the gardens is Japanese), a bar, room service and business services. All rooms have a minibar, satellite TV, internet and telephone.
✉ Calle San Fernando 2, 41004 Seville ☎ 954 91 70 00 ✋ Standard: low €360, high €750; Royal Suite €1,850 excluding breakfast (€25) 🛏 147 (85 non-smoking) 🚭 🚰 Outdoor (Jun–Oct) 🚌 21, 23 🚉 Santa Justa

AMADEUS
www.hotelamadeussevilla.com
A family-run hotel that caters particularly for a musical clientele— some of the rooms are soundproofed and some have pianos. The hotel is close to the Alcázar and La Giralda. Features include internet access and a reading room.
✉ Calle Farnesio 6, 41004 Seville ☎ 954 50 14 43 ✋ €98–€120 excluding breakfast (€8) 🛏 14 🚭 🚌 C3, C4 🚉 Santa Justa

LA CASA DEL REY DE BAEZA
www.hospes.es
This hotel's unique and elegant setting is a well-executed fusion of past and present. The rooms have state-of-the-art features such as CD players and flat screen TVs. There is a rooftop plunge pool, and bicycle rental is available.
✉ Plaza Jesús de la Rendicion 2, 41003 Seville ☎ 954 56 14 96 ✋ €175–€325 excluding breakfast (€18) 🛏 41 (32 non-smoking) 🚭 🚰 Outdoor

LA HOSTERÍA DEL LAUREL
www.hosteriadellaurel.com
This former coach house is in the heart of the Barrio de Santa Cruz. The rooms are bright, well equipped and spotlessly clean, but those overlooking the plaza can be noisy in the high season. All rooms have direct-dial telephone, TV and a private bathroom.
✉ Plaza de los Venerables 5, 41004 Seville ☎ 954 22 02 95 ✋ €85–€145 🛏 20 🚭 🚌 C3, C4 🚉 Santa Justa

BALEARIC ISLANDS

The quartet of Balearic Islands — Mallorca, Menorca, Ibiza and Formentera — may be tiny, but they all have big personalities. Each has a distinct character, appealing to a different kind of visitor.

Mallorca, as the largest of the islands, is probably the most diverse, both geographically and in terms of its attractions. The notoriously built-up resorts around the Bay of Palma may hog the headlines, but the island also boasts a clutch of beautiful rural villages, some of the most luxurious hotels in Spain, and a string of superb beaches and coves which remain surprisingly empty even in high season. The capital, Palma de Mallorca, is a vibrant, enchanting little city on the water's edge, with a buzzy nightlife, a lively tapas culture and some excellent restaurants.

Menorca is quieter than its big sister, with a few relatively low-key resorts along the coast, and a green, hilly hinterland scattered with mellow villages and small towns. The northern coastline is pocked with hard-to-reach but beautiful little coves and the two largest cities, Maó and Ciutadella, are tranquil and elegant.

Ibiza manages to attract everyone from package tourists to celebrities, and offers a mixed bag of rural charm, particularly in the north, and a famously wild nightlife. There are some wonderful, bohemian and chic accommodation options and a few, relatively unspoiled, if hard-to-access, beaches have survived the great influx of mass tourism. Ibiza town has a pretty old quarter, overlooked by a citadel, and, of the larger tourist resorts, Santa Eulària has best preserved its original charm.

Tiny Formentera, with just one road, a couple of lighthouses, a few clusters of white-painted houses, and one of the most beautiful (and emptiest) beaches in the Mediterranean, is the perfect retreat. It gets overcrowded in August, but in June and September it is utterly paradisical.

MALLORCA

ALCÚDIA

www.alcudiamallorca.com

Behind Mallorca's longest beach is this well-preserved medieval city, which has some extensive Roman remains. The heart of Alcúdia is found inside its walled ramparts, through the Portal del Moll, the symbolic entrance to the city. Here, Renaissance palaces shelter in narrow, shady streets. Just outside the walls are the remains of the Roman city of Pollentia (May–Sep Tue–Sun 9.30–8.30; Oct–Apr Tue–Fri 10–4, Sat 10–2), including a forum and a theatre where concerts are still held in summer.

You can learn more about the Roman ruins at the Museu Monogràfic de Pollentia (May–Sep Tue–Sun 11–2, 4–7; Oct–Apr Tue–Sun 10–2), which stands across the road. The old town is not to be confused with the modern resort of Port d'Alcúdia, a short distance away. The latter is a busy commercial and ferry town, with a fishing port, marina and sprawling tourist resort. The beach itself stretches for 10km (6 miles) around the Badia d'Alcúdia.

🚍 475 P6 🛈 Carretera d'Artà 68, 07410 Port d'Alcúdia ☎ 971 89 26 15 🕔 Closed Sun and Nov–Mar 🛈 Carrer Major 17, 07400 Alcúdia (old town) ☎ 971 89 71 00 🚍 From Palma, Pollença and Port de Pollença

ARTÀ

www.arta-web.com

Artà is one of Mallorca's most historic towns, guarded by a hilltop fortress and a sanctuary church, and is well stocked with shops and cafés. The best place to start a visit is Carrer Ciutat, the vehicle-free main street. A 10-minute climb past the imposing parish church leads to an avenue of cypress trees and the sanctuary of Sant Salvador (Apr–Oct daily 8.30–8.30; Nov–Mar daily 8.30–6). This fortress-church was built on the site of an Arab castle and has battlements, towers, medieval walls, a chapel and view.

Just outside Artà is Ses Païsses, a well-preserved settlement dating from the Talaiotic era (c1200BC), with a monumental stone doorway and cyclopean walls. A clearly marked circuit leads around the site (Apr–Oct Mon–Sat 10–1, 2.30–6.30; Nov–Mar Mon–Sat 9–1, 2–5).

🚍 475 Q6 🛈 Carrer Costa i Llobera 6, 07570 Artà ☎ 971 82 92 19 🚍 From Palma

CAP DE FORMENTOR

The sinuous drive from Port de Pollença across this wild and rugged headland has some of the most dramatic scenery in Mallorca, with tall cliffs dropping sheer into the sea beside idyllic, isolated beach coves. The views are spectacular, but it is not a journey for nervous drivers and you must keep your eyes on the road. The first stop is at Mirador des Colomer, where a viewpoint on the left looks out over a rocky islet.

A road opposite the viewpoint climbs to Talaia d'Albercutx, a watchtower with 360-degree views over the bays of Pollença and Alcúdia. The main road continues to Formentor beach, the site of Mallorca's original luxury hotel, Hotel Formentor, which opened in 1926. The white-sand beach here is one of the most attractive on the island, and makes a great place to unwind before you travel through the pine woods to the lighthouse at the end of the cape – from where the island of Menorca is visible on a clear day.

🚍 475 P6 🛈 Passeig Saralegui s/n, 07470 Port de Pollença ☎ 971 86 54 67 🕔 Closed Sun 🚍 From Palma and Port de Pollença to Formentor beach in summer

COVES D'ARTÀ

If you have time to visit only one set of caves in Mallorca, make this the one. The fascinating network of underground caverns at Coves d'Artà, on the island's east coast just 7km (4 miles) southeast of Artà itself, is thought to have inspired the 1864 novel *Journey to the Centre of the Earth* by Jules Verne (1828–1905). The stalactites, stalagmites and huge underground chambers of these limestone caves are certainly the most impressive in Mallorca.

The first serious study of the caves was carried out in 1876 by French geologist Édouard Martel, although the locals had known about them for centuries. Over the years the caves had provided a refuge for smugglers, hermits and Arabs fleeing the Catalán invasion.

The guided tour comes with sound and light effects, and the various chambers are given names – such as Hell, Purgatory and Paradise – to excite the imagination. One particular chamber is as large as the nave of Palma's cathedral (▷ 400).

Do note that the tour is not suitable for visitors with disabilities, young children or those who have trouble with stairs.

🚍 475 Q6 ✉ Carretera Coves d'Artà, 07589 Canyamel ☎ 971 84 12 93 🕔 Jul–Sep daily 10–7, Oct–Jun 10–5 🎫 Adult €10, child (7–12) €5.50, under 7 free 🚍 From Artà and Cala Ratjada in summer

Opposite *The golden-brick Sant Jaume church in Alcúdia*

Below *A viewpoint at Cap de Formentor*

COVES DEL DRAC

The tour of the 'dragon caves' starts with a descent of around 100 steps into the dark and humid grotto, and continues along 1km (0.6 miles) of slippery paths, with stalactites, stalagmites and rocky pools. The climax of the tour is a floating concert on Lake Martel, Europe's largest underground lake, followed by a boat trip to the exit. As with the Coves d'Artà (▷ 397), the caves are not suitable for visitors with disabilities, young children or those who have trouble with stairs.

➕ 475 Q6 ✉ Carretera Cuevas s/n, 07680 Portocristo ☎ 971 82 07 53 ◷ Daily (tour times below) ♿ Adult €11, under 7 free ⛴ Tours on the hour Apr–Oct 10–12, 2–5; Nov–Mar tours at 10.45, 12, 2 and 3.30 🚌 From Palma and from east coast resorts in summer

DEIÀ

This village of ochre-stone houses is surrounded by olive and orange groves and lies in the shadow of the Teix mountain 1,064m (3,491ft) high. Deià has long had a reputation for attracting writers and artists, but it was the British poet and author Robert Graves (1895–1985) who put it on the map. He lived here from 1946 until his death, and summed up its appeal as 'sun, sea, mountains, spring water, shady trees, no politics'. He is buried beneath a simple stone slab in the churchyard of Sant Joan Baptista at the top of the village. His home, Ca n'Alluny (Tue–Sat 10–4.20, Sun 10–2.20; €6) is now a museum, filled with manuscripts and personal mementoes. In recent years Deià has become something of a magnet for film stars and celebrities, who stay at La Residencia hotel (▷ 418).

A 20-minute walk through a wooded ravine leads down to the shingle beach at Cala de Deià, set in a pretty cove. Although attractive, this is definitely not the real Mallorca. Deià has several high-class restaurants, galleries and boutiques.

➕ 475 D6 ℹ Avenida de Palma 6, 07170 Valldemossa ☎ 971 61 20 19 🚌 From Palma, Sòller and Valldemossa

MONESTIR DE LLUC

www.lluc.net

Lluc monastery is an ancient site of pilgrimage and the spiritual heart of Mallorca, set in a fertile valley in the Serra de Tramuntana (▷ 399). The monastery owes its existence to the legend of Lluch, a 13th-century shepherd boy who is said to have discovered a statue of the Virgin Mary hidden in a cleft in the rock. A chapel was built to house the statue, a dark-skinned Mary with the baby Jesus in her arms, and La Moreneta (meaning 'the little dark one') still attracts pilgrims today.

One of the best times to visit is when the boys' choir, Es Blauets, sings (daily 11.15 and 7.30), or come late in the day to avoid the crowds. You can rent a room for the night in one of the former monks' cells. Lluc is also a popular ecological centre, with a botanical garden and mountain walks.

The Way of the Rosary, behind the monastery, features sculptures by Antoni Gaudí (1852–1926); the Museu de Lluc has displays on sacred art and folklore.

➕ 475 P6 ✉ Monestir de Lluc, 07315 Escorca ☎ 971 87 15 25 ◷ Monastery: daily 8.30–8.30. Museum: daily 10–1.30, 2.30–5.15 ♿ Monastery: free. Museum: €4 🚌 One or two buses per day from Palma

PALMA DE MALLORA

▷ 400.

PARC NATURAL DE S'ALBUFERA

www.mallorcaweb.net/salbufera

This protected wetland reserve in the Bahía de Alcúdia is an important birding and ecological site. Cars are not allowed inside the reserve, so park opposite the Hotel Parc Natural and walk or bicycle the 1km (0.6 miles) from the Pont dels Anglesos bridge. All visitors must register at the reception area, where maps and a list of recent sightings can be picked up. There are footpaths, a small museum and birding hides. At the hides you can look for osprey, peregrine and purple gallinule; 200-plus species pass through here during migrations.

➕ 475 P6 ✉ Parc Natural de S'Albufera, 07458 Can Picafort ☎ 971 89 22 50 ◷ Apr–Sep daily 9–6; Oct–Mar daily 9–5 🚌 From Alcúdia and Pollença in summer

POLLENÇA

Pollença is one of the most attractive towns in Mallorca. It is neatly tucked away between two hills, one topped by the Santuari del Puig de Maria monastery (open at all times), the other by the Calvari church (opening times vary), which is reached from the middle of town up a long flight of steps lined with cypress trees.

Many foreigners have homes here and the town is the venue for an international music festival each summer. Pollença comes alive each Sunday morning when the square in front of the church is the setting for a busy and popular market.

➕ 475 P6 ℹ️ Carrer Sant Domingo 17, 07460 Pollença ☎ 971 53 50 77 🕐 Closed Sat and Sun 🚌 From Palma and Port de Pollença

PORT DE POLLENÇA

Some 6km (4 miles) north of Pollença is the picture-perfect resort of Port de Pollença, backed by craggy grey mountains and set around a horseshoe bay.

The main focus is the Passeig Voramar (Pine Walk), a waterfront promenade that leads past old-fashioned villas and hotels where pine trees lean into the sea. South of here, beyond the bay, is the heart of the modern resort, with a huge beach and safe, shallow water for swimming.

➕ 475 P6 ℹ️ Passeig de Sarelegui, 07470 Port de Pollença ☎ 971 86 54 67 🕐 Closed Sun 🚌 From Palma, Pollença and Alcúdia

SERRA DE TRAMUNTANA

The Tramuntana mountain range has walking routes looking over the north coast of Mallorca, where the cliffs drop down into the sea. The 'mountains of the north wind' run for 88km (55 miles) from Andratx to Pollença, with the rocky outcrops of Illa Sa Dragonera and Cap de Formentor marking either end. The best way to appreciate the

variety of scenery is to walk, but you can drive across the sierra in a day. The most dramatic stretch is between Sóller and Lluc (▷ below and 398 respectively): The road passes through tunnels and gorges, and snakes around Mallorca's highest mountain, Puig Major (1,448m/4,751ft). An even more hair-raising drive runs down to the north coast at Sa Calobra. The view from the Mirador de Ses Animes at Banyalbufar is unforgettable.

➕ 475 P6 ℹ️ Ca S'Amitger, Monestir de Lluc ☎ 971 51 70 70 🚌 From Palma to Sóller, Deià and Valldemossa; summer service from Port de Pollença to Port de Sóller via Lluc

SÓLLER

www.sollernet.com

Sóller is a handsome and prosperous town famous for its oranges, with a cosmopolitan atmosphere and excellent shops, cafés and bars. Although a new tunnel through the mountains has brought Sóller within easy driving distance of Palma, most people still arrive on the vintage electric train that rattles over the mountains before making its zigzag descent. A short walk from the rail station leads to the shady main square, as well as the Iglesia de Sant Bartomeu (Mon–Thu 10.30–1, 2.45–4.15, Fri–Sat 10.30–1), designed by the Catalán *modernista* architect Joan Rubió i Bellver (1871–1952). The local ice-cream from Sa Fàbrica de Gelats (Plaça des Mercat, summer daily 10–9) is delicious.

Trams—brought here from San Francisco—lead down to Port de

Sóller, a 3km (2-mile) ride through gardens and orange orchards that ends at a pretty, fish-shaped bay.

Another popular excursion is the easy walk to the dramatically situated village of Fornalutx.

➕ 475 P6 ℹ️ Plaça d'Espanya s/n, 07100 Sóller (in an old rail carriage (car) outside the station) ☎ 971 63 80 08 🕐 Mon–Fri 9.30–2, 3–5, Sat–Sun 10–1 🚆 Sóller 🚌 From Palma, Deià and Valldemossa

VALLDEMOSSA

Mallorca's highest town is set in a mossy vale in the Serra de Tramuntana (see left). Composer Frédéric Chopin (1810–49) and his lover, the French novelist George Sand (1804–76), spent a cold, damp winter together in Valldemossa in 1838–39. At the heart of town is the Real Cartuja (Apr–Sep Mon–Sat 9.30–4.30; Oct–Mar Tue–Sat 9.30–6, Sun 10–1), the former Carthusian monastery where Sand and Chopin rented a cell. It was not a happy experience and their relationship never really recovered; the story is told in Sand's book *Winter in Majorca* (1841). Apart from the couple's cell, you can also visit the old pharmacy, the library and the modern art museum with works by Picasso and Miró. The entrance to the monastery gives access to the next-door palace, where Chopin piano recitals are performed hourly. A newer attraction is Costa Nord (audiovisual exhibit daily 10–5, plus performances), a cultural centre.

➕ 475 P6 ℹ️ Avenida de Palma 7, 07170 Valldemossa ☎ 971 61 20 19 🚌 From Palma, Deià and Sóller

Opposite left *Lake Martel, Coves del Drac*
Opposite right *Lluc-Alcari, near Deià*
Right *The view from the Mirador des Colomar in the Sierra Tramuntana*

INFORMATION
✚ 475 P6 ℹ Plaça de la Reina 2, 07012
Palma de Mallorca ☎ 971 71 22 16
⏱ Mon–Fri 9–8, Sat 9–2 ❓ There are
also visitor offices at Carrer Sant Domingo
11 and beside the rail station in Parc de
les Estacions

INTRODUCTION

Millions of people pass through Palma each year in their rush for the beaches, yet few bother to stop off in the city. For those who take the time to linger, Palma is something of a surprise. This confident city has great restaurants, buzzing cafés and a thriving modern arts scene. It is the only place in the Balearics with a big city feel, yet it has hidden corners that have changed little in centuries, with Renaissance mansions and patios behind wooden doors.

The city was founded by the Romans in 123BC, who named it Palmaria after the palm trees they found growing here. During the period of Arab rule in Mallorca (AD902–1229), it was known as Medina Mayurqa and was one of the most advanced cities in Europe, with streetlights, covered sewers and heated baths. After the Catalán conquest of 1229 a cathedral was built on the site of the main mosque and the Arab governor's fortress became a royal palace.

WHAT TO SEE

LA SEU

Palma sits in the middle of a broad, sheltered bay. A long promenade leads along the waterfront, passing the fishing port, yacht club, restaurants and bars. Viewed from the water, the city is dwarfed by its cathedral, La Seu, a triumph of Gothic architecture whose flying buttresses and sandstone walls seems to rise out of the old city walls. Look for the controversial new chapel of Sant Pere by artist Miquel Barceló, which opened in 2007. The walls are thickly covered in an abstract ceramic mural representing the miracle of the loaves and the fishes. Some of the best views of La Seu are from the Parc de la Mar, whose artificial lake was designed to catch the cathedral's reflection.
⏱ Apr–Oct Mon–Fri 10–6, Sat 10–2; Nov–Mar Mon–Fri 10–3.15, Sat 10–2

Above *The fortified circular walls of Castell de Bellver*

Opposite *The light and airy nave of the 13th-century cathedral*

PALAU DE L'ALMUDAINA

To one side of La Seu is the Palau del l'Almudaina, former residence of the Mallorcan kings. It is still used by the Spanish royal family when they come to Palma (public visits are suspended if they are in residence). Only part of the palace is open to the public, but the real draw is the sea-facing terrace, the Mirador del Mar, which offers splendid sea views.

🕐 Apr–Sep Mon–Fri 10–5.45, Sat 10–1; Oct–Mar Mon–Fri 10–1, 4–5.45, Sat 10–2

AROUND THE OLD CITY

Behind La Seu is a warren of narrow streets leading to the oldest part of town. Here you will find the Museu de Mallorca (Tue–Sat 10–7, Sun 10–2), with archaeological displays, and the 10th-century Baños Àrabes (Arab Baths: Apr–Nov daily 9.30–7.30; Dec–Mar daily 9.30–6).

MORE TO SEE

ES BALUARD

Es Baluard, an excellent contemporary art museum is located in a stunning modern building which incorporates a Renaissance bastion. The fabulous rooftop café offers wonderful views (open to all).

🕐 Mid-Jun to Sep daily 10–10; Oct to mid-Jun 10–8 ✋ €6

CASTELL DE BELLVER

Castell de Bellver is a 14th-century fortress on the outskirts of Palma, and is the only circular castle in Spain. Its name means 'lovely view', and there are indeed superb panoramas over the Bahía de Palma from its roof. The nearby Fundació Pilar i Joan Miró contains the studio of celebrated artist Joan Miró and an extensive collection of his works.

🕐 Apr–Sep Mon–Sat 8am–8.15pm, Sun 10–5; Oct–Mar Mon–Sat 8–7.15, Sun 10–5

TIPS

» As you wander around the old town, peer into the courtyards of the Gothic and Renaissance palaces, with their stone staircases, loggias and arcades. Some of the best examples are found along Carrer Morey, particularly Can Oleza (No. 9).

» At Fundació La Caixa (Tue–Sat 10–9, Sun and festivals 10–2), around Plaça Major, shops sell pottery, carved olive wood, Mallorcan sausages, cheese and wine.

MENORCA

CALA MACARELLA

www.emenorca.org

This idyllic cove to the west of Cala Santa Galdana has a delightful setting where the pine trees reach almost to the sea. You can walk here for 40 minutes over the headland from Cala de Santa Galdana, then following a steep, rocky descent to the beach. The inaccessibility of coves like Cala Macarella has protected them from development, and they remain special places for those prepared to put in the effort to get there. The sand shelves gently at Cala Macarella and the water is clear. In summer there is a popular beach bar here.

A path leads over the cliff to the even more isolated cove of Cala Macarelleta. As with other remote beaches on Menorca's southwestern coast, Cala Macarella can also be reached via a country lane from Ciutadella, although you have to walk the last section.

Another beautiful beach in this area is Cala En Turqueta, which also backs on to pine woods.

➕ 475 Q6 ℹ️ Plaça de Catedral 5, 07760 Ciutadella ☎ 971 38 26 93

CALA PREGONDA

www.emenorca.org

Wherever you are in Menorca, you are never far from an unspoiled cove, and Cala Pregonda is no exception. The beach here is characterized by offshore sandstone stacks and is one of the most peaceful spots on the north coast.

The only way to get to Cala Pregonda is to walk from the west end of Binimel.là beach, itself an attractive and remote spot with reddish dunes and a freshwater lake. Climb the steps over a wall, follow the path across salt flats and around a pebble cove, clamber over a small headland and drop down to Cala Pregonda. The beach is backed by pine and tamarisk trees, and the water is crystal clear. There are no facilities, so take a picnic and plenty of water. But don't expect to be alone unless you come here in winter.

Just offshore is Es Prego, a sandstone outcrop that has been carved by the wind and sea into the shape of a hooded monk. Also off Cala Pregonda is a rocky island with its own tiny beach; in summer there are usually yachts moored nearby.

➕ 475 Q6 ℹ️ Plaça de Catedral 5, 07760 Ciutadella ☎ 971 38 26 93

ES CASTELL

www.emenorca.org

This former garrison town on the edge of Maó bay is a relic of the 18th-century British occupation of Menorca. Originally named Georgetown after King George III, Es Castell retains the feel of a British colonial town. The old parade ground, Plaça de S'Esplanada, is lined with solid Georgian buildings that have features typical of the style, including sash windows and fanlights. The plum-red town hall has a very British clocktower, while opposite it is the Museu Militar (Mon, Thu and 1st Sun of each month 11–1), housed in the former army barracks. The port at Cales Fonts is perfectly placed to catch the lunchtime sun and there is a good choice of restaurants on the waterfront. Nearby, the old British fortress of Fort Marlborough has been turned into an entertaining museum, with special effects such as explosions set off as you walk through the underground tunnels (May–Oct Tue–Sat 10–1, 3–7, Sun 10–1; Nov–Apr Tue–Sun 10–1; festival days 10–1).

➕ 475 R6 ℹ️ Sa Rovellada de Dalt 24, 07703 Maó ☎ 971 36 37 90 ⊗ Closed Sun 🚌 From Maó

CIUTADELLA DE MENORCA

▷ 403.

FERRERIES

Ferreries is one of three towns strung along the main road between Maó and Ciutadella, and has an old quarter of whitewashed houses huddled together in narrow streets. The other two towns, Es Mercadal and Es Migjorn Gran, reward a gentle stroll. The best time to visit Ferreries is on a Saturday morning, when the main square, Plaça d'Espanya, is taken over by a farmers' market with craft stalls and folk-dancing displays. Behind the square are the narrow streets of the old town. Nearby is the Museu de la Natura, an ecological museum (Jan–24 Oct Tue–Sat 10–1, 6–9, Sun 10–1; 25 Oct–19 Dec Wed–Fri 5.30–8.30, Sat 10–1, 5–8; closed on festival days).

Other places of interest close to Ferreries are the manor house of Binisues, with exhibits on traditional rural Menorcan life and a restaurant specializing in Menorcan cuisine (Mon–Sat 11–6), and the magnificent beach at Cala de Santa Galdana, lying at the entrance to the Algendar gorge, framed by limestone cliffs.

➕ 475 Q6 ℹ️ Plaça de Catedral 5, 07760 Ciutadella ☎ 971 38 26 93 🚌 From Maó and Ciutadella

CIUTADELLA DE MENORCA

Ciutadella may not have the status of a capital, but it is by far the most pleasing town on Menorca, with Gothic churches, Renaissance palaces and narrow whitewashed lanes. Its streets are filled with a fine mix of lively cafés, stylish art galleries, jewellery shops and clothing stores.

The Romans established the first town here in 123BC and the Arabs made it the capital of Menorca in AD902, naming the city Medina Minurqa in contrast to Medina Mayurqa (Palma). After the Catalán conquest of Menorca in 1287, Ciutadella became the power base of the Church and nobility, and it retained this role even after the British moved the capital to Maó in 1722. The result is that Ciutadella remains a pure Catalán town, similar in feel to the old quarter of Palma (▷ 401), its handsome stone palaces sporting coats of arms that reflect the power of Menorca's noble families.

THE SIGHTS

The main focus of Ciutadella is Plaça des Born, the old parade ground overlooking the bay. On one side of the square is the crenellated town hall, and on the other are two aristocratic palaces, one of which (Palau Salort) can be visited (Apr–Oct Mon–Sat 10–2). A monument at the heart of the square commemorates those citizens of Ciutadella who were killed during a Turkish raid in 1558. Just off the square are the streets of the old town, clustered around the austere Gothic Catedral de Santa María (closed for restoration). The whitewashed arches of the alley known as Ses Voltes—a reminder of Ciutadella's Moorish past—are home to smart cafés and shops. A market is held in Plaça de la Llibertat (Mon–Sat 9–1).

For a contrast, head to the Passeig Marítim, a waterfront promenade that stretches from the port to the small beach at Cala des Degollador. This makes a pleasant 30-minute walk, especially at dusk, when Mallorca is usually visible on the horizon.

Naveta des Tudons, a Bronze Age burial chamber in the shape of an upturned boat, is 4km (2.5 miles) from Ciutadella on the road to Maó. This is the best preserved of Menorca's various *navetas*.

INFORMATION

www.emenorca.org
www.ciutadella.org
✚ 475 Q6 🛈 Plaça de la Catedral 5
☎ 971 38 26 93 🕐 May–Oct Mon–Sat 9–8.30; Nov–Apr Mon–Fri 9–1, 5–7, Sat 9–1 🚌 From Maó and other main towns ⛴ Ferries from Cala Ratjada and Port d'Alcúdia, Mallorca

TIPS

» For the best sunset views, climb to the rooftop of Castell de Sant Nicolau, halfway around the Passeig Marítim. Mallorca can usually be seen silhouetted on the horizon, often appearing as two separate islands—these are the island's two mountain ranges separated by a flat plain.
» If you fancy a quick visit to Ciutadella from Mallorca, you can get there via the daily ferry services from Cala Ratjada and Port d'Alcúdia.

Opposite *The waterfront of Cales Fonts in Es Castell is lined with cafés and restaurants*
Below *Old buildings in a narrow alleyway in Ciutadella de Menorca*

REGIONS | BALEARIC ISLANDS • SIGHTS

FORNELLS

This classically pretty fishing village has a collection of low, whitewashed cottages clustered around a bay and shady palm trees lining its promenade, and is best known for its restaurants, which serve the local dish, *caldereta de llagosta* (lobster stew). The most celebrated restaurant is Es Plà, popular with King Juan Carlos.

A number of fortifications can still be seen in the area. These were built on the west side of the Bahía de Fornells to protect Menorca's north coast from pirate ships.

One of the towers, Torre de Fornells, has been renovated as a museum and you can climb to the top of the watchtower for superb views out to sea (Tue–Sat 11–2, 5–8; closed on Sun and festival days).
➕ 475 Q6 🛈 Plaça de Catedral 5, 07760 Ciutadella 🕾 971 38 26 93 🚌 Occasional buses from Maó and Es Mercadal

MAÓ (MAHÓN)

www.emenorca.org

Menorca's capital stands on a cliff face overlooking one of the world's great natural harbours. There has been a city here since Roman times (*c*123BC), but the biggest influence on Maó was the period of British rule during the 18th century. It was the British who moved the capital across the island from Ciutadella and who left behind the wealth of Georgian architecture that can still be seen today.

The best place to start a visit is on Plaça de S'Esplanada, a large, open square with palm trees and fountains. From here, narrow streets lead down towards the port and a covered market in the cloisters of an old Carmelite convent (Mon–Sat 9–9). From the foot of the portside steps, you can take a boat trip around Maó bay in summer, or follow the restaurant-lined waterfront promenade. The magnificent port has protected Maó throughout its history.

High above the bay, in the old part of town, 18th-century houses line Carrer Isabel II. The street ends at the Museu de Menorca, in the cloisters of a former monastery, with archaeological finds from the Talaiotic era (*c*1200BC), along with Roman mosaics found on an island in Maó bay and a complete skeleton of the extinct Balearic goat (Apr–Oct Tue–Sat 10–2, 6–9, Sun 10–2; Nov–Mar Tue–Sat 9.30–2, Sun 10–2; closed Mon and festivals).
➕ 475 R6 🛈 Sa Rovellada de Dalt 24, 07703 Maó 🕾 971 36 37 90 🕐 Closed Sun 🚌 From Ciutadella and other main towns

SON BOU

In contrast to the creeks and coves that make up most of Menorca's southern coastline, Son Bou has the longest beach on the island—3km (2 miles) of unbroken sand—making it perfect for summer bathing.

At the eastern end of the beach, almost hidden in the sand, are the ruins of a fifth-century Christian basilica. You can climb the cliffs above the basilica to some prehistoric burial caves, with great views back down over the beach.

Just inland from Son Bou is the well-preserved prehistoric village of Torre d'en Galmés (Tue–Sat 10–2, 5–8, Sun 10–2; closed Mon and festivals), with three *talaiots* (watchtowers).
➕ 475 Q6 🛈 Sa Rovellada de Dalt 24, 07703 Maó 🕾 971 36 37 90 🚌 From Maó in summer

EL TORO

From the highest point on Menorca there are spectacular views across the island. This is also an important place of pilgrimage. El Toro is set right in the middle of Menorca and the views from here extend to the sea in all directions.

The summit is crowned by radar masts, a huge statue of Christ and a peaceful courtyard leading to a simple white-domed church 'Santuario de la Virgen de Monte Toro' (daily 8–sunset). The altarpiece has a venerated statue of La Verge del Toro, a black Madonna cradling Jesus in her arms and with a bull *(toro)* at her feet—a reference to the legend that a bull originally discovered the Virgin statue in the rocks on the hillside.
➕ 475 Q6 🛈 Sa Rovellada de Dalt 24, 07703 Maó 🕾 971 36 37 90

Below left *Fishing boats at rest in the port at Fornells, Menorca*
Below *Remains of a fifth-century basilica, Platje des Son Bou, Menorca*

EIVISSA (IBIZA)

Above *Punta de Sa Torre watchtower at Portinatx on the island of Ibiza*

BENIRRÀS

The enchanting beach cove of Benirràs, on the unspoiled north coast of Ibiza has a beautiful sandy beach set between forested cliffs, with a small rocky island offshore, and is reached along a minor road between Sant Joan and Sant Miquel. There has been comparatively little development here, but the beach still offers every amenity from sun-bed rental to restaurants and beach bars. In the 1960s, when Ibiza's hippy scene was at its height, this was the setting for infamous full-moon parties. Today Benirràs still has a bohemian feel, especially for the annual drumming festival on 28 August. Come here at sunset for a real sense of the magic of the place.

The nearby town of Sant Miquel has a whitewashed fortified church, where displays of folk dancing are held on Thursday afternoons.
✚ 474 N7 ℹ Carrer Mariano Riquer Wallis 4, 07840 Santa Eulària des Riu ☎ 971 33 07 28 ⏣ Closed Sun

CALA D'HORT

This is not only one of the prettiest of Ibiza's rugged bays, with a wide beach backed by pine-studded cliffs overlooking a turquoise sea, but it also has magnificent views of the rocky outcrop of Es Vedrá. This dramatic limestone island is featured in countless legends: It was said to be the lair of sirens, who lured sailors to their deaths, and the home of Tanit, the Carthaginian goddess of fertility, who is still revered in Ibiza today. Cala d'Hort has been the focus of an ongoing battle between developers and environmentalists over plans to build a major tourist resort; The plans have been suspended, but old fears have been resurrected with controversial plans to develop a golf course.
✚ 474 M7 ℹ Carrer Antonio Riquer 2, 07800 Eivissa ☎ 971 30 19 00

CALA SALADA

Just north of the brash resort of Sant Antoni is a succession of beach coves that reveals a different side to the west coast. The beaches are connected by a coastal footpath, from Sant Antoni passing Cala Gració, Cala Gracioneta and Cala Yoga on its way to Cala Salada. This is an idyllic spot, with a few fishermen's huts, a fish restaurant and a wide sand beach.
✚ 474 M7 ℹ Passeig de Ses Fonts s/n, 07820 Sant Antoni ☎ 971 34 33 63

EIVISSA
▷ 406.

FORMENTERA
▷ 407.

PORTINATX

This family-orientated resort sits at Ibiza's remote northern tip and has a romantic setting around a deep bay with a golden crescent of sand. Portinatx is the only sizeable resort on the north coast, a region of pine woods, mountains, olive and citrus groves, and pretty coves under tall cliffs. Reach it via a circular route from Sant Joan, which passes the beautiful beach of Cala Xarraca. Portinatx is separated from this beach by the headland of Punta de Sa Torre, where an old watchtower stands. Portinatx has three beaches, but perhaps the best in the area is at Cala d'en Serrà, 3km (2 miles) east of the resort on the return trip to Sant Joan. Cala de Sant Vicent, at Ibiza's northeastern tip, is a small resort

with a magnificent beach backed by woods and cliffs.
✚ 474 N7 ℹ Plaça de la Catedral, 07800 Eivissa ☎ 971 39 92 32 🚌 From Eivissa

SANTA EULÀRIA DES RIU
www.santaeulalia.net

Santa Eulària strikes a balance between tourism and everyday life, with the result that it retains the feel of a provincial town. Stroll along the waterfront promenade, past the port and crescent-shaped beaches, or down shady Passeig de S'Alamera boulevard, which links the town hall to the sea. A short climb from the town hall leads up to Puig de Missa, 52m (170ft) high, overlooking the town and topped by a 16th-century fortress-church with a magnificent arched porch (daily 9–9). Halfway up Puig de Missa is the Museu Etnològic (Apr–Sep Mon–Sat 10–2, 5.30–8; Oct–Mar Tue–Sat 10–2; all year Sun 11–1.30), in a traditional flat-roofed rural Ibizan house and featuring the folk crafts of Ibiza and Formentera. Santa Eulària has the only river (usually dry) in the Balearic islands; stroll along its banks to see the Pont Vell, a stone-arched bridge originally built by the Romans.

North of Santa Eulària, Sant Carles has a bohemian reputation and is the venue for Ibiza's only year-round 'hippy market', held in the Las Dalias bar on Saturdays.
✚ 474 N7 ℹ Carrer Mariano Riquer Wallis 4, 07840 Santa Eulària des Riu; in summer, there is also an information booth on Passeig de S'Alamera ☎ 971 33 07 28 ⏣ Closed Sun 🚌 From Eivissa

REGIONS BALEARIC ISLANDS • SIGHTS

s

REGIONS BALEARIC ISLANDS • SIGHTS

REGIONS BALEARIC ISLANDS • SIGHTS

REGIONS BALEARIC ISLANDS • SIGHTS

INFORMATION

www.eivissa.es

✚ 474 N7 ℹ Plaça de la Catedral, 07800 Eivissa ☎ 971 39 92 32 🕓 Closed Sun

EIVISSA

The Ibizan capital is a lively, cosmopolitan place where just about anything can happen. Fishermen, businesspeople and drag queens are all found here, and the whole town exudes a sense of excitement and edge that sums up modern Ibiza. It all takes place in the shadow of the old walled city of Dalt Vila (meaning 'high town'), one of the most stunning sights in the Mediterranean.

MEDIEVAL CITY

Eivissa (sometimes known as Ibiza Town) is dominated by its medieval city, set high on a cliff and still surrounded by its 16th-century curtain walls and bastions, which are seen to best effect from the sea.

The main entry to Dalt Vila is through the Portal de Ses Taules, which has a drawbridge and bears the coat of arms of Felipe II. From the colonnaded Patio des Armas there are several routes up to the summit of the town, passing nobles' houses dating from the 15th and 16th centuries on the way to the Gothic cathedral (daily 8.30–8). Opposite the cathedral is the Museu Arqueològic (Apr–Sep Tue–Sat 10–2, 6–8; Oct–Mar Tue–Sat 9–3, Sun 10–2), which displays prehistoric pottery, sculptures of Punic gods and goddesses, Roman amphorae, coins and funerary steles, and gives access to a section of the medieval ramparts. The castle and bishop's palace, behind the cathedral, are slowly undergoing restoration. From the nearby bastion of Sant Bernat there are views across to the island of Formentera, and you can walk most of the way around the outer walls for more views over Eivissa and its bay.

MORE SIGHTS

Outside Dalt Vila, other areas of interest include the old fishermen's district of Sa Penya, now a rather seedy nightlife quarter; the glitzy waterfront at La Marina, where outrageous club parades take place nightly in summer; and the heart of the modern town on the Passeig Vara de Rey promenade.

Finally, don't miss the Punic necropolis at Puig des Molins, probably the most important example of its kind in the world, where 3,000 rock-cut tombs dating from the fourth century BC have been discovered (mid-Mar to mid-Oct Tue–Sat 10–2, 6–8, Sun 10–2; mid-Oct to mid-Mar Tue–Sat 9–3, Sun 10–2).

Above *The old fortified town, Dalt Vila, overlooks La Marina in Eivissa*

FORMENTERA

Although it lies just a short ferry ride from Ibiza, the island of Formentera feels like a world apart, and a visit here can offer a relaxing alternative to the excesses of its larger neighbour. The smallest of the Balearic Islands has a population of just 5,000 people and a peaceful landscape of vineyards, carob trees, saltpans, wheat fields, tiny villages, dramatic cliffs and some of the finest and most unspoiled beaches in Spain.

ES PUJOLS AND CA NA COSTA

Formentera's only real visitor resort is tiny by Balearic standards, and focuses around two sandy beaches backed by dunes, craggy rocks and pine woods. There are watersports here, and if you're looking for Formentera's minimal nightlife, this is the place to come. Just north of Es Pujols is Ca na Costa, a megalithic burial tomb and stone circle dating from around 2000BC (open at all times). This unusually complex site for its period is now recognized as one of the most important sites on the Balearic Islands.

🛈 Es Pujols: Carrer Espalmador (corner with Avinguda Miramar) 🕘 May–Oct daily

PILAR DE MOLA

This sleepy little town lies in the east of the island and only really comes to life for its twice weekly craft markets, on Wednesday and Sunday evenings in summer. Two kilometres (1.2 miles) farther east, the lighthouse of Far de la Mola stands high above the sea; a plaque commemorates the French novelist Jules Verne (1828–1905), who was inspired to write his book *Journey Around the Solar System* while watching the night sky here.

SANT FRANCESC DE FORMENTERA

Formentera's capital lies inland from the arrival port of Sa Savina and, though little more than a village, serves as the island's main commercial and shopping hub, with markets, shops, restaurants and banks. Its main sight is the mighty fortified church, Sa Tanca Vella, in the large plaza at the top of town.

SES SALINES

These disused saltpans in the north of the island, now a nature reserve, are bounded by more superb beaches. Bird enthusiasts can look for herons and flamingos in the reserve itself. The entire area is protected as part of the Ses Salines nature reserve, and apart from a couple of beach huts and bars there has been very little development here.

INFORMATION

www.formentera.es

➕ 475 N8 🛈 Calle Calp s/n, 07870 Port de la Savina ☎ 971 32 20 57

🕘 Mon–Fri 10–2, 5–7, Sat 10–2

🚢 From Eivissa

TIPS

» The only way to get to Formentera is on one of the ferries from Ibiza, which depart regularly throughout the year from Eivissa harbour. The journey takes between 30 minutes and an hour, and provides magnificent views of the town's Dalt Vila and Ibiza's southeastern coast.

» The boats dock at Sa Savina, Formentera's harbour, where you can rent a car, moped or bicycle to explore the island.

» A bicycle is the best option; the island measures only 14km (9 miles) from one end to the other and this gives you the chance to leave the road and explore the network of *circuits verds* (green lanes).

» There are wonderful views from the cliffs beside the La Mola lighthouse.

» To experience the best of Platja de Migjorn, the longest beach on the island, head away from the development at either end and find a good spot in the central dunes.

Below *Cap de la Mola at La Mola*, *Formentera*

SOUTHERN MALLORCA

This gentle half-day drive leads around the cliffs, coves and beaches of Mallorca's southern coast, a sleepy region of almond groves, apricot orchards and small farms dotted with stone walls. *Agroturismo* (rural tourism) is gradually taking off here, and you will pass a number of farmhouses offering country hospitality. In summer there are numerous opportunities to break up the drive, as various minor roads lead off the main route to some of Mallorca's lesser known beaches—a world away from the island's stylish capital of Palma, where the drive begins.

THE DRIVE

Distance: 120km (74 miles)
Allow: 4 hours
Start/end at: Palma de Mallorca, map 475 P6

★ Leave Palma de Mallorca via the highway in the direction of the airport and the beaches of Platja de Palma. When the highway runs out, fork right following signs to Cala Blava, passing Aquacity water park on your left. Ignore the next right to Cala Blava and continue on the main road (MA-6014) towards Cala Pi.

❶ There are splendid views and clifftop walks at the headland of Cap Blanc, although the lighthouse is out of bounds as it is part of a military base.

After 5km (3 miles) there is the option of a right turn to Cala Pi .

❷ Pine trees lean out over the cliffs above this beautiful inlet and steps lead down to a small, sandy beach.

The main road (still the MA-6014) keeps left to the prehistoric village of Capocorb Vell.

❸ Capocorb Vell is one of the largest remaining settlements of the Talaiotic culture, which thrived on Mallorca between 1300 and 800BC. Among the remains here are five ancient *talaiots*, or watchtowers.

After passing the site, stay on this road as it swings right, following signs to Santanyí. When you reach

a crossroads, turn right and then immediately left. Stay on this long, straight road, which passes between almond groves and stone walls and offers fine views of the Serra de Llevant hills up ahead. Various country roads to your right lead down to Platja des Trenc.

❹ This idyllic beach of fine white sand, backed by dunes and pine woods, is popular with local families and nudists in summer.

Eventually you turn right to the small resort and fishing village of Còlonia de Sant Jordi, passing the old spa buildings at Banys de Sant Joan and the saltpans of Salines de Llevant. As you drop to the sea, the island of Cabrera looms on the horizon.

attractive coves, where white-painted fishermen's cottages reach down to the water.

After exploring Santanyí, take the MA-19 and the MA-19A towards Palma, passing through the towns of Campos and Llucmajor on your return to the capital.

WHEN TO GO
The drive is enjoyable at any time of year, but go in summer if you want to combine it with a few hours on one of the south coast's unspoiled beaches.

WHERE TO EAT
There are some good seafood restaurants at Colònia de Sant Jordi, including El Puerto (below). Santanyí is another pleasant place to break the journey, and has several tapas bars and a funky art gallery and internet café clustered together on the square in front of the church.

EL PUERTO
✉ Carrer Lonja 2, 07638 Colònia de Sant Jordi ☎ 971 65 60 47 🕐 Feb–Nov Tue–Sun 12–4, 7–12

PLACE TO VISIT
CAPOCORB VELL
✉ Carretera Cap Blanc–Llucmajor (07639) ☎ 971 18 01 55 🕐 Fri–Wed 10–4.30. Closed Thu ♿ €2

Turn right at the roundabout and follow signs for the port to visit the beach, fishing port and waterfront restaurants.

❺ The waters of Colònia de Sant Jordi, once the haunt of smugglers from the North African coast, are now busy with pleasure boats and glass-bottomed vessels that offer excursions around the coast and south to Cabrera.

After exploring Colònia de Sant Jordi, return to the roundabout outside the village and keep straight ahead through the village of Ses Salines. The road now passes Botanicactus, a large botanical garden, on its way to Santanyí.

In the village of Es Llombards, there is the option of a short drive through the pine woods to the picturesque beach of Cala Llombards. The main route continues to Santanyí.

❻ It is worthwhile stopping in this delightful Mallorcan town built from the mellow local sandstone that was also used in the construction of Palma's cathedral. One of the

original town gates has survived, together with sections of the medieval walls. The main square in front of the church, Plaça Major, is now for pedestrians only and is lined with cafés and bars. A good time to visit is during the Saturday morning market, when local pottery is sold in the square.

From Santanyí you can drive down to Cala Figuera, one of Mallorca's most

---

Opposite Looking over Palma de Mallorca from the Castell de Bellver
Below Talaiotic remains and Bronze Age dwellings at Capocorb Vell

THE BÓQUER VALLEY

This coast-to-coast walk through Mallorca's delightful Valle de Bóquer is easy to follow and can be done by anyone of average fitness. Wear stout shoes and take binoculars for observing the great variety of birdlife, including redstarts and pied flycatchers.

THE WALK

Distance: 6km (3.7 miles)
Allow: 2 hours
Start/end at: Port de Pollença, map 475 P6
Parking: On the waterfront, beside the port

HOW TO GET THERE

Port de Pollença lies at the northern tip of Mallorca on the MA-2200.

★ Start at the roundabout on the waterfront in Port de Pollença and head north along the promenade with the sea to your right.

❶ A bust of the painter Hermenegildo Anglada-Camarasa (1871–1959), a leading figure in the Pollença school of artists, marks the start of the narrow Passeig Voramar, also known as the Pine Walk, where pine trees lean into the sea.

Continue along the Pine Walk to the end of the first small section of beach. Just beyond Los Pescadores restaurant, turn left along Avinguda Bocchoris, then cross the main road and keep straight ahead along an avenue of ageing tamarisk trees to join the signposted Camí de Boquer.

Follow the twisting path uphill towards a large farmhouse. You can pass through the entrance gates despite the forbidding-looking notice, but you must stick to the path. Dogs are not allowed.

❷ As you reach the farmhouse, take a look behind you for a panoramic view over Pollença Bay.

Continue past the farmhouse and through a second gate. Don't forget

to shut the gate behind you, then follow the path around to the right to climb to another gate a few metres farther on.

❸ You are now in the Valle de Bóquer. Sheep graze on the valley floor to your left as you follow a broad, stony trail. On the far side of the valley, the dramatic 360m-high (1,180ft) limestone ridge of Cavall Bernat runs northwards to the sea.

Stay on the path as it passes between huge boulders and through clumps of dwarf palm. It then widens and dips down.

❹ To your left, at the base of one of the boulders, is a cave that was built as a winter shelter for sheep and goats.

After passing through a gap in a dry-stone wall, you will see a derelict stone kiln on your left.

❺ Such kilns were used in Mallorca long ago to fire limestone in the production of lime and whitewash for painting houses. Farther on, also on your left, are the remains of the prehistoric settlement of Bocchoris, today little more than a pile of stones at the foot of Cavall Bernat.

❻ The trail now climbs to a plateau marked by a grove of umbrella pines.

Wild cyclamen and orchids bloom here in spring, and you may also see wild goats.

From the pine grove, the route meanders gently uphill, passing through another old stone wall on its way to the Coll del Moro (Moor's Hill).

❼ The views from the 80m (262ft) Coll del Moro are magnificent: note the rocky outcrop of Es Colomer and the jagged ridge of Cavall Bernat.

The main trail heads down to the sea; ignore this and keep to the right on a narrow path that winds through clumps of rosemary and dwarf palm towards a rocky ledge overlooking the crystal-clear waters of Cala Bóquer.

❽ On a calm summer's day this makes a fine picnic spot, but in winter it can be wild and windswept.

Stay on the path as it turns left along the clifftop before heading inland. At the next meeting of paths, turn right if you want to drop down to the shingle beach. Otherwise, turn left to return to Coll del Moro and retrace your steps to Port de Pollença.

If you still have some energy at the end of the walk, turn left along the waterfront to follow the promenade all the way to its end at the Hotel Illa d'Or.

WHEN TO GO

This walk is pleasant at any time of year, although the best times for birding are during the spring and

Above *Path through the lower slopes*
Opposite *Vine-shaded doorway on the route*
Below *Promenade at Port de Pollença*

autumn migration seasons (April, May and September, October).

WHERE TO EAT

There are no facilities at Cala Bóquer, so take a picnic and plenty of water. There are numerous cafés and restaurants on the waterfront at Port de Pollença near the start and end of the walk.

LOS PESCADORES

A good fish restaurant on the Pine Walk promenade.
✉ Passeig Voramar 45, 07470 Port de Pollença ☎ 971 86 62 74 ⏱ May–Oct daily 12–2, 7–12

MALLORCA

ALCÚDIA

HÍPICA FORMENTOR

www.hipicaformentor.com

This friendly riding centre is located between the Bay of Pollença and the Albufera wetlands, now a wildlife reserve, and offers riding lessons and treks for riders of all abilities. Beginners will enjoy the short excursions around the beautiful reserve, while those with more experience can take longer treks, or even choose from a range of riding holidays (between 3 and 8 days) which explore the whole island. The most popular treks are the fabulous, atmospheric rides along the island's beaches at sunset. Children are welcome and there are horses and ponies of all sizes to accommodate everyone.

✉ Apt 182, 07400 Alcúdia
☎ 609826703 (mobile) ⏰ Year round
🖐 From €20 for a one-hour excursion

ALGAIDA

CASA GORDIOLA

www.gordiola.com

Hand-blown glass is a traditional product of Mallorca. Here glassblowers fashion bottles, bowls and lamps in the traditional style followed by the Gordiola family since 1719. Above the workshop is a small museum; next door are the shops where you can buy glass pieces or other souvenirs.

✉ Km 19, Carretera Palma–Manacor, 07210 Algaida ☎ 971 66 50 46 ⏰ Shop: Mon–Sat 9–7, Sun 9–1.30; glassworks: Mon–Sat 9–1.30, 3–6, Sun 9–12 🚗 2.5km (1.5 miles) northwest of Algaida on C-715

CAPDEPERA

CANYAMEL GOLF

www.canyamelgolf.com

Mallorca boasts scores of spectacular golf courses. Canyamel is beautifully located on the northern coast, between the sea and the hills around Artà, and offers splendid views which can even reach to Menorca

on clear days. This 18-hole, par-73 course is considered one of the trickiest on the island, with plenty to challenge even the finest golfers. Among the facilities are a golf school, driving range, restaurant and bar. The golf club can also arrange accommodation in the area.

✉ Urbanización Canyamel, Avinguda d'es Cap Vermell, 07580 Capdepera ☎ 971 84 13 13 ⏰ Year round 🖐 Green fee €75–€90

INCA

CAMPER FACTORY STORE

www.camper.com

Inca is known primarily for its shoe and leather industry, and the Camper store is a must for anyone looking for comfortable shoes. The company's funky, urban footwear is sold here at a discount.

✉ Polígono Industrial de Inca, 07300 Inca ☎ 971 88 82 33 ⏰ Mon–Sat 10–8 (until 8.30 in summer) 🚆 The Palma–Inca train leaves Palma's Plaça de Espanya hourly 🚗 From Palma, head to Alcúdia along the main highway. Follow signs to Inca

MANACOR
PERLAS MAJORICA
www.majorica.com

Majorica is Spain's largest jewellery company, and its organic, man-made pearls are sold worldwide. Although you can buy them (and other brand pearls) throughout the island, you'll get better prices at this large outlet store. You can also visit the factory.

✉ Ctra Palma-Artá Km 48 ☎ 971 55 09 00
🕐 Mon–Fri 9–7, Sat–Sun 10–1
🚉 Manacor

PALMA DE MALLORCA
AUDITORIUM
www.auditoriumdepalma.com

The Auditorium is a conference centre and performance hall for events such as theatre, opera and orchestral concerts. There's also a cafeteria/bar.

✉ Passeig Marítim 18, 07014 Palma de Mallorca ☎ 971 73 53 28 (information); ticket line: 971 73 47 35 💶 €20–€55
🚌 EMT

LA CASA DEL OLIVO

Olive trees line Mallorca's countryside, and their richly textured, honey-toned wood is prized for decorative use. This shop sells handcarved bowls, dishes and other pieces. The prices aren't low, but the craftsmanship is high.

✉ Carrer Peseateria Vella 4, 07001 Palma de Mallorca ☎ 971 72 70 25 🕐 Mon–Fri 10–1.30, 5–8, Sat 10–1.30. Closed Jul and Aug 🚌 2

PURO BEACH
www.purobeach.com

Hang out with the fashion pack at this bright white beach club, set around a pristine pool on the ocean's edge. During the day, there are various activities, including yoga (11am), but at night, DJs play mellow chill-out music which gets increasingly upbeat as the night wears on. There is a café-restaurant, where you can dine on modern Mediterranean cuisine and even a spa for massage and beauty treatments. Check out the website for a current programme of events.

✉ Carrer de Pagell 1, Cala Estància, 07012 Palma de Mallorca ☎ 971 42 54 50
🕐 11am–midnight

SA GERRERIA
www.sagerreria.es

To find the best Mallorcan handicrafts, make for the Sa Gerreria. Here, you'll find workshops and galleries dedicated to everything from ceramics and glasswork, to pearls and jewellery. Stop at the Interpretation Centre for information on the crafts and the workshops available. The centre also runs various events, including concerts. There's also a café-bar on Plaça Llorenç Bisbal, offering a good value *menu del día* on weekdays.

✉ Carrer d'en Bosc/Plaça Artesania, 07002 Palma de Mallorca ☎ 971 21 36 50 (Interpretation Centre) 🕐 Mon–Fri 11–7

LA PORRASA
AQUALAND
www.aqualand.es

Aqualand has more than 30 water slides, a huge lake and a 'lazy river'. There's a special area for the young. Restaurants, drink stands and baby-changing facilities are all available on site.

✉ Carretera Cala Figuera 1–23, 07182 La Porrasa ☎ 971 13 08 11 🕐 Jul–Aug daily 10–6; May, Sep–Oct 10–5 💶 Adult €20, child €14, under 3 free 🚌 From Santa Pença and Paquera 104; from Palma 104, 105; from Palma Nova Magaluf 104, 105, 106 🚗 Off the main highway between Figuera and Magalluf

PORT DE SOLLER
NAUTIC SOLLER
www.nauticsoller.com

You can rent windsurfing boards, canoes, sailboats or motorboats here hourly or daily. There's also water-skiing, or try the 'ski bus', an inflated tube carrying four people that's pulled behind a boat.

✉ Platja d'En Repic, 07108 Port de Soller ☎ 971 63 30 01, 609 35 41 32
🕐 Easter–Oct daily 9–6 💶 Canoe rental (two places) 1 hour €15, half a day €40, 1 day €60. Lessons (sailing, canoeing, etc) available

🚉 Tren de Soller connects Soller with Port de Soller 🚗 On left off main highway before you reach Port de Soller; indicated by a sign

PORTO CRISTO
COVES DEL DRAC
www.cuevasdeldrach.com

Walking down into this damp underground cave is like entering another world. Follow the trail past stalagmites and stalactites, tree-like rock formations and six underground lakes, including Lake Martel, where classical music concerts are held. A cafeteria, toilets and open-air plaza with tables are just outside the entrance.

✉ Carretera de les Coves s/n, 07680 Porto Cristo ☎ 971 82 07 53 🕐 Daily. Tours: Apr–Oct hourly 10–5; Nov–Mar at 10.45, noon, 2 and 3.30 💶 €12; under 7 free
🚗 From the centre of Porto Cristo, follow Carretera de les Coves for about 20 min; the Coves del Drac are on the left

VALLDEMOSSA
COSTA NORD
www.costanord.com

This cultural centre shows an audiovisual exhibit on Mallorca during the day. The Mediterranean Nights concert series features international musicians. There is a bar and restaurant on site.

✉ Avinguda Palma 6, 07170 Valldemossa ☎ 971 61 24 25 🕐 Daily 9–5, plus special evening events

MENORCA
ALAIOR
COVA D'EN XOROI
www.covadenxoroi.com

Nightclubs don't come much more distinctive than this: The setting is stunning, in a cave on the side of a cliff. It is open early in the morning for visitors to the caves, and until late for drinking and dancing. It's in Cala'n Porter and is signposted.

✉ Cala'n Porter, Ocio, 07730 Alaior
☎ 971 37 72 36 🕐 Caves: summer daily 11am–10pm; winter Sat–Sun 11.30–8.30. Nightclub: Jun–Sep daily 11pm–5am; mid- to end May, Oct Fri–Sat 💶 Caves €6. Nightclub €17–€22

CIUTADELLA

ESFERA
www.esferadisco.com
Menorca doesn't have a big reputation for its nightlife, but this is a fun nightclub in the buzzy port in Ciutadella. It is arranged around five levels, which includes two outdoor terraces, both of which offer stunning views over the old port and the historic quarter. The music covers everything from Spanish pop to house to salsa and Latin rhythms. Entrance is free, and its very popular with young locals.
✉ Port de Ciutadella, 07760 Ciutadella de Menorca ⏰ Daily in summer 11pm–6am ✋ Free

GALERÍA RETXA
Galería Retxa is a small but well-established art gallery. Paintings, etchings and a few sculptures by well-known local artists and some international artists are exhibited and sold here.
✉ Calle 9 de Julio 37, 07760 Ciutadella ☎ 971 38 18 06 ⏰ Mon–Fri 9.30–1.30, 5.30–8, Sat 9.30–1.30

TEATRO MUNICIPAL DES BORN
This is one of Menorca's main theatres, with excellent period features and superb acoustics. International and local groups perform classical and contemporary music, dance and theatre here. Films are screened.
✉ Plaza des Born 20, 07760 Ciutadella ☎ 971 48 44 84 ✋ Free–€25

FERRERIES

ESPECTÁCULO ECUESTRE DE MENORCA
www.showmenorca.com
For an unusual type of entertainment, visit this equestrian school. The show includes a demonstration on how horses are prepared for the island's traditional fiestas.
✉ Km 0.5, Carretera Cala Galdana, 07750 Ferreries ☎ 971 15 50 59 ⏰ Jun–Sep Wed, Sun at 8.30 ✋ €15, under 12 free 🚌 From Ferreries, take Carretera General Maó towards Ciutadella, then the turning towards Cala Galdana on ME-22; the school is 500m (550 yards) down this road

FERRERIES CENTRE
You can buy shoes, handbags (purses), leather goods, ceramics, souvenirs and regional delicacies—local cheeses, honey and gin—at the Racó de Menorca stall. There is a bar and cafeteria. It is in the industrial park, at the entrance to Ferreries.
✉ Calle D, Polígono Industrial Ferreries, 07750 Ferreries ☎ 971 37 38 37 ⏰ 15 Apr–Oct Mon–Sat 9–8.30, Sun 10–2 🚌 On main road from Mão to Ciutadella; take exit at Km27

SON MARTORELLET
www.sonmartorellet.com
This ranch has a spectacular horse show featuring Menorcan-bred horses. For kids, there's a playground area and a train ride during the show's intermission. You can also tour the ranch and see the horses in their stables and pastures.
✉ Km 1.5, Carretera Cala Galdana, 07750 Ferreries ☎ 971 37 40 66, 609 04 94 93 ⏰ Show and visit: May–Oct Tue, Thu 8.30pm and 10pm. Ranch tour: Mon–Fri 10–noon, 3–6 ✋ Show €16–€20, under 10 €7. Ranch visit free 🚌 On the left less than 2km (1.2 miles) after the start of the Carretera Cala Galdana

FORNELLS

WINDSURF FORNELLS
www.windfornells.com
Windsurf Fornells, by the sheltered waters of the Bahía de Fornells, gives windsurfing and sailing lessons. Tuition is tailored to your requirements on a one-to-one basis.
✉ Carrer Nou 33, 07740 Es Mercadal ☎ 971 18 81 50 ⏰ Jul–Aug daily 9.45–12, 12.25–2.40, 4.25–6.40; Apr–Jun, Sep, Oct daily 10.15–1, 3–5.45 ✋ 2 sessions €114, 6 sessions €252 🚌 1km (0.5 mile) south of Fornells between the road and the sea at the entrance to the village

MAÓ (MAHÓN)

SA BARCA
If you take a stroll by Maó's port you'll find Sa Barca, a typically Menorcan fashion shop offering all the musts, including *abarcas* (traditional Menorcan footwear), leather goods and eco-garments in natural fibres

from the renowned Pou Nou brand.
✉ Moll de Llevant 221, 07701 Maó ☎ 971 36 44 29 ⏰ Easter–Sep daily 11am–1am

TEATRE PRINCIPAL DE MAHÓN
www.teatremao.org
One of the most important venues on the island, showcasing classical and contemporary music, dance and theatre, with plays in Spanish and Catalán. There are two bars, open only on performance nights.
✉ Calle Costa d'en Deià 40, 07701 Maó ☎ 971 35 57 76 ⏰ Performances Tue–Sat, times vary ✋ €5–€55

EIVISSA (IBIZA)

EIVISSA

AMNESIA
www.amnesia.es
Amnesia, which started in the 1970s, is one of the oldest and most famous clubs on the island. It is located in an old *finca*, now transformed almost beyond recognition into a fashionable and enormous complex of bars with several dancefloors. There are different parties every night in summer, including foam parties at least twice a week, and the list of celebrity guests is long and glittering. The resident and guest DJs are among the best in Europe and the club regularly hosts live music from international artists such as Fat Boy Slim and the Arctic Monkeys.
✉ Carretera Ibiza-Sant Antoni Km 5, 07820 Eivissa ☎ 971 19 80 41 ⏰ Jun–Sep daily from midnight (check exact dates, which change annually, on the website) ✋ From €35–€55

HOLALA
www.holala-ibiza.com
Holala is a prestigious second-hand and vintage shop specializing in good-quality clothing imported from abroad. Items range from Ibizan fashion to army surplus. The shop's philosophy is to provide 'unique

clothing for unique people' while setting the trends for things to come.
✉ Plaça Mercado Viejo 12, 07800 Eivissa
☎ 971 31 65 37 🕐 Jul–Aug Mon–Sat 11–2, 4–12; Jun Mon–Sat 11–2, 5–10; Apr–May, Sep–Dec Mon–Sat 11–2, 5–8

LIFE CONCEPT IBIZA
www.lifeconceptibiza.com
Highly stylish store for shoppers who are not on a budget. The latest fashion in clothes, shoes, handbags (purses) and other accessories are displayed in a very modern, minimalist environment.
✉ Avenida Bartolomé Roselló 28, 07800 Eivissa ☎ 971 19 11 10 🕐 Jun–Sep Mon–Sat 10.30–3, 6–11; Oct–May Mon–Sat 10–1, 5–9

PRIVILEGE
www.privilegeibiza.es
Privilege is the biggest club in the world and is truly spectacular. It can accommodate up to 10,000 people. Funky with trance and techno music, a garden and a swimming pool. Advance reservations recommended. There are free minibuses from the harbour in Ibiza.
✉ Carretera Sant Antoni de Portmany, 07820 Eivissa ☎ 971 19 81 60 🕐 15 Jun–Sep daily midnight–late 👋 €30–€65
🚌 From Sant Antoni, follow directions to Eivissa; the nightclub is halfway along, near San Rafael

SANT ANTONI DE PORTMANY
AQUARIUM CAP BLANC
An underground saltwater lake is the main feature at this aquarium, in a dark cave at sea-level. The water is lit to showcase the fish and sealife below the surface. Look for the turtles!
✉ Carretera de Cala Gració s/n, 07020 Sant Antoni de Portmany
☎ 971 34 22 06 🕐 10 Apr–Oct daily 10am–dusk; Nov–9 Oct Fri 10–1
👋 Adult €4.50, child €2.50 🚌 1 from Puerto de Sant Antonio 🚌 Follow signs from Sant Antoni

CAFÉ DEL MAR
www.cafedelmarmusic.com
Set on the beach, the main attraction

is its wonderful sunset view, accompanied by chill-out music. You can dance the night away on the beach.
✉ Vara de Rey 27, 07820 Sant Antoni de Portmany ☎ 971 34 75 43 🕐 Jul–Sep daily 6pm–3am; Easter–Jun, Oct 3pm–2am

CASA ALFONSO
This food store has a reputation for quality fresh foods and a wide choice of drinks. It's popular for its great selection of imported goods, and is a good place to stock up on local delicacies.
✉ Carrer Progrés 8, 07820 Sant Antoni de Portmany ☎ 971 34 30 12 🕐 Easter–Oct Mon–Sat 9am–10.30pm; Nov–Easter Mon–Fri 9–2, 5–8, Sat 9–3 🚌 Bus stops about five min from shop

SANTA EULÀRIA DES RIU
LAS DALIAS HIPPY MARKET
www.lasdalias.es
Set in the gardens of La Sala Dalias, and with about 100 stands, this market is the most famous on the island. All kinds of handmade goods are on offer, including clothes, jewellery and handicrafts. In December the unmissable Las Dalias Christmas market sets up here.
✉ Km 12, Carretera a Sant Carles 85, 07850 Santa Eulària des Riu ☎ 971 32 68 25 🕐 Sat 10–8 🚌 Take the road to Sant Carles; the market is 1km (0.5 mile) before the town

JANUARY
FESTES DE SANT SEBASTIA
Mallorca's capital city celebrates its patron saint with fireworks, processions, and more.
✉ Palma de Mallorca

FEBRUARY–MARCH
CARNAVAL
✉ Throughout the islands

MARCH–APRIL
SEMANA SANTA
✉ Throughout the islands

MAY
FESTA DE NOSTRA SENYORA DE LA VICTÒRIA
Mock battles between Moors and Christians commemorate the 1229 conquest of Mallorca by Jaume I el Conqueridor (James I the Conqueror).
✉ Port de Sóller, Mallorca

JUNE
FESTA DE SANT JUAN
Jousting, folk music, parades, dancing and fireworks.
✉ Ciutadella, Menorca

GO-KARTS
www.gokartssantaeularia.com
Pinball, soccer and video games are great on rainy days, but the real fun is the go-cart track. There are special baby and youth carts for kids as young as three years, and a playground on site.
✉ Km 6, Carretera de Santa Eulària, 07840 Santa Eulària des Riu ☎ 971 31 77 44
🕐 Apr–Oct daily 10–dusk; Nov–Mar daily 11–dusk 👋 €8–€25

Below *Brightly decorated bead boxes for sale at a market on Ibiza*

PRICES AND SYMBOLS

The restaurants are listed alphabetically (excluding Le, La and Les). The prices given are the average for a two-course lunch (L) and a three-course dinner (D) for one person, without drinks. The wine price is for the least expensive bottle.

For a key to the symbols, ▷ 2.

MALLORCA

DEIÀ
EL OLIVO

www.hotellaresidencia.com
The not-so-secret hide-out of the rich and famous, Deià is one of Mallorca's prettiest villages and one of the island's (and Spain's) top spots for food. El Olivo is the creation of chef Guillermo Méndez.

✉ Hotel La Residencia, Son Canals s/n, Deià ☎ 971 63 93 92 🕐 Daily 1–3, 7.30–10.30 🍴 L €55, D €85, Tasting menu €105, Vegetarian menu €80, Wine €36

RESTAURANTE JAUME

Fresh, modern Mediterranean cuisine is served in a charming, traditional stone house.

✉ Carrer Arxiduc Lluis Salvador 24, 07179 Deià ☎ 971 63 90 29 🕐 Tue–Sat 1–3.30, 7.30–10.30, Sun 1–3.30 (also open Sun eve mid-Apr to mid-Oct) 🍴 L €30, D €45, Wine €16

FORNALUTX
CA N'ATUNA

Fornalutx is a tiny town in the Serra de Tramuntana mountains. The valley in all its glory is beautifully shown off from Ca N'Atuna's stone terrace, where you can enjoy local dishes in huge portions.

✉ Carrer Arbona Colom 8, 07109 Fornalutx ☎ 971 63 30 68 🕐 Daily 12.30–4, 7.30–11 🍴 L €25, D €35, Wine €10

PALMA DE MALLORCA
LA BÓVEDA

www.restaurantelaboveda.com
This tavern-style tapas bar serves traditional Mallorcan fare such as brown bread with oil, and local olives and sausages. The restaurant has a sister branch at Passeig Sagrera 3.

✉ Carrer Boteria 3, 07012 Palma de Mallorca ☎ 971 71 48 63 🕐 Mon–Sat 1.30–4, 8.30–12. Closed Feb 🍴 L €18, D €28, Wine €10

CELLER SA PREMSA

www.cellersapremsa.com
Enjoy traditional Mallorcan classic dishes such as *tumbet* (aubergine/eggplant) or *frit mallorquí* with bread and green olives as starters.

✉ Plaça Bisbe Berenguer de Palou 8, 07003 Palma de Mallorca ☎ 971 72 35 29 🕐 Mon–Sat 1–4, 7.30–11.30. Closed Sun (also Sat Jul–Aug) 🍴 L €25, D €42, Wine €10

FÀBRICA 23

www.fabrica23restaurante.com
The Santa Catalina neighbourhood is currently the hottest in the city, with excellent restaurants. One of the pioneers, and still going strong, is Fàbrica 23, which combines adventurous Mediterranean cuisine and stylish, although understated, surroundings. It's an excellent dining option on every level—cuisine, style and service. Three British friends, all great fans of Mallorca, are behind the restaurant, which perhaps accounts for the daring cuisine. The menu offers whatever is freshest at the nearby market, and then serves it up in adventurous combinations: Try the clams with sweet-and-sour lentils, or the confit of duck with beetroot purée.

✉ Carrer Cótoner 42–44, 07013 Palma de Mallorca ☎ 971 45 31 25 🕐 Sun–Mon 1–3.30, Tue–Sat 1–3.30, 9–11 🍴 L €38 D €40, Wine €14

PARLAMENT

www.restaurantparlament.com
This old-fashioned, elegant
establishment is very busy at
lunchtime. Famous for its squid and
paella *ciega* (with no bones), it serves
mainly fish and rice dishes, and a
variety of meats.
✉ Carrer Conquistador 11, 07001 Palma
de Mallorca ☎ 971 72 60 26 🕐 Daily 1–4,
8–11. Closed Aug 🖐 L €25, D €45, *Menú
del día* €22, Wine €12.

RESTAURANTE KOLDO ROYO

www.koldoroyo.com
In chic surroundings overlooking
the port, this place serves innovative
cuisine based on Basque classics.
✉ Carrer Ingeniero Gabriel Roca 3, 07012
Palma de Mallorca ☎ 971 73 24 35
🕐 Tue–Sat 1.30–3.30, 8–11 🖐 L €52,
D €70, Wine €16

RESTAURANTE EL PILÓN

http://restepilon.restaurantesok.com
This tiny restaurant specializes in
local seafood platters, but is best
known for its range of tasty tapas.
✉ Carrer C'an Cifré 4, 07012 Palma de
Mallorca ☎ 971 71 75 90 🕐 Mon–Sat
1–4, 6–12 🖐 L €16, D €28, Wine €10

SÓLLER

LUNA 36

www.luna36.net
A 19th-century chocolate factory
in the heart of the attractive little
town of Sóller has been handsomely
converted to house this bright,
light-filled café and restaurant. The
chef, a former pupil of Basque chef
Martin Berasategui (who has three
Michelin stars), prepares delicious
Mediterranean cuisine that excels.
The home-made bread is heavenly,
and perfect for dipping into local olive
oil. The lunch menu is usually light
and simple—soups, salads, pasta
dishes and tapas. In the evenings, a
wider variety of exquisite fresh fish,
meat and shellfish dishes can be
enjoyed on the candlelit terrace.
✉ Carrer de la Luna 36, Sóller ☎ 971 63
47 39 🕐 Mon–Sat 12–3, 7–10 🖐 L €24,
D €40, Wine €12

Opposite Bacchus restaurant, Read's Hotel

MENORCA

FORNELLS

ES PLA

The menu here includes traditional
dishes of outstanding quality, such as
seafood stew, paella and the house
special, *caldereta de langosta* (spiny
lobster stew). The walls are decorated
with photographs of famous people
who have dined here. The several set
meals include a gourmet menu all
year. Parking is nearby.
✉ Pasaje des Pla, 07748 Fornells ☎ 971
37 66 55 🕐 Jun–Aug daily 1–4.30, 7–11;
Sep–May 1–4, 7–10.30. Closed 18 Jan–18
Feb 🖐 L €35, D €55, Wine €16

ES MERCADAL

ES MOLÍ D'ES RACÓ

www.restaurantemolidesraco.com
This charming old restored mill
serves well-cooked and reasonably
priced traditional Menorcan cuisine.
The menu has a selection of fish,
seafood and meats.
✉ C/Major, 53 Carretera General
Mahón–Ciutadella, 07740 Es Mercadal
☎ 971 37 52 75 🕐 Daily 1–4, 7–11.
Closed 15 Jan–15 Feb 🖐 L €26, D €38,
Wine €10

SANT LLUÍS

LA CARABA

http://restaurantelacaraba.com
Reserve early for a table here, one
of the most celebrated restaurants
on Menorca. Set in an attractive
Menorquin-style house, with a
beautiful garden terrace and porch,
it provides a deeply romantic setting
for sophisticated regional cuisine.
As well as the fresh fish dishes,
often served simply grilled to best
appreciate the flavour, you can try
typical *coca* (a kind of local flatbread)
with marinated sardines and roasted
peppers, or more adventurous
dishes such as the quail with sepia
'meatballs' and black olive purée,
or the *brocheta* of langoustines (a
specialty). The wine list is short but
chosen to complement the cuisine.
✉ Carrer S'Uestra 78, 07710 Sant Lluís
☎ 971 15 06 82 🕐 Mid-May to mid-Oct
daily 8–11 🖐 D €45, Wine €16

EIVISSA (IBIZA)

CALA VADELLA

MARÍA LUISA

The María Luisa, one of the few
restaurants on the island open
through the winter, is very popular,
particularly for its paellas. There is
also a good choice of fresh fish,
meats and seafood. Reserve during
weekends and on public holidays.
✉ Carrer San José, 07830 Cala Vadella
☎ 971 80 80 12 🕐 Dec–Oct Tue–Sun
12–12 🖐 L €28, D €45, Wine €14

SAN JORGE

ES CAVALLET CHIRINGUITO

http://el-chiringuito.ibiza4all.es
This fashionable, family-run
restaurant started out more than
two decades ago as a *chiringuito*
(beach bar). The huge and attractively
furnished terrace overlooks the
glorious sands of Es Cavallet. It is
known for its perfectly prepared fresh
fish, rice dishes, abundant salads and
delicious desserts. Expect a long wait
during peak hours in the high season.
✉ Playa Es Cavallet ☎ 971 39 53
55 🕐 Daily 12pm–midnight. Closed
Nov–Easter 🖐 L €28, D €42, Wine €14

SANT ANTONI DE PORTMANY

CAN PUJOL

At Can Pujol you can expect simply
cooked fresh fish. In summer, the
terrace extends on to the beach.
✉ Carretera Vieja Port des Torrent s/n,
07820 Sant Antoni de Portmany ☎ 971 34
14 07 🕐 Thu–Tue 1–4, 7.30–11.30. Closed
Dec 🖐 L €38, D €50, Wine €12

SA CAPELLA

This elegant restaurant serves fresh
fish, superb meat dishes and home-
made desserts. Reserve a table in
advance during high season.
✉ Carretera San Antoni a Santa Agnés
Km 0.6, 07820 Sant Antoni de Portmany
☎ 971 34 00 57 🕐 Jun–Aug daily
8.30pm–12.30am; Apr, May, Sep, Oct daily
8pm–midnight 🖐 D €45, Wine €14

PRICES AND SYMBOLS

The prices are for a double room for one night including breakfast, unless otherwise stated. All the hotels listed accept credit cards unless otherwise stated. Note that rates can vary widely throughout the year.

For a key to the symbols, ▷ 2.

MALLORCA

DEIÀ

LA RESIDENCIA

www.hotel-laresidencia.com

Prepare to be pampered at this 16th-century stone mansion. The hotel's restaurant, El Olivo, is one of the best in the area. There are tennis courts, swimming pools and a beauty salon. The spa is considered one of the best in Europe. The hotel provides a bus to take you to a private beach. A minimum five-night stay is required between May and October; children under 10 are welcome only between 1 July and 15 August, at the end of October and over Christmas. Visit the website for their package range.

✉ Carrer Son Canals, 07179 Deià
☎ 971 63 90 11 💳 €375–€790 (classic and superior); €780–€1,450 (suites, some with private plunge pool) ⓘ 64 ⬛ 🏊 Outdoor and indoor 🛁

SA PEDRISSA

www.sapedrissa.com

A 17th-century farmhouse with elegant rooms and suites, this *casa rural* provides a relaxing retreat, surrounded by olive groves. Meals feature home-grown olive oil and other fresh produce. Set in the hills behind Deià, some of the rooms boast sea views. There's a delightful restaurant, with a summer terrace, and a swimming pool.

✉ Carretera Valldemossa-Deià Km 64.5, 07179 Deià ☎ 971 63 91 11 💳 €135–€355 ⓘ 8 ⬛ 🏊

PALMA DE MALLORCA

BORN

www.hotelborn.com

Hotel Born is a 16th-century palace that has been converted into a charming hotel. It has a traditional Mallorcan-style patio and an elegant lobby. Rooms are simple and a little sparse, but have modern amenities. The bar serves only drinks, but there are many restaurants nearby.

✉ Carrer Sant Jaume 3, 07012 Palma de Mallorca ☎ 971 71 29 42 💳 €95–€145, excluding breakfast ⓘ 29 ⬛

DALT MURADA

www.hotelmurada.com

Chic and charming in equal measure, Dalt Murada is perfectly located in the oldest part of the city, near the cathedral. The 16th-century mansion still belongs to the aristocratic family who have taken pains to transform it into one of the city's most appealing small hotels. The rooms and suites are elegantly furnished with antiques, with bright curtains and crisp white bed linen adding a modern touch. Most of the bathrooms are huge, and some have Jacuzzis. For a special treat, go for the penthouse suite with private sitting room and roof terrace.

✉ Carrer Almudaina 6, 07001 Palma
☎ 971 42 53 00 💳 €150–€290 ⓘ 14 ⬛

GRAN MELIÁ VICTORIA

www.granmeliavictoria.solmelia.com

The Gran Meliá chain is well known for offering quality service. This branch is by the sea, near the heart of Palma. The rooms are plush, though not large, and the bathrooms are new and clean. The restaurant serves food all day. The snack bars are best for drinks and light fare.

✉ Avinguda Joan Miró 21, 07014 Palma de Mallorca ☎ 971 73 25 42 💳 €375–€790 🛏 171 (72 on three floors for non smokers) 🏊 🌊 Outdoor and indoor 🍽

POLLENÇA
DES BRULL

www.desbrull.com

This small, chic boutique hotel is housed in an old 18th-century townhouse, which has been prettily renovated. Contemporary furnishings and amenities are complemented by the wooden beams and other original details. Located in the heart of historic Pollença, in a prime spot in front of the municipal museum, Des Brull makes a great base for exploring the northeast corner of the island. Prices, particularly out of season, are very reasonable.

✉ Carrer Marqués Desbrull 7, 07460 Pollença ☎ 971 53 50 55 💳 €85–€110 🛏 6 🏊

PORT DE SOLLER
MIRAMAR

www.hotelmiramarsoller.com

This small hotel is clean, friendly and close to the sea. Most of the double rooms have tile floors, two twin beds and a balcony. Below is a bar and restaurant. The Tren de Soller, a tram connecting Soller with Port de Soller, passes regularly.

✉ Carrer Marina 12, 07118 Port de Soller ☎ 971 63 13 50 🕐 Closed Dec–15 Jan 💳 €65–€70 (apartments also available €95–€140) 🛏 32

SANTA MARIA DEL CAMÍ
READ'S HOTEL AND RESTAURANT

www.readshotel.com

For sheer comfort, few hotels can compare with Read's, set in a glorious, antique-filled country house just a 20-minute drive from Palma. It's won countless plaudits for its extraordinary attention to detail and superb customer service. The rooms all come with extra-large beds, for example, and the bathrooms are filled with Molton Brown goodies. The celebrated restaurant, Bacchus, under British chef Marc Fosh, is one of the finest on the island (and has been awarded a Michelin star). There is also a more affordable brasserie. A spa is available for special pampering. No children under 14 are allowed in the hotel.

✉ Carretera Santa Maria del Camí-Alaró, 07320 Santa Maria del Camí ☎ 971 14 02 61 💳 €250–€425 🛏 23 🏊 🌊 🍽

VALLDEMOSSA
ES PETIT HOTEL

www.espetithotel-valldemossa.com

Valldemossa, where George Sand and Chopin famously spent a winter at the monastery, is one of Mallorca's prettiest villages. This modest country hotel is located in an old village townhouse, set in its own little gardens, and offers magnificent views of the surrounding hills from the terrace. The dramatic coves and cliffs of western Mallorca are just 6km (4 miles) away, and it's a good base for hiking in the Sierra Tramontana. Each room is simply decorated in pale tones of blue, cream and beige, and some have their own private terrace. There's a good little restaurant, serving reasonably priced local cuisine.

✉ Carrer Uetam 1, 07170 Valldemossa ☎ 971 61 24 79 💳 €110–€185 🛏 8 🏊

MENORCA

ES CASTELL
HOTEL DEL ALMIRANTE

www.hoteldelalmirante.com

This simple yet well kept one-star hotel has retained the character of a bygone era, reflected in its original Georgian (18th-century) facade and tasteful interior furnished with antiques. Some guest rooms in another building overlooking the swimming pool have less charm. Reserve well in advance. There is a tennis court.

✉ Carretera de Mahón Es Castell, 07720 Es Castell ☎ 971 36 27 00 🕐 Closed Nov–Apr 💳 €75–€115 🛏 39 🏊 In common areas; fans in rooms 🌊 Outdoor 🚗 From the airport head towards Mahón and follow signs to Es Castell. Turn right at the sixth roundabout; the hotel is on the left

CIUTADELLA
MORVEDRA NOU

www.morvedranou.es

The charmingly old fashioned, Morvedra Nou occupies a traditional, whitewashed 17th-century *finca*, 8km (5 miles) from Ciutadella. It is relaxed and tranquil, set in extensive gardens dotted with palm trees, and filled with bright pink bougainvillea. The rooms are spacious and classically furnished; all have private terraces. There is a large swimming pool in the gardens and a good restaurant serving local specialties. Activities, such as sailing or horse-riding, can be arranged and the nearest beaches are 7km (4 miles) away. Top prices listed below are for peak season (mid-July to the end of August).

✉ Camí Sant Joan de Missa 7, 07760 Ciutadella ☎ 971 35 95 21 💳 €115–€230 🛏 16 🏊 🌊

FORNELLS
HOSTAL FORNELLS

www.hostalfornells.com

Close to the waterfront in Fornells, this *hostal* has simply yet gracefully decorated bedrooms. All rooms have private bathrooms, telephone, TV and safe. Facilities include a bar and café.

✉ Major 17, 07748 Fornells ☎ 971 37 66 76 🕐 Closed Nov–Apr 💳 €45–€115 🛏 17 🏊 🌊 Outdoor

MAÓ (MAHÓN)
CASA ALBERTÍ

www.casalaberti.com

In this quirky and original little

Opposite *The view from Es Petit Hotel is superb. This small country hotel in Valldemossa is evidence that there is far more to the Balearics than high-rise hotels*

hotel in a handsome 18th-century townhouse, there are just six rooms. Each room is whitewashed and furnished simply with an attractive mixture of antique and new furnishings, and all have private bathrooms. The rooms vary widely in size, which is reflected in the prices. There's a communal kitchen, overlooking a central patio with hammock, and at the top of the staircase is a huge roof terrace, offering dazzling views over the rooftops and out to sea. The highest prices listed here are for a standard double room for stays during the peak holiday season (mid-July to the of August).

✉ Carrer Isabel II 9, 07701 Maó ☎ 971 35 42 10 🕐 Closed Nov–Feb ✋ €105–€230 🛈 6

PORT MAHÓN
www.sethotels.com
This elegant four-star hotel is set right in the middle of Maó's port area. The bedrooms have private bathrooms, telephone, TV, minibar and safe. There are two restaurants, a piano bar and a cafeteria, as well as an outdoor pool.

✉ Fort de l'Eau 13, 07701 Maó ☎ 971 36 26 00 ✋ €175–€325 🛈 73 rooms, 9 suites 🌀 🏊 Outdoor

EIVISSA (IBIZA)

SAN MIGUEL DE BALANSAT
CA'S PLA
www.caspla-ibiza.com
Facilities at this hotel include a helipad, a bar, a spa with sauna, Jacuzzi and beauty treatments, and the convenience of car and boat rental. Horseback-riding, golf and scuba diving can be reserved through the hotel.

✉ 07800 San Miguel de Balansat ☎ 971 33 45 87 ✋ €135–€195 excluding breakfast (€14) 🛈 16 🌀 🏊 Outdoor 🛒 🚗 From the airport, follow signs to San Miguel; take the road to the port. After 14km (9 miles),

take the signposted track to the hotel, which is a farther 1km (0.5 mile) from this intersection

HACIENDA NA XAMENA
www.hotelhacienda-ibiza.com
The hotel has fantastic sea views. There are whirlpool baths in the suites. It serves fine cuisine and special features include beauty treatments. There is tennis and a spa.

✉ 07815 San Miguel de Balansat ☎ 971 33 45 00 🕐 15 Apr–Oct. Closed Nov–Apr ✋ €235–€445 (standard); €750–€1,775 (suites, some with private mini pool) excluding breakfast (€24) 🛈 70 🌀 🏊 Outdoor and indoor 🛒 🚗 From Ibiza Town head 22km (14 miles) northwest to reach San Miguel

SANTA AGNÈS DE CORONA
CAN PUJOLET
www.canpujolet.com
A country house and working farm on a clifftop overlooking Santa Inés, perhaps the loveliest village in Ibiza, this *agriturismo* is surrounded by olive groves and fruit orchards. Guests can dine on home-grown organic produce by prior arrangement with the friendly owners. Each of the rooms is traditionally decorated in pale soothing colours, and all have private terrace. There is also a pool in the gardens. Self-catering accommodation (an apartment and a bungalow) is also available.

✉ 07828 Santa Agnès de Corona ☎ 971 80 51 70 ✋ €165–€235 🛈 10 🌀 🏊

SANTA EULÀRIA DES RIU
LES TERRASSES
www.lesterrasses.com
One of the first of Ibiza's famously bohemian chic *finca* hotels, this one opened in 1987 and remains enduringly popular. The delightful French owner, Françoise, has created a magical retreat, with whitewashed rooms filled with bold artworks and quirky details. The *finca* is arranged higgledy-piggledy in different layers and surrounded by gardens and groves of citrus trees. There are a couple of small outdoor pools for lounging, and a tennis court. Françoise, a superb cook, also

prepares evening meals, which are generally enjoyed family-style at a single, shared table.

✉ Carretera Santa Eulària ☎ 971 33 26 43 🕐 Closed Dec–Mar ✋ €175–€345 🛈 10

TALAMANCA
ROCAMAR
www.rocamaribiza.com
The Rocamar hotel is right by the sandy beach of Talamanca. Rooms have a telephone, satellite TV, safe, minibar, hairdryer and double-glazed windows. Breakfast is served on a terrace overlooking the harbour. A golf course, a diving school and watersports are all nearby. Transportation to Ibiza Town is by ferry, which departs every 15 minutes and stops close to the hotel.

✉ S'Illa Plan s/n, 07800 Talamanca ☎ 971 31 79 22 🕐 Closed Dec ✋ €125–€190 🛈 18 🌀

FORMENTERA

SANT FRANCESC DE FORMENTERA
HOTEL CAP DE BARBARIA
www.capdebarbaria.com
Formentera is the tiniest Balearic island, but has become increasingly fashionable with celebrities looking to get away from it all in recent years. This is the plushest accommodation option on the island, a small and exquisitely renovated traditional stone house in the quietest and most remote corner of Formentera. There are just a handful of luxurious rooms, with contemporary furnishings and modern art providing a chic counterpoint to the original stone and wood. All have lovely views over the surrounding olive groves and vines, and it's a short walk to the superb beaches. In the evenings you can dine on French cuisine in the pretty gardens, and drink in the peace and tranquillity. The hotel was closed for renovation at the time of writing; check the website for opening information.

✉ Carretera de Cap de Barbaria Km 5.8, 07860 Sant Francesc de Formentera ☎ 617 46 06 29 ✋ €475 🛈 6 🌀 🏊 Outdoor

PRACTICALITIES

Practicalities gives you all the important practical information you will need during your visit from money matters to emergency phone numbers.

WEATHER

CLIMATE AND WHEN TO GO

Due to its size and geography, Spain has a very varied climate. Although generally thought of as a hot, dry country (despite the famous rain that falls mainly on the plain), the weather in Spain can change dramatically according to the season and the region you are in at the time.

During the summer months the temperature in the Mediterranean, northern and central regions can be scorching, with up to eight hours of sunshine a day.

There is a huge regional variation in rainfall, which is highest in Galicia and the Cantabrian mountains, and in the central areas the winters can be quite cold, with bitter winds coming in off the sierras.

Cool, refreshing sea breezes moderate the summer heat in the north, while in the south there is sometimes a hot, dry wind blowing in from Africa.

Most people agree that the Spanish climate is at its best in late spring or early autumn when there is plenty of sunshine but the heat is tempered by a delightful warm breeze.

Spring is the season to visit the Balearic Islands and the central regions of Castile, Andalucía and the Mediterranean coast, whereas early autumn is ideal for almost everywhere in the country, with a high percentage of sunny days and blue skies.

Committed sun-lovers flock to Spain from all over the world during high summer (July and August). Although the bars, shops and beaches of the Mediterranean coast are generally packed to bursting point with holidaymakers, the almost guaranteed all-day sunshine and warm, balmy evenings more than compensate.

High summer is also the optimum time to visit the cooler northern Atlantic coast and the mountainous regions.

Spain is an excellent choice if you are looking for winter sunshine in Europe. Head for the southern and eastern coastal resorts, particularly Almería, which holds the winter sunshine record. This is also the best time to visit the much maligned Costa del Sol; it feels like a different place without the crowds. The beautiful mountainous regions are ideal for winter sports.

WEATHER REPORTS

» For information in English on the current weather picture, check the website of your local news network station, such as the BBC (www.bbc.co.uk) or CNN (www.cnn.com), or a specialist website such as www.weather.com, www.idealspain.com or www.onlineweather.com.

» English-language newspapers such as *Daily Spain* (www.dailyspain.com) and *Costa Blanca News* (www.costablanca-news.com) have good weather coverage.

TIME ZONES

Spain is on CET (Central European Time), 1 hour ahead of GMT (Greenwich Mean Time). Daylight Saving Time, when the clocks move forward 1 hour, runs from the morning of the last Sunday in March to the last Sunday in October; consequently Spain is 2 hours ahead of GMT. Compared with Spain, other countries are generally as follows:

Australia: 7–9 hours ahead
Canada: 4.5–9 hours behind
New Zealand: 11 hours ahead
UK and Republic of Ireland: 1 hour behind
US: 6–9 hours behind

DOCUMENTS

PASSPORTS AND VISAS

» All visitors to Spain must carry a valid passport or, in the case of EU nationals (except those from Denmark, Ireland and the UK), a national ID card.

» Once in Spain, you are required by law to carry one of these documents with you at all times.

» EU visitors do not require a visa for entry into Spain.

» Visitors from the US and Canada require a visa for stays exceeding 90 days.

» Always check with the consulate about visa requirements and entry regulations as they are liable to change, often at short notice. For addresses of consulates and embassies in Madrid, ▷ 422.

» See also Loss of passport, ▷ 432.

SPANISH EMBASSIES/CONSULATES ABROAD

Australia and New Zealand	15 Arkana Street, Yarralumla, Canberra, ACT 2600 (tel +61 (0)6-273 3555)
Canada	74 Stanley Avenue, Ottawa, ON K1M 1P4 (tel +1 613/747-2252)
Republic of Ireland	17a Merlyn Park, Ballsbridge, Dublin 4 (tel +353 (0)1 269 1640, 269 2507)
UK	20 Draycott Place, London SW3 2RZ (tel +44 (0)20 7589 8989; visa information 0906 550 8970);
	Suite 1a, Brook House, 70 Spring Gardens, Manchester, M2 2BQ (tel +44 (0)161 236 1262);
	63 North Castle Street, Edinburgh, EH2 3LJ (tel +44 (0)131 220 1843)
USA	30th floor, 150 East 58th Street, New York, NY 10155 (tel +1 212/355-4080);
	2375 Pennsylvania Avenue N.W., Washington, DC 20037 (tel +1 202/728-2340);
	Suite 860, 5055 Wilshire Boulevard, Los Angeles, CA 90036 (tel +1 323/938-0158);
	Suite 1500, 180 North Michigan Avenue, Chicago, IL 60601 (tel +1 312/782-4588/4589)

TRAVEL INSURANCE

» It is important to make sure you have adequate travel insurance including repatriation, baggage and money loss.
» Keep all receipts for expenses.
» Report losses or theft to the police.
» Obtain a signed and date-stamped copy of your formal complaint statement *(denuncia)* from a police station *(comisaría)* to help if you make any insurance claims.

HEALTH INSURANCE

» British visitors are advised to get a European Health Insurance Card (EHIC) (see If You Need Treatment, ▷ 426) before leaving the UK. This entitles UK citizens—like any other EU citizens—to reciprocal health care throughout their stay in Spain.
» Without this card, EU citizens will be charged at private rates, which can be very expensive. Your insurance company may not refund costs you could have saved with an EHIC.
» Private insurance is strongly recommended, particularly if you are visiting from outside the EU.

CUSTOMS

Goods you buy in the EU

The amounts shown below are in line with other EU countries. There is no limit on the amount of foreign currency or euros that you can bring into Spain. Tax-paid goods for personal use (such as video cameras) can be brought in from other EU countries without customs charges being incurred. Guidance levels for tax-paid goods bought in the EU are as follows:
» 800 cigarettes or
» 400 cigarillos or
» 200 cigars or
» 1kg of smoking tobacco
» 10 litres of spirits or
» 20 litres of fortified wine (such as port or sherry) or
» 90 litres of wine (of which only 60 litres can be sparkling wine) or
» 110 litres of beer

MADRID
TEMPERATURE

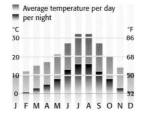

RAINFALL

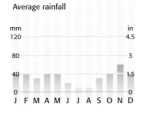

SEVILLA
TEMPERATURE

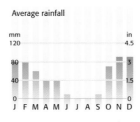

RAINFALL

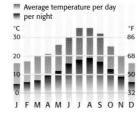

Visiting Spain from outside the EU

You are entitled to the allowances shown below only if you travel with the goods and do not plan to sell them. Check out www.hmce.gov.uk
» 200 cigarettes or
» 100 cigarillos or

BARCELONA
TEMPERATURE

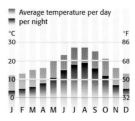

RAINFALL

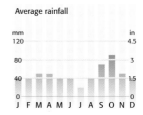

BILBAO
TEMPERATURE

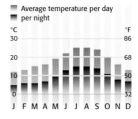

RAINFALL

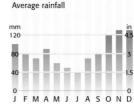

» 50 cigars or
» 250g of smoking tobacco
» 1 litre of spirits or strong liqueurs
» 2 litres of still table wine
» 2 litres of fortified wine, sparkling wine or other liqueurs
» 50cc of perfume
» 250cc/ml of eau de toilette

MONEY

Spain is one of 15 countries in the EU that have adopted the euro as their official currency. Euro notes and coins were introduced in 2002, replacing Spain's former currency, the peseta.

BEFORE YOU GO

It is advisable to use a combination of cash, traveller's cheques and credit cards rather than relying on any one means of payment during your trip. Check with your credit card company that you can withdraw cash from cashpoints (ATMs) in Spain. You should also check what fee will be charged for this, and what number to use if your card is stolen (see panel). Traveller's cheques are a safer way of carrying money as you are insured if they are stolen. Remember to keep a separate note of their numbers.

CREDIT CARDS

All the leading credit cards are recognized in Spain. Should yours get lost or stolen, contact details (in Spain) are:

American Express	tel 902 375 637 (cards)
American Express	tel 900 994 426 (traveller's cheques)
Diners Club	tel 901 10 10 11
MasterCard	tel 900 971 231
Visa	tel 900 991 124

THE EURO

Since 2002 Spain's currency has been the euro (€), along with 11 other European countries: Austria, Belgium, Finland, France, Germany, Greece, Italy, Luxembourg, The Netherlands, Portugal and the Republic of Ireland. Cyprus, Malta and Slovenia later joined the euro.

The euro is also the currency of the principality of Andorra, which is not part of the European Union.

Euro coins have one side dedicated to their country of origin; euro notes are identical across the euro zone.

EXCHANGE RATES

The exchange rate per euro for visitors from the UK, USA and Canada is subject to daily fluctuation, but at the time of printing was approximately £0.85, US$1.23 and C$1.30.

BANKS

There is no shortage of banks (bancos) across Spain. Most have a foreign exchange desk. Look for the cambio or exchange signs.

ATMS

These are widespread throughout Spain. If your card has the Maestro or Cirrus facilities you will be able to pay for goods and services (remember you must show ID) and withdraw cash from machines all over the country, provided you have a four-digit PIN composed of numbers only. Contact your bank in advance if you need to change your PIN.

POST OFFICES

Post offices (correos) are normally located in the middle of town. Poste restante letters can be sent to any Spanish post office. If you use this service, make sure the surname of the recipient is in capitals and underlined, and address the letter to Lista de Correos, followed by the postal code and name of the town and the province. You will need ID to collect it.

CHANGING MONEY

Banks and bureaux de change charge what seems like a hefty commission, but the rates are better than those at airports, hotels and smaller money exchange outlets. It is sensible to make sure you have at least some euros on you before leaving the airport. You will find 24-hour exchange facilities at the bigger train stations in Madrid and Barcelona.

WIRING MONEY

In an emergency money can be wired from your home country, but this can be very expensive and time-consuming. You can send and receive money via agents such as Western Union (www.westernunion.com) or MoneyGram (www.moneygram.com).

TAX REFUNDS

VAT, or sales tax (known as IVA in Spain), of 7 per cent, is

PRACTICALITIES | ESSENTIAL INFORMATION

10 EVERYDAY ITEMS AND HOW MUCH THEY COST

Sandwich	€3
Bottle of water	€1.25–€1.75
Cup of tea or coffee	€1.50–€2
Glass of wine	€2–€3
Glass of beer	€2
Daily newspaper	€1.30
Roll of camera film	€4.75
20 cigarettes	€4.25
Ice cream	€2.50
Litre of petrol	€1.45

added to services such as hotel accommodation and meals in restaurants. This is non-refundable. For all other goods and services 16 per cent is added.

Visitors to Spain who are not EU-residents are entitled to a reimbursement of the 16 per cent tax paid on purchases to the value of more than €90.15 spent in the same store. The store must provide an invoice itemizing all goods, the price paid for them, and the tax charged, and the full address of both the vendor and purchaser. The goods must then be brought out of the EU within three months. The goods and invoice(s) should be taken to the booth provided at Spanish customs on your departure from Spain, prior to checking in your baggage, unless you are moving on to another EU country. If this is the case, tax claims should be processed on departure from your final destination in the EU.

Alternatively, tax can be reclaimed through Global Refund Tax Free Shopping, a service offered by major retailers worldwide. For information see www.globalrefund.com

DISCOUNTS

Seniors can get reductions on some museum entry charges on production of an identity document. An International Student Identity Card (ISIC) may help students obtain reduced entry to many museums and sites as well as other discounts.

TIPPING GUIDE

Although locals rarely tip, tipping is usually expected from foreigners. It is not, however, obligatory.

Restaurants (service not included)	5–10%
Bar service	Change
Tour guides	Optional
Hairdressers	5%
Taxis	3–5%
Chambermaids	€6
Porters	€6

HEALTH

Spain's national health service works alongside the private sector, and its hospitals are generally of a high standard. Visitors from EU countries are entitled to free medical treatment (▷ below).

BEFORE YOU GO

» If you are likely to need a repeat prescription during the time you are away, apply for this well before you travel and ask your doctor to give you a note of any medication you are on in case you lose it.

» Visiting the dentist for a check-up and having an eye test if one is due are also sensible precautions.

» No inoculations are required for visiting Spain, although it is a good idea to check when you were last inoculated against tetanus and, if more than 10 years ago, have a booster before you travel.

» If you are planning a long stay in Spain it makes sense to have a full health check before you travel.

WHAT TO TAKE WITH YOU

» Mosquitoes are plentiful in Spain, so stock up on insect repellent. Citronella candles can repel insects while you eat alfresco during the evening. When in coastal areas, beware of sandflies, which can carry a number of parasitic diseases.

» It is a good idea to carry a first aid box in your car or as part of your hand luggage, particularly when you are accompanied by children. This could include:
After-sun cream to soothe sunburned skin
Antihistamine cream for insect stings or bites
Antiseptic cream or spray
Bandages
Calamine lotion
Cotton wool
Cough mixture
Eye drops
Motion-sickness remedies such as travel bands
Painkillers such as paracetamol or Tylenol
Plasters (Band-Aids)
Rehydration tablets
Wet wipes

IF YOU NEED TREATMENT

The quality of health care in Spain is generally very good, especially in the larger towns and cities.

» Spain has a standard agreement with other EU countries entitling EU citizens to a certain amount of free reciprocal health care, including hospital treatment. To take advantage of this you must complete all the necessary paperwork well before you travel. In the UK, ask for the European Health Insurance Card (EHIC) from the Department of Health or at main post offices. It is still necessary to take out adequate health insurance to cover the costs of emergency treatment, however. You should then be able to use this insurance to claim back the cost of any drugs prescribed. EHIC does not cover any private treatment.

» US visitors may find that their existing health policy stays effective when they travel abroad, but it is very important to check.

EMERGENCY

» In the event of an emergency, go to the casualty department (urgencias) of a major hospital.

» For minor ailments, visit a farmacia (pharmacy) (▷ Pharmacies below).

FINDING A DOCTOR

A doctor (médico) can be found by asking at the local pharmacy or at your hotel.

FINDING A HOSPITAL

Public hospitals are listed in the phone book under Hospital.

PHARMACIES

» Pharmacies usually have a flashing green or red cross displayed outside and can be found in almost every town and village in Spain. They normally offer excellent over-the-counter advice, often in English.

» For minor ailments, it is usually worth consulting a pharmacist before seeing a doctor.

» Many drugs that are prescription-only in other countries are available without one in Spain.

» Ask your doctor to provide you with the chemical name of a prescription drug before you travel, as it may be marketed under another name in Spain.

» A rota system operates so there is always one pharmacy open 24 hours a day; check the pharmacy window for details.

WATER

It is generally safe to drink the tap water in Spain (unless it says no

potable), although it may have a strong taste of chlorine. Unfamiliar water can sometimes cause stomach upsets. Mineral water *(agua mineral)* is inexpensive and widely available. It is sold *sin gas* (still) or *con gas* (carbonated).

SUMMER HAZARDS

Spain is hot and sunny in summer and humidity is high.

» Always protect against sunburn by dressing suitably in loose clothing and covering your head.

» Apply high-factor sunscreen and drink about 2 litres (4 pints) of water a day to avoid dehydration.

» During the hottest part of the day few locals are out and about.

» The most sensible thing is to have a siesta or at least stay in the shade between noon and 2pm.

DENTAL TREATMENT

» Dental treatment is expensive in Spain, so it makes sense to have a dental check-up before you depart.

» Check your medical insurance before you go to see if it covers emergency dental treatment. (Note that dental treatment is not covered by reciprocal healthcare agreements within the EU.)

OPTICIANS

It is a good idea to pack a spare pair of glasses or contact lenses and your prescription in case you lose or break them. Opticians can be found in the yellow pages *(páginas amarillas)* under *Ópticas,* or ask at the nearest pharmacy.

Two of the biggest chains in Spain are Federopticos (www.federopticos. com) and Multiopticas (tel 900 34 35 36; www.multiopticas.es). Both websites are Spanish only.

COMMON AILMENT

The most common ailment among visitors is diarrhoea, caught from contaminated food or water. To avoid this, wash fresh fruit and vegetables in clean water before eating them and don't eat food that you suspect may have been left uncovered for some time.

HEALTHY FLYING

» Visitors to Spain from as far as the USA, Australia or New Zealand may be concerned about the effect of long-haul flights on their health. The most widely publicized concern is deep vein thrombosis, or DVT. Misleadingly called 'economy class syndrome', DVT is the forming of a blood clot in the body's deep veins, particularly in the legs. The clot can move around the bloodstream and could be fatal.

» Those most at risk include the elderly, pregnant women and those using the contraceptive pill, smokers and the overweight. If you are at increased risk of DVT see your doctor before departing. Flying increases the likelihood of DVT because passengers are often seated in a cramped position for long periods of time and may become dehydrated.

To minimize risk:

drink water (not alcohol)

don't stay immobile for hours at a time

stretch and exercise your legs periodically

do wear elastic flight socks, which support veins and reduce the chances of a clot forming.

EXERCISES

Other health hazards for flyers are airborne diseases and bugs spread by the plane's air-conditioning system. These are largely unavoidable, but if you have a serious medical condition seek advice from a doctor before flying.

Ankle rotations	Calf stretches	Knee lifts
Lift feet off the floor. Draw a circle with the toes, moving one foot clockwise and the other counterclockwise	Start with heel on the floor and point foot upward as high as you can. Then lift heels high, keeping balls of feet on the floor	Lift leg with knee bent while contracting your thigh muscle. Then straighten leg, pressing foot flat to the floor

SUNBURN INDEX

SKIN TYPE

Index	Fair, burns	Fair, tans	Brown skin	Black skin
1/2	Low	Low	Low	Low
3/4	Medium	Low	Low	Low
5	High	Medium	Low	Low
6	Very high	Medium	Medium	Low
7	Very high	High	Medium	Medium
8	Very high	High	Medium	Medium
9	Very high	High	Medium	Medium
10	Very high	High	High	Medium

Low risk: the sun is not likely to harm you.

Medium risk: do not stay in direct sunlight for more than 1–2 hours.

High risk: you could burn in 30–60 minutes. Avoid direct sunlight, cover up and use sunscreen of SPF 15+.

Very high risk: you could burn in 20–30 minutes. Avoid direct sunlight, cover up and use sunscreen of SPF 15+.

ALTERNATIVE MEDICINE

Most kinds of alternative medicine, including homeopathy and reflexology, are available in Spain. There are *herbolarios* (part health shop/part herbalist) in most towns. Fundación Europea de Medicinas Alternativas based at Leganitos 35, Madrid (tel 91 532 44 70; www.femalt.com) is a network of alternative practitioners.

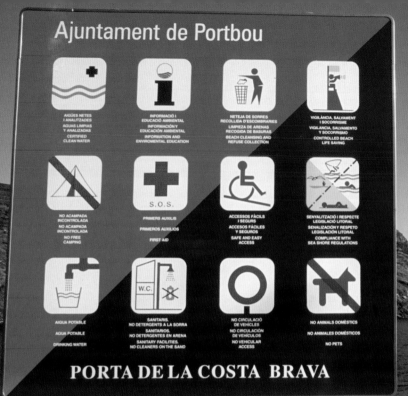

Ajuntament de Portbou

AIGÜES NETES I ANALITZADES / AGUAS LIMPIAS Y ANALIZADAS / CERTIFIED CLEAN WATER	INFORMACIÓ I EDUCACIÓ AMBIENTAL / INFORMACIÓN Y EDUCACIÓN AMBIENTAL / INFORMATION AND ENVIROMENTAL EDUCATION	NETEJA DE SORRES RECOLLIDA D'ESCOMBRARIES / LIMPIEZA DE ARENAS RECOGIDA DE BASURAS / BEACH CLEANSING AND REFUSE COLLECTION	VIGILÀNCIA, SALVAMENT I SOCORRISME / VIGILANCIA, SALVAMENTO Y SOCORRISMO / CONTROLLED BEACH LIFE SAVING
NO ACAMPADA INCONTROLADA / NO ACAMPADA INCONTROLADA / NO FREE CAMPING	S.O.S. PRIMERS AUXILIS / PRIMEROS AUXILIOS / FIRST AID	ACCESSOS FÀCILS I SEGURS / ACCESOS FÁCILES Y SEGUROS / SAFE AND EASY ACCESS	SENYALITZACIÓ I RESPECTE LEGISLACIÓ LITORAL / SENALIZACIÓN Y RESPETO LEGISLACIÓN LITORAL / COMPLIANCE WITH SEA SHORE REGULATIONS
AIGUA POTABLE / AGUA POTABLE / DRINKING WATER	SANITARIS. NO DETERGENTS A LA SORRA / SANITARIOS, NO DETERGENTES EN ARENA / SANITARY FACILITIES. NO CLEANERS ON THE SAND	NO CIRCULACIÓ DE VEHICLES / NO CIRCULACIÓN DE VEHICULOS / NO VEHICULAR ACCESS	NO ANIMALS DOMÈSTICS / NO ANIMALES DOMÉSTICOS / NO PETS

PORTA DE LA COSTA BRAVA

BASICS

ELECTRICITY

» The power supply in Spain is 220 and 225 volts AC.
» Plugs have two round pins, so it is a good idea to bring an adaptor with you, although these are available at hardware stores.
» Visitors from the US should also bring a transformer; these are hard to find in Spain, except in big cities.

LAUNDRY

» The major cities have a scattering of self-service laundromats but these are few and far between.
» You can leave your clothes to be cleaned by staff at a *lavandería*, but this will be costly, though probably not as expensive as having them cleaned at your hotel.

MEASUREMENTS

Spain uses the metric system. Distances are measured in metres and kilometres, fuel is sold by the litre and food is weighed in grams and kilograms.

PUBLIC TOILETS

» Public toilets are variously known as *aseos, baños, sanitarios* or *servicios*, and can be scarce.
» The best lavatories are in large department stores, museums, galleries and places of interest. It is also acceptable to use the facilities in bars and restaurants, though it is polite to buy something before doing so.

SMOKING

Bars and restaurants over 100sq m

(1,076sq ft) in size are now required by law to provide a non-smoking section. In practice, this often means diners are seated side-by-side with nothing more than a velvet rope separating them. Smaller establishments were allowed to choose whether to become smoking or non-smoking, but most voted to remain the former.

LOCAL WAYS

It's a good idea to follow the Spanish custom of having a siesta at lunchtime. All the shops are shut and everything grinds to a halt for a couple of hours at the hottest time of day, particularly in the south of the country. This extends the evening and pushes dinner time to past 9pm; it might be difficult to get an evening neal before that time in some areas.

The informality of the bars and restaurants is not always extended to other places, however. When visiting cathedrals, churches and other religious places of interest you should dress modestly and show respect, especially in the more remote regions where the locals, particularly the older generation, can be less tolerant of visitors.

CHILDREN

Although not generally known for their overt friendliness to strangers, the Spaniards adore children, so if you are touring as a family you are bound to attract some friendly attention in bars, shops and restaurants. Don't be afraid that your children will be unwelcome when you sample the nightlife: the Spanish routinely take their children with them when they go out at night and the whole family eats, talks and stays up late together.

» Children generally receive a warm welcome everywhere in Spain.

» Local tourist boards supply lists of theme parks and other child-friendly attractions, and family rooms, equipped with three or four beds, are quite common in hotels.

CONVERSION CHART

From	To	Multiply by
Inches	Centimetres	2.54
Centimetres	Inches	0.3937
Feet	Metres	0.3048
Metres	Feet	3.2810
Yards	Metres	0.9144
Metres	Yards	1.0940
Miles	Kilometres	1.6090
Kilometres	Miles	0.6214
Acres	Hectares	0.4047
Hectares	Acres	2.4710
Gallons	Litres	4.5460
Litres	Gallons	0.2200
Ounces	Grams	28.35
Grams	Ounces	0.0353
Pounds	Grams	453.6
Grams	Pounds	0.0022
Pounds	Kilograms	0.4536
Kilograms	Pounds	2.205
Tons	Tonnes	1.0160
Tonnes	Tons	0.9842

» Baby supplies and food are available everywhere and children are welcomed in restaurants, where their dietary needs are met.

» Children under four years old travel free on RENFE (Spanish national rail) trains and there is a discount of between 20 and 40 per cent (depending on the type of train) for children aged four to twelve.

VISITORS WITH DISABILITIES

» Spain's facilities for visitors with disabilities are not extensive; however, the situation is improving slowly. Most of the major hotels in the main cities and tourist areas have wheelchair access, but finding properly adapted lavatories and accessible public transportation can still be a problem. In general, the newer the building, the more likely it is to have the benefit of ramps and wide doorways.

» The organization for the blind, ONCE, Calle Prado 24, 28014 Madrid (tel 915 89 46 00, www.once.es), runs a national lottery and is a strong pressure group for people with disabilities.

» COCEMFE, Calle Luis Cabrera 63, 28002 Madrid (tel 917 44 36 00) can provide useful information on accessibility.

» RENFE, Spain's national rail company (www.renfe.es), has wheelchairs available for transfers at mainline stations.

» ECOM, Avinguda Gran Via de les Corts Catalanes 562, 08011 Barcelona (tel 934 51 55 50; www.ecom.es) is the federation of private organizations for people with disabilities.

» The Red Cross (Cruz Roja Española), Calle Rafael Villa s/n, 28023 Madrid (tel 913 35 44 44).

» For information on the accessibility of flights within Spain, check with Iberia Airlines, Calle Velázquez 130, 28006 Madrid (tel 902 40 05 00).

For more information for visitors with disabilities, ▷ 62.

PLACES OF WORSHIP

The Roman Catholic Church still

plays a key role in the everyday life of the average Spanish family, despite the decline in church attendance in recent years. While it is no longer compulsory for boys to be named after saints and girls after manifestations of the Virgin Mary, the numerous religious festivals are still celebrated throughout the year.

Tourist offices can give information on local places of worship and service times. The following are places of worship in Madrid:

Anglican St. George's, Calle Núñez de Balboa 43 (tel 915 76 51 09).

Beth Yaacov Synagogue Calle Balmes 3 (tel 915 91 31 31).

Immanuel Baptist Church Calle Hernández de Tejada 4 (tel 914 07 43 47).

Islamic Centre and Mosque Calle Salvador de Madariaga 4 (tel 913 26 26 10).

Mormon Temple Calle del Templo 2 (tel 913 01 76 08).

North American Catholic Church Avenida Alfonso XIII 165 (tel 914 16 90 09).

COMMUNICATION

The advent of the internet and the ubiquitous mobile phone means that communicating with home from Spain can be easy and instant, provided you've done your homework first.

TELEPHONES

Spain's telephone system is fast and efficient. The state telephone company is Telefónica. International lines may be busy at times and you will get a recorded message rather than an operator; however, this rarely lasts long. The country code for Spain is 34.

To call Spain from the UK, prefix the area code and number with 00 34; from the USA prefix with 011 34. To call the UK from Spain, dial 00 44, then drop the first 0 from the area code; to call the USA from Spain prefix the area code and number with 001.

PUBLIC TELEPHONES

» Public telephone booths are blue and you don't have to walk far to find one. Look for the *Teléfono* signs.
» They operate with both coins and phone cards *(tarjeta telefónica* or *credifone)*, available from newsstands, post offices and tobacconists *(tabacos)*, and have instructions printed in English.
» Be ready to feed in 1 and 2 euro coins as well as 5, 10, 20 and 50 *céntimos* or phone cards of 6 and 12 euros, available from post offices.
» Telefónica also operates public phone stations *(locutorios)* where you pay the attendant at the end of your call.

AREA CODES WITHIN SPAIN

Spanish phone numbers all have nine digits starting with a 9; this includes the area code, which may be two or three digits. You must always dial the whole number (including the area code), even when making a local call.

Madrid	91
Barcelona	93
Bilbao, Vizcaya	94
Sevilla	95
Valencia	96
Santander	942
Navarra	948
Granada	958

USEFUL TELEPHONE NUMBERS

Operator 1009
Directory enquiries (national) 11818
Directory enquiries (international) 11825
International operator (Europe, Algeria, Libya, Morocco, Tunisia and Turkey) 1008
International operator (rest of the world) 1005

INTERNATIONAL DIALLING CODES

To call home from Spain dial the international access code (00) followed by the country code:

UK	44
USA/Canada	1
Republic of Ireland	353
Australia	61
New Zealand	64

CALL CHARGES FROM PUBLIC PAY PHONES (PER MINUTE)

	Peak rate	Reduced rate
Local	€0.06	€0.04
National	€0.10	€0.06
Western Europe	€0.18	€0.18
Eastern Europe	€0.40	€0.40
USA	€0.18	€0.18
North Africa	€0.40	€0.40
Australia	€0.96	€0.96
India	€0.96	€0.96
Japan	€0.96	€0.96
China	€0.96	€0.96

» Cheap rates operate between 10pm and 8am from Monday to Saturday, and all day on Sunday.
» The telephone in your hotel room is bound to be more expensive than using a pay phone.

MOBILE PHONES

» If your mobile phone SIM card is removable, it makes sense to replace it with a Spanish card on arrival. You will then be able to use the Spanish mobile system at local rates.
» Otherwise, check with your phone company before leaving home and make sure you are fully aware what the call charges will be. North American visitors will have to have a triband phone for it to work in Spain without changing the SIM card.

SENDING A LETTER

» Spanish post boxes *(buzones)* are bright yellow.
» Be warned: The postal service is not fast. Letters and postcards to other EU countries will take up to a week to arrive; for those to the USA allow up to two weeks.
» Although stamps *(sellos)* can be bought at post offices *(correos)*, it is sometimes quicker to go to the nearest tobacconist *(tabacos* or *estanco)* where you will see a brown and yellow symbol. Some hotels also sell them.
» Say something is *urgente* if you want to send it express.

POSTAGE RATES FOR LETTERS UP TO 20G

Within Spain	€0.34
To Western Europe	€0.64
To Eastern Europe	€0.64
To America	€0.78
To Africa	€0.78
To Asia	€0.78
To Australia	€0.78

USING A COIN-OPERATED PHONE

1 Lift the receiver and listen for the dial tone.
2 Insert phone card or coins. The coin drops as soon as you insert it. On some phones, you may be required to push a bar on the right-hand side of the phone to make the coin drop.
3 Dial or press the number.
4 If you want to cancel the call before it is answered, or if the call does not connect, press the coin release lever or hang up and take the coins from the coin return.
5 Once your call is answered, the display will show how much money or units you have left. Unused coins will be returned after the call.

INTERNET ACCESS

Internet cafés, where you can access your email, are becoming popular in Spain, particularly in the major towns and cities. Many post offices in provincial capitals offer internet access from 8.30am to 8.30pm, at 50 cents for 20 minutes or €1.50 per hour.

Madrid	Easy Internet Cafe, Calle Montera 10;
	BBigg, Calle Alcalá 21
Barcelona	El Cyber Mundo, Carrer Bergara 3 (tel 933 17 71 42);
	Inetcorner, Carrer Sardenya 306 (tel 932 44 80 80)
Sevilla	Cibercenter, Calle Julio César 8 (tel 954 22 88 99)

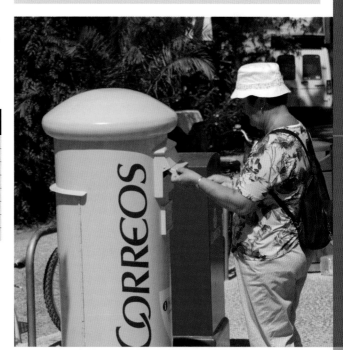

Opposite *The main post office in Barcelona*

FINDING HELP

If you have any concerns about your safety talk to an English-speaking local in your hotel or the nearest tourist information office — they will probably be able to advise you on where to find help.

PERSONAL SECURITY

Spain is generally a safe country and crime against visitors is rare. To be sure, however, take sensible precautions:

» Never carry more cash than you need.

» Place valuables in a hotel safety-deposit box.

» Wear bags and cameras slung diagonally across the chest rather than hanging from a shoulder or in a rucksack-type bag.

» Keep belongings close by in public places and crowded tourist areas.

» Be aware of ploys to distract your attention by thieves working in pairs.

» Be cautious of anyone invading your personal space.

» Stick to brightly lit, main thoroughfares at night.

» Never leave luggage or other belongings on view in a parked car and, if possible, remove the music system and take it with you.

» Never stop the car on a motorway, if another car signals a problem. This

CONTACTING YOUR EMBASSY IN MADRID	
If you lose your passport or are arrested, contact your embassy.	
Australia	Plaza del Descubridor, Diego de Ordas 3 (tel 913 53 66 00)
Canada	Calle Nuñéz de Balboa 35 (tel 914 23 32 50)
Republic of Ireland	Paseo de la Castellana 46 (tel 914 36 40 93)
New Zealand	3rd floor, Plaza de la Lealtad 2 (tel 915 23 02 26)
UK	Calle Fernando el Santo 16 (tel 913 19 02 00 or 917 00 82 72)
USA	Calle Serrano 75 (tel 915 87 22 00)

EMERGENCY NUMBERS

All emergency services: 112; however, the numbers below still provide direct contact with the services indicated.

Police 091
in all cities;
in towns and villages call the operator.

Fire *(bomberos)* 080

Ambulance 061, though it varies from region to region: contact the operator.

is a popular scam—when you leave the car to inspect the damage, your bags will be stolen.

LOST PROPERTY

» If you lose your passport, see below. If you lose money or other items, inform the police, and, depending on the terms of your policy, your travel insurance company as soon as possible.

» If your traveller's cheques have been stolen, notify the issuing company (always keep a record of the first and last numbers of your cheques), as well as the numbers of the cheques you have spent.

» Because of the amount of time and paperwork involved, it's not usually worth reporting the theft or loss of inexpensive items or small amounts of money. However, your insurance company will require a report if you wish to claim.

LOSS OF PASSPORT

» Always keep a separate note of your passport number and a photocopy of the page that carries your details, in case of loss or theft.

» You can also scan the relevant pages of your passport and email

them to yourself at an email account which you can access anywhere (such as www.hotmail.com).

» If you do lose your passport or it is stolen, report it to the police and then contact your embassy or consulate for assistance.

CONTACTING YOUR EMBASSY OR CONSULATE

Most countries are represented by an embassy in Madrid and/or Barcelona, and may operate consulates in other cities or resorts.

SEEKING HELP

» Telephone 112 in an emergency. This number functions anywhere in the EU and can be used for any type of emergency.

POLICE

The emergency telephone number for the police is 112. There are three different types of police force in Spain, each dealing with different aspects of public order.

» Policía Municipal, whose main responsibility is urban traffic, are the local police. They are identifiable by their blue uniforms and the white checked bands on their vehicles.

» Policía Nacional, who wear brown uniforms and berets, deal with law and order and national security.

» Guardia Civil, responsible for border posts, country areas, the coast and highways, wear olive green uniforms.

» Basque police in the Basque country wear red berets. Catalunya has its own police force, too.

» Take the time to report thefts to the police, especially if you intend to make a claim for the loss.

» You will need a police report to pass on to your insurance company.

MEDIA

TELEVISION

In many local bars a TV set tuned into the news or a sports channel is a permanent fixture. The two national state-run channels are TVE1 and TVE2.

Regional authorities also run local stations, such as Canal Sur in Andalucía.

There are several private TV companies, including Tele 5, Antena 3 TV and Canal Plus Satelite Digital.

Most hotels have satellite, cable or digital television, so you can view international channels such as BBC World, CNN and Sky.

RADIO

Throughout the summer season Spanish radio broadcasts regular tourist emergency information, which can be very helpful if you are touring around. Tuning in at the start of each day may help you to plan your route to avoid traffic build-ups.

The state-run public radio company is Radio Nacional de España (RNE), which has a current affairs station (RNE 1), a classical music station (Radio Clásica), a pop music station (Radio 3) and a sports and entertainment station (RNE 5).

There are also many independent radio stations. Check the listings

section of *El País* for further details. It's also possible to pick up the BBC World Service on certain frequencies.

NEWSPAPERS AND MAGAZINES

You will find popular English-language newspapers and magazines on sale in large cities and the main coastal resorts. US publications such as the *International Herald Tribune*, *USA Today* and the *Wall Street Journal* are easily available. Many are now printed in Spain and appear on the newsstands first thing in the morning.

Spain's most popular national papers are *El País* and *El Mundo*, both of which have very informative events listings, particularly in the weekend editions. An English version of *El País* now comes inside the *International Herald Tribune*.

Newspaper readership in Spain is not as high as in other European countries: TV and radio are regarded as more entertaining purveyors of information.

The magazine market is dominated by TV weeklies and star gossip glossies, with the queen of them all, *¡Hola!*, now successfully established as *Hello!* magazine in the UK, where it continues to thrive.

In areas with large expatriate British populations, there are many

English-language newspapers and magazines — both translations of Spanish publications and specially written what's on guides. These have information about local events and entertainment, and on local services.

The *Barcelona Metropolitan* and *The Broadsheet* (Madrid) are two of the best, along with *Essential Marbella* and *Catalonia Today*.

NEWSPAPERS
The following are the most popular Spanish newspapers.
ABC
National daily. Catholic, monarchist, right-of-centre. Broadly aligned to the Popular Party.
El Mundo
National daily. Independent, tending towards tabloid sensationalism.
El País
National daily. Liberal, left-of-centre, broadly aligned to the Socialist Party. There is also a Catalán version.
La Vanguardia Española
Barcelona's most read newspaper, published in Castilian Spanish and widely considered the most balanced reporting in Spain.
La Razon
National daily. Very right wing.
As
Dedicated entirely to sport.
Marca
More sports.

PRACTICALITIES | ESSENTIAL INFORMATION

BOOKS, MAPS AND FILMS

BOOKS

An understanding of Spain's rich history and culture enriches any visit there. These books are an enjoyable read and will whet your appetite either before you go or will engage you while you're there.

South From Granada by Gerald Brenan. The Bloomsbury set in Spain.
The Sun Also Rises, Ernest Hemingway's 1926 account of American and British expatriates on a party in Pampona is a must, while his 1941 **For Whom the Bell Tolls** chronicles the Spanish Civil War.
Spanish Journeys by Adam Hopkins. History and contemporary culture go hand in hand.
As I Walked Out One Midsummer Morning by Laurie Lee. An autobiographical account of Lee's walk through pre-Civil War Spain.
Driving Over Lemons—An Optimist in Andalucia by Chris Stewart. A witty account of life on a remote farm in the Alpujarras by the original drummer in the rock group Genesis.
Ghosts of Spain by Giles Tremlett. An engaging, personal and witty observation of Spain's past and present by the foreign correspondent of *The Guardian*.
The Shadow of the Wind by Carlos Ruiz Zafón captures Barcelona's 1950s and 60s in a novel of romance and intrigue.

MAPS AND OTHER PUBLICATIONS

The Spanish National Tourist Office offers a useful free map of road, rail and air communications in Spain called the *Mapa de Comunicaciones*. It gives detailed practical information on road rescue, local rail stations, airport telephone numbers and border crossings, and also has road maps of Barcelona, Bilbao, Madrid, Seville, Valencia and Zaragoza.

Detailed maps of every major town in Spain can also be found at the local tourist information offices, allowing you to locate major attractions on foot.

In addition, an atlas of Spain can be found (▷ 461–480 of this book), with city plans of Barcelona (▷ 210–211) and Madrid (▷ 66–67). There is a regional map (▷ 8) and Metro maps for Madrid (▷ 69) and Barcelona (▷ 213).

Maps for Hikers

You can obtain large-scale walking maps from Servicio de Publicaciones del Instituto Geográfico Nacional, Calle General Ibáñez de Ibero 3, 28003 Madrid, or any good bookshop in Spain.

FILMS

The restraints of censorship during the Franco years, as well as other political and economical factors, held back the film industry in Spain. However, in 1955 the prestigious film *Alexander the Great* was filmed in Spain and by the mid-1960s American film producers looking for wide, open spaces were not slow to capitalize on the appeal of relatively inexpensive Spanish locations.

More than a hundred of the so-called Spaghetti Westerns were actually shot in Spain. Who can forget Clint Eastwood in *A Fistful of Dollars*, *For a Few Dollars More* and *The Good, The Bad and The Ugly*, squinting in the Spanish sun? And if the parched landscape around Tabernas seems familiar, it may be because it forms the backdrop to a string of classic films, including the epic *Lawrence of Arabia*.

Three former Spanish film sets are now run as mini theme parks, where stunt men re-enact well loved scenes from Westerns, such as gunfights and bank robberies. Another Almería landscape, a beach near the Cabo de Gata, made an appearance in *Indiana Jones and the Last Crusade*, starring Harrison Ford.

With the emergence of auteur directors like Pedro Almodóvar, Alejandro Amenábar (director of the Oscar-awarded *The Sea Inside*) and Fernando León de Aranoa, the native film industry is now in a more than healthy state. Spain is represented in Hollywood by two of its most successful actors: Antonio Banderas, played Zorro and voiced the Puss in Boots in the *Shrek* film series, and Penélope Cruz, who won the Oscar for her role in Almodóvar's *Volver* (2006).

OPENING TIMES AND TICKETS

ADMISSION CHARGES

Many sites charge admission fees, but these are generally moderate or inexpensive, and often there is a free day for EU visitors. The more expensive sites tend to be the large, privately owned attractions, such as the Guggenheim in Bilbao, or the theme parks.

YOUTH AND STUDENT DISCOUNTS

» Full-time students can buy the International Student ID Card (ISIC), which entitles them to special air, rail and bus fares, as well as discounts at some attractions.
» Under 27s can purchase the International Youth Travel Card, which carries similar benefits.

CAMPING DISCOUNTS

The International Camping Carnet (CCI) is an identity card which provides access to organized campsites, controlled by clubs that belong to the Alliance Internationale de Tourisme (AIT), the Fédération Internationale de l'Automobile (FIA) and the Fédération Internationale de Camping et de Caravanning (FICC). It is valid for a total of 12 months from the date of issue and offers discounts on campsite fees, reservation priority, the possibility of being granted permission to camp in state forests and covers you for third-party insurance while camping. It is available from major automobile associations and camping and caravanning organizations.

OPENING TIMES

Most places in Spain close for siesta — usually two hours during the hottest part of the day.

Banks

Banks open Mon–Fri 8.30–2, Sat 8.30–1, though there are regional variations. They may stay open all day in major cities.

Bars

Bars are generally open all day until the early hours and up until between 3am and 5am in the summer; some open until dawn in cities and resorts.

Cafés

Usually from 7am onwards.

Churches

Many churches are kept locked and can be visited only by prior arrangement with a caretaker. Others have specific opening times and may charge a fee.

Museums

Opening times vary across the country and are seasonal; check locally. Many close on Monday.

Offices

Normally 9–2 and 4–7.30.

Post Offices

Post offices in provincial capitals open Mon–Fri 8.30–8.30, Sat 9.30–2; in smaller towns generally Mon–Fri 8.30–2.30, Sat 9.30–1. In major towns and resorts they often open also in the afternoon.

Shops

Spanish shops usually open between 9.30 and 10am, then close for lunch from 1.30 or 2pm until 4.30 or 5pm, a custom that often takes visitors by surprise. The good news is that they generally stay open until 8 in the evening; in coastal regions in high summer they may not close until 10pm. Most shops close on Saturday afternoons and Sundays, though in major resorts a few shops may stay open seven days a week. The larger department stores do not usually close for lunch.

NATIONAL HOLIDAYS
1 January New Year's Day (Año Nuevo)
6 January Epiphany (Epifanía or Reyes)
March/April Good Friday/Easter Monday (Viernes Santo, Lunes Santo)
1 May Labour Day (Fiesta del Trabajo)
15 August Assumption of the Virgin (La Asunción de Nuestra Señora)
12 October National Day (Día de la Hispanidad)
1 November All Saints' Day (Todos los Santos)
6 December Constitution Day (Día de la Constitución)
8 December Feast of the Immaculate Conception (Día de la Inmaculada Concepción)
25 December Christmas Day (Navidad)

The autonomous regions have their own holidays and each town celebrates its patron saint's feast day.

USEFUL WEBSITES

There are thousands of websites with information on Spain. This list contains the addresses of the major organizations that carry information of value to visitors.

BACKPACKERS
www.backpackeurope.com Excellent site for backpackers.

DOCUMENTATION
www.fco.gov.uk Advice from the British Foreign Office on how to get help abroad.
www.travel.state.gov US Department of State Bureau of Consular Affairs.

DRIVING
www.dgt.es Road system and traffic regulations information from Spain's Traffic Authority website.
www.ideamerge.com/ motoeuropa Information on driving anywhere in Europe.

FIESTAS
www.spanish-fiestas.com This site has all kinds of useful tourist information, including when and where to find the best fiestas.

FOOD
www.iberianfoods.co.uk A good introduction to Spanish food, regional specialities, with a food glossary and recipe section. Demystify restaurant menus with Spanish and Catalan dishes translated into English.

GENERAL TOURIST INFORMATION
www.virtualtourist.com Takes you on a virtual tour of well-known tourist attractions.
www.visiteurope.com Advice from the European Travel Commission.
www.spain.info The official website of the Spanish Tourist Office. General information on Spain.

HEALTH
www.cdc.gov Health advice for visitors from the USA.
www.dh.gov.uk/en/healthcare/ healthadvicefortravellers/index. htm Information from the UK's Department of Health.
www.who.int World Health Organization site.

HOTELS
www.hotelsearch.com Comprehensive list of Spanish hotels.
http://interhotel.com/spain Online booking service.
www.madeinspain.net More hotels online.
www.parador.es Central reservations for paradors.
www.rusticae.es Small, 'charming' hotels.

MOTORING ORGANIZATION
www.theaa.com Up-to-date travel advice from Britain's leading motoring organization.

MUSEUMS
www.mcu.es (in Spanish only) Links to Spanish museum websites.

REGIONAL INFORMATION
www.andalucia.org Information on Andalucía.
www.barcelonaturisme.com Information on Barcelona.
www.descubremadrid.com Information on Madrid.
www.euskadi.net Information on the Basque Country
.

VISITORS WITH DISABILITIES
www.access-able.com US-based website.
www.radar.org.uk UK and Republic of Ireland website.
www.afdo.org.au Australian website.
www.dpa.org.nz New Zealand website.

WEATHER
www.met-office.gov.uk UK site giving information about Spain's weather, its climate and five-day forecasts.
www.weather.com US-based site with information on weather in Europe.
www.rainorshine.com Useful weather information.

WINE
www.jrnet.com/vino Spanish wines at a glance.

WORKING HOLIDAYS
www.travelalternatives.org Information for anyone wanting to take a working holiday.

KEY SIGHTS QUICK WEBSITE FINDER

SIGHT	WEBSITE	PAGE
Cuevas de Altamira	http://museodealtamira.mcu.es	136
Picos de Europa	www.picosdeeuropa.com	140–141
Catedral de Santiago	www.santiagoturismo.com	173
Museo Guggenheim	www.guggenheim-bilbao.es	172–173
Parque Nacional Ordesa y Monte Perdido	www.ordesa.net	194–195
L'Aquàrium de Barcelona	www.aquariumbcn.com	215
Casa Milà (La Pedrera)	http://obrasocial.caixacatalunya.es	215
Catedral, Barcelona	www.catedralbcn.org	218
Fundació Joan Miró	www.bcn.fjmiro.es	220
Museu Picasso	www.museupicasso.bcn.es	223
Sagrada Família	www.sagradafamilia.org	228–231
Teatro-Museu Salvador Dalí	www.salvador-dali.org	259
Montserrat	www.abadiamontserrat.net	261
Castillo de Coca	www.coca-ciudaddecauca.org	292
Monasterio de las Descalzas Reales	www.patrimonionacional.es	72
Museo Reina Sofía	www.museoreinasofia.es	77
Museo del Prado	www.museoprado.es	74–75
Museo Thyssen-Bornemisza	www.museothyssen.org	78–79
Alhambra	www.alhambra.org	364–365

TOURIST OFFICES

Throughout Spain you will find branches of the Spanish National Tourist Office (SNTO) in most of the major towns and tourist areas. Called *Turismo*, they offer a vast number of maps, guides and leaflets designed to help visitors make the most of their stay, and are manned by English-speaking staff who should be able to help you to arrange anything from finding somewhere to stay to visiting remote churches. However, they are not travel agencies and do not book or arrange travel packages.

If you're touring Spain, a visit to a *Turismo* each time you enter a new region will provide you with an excellent selection of regional information on activities such as walking, bicycling, birdwatching, skiing, horseback-riding, golf and visiting the Spanish vineyards. Alternatively, before you travel look at the SNTO's website (www.tourspain. es).

Tourist offices in the big resorts tend to stay open all day but in areas less geared to visitors you may find them closed for siesta between 1 and 4pm as well as on weekends. They make a very good first point of contact if you find yourself in any kind of difficulty while in Spain—the staff should be able to reassure you and advise you who to contact.

TOURIST INFORMATION OFFICES IN SPAIN

THE FOLLOWING ARE TOURIST INFORMATION OFFICES IN SPAIN'S PRINCIPAL REGIONAL TOWNS:

Barcelona Ciutat 2, Plaça Sant Jaume (tel 932 85 38 34)

Bilbao (Bilbo) Plaza Ensanche 11 (tel 944 71 13 01)

Logroño Calle Portales bis, 26001 Logroño (tel 941 27 33 53)

Madrid Plaza Mayor 27 (tel 915 88 16 36)

Mérida Avenida José Álvarez Sáez de Buruaga (tel 924 00 97 30)

Murcia Plaza del Cardenal Belluga s/n (tel 968 35 87 49)

Oviedo Plaza de la Constitución 4 (tel 984 08 06 60)

Pamplona (Iruña) Calle Eslava 1 (tel 948 20 65 40)

Santiago de Compostela Rúa do Vilar 63 (tel 981 55 51 29)

Santander Paseo de Pareda (tel 942 20 30 00)

Sevilla Avenida de la Constitución 21B (tel 954 22 14 04)

Toledo Plaza del Consistorio 1 (tel 925 25 40 00)

Valencia Carrer Poeta Querol s/n, Teatro Principal (tel 963 51 49 07)

Valladolid Pabellón de Cristal, Acera de Recoletos 4 (tel 983 21 93 10)

Zaragoza Plaza del Pilar s/n (tel 976 39 35 37)

For information on more specific tourist areas:

Alacant (Alicante) Rambla Méndez Núñez 23 (tel 965 20 00 00)

Alcalá de Henares Callejón de Santa María 1 (tel 918 89 26 94)

Andorra la Vella Plaça de la Rotonda (tel 376 82 71 17)

Ávila Avenida de Madrid 39 (tel 920 22 59 69)

Benidorm Plaza de Canalejas 1 (tel 966 81 54 63)

Burgos Teatro Principal, Paseo del Espolón s/n (tel 947 28 88 74)

Cadaqués Carrer Cotxe 2-A (tel 972 25 83 15)

Cádiz Plaza de San Juan de Dios 11 (tel 956 24 10 01)

Cardona Avenida del Rastrillo s/n (tel 938 69 27 98)

Córdoba Calle Torrijos 10 (tel 957 47 12 35)

Cuenca Calle Alfonso VIII 2 (tel 969 24 10 51)

Donostia (San Sebastián) Calle Reina Regente 3 (tel 943 48 11 66)

Figueres Plaça del Sol (tel 972 50 31 55)

Fuengirola Avenida Jesús Santos Rein 6 (tel 952 46 74 57)

Girona Rambla de la Llibertat 1 (tel 972 22 65 75)

Gijón Rodriguez San Pedro s/n (tel 985 34 17 71)

Granada Plaza Mariana Pineda 10 (tel 958 24 71 28)

Huelva Plaza Alcalde Coto Mora 2 (tel 959 25 74 03)

Jaca Plaza San Pedro 11–13 (tel 974 36 00 98)

León Plaza de Regla 3 (tel 987 23 70 82)

Llanes Calle Alfonso IX, La Torre (tel 985 40 01 64)

Málaga Pasaje de Chinitas 4 (tel 952 21 34 45)

Marbella Plaza de los Naranjos (tel 952 82 35 50)

Montserrat Plaça de la Creu (tel 938 77 77 01)

Peñiscola Passeig Marítim (tel 964 48 02 08)

Roses Avinguda de Rhode 77 (tel 902 10 36 36)

Salamanca Casa de las Conchas, Calle Rúa Mayor 70 (tel 923 26 85 71)

San Lorenzo de El Escorial Calle Grimaldi 2 (tel 918 90 53 13)

Segovia Plaza Mayor 10 (tel 921 46 03 34)

Sigüenza Ermita de Humilladero (tel 949 34 70 07)

Sitges Carrer Sínia Morera (tel 938 94 43 05)

Soria Calle Medinaceli (tel 975 21 20 52)

Tarragona Carrer Major 39 (tel 977 25 07 95)

Torremolinos Plaza Blas Infante 1 (tel 952 37 95 12)

Úbeda Palacio del Marqués del Contadero, Calle Baja del Marqués 4 (tel 953 75 08 97)

Vigo Estación Marítima de Transatlánticos (tel 986 43 05 77)

Vitoria (Gasteiz) Plaza General Loma s/n (tel 945 16 15 98)

SNTO TOURIST INFORMATION OFFICES ABROAD

Contact the SNTO (Spanish National Tourist Office) for general information before leaving home:

Australia

There is no longer an Australia office. The Singapore Office (Orchard Road 541, Liat Tower 09–04, 23881 Singapore, tel +65 6737 3008) has Australia and New Zealand under its area of influence.

Canada

34th Floor, 2 Bloor Street West, Toronto, ON M4W 3E2 (tel +1 416/961-3131, www.tourspain.toronto.on.ca)

UK and Republic of Ireland

2nd Floor, 79 New Cavendish Street, London W1W 6XB (tel +44 (0)20 7486 8077, www.tourspain.co.uk)

USA

Chicago: Water Tower Place, Suite 915 East, 845 N. Michigan Avenue, Chicago, IL 60611 (tel +1 312/642-1992); Los Angeles: 8383 Wilshire Boulevard, Suite 960, Beverly Hills, CA 90211 (tel +1 323/658-7188); Miami: 1221 Brickell Avenue, Suite 1850, Miami FL 33131 (tel +1 305/358-1992); New York: 666 Fifth Avenue, New York, NY 10103 (tel +1 212/265-8822; www. okspain.org).

SHOPPING

Shopping malls are opening up throughout Spain and the Spanish are eagerly embracing the benefits of retail therapy. It's a relatively recent phenomenon; until Spain joined the European Union in 1986, shopping was confined largely to small, old-fashioned stores, with only the biggest cities offering much else. But that's all changed, and Spanish fashion names are as well known outside Spain as they are within the country. Madrid and Barcelona top the list of places to shop, but all regional capitals have excellent facilities.

Side by side with 21st-century consumerism goes Spanish traditional loyalty to the small shops, the *tiendas*. These can range from general outfitters in the most remote *pueblos* (small towns) to the wonderfully quirky and idiosyncratic shops in major cities like Madrid, Barcelona and Seville. In addition almost every Spanish *pueblo* has its daily food market, and a general goods market held at least once a week.

DEPARTMENT STORES
Spain's big name is El Corte Inglés, Europe's second-largest department store chain, after German chain Karstadt. It sells a huge range of quality Spanish and international goods. Most department stores also have excellent supermarkets or food halls selling a variety of Spanish and imported foods. The book departments are a good place to find local guidebooks, often in English, and maps.

MARKETS
The *mercado municipal* (food market) can be an attraction in its own right. Meat, fish, fruit and vegetables, dairy products and groceries are for sale, with bigger markets having as many as 20 or so of each type of stand. Prices are fixed.

General markets, the *mercadillos*, operate on a fixed day once a week, and can be a couple of dozen stands or something as big as Madrid's famous Rastro flea market (▷ 92). You'll find everything from clothes and garden plants to pirated DVDs and handmade jewellery.

SUPERSTORES AND HYPERMARKETS
Most larger cities have *centros commerciales* (retail outlets) on their outskirts. These generally contain huge food hypermarkets, plus aisles of inexpensive clothes, household goods and electrical items. They also have furniture stores, DIY stores and often toy and record stores.

Manufacturing towns sometimes have factory outlets for leather goods and shoes.

OPENING HOURS
Opening hours are flexible, depending on the region, city, town and type of shop.
» Small shops tend to close between 1 or 2 and 4 or 5.
» Big stores and malls often open all day every day.
» Urban shops, souvenir shops in resorts and supermarkets usually open all day 8–8.

PAYMENT
» Credit and debit cards are widely accepted, though not for small sums.
» Food bills and market traders are usually paid in cash.
» Personal cheques are not generally accepted.

TAX REFUNDS AND SALES
» IVA (sales tax) is added at 7 per cent on food and 16 per cent on most other items.
» Non-EU visitors can request a tax-free cheque on major purchases, which can be cashed at customs when leaving Spain to reclaim IVA. Stores taking part display a Tax-Free Shopping sticker.
» Sales run from mid-January to February, and July to August.

WHAT TO BUY
Ceramics and Porcelain
Ceramics and porcelain are excellent value. You'll see them at roadside stores in many regions, and you can buy in bulk direct from the

manufacturers. Tiles are another local product. The best are usually found in the south; retailers will arrange shipping if you're buying a lot. As these costs are high, ask first whether they have an agent in your own country.

The porcelain manufacturers Lladró export their figures worldwide and the selection and prices are better in Spain than overseas. They sell an almost identical though less expensive range, NAO.

Fans and Hair Combs
Spanish women use beautifully made and decorated fans throughout the stifling summers. They range from hand-carved tortoiseshell and lace filigree to cheap and cheerful mass-produced paper ones. There are also traditional hair combs and slides, as well as funkier versions.

Fashion
You will find Zara, Mango (fashion) and Camper (shoes) all over the world, but bear in mind that their stores in Spain are often cheaper and have a wider selection.

Shops in both Madrid and Barcelona are strong on street- and clubwear—cutting-edge style that's well ahead of the pack.

Food and Wine
Every region has its own local food and wine specialities which you'll find in food shops or delicatessens. It's a good idea to buy these when you come across them as they are unlikely to be sold elsewhere.

Spain's traditional cakes and biscuits, produced behind the closed walls of religious convents, are unique; many specialize in a particular variety. You buy on the spot, putting money on a turntable and waiting for the sweets to come back.

The Convento de la Dueñas in Salamanca makes *bizcocho* (a type of pastry), and *yemas* (candied egg yolks) are made by the nuns in Ávila.

Guitars
Guitars are made in Spain for export all over the world, but you'll find a wider choice, better prices and the chance to have one custom made if you buy it here. Andalucía and particularly Seville are noted for guitar-making.

Handicrafts
Spain still has plenty of artisan producers, and handicrafts are among the best buys. The range is large and generally reflects the region, with many products available only in and around the place where they are made.

Some regions have *centros de artesanía*, to show all the local crafts in one place.

Leather Goods
Leather is an excellent buy. Spain has a huge choice of designs and prices right across the board. You'll find great shoes, belts and bags everywhere in the country. Loewe is the big name—expensive and superbly made.

Mantones and *Mantillas*
The exquisite fringed and embroidered shawls, *mantones*, worn by Spanish women on festivals and holidays, are something you won't find elsewhere. Traditionally black or ivory, they now come in all shades.

You can also buy gossamer-fine *mantillas* (lace shawls) at excellent prices.

Religious Articles
Most fair-sized towns in this deeply religious country have shops specializing in religious articles: statues of Christ, the Virgin and the saints, rosaries, prayer books, votive candles of all shapes and sizes.

CHAIN STORES

NAME	LINE OF GOODS	CONTACT NUMBER	WEBSITE
Armand Basi	Fashion		www.armandbasi.com
Camper	Shoes	934 84 64 01	www.camper.com
Custo Barcelona	Fashion designers		www.custo-barcelona.com
El Corte Inglés	Department store	902 12 21 22	www.elcorteisgles.es
Farrutx	Shoes	971 50 18 66	www.farrutx.com
Lladró (NAO)	Porcelain	900 21 10 10	www.lladro.com
Loewe	Leather		www.loewe.es
Mango	Fashion		www.mango.es
Purification Garcia	Fashion designers		www.purificationgarcia.es
Tous	Jewellery, accessories	938 78 44 44	www.tous.es
Zara	Fashion	981 18 54 00	www.zara.com

ENTERTAINMENT AND NIGHTLIFE

There is plenty to keep you entertained in Spain, from cinema and dance to classical music and opera. Flamenco is, of course, the quintessential sound of the country, at least in the south, and it is well worth tracking down an authentic performance. Spain also boasts a lively festival scene (▷ 448). Spanish nightlife is up there with the best in Europe. This is a country that knows how to party, whether it's the annual fiesta in a small *pueblo* (town) or the all-night scene in Madrid or Barcelona. The island of Ibiza is internationally renowned, with people flocking to enjoy one of Europe's most vibrant club scenes. In mainland Spain the big cities—Madrid, Barcelona and Valencia—have the cutting edge, but you'll find something in every Spanish city, whether you're looking for a night's dancing or a late bar with live music. The music is often uniquely Spanish, and music bars can be the best places to discover some of the country's indigenous sounds, often a thrilling fusion of traditional with contemporary. Andalucía, the Basque country and the northern regions are particularly active in this respect.

CINEMA

The Spanish are avid cinema fans, and the country has some of the largest mega-multiplexes in Europe. The good news for visitors is that first-release movies are often shown in their original language with Spanish subtitles. These are indicated in listings in the major cities by the initials VO *(versión original)*.

Performances start later than in other European countries, with the first busy showing between 7.45 and 8.30pm, and the most popular screening time at 10 to 10.30pm. There's generally no need to reserve for the early evening shows, but weekends are very popular, so either get there early or reserve in advance. Matinées usually begin at around 4.30 to 5pm, and in larger cities midnight shows are a feature.

Prices are reasonable and many cinemas have lower charges for the first afternoon show and a reduced price day—the *día del espectador*—usually Monday or Tuesday.

In summer there are open-air *cines de verano*, where you can enjoy a beer while you watch the movie. Parts of Spain where there are big foreign communities occasionally have foreign-language films showing at the local cinemas. Details of films are shown in weekend newspapers and weekly and monthly listings magazines (▷ 433).

CLASSICAL MUSIC, OPERA AND DANCE

There is usually a good selection of classical music concerts and dance performances during the main season, which runs from September to June. The major cities for these branches of the performing arts are Madrid and Barcelona, but other places have their own seasons, where performances are put on by local groups or touring companies. During the summer the arts festivals

VO CINEMAS

Madrid
Renoir Plaza de España
Calle Martín de los Heros 12, Argüelles
Renoir Princesa
Calle de la Princesa 3, Argüelles
Renoir Cuatro Caminos
Calle Raimundo Fernández Villaverde 10, Cuatro Caminos
Renoir Retiro
Calle Narváez 42, El Retir
Alphaville
Calle Martín de los Heros 14, Argüelles

Barcelona
Icària Yelmo Cineplex
Carrer Salvador Espriu 61, Vila Olímpic
Verdi
Carrer Verdi 32, Gràcia

Sevilla
Cine Avenida
Calle Marqués de Paradas 1

Valencia
Filmoteca
Plaza del Ayuntamiento
Albatros Mini-Cines
Plaza Fray Luís Colomer 4
Babel
Calle Vicente Sancho Teller 10

TICKETING IN MADRID

» The Comedia, Maria Guerrero, Teatro dela Zarzuela and Auditorio Nacional have a joint system; you can buy tickets for them all at any of these venues or via the Caja Madrid telesales service (tel 902 22 16 22, www.entradas.com).

» For other theatres, reserve direct from box offices or through Caja Madrid (tel 902 22 16 22, www.entradas.com), Caixa Catalunya (tel 902 10 12 12, www.telentrada.com) or El Corte Inglés (tel 902 40 02 22; www.elcorteingles.es/entradas).

» For the Teatro Real, tel 902 24 48 48.

TICKETING IN BARCELONA

» The savings banks La Caixa and Caixa de Catalunya have ticketing facilities. You can reserve through them by phone (many of the operators speak English), on the internet, over the counter in some branches or via the ticketing machines found next to the cash machines in the bigger branches.

Servi-Caixa — La Caixa
Tel 902 33 22 11
www.serviticket.com

Tel-entrada — Caixa Catalunya
Tel 902 10 12 12
www.telentrada.com

Elsewhere

You can buy tickets direct from the venue or through local agencies. Tourist information offices will be able to help, as will the bigger hotels. A good site for online ticket sales throughout Spain (in English) is www.generaltickets.com.

---

in different Spanish cities may offer something that appeals; check with the local press or tourist offices.

CONTEMPORARY LIVE MUSIC

Major international acts tend to concentrate on Madrid and Barcelona, where concerts are often staged in the huge soccer stadiums.

Local rock is performed all over Spain, and is at its best in the university cities. There are several jazz festivals; among them those in Barcelona, Santander, Donostia (San Sebastián) and Sitges are the liveliest.

All the major music festivals are listed at www.festivals.com

FLAMENCO

The best place to hear flamenco is in its birthplace, Andalucía. It is composed of three elements—the guitar, the human voice and dance—and is more likely to express pain than joie de vivre.

To experience the real thing you have to get off the tourist track or visit one of the summer flamenco festivals. The Biennial Flamenco Festival in Seville is the best known, but there are excellent examples in Cartageña, Jerez and Granada. Look for local information in the press and at tourist offices.

If you can gain access to a *peña* (club) you'll find the standard here extremely high and the flamenco totally genuine. The tourist flamenco shows in Madrid, Barcelona and the Andalucían cities may be fun, but are also overpriced and often less than genuine.

Flamenco is evolving all the time and you may get the chance to hear some of the new-style artists who combine rock and jazz elements into the art; Madrid is a good place to experience this.

FOLK AND REGIONAL MUSIC

Regional music is alive and well in Spain, as the autonomous regions proclaim their sense of identity through their music. This is particularly strong in northern

Spain, where Galicia and Euskadi lead the field. Galician music features bagpipes, drums and pipes, and is Celtic in origin, while Basques go for *trikitrixa* — wild accordion music.

There are major summer festivals at Ortigueira and Oviedo, and local festivals throughout Galicia, Asturias and the Basque country. You'll find regional music in Catalonia and the Balearics, such as Catalonia'a native dance rhythm, the *sardana*, as well as traditional dance music performed by specialist orchestras. All of this is advertised in the local press, with more information available at the local tourist offices.

THEATRE
Unless you are a Spanish-speaker you are unlikely to want to go to the theatre in Spain, but many places double up as venues for music, ballet and dance, so it's worth checking the listings. Apart from Madrid and Barcelona, other cities with a good live scene include Seville, Bilbao, Zaragoza and Valencia. During the summer there are open-air festivals, which include theatre as well as music and dance.

BARS
Nightlife in big cities tends to be concentrated in certain areas. In Madrid things hot up first in the Huertas area, moving on to Malasaña, Conde Duque, Lavapiés and Sol, while Barcelonins congregate on the Raval, El Born, the Barri Gòtic and the port areas. Valencia's bar scene is quite diffused and you'll have to move around the city to find the action; the Barrio del Carmèn and across the River Turia are good places to start. Late-night bars often have live music, a small dance floor and a resident or guest DJ at different times. Entrance is generally free, but drinks cost more than in ordinary bars.

CLUBS
Outside the main cities, the best places for good nightlife are university cities such as Salamanca and Zaragoza. Smaller cities tend

to be sedate during the week but let their hair down on Fridays and Saturdays. If you're an enthusiastic clubber, you may find that there's not much choice outside mainstream rock in small towns, but the atmosphere will be great. Spain goes to bed very late, and nightlife means what it says, with things getting going only around midnight or later and some clubs actually opening at dawn. There's even a Spanish word, *madrugada*, which means the hours between midnight and dawn, and events will be advertised as starting at *dos de la madrugada* — which may help explain why it's possible to be caught in a traffic jam at 4am in Madrid. The 24-hour clubs operate over the weekend and through to Monday afternoon. Late-night clubs sometimes have early evening sessions for teenagers. Smaller towns inland may have just one club, open at weekends only, with a less than exciting choice of chart music.

Hard-core ravers head for Ibiza, where world-class venues are strung along the south coast, with Sant Antoní, Sant Rafel, Eivissa town and Platja d'en Bossa having the best. Promoters can move from venue to

venue and things change rapidly, so check up-to-date information.

GAY AND LESBIAN SCENE
Attitudes to gays and lesbians have changed over the past decade or so in Spain. There's a relaxed welcome in all the major cities and many coastal resorts, where you'll find a thriving scene and, in places such as Madrid, Barcelona, Sitges and Cádiz, a large resident community. It may be best to keep a low profile, though, in staunchly conservative, church-going country places.

GOOD PLACES FOR LATE, LATE NIGHTS

A Coruña	Málaga
Barcelona	Murcia
Bilbao	Oviedo
Cáceres	Salamanca
Córdoba	Santander
Cuenca	Seville
Donostia	Sitges
Granada	Valencia
Ibiza	Zaragoza
Madrid	

HOW TO FIND OUT MORE
Most major cities publish listings for what's on locally, which are sold at newsstands. It's also worth checking the listings in the papers for up-to-the-minute information, particularly for late-night music and the club scene. In smaller places, tourist information offices will help, and bars are good places to pick up flyers. An online listings service www.lanetro.com, has comprehensive listings and information for all the major cities (Spanish only).

MADRID
» *El País* and *El Mundo* newspapers have separate listings sections in Friday's editions, and daily listings as well.
» *Guía del Ocio*, a weekly Spanish-language listings magazine, is available at newsstands.
» *En Madrid* is a monthly what's on pamphlet published by the town hall and is available from tourist information offices.
» *In Madrid* is a free English-language monthly listings magazine, available in many bars.
» www.webmadrid.com is a complete guide in English.

BARCELONA
» *El País* and *La Vanguardia* newspapers are best for listings; they're published daily, with a separate section on Fridays.
» *Guía del Ocio* (see Madrid above).
» Posters and flyers for one-off events are displayed in bars
» *Time Out* publishes a weekly guide to Barcelona. It's in Catalán only, but is nonetheless fairly accessible to non-Catalán speakers..

SPORTS AND ACTIVITIES

The 1990s saw an upswing in the popularity of spectator sports in Spain, driven by the immense success of the Barcelona Olympics and the advent of cable and satellite TV. Millions of Spaniards tune into the fortunes of their home-grown heroes and teams, following their ups and downs in the fields of everything from soccer to bicycling and tennis. If there's something happening during your visit and you're a sports fan, join the crowds for a real Spanish experience. Compared to many other southern European nations, the Spanish are relatively sports-conscious, and most Spanish towns have excellent sporting facilities, particularly in resort areas and larger cities. In high summer temperatures thoughts turn to swimming and watersports, and you'll find plenty of opportunities along the coast. Inland, even small towns have a pool. The classier hotels in resort areas usually have good facilities, certainly a pool and tennis courts and often easy access to one of Spain's superb golf courses. Some hotels are equipped with gyms and exercise rooms, and resort hotels may have aerobic and exercise classes. If you're visiting in the countryside, there may be horseback-riding, a great way to explore the countryside and exercise at the same time.

BASKETBALL

Basketball holds second place to soccer in terms of popularity, and Spanish teams are among the best in Europe. The season runs from September to May, and teams play in a league system. Most games take place on weekend evenings.

BICYCLING

Competitive bicycling is closely followed in Spain. It has its own Tour, La Vuelta de España, in September (check out www.lavuelta.com). Starting in Gijón, it runs along the north coast, down to Barcelona, then through Castile to finish in Madrid on the third weekend of the month. On Sundays you'll see local teams out everywhere.

BIRDING

The lonely, sparsely inhabited stretches of inland and coastal Spain have some of the best birding in Europe, where you can see everything from the great raptors to over-wintering waterfowl and summer visitors.

Habitats range from the high mountains of the Pyrenees and Picos de Europa to wetlands such as the Donaña in Andalucía. Wooded national parks are the places to spot rollers, hoopoes and bee-eaters. Excellent birding areas include:

Ebro Delta (Catalonia)
Lagoon and wetlands with woodlands and rice paddies, at its best during the spring and autumn migration seasons.

Picos de Europa (Asturias) is a
prime site for eagles, griffon vultures and rare mountain species such as choughs, snow finches and citrils. It's best from May to October, but can be wet and misty at any time.

Donaña National Park (Andalucía),
a superb wetland region, is the place to look for over-wintering wildfowl during migration and in winter. Access can be difficult.

Monfragüe Natural Park
(Extremadura), with its wooded hills and gorges, is at its best in summer, when there are huge numbers of raptors and migrants.

Ordesa National Park (Aragón),
in the Pyrenees, is renowned for its high-altitude birds. Access is easiest in the summer.

BULLFIGHTING
Bullfights are covered on the arts pages of the Spanish press, along with the theatre and ballet. For most foreigners, however, the *corrida* is erroneously perceived as a type of sport, and an overwhelmingly alien one at that.

Throughout Spain, major summer festivals include bullfights, and all cities and towns of any size have a bullring. Outsiders may see only death and cruelty but aficionados see grace, courage and beauty, a combination of *arte*, *ética y estética*.

It's an intensely Spanish experience, and gives more insight into the Spanish national psyche.

Six bulls are killed during a *corrida*; they will never have seen an unmounted man, having grown up running free on huge ranches, until the moment they enter the ring. Once the bull is in the ring, it has to be weakened before the *torero* can get close enough to control it with the capework and finally kill it. This is the work of the *picadores*, with their lances, and the *bandilleros*, who plant barbed sticks in the bull's neck. It's the prelude to the final act, the *faena*, when the matador draws the bull across his body in a series of passes, then kills the bull with a clean thrust over the horns, between the shoulder blades and through the aorta.

The season runs from March to October. The *corrida* traditionally starts at 5pm, but 7pm is becoming the norm. Prices vary enormously but can start from around €12. Buy your ticket at the bullring box office. Seats are divided into *sol* (sun), *sombra* (shade) and *sol y sombra* (sun and shade). In the height of summer it's worth paying extra to sit in the shade; pay for a cushion, too, as stone benches often form the seating. You can explore the world of the *corrida* at www.mundo-taurino.org

For the anti-bullfighting message, see www.pacma.es (also in English). Attitudes are changing in Spain—bullfights are no longer shown on state television, as they are deemed unsuitable for children.

FISHING
Northern Atlantic Spain and the Pyrenees have very good trout and salmon fishing, and lakes all over the country are stocked with carp, bream and other freshwater fish. The delta of the River Ebro is noted for catfish, and catches of 45kg (100lb) are fairly common. You will need a permit, available from the local ICONA office in larger towns or local tourist information offices. If you want a fishing trip to Spain, check out www.fishing-guides.co.uk which lists fishing holiday specialists.

GOLF
Golf is big business in Spain, and there are more than 150 courses to choose from. Beautifully designed, and often challenging, courses have proliferated in recent years, with country-club facilities around them, and sometimes entire housing and villa developments within the complex. You'll find this type of golf facility mainly on the Mediterranean coast; the Costa del Sol, the Costa Blanca, the Costa Brava, Almería, La Manga, on the Mar Menor, and the Costa de la Luz all provide a wide choice.

Golfers can reserve a golfing holiday, the cost of which includes flights and hotels as well as green fees on a specified number and selection of courses. Professional instruction is also available, usually with an English or English-speaking professional.

If you just want a game of golf, ask at the local tourist information office for details of the nearest course. Spanish golf clubs are private and can be very exclusive, but it's often possible to play a round and rent clubs and a trolley and use the driving range.

Many courses arrange a day membership, although it can be extremely expensive.

GYMS
There are two types of fitness complex in Spain—the simple *gimnasio* and the *polideportivo*.

At a *gimnasio* you'll find health-club facilities with weights, exercise machines, aerobic classes and sometimes a pool, Jacuzzi or sauna. Such clubs are usually private and can be mixed or single sex. Some hotels have reciprocal arrangements with the nearest *gimnasio*.

Polideportivos are public sports complexes, run by the local government. You'll find them all over the country. Facilities vary enormously, with some offering little more than gym equipment, while others may include pools and tennis courts. Unlike a *gimnasio*, where the price—often quite high—includes

the use of all that's on offer, at a *polideportivo* you pay only for the facilities you actually use; normally, the rates are more than reasonable.

To find out more, ask at your hotel or the local tourist information office.

HORSEBACK-RIDING

You will find riding opportunities all over the country, with specialized tour operators offering guided riding holidays through some of the most beautiful areas. If you want just a gentle day's trekking or hacking, contact the local tourist office; for a riding holiday in the Alpujarras, one of Spain's most beautiful and unspoiled regions, you could try:

Rancho Ferrer
Rubite 18711, Granada
(tel 958 34 91 16,
www.ranchoferrer.com)

Dallas Love
18412 Bubíon (tel 958 76 30 38,
www.spain-horse-riding.com)

SOCCER

Soccer *(fútbol)* is Spain's most popular spectator sport. The country's two most dominant teams are Real Madrid and FC Barcelona, though they're challenged by clubs like Atlético Madrid, Deportivo A Coruña, Valencia FC, Athletic de Bilbao, Sevilla and Villareal.

The season runs from the end of August/September until May and matches are normally played on Sunday afternoons, with some midweek and Saturday evening games. Except for the big matches, tickets are fairly easy to obtain, either direct from the ground or from agencies.

FC Barcelona
Camp Nou, Avinguda Arístides Maillol, Les Corts (tel 902 18 99 00 in Spain, 934 96 36 00 from abroad. Ticket office Mon–Thu 9–1.30, 3.30–6, Fri 9–2.30; also Sat 9–1.30 when there are weekend matches, www.fcbarcelona.com).

Real Madrid
Estadio Santiago Bernabéu, Paseo de la Castellana 144, Chamartín (tel 913 98 43 00. Ticket office 6–9pm daily, www.realmadrid.es).

SWIMMING
With summer temperatures pushing 40°C (104°F), pools are practically a necessity in Spain, particularly inland. Along the coast, many seaside hotels also have their own pools.

Spanish beach standards are high; water is clean and beaches display the rating given by the international beach standards authority.

Popular beaches normally have freshwater showers, bars, restaurants and toilet facilities nearby, as well as sunbeds and umbrellas for rent. If the beach is sandy, it is usually cleaned and raked overnight, and you are expected to deposit litter in the trash cans provided.

Away from the coast, there are plenty of opportunities for swimming. Many good hotels, particularly those in rural areas, have a pool. The cities often have superb amenities; Barcelona is particularly well served with the pools that were built for the 1992 Olympics.

Spanish public pools are often attractively landscaped, and may have topless sunbathing areas, water chutes for kids, and bars and cafés. For details of the locations and opening times of swimming pools, ask at your hotel or the local tourist information office.

TENNIS
Early morning or after dark on a floodlit court is the time to play tennis in summer in Spain. Many hotels in resort areas often have a clay or hard-surface court for guests, and many *polideportivos* (see Gyms) include

tennis courts. Along the Atlantic and Mediterranean coasts, courts are often part of a golf complex and non-members can play for a fixed price per hour. Most tennis venues rent out balls, and racquets. Instruction is available in Mediterranean resorts, often with an English or Australian coach.

Local tourist offices have details of what's available in resort areas; in cities, head for the tourist office or nearest *polideportivo*.

WALKING AND HIKING
The Camino de Santiago
Spain's ultimate experience for walkers has to be the Camino de Santiago—the Way of St. James—a long-distance, ancient footpath that runs across northern Spain from the Pyrenees to the city of Santiago de Compostela in Galicia (▷ 144–146). This medieval pilgrim route was revived in the 1880s, but over the last 20 years there has been a huge increase in the number of pilgrims, with people walking the Camino for very different reasons from that of the medieval wayfarers.

Local governments have invested heavily in upgrading the paths, making new ones to keep pilgrims off the horribly busy main roads, building hostels and restoring some of the historic churches and buildings along the way. From the Pyrenees to Santiago the distance is around 760km (470 miles), traversing wild and beautiful country of immense diversity, as well as some of northern Spain's most historic and beautiful cities.

You can do the Camino on foot, by bicycle or on horseback, all recognized as means of gaining the *compostela*, the certificate issued by the Cathedral authorities in Santiago, which confirms the completion of the pilgrimage. At the start, people are issued with the *credencial*, the pilgrim's passport, a multi-page folder which must be stamped by the authorities in the towns along the route. Possession of the *credencial* also entitles you to stay for a small fee at the hostels en route.

To find out more contact one of the following:

The Confraternity of St. James is an English-based, non-denominational charity dedicated to helping English-speaking pilgrims and promoting the Camino. 1 Talbot Yard, Borough High Street, London SE1 1YP, UK (www.csj.org.uk; www.jacobeo.net).

The American Pilgrims on the Camino Association, 1514 Channing Avenue, Palo Alto CA 94303-2801 (www.americanpilgrims.com).

Other countries also have pilgrim associations; check the website www.csj.org.uk.

Other options

Gentler but still superb walking can be found all over Spain, whether it's seaside strolls or upland paths through mountainous landscape.

Green tourism is becoming more widespread and local tourist boards are trying to interest visitors in the natural beauty of their areas, which can be enjoyed on foot, by bicycle or on horseback. The choice is biggest in the areas covered by the national parks (parques nacionales).

There are natural parks (parques naturales) and regional parks, which vary tremendously in size.

NATIONAL PARKS

Los Picos de Europa, straddling Asturias, Cantabria and León (▷ 74–75). Information offices at Casa Dago, Cangas de Onís, Asturias (tel 985 84 86 14); Camaleño, Cantabria (tel 942

73 30 20); Posada de Valdeón, León (tel 987 74 05 49).

Ordesa y Monte Perdido, Aragón (▷ 194–195). Information office at Ordesa (tel 974 48 64 21).

Aigüestortes i Estany de Sant Maurici, Catalonia (▷ 263). Boi information office (tel 973 69 61 89).

Tablas de Daimiel, Castile-La Mancha. Information office 11km (7 miles) north of Daimiel at park entrance (tel 926 69 31 18).

Cabañeros, Castile-La Mancha. Information office near Pueblo Nuevo del Bullaque (tel 926 78 32 97).

Doñana, Andalucía (▷ 368–369). Information office at Acebuche (tel 959 44 87 11); La Rocina (tel 959 44 23 40); www.parquenacionaldonana.com

Cabrera, south of Mallorca, a maritime park. c/o ICONA, Palma de Mallorca (tel 971 72 50 10).

There is a complete list of Spain's 14 National Parks at www.mma.es (Spanish only), or www.spain.info (several languages). Also check out www.spainmountains.com.

WATERSPORTS

With practically year-round good weather, Spain's Mediterranean coasts draw thousands of watersports enthusiasts for sailing, windsurfing, scuba diving, surfing and jet skiing.

Head for the Costas for the full range, where there are excellent tuition and rental facilities.

The Costa Blanca has particularly good options, followed by the Costa Brava and the Costa del Sol; surfers and windsurfers are drawn to the magnificent coast west of Gibraltar, the Costa de la Luz.

Surfing instructors speak good English and you can sign up for a day's lesson or a full course.

Local tourist information offices and foreign-language newspapers have full details and you'll find plenty of flyers in seaside resorts.

River watersports are gaining in popularity, particularly canoeing and white-water rafting, which are best in the Pyrenees and along the north coast into the Picos de Europa.

WINTER SPORTS

Spain is a high country (average altitude over 600m/1,970ft). There is serious skiing in the Pyrenees and Sierra Nevada, with weekend possibilites near Madrid and Santander. Skiing in Spain is less expensive than in the Alps; the infrastructure is adequate and improving. The clientele tends to be Spanish, and there's a friendly, low-key atmosphere.

» Some resorts can be reserved through overseas agencies, but you'll usually get a better deal by reserving a package in Spain or on www.viajeselcorteingles.es
» Local tourist offices offer on-the-spot mini-packages.
» The official tourist website, www.spain.info, has comprehensive information on Spain's 36 ski resorts.
» For up-to-date information on Sierra Nevada, go to www.sierranevadaski.com

Pyrenees

The town of Jaca in the province of Aragón missed out on hosting the 2010 Winter Olympics to Vancouver but they're back in the hunt for 2022. Aragón's main resorts are Candanchu and Astun; Formigal is another good bet; and Panticosa and Cerler are both intermediate areas.

Andorra has several resorts; Pal and Arinsal both give access to the main areas of Soldeu el Tarter and Pas de la Casa/Grau Roig.

Catalonia

Family resorts worth considering are Port-Ainé, Núria and Super Espot. Intermediate and advanced skiers can head for Boí-Taüll, La Masella and Baqueira-Beret, the largest ski resort in Spain. There is good cross-country skiing at Lles de Cerdanya and in the Sierra del Cadí.

Sierra Nevada

The ski slopes are at Solynieve, 28km (17 miles) away from Granada. This makes weekend skiing crowded. It's best to go mid-week, and aim to arrive early in the seaon; January and February are the best months.

HEALTH AND BEAUTY

SPAS

Spain's spas (*balnearios*) may not be the five-star beauty-farm type—though these are starting to appear—but as a totally Spanish experience and a quick, inexpensive route to physical wellbeing, they're hard to beat.

The Spanish have a long tradition of using mineral water to improve their health, either by drinking it or by using its beneficial qualities as a source of treatment for everything from allergies and skin problems to liver complaints, rheumatism and arthritis.

Some spas are in remote areas, so you may find yourself well off the beaten track. Some have a range of hotels in the town or village, others comprise just one hotel built around a single water source.

If you're seeking to alleviate a medical condition, you will see a doctor who will work out a regime for you when you arrive. If not, and you just want to wallow in steaming water in a marble tub, make a reservation and enjoy. Bathing usually takes place in the first half of the morning, leaving the rest of the day to pursue other pleasures.

Also worth mentioning are the Arab Baths, which you can enjoy in Seville and Granada:

» Seville: www.airedesevilla.com
» Granada: tel 958 22 99 78
www.hammamspain.com

FOR CHILDREN

THEME PARKS

Given the vast numbers of visitors staying along Spain's Mediterranean coast, it's not surprising that theme parks have sprung up in recent years. Most of them are within easy reach of the main resort areas.

TAKING YOUR KIDS

» Children are welcome everywhere in Spain; the Spanish love kids and are indulgent towards them, but their own are brought up strictly.
» Spanish children stay up late—if parents are eating out, the kids go, too. This means that most hotels do not offer a baby-sitting service.
» Budget hotels and *hostales* (boarding houses) are often unheated. This is worth knowing if you're touring in the north or out of season.
» Family-run *hostales* will often let you use the kitchen if you need to prepare baby food.
» Baby needs are readily available, but you might want to bring formula.
» Most *hostales* and *pensiones* will put up to four beds in a room so that families can stay together. Just ask.
» Reductions for children are available on RENFE trains: children under 4 travel free, children between 4 and 12 get a 40 per cent discount.
» Barcelona and Madrid tourist offices have good information on attractions for children.
» It's also worth asking at other tourist information offices, particularly in the coastal areas.
» Remember the strength of the sun in Spain; apply high-factor suncream liberally and keep children covered up until they acclimatize.
» Keep them in the shade during the middle of the day, when the sun is at its hottest.
» If they're swimming, persuade them to cover up—it's better to have a wet T-shirt than a sunburned and miserable child.

WHAT TO DO

PRACTICALITIES

THE BIGGEST AND BEST THEME PARKS

Parque Warner
www.parquewarner.com
A vast theme park dedicated to Warner Bros cartoon characters and superheroes, this is Spain's newest megapark. Exciting rides, shows, water park and much more. (Check online for hotel-plus-ride deals.)
✉ Carretera A4, km 22, 28330 San Martín de la Vega ☎ 902 02 41 00, 918 21 13 00 (from outside Spain) 🕐 Summer daily; winter weekends only

Terra Mítica
www.terramiticapark.com
A huge park near Benidorm, its theme is the World of Myths. There are rides, shows and events based on past Mediterranean civilizations, such as Egypt, Greece and Rome. Rides include a great log flume and Europe's largest wooden roller-coaster.
✉ Carretera Benidorm a Finstrat, Camino del Moralet s/n ☎ 902 02 02 20 🕐 Summer 10am–midnight; mid-Sep to end Oct 10am–8pm; closed Nov–end Feb

Universal's Port Aventura
www.portaventura.es
Another massive park, this one is outside Salou, complete with its own rail station. It has five themed areas—Polynesia, the Mediterranean, the Far West, Mexico and China—and is constantly expanding. There are themed shows and rides to suit all ages and tastes.
✉ Salou, Tarragona ☎ 902 202 200; 0870 700 5122 (from UK); 00 34 977 77 90 90 (from other countries) 🕐 Mid-Jun to mid-Sep 10am–midnight; rest of year 10–8; closed Jan–mid-Mar

Other Parks
Cortylandia, Puerto Banús, Marbella.
Isla Mágica, Seville.
Tibidabo Parc d'Atraccions, Barcelona
Parque de Atracciones, Madrid
Parque de Atracciones de Monte Igueldo, Donostia (San Sebastián).
Tivoli World, Arroyo de la Miel, Benalmádena, Málaga.

FESTIVALS AND EVENTS

Like all European countries, Spain has an active arts scene and stages arts festivals of different types throughout the year. These take place mainly in the larger cities and can be focused on classical music, opera, jazz, folk and contemporary music, theatre, ballet and dance. Where the country differs is in the enormous range of fiestas, uniquely Spanish celebrations involving the whole community. During the year, even the tiniest and most remote villages dedicate at least one day to staging the biggest, noisiest, best fiesta they can afford, while the celebrations in larger cities and towns can continue for days on end.

Every fiesta is different, but the common strand of many is usually a key point in the Christian year. This can range from the great religious feasts of Lent, Easter and Corpus Christi, celebrated right across Spain, to individual feast days dedicated to the Virgin or the patron saint of a local community. Most fiestas include a procession or parade, feasting and drinking, fireworks, music and dance—all elements which unite a community and re-affirm local ties and culture.

For a real insight into Spain, try and take in a fiesta if you have the chance while you are there.

They often occur over the weekend nearest to the feastday itself. If you're planning to attend one of the major festivals such as the Valencia Fallas, San Fermín in Pamplona or Semana Santa in Seville, reserve a hotel room well in advance.

Local tourist offices supply up-to-date information on festivals in their area. You'll also see posters and flyers; these normally give a full schedule of events, timings and venues throughout the fiesta period.

You can also check out www.festivals.com for more information.

THE BIGGEST AND THE BEST FESTIVALS

Carnavales Celebrates the run-up to Lent with processions, floats, music, fireworks and frenzied partying. It is celebrated all over Spain, but experts agree that Sitges in Catalonia, Galicia and Cádiz in Andalucía have the edge (February–March).

Fallas de San José (Valencia) Dedicated to the feast of San José, a week-long party focused on giant satirical caricatures, the *fallas*. These are judged before being set alight on the *Nit de Foc*. Processions, fireworks and feasting daily (19 March).

Semana Santa The most important religious event of the year, the week leading up to Easter is celebrated throughout Spain with penitential processions of great drama and intensity. Those at Seville, Málaga,

Córdoba and Granada are considered the best (March–April).

Feria de Abril (Seville) Week-long fair, the largest in Spain, with music, dance, horses, eating and drinking (April).

Feria de Caballo (Jerez de la Frontera) Spain's biggest horse fair is a chance to see superb riders and their mounts and much more (April/May).

Romería del Rocio (Huelva) Enormous, atmospheric fiesta in the form of a pilgrimage to the shrine of the Virgin at El Rocío in Andalucía. Horse-drawn carriages and processions converge on a tiny and remote village from all over southern Spain (Whitsun week).

Fiesta de San Fermín (Pamplona) Huge

fiesta during which members of the public run through the streets of the town ahead of six bulls. Processions, bullfights, feasting, dancing and fireworks every day for a week (July).

Fiesta de Santiago (Santiago de Compostela) Enormous celebration in honour of St. James, patron saint of Spain, and celebrating Galician history and culture. Stupendous fireworks and processions (July).

Misteri d'Elx (Elx) Unique medieval mystery plays performed by townspeople to celebrate the life of the Virgin, with general partying (August).

Enjoying a good meal and sampling some of a country's special dishes is a major pleasure when you're abroad, and there's something to satisfy most tastes in Spain. Apart from paella (saffron rice, chicken and seafood), *tortilla* (potato omelette) and *gazpacho* (tomato- and pepper-based chilled soup), the country has no single national cuisine; rather, each region takes pride in its own local produce and culinary traditions. Spain's diversity shines through as much in its cooking as in its cities, towns, languages and landscape.

The accent everywhere is on local, seasonal and fresh produce, so you'll find rice and seafood on the coasts and baby roast meats in the interior, while hearty soups and stews in the misty north contrast with cooling salads and a multitude of vegetables in the more southerly areas. The larger cities have restaurants specializing in dishes from different regions, so visitors to Madrid and Barcelona can sample the cooking of the entire country. Fast food, in the form of tapas, is some of the best in Europe, but if you yearn for a burger, a taste of home or a sandwich, you'll find it here too.

MEALS AND MEALTIMES

» Breakfast *(desayuno)* is usually eaten between 9 and 10, often after they've started work; they'll have had a quick coffee to start the day. If you're staying in a hotel, a Continental-type breakfast, with fruit juice, cereal, bread, cold cuts and cheese, may be included in the room price; if not, head for a bar or café.
» The quintessential Spanish breakfast is *chocolate con churros* — thick, sweet chocolate served with strips of deep-fried dough, which you dip in the chocolate. It's also a popular snack in bars at the end of a hard day (or a long night's partying!).
» *Tostadas* (toast) with coffee is the other main choice for breakfast. The toast can be eaten with olive oil *(con aceite)*, butter *(con mantequilla)*, jam *(con mermelada)* or *manteca* — pork lard with crushed paprika; not for the faint-hearted first thing in the morning.
» Lunch *(almuerzo)*, the main meal, is served between 2 and 4, and is traditionally the most important meal of the day. It generally consists of three or four courses, starting with soup, hors d'oeuvres *(entremeses)* and/or salad, followed by the main course with vegetables.
» Dessert choices are limited — fruit, ice cream or the ubiquitous *flan* (baked egg custard). The wonderful pastries found in the *pastelerías* are eaten as snacks rather than as part of a restaurant meal.
» The Spanish eat dinner *(cena)* any time after 9, right through until midnight. It's a lighter meal than lunch, usually vegetable soup, egg dishes and rice, with lighter meats and fish as popular choices.
» In resort areas, restaurants are used to foreign eating habits and you can order dinner earlier, but don't

expect this in the interior. Dinner time varies across the country but it's never much before 8.30, and in Madrid restaurants open for dinner at 9 at the earliest.

WHERE TO EAT
» *Comedores*, family-run eating houses usually attached to bars serving all-inclusive menus, are the best budget choice. These serve the *menú del día*, sometimes called the *cubierto* or *menú de la casa*—a three-course meal with bread and wine between €10 and €14. You'll find them all over the provinces, often in a room behind a bar, or behind an unmarked doorway.

» *Cafeterías* are a more modern equivalent and are often self-service; good if you're in a hurry. They usually offer *platos combinados*, a combined plate, with bread and a drink included. Prices are similar to those charged in *comedores*.

» *Restaurantes* are graded by the local authorities with one to five forks, and range from simple places serving up the trusty *menú del día* to something very grand indeed, with prices to match. In resort areas, restaurants serve food mainly with a distinctly international twist, which can mean anything from British staples like steak and kidney pie or a huge fry-up to bland re-workings of haute cuisine. On the Mediterranean in particular, if you're looking for truly Spanish cooking, it's better to head well away from your hotel. Resort restaurants also tend to be more expensive, and you're unlikely to find a fixed-price menu.

» *Marisquerías* are restaurants serving fish and seafood exclusively. You'll find them all over Spain, which has a tradition of transporting fish quickly from the coast into the heart of the interior. Fish is not cheap, but bear in mind that the price quoted on the menu is often per kilo; your portion is weighed and priced accordingly. There's little difference between prices at *marisquerías* on the coast and inland.

» It's customary for tourists to leave a small tip; 5 to 10 per cent of the bill is the norm.

» Most restaurants add a 7 per cent IVA tax; the menu states if this is the case.

TAPAS
Tapas are Spain's great contribution to the European culinary scene, found in bars in every corner of the country. These snacks, once traditionally served free with a drink, range from a few olives or almonds to *tortilla*, chunks of meat and fish, *jamón ibérico* (cured raw ham) or its less expensive cousin *jamón Serrano*, shellfish, anchovies, salads, meat croquettes and wonderful vegetable dishes laced with garlic and chilli. Tapas can be hot or cold, and are laid out on the counter or listed on a board behind it. Some hot tapas are cooked to order. If you want more than a mouthful or two, ask for a *ración*, a larger serving.

» All tapas bars have their own special dishes. Locals move from place to place, ordering the dish that each bar does particularly well.

» Tapas are found in bars, *tabernas*, bodegas, *cervecerías* and *tascas*.

» Half a dozen tapas and three or four *raciones* make a varied and delicious meal for two or three people.

» The bartender normally keeps track of what you've had to eat.

» It's quite acceptable to discard paper napkins, toothpicks, etc on the floor in many bars—follow what others do.

OTHER FAST FOOD
» International burger chains, such as McDonald's and Burger King, are found in most cities and larger towns.

» The word sandwich in Spain means toasted cheese and ham, made using sliced white bread; the real thing is a *bocadillo*, a crusty roll bursting with filling.

» Two nationwide chains, Pans & Co and Bocatta, serve *bocadillos* and other snacks.

» Some grocery shops will make you up a sandwich for a picnic, or you can buy what you need at the market. Bakers' stalls often sell *empanadas* (small savoury pies) and other bread and pastry snacks.

INTERNATIONAL CUISINE
» Restaurants in the Mediterranean coast resort areas serve pan-European food, international dishes familiar to everyone. Many resorts

have restaurants owned by foreign nationals serving dishes from their own country, where they'll rustle up a full English breakfast or a traditional Sunday lunch.

» Major cities have French, Italian and other restaurants. The number of Chinese establishments is increasing, and you'll find them in even relatively off-the-beaten-track towns. The widest choice of international restaurants is in Madrid, Barcelona and along the Mediterranean coast.

WHAT TO DRINK

» Beer (cerveza) is widely drunk in Spain, and can be more expensive than house wine. It comes in bottles or on draught; ask for a caña, or caña doble or tubo for a larger glass. Spain produces national and local beers, and many foreign brands are imported or made under licence in Spain. San Miguel is probably the most popular brand.

» You'll find cider (sidra) in northern Spain, particularly the Basque country and Asturias.

» Wine (vino) is the normal meal-time drink, either red (tinto), white (blanco) or rosé (rosado). The most common bottled wines found throughout the country are Valdepeñas and Rioja, but there are presently over 65 denomination areas in Spain, and local wines can be excellent. On the whole, house wine (vino de la casa) is the norm, either specially bottled or straight from the barrel. There are three categories of higher-grade bottled wine: crianza, reserva and gran reserva. Label laws specify that this must be shown on the bottle. Crianza means aged in wood, and it's this that gives good-quality Spanish wine its distinctive taste. Reservas will have spent anything from six months to two years in oak casks. The gran reservas are the best; aged for at least two years in oak, they may not be sold until six years after harvest and can be of exceptional quality.

» Sherry is produced around Jerez de la Frontera in Andalucía. It's served in a large copa (glass), often chilled, and makes a perfect accompaniment to tapas. Ask for it fino (dry), amontillado (medium) or oloroso (sweet).

» Montilla and manzanilla, also from Andalucía, are similar to sherry and well worth trying.

» For bottled water in restaurants, ask for agua mineral con gas (sparkling) or sin gas (still).

» Spirits are much cheaper in Spain than many other countries, and are served in generous measures. Nationally produced brands are the least expensive and, except for whisky, are generally of good quality. Specify the brand when ordering. Spanish brandy (coñac) is popular; try Osborne, Fundador, Veterano or Soberano to get an idea of the range. The most popular liqueur is anís, with the taste of aniseed.

» The full range of international soft drinks, including Coca-Cola, Seven-Up and Sprite, can be found everywhere in Spain. Local drinks worth sampling are fresh zumo (fruit juice), granizado (slush) and horchata (a milky drink made from tiger nuts).

» Coffee is served in bars, cafés and heladerías (ice-cream shops) throughout the day. It's normally good, strong espresso served black (café solo). If you want black coffee, ask for a café americano, which is an espresso topped up with hot water. If you want milk, ask for a café cortado, a small cup with a drop of milk; a café con leche is made with lots of hot milk; and for a drop of coffee and lots of milk, ask for a manchada. If you want tea (té) with milk, ask for the milk when the tea arrives, or you could end up with a tea bag in a glass of hot milk.

SPECIAL REQUIREMENTS

» If you need to watch what you're eating, be sure to tell the waiters when you're ordering—they'll do their best to help (▷ 459).

» Vegetarians should be careful when choosing a meal, as seemingly innocuous soups, rice and and vegetable dishes are usually made with meat stock and pieces of bacon or sausage. Even straightforward vegetables may contain pork fat. It's always best to ask.

» Gluten-free diets are best achieved by sticking to plain grills, roasts and rice dishes. As bread is the traditional accompaniment to meals, main dishes are normally served without vegetables, so order a side dish of potatoes to provide some bulk. Flour and bread are used as a thickener in sauces and soups, so watch out here. Some tapas, such as bolas and buñuelos, are pastry- or bread-based or made using flour-thickened béchamel sauce. On the whole, it's safer to stick to the most simple dishes, salads and fruit.

» If you can't tolerate milk you should have few problems as it is used little in Spanish cooking. Avoid wine and cream sauces, particularly if you're touring in the north where cream features in some special dishes. Creamy puddings are based on egg yolks and almonds rather than dairy products.

CHILDREN'S FOOD

» Spanish children eat out with their parents from an early age and are expected to behave properly and eat what's on offer. They're welcome at most restaurants, and will be fussed over by waiters. If your children are picky eaters with small appetites, tapas are ideal, and every restaurant will rustle up a plate of fries to go with the fried eggs, omelette or fish.

» Very small children can share their parents' plates and finish off with an ice-cream. If you want to feed them early in the evening, cafés and bars are a good bet before they fill up with evening drinkers around 7pm.

Each region of Spain has its own dishes, based on the best locally available ingredients and served with regional wines or other drinks. If you don't speak Spanish it can be a daunting experience working out what's on the menu. Below is a menu reader that helps you familiarize yourself with some of the dishes and foods you are likely to come across.

COMIDAS – MEALS

desayuno breakfast
almuerzo lunch
cena/comida dinner

PLATOS – COURSES

entremés/entrantes starter
el primero first course
el segundo/plato principal course
postre dessert

CARNE – MEAT

beicón bacon
bistec/k steak
morcilla blood sausage or black pudding
ternera beef up to two years old
cerdo pork
chorizo spicy sausage
chuleta chop
conejo rabbit
cordero lamb
hígado liver
jamón de York cooked ham
jamón serrano cured raw ham
lengua tongue
lomo de cerdo pork tenderloin
pato duck
pavo turkey
perdiz partridge
pollo chicken
salchicha cured, ready-to-eat sausage
solomillo de ternera fillet of beef
ternera veal, but can be up to two years old

PESCADO – FISH

anchoas preserved anchovies
atún tuna
bacalao salted, dried cod
boquerones fresh anchovies
lenguado sole
lubina sea bass
merluza hake
mero grouper
pez espada swordfish
rape monkfish
raya skate
salmón salmon
salmonete red mullet
trucha trout

MARISCOS – SEAFOOD

anguila eel
calamares squid
cangrejo crab
cigalas scampi
concha/vieras scallops
gamba prawn (shrimp)
langosta lobster

mejillón mussel
ostra oyster
pulpo octopus

VERDURAS – VEGETABLES
aguacate avocado
ajo garlic
apio celery
berenjena aubergine (eggplant)
berza green cabbage
brócoli broccoli
calabacín courgette (zucchini)
cebolla onion
champiñones mushrooms
coliflor cauliflower
espárragos asparagus
espinacas spinach
garbanzos chick peas
guisantes peas
habas broad beans
judías dried beans
judías verdes green beans
lechuga lettuce
patata potato
pepinillo pickled gherkin
pepino cucumber
pimientos red/green peppers
verduras vegetables
zanahorias carrots

FRUTA – FRUIT
albaricoque apricot
cereza cherry
chirimoya custard apple
frambuesa raspberry
fresa strawberry
limón lemon
manzana apple
melocotón peach
melón melon
naranja orange
pera pear
piña pineapple
platano banana
uva grape

COOKING METHODS
a la brasa flame-grilled (broiled)
a la plancha grilled on a griddle
al horno baked, roasted
asado roast
crudo raw
frito fried
poché poached
relleno filled/stuffed

ESPECIALIDAD – SPECIAL DISHES
ajo blanco con uvas de Málaga chilled almond cream soup with garlic and muscat grapes
ajo de la mano potatoes cooked with chillies, dressed with pounded garlic, cumin, oil and vinegar
albóndigas en salsa meatballs in sauce, usually tomato
alioli emulsion of garlic and olive oil
arroz/arroces (plural) rice dishes, some cooked with fish, others with vegetables, meat or sausages
bacalao a la vizcaína salted cod in a sauce of piquant peppers and sweet chillies
canelones similar to cannelloni, but stuffed with tuna or spinach as well as meat and covered in a white sauce, rather than tomato sauce
cocido slow-cooked meat, sausage, legume and vegetable stew; the ingredients vary from region to region
churros strips of fried dough covered in sugar
crema catalana a creamy sweet custard, served cold with a crackling layer of caramelized sugar on top
ensalada mixta salad that can include a wide range of vegetables
ensalada ruso or ensaladilla Russian or little salad made of potato, peas, carrots and mayonnaise
escalivada a dish of peppers, aubergine (eggplant) and courgette (zucchini)
escudella meat, vegetable, bean, and noodle stew
fideuà paella with fine noodles instead of rice
gazpacho chilled soup made from puréed bread and garlic, with raw peppers, tomatoes and cucumber
pa amb tomàquet bread rubbed with tomato, sprinkled with salt and drizzled with olive oil; a Catalán dish
paella the most famous of the *arroces*, but saffron is less used than in the traditional Valencian dish
patatas bravas potatoes in a spicy tomato sauce
tortilla española Spanish omelette made with potatoes
tortilla francesa plain omelette

ENTREMÉS – SIDE DISHES
ensalada salad
huevo egg
mantequilla butter
pan bread
patatas fritas chips (french fries)
queso cheese

POSTRE–CAKES AND DESSERTS
bizcocho, galleta biscuit
el bizcocho de chocolate chocolate cake
buñuelos warm, sugared, deep-fried doughnuts, sometimes cream-filled
con nata with cream
flan crème caramel
helado ice cream
pastel cake
pijama ice cream with fruit and syrup
postre de músico dessert of dried fruit and nuts
la tarta de queso cheesecake
la tartaleta de frutas fruit tart

BEBIDAS – DRINKS
agua con gas sparkling water
agua sin gas still water
café coffee
cerveza beer
hielo ice
zumo fruit juice
leche milk
sidra cider
té tea
vino blanco white wine
vino rosado rosé wine
vino tinto red wine
zumo de naranja orange juice

ADREZO DE MESA – CONDIMENTS
aceite de oliva olive oil
ajo garlic
azúcar sugar
mermelada jam
miel honey
pimiento pepper
sal salt
salsa sauce
vinagre vinegar

CUENTA – THE BILL
servicio está incluido service included
servicio no está incluido service not included

Accommodation options in Spain range from luxury suites in world-class resort hotels and historic, state-run *paradores* to simple village rooms in remote areas. This is still a country where you still get value for money, and there's something to suit all pockets. On the whole, rooms are more expensive in the big cities and at the popular resorts, particularly in high season. If you're heading for the remoter areas, you may be pleasantly surprised at how far your euros go.

Reserve in advance in the main resort areas, and, in summer, in off-the-beaten-track regions that aren't as well served with hotels. If you are touring, reserve ahead the night before, or aim to get to your destination in the afternoon, to give yourself time to find somewhere to stay. Remember that the Spanish take a holiday break in summer, and they too will be pouring into the popular areas.

PARADORES

The *paradores*, Spain's state-run chain of top-quality hotels, are wonderful places to stay.

Most are in historic buildings—castles, monasteries and palaces—lovingly converted to luxurious standards while still retaining their character. Often beautifully furnished with antiques, they are oases of calm, with restaurants where the accent is firmly on the best of local ingredients and cuisine. Some *paradores* are modern, purpose-built hotels, and some, even the historic ones, retain a distinctly institutional feel.

Prices at *paradores* vary considerably depending on their situation, so there's no need to dismiss the idea even if you're on a tight budget.

HOTELS

Hotels in Spain are classified and regularly inspected by the various regional authorities. They are awarded one to five stars *(estrellas)*, according to the amenities they provide. You can expect five-star hotels to be truly luxurious, with superb facilities and a high level of service. The 4-star listings are almost as good and the standard is high. A 3-star hotel costs appreciably less, but can be lovely, particularly in rural areas. Rooms in these hotels will have TV and air-conditioning, but the public areas are less imposing. One- and two-star hotels are relatively inexpensive, but are clean and comfortable, and rooms almost always have private bathrooms in 2-star places. Simpler hotels rarely have restaurants, and some do not provide breakfast.

HOSTALES
At first glance there's little to distinguish many *hostales* from small hotels, and they're often nicer and better value for money. They tend to be family run, and are graded from one to three stars; a three-star *hostal* is generally on a par with a two-star hotel.

PENSIONES
These family-run establishments with simple, clean rooms and shared bathrooms are a good choice for budget visitors. Their only drawback is that the owner sometimes expects you to take either full- or half-board, eating your meals in the *pensión,* cutting out the chance to sample the local restaurants. Check when you make your reservation.

CAMAS
Camas, sometimes advertised as *habitaciones*, are rooms in private houses or above bars and restaurants in country towns and villages and on the coast. They are inexpensive and simple, with shared bathrooms.

FONDAS
You'll find these small inns with basic rooms for rent in rural localities.

CASAS RURALES
These are country houses, often farms or working estates, that rent rooms and provide breakfast and sometimes dinner. They are gaining in popularity. Staying in a private country house is an eye-opener to the 'real Spain', and is excellent value. Local tourist offices have details and will often help with reservations. Some regions are far better endowed than others; they are particularly strong in the north and Catalonia.

MONASTERIOS Y CONVENTOS
With religious orders shrinking even in this deeply Catholic country, monasteries and convents often have surplus space, particularly in more remote areas. You will be offered a simple cell, often in a wonderfully historic building. Turn up and ask, or ask the local tourist office *(Turismo)* to phone ahead. The best places for this type of arrangement are Catalonia, Galicia and Mallorca.

CAMPSITES
There are more than 350 authorized campsites in Spain, mostly along the coasts, and all are regularly inspected and graded into four categories— from 3rd-class to luxury. The better sites have swimming pools, bars, restaurants and shops, and cater for people with caravans (RVs), so if you are camping with a tent, stick to the smaller sites.

SELF-CATERING
If you want total independence, or have young children, self-catering might be an attractive option. Tour operators offer villa packages to many areas of Spain, all-in deals that can include flights and car rental. If you want to arrange details yourself, contact the local *Turismo* in advance. You can do this via the internet, where you'll also find sites devoted to private house rentals. Check out www. holidayrentals.com for further information.

FINDING A ROOM
» If you haven't reserved in advance, the best place to start looking is around the main plaza, where you'll find the greatest concentration of hotels and *hostales*. The local *Turismo*, if there is one, will have lists of possibilities and may be willing to phone on your behalf.
» It's perfectly acceptable to ask to see a hotel room before you make up your mind.
» You will be asked to leave your passport for registration.
» Check-out is normally noon, although at some *hostales* and *pensiones* it may be 11am.

» Hotels will often store your luggage till the end of the day.

PRICING
» Room rates vary according to the season by as much as 25 per cent, and during national holidays or local fiestas, such as *Semana Santa* (Holy Week) and the April *feria* in Seville or the *Fallas* in Valencia.
» Hotels often quote their most expensive prices; you could ask if they have less expensive rooms. They often have weekend reductions. The best deals can usually by found by shopping around on the internet.
» Smaller hotels are usually open to a little gentle bargaining, particularly during quieter times.
» Some establishments will put an extra bed in a room for a small charge; ideal for families.
» If you have problems, ask to see the *libro de reclamaciones*—the complaints book, which all establishments are legally required to keep. Such a request generally produces instant results.

TIPS
» If you're touring around Spain the best guide is the *Guía Oficial de Hoteles,* published annually by Turespaña, and on sale (€14) from January/February. This gives a complete list of hotels, *hostales* and *pensiones*, arranged alphabetically in regions. Addresses, telephone and fax numbers, and websites where applicable, are given as well as information on rooms and services. Pamphlets with the same information for separate regions are also available from tourist offices.
» Campers can buy *Guía de Campings*, which is laid out similarly, from most bookshops (€11).
» If you want to book a *parador* try: Central de Reservas, Requena 3, 28013 Madrid (tel 915 16 66 66; www.parador.es).
» Other online reservation sites include: www.madeinspain.net www.travelweb.com www.interhotel.com/spain/es www.all-hotels.com

Once you have mastered a few basic rules, Spanish is an easy language to speak: It is phonetic and, unlike English, particular combinations of letters are always pronounced the same way. When a word ends in a vowel, an n or an s, the stress is usually on the penultimate syllable; otherwise, it falls on the last syllable. If a word has an accent, this is where the stress falls.

a	as in	pat
e	as in	set
i	as **e** in	be
o	as in	hot
u	as in	flute
ai, ay	as **i** in	side
au	as **ou** in	out
ei, ey	as **ey** in	they
oi, oy	as **oy** in	boy

Consonants as in English except:
c before **i** and **e** as **th**, although some Spaniards say it as **s**
ch as **ch** in church
d at the end of a word becomes **th**
g before **i** or **e** becomes **ch** as in loch
h is silent
j as **ch** in loch
ll as **lli** in million
ñ as **ny** in canyon
qu is hard like a **k**
r usually rolled
v is a **b**
z is a **th**, but **s** in parts of Andalucía

COLOURS
black ....negro
blue ....azul
brown ....marrón
cerise ....cereza
gold ....oro
green .... verde
grey .... gris
mauve ....malva
orange ....naranja
pink .... rosa
purple ....purpúreo
red ....rojo
silver .... plata
turquoise ....turquesa

white .... blanco
yellow ....amarillo

CONVERSATION
What is the time?
¿Qué hora es?
I don't speak Spanish
No hablo español
Do you speak English?
¿Habla inglés?
I don't understand
No entiendo
Please repeat that
Por favor repita eso
Please speak more slowly
Por favor hable más despacio
What does this mean?
¿Qué significa esto?
Can you write that for me?
¿Me lo puede escribir?
My name is...
Me llamo...
What's your name?
¿Como de llama?
Hello, pleased to meet you
Hola, encantado
I'm from...
Soy de...
I live in...
Vivo en...
Where do you live?
¿Dónde vive usted?
Good morning/afternoon
Buenos días/buenas tardes
Good evening/night
Buenas noches
Goodbye
Adiós
This is my wife/husband/son/ daughter/friend
Esta es mi mujer/marido/ hijo/hija/ amigo
See you later
Hasta luego
That's all right
Está bien
I don't know
No lo sé
You're welcome
De nada
How are you?
¿Cómo estás?

USEFUL WORDS
yes ....sí
no .... no
please .... por favor
thank you ....gracias
fine .... bueno
there .... allí
where .... dónde
here .... aquí
when .... cuándo
who .... quien
how ....cómo
free (no charge) .... gratis
I'm sorry .... Lo siento
excuse me .... perdone
large ....grande
small .... pequeño
good .... bueno
bad .... malo

TIMES/DAYS/MONTHS/ HOLIDAYS
morning ....la mañana
afternoon .... la tarde
evening .... la tarde/noche
day ....el día
night ....la noche
today .... hoy
yesterday ....ayer
tomorrow .... mañana
now .... ahora
later .... más tarde
spring .... primavera
summer .... verano
autumn ....otoño
winter .... invierno
Monday ....lunes
Tuesday .... martes
Wednesday .... miércoles
Thursday .... jueves
Friday ....viernes
Saturday ....sábado
Sunday .... domingo
month ....el mes
year ....el año
January .... enero
February ....febrero
March .... marzo
April .... abril
May .... mayo
June .... junio
July ....julio

August	agosto
September	septiembre
October	octubre
November	noviembre
December	diciembre
Easter	Semana Santa
Christmas	Navidad
New Year	Nuevo Año
All Saints' Day	Todos los Santos
holiday (vacation)	vacaciones
pilgrimage	romería

MONEY

Is there a bank/bureau de change nearby?
¿Hay un banco/una oficina de cambio cerca?

Can I cash this here?
¿Puedo cobrar esto aquí?

I'd like to change sterling/dollars into euros
Quiero cambiar libras/dólares a euros

Can I use my credit card to withdraw cash?
¿Puedo usar la tarjeta de crédito para sacar dinero?

What is the exchange rate?
¿Cómo está el cambio?

GETTING AROUND

Where is the information desk?
¿Dónde está el mostrador de información?

What street is this?
¿Qué calle es esta?

I want to get off at...
¿Quiero bajarme en...

Which line do I take for...?
¿Que línea cojo para...

How far is...?
¿A qué distancia está...?

This is the hotel address?
¿Esta es la dirección del hotel

Where is the timetable?
¿Dónde está el horario?

Does this train/bus go to...?
¿Va este tren/autobús a...?

Does this train/bus stop at...?
¿Para este tren/autobús en...?

Do I have to get off here?
¿Me tengo que bajar aquí?

Do you have a subway/ bus map?
¿Tiene un mapa del metro/de los autobuses?

Can I have a one-way/return ticket to...?
¿Me da un billete sencillo/de ida y vuelta para...?

Can I have a standard/first-class ticket to...?
¿Quiero un billete de segunda/ primera clase para...?

I'd like to rent a car
Quiero alquilar un coche

Where are we?
¿Dónde estamos?

I'm lost
Me he perdido

Is this the way to...?
¿Es éste el camino para ir a...?

I am in a hurry
Tengo prisa

Where can I find a taxi?
¿Dónde puedo encontrar un taxi?

Please take me to...
A..., por favor

Please slow down
Vaya más despacio por favor

Can you turn on the meter?
¿Baje la bandera, por favor?

How much is the journey?
¿Cuánto cuesta esta carrera?

Could you wait for me?
¿Puede esperar aquí?

POST AND TELEPHONES

Where is the nearest post office/ mail box?
¿Dónde está la oficina de correos más cercana/el buzón más cercano?

What is the postage to...?
¿Cuánto vale mandarlo a...?

I'd like to send this by air mail
Quiero mandar esto por correo aéreo

Hello this is...
Hola, ... al habla

I'd like to speak to...
Me puede poner con...

Who is speaking?
¿Con quién hablo?

What is the number for...?
¿Cuál es el número de...?

Please put me through to...
Póngame con..., por favor

Where can I buy a phone card?
¿Dónde puedo comprar una tarjeta de teléfono?

How do I make an outside call?
¿Como hago una llamada exterior?

What is the area code?
¿Cual es el prefijo?

I'd like to make an international call
Quiero hacer una llamada internacional

It's just a local call
Solo es una llamada local

I'd like a wake-up call for 8 tomorrow morning.
Quiero que me despierten a las ocho de la mañana

SHOPPING

Could you help me please?
¿Me atiende por favor?

How much is this?
¿Cuánto vale esto?

I'm looking for...
Busco...

When does the shop open/close?
¿A qué hora abre/cierra la tienda?

I'm just looking
Sólo estoy mirando

Do you have anything less expensive/smaller/larger?
¿Tiene algo más barato/pequeño/ grande?

Do you have this in...?
¿Tienen esto en...?

This is the right size
Esta talla está bien

I'll take this
Me llevo esto

Do you have a bag for this?
¿Tiene una bolsa para esto?

Can you gift wrap this?
¿Me lo envuelve para regalo?

Do you accept credit cards?
¿Aceptan tarjetas de crédito?

I'd like ... grams
Póngame ... gramos, por favor

I'd like a kilo of ...
Póngame un kilo de...

I'd like ... slices of that
Me pone ... lonchas de eso

This isn't what I want
No es lo que quiero

Can I help myself?
¿Puedo servirme?

bakery
la panadería

pharmacy
la farmacia

supermarket
el supermercado

market
el mercado
sale
las rebajas

NUMBERS

1	uno
2	dos
3	tres
4	cuatro
5	cinco
6	seis
7	siete
8	ocho
9	nueve
10	diez
11	once
12	doce
13	trece
14	catorce
15	quince
16	dieciséis
17	diecisiete
18	dieciocho
19	diecinueve
20	veinte
21	veintiuno
30	treinta
40	cuarenta
50	cincuenta
60	sesenta
70	setente
80	ochenta
90	noventa
100	cien
1,000	mil

HOTELS

Do you have a room?
¿Tiene una habitación?
I have a reservation for ... nights
Tengo una reserva para ... noches
How much per night?
¿Cuánto por noche?
Double room
Habitación doble con cama de matrimonio
Single room
Habitación individual
Twin room
Habitación doble con dos camas
With bath/shower
Con bañera/ducha
Swimming pool
La piscina

Air-conditioning
aire acondicionada
Non-smoking
Se prohibe fumar
Is breakfast included?
¿Está el desayuno incluido?
When is breakfast served?
¿A qué hora se sirve el desayuno?
May I see the room?
¿Puedo ver la habitación?
Is there a parking area?
¿Tiene aparcamiento?
Is there a lift (elevator)?
¿Hay ascensor?
I'll take this room
Me quedo con la habitación
The room is dirty
La habitación está sucia
The room is too hot/cold
Hace demasiado calor/frío en la habitación
Can I pay my bill, please?
¿La cuenta, por favor?
Could you order a taxi for me?
¿Me pide un taxi por favor?

RESTAURANTS

See also the menu reader
▷ 452–453.
I'd like to reserve a table for ... people at...
Quiero reservar una mesa para ... personas para las...
A table for ... please
Una mesa para ... por favor
We'd like to wait for a table
Queremos esperar a que haya una mesa
Could we sit here?
¿Nos podemos sentar aquí?
Is this table free?
¿Está libre esta mesa?
Waiter/waitress
El camarero/la camarera
Is there a parking area?
¿Hay aparcamiento?
Where are the toilets?
¿Dónde están los aseos?
Can I have an ashtray?
¿Me da un cenicero?
I prefer non-smoking
Prefiero no fumadores
Could we see the menu/ wine list?
¿Podemos ver la carta/carta de vinos?

We would like something to drink
Quisieramos algo de beber
What do you recommend?
¿Qué nos recomienda?
Can you recommend a local wine?
¿Puede usted récomendar un vino de la región?
Is there a dish of the day?
¿Tiene un plato del día?
I can't eat wheat/sugar/salt/pork/ beef/dairy/nuts
No puedo tomar trigo/azúcar/ cerdo/ ternera/productos lácteos/nueces
Could I have a bottle of still/ sparkling water?
¿Podría traerme una botella de agua mineral sin/con gas?
Could we have some more bread?
¿Podría traernos más pan?
Could we have some salt and pepper?
¿Podría traernos sal y pimienta?
This is not what I ordered
Esto no es lo que yo he pedido
I ordered...
Yo pedí...
I'd like...
Quiero...
May I change my order?
¿Puedo cambiar el pedido?
How is it cooked?
¿Cómo se hace?
The food is cold
La comida está fría
... is too rare/overcooked
... está muy cruda/ demasiado hecha
We would like a coffee
Quisieramos tomar café
May I have the bill, please?
¿La cuenta, por favor?
Is service included?
¿Está incluido el servicio?
What is this charge?
¿Qué es esta cantidad?
The bill is not right
La cuenta no está bien
Do you accept this credit card (traveller's cheques)?
¿Acepta usted esta tarjeta de crédito (cheques de viajer)?
I'd like to speak to the manager
Quiero hablar con el encargado
The food was excellent
La comida ha sido excelente
We enjoyed it, thank you
Nos ha gustado, muchas gracias

knife/fork/spoon
el cuchillo/tenedor/la cuchara

SPECIAL REQUIREMENTS
Do you have vegetarian dishes?
¿Tiene platos vegetarianos?
I'd prefer a salad
Prefiero una ensalada
I have to keep to a diet
Estoy a régimen
I am allergic to mussels (shellfish)
Soy alérgico(a) a los mejillones
(mariscos)
I can't eat fried food
No puedo comer los platos fritos
I am diabetic
Soy diabético(a)
Is there any meat in it?
¿Hay carne en este plato?
I can't eat it because I'm on a diet
No puedo comerlo porque estoy a régimen
Is it very spicy (hot)?
¿Es picante?
Can you bring some (a few) serviettes?
¿Puede traernos (algunas) servilletas?
Another plate, please
Otro plato, por favor
Some (two) spoons
Unas (dos) cucharas
Some (two) teaspoons
Unas (dos) cucharillas
Have you got a high chair, please?
¿Tiene una silla alta, por favor?
Please could you warm up the baby's bottle?
¿Puede calentar el biberón de bebé?

TOURIST INFORMATION
Where is the tourist information office?
¿Dónde está la oficina de información?
Do you have a city map?
¿Tiene un plano de la ciudad?
Can you give me some information about...?
¿Tiene alguna información sobre...?
What sights/hotels/restaurants can you recommend?
¿Qué visitas/hoteles/ restaurantes nos recomienda?

Can you point them out on the map?
¿Me los puede señalar en el plano?
What time does it open/close?
¿A qué hora abre/cierra?
Are there guided tours?
¿Hay visitas con guía?
Is there an English-speaking guide?
¿Hay algún guía que hable inglés?
Can we make reservations here?
¿Podemos hacer las reservas aquí?
What is the admission price?
¿Cuánto cuesta la entrada?
Is photography allowed?
¿Se pueden hacer fotos?
Is there a discount for senior citizens/students?
¿Hacen descuento para la tercera edad/los estudiantes?
Do you have a brochure in English?
¿Tiene un folleto en inglés?
What time does the show start?
¿A qué hora empieza la función?
How much is a ticket?
¿Cuánto vale una entrada?

IN THE TOWN
church .... la iglesia
castle .... el castillo
museum ....el museo
park...................................... el parque
cathedral ....la catedral
bridge .... el puente
gallery....................la galería de arte
river... el río
no entry.................prohibido el paso
entrance .... entrada
exit .... salida
toilets................................ los aseos
men/women ..... caballeros/señoras
open.. abierto
closed .... cerrado

ILLNESS AND EMERGENCIES
I don't feel well
No me encuentro bien
Could you call a doctor?
¿Puede llamar a un médico?
I feel nauseous
Tengo ganas de vomitar
I have a headache

Me duele la cabeza
I am allergic to...
Soy alérgico a...
I am on medication
Estoy con medicación
I am diabetic
Soy diabético
I am pregnant
Estoy embarazada
I have asthma
Soy asmático
hospital
el hospital
How long will I have to stay in bed/hospital?
¿Cuánto tiempo tengo que estar en cama/el hospital?
How many tablets a day should I take?
¿Cuántas pastillas tengo que tomar al día?
Can I have a painkiller?
¿Me da un analgésico?
I need to see a doctor/dentist
Necesito un médico/dentista
I have a bad toothache
Tengo un dolor de muelas horrible
A filling has come out
Se me ha caído un empaste
Help!
¡Socorro!
Stop thief!
¡Al ladrón!
Call the fire brigade/police/ambulance
Llame a los bomberos/la policía/una ambulancia
I have lost my passport/wallet/purse/bag
He perdido el pasaporte/la cartera/el monedero/el bolso
Is there a lost property office?
¿Hay una oficina de objetos perdidos?
I have had an accident
He tenido un accidente
I have been robbed
Me han robado
Where is the police station?
¿Dónde está la comisaría?

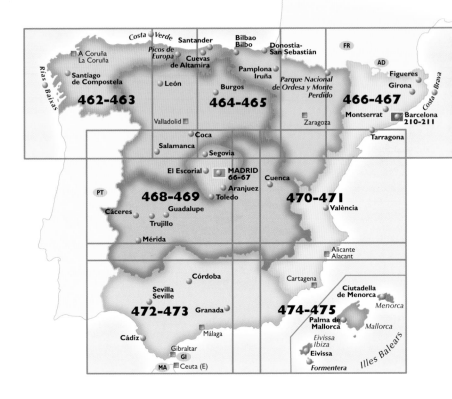

Costa Verde Santander Bilbao / Bilbo
A Coruña / La Coruña Pícos de Europa Cuevas de Altamira Donostia-San Sebastián FR
Rías Baixas Santiago de Compostela León Pamplona / Iruña Parque Nacional de Ordesa y Monte Perdido AD
462-463 Burgos **466-467** Figueres / Girona Costa Brava
Valladolid **464-465** Zaragoza Montserrat Barcelona **210-211**
Coca Tarragona
Salamanca Segovia
El Escorial MADRID **66-67** Cuenca
PT Aranjuez València
468-469 Toledo
Cáceres Guadalupe **470-471**
Trujillo
Mérida Alicante / Alacant
Córdoba Cartagena Ciutadella de Menorca
Sevilla / Seville Menorca
472-473 Granada **474-475** Palma de Mallorca Mallorca
Cádiz Málaga Eivissa / Ibiza Illes Balears
Gibraltar GI Eivissa
MA Ceuta (E) Formentera

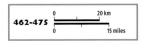

462-475 0 — 20 km / 0 — 15 miles

▨▨ Toll motorway (Turnpike)	◉ Featured place of interest
═══ Motorway (Expressway)	▪ City / Town
➋ ● Motorway junction with and without number	National / Natural park
⇒ National road	✈ Airport
— Regional road	621 ▲ Height in metres
— Local road	⚓ Port / Ferry route
— Railway	▨▨ International boundary
	-- Regional boundary

MAPS

Map references for the sights refer to the atlas pages within this section or to the individual town plans within the regions. For example, Madrid has the reference ✚ 469 G6, indicating the page on which the map is found (469) and the grid square in which Madrid sits (G6).

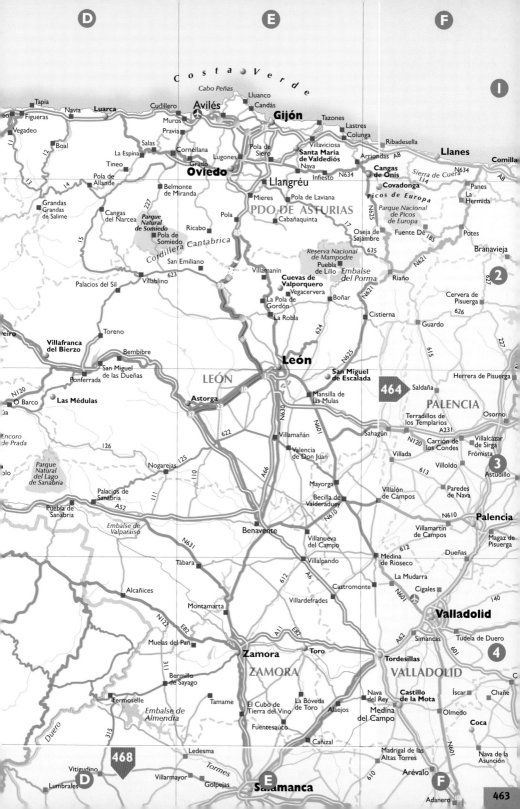

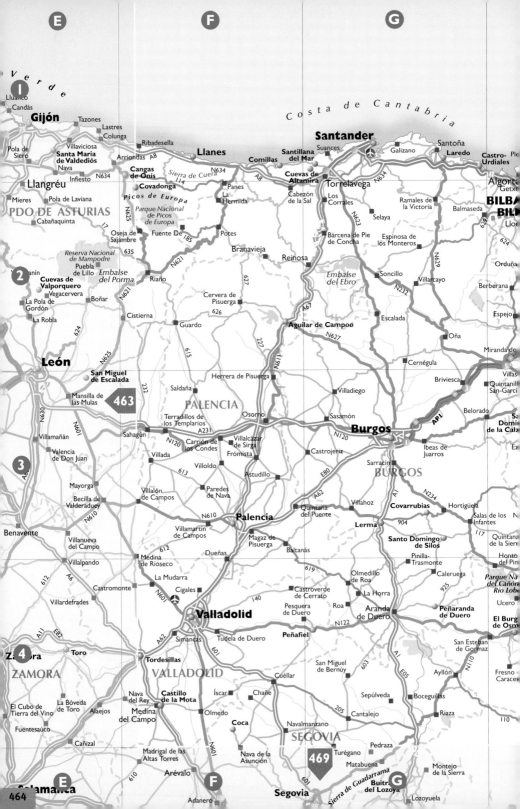

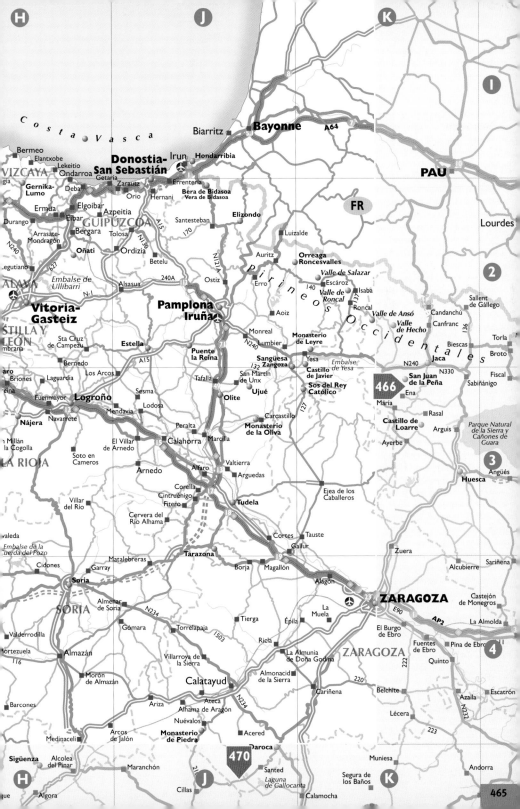

Carcassonne   Narbonne

FR

PERPIGNAN

AD

dorra
a Vella

la Seu
d'Urgell

Coll de Nargó

Oliana

Solsona

Cardona

Súria

25   Calaf
Cervera

Coloma
e Queralt

ntblanc   Vila-
rodona

over   N240

TARRAGONA

Costa   Daurada

Llívia
Puigcerdà
La Cerdanya
Alp   la Molina
Bellver de
Cerdanya   Ribes de
Freser

Berga

26   Sant Quirze
de Besora
Gironella   **Torelló**

Balsareny

BARCELONA

Manresa
37
Caldes de
Montbui
Igualada

Montserrat

Martorell
Sant Sadurní
d'Anoia   Gelida
Vilafranca
del Penedès   **Sant Boi
de Llobregat**
Castelldefels
Sitges   Garraf
El Vendrell   Vilanova i la Geltrú
Calafell
Torredembarra

Pirineos   Orientales

Castellfollit
de la Roca
Olot
Sant Pere
de Torelló
Sta Maria
de Corcó
Manlleu
Sant Hilari
Sacalm
**Vic
Vich**
Santa Coloma
de Farners
Tona
Montseny
Sant Celoni
Cardedeu
Granollers
Vilassar
de Mar
TERRASSA **SABADELL**
BADALONA
BARCELONA
El Prat de Llobregat

 Einssa, Palma de Mallorca

*Parc
Natural de la
Zona Volcànica
de la Garrotxa*
GIRONA
les Planes
d'Hostoles
Banyoles

La Jonquera
Llançà
Portbou
el Port de
la Selva
Sant Pere
de Rodes
Cap de Creus
**Figueres
Figueras**
Sant Pere
Pescador
Empúries
Viladamat

N260
Besalú

**Roses
Rosas**
Golf de Roses
*Parc Natural del
Cap de Creus*
Cadaqués

*Parc Natural
dels Aiguamolls
de l'Empordà*
L'Escala
L'Estartit
**Torroella
de Montgrí**
Begur
Calella de
Palafrugell
Palamós
Platja d'Aro

**Girona
Gerona**
Cassà de
la Selva
Llagostera
Palafrugell

Maçanet de la Selva
Sils
Tordera
Blanes
Pineda de Mar
Sant Pol de Mar
Canet de Mar
Calella
Malgrat de Mar
Tossa de Mar
Lloret de Mar
**Sant Feliu
de Guíxols**

Costa   Brava

**Arenys
de Mar**
Premià de Mar
MATARÓ

Génova

Livorno

467

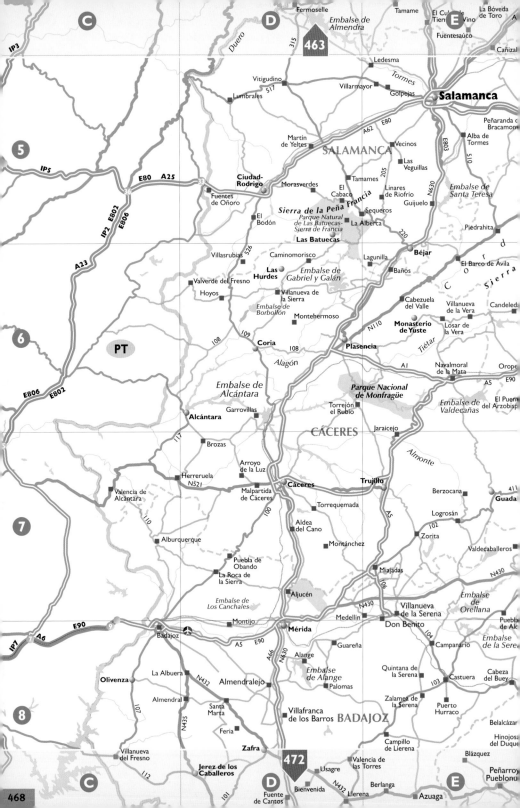

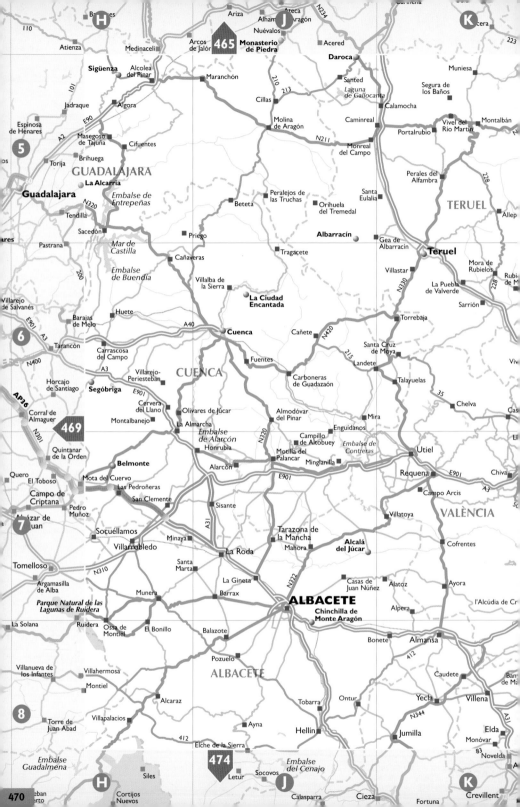

Escatrón
Caspe
466 L
Maella
Alcañiz
Valdeltormo
Castelserás
Alcorisa
Valderrobres
Monroyo
Forcall
Morella
Cinctorres
la Vallivana
Cantavieja
Ares del Maestre
del Maestrazgo
strazgo
Albocàsser
stabella
strazgo
La Torre
d'En Besora
ASTELLÓ
L'Alcora
nejos
Onda
Vila-Real
Nules
orbe La Vall
d'Uixó

Flix
12
Móra
d'Ebre
Móra la Nova
Falset
Gandesa
Miravet
Prat de
Comte
L'Ametlla de Mar
el Perelló
Tortosa
Amposta
Parc
Natural del
Delta de l'Ebre
Sant Carles
de la Ràpita
Ulldecona
Alcanar
Vinaròs
Benicarló
Peñíscola
Alcalà
de Xivert
Torreblanca
Torrenostra
la Pobla
Tornesa
Benicàssim
CASTELLÓ
DE LA PLANA
Almassora
Burriana

N420
Pla
N240
El Vendrell
Calafell
Vilanova i la Geltru
Torredembarra
TARRAGONA 467 N
Cambrils
Salou
l' Almadrava
l'Ampolla
Riumar

Costa Dau
a

N240

Costa del Azahar

Costa Dau

5

6

Sagunt
Sagunto
Puçol

Costa de València

VALÈNCIA
Silla
Parc Natural
de l'Albufera
el Perelló
Sueca
Cullera
Alzira Favara
Carcaixent
Xeraco
Xàtiva
als
Gandía
Oliva
Albaida
Pego
ent
Cocentaina
oi
70
Benissa
Xàbia
Jávea
Teulada
Moraira
Calp
Calpe
Altea
Benidorm
La Villa Joiosa
Villajoyossa
el Campello
speig
S Joan d'Alacant
ALICANTE
ALACANT
Santa Pola

Costa de València

Costa Blanca

Salerno,
Palermo,
Palma de Mallorca

474

Eivissa
Ibiza
Benirras
Sant Miquel
de Balansat
Cala Salada
Sant Antoni
de Portmany
Cala d'Hort
Illa es
Vedrà

Portinatx

Santa Eulària des Riu

Eivissa

I S'Espalmador
Sant Francesc
de Formentera
Sa Savina
Formentera
Platja
de Migjorn
El Pilar
de la Mola

Palma de Mallorca

Palma de Mallorca

7

8

475 M

L

M

N

471

Alcaraz
Tobarra
Óntur
Yecla
Villena

lacios
J
470
N344
Elda
Monóvar
83
Novelda

Torre de
Juan Abad
412
Ayna
Jumilla
K
As

8
Elche de la Sierra
Embalse
del Cenajo

Embalse
Guadalmena
Siles
Letur
Socovos
Calasparra
Cieza
Fortuna
Crevillent
El

Santisteban
del Puerto
Cortijos
Nuevos
El Sabinar
Moratalla
3314
Caravaca
de la Cruz
Cehegín
Archena
Almóradi
Dol

Villanueva del
Arzobispo
Parque Natural
de las Sierras de
Cazorla,
Segura
y las
Villas
Bullas
Mula
415
Santomera
Orihuela
Torrev

Villacarrillo
Embalse de
El Tranco
de Beas
330
MURCIA
Murcia
Dehesa
Campoan

Peal de
Becerro
Santo
Tomé
Mogón
Puebla de
Don Fadrique
La Paca
Alhama de Murcia
Alcantarilla
San Pedro
del Pinatar
San Javier

9
Cazorla
315
Huéscar
317
Parque Natural
de Sierra
María-Los Vélez
Totana
Lorca
3211
Balsicas
San Javier
San
de I
Ribe

Quesada
Embalse de
San Clemente
Pozo Alcón
330
Puerto
Lumbreras
Torre-
Pacheco
Los Alcázares

Embalse de
Negratín
A91
Mazarrón
Cartagena
La Uníc

GRANADA
A92N
Baza
473
Caniles
334
Albox
Huércal-
Overa
Águilas
AP7
Golfo de Mazarrón
Costa Cálida

Guadix
A92
Serón
Cantoria
Cuevas del
Almanzora
Vera

10
Sierra Nevada
Abla
Gérgal
Sorbas
Turre
Garrucha
Mojácar

Ugíjar
Alboloduy
348
ALMERÍA
Tabernas
Níjar
Carboneras
N341

Las Alpujarras
347
Canjáyar
Illar
Sierra de Alhamilla
E15

Berja
Dalías
Aguadulce
Almería
Parque Natural
Cabo de
Gata-Níjar

Albuñol
El Ejido
N7
Golfo de
Almería
Cabo
de
Gata

N340
Adra
Roquetas
de Mar
Almerimar

11

Salerno,
Palermo,
València

Eivissa
Ibiza
Benirràs
Portinatx
Sant Miquel
de Balansat
Cala Salada
Sant Antoni
de Portmany
Santa Eulària
des Ríu

Cala d'Hort
Dénia
Eivissa

I S'Espalmador
Sant Francesc
de Formentera
El Pilar
de la Mola

12
Melilla
Illa es
Vedrà
Sa Savina
Formentera
Platja de
Migjorn

J
M

N340

Altea

Jorm

La Villajoyosa
Villajoyossa

icente
aspeig

S Joan d'Alacant
el Campello

ALICANTE
ALACANT

Santa Pola

damar
egura

Costa Blanca

Oran

Alger

de Palos

5

Barcelona

Menorca

Cala Pregonda   Fornells

Ciutadella   Es Mercadal   El Toro   Es Grau
de Menorca   Ferreries   Maó
                 Cap d'Artrutx   Mahón
Cap de Formentor   Cala   Son Bou   Es Castell
Port de   Macarella   de Baix
Pollença

Pollença   Badia de Pollença

Monestir de Lluc   Alcúdia
                   Port de   *Badia*
                   d'Alcúdia   *d'Alcúdia*
Port de Sóller   ▲1445
              Puig Major   P N de
Deià   Sóller   Inca   S'Albufera   Can Picafort
Valldemossa   Artà   Cala Rajada
Banyalbufar   *Serra de*   Santa   Coves d'Artà
              Traumuntana   Sinéu   Margalida
I Sa   Son Servera
Dragonera   Vilafranca   Cala Millor
Palma de   de Bonany   Portocristo
Mallorca   Manacor
Andratx   Coves del Drac
Port   Magaluf   S'Arenal   Felanitx
d'Andratx   Peguera   Llucmajor
          Badia   Campos
          de Palma
          Sa Ràpita   Cala d'Or
          Cap   Santanyí
          Blanc   Ses Salines
                    Colònia de
          Mallorca   Sant Jordi

Ma-13
Ma-1

Palma de Mallorca

I de Cabrera

6

7

8

478

SPAIN INDEX

INDEX SPAIN

489

PICTURES

The Automobile Association would like to thank the following photographers, companies and picture libraries for their assistance in the preparation of this book.

Abbreviations for the picture credits are as follows: (t) top; (b) bottom; (l) left; (r) right; (AA) AA World Travel Library.

2 AA/M Jourdan;
3t AA/P Wilson;
3tc AA/M Chaplow;
3bc AA/M Chaplow;
3b AA/P Enticknap;
4 AA/P Wilson;
5 AA/P Enticknap;
6 AA/M Chaplow;
7bl AA/S Day;
7br AA/M Jourdan;
9tl AA/P Wilson;
9tr AA/P Wilson;
9b AA/M Jourdan;
10 AA/S Day;
11 AA/M Chaplow;
12tl AA/S Watkins;
12tr AA/M Jourdan;
12b AA/J Edmanson;
13 AA/M Chaplow;
14 Bjorn Svensson/ age fotostock/ Photolibrary.com;
15bl AA/P Wilson;
15br AA/R Strange;
16 AA/P Enticknap;
17t AA/M Chaplow;
17b AA/M Chaplow;
18 © Nature Picture Library/Alamy;
19t © JAVIER SORIANO/AFP/Getty Images;
19b © Hulton Archive/Getty Images;
20 © Chris Knapton / Alamy;
21bl © PEDRO ARMESTRE/AFP/Getty Images;
21br AA/P Wilson;
22 AA/M Jourdan;
23cl AA/J Poulsen;
23bl AA/S McBride;
23t A/C Sawyer;
24 AA/M Chaplow;
25bl AA/M Jourdan;
25br Redferns/ Getty Images;
26tl Photolibrary Group;
26tr Photolibrary Group;
27 AA/D Robertson;
28 © Gianni Dagli Orti/CORBIS;
29t AA/M Chaplow;
29b AA/P Enticknap;
30 AA/J Edmanson;

31t AA/P Enticknap;
31b AA/P Wilson;
32 Fol.53r Departure of a Boat for the Crusades, written in Galacian for Alfonso X (1221-84) (vellum) by Spanish School, (13th century), Biblioteca Monasterio del Escorial, Madrid, Spain/ Giraudon/ The Bridgeman Art Library;
33bl AA/M Chaplow;
33br AA/J Edmanson;
34 AA/S Day;
35t AA;
35b Mary Evans Picture Library;
36 AA/M Chaplow;
37bl AA/M Chaplow;
37br Mary Evans Picture Library;
38 The Battle of Trafalgar, October 21st 1805, engraved by Thomas Sutherland for J. Jenkins's 'Naval Achievements', 1816 (colour engraving) by Whitcombe, Thomas (c.1752-1824) (after) Private Collection/ The Stapleton Collection/ The Bridgeman Art Library;
39t Charles III (1716-88) signs the decree authorising trade with Asia and the Philipines, 18th century (oil on canvas) by Muntanya, Pere Pau (18th century), Palacio de la Aduana, Barcelona, Spain/ Index/ The Bridgeman Art Library;
39cr AA/J Edmanson;
39br The Naked Maja, c.1800 (oil on canvas) by Goya y Lucientes, Francisco Jose de (1746-1828), Prado, Madrid, Spain/ The Bridgeman Art Library;
40 Guernica, 1937 (oil on canvas) by Picasso, Pablo (1881-1973), Museo Nacional Centro de Arte Reina Sofia, Madrid, Spain/ The Bridgeman Art Library/ © Succession Picasso/DACS 2008;
41bl AA/M Jourdan;
41br AA/P Enticknap;
42tl AA/M Chaplow;
42tr © Central Press/Hulton Archive/ Getty Images;
43 AA/M Jourdan;
44 Digitalvision;
46 AA/C Sawyer;
47 AA/C Sawyer;
48 AA/M Chaplow;
49 AA/M Chaplow;
50 AA/R Strange;
51 AA/M Chaplow;
52 AA/P Baker;
53 AA/C Sawyer;
55 AA/A Molyneux;

56 AA/S Watkins;
57 AA/M Chaplow;
61 David R. Frazier Photolibrary, Inc./ Alamy;
62 AA/S Watkins;
63 AA/J Edmanson;
64 AA/M Jourdan;
70 AA/R Strange;
71 AA/R Strange;
72 AA/M Chaplow;
73 AA/R Strange;
74 AA/M Jourdan;
75bl AA/T Oliver;
75br AA/M Jourdan;
76tl AA/M Jourdan;
76tr Las Meninas or The Family of Philip IV, c.1656 (oil on canvas) by Velazquez, Diego Rodriguez de Silva y (1599-1660), Prado, Madrid, Spain/ Giraudon/ The Bridgeman Art Library;
77 AA/M Jourdan;
78 AA/M Jourdan/ © The Estate of Roy Lichtenstein/DACS 2008;
79tl AA/R Strange;
79tr AA/M Jourdan;
80 AA/R Strange;
81 AA/J Edmanson;
82bl AA/M Jourdan;
82br AA/M Jourdan;
83 AA/M Chaplow;
84 AA/M Jourdan;
85bl AA/M Jourdan;
85br AA/R Strange;
86 AA/M Chaplow;
87 AA/M Chaplow;
88 AA/M Chaplow;
89 AA/R Strange;
90 AA/M Chaplow;
93 Siroco/Madrid;
95 AA/R Strange;
96 AA/M Chaplow;
99 AA/P Wilson;
100 Casa de Madrid;
102 Kevin George/Alamy;
103 AA/C Sawyer;
104 AA/J Edmanson;
106 Kevin George/ age fotostock/ Photolibrary.com;
107 AA/P Enticknap;
108 Photolibrary Group;
108bl AA/P Enticknap;
108br AA/P Enticknap;
109 AA/M Chaplow;
110tl AA/M Chaplow;
110tr AA/P Enticknap;
111 AA/M Chaplow;
112 AA/M Chaplow;
113bl AA/P Enticknap;
113br AA/M Chaplow;
114 AA/M Chaplow;

115tl AA/M Chaplow;
115tr AA/M Chaplow;
116 AA/J Edmanson;
117 AA/M Chaplow;
118 AA/P Enticknap;
119t A Mockford & N Bonetti;
119b AA/P Enticknap;
120 AA/M Chaplow;
121 AA/M Chaplow;
122 AA/J Edmanson;
124 AA/P Enticknap;
126 Paradores de Turismo, S.A;
128 AA/M Chaplow;
130 AA/P Enticknap;
132 AA/M Jourdan;
133 AA/M Jourdan;
134tl AA/M Jourdan;
134tr AA/S Watkins;
135 AA/S Watkins;
136 Bisons, from the Caves at
Altamira, c.15000 BC (cave painting)
by Prehistoric Altamira, Spain/
Giraudon / The Bridgeman Art Library;
137bl Photolibrary Group;
137br Photolibrary Group;
138bl AA/S Watkins;
138br AA/S Watkins;
139tl AA/S Watkins;
139tr AA/M Jourdan;
140t AA/M Jourdan;
140b AA/M Jourdan;
141bl AA/M Jourdan;
141br AA/M Jourdan;
142 AA/S Watkins;
143t AA/S Watkins;
143b © Carmen Sedano / Alamy;
144 Photolibrary Group;
145cr AA/M Jourdan;
145br Toni Vilches / Alamy;
146 AA/S Watkins;
147tl AA/M Jourdan;
147tr AA/P Enticknap;
148 AA/S Watkins;
149 Turgalicia;
150 AA/ Steve Watkins;
151 AA/S Watkins;
152 AA/S Watkins;
153 AA/S Watkins;
154 Photolibrary Group;
155 Photodisc;
156 AA/S Watkins;
157 AA/S Watkins;
158 AA/S Watkins;
160 AA/C Sawyer;
162 AA/C Sawyer;
165 AA/C Sawyer;
166 Paradores de Turismo, S.A;
168 AA/M Jourdan;
170 © Geoffrey Grace / Alamy;
171 AA/S Watkins;

172 AA/M Jourdan;
173bl AA/M Jourdan;
173br AA/M Jourdan;
173t AA/S Watkins;
174 AA/M Jourdan;
175bl AA/S Watkins;
175br AA/M Jourdan;
176bl AA/P Enticknap;
176br AA/P Enticknap;
177 AA/S Watkins;
178 AA/S Watkins;
179bl AA/S Watkins;
179br AA/P Enticknap;
180tl AA/S Watkins;
180tr AA/S Watkins;
181 AA/P Enticknap;
182 © Chris McLennan/Alamy;
183 AA/S Watkins;
184 AA/S Watkins;
185tl AA/S Watkins;
185tr AA/S Watkins;
186 AA/S Watkins;
187bl AA/S Watkins;
187br AA/S Watkins;
188 AA/M Jourdan;
190 AA/S Watkins;
191 AA/S Watkins;
192 AA/S Watkins;
193tl AA/S Watkins;
193tr AA/S Watkins;
194 AA/P Enticknap;
195 AA/S Watkins;
196 AA/S Watkins;
197bl AA/S Watkins;
197br AA/S Watkins;
198 Aquarium Donostia;
200 Bataplan of San Sebastian;
202 Luxury Collection Hotels;
205 AA/C Sawyer;
206 AA/Max Jourdan;
208 AA/S Day;
214 AA/M Chaplow;
215 AA/M Jourdan;
216t AA/S Day;
216b AA/S Day;
217bl AA/M Chaplow;
217br AA/M Jourdan;
218 AA/P Wood;
219 © CosmoCaixa Barcelona/Ronald
Stallard;
220t AA/S Day;
220b AA/P Wilson © Succession
Miro/ADAGP, Paris and DACS,
London 2008;
221 AA/M Jourdan;
222tl AA/S Day;
222tr AA/M Jourdan;
223 AA/P Wilson;
224 AA/M Jourdan;
225tl AA/S Day;

225tr AA/S Day;
226t AA/M Chaplow;
226b AA/S Day;
227 AA/P Wilson;
228 AA/M Jourdan;
229 AA/S Day;
231 AA/S Day;
232 AA/S Day;
233 AA/M Chaplow;
234 AA/M Jourdan/© Foundation
Antoni Tapies, Barcelone/VEGAP,
Madrid and DACS, London 2008;
235 AA/M Jourdan;
236 AA/ Simon McBride;
239 AA/M Chaplow;
240 AA/ Myriam Bonnet;
242 Rafael Vargas/ Casa Calvet;
245 AA/S McBride;
246 AA/S McBride;
248 NN Hotels;
251 Granados 83/ Derby Hotels;
252 AA/J Edmanson;
254 AA/P Enticknap;
255bl AA/M Chaplow;
255br AA/M Chaplow;
256 AA/M Chaplow;
257t AA/M Chaplow;
257b AA/M Chaplow;
258tl AA/M Chaplow;
258tr AA/P Enticknap;
259 AA/S Watkins/ © Salvador Dali,
Gala-Salvador Dali Foundation, DACS,
London 2008;
260 AA/P Enticknap;
261 AA/P Wilson;
262t AA/S Watkins;
262b AA/S Watkins;
263t AA/M Chaplow;
263b AA/S Watkins;
264 AA/M Chaplow;
265t AA/M Chaplow;
265b AA/M Chaplow;
266 AA/P Enticknap;
267 AA/P Enticknap;
268 AA/J Edmanson;
269tl AA/M Chaplow;
269tr AA/M Chaplow;
270 AA/S Watkins;
271tl AA/S Watkins;
271tr AA/M Chaplow;
272 AA/M Chaplow;
274 © guichaoua / Alamy;
276 Digitalvision;
278 Artesania Huerta de San Vicente/
Equipo Singular, tiendapalma;
280 Torrijos Restaurant;
283 Copyright IVAM;
284 Hotel Lauria;
286 AA/S Watkins;
288 AA/S Watkins;

289 AA/M Chaplow;
290 AA/S Watkins;
291t AA/S Watkins;
291b AA/S Watkins;
292 AA/M Chaplow;
293tl AA/S Watkins;
293tr AA/P Enticknap;
294t AA/S Watkins;
294b AA/S Watkins;
295 AA/S Watkins;
296bl AA/S Watkins;
296br AA/P Enticknap;
297tl AA/M Jourdan;
297tr AA/P Enticknap;
298t AA/S Watkins;
298b © LOOK Die Bildagentur der Fotografen GmbH / Alamy;
299 AA/S Watkins;
300 AA/M Chaplow;
301bl AA/M Chaplow;
301br AA/M Chaplow;
302 AA/P Enticknap;
303 AA/M Chaplow;
304t AA/S Watkins;
304b AA/S Watkins;
305 AA/S Watkins;
306 AA/S Watkins;
307bl AA/S Watkins;
307br AA/S Watkins;
308 © Peter Eastland / Alamy;
310 AA/M Chaplow;
311 AA/M Chaplow;
312 AA/S Watkins;
314 Museo Art Nouveau y Art Deco de Salamanca;
316 AA/ S McBride;
319 AA/S McBride;
320 Landa Palace;
322 AA/M Chaplow;
324 AA/J Edmanson;
325 AA/M Chaplow;
326l AA/M Chaplow;
326r AA/J Edmanson;
327 AA/M Chaplow;
328t AA/M Chaplow;
328b AA/M Chaplow;
329bl AA/M Chaplow;
329br AA/M Chaplow;
330 AA/M Chaplow;
331t Michele Bella/ Cuboimages/ Photolibrary.com;
331b AA/M Chaplow;
332 AA/M Chaplow;
333bl AA/M Chaplow;
333br AA/M Chaplow;
334 AA/M Chaplow;
335 AA/M Chaplow;
336 AA/M Chaplow;
337tl AA/M Chaplow;
337tr AA/M Chaplow;

338 AA/M Chaplow;
339 AA/J Edmanson;
340 Photolibrary;
341bl © NHPA/Bill Coster;
341br Oficina de Turismo Valle del Jerte;
342 AA/S McBride;
344 AA/S McBride;
346 Hotel Cueva del Fraile;
348 AA/P Wilson;
350 AA/P Wilson;
351tl AA/J Poulsen;
351tr AA/D Robertson;
352 AA/P Wilson;
353t AA/D Robertson;
353b AA/P Wilson;
354 AA/M Chaplow;
355bl AA/M Chaplow;
355br AA/M Chaplow;
356 AA/M Chaplow;
357t AA/M Chaplow;
357b AA/M Chaplow;
358bl AA/M Chaplow;
358br AA/M Chaplow;
359 AA/M Chaplow;
360 AA/M Chaplow;
361bl AA/M Chaplow;
361br AA/M Chaplow;
362bl AA/M Chaplow;
362br AA/M Chaplow;
363 AA/D Robertson;
364 AA/M Chaplow;
365 AA/M Chaplow;
366tl AA/M Chaplow;
366tr AA/M Chaplow;
367 AA/M Chaplow;
368bl AA/M Chaplow;
368br AA/M Chaplow;
369 AA/M Chaplow;
370 AA/P Wilson;
371 AA/M Chaplow;
372 AA/A Molyneux;
373 AA/P Wilson;
375t AA/J Edmanson;
375b AA/M Chaplow;
376 AA/M Chaplow;
377 AA/M Chaplow;
378 AA/D Robertson;
380 AA/P Wilson;
381bl AA/P Wilson;
381br AA/D Robertson;
382 AA/S McBride;
385 Photodisc;
386 La Oliva, Granada;
388 AA/M Chaplow;
391 Photodisc;
392 AA/M Chaplow;
394 AA/J Tims;
396 Bildagentur RM/ Tips Italia/ Photolibrary.com;

397 AA/P Baker;
398tl AA/K Paterson;
398tr AA/K Paterson;
399 AA/K Paterson;
400 AA/K Paterson;
401 AA/K Paterson;
402 AA/J Tims;
403 AA/J Tims;
404bl AA/J Tims;
404br AA/J Tims;
405 AA/C Sawyer;
406 AA/J Tims;
407 AA/C Sawyer;
408 AA/K Paterson;
409 AA/K Paterson;
410 AA/K Paterson;
411t AA/K Paterson;
411b AA/J Cowham;
412 AA/J Tims;
415 AA/C Sawyer;
416 Fernando Esteva Medina/ Copyright READS HOTEL.S.L;
418 Es Petit Hotel de Valldemossa;
421 AA/S Day;
424 AA/A Molyneux;
425 AA/M Jourdan;
426 AA/C Sawyer;
428 AA/S Watkins;
429 AA/M Chaplow;
430 AA/ Myriam Bonnet;
431t AA/M Chaplow;
431b AA/C Sawyer;
432 AA/J Edmanson;
433 AA/M Jourdan;
434 AA/K Paterson;
435 AA/S McBride;
438 AA/C Sawyer;
439 A/M Chaplow;
440 Digitalvision;
441 AA/A Molyneux;
443 AA/S Day;
444 AA/M Jourdan;
445 Photodisc;
446 AA/M Jourdan;
447 AA/A Molyneux;
448 Granada Provincial Tourist Board;
449 AA/E Meacher;
450tl AA/C Sawyer;
450tr AA/S McBride;
451 AA/M Chaplow;
452 AA/S McBride;
454 AA/C Sawyer;
457 AA/P Enticknap.

Every effort has been made to trace the copyright holders, and we apologise in advance for any accidental errors. We would be happy to apply the corrections in the following edition of this publication.

SPAIN

ACKNOWLEDGMENTS

CREDITS

Series editor
Sheila Hawkins

Project editor
Bookwork Creative Associates Ltd

Design
Low Sky Design Ltd

Cover design
Chie Ushio

Picture research
Paula Boyd-Barrett

Image retouching and repro
Sarah Montgomery

Mapping
Maps produced by the Mapping Services
Department of AA Publishing

See It Spain
ISBN 978-1-4000-0556-7
Fourth Edition

Main contributors
Daniel Campi, The Content Works, Donna Dailey,
Mary-Ann Gallagher, Paul Grogan, Alex Johnson,
Clare Jones, Tony Kelly, Chris and Melanie Rice,
Sally Roy, Damien Simonis, Suzanne Wales,
Steve Watkins

Updater
George Semler

Indexer
Marie Lorimer

Production
Lorraine Taylor

Published in the United States by Fodor's Travel and simultaneously in Canada by Random House of Canada Limited, Toronto.
Published in the United Kingdom by AA Publishing.
Fodor's is a registered trademark of Random House, Inc., and Fodor's See It is a trademark of Random House, Inc.
Fodor's Travel is a division of Random House, Inc.

Color separation by AA Digital Department
Printed and bound by Leo Paper Products, China
10 9 8 7 6 5 4 3 2 1

Special Sales: This book is available for special discounts for bulk purchases for sales promotions or premiums. Special editions, including personalized covers, excerpts of existing books, and corporate imprints, can be created in large quantities for special needs. For more information, write to Special Markets/Premium Sales, 1745 Broadway, New York, NY 10019 or e-mail specialmarkets@randomhouse.com

Important Note: Time inevitably brings changes, so always confirm prices, travel facts, and other perishable information when it matters. Although Fodor's cannot accept responsibility for errors, you can use this guide in the confidence that we have taken every care to ensure its accuracy.

A04411
Maps in this title produced from: Mapping © MAIRDUMONT / Falk Verlag 2011.
Mapping © ISTITUTO GEOGRAFICO DE AGOSTINI S.p.A., NOVARA 2008
Transport map © Communicarta Ltd, UK
Weather chart statistics © Copyright 2004 Canty and Associates, LLC.

Unleash the Possibilities of Travel With Fodor's

Read before you get there, navigate your picks while you're there – make your trip unforgettable with Fodor's guidebooks. Fodor's offers the assurance of our expertise, the guarantee of selectivity, and the choice details that truly define a destination. Our books are written by local authors, so it's like having a friend wherever you travel.

With more than 10 different types of guidebooks to more than 150 destinations around the world, Fodor's has choices to meet every traveler's needs.

Visit **www.fodors.com** to find the guidebooks and connect with a like-minded community of selective travelers – living, learning, and traveling on their terms.

Fodor's For Choice Travel Experiences

Dear Traveler,

From buying a plane ticket to booking a
room and seeing the sights, a trip goes much
more smoothly when you have a good travel
guide. Dozens of writers, editors, designers,
and cartographers have worked hard to
make the book you hold in your hands a
good one. Was it everything you expected?
Were our descriptions accurate? Were our
recommendations on target? And did you find
our tips and practical advice helpful? Your
ideas and experiences matter to us. If we have
missed or misstated something, we'd love
to hear about it. Fill out our survey at www.
fodors.com/books/feedback/, or e-mail us at
seeit@fodors.com. Or you can snail mail to the
See It Editor at Fodor's, 1745 Broadway, New
York, New York 10019. We'll look forward to
hearing from you.

Tim Jarrell
Publisher